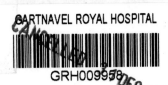

ALCOHOL-USE DISORDERS

DIAGNOSIS, ASSESSMENT AND MANAGEMENT OF HARMFUL DRINKING AND ALCOHOL DEPENDENCE

National Clinical Practice Guideline 115

National Collaborating Centre for Mental Health
commissioned by the

National Institute for Health & Clinical Excellence

published by
The British Psychological Society and The Royal College of Psychiatrists

British Library Cataloguing-in-Publication Data

A catalogue record for this book is available from
the British Library.

ISBN-: 978-1-904671-26-8

Printed in Great Britain by Stanley L. Hunt (Printers) Ltd.

Additional material: data CD-Rom created by Pix18
(www.pix18.co.uk)

developed by   National Collaborating Centre for Mental Health
The Royal College of Psychiatrists
4th Floor, Standon House
21 Mansell Street
London
E1 8AA
www.nccmh.org.uk

commissioned by   National Institute for Health and Clinical Excellence
MidCity Place, 71 High Holborn
London
WCIV 6NA
www.nice.org.uk

published by   The British Psychological Society
St Andrews House
48 Princess Road East
Leicester
LE1 7DR
www.bps.org.uk

and

The Royal College of Psychiatrists
17 Belgrave Square
London
SW1X 8PG
www.rcpsych.ac.uk

CONTENTS

Contents

4

Contents

GUIDELINE DEVELOPMENT GROUP MEMBERS

Professor Colin Drummond (Chair, Guideline Development Group)
Professor of Addiction Psychiatry and Honorary Consultant Addiction Psychiatrist,
National Addiction Centre, Institute of Psychiatry, King's College London, and
South London and Maudsley Foundation NHS Trust

Professor Stephen Pilling (Facilitator, Guideline Development Group)
Director, National Collaborating Centre for Mental Health
Director, Centre for Outcomes Research and Effectiveness, University College
London

Mr Adrian Brown
Alcohol Nurse Specialist, Addiction Services, Central and North West London NHS
Foundation Trust, and St Mary's Hospital, Imperial College

Professor Alex Copello
Professor of Addiction Research, University of Birmingham, and
Consultant Clinical Psychologist, Addiction Services, Birmingham and Solihull
Mental Health Foundation NHS Trust

Dr Edward Day
Senior Lecturer and Consultant in Addiction Psychiatry, University of
Birmingham/Birmingham and Solihull Mental Health NHS Foundation Trust

Mr John Dervan
Lay member and retired Alcohol Treatment Agency CEO

Mr Matthew Dyer
Health Economist (2008 to 2010), National Collaborating Centre for Mental Health

Ms Esther Flanagan
Guideline Development Manager (2008 to 2010), National Collaborating Centre
for Mental Health

Ms Jan Fry
Carer Representative and Voluntary Sector Consultant

Mr Brendan Georgeson
Treatment Coordinator, Walsingham House, Bristol

7

Guideline Development Group members

Dr Eilish Gilvarry
Consultant Psychiatrist (with specialist interest in adolescent addictions), and Assistant Medical Director, Northumberland, Tyne and Wear NHS Foundation Trust

Ms Naomi Glover
Research Assistant (from 2010), National Collaborating Centre for Mental Health

Ms Jayne Gosnall
Service User Representative, and Treasurer of Salford Drug and Alcohol Forum

Dr Linda Harris
Clinical Director, Wakefield Integrated Substance Misuse Services and Director, RCGP Substance Misuse Unit

Dr John Lewis (Co-opted specialist paediatric adviser)
Consultant Community Paediatrician, Royal Cornwall Hospitals Trust

Professor Anne Lingford-Hughes
Professor of Addiction Biology, Imperial College London and Honorary Consultant, Central North West London NHS Foundation Trust

Dr Ifigeneia Mavranezouli
Senior Health Economist, National Collaborating Centre for Mental Health

Mr Trevor McCarthy
Independent Addictions Consultant and Trainer

Dr Marsha Morgan
Reader in Medicine and Honorary Consultant Physician, University of London Medical School

Mrs Stephanie Noble
Registered Manager/Nursing Manager, Broadway Lodge

Dr Suffiya Omarjee
Health Economist (2008 to 2010), National Collaborating Centre for Mental Health

Mr Tom Phillips
Consultant Nurse in Addiction, Humber NHS Foundation Trust

Dr Pamela Roberts
Consultant Clinical and Forensic Psychologist, Cardiff Addictions Unit

Mrs Kate Satrettin
Guideline Development Manager (from 2010), National Collaborating Centre for Mental Health

Mr Rob Saunders
Research Assistant (2008 to 2010), National Collaborating Centre for Mental Health

Ms Laura Shields
Research Assistant (2009 to 2010), National Collaborating Centre for Mental Health

Dr Julia Sinclair
Senior Lecturer in Psychiatry, University of Southampton and Honorary Consultant in Addiction Psychiatry, Hampshire Partnership NHS Foundation Trust

Ms Sarah Stockton
Senior Information Scientist, National Collaborating Centre for Mental Health

Dr Clare Taylor
Senior Editor, National Collaborating Centre for Mental Health

Dr Amina Yesufu-Udechuku
Systematic Reviewer, National Collaborating Centre for Mental Health

ACKNOWLEDGEMENTS

The Guideline Development Group would like to thank the following:

Editorial assistance
Ms Nuala Ernest, Assistant Editor, National Collaborating Centre for Mental Health

1 PREFACE

This guideline is one of three pieces of the National Institute for Health and Clinical Excellence's (NICE) guidance developed to advise on alcohol-use disorders. The present guideline addresses the management of alcohol dependence and harmful alcohol use in people aged 10 years and older, including assessment, pharmacological interventions, psychological and psychosocial interventions, and settings of assisted withdrawal and rehabilitation. The two other NICE guidelines address: (1) the prevention of alcohol-use disorders in people aged 10 years and older, which is public health guidance on the price of alcohol, advertising and availability of alcohol, how best to detect alcohol misuse both in and out of primary care and brief interventions to manage alcohol misuse in these settings (NICE, 2010a); and (2) the assessment and clinical management in people aged 10 years and older of acute alcohol withdrawal, including delirium tremens (DTs), liver damage, acute and chronic pancreatitis, and the management of Wernicke's encephalopathy (WE) (NICE, 2010b).

This guideline will sometimes use the term alcohol misuse, which will encompass both people with alcohol dependence and harmful alcohol use.

The guideline recommendations have been developed by a multidisciplinary team of healthcare professionals, a lay member, service users and carer representatives, and guideline methodologists after careful consideration of the best available evidence. It is intended that the guideline will be useful to clinicians and service commissioners in providing and planning high-quality care for people who misuse alcohol while also emphasising the importance of the experience of care for them and their carers (see Appendix 1 for more details on the scope of the guideline).

Although the evidence base is rapidly expanding there are a number of gaps and future revisions of this guideline will incorporate new scientific evidence as it develops. The guideline makes a number of research recommendations specifically to address gaps in the evidence base. In the meantime, it is hoped that the guideline will assist clinicians, people who misuse alcohol and their carers by identifying the merits of particular treatment approaches where the evidence from research and clinical experience exists.

1.1 NATIONAL CLINICAL GUIDELINES

1.1.1 What are clinical guidelines?

Clinical guidelines are 'systematically developed statements that assist clinicians and service users in making decisions about appropriate treatment for specific conditions' (Mann, 1996). They are derived from the best available research evidence, using predetermined and systematic methods to identify and evaluate the evidence relating to the specific condition in question. Where evidence is lacking, the guidelines incorporate statements and recommendations based upon the consensus statements developed by the Guideline Development Group (GDG).

Clinical guidelines are intended to improve the process and outcomes of healthcare in a number of different ways. They can:

- provide up-to-date evidence-based recommendations for the management of conditions and disorders by healthcare professionals
- be used as the basis to set standards to assess the practice of healthcare professionals
- form the basis for education and training of healthcare professionals
- assist service users and their carers in making informed decisions about their treatment and care
- improve communication between healthcare professionals, service users and their carers
- help identify priority areas for further research.

1.1.2 Uses and limitations of clinical guidelines

Guidelines are not a substitute for professional knowledge and clinical judgement. They can be limited in their usefulness and applicability by a number of different factors: the availability of high-quality research evidence, the quality of the methodology used in the development of the guideline, the generalisability of research findings and the uniqueness of individuals.

Although the quality of research in this field is variable, the methodology used here reflects current international understanding on the appropriate practice for guideline development (Appraisal of Guidelines for Research and Evaluation Instrument [AGREE]; www.agreetrust.org; AGREE Collaboration, 2003), ensuring the collection and selection of the best research evidence available, and the systematic generation of treatment recommendations applicable to the majority of people who misuse alcohol. However, there will always be some people and situations for which clinical guideline recommendations are not readily applicable. This guideline does not, therefore, override the individual responsibility of healthcare professionals to make appropriate decisions in the circumstances of the individual, in consultation with the person with alcohol dependence and harmful alcohol use or their carer.

In addition to the clinical evidence, cost-effectiveness information, where available, is taken into account in the generation of statements and recommendations of the clinical guidelines. While national guidelines are concerned with clinical and cost effectiveness, issues of affordability and implementation costs are to be determined by the National Health Service (NHS).

In using guidelines, it is important to remember that the absence of empirical evidence for the effectiveness of a particular intervention is not the same as evidence for ineffectiveness. In addition, and of particular relevance in mental health, evidence-based treatments are often delivered within the context of an overall treatment programme including a range of activities, the purpose of which may be to help engage the person and provide an appropriate context for the delivery of specific interventions. It is important to maintain and enhance the service context in which these interventions are delivered; otherwise the specific benefits of effective interventions will be lost. Indeed, the importance of organising care in order to support and encourage a good therapeutic relationship is at times as important as the specific treatments offered.

1.1.3   Why develop national guidelines?

NICE was established as a Special Health Authority for England and Wales in 1999, with a remit to provide a single source of authoritative and reliable guidance for service users, professionals and the public. NICE guidance aims to improve standards of care, diminish unacceptable variations in the provision and quality of care across the NHS, and ensure that the health service is patient centred. All guidance is developed in a transparent and collaborative manner, using the best available evidence and involving all relevant stakeholders.

NICE generates guidance in a number of different ways, three of which are relevant here. First, national guidance is produced by the Technology Appraisal Committee to give robust advice about a particular treatment, intervention, procedure or other health technology. Second, NICE commissions public health intervention guidance focused on types of activity (interventions) that help to reduce people's risk of developing a disease or condition or help to promote or maintain a healthy lifestyle. Third, NICE commissions the production of national clinical practice guidelines focused upon the overall treatment and management of a specific condition. To enable this latter development, NICE has established four National Collaborating Centres in conjunction with a range of professional organisations involved in healthcare.

1.1.4   The National Collaborating Centre for Mental Health

This guideline has been commissioned by NICE and developed within the National Collaborating Centre for Mental Health (NCCMH). The NCCMH is a collaboration of the professional organisations involved in the field of mental health, national service user and carer organisations, a number of academic institutions and NICE. The NCCMH is funded by NICE and is led by a partnership between the Royal College of Psychiatrists and the British Psychological Society's Centre for Outcomes Research and Effectiveness, based at University College London.

1.1.5   From national clinical guidelines to local protocols

Once a national guideline has been published and disseminated, local healthcare groups will be expected to produce a plan and identify resources for implementation, along with appropriate timetables. Subsequently, a multidisciplinary group involving commissioners of healthcare, primary care and specialist mental health professionals, service users and carers should undertake the translation of the implementation plan into local protocols taking into account both the recommendations set out in this guideline and the priorities set in the National Service Framework for Mental Health (Department of Health, 1999) and related documentation. The nature and pace of the local plan will reflect local healthcare needs and the nature of existing services; full implementation may take considerable time, especially where substantial training needs are identified.

1.1.6 Auditing the implementation of clinical guidelines

This guideline identifies key areas of clinical practice and service delivery for local and national audit. Although the generation of audit standards is an important and necessary step in the implementation of this guidance, a more broadly-based implementation strategy will be developed. Nevertheless, it should be noted that the Care Quality Commission will monitor the extent to which Primary Care Trusts, trusts responsible for mental health and social care, and Health Authorities have implemented these guidelines.

1.2 THE NATIONAL ALCOHOL DEPENDENCE AND HARMFUL ALCOHOL USE GUIDELINE

1.2.1 Who has developed this guideline?

The GDG was convened by the NCCMH and supported by funding from NICE. The GDG included alcohol misusers and carers, and professionals from psychiatry, clinical psychology, general practice, nursing and psychiatric pharmacy.

Staff from the NCCMH provided leadership and support throughout the process of guideline development, undertaking systematic searches, information retrieval, appraisal and systematic review of the evidence. Members of the GDG received training in the process of guideline development from NCCMH staff, and the service users and carers received training and support from the NICE Patient and Public Involvement Programme. The NICE Guidelines Technical Advisor provided advice and assistance regarding aspects of the guideline development process.

All GDG members made formal declarations of interest at the outset, which were updated at every GDG meeting. The GDG met a total of 12 times throughout the process of guideline development. It met as a whole, but key topics were led by a national expert in the relevant topic. The GDG was supported by the NCCMH technical team, with additional expert advice from special advisors where needed. The group oversaw the production and synthesis of research evidence before presentation. All statements and recommendations in this guideline have been generated and agreed by the whole GDG.

1.2.2   For whom is this guideline intended?

This guideline is relevant for adults and young people with alcohol dependence and harmful alcohol use as the primary diagnosis, and covers the care provided by primary, community, secondary, tertiary and other healthcare professionals who have direct contact with, and make decisions concerning the care of, adults and young people with alcohol dependence and harmful alcohol use.

The guideline will also be relevant to the work, but will not specifically cover the practice, of those in:
● occupational health services
● social services
● forensic services
● the independent sector.

The experience of alcohol misuse can affect the whole family and often the community. The guideline recognises the role of both in the treatment and support of people with alcohol dependence and harmful alcohol use.

1.2.3   Specific aims of this guideline

The guideline makes recommendations for the treatment and management of alcohol dependence and harmful alcohol use. It aims to:
● improve access and engagement with treatment and services for people who misuse alcohol
● evaluate the role of specific psychological, psychosocial and pharmacological interventions in the treatment of alcohol dependence and harmful alcohol use
● evaluate the role of psychological and psychosocial interventions in combination with pharmacological interventions in the treatment of alcohol dependence and harmful alcohol use
● integrate the above to provide best-practice advice on the care of individuals throughout the course of their alcohol dependence and harmful alcohol use
● promote the implementation of best clinical practice through the development of recommendations tailored to the requirements of the NHS in England and Wales.

1.2.4   The structure of this guideline

The guideline is divided into chapters, each covering a set of related topics. The first three chapters provide a summary of the clinical practice and research recommendations, and a general introduction to guidelines and to the methods used to develop them. Chapter 4 provides the evidence for the experience of care of individuals who misuse alcohol and their carers. Chapters 5 to 7 provide the evidence that underpins the recommendations about the treatment and management of alcohol misuse.

Each evidence chapter begins with a general introduction to the topic that sets the recommendations in context. Depending on the nature of the evidence, narrative reviews or meta-analyses were conducted, and the structure of the chapters varies accordingly. Where appropriate, details about current practice, the evidence base and any research limitations are provided. Where meta-analyses were conducted, information is given about both the interventions included and the studies considered for review. Clinical summaries are then used to summarise the evidence presented. Health economic evidence is then presented (where appropriate), followed by a section (from evidence to recommendations) that draws together the clinical and health economic evidence, and provides a rationale for the recommendations. On the CD-ROM, full details about the included studies can be found in Appendix 16. Where meta-analyses were conducted, the data are presented using forest plots in Appendix 17 (see Table 1 for details).

Table 1: Appendices on CD-ROM

Clinical study characteristics tables	Appendix 16
Clinical evidence forest plots	Appendix 17
GRADE evidence profiles	Appendix 18
Evidence tables for economic studies	Appendix 19

2 ALCOHOL DEPENDENCE AND HARMFUL ALCOHOL USE

2.1 INTRODUCTION

This guideline is concerned with the identification, assessment and management of alcohol dependence and harmful alcohol use[1] in people aged 10 years and older. In 2008, alcoholic beverages were consumed by 87% of the population in England, which is equivalent to 36 million people (adults aged 16 years or over) (Fuller, 2009). Drinking alcohol is widely socially accepted and associated with relaxation and pleasure, and some people drink alcohol without experiencing harmful effects. However, a growing number of people experience physical, social and psychological harmful effects of alcohol. Twenty-four per cent[2] of the adult population in England, including 33% of men and 16% of women, consumes alcohol in a way that is potentially or actually harmful to their health or well-being (McManus *et al.*, 2009). Four per cent of adults in England are alcohol dependent[3] (6% men; 2% women), which involves a significant degree of addiction to alcohol, making it difficult for them to reduce their drinking or abstain despite increasingly serious harm (Drummond *et al.*, 2005). Alcohol dependence and harmful alcohol use are recognised as mental health disorders by the World Health Organization (WHO, 1992; see Section 2.2). Although not an official diagnostic term, 'alcohol misuse' will be used as a collective term to encompass alcohol dependence and harmful alcohol use throughout this guideline.

The physical harm related to alcohol is a consequence of its toxic and dependence-producing properties. Ethanol (or ethyl alcohol) in alcoholic beverages is produced by the fermentation of sugar by yeast. It is a small molecule that is rapidly absorbed in the gut and is distributed to, and has effects in, every part of the body. Most organs in the body can be affected by the toxic effects of alcohol, resulting in more than 60 different diseases. The risks of developing these diseases are related to the amount of alcohol consumed over time, with different diseases having different levels of risk. For example, the risk of developing breast cancer increases in a linear way, in which even small amounts of alcohol increase risk. With alcoholic liver disease the risk is curvilinear, with harm increasing more steeply with increasing alcohol consumption. In the case of cardiovascular disease a modest beneficial effect has been reported with moderate amounts of alcohol, although recent research

---

[1]Several terms including 'alcoholism', 'alcohol addiction', 'alcohol abuse' and 'problem drinking' have been used in the past to describe disorders related to alcohol consumption. However, 'alcohol dependence' and 'harmful alcohol use' are used throughout this guideline to be consistent with WHO's *International Classification of Mental Disorders*, 10th Revision (WHO, 1992).
[2]Defined as scoring 8 or more on the Alcohol Use Disorders Identification Test (AUDIT).
[3]Defined as scoring 16 or more on the AUDIT.

suggests this effect may have been overestimated (Ofori-Adjei *et al.*, 2007). During pregnancy alcohol can cause harm to the foetus, which can cause prematurity, stillbirth and the developmental disorder fetal alcohol syndrome.

Alcohol is rapidly absorbed in the gut and reaches the brain soon after drinking. This quickly leads to changes in coordination that increase the risk of accidents and injuries, particularly when driving a vehicle or operating machinery, and when combined with other sedative drugs (for example, benzodiazepines). Its adverse effects on mood and judgement can increase the risk of violence and violent crime. Heavy chronic alcohol consumption increases the risk of mental health disorders including depression, anxiety, psychosis, impairments of memory and learning, alcohol dependence and an increased risk of suicide. Both acute and chronic heavy drinking can contribute to a wide range of social problems including domestic violence and marital breakdown, child abuse and neglect, absenteeism and job loss (Drummond, 1990; Head *et al.*, 2002; Velleman & Orford, 1999).

The physical harm related to alcohol has been increasing in the UK in the past three decades. Deaths from alcoholic liver disease have doubled since 1980 (Leon & McCambridge, 2006) compared with a decrease in many other European countries. Alcohol related hospital admissions increased by 85% between 2002/03 and 2008/09, accounting for 945,000 admissions with a primary or secondary diagnosis wholly or partly related to alcohol in 2006/07 and comprising 7% of all hospital admissions (North West Public Health Observatory, 2010).

Alcohol is a psychoactive substance with properties known to cause dependence (or addiction). If compared within the framework of the 1971 Convention on Psychotropic Substances, alcohol would qualify as a dependence-producing substance warranting international control (United Nations, 1977; Ofori-Adjei *et al.*, 2007). Alcohol shares some of its dependence-producing mechanisms with other psychoactive addictive drugs. Although a smaller proportion of the population who consume alcohol become dependent than is the case with some illegal drugs such as cocaine, it is nevertheless a significant problem due to much the larger number of people who consume alcohol (Kandel *et al.*, 1997).

Alcohol presents particularly serious consequences in young people due to a higher level of vulnerability to the adverse effects of alcohol (see Section 2.12 on special populations).

Heavy drinking in adolescence can affect brain development and has a higher risk of organ damage in the developing body (Zeigler *et al.*, 2005). Alcohol consumption before the age of 13 years, for example, is associated with a four-fold increased risk of alcohol dependence in adulthood (Dawson *et al.*, 2008; Hingson & Zha, 2009).

Other groups who are also at higher risk of alcohol-related harm include: the elderly, those with pre-existing illnesses or who are taking a range of medicines that interact with alcohol, and the socially disadvantaged (Marmot *et al.*, 2010; O'Connell *et al.*, 2003). A given amount of alcohol will also be more harmful in women compared with men due to differences in body mass and composition, hence the government's recommended sensible-drinking guidelines are lower for women than men. Nevertheless, or perhaps as a consequence, women tend to seek help for alcohol misuse earlier in their drinking career than do men (Schuckit, 2009).

2.2   DEFINITIONS

The definition of harmful alcohol use in this guideline is that of WHOs *International Classification of Diseases, 10th Revision (The ICD–10 Classification of Mental and Behavioural Disorders)* (ICD–10; WHO, 1992):

> *a pattern of psychoactive substance use that is causing damage to health. The damage may be physical (e.g. hepatitis) or mental (e.g. depressive episodes secondary to heavy alcohol intake). Harmful use commonly, but not invariably, has adverse social consequences; social consequences in themselves, however, are not sufficient to justify a diagnosis of harmful use.*

The term was introduced in ICD–10 and replaced 'non-dependent use' as a diagnostic term. The closest equivalent in other diagnostic systems (for example, the *Diagnostic and Statistical Manual of Mental Disorders* of the American Psychiatric Association [APA, 1994], currently in its fourth edition [DSM–IV]) is 'alcohol abuse', which usually includes social consequences.

The term 'hazardous use' appeared in the draft version of ICD–10 to indicate a pattern of substance use that increases the risk of harmful consequences for the user. This is not a current diagnostic term within ICD–10. Nevertheless it continues to be used by WHO in its public health programme (WHO, 2010a and 2010b).

In ICD–10 the 'dependence syndrome' is defined as:

> *a cluster of behavioural, cognitive, and physiological phenomena that develop after repeated substance use and that typically include a strong desire to take the drug, difficulties in controlling its use, persisting in its use despite harmful consequences, a higher priority given to drug use than to other activities and obligations, increased tolerance, and sometimes a physical withdrawal state.*

In more common language and in earlier disease-classification systems this has been referred to as 'alcoholism'. However, the term 'alcohol dependence' is preferred because it is more precise, and more reliably defined and measured using the criteria of ICD–10 (Text Box 1).

Alcohol dependence is also a category of mental disorder in DSM–IV (APA, 1994), although the criteria are slightly different from those used by ICD–10. For example a strong desire or compulsion to use substances is not included in DSM–IV, whereas more criteria relate to harmful consequences of use. It should be noted that DSM is currently under revision, but the final version of DSM–V will not be published until 2013 (APA, 2010).

Text Box 1: ICD–10 diagnostic guidelines for the dependence syndrome (WHO, 1992)

A definite diagnosis of dependence should usually be made only if three or more of the following have been present together at some time during the previous year:

(a) a strong desire or sense of compulsion to take the substance;

(b) difficulties in controlling substance-taking behaviour in terms of its onset, termination, or levels of use;

(c) a physiological withdrawal state when substance use has ceased or been reduced, as evidenced by: the characteristic withdrawal syndrome for the substance; or use of the same (or a closely related) substance with the intention of relieving or avoiding withdrawal symptoms;

(d) evidence of tolerance, such that increased doses of the psychoactive substances are required in order to achieve effects originally produced by lower doses (clear examples of this are found in alcohol- and opiate-dependent individuals who may take daily doses sufficient to incapacitate or kill non-tolerant users);

(e) progressive neglect of alternative pleasures or interests because of psycho-active substance use, increased amount of time necessary to obtain or take the substance or to recover from its effects;

(f) persisting with substance use despite clear evidence of overtly harmful conse-quences, such as harm to the liver through excessive drinking, depressive mood states consequent to periods of heavy substance use, or drug-related impairment of cognitive functioning; efforts should be made to determine that the user was actually, or could be expected to be, aware of the nature and extent of the harm.

Narrowing of the personal repertoire of patterns of psychoactive substance use has also been described as a characteristic feature (for example, a tendency to drink alcoholic drinks in the same way on weekdays and weekends, regardless of social constraints that determine appropriate drinking behaviour).

It is an essential characteristic of the dependence syndrome that either psycho-active substance taking or a desire to take a particular substance should be pres-ent; the subjective awareness of compulsion to use drugs is most commonly seen during attempts to stop or control substance use.

Although alcohol dependence is defined in ICD–10 and DSM–IV in categorical terms for diagnostic and statistical purposes as being either present or absent, in real-ity dependence exists on a continuum of severity. Therefore, it is helpful from a clin-ical perspective to subdivide dependence into categories of mild, moderate and severe. People with mild dependence (those scoring 15 or less on the Severity of Alcohol Dependence Questionnaire [SADQ]) usually do not need assisted alcohol withdrawal. People with moderate dependence (with an SADQ score of between 15 and 30) usually need assisted alcohol withdrawal, which can typically be managed in a community setting unless there are other risks. People who are severely alcohol dependent (with an SADQ score of 31 or more) will need assisted alcohol withdrawal, typically in an inpatient or residential setting. In this guideline these definitions of severity are used to guide the selection of appropriate interventions.

2.3   EPIDEMIOLOGY OF ALCOHOL

2.3.1   Prevalence

Alcohol was consumed by 87% of the UK population in the past year (Fuller, 2009). Amongst those who are current abstainers, some have never consumed alcohol for religious, cultural or other reasons, and some have consumed alcohol but not in the past year. This latter group includes people who have been harmful drinkers or alcohol dependent in the past and who have stopped because of experiencing the harmful effects of alcohol.

Amongst those who currently consume alcohol there is a wide spectrum of alcohol consumption, from the majority who are moderate drinkers through to a smaller number of people who regularly consume a litre of spirits per day or more and who will typically be severely alcohol dependent. However, it is important to note that most of the alcohol consumed by the population is drunk by a minority of heavy drinkers.

The Department of Health has introduced definitions that relate to different levels of drinking risk. One UK unit of alcohol is defined as 8 g (or 10 ml) of pure ethanol.[4] The Department of Health recommends that adult men should not regularly drink more than four units of alcohol per day and women no more than three units (Department of Health, 1995). This definition implies the need for alcohol free or lower alcohol consumption days. Below this level alcohol consumption is regarded a 'low risk' in terms of health or social harms. The government's advice on alcohol in pregnancy is to abstain (Department of Health, 2008a). The Royal College of Psychiatrists' advice is to drink less than 21 units of alcohol per week in men and 14 units in women, which is consistent with government advice if alcohol-free days are included in the weekly drinking pattern (Royal College of Psychiatrists, 1986). Those people who drink above these levels but have not yet experienced alcohol-related harm are regarded as hazardous drinkers: that is, their drinking is at a level which increases the risk of harm in the future. These recommendations are based on longitudinal research on the impact of different levels of alcohol consumption on mortality. Above 50 units of alcohol per day in men and 35 units in women is regarded as 'definitely harmful' (Royal College of Psychiatrists, 1986). Those drinking more than eight units per day in men and six units in women are regarded by the government as 'binge drinkers' (Prime Minister's Strategy Unit, 2004). Again these definitions are based on longitudinal research on the effects of alcohol consumption on adverse consequences including accidents, injuries and other forms of harm.

---

[4]The UK unit definition differs from definitions of standard drinks in some other countries. For example, a UK unit contains two thirds of the quantity of ethanol that a US 'standard drink' has.

Most of the data on the English population's drinking patterns comes from the General Household Survey, the Health Survey for England and the Psychiatric Morbidity Survey (Craig *et al.*, 2009; McManus *et al.*, 2009; Robinson & Bulger, 2010). In terms of hazardous drinking, in 2008, 21% of adult men were drinking between 22 and 50 units per week, and 15% of adult women were drinking between 15 and 35 units; a further 7% of men and 5% of women were harmful drinkers, drinking above 50 and 35 units per week, respectively. In addition, 21% of adult men and 14% of women met the government's criteria for binge drinking. There were regional variations in the prevalence of these drinking patterns. Hazardous drinking among men varied from 24% in the West Midlands to 32% in Yorkshire and Humber, and in women from 15% in the East of England to 25% in the North East. Harmful drinking in men varied from 5% in the East Midlands to 11% in Yorkshire and Humber, and in women from 2% in the East of England to 7% in Yorkshire and Humber. Binge drinking among men varied from 19% in the West Midlands to 29% in Yorkshire and Humber and among women from 11% in East of England to 21% in Yorkshire and Humber (Robinson & Bulger, 2010).

There is a lack of reliable data on the prevalence of alcohol dependence because UK general-population surveys do not include questionnaires that provide an ICD–10 diagnosis of alcohol dependence (for example, the WHO Composite International Diagnostic Interview [CIDI]). Instead the most reliable estimate of alcohol dependence comes from the Psychiatric Morbidity Survey, which used a WHO measure of alcohol-use disorders: the Alcohol Use Disorders Identification Test (AUDIT; Babor *et al.*, 2001). A score of 16 or more on this questionnaire is indicative of possible alcohol dependence (Drummond *et al.*, 2005). The Alcohol Needs Assessment Research Project (ANARP) in England found the prevalence of alcohol dependence to be 4% in 16- to 64-year-old adults: 6% of men and 2% of women (Drummond *et al.*, 2005). This equates to a population of 1.1 million people in England with alcohol dependence in 2000. This population increased to 1.6 million in 2007 (McManus *et al.*, 2009). There was considerable regional variation in the prevalence of alcohol dependence, from 2% in the East Midlands to 5% in the North West. The prevalence of hazardous and harmful drinking and dependence is highest in 16- to 24-year-olds and decreases steadily with age. Hazardous and harmful drinking is 1.6 times greater in the white population than in the black and minority ethnic population. However, alcohol dependence is approximately equally prevalent in these two populations (see Section 2.12 on special populations).

Whilst the government and Royal Colleges' definitions of harmful drinking and risk levels of alcohol consumption provide useful benchmarks to estimate the prevalence of alcohol-use disorders in the general population and monitor trends over time, they have a number of limitations. This is particularly apparent when examining an individual's risk of alcohol-related harm at a given level of alcohol consumption.

According to WHO, alcohol is implicated as a risk factor in over 60 health disorders including high blood pressure, stroke, coronary heart disease, liver cirrhosis and various cancers. The extent to which these disorders are attributable to alcohol varies. This is known as the alcohol-attributable fraction (AAF). The AAF for alcoholic liver disease and alcohol poisoning is 1 (or 100% alcohol attributable) (WHO,

2000). For other diseases such as cancer and heart disease the AAF is less than 1 (that is, partly attributable to alcohol) or 0 (that is, not attributable to alcohol). Further, the AAF varies with age and gender. Also, as noted earlier, the risk with increasing levels of alcohol consumption is different for different health disorders. Risk of a given level of alcohol consumption is also related to gender, body weight, nutritional status, concurrent use of a range of medications, mental health status, contextual factors and social deprivation, amongst other factors. Therefore it is impossible to define a level at which alcohol is universally without risk of harm.

2.3.2   Mental health

Alcohol is strongly associated with a wide range of mental health problems. Depression, anxiety, drug misuse, nicotine dependence and self-harm are commonly associated with excessive alcohol consumption. Up to 41% of suicides are attributable to alcohol and 23% of people who engage in deliberate self-harm are alcohol dependent (Demirbas *et al.*, 2003; Merrill *et al.*, 1992). Amongst adults admitted to inpatient mental health services, hazardous and harmful alcohol use increased the risk of a suicidal presentation by a factor of three, and alcohol dependence increased the risk by a factor of eight (McCloud *et al.*, 2004). In the same study 49% of patients admitted were hazardous and harmful drinkers, including 53% of men and 44% of women, and 22% of the total population were alcohol dependent (Barnaby *et al.*, 2003). These prevalence rates are considerably higher than the general population, particularly in women.

A UK study found 26% of community mental health team patients were hazardous or harmful drinkers and 9% were alcohol dependent (Weaver *et al.*, 2003). In the same study examining patients attending specialist alcohol treatment services, overall 85% had a psychiatric disorder in addition to alcohol dependence. Eighty-one per cent had an affective and/or anxiety disorder (severe depression, 34%; mild depression, 47%; anxiety, 32%), 53% had a personality disorder and 19% had a psychotic disorder.

2.3.3   Social problems

Alcohol is implicated in relationship breakdown, domestic violence and poor parenting, including child neglect and abuse. It is estimated that over 1 million children are affected by parental alcohol misuse and up to 60% of child protection cases involve alcohol (Prime Minister's Strategy Unit, 2003). Alcohol also contributes to unsafe sex and unplanned pregnancy, financial problems and homelessness. Up to half of homeless people are alcohol dependent (Gill *et al.*, 1996).

In terms of productivity, alcohol contributes to absenteeism, accidents in the workplace and decline in work performance. Up to 17 million working days are lost annually in the UK due to alcohol-related absences and 58,000 working years are lost annually due to premature deaths related to alcohol (Leontaridi, 2003). Alcohol misuse can also lead to job loss and over 38,000 people of working age in England were claiming Incapacity Benefit with a diagnosis of 'alcoholism' – nearly 2% of all claimants (Deacon *et al.*, 2007).

2.3.4   Criminality

There were 986,000 violent incidents in England and Wales in 2009/10 where the victim believed the offender to be under the influence of alcohol, accounting for 50% of all violent crimes (Flatley *et al.*, 2010). Nearly half of all offences of criminal damage are alcohol related and alcohol is implicated in domestic violence, sexual assaults, burglary, theft, robbery and murder (Prime Minister's Strategy Unit, 2003). In 2008, it was estimated that 13,020 reported road casualties (6% of all road casualties) occurred when someone was driving whilst over the legal alcohol limit. The provisional number of people estimated to have been killed in drink-driving accidents was 430 in 2008 (17% of all road fatalities) (Department of Transport, 2009).

Approximately two thirds of male prisoners and over one third of female prisoners are hazardous or harmful drinkers, and up to 70% of probation clients are hazardous or harmful drinkers (Singleton *et al.*, 1998).

2.3.5   Public health impact

WHO has estimated the global burden of disease due to alcohol using AAFs, as described above, and found that alcohol accounts for 4% of all disease burden worldwide (Rehm *et al.*, 2004). Alcohol is the third leading cause of disability in the developed world after smoking and hypertension. Using the same methodology, nearly 15,000 deaths in England are caused by alcohol per annum – 3% of all deaths (Jones *et al.*, 2008). Men had more than double the risk of alcohol attributable deaths compared with women, and deaths of 16- to 24–year-olds are 20 times more likely to be the result of alcohol compared with deaths of those aged 75 years and over (23% of all deaths in 16- to 24-year-olds), mostly due to acute effects of alcohol: intentional self-harm and road traffic accidents. In those over 35 years old, alcohol-related deaths are more commonly due to chronic physical illness from alcohol, for example alcoholic liver disease, malignant cancers of the oesophagus and breast, and hypertension.

The health consequences of alcohol, including deaths from alcoholic liver disease, have been increasing in the UK compared with a reduction in many other European countries (Leon & McCambridge, 2006). Further, the age at which deaths from alcoholic liver disease occur has been falling in the UK, which is partly attributable to increasing alcohol consumption in young people (Office for National Statistics, 2003).

Alcohol-related hospital admissions increased by 85% between 2002/03 and 2008/09. For conditions directly attributable to alcohol, admissions increased by 81% between 2002/03 and 2008/09. In 2008/09, there were 945,000 hospital admissions in England where alcohol was either a primary or secondary diagnosis (North West

Public Health Observatory, 2010). Alcohol related admissions increase steeply with age, peaking in the 60- to 64-year-old age group (Deacon *et al.*, 2007).

Data on alcohol-related attendances at accident and emergency departments are not routinely collected nationally in England. However, a 24-hour weekend survey of 36 accident and emergency departments found that 40% of attendances were alcohol related and at peak times (midnight to 5 a.m. at weekends) this rises to 70% (Drummond *et al.*, 2005). Harmful and dependent drinkers are much more likely to be frequent accident and emergency department attenders, attending on average five times per annum. Between 20 and 30% of medical admissions, and one third of primary care attendances, are alcohol related (Coulton *et al.*, 2006; Kouimtsidis *et al.*, 2003; Royal College of Physicians, 2001). Further, people who are alcohol dependent are twice as likely as moderate drinkers to visit their general practitioner (GP) (Fuller *et al.*, 2009).

2.4   AETIOLOGY

There is no single factor that accounts for the variation in individual risk of developing alcohol-use disorders. The evidence suggests that harmful alcohol use and alcohol dependence have a wide range of causal factors, some of which interact with each other to increase risk.

2.4.1   Family history

It is well established that alcohol dependence runs in families. In general, offspring of parents with alcohol dependence are four times more likely to develop alcohol dependence. Evidence from genetic studies, particularly those in twins, has clearly demonstrated a genetic component to the risk of alcohol dependence. A meta-analysis of 9,897 twin pairs from Australian and US studies found the heritability of alcohol dependence to be in excess of 50% (Goldman *et al.*, 2005). However, a meta-analysis of 50 family, twin and adoption studies showed the heritability of alcohol misuse to be at most 30 to 36% (Walters, 2002). Whatever the true heritability, these studies indicate that genetic factors may explain only part of the aetiology of alcohol dependence. The remaining variation is accounted for by environmental factors and their interaction with genetic factors. While no single gene for alcohol dependence has so far been identified, a range of genes that determine brain function have been implicated (Agrawal *et al.*, 2008).

2.4.2   Psychological factors

There is good evidence that a range of psychological factors contribute to the risk of developing alcohol-use disorders. Various learning theories have provided evidence of an important role of learning in alcohol dependence. Conditioning theories provide an explanation for the development of alcohol dependence. Alcohol, being a psychoactive drug, has reinforcing properties, for example through its pleasurable effects and its ability to relieve negative mood states such as anxiety. Conditioning can also explain why people become particularly sensitive to stimuli or cues associated with alcohol consumption, for example the sight and smell of a favourite drink, such that these cues can trigger craving for and continued use of alcohol, including relapse after a period of abstinence (Drummond *et al.*, 1990).

Social learning theory also provides some explanations of increased risk of excessive drinking and the development of alcohol dependence. People can learn from families and peer groups through a process of modelling patterns of drinking and expectancies (beliefs) about the effects of alcohol. Teenagers with higher positive expectancies (for example, that drinking is pleasurable and desirable) are more likely to start drinking at an earlier age and to drink more heavily (Christiansen *et al.*, 1989; Dunn & Goldman, 1998).

2.4.3   Personality factors

The idea that a particular 'addictive personality' leads to the development of alcohol dependence is popular with some addiction counsellors, but does not have strong support from research. Often with patients in treatment for alcohol dependence, it is difficult to disentangle the effects of alcohol on the expression of personality and behaviour from those personality factors that preceded alcohol dependence. Nevertheless, people who are alcohol dependent have a 21-fold higher risk of also having antisocial personality disorder (ASPD; Regier *et al.*, 1990), and people with ASPD have a higher risk of severe alcohol dependence (Goldstein *et al.*, 2007). Recent evidence points to the importance of disinhibition traits, such as novelty and sensation seeking, and poor impulse control, as factors related to increased risk of both alcohol and drug dependence, which may have a basis in abnormal brain function in the pre-frontal cortex (Dick *et al.*, 2007; Kalivas & Volkow, 2005).

2.4.4   Psychiatric comorbidity

As noted earlier, people who are alcohol dependent have higher rates of comorbidity with other psychiatric disorders, particularly depression, anxiety, post-traumatic stress disorder (PTSD), psychosis and drug misuse, than people in the general population. Alcohol can, temporarily at least, reduce the symptoms of anxiety and depression, leading to the theory that alcohol use in this situation is a form of 'self-medication'. This theory, however, lacks clear experimental support, and the longer-term effects of alcohol worsen these disorders.

2.4.5   Stress, adverse life events and abuse

There is clear evidence that adverse life events can trigger excessive drinking and may predispose to the development of alcohol dependence. This is particularly apparent in alcohol dependence developing later in life following, for example, a bereavement or job loss. Stressful life situations or events can also trigger heavy drinking. People who are alcohol dependent also report much higher levels of childhood abuse and neglect, particularly sexual abuse. One UK study found 54% of female and 24% of male alcohol dependent patients identified themselves as victims of sexual abuse, mostly before the age of 16 years (Moncrieff *et al.*, 1996). Further, they were more likely to have a family history of alcohol misuse, and began drinking and developed alcohol dependence earlier than those without such a history.

2.4.6 Other environmental and cultural factors

There is a wide range of other environmental factors that predispose to the development of alcohol-use disorders (Cook, 1994). These include the affordability and availability of alcohol, high consumption rates in the general population, occupational risk factors (such as working in the alcohol or hospitality industries), social pressure to drink, and religious- and culturally-related attitudes towards alcohol.

2.5 COURSE OF HARMFUL ALCOHOL USE AND DEPENDENCE

Harmful alcohol use and dependence are relatively uncommon before the age of 15 years, but increase steeply to reach a peak in the early 20s, this being the period when alcohol use-disorders are most likely to begin. One US general population study found the prevalence of alcohol dependence to be 2% in 12- to 17-year-olds, rising to 12% in 18- to 20–year-olds (Grant *et al.*, 2004a). Thereafter, the prevalence of alcohol-use disorders declines steadily with age. The same US study found the prevalence of dependence was 4% in 30- to 34-year-olds and 1.5% in 50- to 54-year-olds. A similar UK study found the prevalence of alcohol dependence to be 6% in 16- to 19-year-olds, 8.2% in 20- to 24–year-olds, 3.6% in 30- to 34-year-olds and 2.3% in 50- to 54–year-olds (Drummond *et al.*, 2005). Therefore, it is clear that there is substantial remission from alcohol-use disorders over time. Much of this remission takes place without contact with alcohol treatment services (Dawson *et al.*, 2005a).

However, it is also known that people who develop alcohol dependence at a younger age tend to have a more chronic course (Dawson *et al.*, 2008). Further, while a large proportion of those who meet the criteria for alcohol dependence in their 20s will remit over the following two decades, those who remain alcohol dependent in their 40s will tend to have a more chronic course. This is the typical age group of people entering specialist alcohol treatment. Most studies examining the outcome of people attending alcohol treatment find that 70 to 80% will relapse in the year following treatment, with the highest rate of relapse taking place in the first 3 months after completing treatment (Hunt *et al.*, 1971; Raistrick *et al.*, 2006). Those who remain abstinent from alcohol for the first year after treatment have a relatively low risk of relapse thereafter (Schuckit, 2009). Factors associated with a worse outcome include having less social stability and support (for example, those without jobs, families or stable housing), lacking a social network of non-drinkers, a family history of alcohol dependence, psychiatric comorbidity, multiple previous treatment episodes and history of disengagement from treatment.

In contrast with the relatively positive prognosis in younger people who are alcohol dependent in the general population, the longer term prognosis of alcohol dependence for people entering specialist treatment is comparatively poor. Over a 10-year period about one third have continuing alcohol problems, a third show some improvement and a third have a good outcome (either abstinence or moderate drinking) (Edwards *et al.*, 1988). The mortality rate is high in this population, nearly four times the age-adjusted rate for people without alcohol dependence. Those who are more severely alcohol dependent are less likely to achieve lasting stable moderate drinking and have a higher mortality than those who are less dependent (Marshall *et al.*, 1994). It is important to note that most of the excess mortality is largely accounted for by lung cancer and heart disease, which are strongly related to continued tobacco smoking.

2.6   PHARMACOLOGY OF ALCOHOL

Following ingestion, alcohol is rapidly absorbed by the gut and enters the bloodstream with a peak in blood alcohol concentration after 30 to 60 minutes. Alcohol is then distributed around every part of the body. It readily crosses the blood–brain barrier to enter the brain where it causes subjective or psychoactive and behavioural effects, and, following high levels of chronic alcohol intake, it can cause cognitive impairment and brain damage.

Alcohol is excreted in urine, sweat and breath, but the main method of elimination from the body is by metabolism in the liver where it is converted to acetaldehyde and acetate. These metabolites are then excreted from the body, primarily in urine. The rate at which alcohol is metabolised and the extent to which an individual is affected by a given dose of alcohol is highly variable from one individual to another. These individual differences affect drinking behaviour and the potential for alcohol-related harm and alcohol dependence. Also, the effects of alcohol vary in the same individual over time depending on several factors including whether food has been consumed, rate of drinking, nutritional status, environmental context and concurrent use of other psychoactive drugs. Therefore, it is very difficult to predict the effects of a given amount of alcohol both between individuals and within individuals over time. For instance, the impact on the liver varies clinically so that some experience liver failure early on in their drinking career, whilst in others drinking heavily liver function is relatively normal.

Alcohol is a toxic substance and its toxicity is related to the quantity and duration of alcohol consumption. It can have toxic effects on every organ in the body. In the brain, in a single drinking episode, increasing levels of alcohol lead initially to stimulation (experienced as pleasure), excitement and talkativeness. At increasing concentrations alcohol causes sedation leading to sensations of relaxation, then later to slurred speech, unsteadiness, loss of coordination, incontinence, coma and ultimately death through alcohol poisoning, due to the sedation of the vital brain functions on breathing and circulation.

The dependence-producing properties of alcohol have been studied extensively in the last 20 years. Alcohol affects a wide range of neurotransmitter systems in the brain, leading to the features of alcohol dependence. The main neurotransmitter systems affected by alcohol are *gamma*-aminobutyric acid (GABA), glutamate, dopamine and opioid (Nutt, 1999). The action of alcohol on GABA is similar to the effects of other sedatives such as benzodiazepines and is responsible for alcohol's sedating and anxiolytic properties (Krystal *et al.*, 2006). Glutamate is a major neurotransmitter responsible for brain stimulation, and alcohol affects glutamate through its inhibitory action on N-methyl D-aspartate (NMDA)-type glutamate receptors, producing amnesia (for example, blackouts) and sedation (Krystal *et al.*, 1999).

Chronic alcohol consumption leads to the development of tolerance through a process of neuroadaptation: receptors in the brain gradually adapt to the effects of alcohol, to compensate for stimulation or sedation. This is experienced by the individual as the same amount of alcohol having less effect over time. This can lead to an individual increasing alcohol consumption to achieve the desired psychoactive effects. The key neurotransmitters involved in tolerance are GABA and glutamate, with chronic alcohol intake associated with reduced GABA inhibitory function and increased NMDA-glutamatergic activity (Krystal *et al.*, 2003 and 2006). This GABA–glutamate imbalance is acceptable in the presence of alcohol, which increases GABA and reduces NMDA-glutamate activity. However, when the alcohol-dependent individual stops drinking, the imbalance between these neurotransmitter systems results in the brain becoming overactive after a few hours leading to unpleasant withdrawal symptoms such as anxiety, sweating, craving, seizures and hallucinations. This can be life threatening in severe cases and requires urgent medical treatment. Repeated withdrawal is also thought to underlie the toxic effect of alcohol on neurons, leading to cognitive impairment and brain damage (Loeber *et al.*, 2009). The effects of alcohol withdrawal can take up to between 3 months and 1 year to fully recover from (referred to as the protracted withdrawal syndrome). Even then, the brain remains abnormally sensitive to alcohol and, when drinking is resumed, tolerance and withdrawal can return within a few days (known as reinstatement) (Edwards & Gross, 1976). This makes it extremely difficult for a person who has developed alcohol dependence to return to sustained moderate drinking.

The brain's endogenous opioid system is also affected by alcohol (Oswald & Wand, 2004). Alcohol stimulates endogenous opioids, which are thought to be related to the pleasurable, reinforcing effects of alcohol. Opioids in turn stimulate the dopamine system in the brain, which is thought to be responsible for appetite for a range of appetitive behaviours including regulation of appetite for food, sex and psychoactive drugs. The dopamine system is also activated by stimulant drugs such as amphetamines and cocaine, and it is through this process that the individual seeks more drugs or alcohol (Everitt *et al.*, 2008; Robinson & Berridge, 2008). There is evidence that drugs which block the opioid neurotransmitters, such as naltrexone, can reduce the reinforcing or pleasurable properties of alcohol and so reduce relapse in alcohol-dependent patients (Anton, 2008).

2.7 IDENTIFICATION AND DIAGNOSIS

People with alcohol-use disorders commonly present to health, social and criminal justice agencies, often with problems associated with their alcohol use, but they less often seek help for the alcohol problem itself. Further, alcohol-use disorders are seldom identified by health and social care professionals. One recent study found that UK GPs routinely identify only a small proportion of people with alcohol-use disorders who present to primary care (less than 2% of hazardous or harmful drinkers and less than 5% of alcohol-dependent drinkers) (Cheeta *et al.*, 2008). This has important implications for the prevention and treatment of alcohol-use disorders. Failure to identify alcohol-use disorders means that many people do not get access to alcohol interventions until the problems are more chronic and difficult to treat. Further, failure to address an underlying alcohol problem may undermine the effectiveness of treatment for the presenting health problem (for example, depression or high blood pressure).

Screening and brief intervention delivered by a non-specialist practitioner is a cost-effective approach for hazardous and harmful drinkers (NICE, 2010a). However, for people who are alcohol dependent, brief interventions are less effective and referral to a specialist service is likely to be necessary (Moyer *et al.*, 2002). It is important, therefore, that health and social care professionals are able to identify and appropriately refer harmful drinkers who do not respond to brief interventions, and those who are alcohol dependent, to appropriate specialist services. In acute hospitals, psychiatry liaison teams or specialist addiction liaison psychiatry staff can provide a useful in-reach service including the provision of staff training in alcohol identification and brief interventions, advice on management of alcohol withdrawal and referral to specialist alcohol services in the community (Moriarty *et al.*, 2010). Addiction psychiatrists also have an important role in liaison with general psychiatrists in the optimal management of people with alcohol and mental health comorbidity (Boland *et al.*, 2008).

Around one third of people presenting to specialist alcohol services in England are self-referred and approximately one third are referred by non-specialist health or social care professionals (Drummond *et al.*, 2005). The majority of the remainder are referred by other specialist addiction services or criminal justice services. At the point of entry to treatment it is essential that patients are appropriately diagnosed and assessed in order to decide on the most appropriate treatment and management, assess the level of risk, such as self-harm and risk to others, and identify co-occurring problems that may need particular attention, for example psychiatric comorbidity, physical illness, problems with housing, vulnerability and pregnancy (National Treatment Agency for Substance Misuse, 2006). Therefore assessment should not be narrowly focused on alcohol consumption, but should include all areas of physical, psychological and social functioning.

Because alcohol dependence is associated with a higher level of problems and a more chronic course, and requires a higher level of medical and psychiatric intervention, it is essential that practitioners in specialist alcohol services are able to appropriately diagnose and assess alcohol dependence.

2.8   THE ROLE OF TREATMENT AND MANAGEMENT

As noted above, many people will recover from alcohol-use disorders without specialist treatment and many will reduce their alcohol intake following a change in circumstances, such as parenthood, marriage or taking on a responsible job. Hazardous and harmful drinkers may respond to a brief intervention provided in primary care without requiring access to specialist treatment (NICE, 2010a). For others, their alcohol problems are overcome with the help of a mutual aid organisation, such as Alcoholics Anonymous (AA; see Section 2.10). Nevertheless, many will require access to specialist treatment by virtue of having more severe or chronic alcohol problems, or a higher level of complications of their drinking (for example, social isolation, psychiatric comorbidity and severe alcohol withdrawal).

The primary role of specialist treatment is to assist the individual to reduce or stop drinking alcohol in a safe manner (National Treatment Agency for Substance Misuse, 2006). At the initial stages of engagement with specialist services, service users may be ambivalent about changing their drinking behaviour or dealing with their problems. At this stage, work on enhancing the service user's motivation towards making changes and engagement with treatment will be particularly important.

For most people who are alcohol dependent the most appropriate goal in terms of alcohol consumption should be to aim for complete abstinence. With an increasing level of alcohol dependence a return to moderate or 'controlled' drinking becomes increasingly difficult (Edwards & Gross, 1976; Schuckit, 2009). Further, for people with significant psychiatric or physical comorbidity (for example, depressive disorder or alcoholic liver disease), abstinence is the appropriate goal. However, hazardous and harmful drinkers, and those with a low level of alcohol dependence, may be able to achieve a goal of moderate alcohol consumption (Raistrick *et al.*, 2006). Where a client has a goal of moderation but the clinician believes there are considerable risks in doing so, the clinician should provide strong advice that abstinence is most appropriate but should not deny the client treatment if the advice is unheeded (Raistrick *et al.*, 2006).

For people who are alcohol dependent, the next stage of treatment may require medically-assisted alcohol withdrawal, if necessary with medication to control the symptoms and complications of withdrawal. For people with severe alcohol dependence and/or significant physical or psychiatric comorbidity, this may require assisted alcohol withdrawal in an inpatient or residential setting, such as a specialist NHS inpatient addiction treatment unit (Specialist Clinical Addiction Network, 2006). For the majority, however, alcohol withdrawal can be managed in the community either as part of shared care with the patient's GP or in an outpatient or home-based assisted alcohol withdrawal programme, with appropriate professional and family support (Raistrick *et al.*, 2006). Treatment of alcohol withdrawal is, however, only the beginning of rehabilitation and, for many, a necessary precursor to a longer-term treatment process. Withdrawal management should therefore not be seen as a standalone treatment.

People who are alcohol dependent and who have recently stopped drinking are vulnerable to relapse, and often have many unresolved co-occurring problems that predispose to relapse (for example, psychiatric comorbidity and social problems) (Marlatt & Gordon, 1985). In this phase, the primary role of treatment is the prevention of relapse. This should include interventions aimed primarily at the drinking behaviour, including psychosocial and pharmacological interventions, and interventions aimed at dealing with co-occurring problems. Interventions aimed at preventing relapse include individual therapy (for example, motivational enhancement therapy [MET], cognitive behavioural therapy [CBT]), group and family based therapies, community-based and residential rehabilitation programmes, medications to attenuate drinking or promote abstinence (for example, naltrexone, acamprosate or disulfiram) and interventions promoting social support and integration (for example, social behaviour and network therapy [SBNT] or 12-step facilitation [TSF]) (Raistrick *et al.*, 2006).

Although psychiatric comorbidity is common in people seeking help for alcohol-use disorders, this will usually resolve within a few weeks of abstinence from alcohol without formal psychiatric intervention (Petrakis *et al.*, 2002). However, a proportion of people with psychiatric comorbidity, usually those in whom the mental disorder preceded alcohol dependence, will require psychosocial or pharmacological interventions specifically for the comorbidity following assisted withdrawal. Self-harm and suicide are relatively common in people who are alcohol dependent (Sher, 2006). Therefore, treatment staff need to be trained to identify, monitor and if necessary treat or refer to an appropriate mental health specialist those patients with comorbidity which persists beyond the withdrawal period, and/or are at risk of self-harm or suicide. Patients with complex psychological issues related to trauma, sexual abuse or bereavement will require specific interventions delivered by appropriately trained personnel (Raistrick *et al.*, 2006).

Often, people who are alcohol dependent (particularly in the immediate post-withdrawal period) find it difficult to cope with typical life challenges such as managing their finances or dealing with relationships. They will therefore require additional support directed at these areas of social functioning. Specific social problems such as homelessness, isolation, marital breakdown, child care issues including parenting problems, child abuse and neglect will require referral to, and liaison with, appropriate social care services (National Treatment Agency for Substance Misuse, 2006). A proportion of service users entering specialist treatment are involved with the criminal justice system and some may be entering treatment as a condition of a court order. Therefore, appropriate liaison with criminal justice services is essential for this group.

People who are alcohol dependent are often unable to take care of their health during drinking periods and are at high risk of developing a wide range of health problems because of their drinking (Rehm *et al.*, 2003). Treatment staff therefore need to be able to identify and assess physical health consequences of alcohol use, and refer patients to appropriate medical services.

In the later stages of treatment, the focus will be more on reintegration into society and restoration of normal function, including establishing a healthy lifestyle, finding stable housing, re-entering employment, re-establishing contact with their families, and forming appropriate and fulfilling relationships (National Treatment Agency for Substance Misuse, 2006). All of these factors are important in promoting longer term stable recovery.

2.9   CURRENT CARE IN THE NATIONAL HEALTH SERVICE

A recent alcohol needs assessment in England identified nearly 700 agencies providing specialist alcohol treatment, with an estimated workforce of 4,250 and an annual spend of between £186 million and £217 million (Drummond *et al.*, 2005; National Audit Office, 2008). The majority of agencies (70%) were community based and the remainder were residential, including inpatient units in the NHS, and residential rehabilitation programmes mainly provided by the non-statutory or private sector. Overall, approximately half of all alcohol services are provided by the non-statutory sector but are typically funded by the NHS or local authorities. Approximately one third of specialist alcohol services exclusively provide treatment for people with alcohol problems, but the majority (58%) provide services for both drug and alcohol misuse.

In terms of services provided by community specialist agencies, the majority (63%) provide structured psychological interventions either on an individual basis or as part of a structured community programme (Drummond *et al.*, 2005). There is considerable variation in the availability and access to specialist alcohol services both in community settings and in inpatient settings where provision of specialist psychiatric liaison services with responsibility for alcohol misuse is also very variable. Only 30% provide some form of assisted alcohol-withdrawal programme, and less than 20% provide medications for relapse prevention. Of the residential programmes, 45% provide inpatient medically-assisted alcohol withdrawal and 60% provide residential rehabilitation with some overlap between the two treatment modalities. The alcohol withdrawal programmes are typically of 2 to 3 weeks duration and the rehabilitation programmes are typically of 3 to 6 months duration.

It is estimated that approximately 63,000 people entered specialist treatment for alcohol-use disorders in 2003–04 (Drummond *et al.*, 2005). The recently established National Alcohol Treatment Monitoring System (NATMS) reported 104,000 people entering 1,464 agencies in 2008–09, of whom 70,000 were new presentations (National Treatment Agency, 2009a). However, it is not possible to identify what proportion of services is being provided by primary care under the enhanced care provision as opposed to specialist alcohol agencies.

The 2004 ANARP found that only one out of 18 people who were alcohol dependent in the general population accessed treatment per annum. Access varied considerably from one in 12 in the North West to one in 102 in the North East of England (Drummond *et al.*, 2005).

Although not directly comparable because of different methodology, a low level of access to treatment is regarded as one in ten (Rush, 1990). A recent Scottish national alcohol needs-assessment using the same methods as ANARP found treatment access to be higher than in England, with one in 12 accessing treatment per annum. This level of access may have improved in England since 2004 based on the NATMS data. However, the National Audit Office (2008) reported that the spending on specialist alcohol services by Primary Care Trusts was not based on a clear understanding of the level of need in different parts of England. There is therefore some further progress needed to make alcohol treatment accessible throughout England.

2.10   SERVICE USER ORGANISATIONS

There are several organisations available in England to provide mutual aid for service users and their families. The largest and longest established such organisation is Alcoholics Anonymous. Founded in the US in the 1930s, AA is based on a '12-step' programme, and the '12 traditions' of AA. The programme includes acceptance that one is powerless over alcohol, acceptance of the role of a higher power and the role of the support of other members. AA is self-financing and the seventh tradition is that AA groups should decline outside contributions. In 2010, AA membership worldwide was reported as nearly 2 million (Alcoholics Anonymous, 2010). While AA might not suit all people who misuse alcohol, its advantages include its wide availability and open access.

Allied to AA are Al-anon and Alateen, jointly known as Al-anon Family Groups. Al-anon uses the same 12 steps as AA with some modifications and is focused on meeting the needs of friends and family members of alcoholics. Again, meetings are widely available and provide helpful support beyond what can be provided by specialist treatment services.

Another organisation developing England is Self-Management and Recovery Training (SMART). Its development is being supported by Alcohol Concern, a leading UK alcohol charity, and the Department of Health. SMART is another mutual aid organisation but is based more on cognitive behavioural principles and provides an alternative or adjunct to AA.[5]

2.11   IMPACT ON FAMILIES

The adverse effects of alcohol dependence on family members are considerable. Marriages where one or both partners have an alcohol problem are twice as likely to end in divorce as those in which alcohol is not a problem. Nearly a million children live with one or more parents who misuse alcohol and 6% of adults report having grown up in such a family. Alcohol is implicated in a high proportion of cases of child neglect and abuse, and heavy drinking was identified as a factor in 50% of child protection cases (Orford *et al.*, 2005).

Partners of people with harmful alcohol use and dependence experience higher rates of domestic violence than where alcohol misuse is not a feature. Some 70% of men who assault their partners do so under the influence of alcohol (Murphy *et al*, 2005). Family members of people who are alcohol dependent have high rates of psychiatric morbidity, and growing up with someone who misuses alcohol increases the likelihood of teenagers taking up alcohol early and developing alcohol problems themselves (Latendresse *et al.*, 2010).

All of this points to the importance of addressing the needs of family members of people who misuse alcohol. This includes the need for specialist treatment services to assess the impact of the individual's drinking on family members and the need to ensure the safety of children living with people who misuse alcohol.

---

[5]See www.smartrecovery.org.

2.12   SPECIAL POPULATIONS

There are several special populations which require separate consideration because they have particular needs that are often not well met by mainstream services, or require particular considerations in commissioning or delivering care, or who require modification of general treatment guidelines. This section provides an overview of the issues for each special population. Specific guidance applying to special populations will be referred to in the appropriate section in subsequent chapters.

2.12.1   Children and young people

While drinking and alcohol-use disorders are relatively rare under the age of 10 years, the prevalence increases steeply from the teens to peak in the early 20s. The UK has the highest rate of underage drinking in Western Europe (Hibell *et al.*, 2009). This is of particular concern because alcohol presents particularly serious consequences in young people due to a higher level of vulnerability to the adverse effects of alcohol. Heavy drinking in adolescence can affect brain development and has a higher risk of organ damage in the developing body (Brown *et al.*, 2008).

The number of adolescents consuming alcohol has shown a reduction from 60 to 65% between 1988 and 1998 to 54% in 2007, but the amount consumed by those drinking doubled over the same period to 12.7 units per week (Fuller, 2008). Regular alcohol consumption in adolescence is associated with increased accidents, risky behaviour (including unprotected sex, antisocial behaviour and violence) and decreased family, social and educational functioning. There is evidence of an association between hazardous alcohol consumption in adolescence and increased level of alcohol dependence in early and later adulthood (Hingson *et al.*, 2006). For example, alcohol consumption before the age of 13 years is associated with a four-fold increased risk of alcohol dependence in adulthood. Adolescents with early signs of alcohol misuse who are not seeking treatment are a critical group to target interventions towards. Adolescent alcohol-related attendances at accident and emergency departments saw a tenfold increase in the UK since 1990 and a recent audit estimates that 65,000 alcohol-related adolescent attendances occur annually.

Comorbid psychiatric disorders are considered to be 'the rule, not the exception' for young people with alcohol-use disorders (Perepletchikova *et al.*, 2008). Data from the US National Comorbidity study demonstrated that the majority of lifetime disorders in their sample were comorbid disorders (Kessler *et al.*, 1996). This common occurrence of alcohol-use disorders and other substance-use disorders along with other psychiatric disorders notes the importance of a comprehensive assessment and management of all disorders. Disruptive behaviour disorders are the most common comorbid psychiatric disorders among young people with substance-use disorders. Those with conduct disorder and substance-use disorders are more difficult to treat, have a higher treatment dropout rate and have a worse prognosis. This strong association between conduct disorder and substance-use disorders is considered to be reciprocal, with each exacerbating the expression of the other. Conduct disorder usually precedes or coincides with the onset of substance-use disorders, with conduct disorder severity found to predict substance-use severity. Significantly higher rates of attention deficit hyperactivity disorder (ADHD) have been reported in young people with substance-use disorders; data from untreated adults with ADHD indicate a higher risk of developing substance-use disorders and at an earlier age compared with treated controls as well as a more prolonged course of substance-use disorders. However, those young people with ADHD and co-occurring conduct or bipolar disorders are at highest risk of development of substance-use disorders.

High rates of depression and anxiety have been reported in adolescents with alcohol-use disorders, with increased rates of suicidality. Among clinical populations for alcohol-use disorders there was an increased rate of anxiety symptoms and disorder, PTSD and social phobias (Clark *et al.*, 1997a and 1997b). For young people the presentation may be different because dependence is not common, with binge drinking being the pattern seen more often, frequently alongside polydrug use. Criminality and offending behaviour are often closely related to alcohol misuse in children and adolescents. Liaison with criminal justice services is necessary to ensure that appropriate co-ordination of care and effective communication and information-sharing protocols are in place.

In addition to the problems presented by comorbid disorders, the concept of dependence and criteria for diagnosis (DSM–IV or ICD–10) has limitations when applied to adolescents because of the low prevalence of withdrawal symptoms and the low specificity of tolerance in this age group (Chung *et al.*, 2001). The adolescent therefore may continue drinking despite problems, which manifest as difficulties with school attendance, co-morbid behavioural difficulties, peer affiliation and arguments at home.

As has been noted previously, relationships with parents, carers and the children in their care are often damaged by alcohol misuse (Copello *et al.*, 2005). The prevalence of alcohol-use disorders in the victims and perpetrators of domestic violence provides an important rationale for the exploration of these issues. Sexual abuse has been found to be prevalent in alcohol dependent drinkers seeking treatment and may be a particular concern with young people with alcohol misuse problems (Moncrieff *et al.*, 1996). For young people, both their own alcohol misuse and that of their parents or carers may be a safeguarding concern. The Children Act 2004 places a statutory duty on services providing assessments to make arrangements to ensure that their functions are discharged with regard to the need to safeguard and promote the welfare of children. Services that are involved with those who misuse alcohol fit into a wider context of safeguarding young people from harm and need to work to ensure that the rights of children, young people and their parents are respected. Local protocols between alcohol treatment services and local safeguarding and family services determine the specific actions to be taken (Department for Children, Schools and Families, National Treatment Agency & Department of Health, 2009).

2.12.2   Current service provision for children and young people

In the UK, most treatment is community based and provided as part of a range of services and models. These can be services provided by child and adolescent mental health services (CAMHS) in Tier 2 and Tier 3 services, specific CAMHS addiction services and other commissioned specialist services that are formed by a range of practitioners (generally Tier 2 and Tier 3 collaborating from the youth offending teams, looked-after teams and voluntary sector). Much of the focus is on engagement, health promotion and retention in services. In addition, in the UK, services that offer treatment tend to prioritise drug misuse such as opiate or cannabis misuse and not alcohol. Given the comorbidity noted above, many adolescents having treatment for alcohol-use disorders are often seen in specialist services, such as Youth Offending Teams, or specialist services for young people with conduct disorders, such as the newly-developed multisystemic therapy teams (Department of Health, 2007), although identification and treatment of their dependence and/or harmful use may not be fully explored. In the US, adolescents with substance-use disorders receive treatment in a variety of settings including community, residential and criminal justice settings, and home-based treatment. However, there is little research evaluating the differences between these settings. As a consequence there is little clear evidence to determine the most appropriate treatment environments. The American Academy of Child and Adolescent Psychiatry (2005) recommend that factors affecting the choice of setting should include: the need to provide a safe environment; motivation of the adolescent and his/her family to cooperate with treatment; the need for structure and limit-setting; the presence of additional medical or psychiatric conditions and the associated risks; the availability of specific types of treatment settings for adolescents; preferences for treatment in a particular setting; and treatment failure in a less restrictive/intensive setting in the past.

2.12.3   Older people

The prevalence of alcohol-use disorders declines with increasing age, but the rate of detection by health professionals may be underestimated in older people because of a lack of clinical suspicion or misdiagnosis (O'Connell *et al.*, 2003). Nevertheless, the proportion of older people drinking above the government's recommended levels has recently been increasing in the UK. The proportion of men aged 65 to 74 years who drank more than four units per day in the past week increased from 18 to 30% between 1998 and 2008 (Fuller *et al.*, 2009). In women of the same age, the increase in drinking more than three units per day was from 6 to 14%. Also, as noted earlier, alcohol-related admissions to hospital increase steeply with age although the prevalence of heavy drinking is lower in this group. This may partly reflect the cumulative effects of lifetime alcohol consumption as well as the general increasing risk of hospital admission with advancing age.

Further, it is important to note that due to age-related changes in metabolism, intercurrent ill health, changing life circumstances and interactions with medications, sensible drinking guidelines for younger adults may not be applicable to older people (Reid & Anderson, 1997). Equivalent levels of alcohol consumption will give rise to a higher blood alcohol concentration in older people compared with younger people (Reid & Anderson, 1997). The US National Institute of Alcohol Abuse and Alcoholism (NIAAA) has therefore recommended people over the age of 65 years should drink no more than one drink (1.5 UK units) per day and no more than seven drinks (10.5 UK units) per week. There are no similar recommendations for older people in the UK. A related issue is that standard alcohol screening tools such as the AUDIT may require a lower threshold to be applied in older people (O'Connell *et al.*, 2003).

Older people are at least as likely as younger people to benefit from alcohol treatment (Curtis *et al.*, 1989). Clinicians therefore need to be vigilant to identify and treat older people who misuse alcohol. As older people are more likely to have comorbid physical and mental health problems and be socially isolated, a lower threshold for admission for assisted alcohol withdrawal may be required (Dar, 2006). Further, in view of changes in metabolism, potential drug interactions and physical comorbidity, dosages for medications to treat alcohol withdrawal and prevent relapse may need to be reduced in older people (Dar, 2006). These issues are dealt with in more detail in the relevant chapters.

2.12.4 Homeless people

There is a high prevalence of alcohol misuse (as well as mental and physical health, and social problems) amongst people who are homeless. The prevalence of alcohol-use disorders in this population has been reported to be between 38 and 50% in the UK (Gill *et al.*, 1996; Harrison & Luck, 1997). In the US, studies of this population typically report prevalence rates of 20 to 45%, depending on sampling methods and definitions (Institute of Medicine, 1988).

Homeless people who misuse alcohol have particular difficulties in engaging mainstream alcohol services, often due to difficulties in attending planned appointments.

Homelessness is associated with a poorer clinical outcome, although this may also be due to the higher levels of comorbidity and social isolation in this population rather than the homelessness *per se*. Hence services need to be tailored to maximise engagement with this population.

This has led to the development of specific alcohol services for homeless drinkers, including assertive outreach and 'wet' hostels. In wet hostels, residents are able to continue drinking, but do so in an environment that aims to minimise the harm associated with drinking and address other issues including homelessness (Institute of Medicine, 1988; Harrison & Luck, 1997). Such hostels tend to be located in urban centres where there is a higher concentration of homeless drinkers. Assertive outreach and 'crisis' centres have been developed to attract homeless people who misuse alcohol into treatment (Freimanis, 1993). Further, a lower threshold for admission for assisted alcohol withdrawal and residential rehabilitation will often be required with this population.

2.12.5 People from ethnic minority groups

It is often asserted that people from ethnic minority groups are under-represented in specialist alcohol treatment services (Harrison & Luck, 1997). The reality is that the situation is likely to be more complex and depends on which specific ethnic group and the prevalence of alcohol misuse in that group (Drummond, 2009). Based on the Psychiatric Morbidity Survey, the ANARP study found that people from ethnic minority groups as a whole had a lower prevalence of hazardous and harmful drinking compared with the white population (ratio of 1:1.7) whereas alcohol dependence was approximately equal in prevalence (ratio of 1:1.1) (Drummond *et al.*, 2005). However this study was unable to compare different ethnic minority groups. Nevertheless, because people from ethnic minority groups have approximately the same prevalence of alcohol dependence as the white population, if access to treatment is equal one would expect the population in treatment to have approximately the same proportion of people for ethnic minorities. The ethnic minority population in England was 13% in the 2001 census. The NATMS found that in 2008–09 the proportion of people from ethnic minorities with alcohol dependence is 9%, suggesting some under-representation (National Treatment Agency and Department of Health, 2010). However, it is not clear what proportion of NATMS attenders were hazardous/harmful or dependent drinkers, which may account for the difference in proportions.

Adelstein and colleagues (1984) found that cirrhosis mortality rates are higher than the national average for men from the Asian subcontinent and Ireland, but lower than average for men of African–Caribbean origin. Cirrhosis mortality was lower in Asian and African–Caribbean women but higher in Irish women. However, because there were few total deaths in ethnic minority groups this may lead to large errors in estimating prevalence in this population. Studies in England have tended to find over-representation of Indian-, Scottish- and Irish-born people and under-representation in those of African–Caribbean or Pakistani origin (Harrison & Luck, 1997). This may partly be due to differences in prevalence rates of alcohol misuse, but differences in culturally-related beliefs and help-seeking as well as availability of interpreters or treatment personnel from appropriate ethnic minority groups may also account for some of these differences (Drummond, 2009). There are relatively few specific specialist alcohol services for people from ethnic minority groups, although some examples of good practice exist (Harrison & Luck, 1997).

2.12.6   Women

Thom and Green (1996) identified three main factors that may account for a historical under-representation of women in specialist alcohol services. Women tend to perceive their problems differently from men, with a greater tendency not to identify themselves as 'alcoholic'. They are more likely to experience stigma in relation to their drinking than men and have concerns about their children being taken into care. Also, women regard the services as less suited to their needs than men do. Few services tend to provide childcare facilities or women-only services. Nevertheless, more women are now accessing treatment. The ANARP study found that, taking account of the lower prevalence of alcohol dependence in women compared with men (ratio of 1:3), they were 1.6 times more likely to access treatment (Drummond *et al.*, 2005). Women are also more likely to seek help for alcohol misuse than men in the US (Schuckit, 2009). This may indicate that some of the barriers identified by Thom and Green (1996) may have been overcome. However, services need to be sensitive to the particular needs of women. There is also a need to develop services for pregnant women. This is the subject of a separate NICE guideline on complex pregnancies (NICE, 2010c).

2.13   ECONOMIC IMPACT

Alcohol misuse and the related problems present a considerable cost to society. Estimates of the economic costs attempt to assess in monetary terms the damage that results from the misuse of alcohol. These costs include expenditures on alcohol-related problems and opportunities that are lost because of alcohol (NIAAA, 1991).

Many challenges exist in estimating the costs required for cost-of-illness studies in health; there are two such challenges that are particularly relevant to alcohol misuse. First, researchers attempt to identify costs that are caused by and not merely associated with alcohol misuse, yet it is often hard to establish causation (Cook, 1990; NIAAA, 1991). Second, many costs resulting from alcohol misuse cannot be measured directly. This is especially true of costs that involve placing a value on lost productivity. Researchers use mathematical and statistical methods to estimate such costs, yet recognise that this is imprecise. Moreover, costs of pain and suffering of both people who misuse alcohol and people affected by them cannot be estimated in a reliable way, and are therefore not considered in most cost studies. These challenges highlight the fact that although the economic cost of alcohol misuse can be estimated, it cannot be measured precisely. Nevertheless, estimates of the cost provide an idea of the dimensions of the problem and the breakdown of costs suggests which categories are most costly (NIAAA, 1991).

The first category of costs is that of treating the medical consequences of alcohol misuse and treating alcohol misuse. The second category of health-related costs includes losses in productivity by workers who misuse alcohol. The third category of health-related costs is the loss to society because of premature deaths due to alcohol misuse. In addition to the health-related costs of alcohol misuse are costs involving the criminal justice system, social care, property losses from alcohol-related motor vehicle crashes and fires, and lost productivity of the victims of alcohol-related crime and individuals imprisoned as a consequence of alcohol-related crime (NIAAA, 1991).

The UK Cabinet Office recently estimated that the cost of alcohol to society was £25.1 billion per annum (Department of Health, 2007). A recent report by the Department of Health estimated an annual cost of £2.7 billion attributable to alcohol harm to the NHS in England (Department of Health, 2008a). Hospital inpatient and day visits accounted for 44% of these total costs, whilst accident and emergency department visits and ambulance services accounted for 38%. However, crime and disorder costs amount to £7.3 billion per annum, including costs for policing, drink driving, courts and the criminal justice system, and costs to services both in anticipation and in dealing with the consequences of alcohol-related crime (Prime Minister's Strategy Unit, 2003). The estimated costs in the workplace amount to some £6.4 billion through lost productivity, absenteeism, alcohol-related sickness and premature deaths (Prime Minister's Strategy Unit, 2003).

For the European Union, the US and Canada, social costs of alcohol were estimated to be around €270 billion (2003 prices; Anderson and Baumberg, 2005), US$185 billion (1998 prices; WHO, 2004), and CA$14.6 billion (2002 prices; Rehm *et al.*, 2006), respectively.

3   METHODS USED TO DEVELOP THIS GUIDELINE

3.1   OVERVIEW

The development of this guideline drew upon methods outlined by NICE (further information is available in *The Guidelines Manual*; NICE, 2009a). A team of health professionals, lay representatives and technical experts known as the Guideline Development Group (GDG), with support from the NCCMH staff, undertook the development of a patient-centred, evidence-based guideline. There are six basic steps in the process of developing a guideline:

- Define the scope, which sets the parameters of the guideline and provides a focus and steer for the development work.
- Define review questions considered important for practitioners and service users.
- Develop criteria for evidence searching and search for evidence.
- Design validated protocols for systematic review and apply to evidence recovered by search.
- Synthesise and (meta-) analyse data retrieved, guided by the review questions, and produce Grading of Recommendations: Assessment, Development and Evaluation (GRADE) evidence profiles and summaries.
- Answer review questions with evidence-based recommendations for clinical practice.

The clinical practice recommendations made by the GDG are therefore derived from the most up-to-date and robust evidence base for the clinical and cost effectiveness of the treatments and services used in the treatment and management of alcohol dependence and harmful alcohol use. In addition, to ensure a service user and carer focus, the concerns of service users and carers regarding health and social care have been highlighted and addressed by recommendations agreed by the whole GDG.

3.2   THE SCOPE

Guideline topics are selected by the Department of Health and the Welsh Assembly Government, which identify the main areas to be covered by the guideline in a specific remit (see *The Guidelines Manual* [NICE, 2009a] for further information). The NCCMH developed a scope for the guideline based on the remit. The purpose of the scope is to:

- provide an overview of what the guideline will include and exclude
- identify the key aspects of care that must be included
- set the boundaries of the development work and provide a clear framework to enable work to stay within the priorities agreed by NICE and the National Collaborating Centre, and the remit from the Department of Health/Welsh Assembly Government

- inform the development of the review questions and search strategy
- inform professionals and the public about expected content of the guideline
- keep the guideline to a reasonable size to ensure that its development can be carried out within the allocated period.

An initial draft of the scope was sent to registered stakeholders who had agreed to attend a scoping workshop. The workshop was used to:

- obtain feedback on the selected key clinical issues
- identify which patient or population subgroups should be specified (if any)
- seek views on the composition of the GDG
- encourage applications for GDG membership.

The draft scope was subject to consultation with registered stakeholders over a 4-week period. During the consultation period, the scope was posted on the NICE website (www.nice.org.uk). Comments were invited from stakeholder organisations and the Guideline Review Panel (GRP). Further information about the GRP can also be found on the NICE website. The NCCMH and NICE reviewed the scope in light of comments received, and the revised scope was signed off by the GRP.

3.3 THE GUIDELINE DEVELOPMENT GROUP

The GDG consisted of: professionals in psychiatry, clinical psychology, nursing, social work, and general practice; academic experts in psychiatry and psychology; and service user, lay member and carer representatives. The guideline development process was supported by staff from the NCCMH, who undertook the clinical and health economic literature searches, reviewed and presented the evidence to the GDG, managed the process and contributed to drafting the guideline.

3.3.1 Guideline Development Group meetings

Twelve GDG meetings were held between March 2009 and September 2010. During each day-long GDG meeting, in a plenary session, review questions and clinical and economic evidence were reviewed and assessed, and recommendations formulated. At each meeting, all GDG members declared any potential conflicts of interest, and service user and carer concerns were routinely discussed as part of a standing agenda.

3.3.2 Topic groups

The GDG divided its workload along clinically relevant lines to simplify the guideline development process, and GDG members formed smaller topic groups to undertake guideline work in that area of clinical practice. Topic group membership was decided after a discussion between all GDG members, and each topic group was chaired by a GDG member with expert knowledge of the topic area (one of the healthcare professionals). Topic Group 1 covered questions relating to pharmacological intervention. Topic Group 2 covered psychological and psychosocial interventions. Topic Group 3 covered assessment of alcohol misuse, Topic Group 4 covered service user and carer experiences of care, and Topic Group 5 covered delivery settings for treatment. These groups were designed to efficiently manage the large volume of evidence appraisal prior to presenting it to the GDG as a whole. Topic groups refined the review questions and the clinical definitions of treatment interventions, reviewed and prepared the evidence with the systematic reviewer before presenting it to the GDG as a whole, and helped the GDG to identify further expertise in the topic. Topic group leaders reported the status of the group's work as part of the standing agenda. They also introduced and led the GDG discussion of the evidence review for that topic and assisted the GDG Chair in drafting the section of the guideline relevant to the work of each topic group. All statements and recommendations in this guideline have been agreed by the whole GDG.

3.3.3 Service users and carers

Individuals with direct experience of services gave an integral service-user focus to the GDG and the guideline. The GDG included service user, carer and lay member representatives who contributed as full GDG members to writing the review questions, helping to ensure that the evidence addressed their views and preferences, highlighting sensitive issues and terminology relevant to the guideline, and bringing service-user research to the attention of the GDG. In drafting the guideline, they contributed to writing Chapter 4 and identified recommendations from the service user and carer perspective.

3.3.4 Special advisors

Special advisors, who had specific expertise in one or more aspects of treatment and management relevant to the guideline, assisted the GDG, commenting on specific aspects of the developing guideline and making presentations to the GDG. Appendix 3 lists those who agreed to act as special advisors.

3.3.5 National and international experts

National and international experts in the area under review were identified through the literature search and through the experience of the GDG members. These experts were contacted to recommend unpublished or soon-to-be published studies to ensure that up-to-date evidence was included in the development of the guideline. They informed the group about completed trials at the pre-publication stage, systematic reviews in the process of being published, studies relating to the cost effectiveness of treatment, and trial data if the GDG could be provided with full access to the complete trial report. Appendix 6 lists researchers who were contacted.

3.3.6 Integration of other guidelines on alcohol-use disorders

In addition to this guideline, there are two other pieces of NICE guidance addressing alcohol-use disorders outlined in Chapter 1. During development, steering group meetings were held in which representatives from the three development groups met to discuss any issues, such as overlapping areas of review work and integration of the guidelines.

3.4 REVIEW QUESTIONS

Review (clinical) questions were used to guide the identification and interrogation of the evidence base relevant to the topic of the guideline. The draft review questions were discussed by the GDG at the first few meetings and amended as necessary. Where appropriate, the questions were refined once the evidence had been searched and, where necessary, subquestions were generated. Questions submitted by stake-holders were also discussed by the GDG and the rationale for not including any questions was recorded in the minutes. The final list of review questions can be found in Appendix 7.

For questions about interventions, the Patient, Intervention, Comparison and Outcome (PICO) framework was used (see Table 2).

Questions relating to assessment and diagnosis do not involve an intervention designed to treat a particular condition, therefore the PICO framework was not used. Rather, the questions were designed to identify key issues specifically relevant to diagnostic tests, for example their accuracy, reliability and safety.

Table 2: Features of a well-formulated question on effectiveness intervention – the PICO guide

Patients/population	Which patients or population of patients are we interested in? How can they be best described? Are there subgroups that need to be considered?
Intervention	Which intervention, treatment or approach should be used?
Comparison	What is/are the main alternative/s to compare with the intervention?
Outcome	What is really important for the patient? Which outcomes should be considered: intermediate or short-term measures; mortality; morbidity and treatment complications; rates of relapse; late morbidity and readmission; return to work, physical and social functioning and other measures such as quality of life; general health status?

In some situations, the prognosis of a particular condition is of fundamental importance, over and above its general significance in relation to specific interventions. Areas where this is particularly likely to occur relate to assessment of risk, for example in terms of behaviour modification or screening and early intervention. In addition, review questions related to issues of service delivery are occasionally specified in the remit from the Department of Health/Welsh Assembly Government. In these cases, appropriate review questions were developed to be clear and concise.

To help facilitate the literature review, a note was made of the best study design type to answer each question. There are four main types of review question of relevance to NICE guidelines. These are listed in Table 3. For each type of question the best primary study design varies, where 'best' is interpreted as 'least likely to give misleading answers to the question'.

However, in all cases a well-conducted systematic review (of the appropriate type of study) is likely to yield a better answer than a single study.

Deciding on the best design type to answer a specific review question does not mean that studies of different design types addressing the same question were discarded.

The GDG classified each review question into one of three groups: (1) questions concerning good practice; (2) questions likely to have little or no directly relevant evidence; and (3) questions likely to have a good evidence base. Questions concerning good practice were answered by the GDG using informal consensus. For questions that were unlikely to have a good evidence base, a brief descriptive review was initially undertaken and then the GDG used informal consensus to reach a decision (see Section 3.5.7). For questions with a good evidence base, the review process followed the methods outlined in Section 3.5.1.

Table 3: Best study design to answer each type of question

Type of question	Best primary study design
Effectiveness or other impact of an intervention	Randomised controlled trial (RCT); other studies that may be considered in the absence of RCTs are the following: internally/externally controlled before-and-after trial, interrupted time-series
Accuracy of information (for example, risk factor, test, prediction rule)	Comparing the information against a valid gold standard in a randomised trial or inception cohort study
Rates (of disease, patient experience, rare side effects)	Prospective cohort, registry, cross-sectional study

3.5 CLINICAL EVIDENCE METHODS

The aim of the clinical evidence review was to systematically identify and synthesise relevant evidence from the literature to answer the specific review questions developed by the GDG. Thus, clinical practice recommendations are evidence-based where possible and, if evidence is not available, informal consensus methods are used (see Section 3.5.7) and the need for future research is specified.

3.5.1 The search process

Scoping searches
A broad preliminary search of the literature was undertaken in September 2008 to obtain an overview of the issues likely to be covered by the scope and to help define key areas. Searches were restricted to clinical guidelines, health technology assessment (HTA) reports, key systematic reviews and RCTs, and conducted in the following databases and websites:

- British Medical Journal Clinical Evidence
- Canadian Medical Association (CMA) Infobase (Canadian guidelines)
- Clinical Policy and Practice Program of the New South Wales Department of Health (Australia)
- Clinical Practice Guidelines (Australian Guidelines)
- Cochrane Central Register of Controlled Trials (CENTRAL)
- Cochrane Database of Abstracts of Reviews of Effects (DARE)
- Cochrane Database of Systematic Reviews (CDSR)
- Excerpta Medica Database (EMBASE)
- Guidelines International Network (G-I-N)
- Health Evidence Bulletin Wales
- Health Management Information Consortium (HMIC)
- HTA database (technology assessments)
- Medical Literature Analysis and Retrieval System Online (MEDLINE)/MEDLINE in Process
- National Health and Medical Research Council (NHMRC)
- National Library for Health (NLH) Guidelines Finder
- New Zealand Guidelines Group
- NHS Centre for Reviews and Dissemination (CRD)
- OmniMedicalSearch
- Scottish Intercollegiate Guidelines Network (SIGN)
- Turning Research Into Practice (TRIP)
- US Agency for Healthcare Research and Quality (AHRQ)
- Websites of NICE and the National Institute for Health Research (NIHR) HTA Programme for guidelines and HTAs in development.

Existing NICE guidelines were updated where necessary. Other relevant guidelines were assessed for quality using the AGREE instrument (AGREE Collaboration, 2003). The evidence base underlying high-quality existing guidelines was utilised and updated as appropriate. Further information about this process can be found in *The Guidelines Manual* (NICE, 2009a).

Systematic literature searches

After the scope was finalised, a systematic search strategy was developed to locate all the relevant evidence. The balance between sensitivity (the power to identify all studies on a particular topic) and specificity (the ability to exclude irrelevant studies from the results) was carefully considered, and a decision made to utilise a broad approach to searching, to maximise the retrieval of evidence to all parts of the guideline. Searches were restricted to: systematic reviews, meta-analyses, RCTs, observational studies, quasi-experimental studies and qualitative research. Searches were conducted in the following databases:

- Allied and Complementary Medicine Database (AMED)
- Cumulative Index to Nursing and Allied Health Literature (CINAHL)
- EMBASE
- MEDLINE/MEDLINE In-Process
- Psychological Information Database (PsycINFO)
- DARE
- CDSR
- CENTRAL
- HTA database.

For standard mainstream bibliographic databases (AMED, CINAHL, EMBASE, MEDLINE and PsycINFO), search terms for alcohol dependence and harmful alcohol use were combined with study design filters for systematic reviews, RCTs and qualitative research. For searches generated in databases with collections of study designs at their focus (DARE, CDSR, CENTRAL and HTA), search terms for alcohol dependence and harmful alcohol use were used without a filter. The sensitivity of this approach was aimed at minimising the risk of overlooking relevant publications, due to inaccurate or incomplete indexing of records, as well as potential weaknesses resulting from more focused search strategies (for example, for interventions).

For focused searches, terms for case management and assertive community treatment (ACT) were combined with terms for alcohol dependence and harmful alcohol use, and filters for observational and quasi-experimental studies.

Reference manager

Citations from each search were downloaded into Reference Manager (a software product for managing references and formatting bibliographies) and duplicates removed. Records were then screened against the inclusion criteria of the reviews before being quality appraised (see Section 3.5.2). To keep the process both replicable and transparent, the unfiltered search results were saved and retained for future potential re-analysis.

Search filters

The search filters for systematic reviews and RCTs are adaptations of filters designed by the CRD and the Health Information Research Unit of McMaster University,

Ontario. The qualitative, observational and quasi-experimental filters were developed in-house. Each filter comprised index terms relating to the study type(s) and associated text words for the methodological description of the design(s).

Date and language restrictions

Date restrictions were not applied, except for searches of systematic reviews, which were limited to research published from 1993 onwards. Systematic database searches were initially conducted in June 2008 up to the most recent searchable date. Search updates were generated on a 6-monthly basis, with the final re-runs carried out in March 2010 ahead of the guideline consultation. After this point, studies were only included if they were judged by the GDG to be exceptional (for example, if the evidence was likely to change a recommendation).

Post-guideline searching: following the draft guideline consultation, searches for observational and quasi-experimental studies were conducted for case management and ACT.

Although no language restrictions were applied at the searching stage, foreign language papers were not requested or reviewed unless they were of particular importance to a review question.

Other search methods

Other search methods involved: (1) scanning the reference lists of all eligible publications (systematic reviews, stakeholder evidence and included studies) for more published reports and citations of unpublished research; (2) sending lists of studies meeting the inclusion criteria to subject experts (identified through searches and the GDG) and asking them to check the lists for completeness, and to provide information of any published or unpublished research for consideration (see Appendix 3); (3) checking the tables of contents of key journals for studies that might have been missed by the database and reference list searches; (4) tracking key papers in the Science Citation Index (prospectively) over time for further useful references.

Full details of the search strategies and filters used for the systematic review of clinical evidence are provided in Appendix 9.

Study selection and quality assessment

All primary-level studies included after the first scan of citations were acquired in full and re-evaluated for eligibility at the time when they were being entered into the study information database. More specific eligibility criteria were developed for each review question and are described in the relevant clinical evidence chapters. Eligible systematic reviews and primary-level studies were critically appraised for methodological quality (see Appendix 11 for methodology checklists). The eligibility of each study was confirmed by at least one member of the appropriate topic group.

For some review questions, it was necessary to prioritise the evidence with respect to the UK context (that is, external validity). To make this process explicit, the topic groups took into account the following factors when assessing the evidence:

- participant factors (for example, gender, age and ethnicity)
- provider factors (for example, model fidelity, the conditions under which the intervention was performed and the availability of experienced staff to undertake the procedure)
- cultural factors (for example, differences in standard care and the welfare system).

It was the responsibility of each topic group to decide which prioritisation factors were relevant to each review question in light of the UK context. Any issues and discussions within topic groups were brought back to the wider GDG for further consideration.

Unpublished evidence
The GDG used a number of criteria when deciding whether or not to accept unpublished data. First, the evidence must have been accompanied by a trial report containing sufficient detail to properly assess the quality of the data. Second, the evidence must have been submitted with the understanding that data from the study and a summary of the study's characteristics would be published in the full guideline. Therefore, the GDG did not accept evidence submitted as commercial in confidence. However, the GDG recognised that unpublished evidence submitted by investigators might later be retracted by those investigators if the inclusion of such data would jeopardise publication of their research.

3.5.2   Data extraction

Study characteristics and outcome data were extracted from all eligible studies that met the minimum quality criteria using a Microsoft Word-based form (see Appendix 11).

In most circumstances, for a given outcome (continuous and dichotomous), where more than 50% of the number randomised to any group were lost to follow-up, the data were excluded from the analysis (except for the outcome 'leaving the study early', in which case the denominator was the number randomised). Where possible, dichotomous efficacy outcomes were calculated on an intention-to-treat basis (that is, a 'once-randomised-always-analyse' basis). Where there was good evidence that those participants who ceased to engage in the study were likely to have an unfavourable outcome, early withdrawals were included in both the numerator and denominator. Adverse effects were entered into Review Manager, as reported by the study authors, because it is usually not possible to determine whether early withdrawals have had an unfavourable outcome. Where there was limited data for a particular review, the 50% rule was not applied. In these circumstances the evidence was downgraded due to the risk of bias.

Where some of the studies failed to report standard deviations (for a continuous outcome) and where an estimate of the variance could not be computed from other reported data or obtained from the study author, the following approach was taken.[6]

---

[6]Based on the approach suggested by Furukawa and colleagues (2006).

When the number of studies with missing standard deviations was less than one third and when the total number of studies was at least ten, the pooled standard deviation was imputed (calculated from all the other studies in the same meta-analysis that used the same version of the outcome measure). In this case, the appropriateness of the imputation was made by comparing the standardised mean differences (SMDs) of those trials that had reported standard deviations against the hypothetical SMDs of the same trials based on the imputed standard deviations. If they converged, the meta-analytical results were considered to be reliable.

When the conditions above could not be met, standard deviations were taken from another related systematic review (if available). In this case, the results were considered to be less reliable.

The meta-analysis of survival data, such as time to any drinking episode, was based on log hazard ratios and standard errors. Since individual patient data were not available in included studies, hazard ratios and standard errors calculated from a Cox proportional hazard model were extracted. Where necessary, standard errors were calculated from confidence intervals (CIs) or p-value according to standard formulae (see *Cochrane Handbook for Systematic Reviews of Interventions*, 5.0.2, Higgins *et al.*, 2009). Data were summarised using the generic inverse variance method, using Review Manager.

Consultation with another reviewer or members of the GDG was used to overcome difficulties with coding. Data from studies included in existing systematic reviews were extracted independently by one reviewer and cross-checked with the existing data set. Where possible, two independent reviewers extracted data from new studies. Where double data extraction was not possible, data extracted by one reviewer was checked by the second reviewer. Disagreements were resolved through discussion. Where consensus could not be reached, a third reviewer or GDG members resolved the disagreement. Masked assessment (that is, blind to the journal from which the article comes, the authors, the institution and the magnitude of the effect) was not used since it is unclear that doing so reduces bias (Berlin, 2001; Jadad *et al.*, 1996).

3.5.3   Synthesising the evidence

Meta-analysis
Where possible, meta-analysis was used to synthesise the evidence using Review Manager. If necessary, reanalyses of the data or sub-analyses were used to answer review questions not addressed in the original studies or reviews.

Dichotomous outcomes were analysed as relative risks (RR) with the associated 95% CI (for an example, see Figure 1). A relative risk (also called a risk ratio) is the ratio of the treatment event rate to the control event rate. An RR of 1 indicates no difference between treatment and control. In Figure 1, the overall RR of 0.73 indicates that the event rate (that is, non-remission rate) associated with intervention A is about three quarters of that with the control intervention or, in other words, the RR reduction is 27%.

Figure 1: Example of a forest plot displaying dichotomous data

Review: NCCMH clinical guideline review (example)
Comparison: 01 Intervention A compared with a control group
Outcome: 01 Number of people who did not show remission

Study or sub-category	Intervention A n/N	Control n/N	RR (fixed) 95% CI	Weight %	RR (fixed) 95% CI
01 Intervention A versus control					
GRIFFITHS1994	13/23	27/28		38.79	0.59 [0.41, 0.84]
LEE1986	11/15	14/15		22.30	0.79 [0.56, 1.10]
TREASURE1994	21/28	24/27		38.92	0.84 [0.66, 1.09]
Subtotal (95% CI)	45/66	65/70		100.00	0.73 [0.61, 0.88]

Test for heterogeneity: Chi² = 2.83, df = 2 (P = 0.24), I² = 29.3%
Test for overall effect: Z = 3.37 (P = 0.0007)

```
        0.2    0.5    1    2    5
       Favours intervention  Favours control
```

The CI shows a range of values within which we are 95% confident that the true effect will lie. If the effect size has a CI that does not cross the 'line of no effect', then the effect is commonly interpreted as being statistically significant.

Continuous outcomes were analysed using the SMD because different measures were used in different studies to estimate the same underlying effect (for an example see Figure 2). If reported by study authors, intention-to-treat data using a valid method for imputation of missing data were preferred over data only from people who completed the study.

The number needed to treat for benefit (NNTB) or the number needed to treat for harm (NNTH) was reported for each outcome where the baseline risk (that is, the control group event rate) was similar across studies. In addition, numbers needed to treat (NNTs) calculated at follow-up were only reported where the length of follow-up was similar across studies. When the length of follow-up or baseline risk varies (especially with low risk), the NNT is a poor summary of the treatment effect (Deeks, 2002).

Heterogeneity

To check for consistency of effects among studies, both the I^2 statistic and the chi-squared test of heterogeneity as well as a visual inspection of the forest plots were used. The I^2 statistic describes the proportion of total variation in study estimates that is due to heterogeneity (Higgins & Thompson, 2002). The I^2 statistic was interpreted in the following way based on Higgins and Green (2009):

Figure 2: Example of a forest plot displaying continuous data

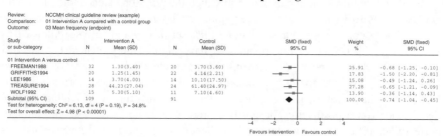

Review: NCCMH clinical guideline review (example)
Comparison: 01 Intervention A compared with a control group
Outcome: 03 Mean frequency (endpoint)

Study or sub-category	N	Intervention A Mean (SD)	N	Control Mean (SD)	SMD (fixed) 95% CI	Weight %	SMD (fixed) 95% CI
01 Intervention A versus control							
FREEMAN1988	32	1.30(3.40)	20	3.70(3.60)		25.91	-0.68 [-1.25, -0.10]
GRIFFITHS1994	20	1.25(1.45)	22	4.14(2.21)		17.83	-1.50 [-2.20, -0.81]
LEE1986	14	3.70(4.00)	14	10.10(17.50)		15.08	-0.49 [-1.24, 0.26]
TREASURE1994	28	44.23(27.04)	24	61.40(24.97)		27.28	-0.65 [-1.21, -0.09]
WOLF1992	15	5.30(5.10)	11	7.10(4.60)		13.90	-0.36 [-1.14, 0.43]
Subtotal (95% CI)	109		91			100.00	-0.74 [-1.04, -0.45]

Test for heterogeneity: Chi² = 6.13, df = 4 (P = 0.19), I² = 34.8%
Test for overall effect: Z = 4.98 (P < 0.00001)

```
       -4    -2    0    2    4
      Favours intervention  Favours control
```

- 0 to 40%: might not be important
- 30 to 60%: may represent moderate heterogeneity
- 50 to 90%: may represent substantial heterogeneity
- 75 to 100%: considerable heterogeneity.

Two factors were used to make a judgement about importance of the observed value of I^2: first, the magnitude and direction of effects, and second, the strength of evidence for heterogeneity (for example, p-value from the chi-squared test, or a CI for I^2).

Publication bias

Where there was sufficient data, we intended to use funnel plots to explore the possibility of publication bias. Asymmetry of the plot would be taken to indicate possible publication bias and investigated further. However, due to a paucity of data, funnel plots could not be used.

Where necessary, an estimate of the proportion of eligible data that were missing (because some studies did not include all relevant outcomes) was calculated for each analysis.

3.5.4 Summary statistics used to evaluate assessment instruments

The main outcomes that need to be extracted from diagnostic accuracy studies are sensitivity, specificity, positive predictive validity and negative predictive validity. These are discussed in detail below. Negative likelihood ratios, positive likelihood ratios and area under the curve will also be briefly described. In addition, definitions of relevant validation and reliability assessment strategies will be provided below.

The sensitivity of an instrument refers to the proportion of those with the condition who test positive. An instrument that detects a low percentage of cases will not be very helpful in determining the numbers of patients who should receive a known effective treatment because many individuals who should receive the treatment will not do so. This would make for poor planning, and underestimate the prevalence of the disorder and the costs of treatments to the community. As the sensitivity of an instrument increases, the number of false negatives it detects will decrease.

The specificity of an instrument refers to the proportion of those without the condition who test negative. This is important so that well individuals are not given treatments they do not need. As the specificity of an instrument increases, the number of false positives will decrease.

To illustrate this: from a population in which the point prevalence rate of alcohol dependence is 10% (that is, 10% of the population has alcohol dependence at any one time), 1000 people are given a test that has 90% sensitivity and 85% specificity. It is known that 100 people in this population have alcohol dependence, but the test detects only 90 (true positives), leaving ten undetected (false negatives). It is also known that 900 people do not have alcohol dependence and the test correctly identifies 765 of these (true negatives), but classifies 135 incorrectly as having alcohol dependence (false positives). The positive predictive value of the test (the number correctly identified as having alcohol dependence as a proportion of positive tests) is

40% (90/90 + 135) and the negative predictive value (the number correctly identified as not having alcohol dependence as a proportion of negative tests) is 98% (765/765 + 10). Therefore, in this example a positive test result is correct in only 40% of cases whilst a negative result can be relied upon in 98% of cases.

The example above illustrates some of the main differences between positive predictive values and negative predictive values in comparison with sensitivity and specificity. For both positive predictive values and negative predictive values, prevalence explicitly forms part of their calculation (see Altman & Bland, 1994a). When the prevalence of a disorder is low in a population this is generally associated with a higher negative predictive value and a lower positive predictive value. Therefore, although these statistics are concerned with issues probably more directly applicable to clinical practice (for example, the probability that a person with a positive test result actually has alcohol dependence), they are largely dependent on the characteristics of the populations sampled and cannot be universally applied (Altman & Bland, 1994a).

In contrast, sensitivity and specificity do not theoretically depend on prevalence (Altman & Bland, 1994b). For example, sensitivity is concerned with the performance of an identification test conditional on a person having depression. Therefore the higher false positives often associated with samples of low prevalence will not affect such estimates. The advantage of this approach is that sensitivity and specificity can be applied across populations (Altman & Bland, 1994b). However, the main disadvantage is that clinicians tend to find such estimates more difficult to interpret.

Criterion validity (or predictive validity) is evaluated when the purpose is to use an instrument to estimate some important form of behaviour that is external to the measuring instrument itself, the latter being referred to as the criterion (Nunnally, 1978). Criterion validity evaluates how well scores on a measure relate to real-world behaviours such as motivation for treatment and long-term treatment outcomes. The degree of correspondence between the test and the criterion is estimated by the size of their correlation.

Construct validity refers to the experimental demonstration that a test is measuring the construct it was intended to measure. Relationships among items, domains and concepts conform to *a priori* hypotheses concerning logical relationships that should exist with other measures or characteristics of patients and patient groups (Brown, 1996).

Content validity is derived from the degree to which a test is a representative sample of the content of whatever objectives or specifications the test was originally designed to measure (Brown, 1996).

Inter-rater reliability refers to the degree to which observers, or raters, are consistent in their scoring on a measurement scale. Internal reliability gives an indication of how much homogeneity or consensus there is amongst the raters (Allen, 2003).

Test–retest reliability is determined by administering the measurement instrument two or more times to each subject. If the correlation between scores is high, the measurement instrument can be said to have good test–retest reliability. This is desirable when measuring constructs that are not expected to change over time, for example family history of alcoholism, age of onset of problem drinking and general expectancies of alcohol effects. In contrast, when measuring more transient constructs such as cravings and treatment motivation, the test–retest reliability would be expected to be lower (Allen, 2003).

Internal consistency is a measure based on the correlation between different items within the scale itself. For instruments designed to measure a single phenomenon, these correlation coefficients should be high (Allen, 2003).

3.5.5   Presenting the data to the Guideline Development Group

Study characteristics tables and, where appropriate, forest plots generated with Review Manager were presented to the GDG.

Where meta-analysis was not appropriate and/or possible, the reported results from each primary-level study were included in the study characteristics table (and, where appropriate, in a narrative review).

Evidence profile tables

A GRADE[7] evidence profile was used to summarise both the quality of the evidence and the results of the evidence synthesis (see Table 4 for an example of an evidence profile). The GRADE approach is based on a sequential assessment of the quality of evidence followed by judgement about the balance between desirable and undesirable effects and subsequent decision about the strength of a recommendation.

For each outcome, quality may be reduced depending on the following factors:

● **study design** (randomised trial, observational study, or any other evidence)
● **limitations** (based on the quality of individual studies)
● **inconsistency** (see Section 3.5.3 for how consistency was assessed)
● **indirectness** (that is, how closely the outcome measures, interventions and participants match those of interest)
● **imprecision** (based on the CI around the effect size).

For observational studies the quality may be increased if there is a large effect, plausible confounding would have changed the effect, or there is evidence of a dose–response gradient (details would be provided under the other considerations column). Each evidence profile also included a summary of the findings: number of patients included in each group, an estimate of the magnitude of the effect and the overall quality of the evidence for each outcome.

3.5.6   Forming the clinical summaries and recommendations

Once the GRADE evidence profiles relating to a particular review question were completed, summary evidence tables were developed (these tables are presented in

---

[7]For further information about GRADE, see www.gradeworkinggroup.org.

Table 4: Example of GRADE evidence profile

Quality assessment							Summary of findings				Quality
							Number of patients		Effect		
No. of studies	Design	Limitations	Inconsistency	Indirectness	Imprecision	Other	Intervention	Control	Relative (95% CI)	Absolute	
Outcome 1											
6	Randomised trial	No serious limitations	No serious inconsistency	No serious indirectness	Very Serious[1,2]	None	8/191	7/150	RR 0.94 (0.39 to 2.23)	0 fewer per 100 (from 3 fewer to 6 more)	⊕⊕⊕○ LOW
Outcome 2											
6	Randomised trial	No serious limitations	No serious inconsistency	No serious indirectness	No serious imprecision	None	120/600	220/450	RR 0.39 (0.39 to 0.65)	30 fewer per 100 (from 17 fewer to 38 fewer)	⊕⊕⊕○ LOW
Outcome 3											
3	Randomised trial	No serious limitations	No serious inconsistency[3]	No serious indirectness	Very Serious[1,2]	None	83	81	–	MD −1.51 (−3.81 to 0.8)	⊕⊕⊕ VERY LOW
Outcome 4											
3	Randomised trial	No serious limitations	No serious inconsistency	No serious indirectness	Serious[1]	None	88	93	–	SMD −0.26 (−0.56 to −0.03)	⊕⊕⊕ MODERATE
Outcome 5											
4	Randomised trial	No serious limitations	No serious inconsistency	No serious indirectness	Very Serious[1,2]	None	109	114	–	SMD −0.13 (−0.6 to 0.34)	⊕⊕⊕ LOW

[1] Optimal information size not met.
[2] The CI includes both (a) no effect and (b) appreciable benefit or appreciable harm.
[3] Considerable heterogeneity.

the evidence chapters). Finally, the systematic reviewer in conjunction with the topic group lead produced a clinical evidence summary.

After the GRADE profiles and clinical summaries were presented to the GDG, the associated recommendations were drafted. In making recommendations, the GDG took into account the trade-off between the benefits and downsides of treatment as well as other important factors, such as economic considerations, social value judgements[8], the requirements to prevent discrimination and to promote equality[9], and the group's awareness of practical issues (Eccles *et al.*, 1998; NICE, 2009a).

3.5.7 Method used to answer a review question in the absence of appropriately designed, high-quality research

In the absence of appropriately designed, high-quality research, or where the GDG were of the opinion (on the basis of previous searches or their knowledge of the literature) that there were unlikely to be such evidence, an informal consensus process was adopted. This process focused on those questions that the GDG considered a priority.

Informal consensus
The starting point for the process of informal consensus was that a member of the topic group identified, with help from the systematic reviewer, a narrative review that most directly addressed the review question. Where this was not possible, a brief review of the recent literature was initiated.

This existing narrative review or new review was used as a basis for beginning an iterative process to identify lower levels of evidence relevant to the review question and to lead to written statements for the guideline. The process involved a number of steps:
1. A description of what was known about the issues concerning the review question was written by one of the topic group members.
2. Evidence from the existing review or new review was then presented in narrative form to the GDG and further comments were sought about the evidence and its perceived relevance to the review question.
3. Based on the feedback from the GDG, additional information was sought and added to the information collected. This may include studies that did not directly address the review question but were thought to contain relevant data.
4. If, during the course of preparing the report, a significant body of primary-level studies (of appropriate design to answer the question) were identified, a full systematic review was done.
5. At this time, subject possibly to further reviews of the evidence, a series of statements that directly addressed the review question were developed.

---

[8]See NICE (2008b).
[9]See NICE's equality scheme: www.nice.org.uk/aboutnice/howwework/NICEEqualityScheme.jsp.

6. Following this, on occasions and as deemed appropriate by the development group, the report was then sent to appointed experts outside of the GDG for peer review and comment. The information from this process was then fed back to the GDG for further discussion of the statements.
7. Recommendations were then developed and could also be sent for further external peer review.
8. After this final stage of comment, the statements and recommendations were again reviewed and agreed upon by the GDG.

3.6   HEALTH ECONOMICS METHODS

The aim of health economics was to contribute to the guideline's development by providing evidence on the cost effectiveness of interventions for alcohol misuse covered in the guideline. This was achieved by:
● a systematic literature review of existing economic evidence
● decision-analytic economic modelling.
    Systematic reviews of economic literature were conducted in all areas covered in the guideline. Economic modelling was undertaken in areas with likely major resource implications, where the current extent of uncertainty over cost effectiveness was significant and economic analysis was expected to reduce this uncertainty, in accordance with *The Guidelines Manual* (NICE, 2009a). Prioritisation of areas for economic modelling was a joint decision between the health economist and the GDG. The rationale for prioritising review questions for economic modelling was set out in an economic plan agreed between NICE, the GDG, the health economist and the other members of the technical team. The following economic questions were selected as key issues that were addressed by economic modelling:
1. What is the preferred method of medically-assisted withdrawal, in terms of clinical and cost effectiveness (taking into consideration the benefits/adverse effects) and for which people and in which setting (taking into account the nature of intervention in each setting)?
    – Community (taking into account levels of supervision: structured versus unstructured day programme)
    – Residential
    – Inpatient: mental health or acute hospital
    – Prisons.
2. For people who are alcohol dependent or harmful drinkers, which pharmacological interventions aimed at attenuation of drinking/maintenance of abstinence are clinically and cost-effective?
3. For people who are alcohol dependent or harmful drinkers, which psychological and psychosocial interventions aimed at attenuation of drinking/maintenance of abstinence are clinically and cost-effective?
4. For people who are alcohol dependent or harmful drinkers, which combination of psychological/psychosocial and pharmacological interventions aimed at attenuation of drinking/maintenance of abstinence are clinically and cost-effective?

In addition, literature on the health-related quality of life of people with alcohol-use disorders was systematically searched to identify studies reporting appropriate utility scores that could be utilised in a cost-utility analysis.

The rest of this section describes the methods adopted in the systematic literature review of economic studies. Methods employed in economic modelling are described in the respective sections of the guideline.

3.6.1 Literature search strategy for economic evidence

Scoping searches

A broad preliminary search of the literature was undertaken in September 2008 to obtain an overview of the issues likely to be covered by the scope and help define key areas. Searches were restricted to economic studies and HTA reports, and conducted in the following databases:

- EMBASE
- MEDLINE/MEDLINE In-Process
- HTA database (technology assessments)
- NHS Economic Evaluation Database (NHS EED).

Systematic literature searches

After the scope was finalised, a systematic search strategy was developed to locate all the relevant evidence. The balance between sensitivity (the power to identify all studies on a particular topic) and specificity (the ability to exclude irrelevant studies from the results) was carefully considered, and a decision made to utilise a broad approach to searching to maximise retrieval of evidence to all parts of the guideline. Searches were restricted to economic studies and HTA reports, and conducted in the following databases:

- CINAHL
- EconLit
- EMBASE
- MEDLINE/MEDLINE In-Process
- PsycINFO
- HTA database (technology assessments)
- NHS EED.

Any relevant economic evidence arising from the clinical scoping searches was also made available to the health economist during the same period.

For standard mainstream bibliographic databases (CINAHL, EMBASE, MEDLINE and PsycINFO), search terms on alcohol dependence and harmful alcohol use were combined with a search filter for health economic studies. For searches generated in topic-specific databases (HTA, NHS EED), search terms on alcohol dependence and harmful alcohol use were used without a filter. The sensitivity of this approach was aimed at minimising the risk of overlooking relevant publications, due to inaccurate or incomplete indexing of records on the databases, as well as potential weaknesses resulting from more focused search strategies (for example, for interventions).

Reference manager

Citations from each search were downloaded into Reference Manager and duplicates removed. Records were then screened against the inclusion criteria of the reviews before being quality appraised. To keep the process both replicable and transparent, the unfiltered search results were saved and retained for future potential re-analysis.

Search filters

The search filter for health economics is an adaptation of a filter designed by the CRD. The filter comprises a combination of controlled vocabulary and free-text retrieval methods.

Date and language restrictions

All of the searches were restricted to research published from 1993 onwards. Systematic database searches were initially conducted in June 2008 up to the most recent searchable date. Search updates were generated on a 6-monthly basis, with the final re-runs carried out in March 2010 ahead of the guideline consultation. After this point, studies were included only if they were judged by the GDG to be exceptional (for example, if the evidence was likely to change a recommendation).

Although no language restrictions were applied at the searching stage, foreign language papers were not requested or reviewed unless they were of particular importance to an area under review.

Other search methods

Other search methods involved scanning the reference lists of all eligible publications (systematic reviews, stakeholder evidence and included studies from the economic and clinical reviews) to identify further studies for consideration.

Full details of the search strategies and filter used for the systematic review of health economic evidence are provided in Appendix 12.

3.6.2   Inclusion criteria for economic studies

The following methods were applied to select studies identified by the economic searches for further consideration:

- No restriction was placed on language or publication status of the papers.
- Studies published from 1998 onwards that reported data from financial year 1997–98 onwards were included. This date restriction was imposed in order to obtain data relevant to current healthcare settings and costs.
- Only studies from Organisation for Economic Co-operation and Development member-countries were included, because the aim of the review was to identify economic information transferable to the UK context.
- Selection criteria based on types of clinical conditions and patients as well as interventions assessed were identical to the clinical literature review.
- Studies were included provided that sufficient details regarding methods and results were available to enable the methodological quality of the study to be

assessed, and provided that the study's data and results were extractable. Poster presentations of abstracts were excluded; however, they were included if they reported utility data required for a cost-utility analysis when no other data were available.

- Full economic evaluations that compared two or more relevant options and considered both costs and consequences (that is, cost-consequence analysis, cost effectiveness analysis, cost-utility analysis or cost-benefit analysis) as well as cost analyses that compared only costs between two or more interventions were included in the review.
- Economic studies were included if they used clinical effectiveness data from an RCT, a prospective cohort study, or a systematic review and meta-analysis of clinical studies. Studies that had a mirror-image or other retrospective design were excluded from the review.
- Studies were included only if the examined interventions were clearly described. This involved the dosage and route of administration and the duration of treatment in the case of pharmacological therapies, and the types of health professionals involved, as well as the frequency and duration of treatment in the case of psychological interventions. Evaluations in which medications were treated as a class were excluded from further consideration.
- Studies that adopted a very narrow perspective, ignoring major categories of costs to the NHS, were excluded; for example, studies that estimated exclusively drug acquisition costs or hospitalisation costs were considered non-informative to the guideline development process.

3.6.3   Applicability and quality criteria for economic studies

All economic papers eligible for inclusion were appraised for their applicability and quality using the methodology checklist for economic evaluations recommended by NICE (NICE, 2009a), which is shown in Appendix 13 of this guideline. The methodology checklist for economic evaluations was also applied to the economic models developed specifically for this guideline. All studies that fully or partially met the applicability and quality criteria described in the methodology checklist were considered during the guideline development process, along with the results of the economic modelling conducted specifically for this guideline.

3.6.4   Presentation of economic evidence

The economic evidence considered in the guideline is provided in the respective evidence chapters, following presentation of the relevant clinical evidence. The references to included studies and to those that were potentially relevant but did not meet the inclusion criteria can be found in Appendix 19, as well as the evidence tables with the characteristics and results of economic studies included in the review. Methods and results of economic modelling undertaken alongside the guideline development process are presented in the relevant evidence chapters. Characteristics and results of all economic studies considered during the guideline development process (including modelling studies conducted for this guideline) are summarised in economic evidence profiles accompanying respective GRADE clinical evidence profiles in Appendix 18.

3.6.5 Results of the systematic search of economic literature

Publications that were clearly not relevant to the topic (that is, economic issues and information on health-related quality of life in harmful drinkers and people with alcohol dependency) were excluded at the sifting stage first. The abstracts of all potentially relevant publications were then assessed against the inclusion criteria for economic evaluations by the health economist. Full texts of the studies potentially meeting the inclusion criteria (including those for which eligibility was not clear from the abstract) were obtained. Studies that did not meet the inclusion criteria, were duplicates, were secondary publications of one study, or had been updated in more recent publications were subsequently excluded. Economic evaluations eligible for inclusion were then appraised for their applicability and quality using the methodology checklist for economic evaluations. Finally, economic studies that fully or partially met the applicability and quality criteria were considered at formulation of the guideline recommendations.

3.7 STAKEHOLDER CONTRIBUTIONS

Professionals, service users and companies have contributed to and commented on the guideline at key stages in its development. Stakeholders for this guideline include:
● service user and carer stakeholders: the national service-user and carer organisations that represent people whose care is described in this guideline
● professional stakeholders: the national organisations that represent healthcare professionals who are providing services to service users
● commercial stakeholders: the companies that manufacture medicines used in the treatment of alcohol dependence and harmful alcohol use
● primary care trusts
● Department of Health and Welsh Assembly Government.
    NICE clinical guidelines are produced for the NHS in England and Wales, so a 'national' organisation is defined as one that represents England and/or Wales, or has a commercial interest in England and/or Wales.
    Stakeholders have been involved in the guideline's development at the following points:
● commenting on the initial scope of the guideline and attending a briefing meeting held by NICE
● contributing possible review questions and lists of evidence to the GDG during the initial scoping phase of the guideline
● commenting on the draft of the guideline
● highlighting factual errors in the pre-publication check.

3.8 VALIDATION OF THE GUIDELINE

Registered stakeholders had an opportunity to comment on the draft guideline, which was posted on the NICE website during the consultation period. Following the consultation, all comments from stakeholders and others were responded to, and the guideline updated as appropriate. The GRP also reviewed the guideline and checked that stakeholders' comments had been addressed.

Following the consultation period, the GDG finalised the recommendations and the NCCMH produced the final documents. These were then submitted to NICE for the pre-publication check where stakeholders were given the opportunity to highlight factual errors. Any errors are corrected by the NCCMH, then the guideline is formally approved by NICE and issued as guidance to the NHS in England and Wales.

4 EXPERIENCE OF CARE

4.1 INTRODUCTION

This chapter provides an overview of the experience of people who misuse alcohol and their families/carers in the form of a review of the qualitative literature. As part of the process of drafting this chapter, the GDG and review team elicited personal accounts from people who misuse alcohol and their family/carers. The personal accounts that were received from service users were from people who had experienced long-standing (almost life-long) problems with alcohol and identified themselves as 'alcoholic'. For this reason, the GDG judged that it could not include them in this chapter because they did not illustrate the breadth of experience covered by this guideline, which ranges from occasional harmful drinking to mild, moderate and severe dependence. (The personal accounts that were received and the methods used to elicit them can be found in Appendix 14.)

As the guideline also aims to address support needs for families/carers, a thematic analysis was conducted using transcripts from people with parents who misuse alcohol. These were accessed from the National Association for Children of Alcoholics (NACOA) website (www.nacoa.org.uk). NACOA provides information and support to people (whether still in childhood or in adulthood) of parents who misuse alcohol and the website includes personal experiences from such people in narrative form. However, there were some limitations to the thematic analysis. Because the review team relied only on transcripts submitted to NACOA, information on other issues that could be particularly pertinent for children with parents who misuse alcohol may not have been identified. Moreover, people who have visited the NACOA website to submit their accounts may over-represent a help-seeking population. Finally, while some accounts are based on experiences that occurred recently, others occurred a long time ago; therefore there may be differences in attitudes, information and services available. For these reasons this analysis was not included in Chapter 4, but it can be found in Appendix 14.

4.2 REVIEW OF THE QUALITATIVE LITERATURE

4.2.1 Introduction

A systematic search for published reviews of relevant qualitative studies of people who misuse alcohol was undertaken. The aim of the review was to explore the experience of care for people who misuse alcohol and their families and carers in terms of the broad topics of receiving a diagnosis, accessing services and having treatment.

4.2.2 Review questions

For people who misuse alcohol, what are their experiences of having problems with alcohol, of access to services and of treatment?

For families and carers of people who misuse alcohol, what are their experiences of caring for people with an alcohol problem and what support is available for families and carers?

4.2.3 Evidence search

Reviews were sought of qualitative studies that used relevant first-hand experiences of people who misuse alcohol and their families/carers. For more information about the databases searched, see Table 5.

4.2.4 Studies considered

Based on the advice of the GDG, this review was focused on qualitative research only because it was felt to be most appropriate to answer questions about the experience of care of those with alcohol dependence or alcohol misuse. Because good quality qualitative research exists within the literature, quantitative and survey studies were excluded.

The search found 32 qualitative studies which met the inclusion criteria (Aira *et al.*, 2003; Allen *et al.*, 2005; Bacchus, 1999; Beich *et al.*, 2002; Burman, 1997; Copeland, 1997; Dyson, 2007; Gance-Cleveland, 2004; Hartney *et al.*, 2003; Hyams *et al.*, 1996; Jethwa, 2009 [10]; Kaner *et al.*, 2006; Lock, 2004; Lock *et al.*, 2002;

Table 5: Databases searched and inclusion/exclusion criteria for clinical evidence

Electronic databases	CINAHL, EMBASE, MEDLINE, PsycINFO
Date searched	Database inception to March 2010
Study design	Systematic reviews and narratives of qualitative studies, qualitative studies
Population	People who are alcohol dependent or harmful drinkers, families and carers, staff who work in alcohol services
Outcomes	None specified - any narrative description of service user/carer experience of alcohol misuse

---

[10]It should be noted that the qualitative patient interviews from the Jethwa (2009) study were not published with the paper, but were received from a member of the GDG. The review team received written permission from the author to use the interviews to identify any themes relevant to this section.

In the ambivalent stage, people want to seek help but the will to drink is stronger than to remain abstinent. In the attempt phase, people try to remain abstinent but, due to a lack of coping strategies in situations that trigger alcohol consumption, many relapse.

Dyson (2007) found that recovery from alcohol dependence arose from a culmination or combination of consequences, coupled with the realisation that life was unbearable as it was:

> *My real recovery began when I admitted that my life had become unmanageable and that I could not control the drink. I experienced a deep change in thinking – sobriety had to be the most important thing in my life.*

Several participants pointed out that their decision to pursue recovery and abstinence had to be made on their own and could not be made or influenced much by others: '*It was something I had to do on my own and I had to do it for me, not for anyone else*'. Evidently this personal decision has important implications for the carers around them. The key to begin recovery appears to be the individual's willingness and readiness to stop drinking (Dyson, 2007).

An earlier study by Orford and colleagues (1998) looked at social support in coping with alcohol and drug problems at home, using a cross-cultural comparison between Mexican and English families. The main cross-cultural differences were that positive social support for Mexican relatives stemmed mostly from family, whereas English relatives mentioned self-help sources, professionals and friends in addition to family. The accounts from the participants mentioned family and friend support as more unsupportive or more negative for the English families. Conversely, the Mexican families often mentioned their family and neighbours as significant contributors of support. The researchers explored the participant's perceptions of the positive and negative drawbacks to their heavy drinking. The negative aspects included increased vulnerability to arguments and fights, and the unpleasant physical effects of drinking (such as waking up tired, stomach upsets and headaches). Many participants mentioned the adverse effects alcohol had had on their physical and mental health. Interestingly, several participants mentioned drinking in order to cope with difficult life events, but masked this association between coping and alcohol by terming it as being 'relaxed'. Many submerged the notion of coping by using the fact that alcohol helped them relax in distressing situations. Thus, the long-term psychological and short-term physical consequences were noted as the principle drawbacks of harmful alcohol consumption, whereas coping, and feelings of being carefree and relaxed, seem to constitute the positive aspects of drinking.

4.2.6   Access and engagement

In the review of the qualitative literature, several themes emerged under the broad heading of 'access and engagement' to services for alcohol misuse, including factors that may act as barriers to accessing treatment services such as external and internal stigma, ethnicity and gender. This review also identified 'reasons for seeking help' as a theme emerging from the included studies. There were eight studies from which themes of access and engagement emerged (Copeland, 1997; Dyson, 2007; Lock, 2004; Nelson-Zlupko *et al.*, 1996; Orford *et al.*, 2006; Rolfe *et al.*, 2009; Vandermause & Wood, 2009; Vandevelde *et al.*, 2003; Vargas & Luis, 2008).

Stigma

Dyson (2007) found that all participants used strategies to hide their alcohol dependence, including covering up the extent of their alcohol consumption. This was primarily due to the fear of being judged or stigmatised: '*I knew that I was ill but was too worried about how other people would react. I felt I would be judged*'. All participants in the study had some contact with healthcare professionals in an attempt to control or reduce their drinking. GPs were described as being particularly helpful and supportive, and nurses and other healthcare workers as less understanding and more dismissive, especially those in accident and emergency departments; this contrasts with another study (Lock, 2004), where people who misuse alcohol found primary care nurses to be helpful. Social stigma can also occur from groups in the community. For example, Morjaria and Orford (2002) highlight in their study that South Asian men in the UK often perceive that members of their religious community could influence their desire to consume alcohol, and furthermore, once religious leaders in the community expressed disapproval of alcohol consumption, there was more encouragement towards being abstinent from alcohol.

Ethnicity

Vandevelde and colleagues' (2003) study of treatment for substance misuse looked at cultural responsiveness from professionals and clients' perspectives in Belgium. People from minority groups found it difficult to openly discuss their emotional problems due to cultural factors, such as cultural honour and respect. Participants stressed the absence of ethno-cultural peers in substance misuse treatment facilities, and how this made it hard to maintain the motivation to complete treatment. Although this study had a focus on substance misuse (that is, both drugs and alcohol), it is important to note its generalisability to alcohol services and treatment.

Gender

Vandermause and Wood (2009) and Nelson-Zlupko and colleagues (1996) both looked at experiences and interactions of women with healthcare practitioners in the US. Many women described waiting until their symptoms were severe before they would seek out healthcare services:

> *... it's hard for me to go in ... and it's not someplace that I want to be, especially when I know that I have to be there. I know that I'm ill, I don't want to admit it... I have to get my temperature taken and my blood pressure and they gotta look at my eyes and my ears ... find out what it is that I've got from somebody else sharing a bottle you know.*

Once the women sought help from a healthcare professional, several felt angry and frustrated after repeated clinic visits resulted in being turned away, treated poorly, or silenced by comments from healthcare professionals. Some women would go in needing to be treated for a physical health problem and the practitioner would address the alcohol problem while ignoring the primary physical complaint.

Conversely, other women were satisfied about how they were treated in interactions with their practitioners, which influenced perceptions of the healthcare services, seeking out treatment and feeling comfortable about disclosing their alcohol use:

> *I was confused and angry, and the doctor made me feel comfortable, even though I was very very ill ... he let me know that I was an individual person but I had a problem that could be arrested. He was very compassionate very empathetic with me and told me the medical facts about what was happening to me, why I was the way I was and he told me a little bit about treatment, what it would do ... so I was able to relax enough and stop and listen rather than become defensive ...*

When women specifically sought treatment for their alcohol use, the authors suggested that there was a crucial need for healthcare practitioners to make the patient feel comfortable and acknowledge their alcohol problem in addition to addressing any other physical health problems.

Nelson-Zlupko and colleagues (1996) found that individual counselling might be important in determining whether a woman is retained or drops out of treatment. Many women felt that what they wanted from treatment was someone to 'be there for them' and lend support. A therapist's ability to treat their patients with dignity, respect and genuine concern was evaluated as more important than individual therapist characteristics (such as ethnicity or age). Some women mentioned that good counsellors were those who:

> *... view you as a person and a woman, not just an addict. They see you have a lot of needs and they try to come up with some kind of a plan.*

Both Nelson-Zlupko and colleagues (1996), and Copeland (1997), highlighted that childcare was a particular need for women because it was not widely available in treatment. When childcare was available, this was perceived to be among one of the most helpful services in improving attendance and use of treatment and drug/alcohol services. In addition, women felt strongly about the availability and structure of outpatient services offered and felt there should be more flexible outpatient programmes taking place, for example, in the evenings or at weekends.

Copeland's (1997) Australian study was of women who self-managed change in their alcohol dependence and the barriers that they faced in accessing treatment. One of the central themes of the study was the social stigma that women felt as being drug or alcohol dependent. Seventy-eight per cent of participants felt that women were more 'looked down upon' as a result of their drinking and the additional burden of an alcohol or drug problem only increased the stigma. Some women reported that the feeling of being stigmatised impacted on their willingness to seek treatment:

> *There is the whole societal thing that women shouldn't show themselves to be so out of control ... that stigma thing was part of the reason for not seeking treatment.*

Experience of care

In line with this, Rolfe and colleagues (2009) interviewed women in the UK about their own perceptions of their heavy alcohol consumption and its relation to a wider social perspective. Many women claimed that stigma was a major obstacle to accessing treatment services and that, while men did carry stigma as heavy drinkers, there was an additional stigma for women due to the way a 'heavy drinking woman' was perceived within society. The interviews emphasised that women need to perform a 'balancing act' to avoid being stigmatised as a 'manly' woman or as someone with alcohol dependence. These discourses are important in understanding the perception of gender differences in heavy alcohol consumption and ways in which stigma can affect women, and their ability and willingness to seek treatment for their alcohol use.

Reasons for seeking help
A study conducted by Orford and colleagues (2006b) investigated the reasons for entering alcohol treatment in the UK. The study was based on pre-treatment interviews from participants who were about to commence the UK Alcohol Treatment Trial (UKATT) and receive either MET or social network behavioural therapy (SNBT) for alcohol dependence or harmful alcohol use. Reasons for entering alcohol treatment included the realisation of worsening problems and accumulating multiple problems relating to alcohol use, which had a negative impact on both family members and the participants' health. Participants were also interviewed about reasons for seeking professional treatment as opposed to unaided or mutual self-help. Common reasons for seeking formal help included such help being suggested by primary care workers, a strong belief in the medical model and in counselling or psychological therapy, or feelings of helplessness.

Accessing help: reasons and preferences
Lock (2004) conducted a focus group study with patients registered with general practices in England. Participants were classified as 'sensible' or 'heavy/binge drinkers'. Participants responded positively to advice delivered in an appropriate context and by a healthcare professional with whom they had developed a rapport. Overall, the GP was deemed to be the preferred healthcare professional with whom to discuss alcohol issues and deliver brief alcohol interventions. Practice nurses were also preferred due to the perception that they were more understanding and more approachable than other healthcare workers. Most said they would rather go straight to their GP with any concern about alcohol, either because the GP had a sense of the patient's history, had known them for a long time or because they were traditionally whom the person would go to see. It was assumed that the GP would have the training and experience to deal with the problem, and refer to a specialist if necessary. Alcohol workers were perceived by many as the person to go to with more severe alcohol misuse because they were experts, but this also carried the stigma of being perceived to have a severe alcohol problem. Seeing a counsellor was also perceived as negative in some ways, as there would be a stigma surrounding mental health problems and going to therapy.

4.2.7   Experience of assessment and treatment for alcohol misuse

In the review of the qualitative literature, several themes emerged under the broad heading of 'experience of treatment for alcohol misuse', including experience of assessment (pre-treatment), assisted withdrawal, other treatments (such as psychological interventions) and treatment setting (inpatient). In this review of assessment and treatment, there were six studies included (Allen *et al.*, 2005; Bacchus, 1999; Dyson, 2007; Hyams *et al.*, 1996; Orford *et al.*, 2006a; Smith, 2004).

Experience of assessment (pre-treatment)
Hyams and colleagues (1996) interviewed service users about their experience and satisfaction with the assessment interview prior to engagement in alcohol treatment. The study had both a quantitative and qualitative aspect to it. The qualitative component assessed the best and worst aspects of the assessment interview. Thirty-three of the 131 participants said that the therapeutic relationship with the interviewer was most beneficial (as assessed by 'The interviewer's understanding of the real me', 'Friendliness of the interviewer' and 'A feeling of genuine care about my problems'). Twenty participants appreciated the ability to talk generally and therapeutically to the interviewer about their problems. Eight participants reported that the assessment interview provided them with a sense of increased awareness about their alcohol use and its impact on their lives: '*I found insight into why I drink …*' Others found that the assessment interview was crucial in taking the first step into treatment: '*Glad that I did attend the interview*' and '*Given me some hope*'.

Although participants identified few drawbacks regarding the interview, they did cite general nervousness particularly about starting the interview. Some criticised the interviewer for not giving enough feedback or not having enough time to talk. Several participants felt that it was distressing to have to reveal so much information about their drinking problems and to come to a state of painful awareness about their problem. This study is noteworthy because it highlights the importance of a thorough assessment prior to entering alcohol treatment that allows participants to speak freely to an accepting, empathetic interviewer and that, if a positive experience for the service user, will increase engagement and motivation to change in subsequent alcohol treatment programmes.

In line with these findings, Orford and colleagues (2006a) found that a comprehensive pre-treatment assessment was perceived by participants to have motivational and self-realising aspects to it. Many participants expressed that this assessment was influential in increasing motivation to undergo their alcohol treatment.

Experience of assisted withdrawal
Two studies, Allen and colleagues (2005) and Smith (2004), captured the patient experience of medically-assisted withdrawal programmes for alcohol misuse in both the UK and Australia. Both studies found that participants expressed fears about the

future and a hesitation about coping with life events that had previously been associated with alcohol consumption:

> *I feel safe in the environment but I don't feel safe with my thoughts at the moment because I can't use alcohol or any drug to cope with it ...*

The most common themes emerged around fears regarding social environment, the physical effects of withdrawal and medication prescribed during detoxification. Participants discussed fears about returning to their homes after detoxification and how to lead a life without alcohol:

> *When you've done the first few days [of detoxification], you get your head back together and start to think, How am I going to be able to cope outside? You know you've got to leave here sometime, so how am I going to cope?*

Participants also expressed significant concerns about the effects of medication, although there were also a number of positive experiences of medication which were referred to but were not described in detail. Some participants feared that their medication would be addictive:

> *I didn't want another problem of having to get off something as well as the booze. I was worried that I could get addicted to the tablets as well and then start craving for those.*

Nearly all participants were apprehensive about the transmission of information about medication between the staff and themselves; they felt they had inadequate information about what medication they were taking, why they were taking it and the effects it may have on them:

> *I didn't know what they were, what they were going to do to me ... they didn't tell me why I was taking them.*

It is clear from this study that providing adequate information about assisted withdrawal and medication procedures needs to be ensured in alcohol services.

A significant proportion of participants also expressed fears about the physical effects of withdrawal, and any pain and/or distress that may be a side effect of the detoxification programme. Those who had had previous medically-assisted withdrawals prior to this study seemed to have the greatest fears. Lastly, participants discussed fears about their future and were concerned about their ability to cope once completing the detoxification programme. These fears mostly stemmed from difficult interpersonal situations and coping strategies:

> *I'm worried about having too much time on my hands; the day goes so much quicker with a few drinks inside you.*

In both studies, participants expressed a lack of confidence and an inability to resist temptation; they also felt that they were not being accepted back into their original social networks where heavy drinking was perceived as the norm. Additionally, fears about the future were related to a feeling that the hospital setting was too far removed from real life:

> *It's nice and safe in here. You are secure in here. But it's not real life is it? And it tells you nothing about how you are going to cope when you are back in the same old situations with the same old problems.*

Participants in the Smith (2004) study also articulated feelings of being out of control during their admission to treatment. These feelings of distress revolved around the difficulty to alter their alcohol consumption, and stick to a reduced consumption level or abstinence:

> *You get well physically and you start thinking clearly ... you start telling yourself you're over it ... you might maintain some kind of normal drinking activity for a short period of time. I just believe that I can't keep doing it. I don't want to.*

With each medically-assisted withdrawal, the goal of abstinence seemed more distant – the thought of this was anxiety-provoking for many participants because they felt they would be unable to maintain abstinence in the future. After medically-assisted withdrawal, they would have to return to a life where all their personal, professional and relationship difficulties still existed but were previously associated with alcohol.

Conversely, there were positive feelings about treatment because most felt they had taken steps to bring about positive changes in their lives by seeking treatment. The facility enabled participants to have respite from their lives as well as social and emotional support from other participants in the programme. The authors suggested that nurses could assist participants in reducing negative feelings (such as shame) by closely observing behaviour and being more sensitive and empathetic to service users' feelings, thereby strengthening therapeutic communication between staff and patients.

Experience of psychological treatment
Orford and colleagues (2005 and 2008) carried out a content analysis of service users' perspectives on change during a psychological intervention for their alcohol dependence in UKATT. Participants highlighted that psychological treatment had helped them to think differently, for example about fearing the future and focusing on the downside of drinking. Others talked of adopting a more positive outlook or more alcohol-focused thinking (for example, paying attention to the physical consequences such as liver disease or brain damage). Several participants mentioned that, '*the questions, the talking, being honest, being open – that was positive [of treatment]*'. Other factors to which change was attributed to were awareness of the consequences of drinking and feeling comfortable talking about their alcohol consumption.

73

Experience of support from family and voluntary organisations
Orford and colleagues (2005) also found that the influence of family and friends helped in promoting change in alcohol consumption. Treatment seemed to assist participants in finding non-drinking-related activities and friends, and seeking out more support from their social networks to deal with problematic situations involving alcohol. Supportive networks provided by AA and the 12-step programme facilitated recovery for participants in the Dyson (2007) study as well, because they were able to be with others who genuinely understood their experiences and fostered a sense of acceptance: '*Here was a bunch of people who really understood where I was coming from*'.

Experience of treatment setting – inpatient
Bacchus (1999) carried out a study about opinions on inpatient treatment for drug and alcohol dependence. Over one third of participants reported that they would have preferred to enter treatment sooner because there was an urgent need to maintain treatment motivation and receive acute medical care:

> *When you make that decision to ask for help, you need it straight away. If you have to wait a long time to get in you just lose your motivation and you might just give up.*

Participants also felt frustrated about the lack of communication and liaison from the referring agency during the waiting period. The structured individual and group counselling treatment programme was seen as a generally effective way of improving self-confidence and self-esteem. Educational group discussions about substance use and risks were particularly positively regarded. Recreational groups (for example, art therapy, exercise and cookery) also proved to be beneficial in terms of engaging in other non-drinking-related activities. One of the most positive aspects of treatment noted by participants was the quality of the therapeutic relationships. Staff attitudes, support, and being non-judgemental and empathetic were all mentioned as crucial components of a positive experience in treatment. Sixty-two per cent of patients had made prior arrangements with staff for aftercare treatment and expressed satisfaction with the arrangements. The only exception was that patients wished for more detailed information about the next phase of their treatment.

4.2.8   Experience of recovery

Four studies (Burman, 1997; Mohatt *et al.*, 2007; Morjaria & Orford, 2002; Yeh *et al.*, 2009) looked at the experience and process of recovery for people who misuse alcohol. All studies with the exception of Yeh and colleagues (2009) looked at recovery from the standpoint of drinkers who were untreated. Nearly all the studies highlighted the importance of utilising active coping and moderation strategies in order to stop consuming alcohol, and a number of the studies touch on the importance of positive social support networks, faith and self-help groups.

Morjaria and Orford (2002) examined the role of religion and spirituality in promoting recovery from drinking problems, specifically in AA programmes and in South Asian men. Both South Asian men and men in AA began recovery once there was a feeling of hitting 'rock bottom' or of reaching a turning point where they felt their drinking must stop. Both groups drew on faith to help promote recovery, but the South Asian men already had a developed faith from which to draw upon, whereas the men in AA had to come to accept a set of beliefs or value system and develop religious faith to help promote abstinence.

In terms of self-recovery strategies, participants in Burman (1997), Mohatt and colleagues (2007) and Yeh and colleagues (2009) often utilised recovery strategies that mirrored those in formal treatment, consisting of drawing on social support networks and avoiding alcohol and alcohol-related situations. Seeing another person giving up alcohol also helped to promote abstinence and motivation, again highlighting the necessity of positive support networks. Another stage of sobriety for participants in Mohatt's study (2007) involved a more gradual acceptance of their vulnerability towards consuming alcohol and continuing to strategise and resist the urge to drink. Additional coping strategies outlined by Burman (1997) were: setting a time limit for recovery; discussing their goals and plans with others to help keep them on track; and keeping reminders of negative experiences to help prevent further relapse.

Similar to those in formal treatment programmes, once in the midst of self-recovery, participants reported a number of positive changes since abstaining (for example, increased energy and memory, self-awareness and empowerment), and more external benefits including regaining trust from their social networks and reintegrating into society. Negative consequences of abstinence included edginess and physical side effects, family problems, struggles with craving and a loss of a specific social circle or group previously related to alcohol.

Taken together, the self-recovery studies highlight the process of abstinence for alcoholics, stressing that the path is not straightforward, and assistance from self-help groups and social support networks are crucial to help ensure a better recovery.

4.2.9   Carer experiences

Four studies (Gance-Cleveland, 2004; Murray, 1998; Orford *et al.*, 1998a; Orford *et al.*, 2002) were found that could be categorised under the heading 'carer experiences'.

Orford and colleagues (1998) conducted cross-sectional interview and questionnaire studies with a series of family members in two sociocultural groups, in Mexico City and in the west of England. They found that there were three approaches to interacting with their family members who misuse alcohol: (1) tolerating; (2) engaging; and (3) withdrawing. In the first approach, the carer would tolerate inaction and support the person in a passive way. Some carers mentioned taking the 'engaging' position with their family members in an attempt to change unacceptable and excessive substance use. Some forms of engagement were more controlling and emotional in nature; others more assertive and supportive. Lastly, some carers mentioned emotionally and physically withdrawing from their family members with an alcohol problem (for example, asking their alcohol-using family member to leave the house). This was seen as a way to detach oneself from the alcohol problem of their family member. One form of coping that carers also mentioned was that one needs to enforce supportive and assertive coping:

> *You need to be very strong, to be there and talk to him but still stick to your own values and beliefs in life.*

There was significant overlap between the coping strategies outlined by both families from England and from Mexico. Families in both countries used assertive and supportive ways of coping with their family member's alcohol problem, either through direct confrontation, financial or emotional sacrifice. Thus, even given a different sociocultural context, there are several common ways for carers to cope and interact with a family member with an alcohol problem.

Orford and colleagues (2002) interviewed the close relatives of untreated heavy drinkers. Most relatives recognised the positive aspects of their family member consuming alcohol (for example, social benefits) and reported a few drawbacks to drinking. Many family members contrasted their family member's current problem with how their problem used to be. Other family members used controlling tactics (for example, checking bottles) as a way to monitor their family members, while others tried to be tolerant and accepting of their family member's drinking behaviour.

There are two qualitative studies that have looked at the perspectives and experiences of people whose parents misuse alcohol. Murray (1998) conducted a qualitative analysis of five in-depth accounts of adolescents with parents who misuse alcohol and found four main themes: (1) 'The nightmare', which includes betrayal (abuse/abandonment), over-responsibility, shame, fear, anger, lack of trust and the need to escape; (2) 'The lost dream', which consists of loss of identity and childhood (lack of parenting, comparing oneself with others, unrealistic expectations); (3) 'The dichotomies', which is the struggle between dichotomies, for example, love and hate (towards parents), fear and hope (towards the future) and denial and reality; (4) 'The awakening', which is gaining an understanding of the problem, realising alcohol is not an answer (possibly through their own experiences), realising they were not to blame and regaining a sense of self.

Another qualitative study (Gance-Cleveland, 2004) investigated the benefit of a school-based support group for children with parents who misuse alcohol and found that the group helped them to identify commonalities with each other, feel that they were understood, support and challenge each other, and share coping strategies. The children who took part also felt that the group was a trusted and safe place in which they could reveal secrets and feel less isolated and lonely, that it enabled them to be more aware of the impact of addiction on family dynamics and helped them increase resilience and do better at school (Gance-Cleveland, 2004). In conclusion, talking to others (especially with those who have had similar experiences) was found to be helpful in terms of coping, making friendships and understanding more about alcohol misuse.

4.2.10   Staff experiences

There were six studies (Aira *et al.*, 2003; Beich *et al.*, 2002; Kaner *et al.*, 2006; Lock *et al.*, 2002; Vandermause, 2007; Vandevelde *et al.*, 2003, Vargas & Luis, 2008) looking at the experience of staff who work with people who misuse alcohol. There were several themes emerging from staff experiences, the first being hesitancy in delivering brief interventions to people who misuse alcohol. Staff implementing the WHO screening and brief intervention programme in Denmark found that it was difficult to establish a rapport with patients who screened positive for alcohol misuse and ensure adherence with the intervention (Beich *et al.*, 2002). In England, primary care practitioners had little confidence in their ability to deliver brief interventions and override negative reactions from patients (Lock *et al.*, 2002). Furthermore, because alcohol misuse can be a sensitive and emotional topic, a significant proportion of the staff in the studies expressed a lack of confidence about their ability to counsel patients effectively on lifestyle issues (Aira *et al.*, 2003; Beich *et al.*, 2002; Lock *et al.*, 2002):

> *The patient does not bring it up and obviously is hiding it ... [Alcohol] is a more awkward issue; which of course must be brought up...*

Approaching emotional problems related to substance misuse through the medical dimension might facilitate the treatment of minority groups, because it was perceived that emotional problems were more often expressed somatically (Vandevelde *et al.*, 2003).

A positive experience with a service user involved an assessment using effective diagnostic tools where staff were able to employ an indirect, non-confrontational approach and service users were able to discuss their problems and tell their story at their own pace (Vandermause, 2007).

Both Beich and colleagues (2002) and Lock and colleagues (2002) highlighted that brief interventions and confronting service users regarding their alcohol consumption was important; there were, however, a number of significant barriers to delivering these interventions effectively (for example, the fear of eliciting negative reactions from their patients). Staff interviewed in the Vandermause (2007) qualitative study also found that staff had concerns about defining alcohol as problematic for their patients.

Aira and colleagues (2003) found that staff were not ready to routinely inquire about alcohol consumption in their consultations, unless an alcohol problem was specifically indicated (for example, the service user was experiencing sleeplessness, high blood pressure or dyspepsia). Even when they were aware of alcohol misuse in advance, staff still had significant difficulty in finding the ideal opportunity to raise the issue with their patients. If they did not know in advance about a drinking problem, they did not raise the issue.

Kaner and colleagues (2006) looked at GPs' own drinking behaviour in relation to recognising alcohol-related risks and problems in their patients. The interviews indicated that GPs' perceived their own drinking behaviour in two ways. Some GPs drew on their own drinking behaviour when talking to patients because it could be seen as an opportunity to enable patients to gain insight into alcohol issues, facilitate discussion and incorporate empathy into the interaction. Other GPs separated their own drinking behaviour from that of 'others', thereby only recognising at-risk behaviours in patients who were least like them.

Vargas and Luis (2008) interviewed nurses from public district health units in Brazil and discovered that despite alcoholism being perceived as a disease by most of the nurses, the patients who misuse alcohol who seek treatment are still stigmatised:

> *We generally think the alcohol addict is a bum, an irresponsible person, we give them all of these attributes and it doesn't occur to you that [he/she] is sick.*

Furthermore, the nurses interviewed seemed to express little hope and optimism for their patients because they believed that after being assisted and detoxified, they would relapse and continue drinking:

> *... he comes here looking for care, takes some glucose and some medications, and as soon as he is discharged he goes back to the ... drink.*

This study highlights the extent of external stigma that those who misuse alcohol can face within the healthcare setting, and how it could prevent positive change due to an apprehension about continually accessing services or seeking help.

All six studies made recommendations for improving staff experience when engaging with people who misuse alcohol, with an emphasis on training, communication skills and engaging patients about alcohol consumption, combined with a flexible approach to enhance dialogue and interaction. However, although many healthcare professionals received training about delivering brief interventions, many lacked the confidence to do so and questioned their ability to motivate their patients to reduce their alcohol consumption. Staff also frequently cited a lack of guidance concerning alcohol consumption and health. Clear health messages, better preparation and training, and more support were cited as recommendations for future programmes. As many healthcare professionals found screening for excessive alcohol use created more problems than it solved, perhaps improving screening procedures could improve the experience of staff delivering these interventions.

4.2.11   Summary of the literature

The evidence from the qualitative literature provides some important insights into the experience of people who misuse alcohol, their carers and staff. Problematic alcohol consumption appears to stem from a range of environmental and social factors, including using alcohol to cope with stressful life events, having family members with alcohol or drug problems and/or social situations that encourage the consumption of alcohol. A cycle of dependence then begins wherein the person goes through stages of indulgence in, ambivalence towards and attempts to abstain from alcohol

(Yeh *et al.*, 2009), resulting in a loss of control over their alcohol consumption. This leads to the consumption of more alcohol to counteract unpleasant physical or mental states. As the alcohol consumption becomes harmful, there seems to be an accumulation of negative alcohol-related events. These can become the catalyst for change in the person's life, when the person realises that their alcohol problem requires further assistance and/or treatment. This readiness or willingness to change needs to be determined by the person who misuses alcohol, sometimes with support and insight from their social networks – readiness to change cannot be imposed externally. These differing patterns of alcohol consumption and reasons for deciding to engage in treatment or change one's behaviour mean that treatment services need to understand an individual's reasons for drinking and how this may influence treatment.

With regard to access and engagement in treatment, once people who misuse alcohol had made the conscious decision to abstain from or reduce their drinking, they were more willing to access treatment, although external factors and the motivational skills of healthcare professional may also play a part. Barriers to treatment included internal and external stigma, an apprehension towards discussing alcohol-related issues with healthcare professionals, and a fear of treatment and the unpleasant effects of stopping drinking. As a group, women felt that they faced additional barriers to treatment in the form of more social stigma, and the need for childcare while seeking and undergoing treatment. In addition, women felt that they received less support from treatment providers, and would benefit from a more empathetic and therapeutic approach. The studies focusing on women and alcohol problems emphasise that a non-judgemental atmosphere in primary care is necessary in order to foster openness and willingness to change with regard to their alcohol problems.

In one study looking at the impact of ethnicity and culture on access to treatment, participants from an ethnic minority report having mostly positive experiences with healthcare practitioners, but improvements could be made to the system in the form of more ethno-cultural peers and increased awareness of culture and how it shapes alcohol consumption and misuse.

The literature strongly suggests that assessments that incorporate motivational cues are crucial in ensuring and promoting readiness to change early on in the treatment process. Having open and friendly interviewers conducting the assessments also seems to have an effect on increasing disclosure of information and the person's willingness to enter into subsequent alcohol treatment.

Although there were some positive experiences of medication, the qualitative literature highlights consistent fears surrounding assisted withdrawal and the unpleasant effects one may experience while in treatment. Many participants across studies fear the future and not being able to adopt appropriate coping strategies that will assist in preventing relapse once they return to their familiar social milieu. More information from staff in alcohol services may be beneficial in alleviating patient's fears about treatment.

Psychological treatment was seen to facilitate insight into one's drinking behaviour and understand the downsides of drinking. Talking with a therapist honestly and openly about alcohol helped in alleviating fears about the future and developing coping strategies. Within a residential treatment programme setting, a therapeutic ethos and a strong therapeutic relationship were regarded as the most positive aspects of alcohol treatment.

Active coping and moderation strategies, self-help groups, rehabilitation programmes and aftercare programmes were found to be helpful in preventing relapse post-treatment, and social support networks may serve as an additional motivation to change and can help promote long-term recovery. It should be noted that these findings were from studies of untreated drinkers, so this should be interpreted with caution if generalising to a population formally in treatment. Emphasis on a therapeutic relationship between healthcare practitioners and patients and good communication seem integral to promoting recovery. Social support, empathic feedback, and adequate information provision also facilitate the recovery process.

Family and friends can have an important role in supporting a person with an alcohol problem to promote and maintain change, but to do this they require information and support from healthcare professionals. But the strain on carers can be challenging and they may require a carer's assessment.

From a staff perspective, the qualitative studies suggest that many staff in primary care have feelings of inadequacy when delivering interventions for alcohol misuse and lack the training they need to work confidently in this area. An improvement in staff training is required to facilitate access and engagement in treatment for people with alcohol problems. When interventions were successfully delivered, assessment and diagnostic tools were seen as crucial. In addition, thorough assessment and diagnostic tools may aid in the process of assessing and treating patients with alcohol-use disorders.

Even if they were aware of a problem, many healthcare professionals felt they had inadequate training, lack of resources, or were unable to carry out motivational techniques themselves. More training about harmful drinking populations and associated interventions, as well as more awareness about how to interact with these populations from a primary care perspective, should be considered.

4.3   FROM EVIDENCE TO RECOMMENDATIONS

In reviewing the qualitative literature, the GDG were able to make a number of recommendations addressing experience of care. However, it should be noted that some of the evidence reviewed in this chapter contributed to the formulation of recommendations in other chapters, in particular Chapter 5.

Stigma was a prevalent theme in the literature review. It was experienced both externally (mostly from healthcare professionals) and internally; internal stigma could result in concealment of the person's alcohol problem from others due to fear or shame, therefore healthcare professionals should take this into account when working with people who misuse alcohol and ensure that the setting is conducive to full disclosure of the person's problems. The positive aspects and benefits of a therapeutic relationship both in a treatment setting and in assessment procedures were cited frequently. This highlights the need for healthcare professionals to interact with people who misuse alcohol in an encouraging and non-judgemental manner. A number of studies also focused on the importance of good information about alcohol misuse and about its treatment (particularly assisted withdrawal), and the GDG makes a detailed recommendation about provision of comprehensive and accessible information.

The GDG also makes a number of recommendations regarding working with families and carers. Given the challenges of caring for someone with an alcohol problem, as described in the review of the literature, more information and support should be available to carers and there should be an emphasis on including them in the treatment process, if this is appropriate and the service user agrees. Furthermore, with the understanding of how important positive social support networks are in maintaining positive change, helping carers supporting their supportive role is crucial so as to promote change.

Children of parents who have alcohol problems will have specific needs that should be recognised. They may struggle to form stable relationships and their education and own mental health may be affected. More opportunities to support those who have parents with alcohol problems, as well as finding ways for them to talk about their emotions, would be beneficial and may help prevent the child or young person developing their own alcohol problems later in life.

4.4   RECOMMENDATIONS

Building a trusting relationship and providing information
4.4.1.1   When working with people who misuse alcohol:
- build a trusting relationship and work in a supportive, empathic and non judgmental manner
- take into account that stigma and discrimination are often associated with alcohol misuse and that minimising the problem may be part of the service user's presentation
- make sure that discussions take place in settings in which confidentiality, privacy and dignity are respected.

4.4.1.2   When working with people who misuse alcohol:
- provide information appropriate to their level of understanding about the nature and treatment of alcohol misuse to support choice from a range of evidence-based treatments
- avoid clinical language without explanation
- make sure that comprehensive written information is available in an appropriate language or, for those who cannot use written text, in an accessible format
- provide independent interpreters (that is, someone who is not known to the service user) if needed.

Working with and supporting families and carers
4.4.1.3   Encourage families and carers to be involved in the treatment and care of people who misuse alcohol to help support and maintain positive change.

4.4.1.4   When families and carers are involved in supporting a person who misuses alcohol, discuss concerns about the impact of alcohol misuse on themselves and other family members, and:

- provide written and verbal information on alcohol misuse and its management, including how families and carers can support the service user
- offer a carer's assessment where necessary
- negotiate with the service user and their family or carer about the family or carer's involvement in their care and the sharing of information; make sure the service user's, family's and carer's right to confidentiality is respected.

4.4.1.5   All staff in contact with parents who misuse alcohol and who have care of or regular contact with their children, should:

- take account of the impact of the parent's drinking on the parent-child relationship and the child's development, education, mental and physical health, own alcohol use, safety and social network
- be aware of and comply with the requirements of the Children Act (2004).

5 ORGANISATION AND DELIVERY OF CARE

SECTION 1 – INTRODUCTION TO THE

ORGANISATION AND DELIVERY OF CARE

5.1 INTRODUCTION

This chapter provides an overview of the types of services available for people who misuse alcohol and how they are currently organised, and reviews the evidence to guide future development and improvements in service provision. The key concepts underpinning service organisation and delivery will be explained and their nature and role will be defined. These concepts will build on existing guidance in the field, notably *Models of Care for Alcohol Misusers* (MoCAM) developed by the National Treatment Agency and the Department of Health (Department of Health, 2006b) and the *Review of the Effectiveness of Treatment for Alcohol Problems* (Raistrick *et al.*, 2006). Where relevant, parallel guidance from NICE on alcohol services will be referred to, in particular the NICE guideline on prevention and early detection (NICE, 2010a) and the NICE guideline on management of alcohol-related physical complications (NICE, 2010b). Because this guideline was the last in the suite of NICE guidelines on alcohol misuse to be developed, this chapter aims to integrate and provide an overview of how the various guidelines are related in order to support the development of a comprehensive pathway for the care and treatment of alcohol misuse.

In Chapter 2 it was highlighted that alcohol service commissioning and provision across England is variable and in some cases poorly integrated (National Audit Office, 2008). Hence the availability of alcohol services and the extent to which they meet the needs of people who misuse alcohol vary across England (Drummond *et al.*, 2005). The GDG also took the view that there is a lack of clarity in the field about which kinds of alcohol services are most beneficial for which people – for example, who should be treated in a community setting compared with a residential setting, what constitutes an adequate assessment of individual's presenting needs and how an individual's care can be most appropriately coordinated. These are all key questions that need to be addressed. This lack of clarity has resulted in diverse commissioning and provision of alcohol services.

This chapter will also highlight that the provision of care for people who misuse alcohol is not solely the responsibility of the agencies and staff who specialise in alcohol treatment. Staff across a wide range of health, social care and criminal justice services who are not exclusively working with people who misuse alcohol but regularly come into contact with them in the course of providing other services also have a crucial role to play in helping people to access appropriate care. In some cases, staff that are not alcohol treatment specialists (most notably those working in primary care) will have a role in delivering key elements of an integrated care pathway for this population.

The chapter begins by describing the organising principles of care for people who misuse alcohol, followed by a description of the different types of services and how they are currently organised; where relevant, existing definitions and frameworks will be referred to. The principles and methods of care delivery, including assessment, care coordination, integrated care pathways and stepped care, will then be reviewed. Evidence on case management, stepped care, ACT, assessment, assisted alcohol withdrawal and care delivered in residential versus community settings will also be reviewed. The chapter will conclude with a description of the main care pathways stemming from the findings of the evidence review.

5.2   ORGANISING PRINCIPLES OF CARE

The introductory chapter highlighted the diverse range and severity of alcohol misuse that exist in the general population, from hazardous and harmful drinking through to alcohol dependence of varying degrees of severity. Alcohol misuse is associated with a wide range of physical, psychological and social problems, some of which are a direct consequence of drinking and others are incidental, but often highly relevant, in planning and delivering individual care. For example, a harmful alcohol user who is homeless and suffering from mental health problems may have more significant care needs than a more severely dependent drinker who has stable accommodation and employment and no psychiatric comorbidity.

It was also noted in Chapter 2 that in many cases alcohol misuse remits without any form of formal intervention or contact with the health or social care system, let alone specialist alcohol treatment. Studies of what has been referred to as 'spontaneous remission' from alcohol misuse find that this is often attributed, by individuals, to both positive and negative life events, such as getting married, taking on childcare responsibilities, or experiencing a negative consequence of drinking such as being arrested, having an accident or experiencing alcoholic hepatitis. It therefore follows that not everyone in the general population who meets the criteria for a diagnosis of an alcohol-use disorder requires specialist treatment. Often a brief intervention from a GP, for example, may be sufficient to help an individual reduce their drinking to a less harmful level (see NICE guideline on prevention and early detection; NICE, 2010a).

Nevertheless, the level of alcohol consumption, and the severity of alcohol dependence and alcohol-related problems, are positively correlated such that people with more severe alcohol dependence usually have more severe problems and greater care needs (Wu & Ringwalt, 2004). Also, a proportion of people will require professional intervention to achieve sufficient change in their drinking behaviour, or to shorten the course of their alcohol-use disorder.

A useful framework for this spectrum of need and the intensity of professional responses was provided by Raistrick and colleagues (2006), adapted from work

ASAM Levels III and IV both fit within MoCAM Tier 4 interventions. Level III is residential (medically monitored) treatment which is closest to residential rehabilitation in England and provides medical cover, often by local GPs who are not necessarily specialists in alcohol treatment. Level IV is medically managed intensive inpatient treatment which is closest to NHS provided inpatient treatment and is usually led by specialist addiction psychiatrists in England.

Text Box 2: Levels of care for addiction treatment (Mee-Lee *et al.*, 2001)

Level I – Outpatient treatment
Treatment provided in regularly scheduled sessions at a treatment centre, designed to help the individual achieve changes in their alcohol use and physical, psychological and social functioning

Level II – Intensive outpatient treatment/partial hospitalisation
An organised outpatient service that delivers treatment services during the day, before or after work or school, in the evenings or on weekends. Such treatment may include medical and psychiatric assessment and treatment, medication, psychological interventions, and educational, housing and employment support.

Level III – Residential (medically-monitored) treatment
Organised services staffed by designated addiction treatment and mental health personnel who provide a planned regimen of care in a 24-hour live-in setting. Such services adhere to defined sets of policies and procedures. They are housed in, or affiliated with, permanent facilities where patients can reside safely. They are staffed 24 hours a day. They all serve individuals who need safe and stable living environments in order to develop their recovery skills. Such living environments may be housed in the same facility where treatment services are provided or they may be in a separate facility affiliated with the treatment provider

Level IV – Medically-managed intensive inpatient treatment
Provide a planned regimen of 24-hour medically directed evaluation, care and treatment of mental and substance-related disorders in an acute care inpatient setting. They are staffed by designated addiction specialist doctors, including psychiatrists, as well as other mental-health and specialist addiction clinicians. Such services are delivered under a defined set of policies and procedures and have permanent facilities that include inpatient beds. They provide care to patients whose mental and substance-related problems are so severe that they require primary biomedical, psychiatric and nursing care. Treatment is provided 24 hours a day, and the full resources of a general acute care hospital or psychiatric hospital are available. The treatment is specific to mental and substance-related disorders – however, the skills of the interdisciplinary team and the availability of support services allow the conjoint treatment of any co-occurring biomedical conditions that need to be addressed.

In England, generic agencies providing interventions for people who misuse alcohol are also diverse. Important among these are general NHS services and criminal justice agencies. Within the NHS, GPs frequently come into contact with people who misuse alcohol and have an important role to play in providing Tier 1 interventions, including early identification, advice, brief intervention and referral of patients to specialist alcohol agencies. Some primary care staff, including GPs, practice nurses and counsellors, also provide more complex alcohol interventions including assisted alcohol withdrawal, and psychological and pharmacological interventions. Sometimes this is provided in a collaborative shared care arrangement with a specialist alcohol treatment agency in liaison with specialist addiction psychiatrists and nurses. Some GPs also provide medical support to residential non-statutory agencies such as assisted alcohol withdrawal.

In relation to the criminal justice system, forensic medical examiners are often called upon to provide assessment and management of detainees in police custody who misuse alcohol. This often includes the management of acute conditions, such as severe alcohol intoxication or alcohol withdrawal. Prison health services also have a key role in the assessment and management of prisoners who misuse alcohol, including assessment and management of assisted alcohol withdrawal.

In acute hospitals a wide range of healthcare professionals come into contact with people who misuse alcohol. In particular, staff in accident and emergency departments often encounter patients with alcohol-related presentations, such as accidents and injuries sustained whilst intoxicated with alcohol, and can play an important role in early identification and intervention. Alcohol-misusing patients admitted to acute hospitals, either in an emergency or for elective treatment, present an opportunity for early identification and intervention. Some acute hospitals will have specialist alcohol liaison teams, often led by addiction psychiatrists or nurses, who support the acute care staff and provide staff training, assessment, intervention and referral to specialist alcohol agencies. Accident and emergency department staff also encounter patients presenting in acute unplanned alcohol withdrawal (NICE, 2010b) and some of these patients will require assisted alcohol withdrawal.

Alcohol misuse is common in clients attending mental health services, particularly among the severely mentally ill (Weaver *et al.*, 2003), but seldom identified by mental health staff (Barnaby *et al.*, 2003). This represents an important missed opportunity to provide early alcohol intervention or referral to specialist services. Also, mental health clients attending both inpatient and community mental health services will often require assisted alcohol withdrawal. Given the wide range of physical co-morbidities associated with alcohol use, there are also potential benefits from improving generic staff competencies in a wider range of healthcare settings. Staff working in these generic settings need to be competent to identify, assess and manage the complications of alcohol misuse. Some mental health trusts have an addiction liaison service provided by specialist addiction psychiatrists and nurses in a model similar to that described above for acute hospitals.

5.3.5 Coordination and organisation of care

From the foregoing, it is apparent that the range of interventions and the agencies that provide them are highly complex and diverse, with considerable geographic variation. This diversity presents challenges both for the person who misuses alcohol and at a treatment system level. For the person entering treatment for the first time, the array of interventions, agencies and staff can be bewildering. Service users, therefore, need considerable help in orientation and understanding what is available to them and what services they might require. Also, the alcohol interventions that an individual requires may be provided by several different agencies in the course of an episode of care, as well as needing care from a range of generic agencies for physical, psychological or social problems. As clients move between different agencies there is considerable potential for premature disengagement. There is therefore the care of an individual client's needs to be planned and coordinated.

5.3.6 Care coordination

Several terms have been used to describe the coordination of care within specialist alcohol services, including case management, keyworking, care coordination, care planning and assertive outreach. In MoCAM (Department of Health, 2006a) there is an expectation that all cases would be care coordinated. These include harmful drinkers who respond to a brief intervention but do not usually require more intensive form of care coordination such as case management. More severely dependent drinkers with complex mental or physical comorbidities or social needs usually require considerable case management due to the complex nature of their problems and/or the wide range of agencies involved. Some studies reviewed in this chapter include more assertive approaches in supporting clients, including ACT.

In this guideline, two terms are mainly used: care coordination and case management. Care coordination describes the coordination of an individual's care whilst in a treatment episode. It is limited in its responsibilities and may involve little or no direct contact with the patient, but rather the focus is on assuring all agreed elements of the care package are linked together and communicated in a clear and effective manner. Case management, as defined in this guideline, is a more substantial endeavour and has several elements. The individual case manager is responsible for assessment of the individual client's needs, development of a care plan in collaboration with the client and relevant others (including relatives and carers, other staff in specialist and generic agencies involved in the client's care), coordination of the delivery of interventions and services, providing support to the client to assist in access to and engagement with services and interventions. The case manager will often use psychological interventions such as motivational interviewing to enhance the client's readiness to engage with treatment. The case manager is also responsible for monitoring the outcome of interventions and revising the care plan accordingly. Case management is a skilled task which requires appropriately competent clinical staff to deliver it effectively. Further, to discharge this function effectively, case managers need to limit the number of clients they can support at any one time. Case management is a Tier 3/4 intervention within MoCAM and should begin with a comprehensive specialist clinical assessment.

5.3.7 Integrated care pathways and stepped care

An integrated care pathway 'describes the nature and anticipated course of treatment for a particular client and a predetermined plan of treatment' (National Treatment Agency, 2002). Integrated care pathways have a function at both an individual and a treatment system level. At the individual level the care plan should describe the client's personalised care pathway, designed to meet the assessed needs, the planned interventions, and the agencies and staff intended to deliver them. The pathway needs to be integrated so that it shows a logical progression of steps with interventions being provided at the appropriate stages. For example, an alcohol-dependent client may initially require inpatient assisted alcohol withdrawal followed by a structured psychosocial intervention in an alcohol day programme, followed by specialised psychotherapy for PTSD, followed by vocational services to support a return to work. Each of these elements of care may be delivered by different agencies in different locations, and the pathway needs to be integrated to deliver maximum benefit and minimise the client's premature disengagement.

Stepped care is a method of organising and providing services in the most cost efficient way to meet individual needs (Sobell & Sobell, 2000). Two defining characteristics are common to all stepped-care systems (Davison, 2000). The first concerns the provision of the least restrictive and least costly intervention (including assessments) that will be effective for an individual's presenting problems, and the second is concerned with building in a self-correcting mechanism. Escalating levels of response to the complexity or severity of the disorder are often implicit in the organisation and delivery of many healthcare interventions, but a stepped-care system is an explicit attempt to formalise the delivery and monitoring of patient flow through the system. In establishing a stepped-care approach, consideration should not only be given to the degree of restrictiveness associated with a treatment, and its costs and effectiveness, but also the likelihood of its uptake by a patient and the likely impact that an unsuccessful intervention will have on the probability of other interventions being taken up.

Within this approach people who misuse alcohol are initially offered the least intensive intervention that is acceptable and most likely to be effective for them, followed by increasingly intensive interventions for those not responding to the less intensive interventions. A stepped-care algorithm effectively describes an integrated care pathway that accommodates individual needs and responses to interventions (Drummond *et al.*, 2009). This approach has gained increasing currency in other mental health disorders, including depression (NICE, 2009b). The stepped-care approach has also been supported by recent guidance from the National Treatment Agency and the Department of Health (National Treatment Agency for Substance Misuse, 2002; Raistrick *et al.*, 2006). The evidence for stepped care for alcohol misuse is reviewed later in this chapter.

5.3.8   Relationship of this guidance to other NICE guidelines

This guideline is focused on the identification, assessment and management of harmful alcohol use and alcohol dependence (alcohol misuse). The NICE guideline on prevention and early detection (NICE, 2010a) is concerned with a range of preventive strategies for alcohol-use disorders. This includes alcohol screening and brief intervention, which is not only a Tier 1 alcohol intervention but also potentially acts as a gateway to other more intensive interventions for alcohol misuse. The NICE guideline on management of alcohol-related physical complications (NICE, 2010b) is focused on the management of a wide range of physical consequences of alcohol misuse. These include the management of assisted alcohol withdrawal in acute hospital settings, which are Tier 4 interventions. However, the guideline is restricted to the management of unplanned assisted alcohol withdrawal – that is, in circumstances where a patient presents to hospital already in a state of alcohol withdrawal. This guideline is concerned with a much wider range of potential scenarios where people who misuse alcohol may require assisted alcohol withdrawal, including where assisted withdrawal is provided in a planned way as part of an integrated programme of alcohol specialist care, and where people are identified as being at risk of developing alcohol withdrawal in acute hospitals or prison settings and therefore require planned assisted alcohol withdrawal.

SECTION 2 – EVALUATING THE ORGANISATION OF CARE

FOR PEOPLE WHO MISUSE ALCOHOL

5.4   REVIEW QUESTION

In adults with alcohol misuse, what is the clinical efficacy, cost-effectiveness, safety of and patient satisfaction associated with different systems for the organisation of care?

5.5   INTRODUCTION

This section presents reviews of the evidence for case management, ACT and stepped care. The reviews and evidence summaries are presented separately, but a combined section on evidence into recommendation is presented at the end of this section along with the recommendations developed by the GDG. In reviewing the evidence for the effectiveness of different service delivery models, the GDG initially decided to focus on RCTs. The use of this type of study design to evaluate service-level interventions gives rise to a number of problems, including the definition of the interventions, the specification of the comparator and the interpretation of results of trials of complex healthcare interventions across different healthcare systems (Campbell *et al.*, 2007). As demonstrated in the section below, the use of RCTs was further complicated by the limited number of studies identified. This led the GDG to include a range of observational studies in a review of the service delivery models, both to increase the available evidence base and also because some observational studies may provide richer data on what services do, how they do it, and how they differ from alternative types of service and the standard care they hope to replace. Given the nature of the studies identified, a narrative synthesis of observational and RCT studies that were relevant to the review question but could not be meta-analysed was conducted after the review of RCTs.

5.6   CASE MANAGEMENT

5.6.1   Introduction

For the purposes of the guideline, case management is defined as the bringing together of the assessment, planning, coordination and monitoring of care under one umbrella. In a number of cases all four of these activities will be undertaken by one individual, but in other cases some of the above functions will be undertaken by other team members or health professionals and coordinated by one individual. In some case management interventions the case manager adopts largely a brokerage role, while at other times they take on an active and direct clinical role. Where the case manager takes on an active clinical role using a specific intervention (for example, CBT), such interventions were excluded from the case management review and included in another relevant review within this guideline. Case management may also vary in its duration and intensity. For the purposes of this guideline, the GDG took the view that the intervention should be of sufficient duration to allow for all four functions to be undertaken.

5.6.2   Clinical review protocol

Information about the databases searched and the inclusion/exclusion criteria used for this section of the guideline can be found in Table 6.

5.6.3   Studies considered[11]

The review team conducted a new systematic search for RCTs and systematic reviews that assessed the benefits and downsides of case management and related health economic evidence.

---

[11]Here and elsewhere in the guideline, each study considered for review is referred to by a study ID in capital letters (primary author and date of study publication, except where a study is in press or only submitted for publication, then a date is not used).

**Table 6: Databases searched and inclusion/exclusion criteria for
clinical evidence**

Electronic databases	CINAHL, EMBASE, MEDLINE, PsycINFO, Cochrane Library
Date searched	Systematic reviews from 1993 to March 2010; RCTs from database inception to March 2010; observational and quasi-experimental studies from database inception to October 2010
Study design	Systematic reviews, RCTs, observational studies, quasi-experimental studies
Patient population	Alcohol dependence or harmful drinking
Interventions	Case management versus other treatment Case management versus treatment as usual (TAU)
Outcomes	Aftercare attendance; engagement in aftercare; abstinence; drinking frequency measures (for example, number of days drinking in the past month); quantity of alcohol consumption measures (for example, drinks per drinking day [DDD]); number retained in treatment; relapse; lapse

Five trials (three RCTs and two observational studies) relating to clinical evidence met the eligibility criteria set by the GDG, providing data on 1,261 participants. Of these trials, all five were published in peer-reviewed journals between 1983 and 1999. In addition, 13 studies were excluded from the analysis. The most common reason for exclusion was no usable outcome data, or the intervention was aimed at a primarily drug misusing population rather than alcohol misuse. Summary study characteristics of the included studies are presented in Table 7. (further information about both included and excluded studies can be found in Appendix 16b).

Case management versus treatment as usual
There were three RCTs and two observational studies involving comparisons of case management and treatment as usual (AHLES1983; CONRAD1998; COX1998; MCLELLAN1999; PATTERSON1997). AHLES1983 compared case management with treatment as usual (standard aftercare arrangements), where the importance of attending aftercare was emphasised but not enforced. Patients were scheduled for one aftercare session at discharge and aftercare consisted of individual problem-oriented counselling. COX1998 compared case management with treatment as usual (there was no further description of treatment as usual). CONRAD1998 compared two types of residential inpatient care; the experimental group was case managed, whereas the control group participated in the residential care programme without case management.

Two observational were also included in the review. PATTERSON1997 compared the addition of a community psychiatric nurse (CPN) to aftercare with standard hospital care. Standard hospital care consisted of an offer of review appointments every 6 weeks following discharge. Lastly, MCLELLAN1999 compared case management with treatment as usual (no case management). In the standard-care condition, participants received group abstinence-oriented outpatient drug-misuse counselling twice weekly. In the case management condition, participants received a clinical case manager to provide support for housing, medical care, legal advice and parenting classes in addition to the drug counselling programme. For a graphical representation of the data, these two studies were inputted into the forest plots for comparison with the results of the RCTs; however, it should be noted that the outcomes and data were not pooled with the data found in the RCTs.

Table 7: Study information table for trials of case management

	Case management versus TAU
Total number of trials (total number of participants)	5 RCTs (N = 1262)
Study ID	(1) AHLES1983 (2) COX1998 (3) CONRAD1998 (4) MCLELLAN1999 (observational) (5) PATTERSON1997 (observational)

Baseline severity (mean [standard deviation; SD])	(1) 80% admitted to levels of drinking within the abusive range
	(2) Days of drinking (any alcohol use) in last 30 days:
	      Case management: 23.6 (9.2)
	      Control: 23 8 (9.1)
	(3) Days of alcohol use in past 30 days (mean): 18.4 for control group; 19.0 for experimental group
	(4) Whole sample on average reported 13.4 years of problem alcohol use (12.1)
	(5) Daily alcohol (units) (mean [SD])
	      CPN aftercare: 39.4 (18.3)
	      Standard aftercare: 42.9 (16.6)

Length of follow-up	(1) 6- and 12-month (2) Assessed in 6-month intervals up to 2-year follow-up (3) 3, 6 and 9 months during enrolment and 12, 18 and 24 months after completion of treatment. (4) 6-month (5) Assessed at 1, 2, 3, 4 and 5 years post-treatment

5.6.4   Clinical evidence for case management

Evidence from the important outcomes and overall quality of evidence are presented in Table 7 and Table 8. The associated forest plots can be found in Appendix 17a.

Table 8: Case management versus TAU

Outcome or subgroup	K	Total N	Statistics	Effect (95% CI)	Quality of the evidence (GRADE)
Lapse (non-abstinence)					
At 6-month follow-up	1	36	RR (M-H, Random, 95% CI)	0.27 (0.11,0.65)	⊕⊕⊕O MODERATE
At 12-month follow-up (RCT)	1	36	RR (M-H, Random, 95% CI)	0.75 (0.52,1.08)	⊕⊕⊕O MODERATE
At 2-year follow-up (non-RCT)	1	122	RR (M-H, Random, 95% CI)	0.88 (0.69,1.12)	⊕OOO VERY LOW
At 3-year follow-up	1	122	RR (M-H, Random, 95% CI)	0.68 (0.53,0.85)	⊕OOO VERY LOW
At 4-year follow-up	1	122	RR (M-H, Random, 95% CI)	0.57 (0.45,0.73)	⊕OOO VERY LOW
At 5-year follow-up	1	122	RR (M-H, Random, 95% CI)	0.49 (0.37,0.63)	⊕OOO VERY LOW
Drinking frequency					
Mean days of alcohol intoxication (non-RCT)	1	537	SMD (IV, Random, 95% CI)	−0.07 (−0.25,0.11)	⊕⊕OO LOW
Days any alcohol use at 6-month follow-up	2	551	SMD (IV, Random, 95% CI)	−0.10 (−0.40,0.20)	⊕⊕⊕⊕ HIGH
Days using alcohol since last interview at 6-month follow-up	1	193	SMD (IV, Random, 95% CI)	−0.34 (−0.63,-0.05)	⊕⊕⊕⊕ HIGH
Days drinking any alcohol in last 30 days at 9-month follow-up	1	358	SMD (IV, Random, 95% CI)	−0.13 (−0.34,0.08)	⊕⊕⊕⊕ HIGH
Days drinking any alcohol in last 30 days at 12-month follow-up	1	193	SMD (IV, Random, 95% CI)	−0.21 (−0.49,0.08)	⊕⊕⊕⊕ HIGH
Days using any alcohol since last interview at 12-month follow-up	1	193	SMD (IV, Random, 95% CI)	−0.30 (−0.59,-0.01)	⊕⊕⊕⊕ HIGH
Days drinking any alcohol in last 30 days at 18-month follow-up	1	193	SMD (IV, Random, 95% CI)	−0.33 (−0.62,-0.05)	⊕⊕⊕⊕ HIGH
Days using alcohol since last interview at 18-month follow-up	1	193	SMD (IV, Random, 95% CI)	−0.49 (−0.78,-0.20)	⊕⊕⊕⊕ HIGH

Note. M-H = Mantel-Haenszel estimate; IV = inverse variance.

5.6.5   Evidence summary

Case management versus treatment as usual
There was a significant difference in lapse (non-abstinence) at 6-month follow-up, in favour of case management, with a small effect size; however, this effect was not significant at 12-month follow-up. There was a significant difference favouring case management found at 3-, 4- and 5-year follow-up, with the largest effect size occurring at 3-year follow-up and decreasing to a moderate effect size at 4- and 5-year follow-up, respectively. It is important to note that these results are based on one observational study (PATTERSON1997).

On measures of drinking frequency, when considering the number of days drinking any alcohol (in the last 30 days) or mean days of intoxication, there were no significant differences between case management or treatment as usual at either 6-, 9- or 12-month follow-up. Interestingly, there was a significant effect observed at 18-month follow-up in favour of case management (small effect size) based on the results of one study (COX1998).

When considering the number of days using alcohol since the last interview (COX1998), there was a significant difference observed, favouring case management over treatment as usual at all follow-up points (small to moderate effect sizes): 6-, 12- and 18-month follow-up.

Based on the GRADE methodology outlined in Chapter 3, the quality of this evidence is *moderate*, therefore further research is likely to have an important impact on the confidence in the estimate of the effect (see Table 8).

Due to the heterogeneous nature of studies within case management, it was not possible to combine the outcome data provided across studies. As a result, there are a number of RCTs which add value to the meta-analysis presented. For the purpose of this guideline and to obtain a better overview of the available literature, four RCTs (Chutuape *et al.*, 2001; Gilbert, 1988; Krupski *et al.*, 2009; Sannibale *et al.*, 2003; Stout *et al.*, 1999), which met methodological criteria but did not have outcomes that could be used in meta-analyses for this review, are described below.

Gilbert (1988) conducted an RCT comparing case management, a home visit and treatment as usual for those with alcohol dependence. After receiving inpatient or outpatient treatment, patients were scheduled to be assigned a case manager or have a home visit, which consisted of appointments scheduled not at the hospital but at a convenient location for the patient. Patients in the home visit condition were contacted with follow-up letters to reschedule aftercare appointments. In the traditional treatment (treatment as usual), no active attempts were made to improve attendance at aftercare appointments. On appointment keeping measures, results from an analysis of variance (ANOVA) revealed a significant group by time interaction $F = 4.56$ (6,240), $p < 0.01$, and post-hoc Tukey's Honestly Significant Difference (HSD) test revealed significant differences between home visit and case manager groups at 6- ($p < 0.05$), 9- and 12-month follow-up ($p < 0.01$). Both active treatment groups showed a decline in appointment keeping rates after the therapists stopped making active attempts to encourage the patient to attend therapy. On drinking outcomes, there were no significant differences between groups at any follow-up point.

Stout and colleagues (1999) conducted an RCT comparing case monitoring versus treatment as usual for those with alcohol dependence. The results indicated a significant difference on percentage of days heavy drinking at 3-year follow-up, where the frequency of heavy drinking was twice as high in the controls as in the case monitored participants. In addition, survival analysis indicated that case monitoring was significantly better at prolonging time to lapse and relapse (p = 0.05), as well as in reducing the severity of the relapse. There was no significant difference between the two groups for time to first heavy drinking day (p = 0.1). It should be noted that 66% of this sample had a comorbid Axis 1 diagnosis.

Chutuape and colleagues (2001) looked at the transition from an assisted-withdrawal programme to aftercare. Participants were randomly assigned to one of three conditions: incentive and escort to aftercare; incentive only; or standard treatment. Standard treatment participants only received referral instructions and were told to go to aftercare following discharge. Results from a logistic regression analysis indicated that aftercare contact rates differed significantly by referral condition (p = 0.001). Post hoc tests indicated that participants in the escort and incentive and incentive only conditions completed intake at aftercare more (p <0.05) than those receiving standard treatment.

When comparing a structured aftercare programme with an unstructured aftercare programme, Sannibale and colleagues (2003) found that structured programmes had a fourfold increase in aftercare attendance (odds ratio [OR] 4.3, 95% CI 1.7 to 11.2) and a reduced rate of uncontrolled substance use at follow-up (OR 0.3, 95% CI 0.1 to 0.9). Furthermore, participants in either aftercare condition relapsed later than those who attended no aftercare programme; however, this significant difference did not emerge for time to lapse.

More recently, Krupski and colleagues (2009) evaluated the impact of recovery support services (including case management) provided through an access to recovery programme in the US for clients undergoing substance-misuse treatment. Standard treatment consisted of 'chemical dependency treatment'. The comparison group was a multi-modal programme entitled Access to Recovery (ATR), which included a case management component. They found that in comparison with standard care the ATR programme was associated with increased length of stay in treatment and completion of treatment (42.5 days longer). Further, multivariate survival analysis indicated the risk of ending treatment was significantly lower (hazard ratio = 0.58, p <0.05) among the ATR clients.

5.6.6 Special populations

No studies that evaluated the efficacy of case management for children and young people or older people and met inclusion criteria were identified.

5.6.7 Health economic evidence

No studies were identified in the systematic literature review that considered the cost effectiveness of case management in the treatment of alcohol misuse. Details on the methods used for the systematic review of the health economic literature for this guideline are described in Chapter 3.

5.7   ASSERTIVE COMMUNITY TREATMENT

5.7.1   Introduction

ACT is a method of delivering treatment and care which was originally developed for people with serious mental illness in the community (Thompson *et al.*, 1990). The intention is to prevent or reduce admission to hospital. The model of care has been defined and validated, based upon the consensus of an international panel of experts (McGrew *et al.*, 1994; McGrew & Bond, 1995). Over time, the focus has shifted to provide for effective support in the community to those with severe, long-term mental illness who may previously have spent many years as hospital inpatients. ACT now aims to support continued engagement with services, reduce the extent (and cost) of hospital admissions and improve outcomes (particularly quality of life and social functioning).

The evidence for effectiveness in the international literature is strong for severe mental illness (Marshall & Lockwood, 2002), although this may in part be due to the comparator used (essentially poor quality standard care). For example, ACT has been shown to be effective in the US (Marshall & Lockwood, 2002), but less so in the UK where standard care is of a better quality (Killaspy *et al.*, 2006). There is little evidence for the effectiveness of ACT in alcohol disorders and the evidence from the field of dual diagnosis (psychosis and substance misuse) is currently rather weak (NICE, 2011a).

5.7.2   Clinical review protocol

Information about the databases searched and the inclusion/exclusion criteria used for this section of the guideline can be found in Table 9.

5.7.3   Studies considered[12]

For the purposes of this guideline the GDG adopted the definition of ACT used by Marshall and Lockwood (2002), which identified the following key elements:
- care is provided by a multidisciplinary team (usually involving a psychiatrist with dedicated sessions)
- care is exclusively provided for a defined group of people (those with severe and chronic problem)

---

[12]Here and elsewhere in the guideline, each study considered for review is referred to by a study ID in capital letters (primary author and date of study publication, except where a study is in press or only submitted for publication, then a date is not used).

Table 9: Databases searched and inclusion/exclusion criteria for clinical evidence

Electronic databases	CINAHL, EMBASE, MEDLINE, PsycINFO, Cochrane Library
Date searched	Systematic reviews from 1993 to March 2010; RCTs from database inception to March 2010; observational and quasi-experimental studies from database inception to October 2010.
Study design	Systematic reviews, RCTs, observational studies, quasi-experimental studies
Patient population	Diagnosed with an alcohol-use disorder (alcohol dependence) or alcohol misuse
Interventions	ACT versus other active interventions ACT versus TAU
Outcomes	None specified

- team members share responsibility for clients, so that several members may work with the same client, and members do not have individual caseloads (unlike case management)
- the team attempts to provide all psychiatric and social care for each service user, rather than making referrals to other agencies
- care is provided at home or in the workplace, as far as possible
- treatment and care are offered assertively to individuals who are uncooperative or reluctant ('assertive outreach')
- medication concordance is emphasised.

The review team conducted a new systematic search for RCTs and systematic reviews that assessed the benefits and downsides of ACT methods.

Four trials relating to clinical evidence met the eligibility criteria set by the GDG, providing data on 706 participants. Of these, none were unpublished and three were published in peer-reviewed journals between 1991 and 2008. In addition, two studies were excluded. The most common reason for exclusion was due to a comorbid sample population of psychosis (where this was the primary diagnosis) and alcohol dependence/misuse. Summary study characteristics of the included studies are presented Table 10 (further information about both included and excluded studies can be found in Appendix 16b).

A meta-analysis was not performed as there was only one non-randomised study which concerned people who misuse alcohol as the primary group (Passetti *et al.*, 2008). The three RCTs, Bond and McDonel (1991), Drake and colleagues (1998) and Essock and colleagues (2006), include populations with co-existing and primary

Table 10: Characteristics of studies evaluating assertive methods

Study	Study design	Comparisons	Outcomes	Baseline severity	Treatment characteristics	Results
PASSETTI2008 (UK)	Non-randomised parallel cohort pilot study	Flexible access clinic (ACT methods) Usual care clinic	Percentage completed assessment Percentage completed aftercare Percentage completed medically assisted withdrawal	Alcohol units per week (mean [SD]): Flexible access: 143 (111) Usual care: 177 (120)	Flexible access clinic (n = 188): two walk-in weekly slots, each of 3 hours; two full-time CPNs, social workers, clinical psychologists and medical cover provided by staff of community alcohol team. Offered community-based assessments whenever patients had failed to attend. Modelled on ACT in the sense that it targeted patients with a history of disengagement; maintained a small case load; operated proactively and engaged assertively; it offered flexible access including assessment and treatment in the community where required; run by a CPN care coordinator working within a multidisciplinary team that met frequently, typically after each assessment or review. Usual care clinic (n = 223): two full-time specialist CPNs and two social workers. Full time medical staff; large caseload (25 to 30), multidisciplinary case discussion took place once weekly or less, community-based assessments were not offered and limited integration of health and social care staff work.	No significant differences between the two groups on percentage completing assessment. Significant differences found between two groups on percentage completed withdrawal programmes, $p < 0.05$ (in favour of flexible access clinic) and percentage entered aftercare, $p < 0.02$

diagnosis psychosis and substance misuse, and thus have been covered in another NICE guideline on psychosis and substance misuse (NICE, 2011a). It is important to note that in the Bond and McDonel (1991) study, 70% had a primary diagnosis of schizophrenia or schizoaffective disorder and 61% reported their primary substance misuse problem was with alcohol. Conversely, in the Essock and colleagues' (2006) study, 76% had a primary diagnosis of schizophrenia or schizoaffective disorder, and 74% misused alcohol while 81% used other substances. In the Drake and colleagues' (1998) study, 53.4% had a primary diagnosis of schizophrenia, 22.4% of schizoaffective disorder, 24.2% of bipolar and 72.6% of the sample misused alcohol. No differences were reported in any of the three trials on relapse outcomes, and there were no significant differences reported on hospitalisation or relapse rates in the Essock and colleagues' (2006) or Drake and colleagues' (1998) trials, both comparing ACT with case management. In the Bond and McDonel (1991) trial, there were significant differences in treatment engagement and completion of assessment, but no significant differences between groups on drinking outcomes.

5.7.4   Evidence summary

Passetti and colleagues (2008) conducted a parallel cohort trial comparing a flexible access clinic (based on ACT principles) with a usual care clinic. Treatment as usual (usual care clinic) consisted of two specialist alcohol community nurses and social workers. Medical cover was provided by a consultant, an associate specialist and a junior doctor. Care coordinators had a relatively large caseload and there was limited integration of health and social care staff, along with less community-based assessments and case discussions. The trial found that participants in the flexible access clinic were significantly more likely to complete withdrawal (Pearson's Chi square test, $\chi^2 = 4.43$ p $= 0.05$) and enter an aftercare programme earlier (Student's t-test, $t = 2.61$, p $= 0.02$). No significant difference between the two groups was found on completion of assessment and drinking outcomes were not measured.

5.7.5   Special populations

No studies evaluating the efficacy of ACT for children and young people or older people which met inclusion criteria could be identified.

5.7.6   Health economic evidence

No studies were identified in the systematic literature review that considered the cost effectiveness of ACT for alcohol misuse. Details on the methods used for the systematic review of the health economic literature for this guideline are described in Chapter 3.

5.8 STEPPED CARE

5.8.1 Introduction

The stepped-care approach to care is based on two key principles (Davison, 2000; Sobell & Sobell, 2000):

- The provision of the least restrictive and least costly intervention that will be effective for a person's presenting problems.
- The use of a self-correcting mechanism which is designed to ensure that if an individual does not benefit from an initial intervention, a system of monitoring is in place to identify a more appropriate and intensive intervention is provided.

Stepped-care models, which have their origins in the treatment of tobacco addiction (Sobell & Sobell, 2000), provide for escalating levels of response to the complexity or severity of the disorder and are an explicit attempt to formalise the delivery and monitoring of patient flow through the system. In establishing a stepped-care approach, consideration should be given not only to the degree of restrictiveness associated with a treatment, and its costs and effectiveness, but also to the likelihood of its uptake by a patient and the likely impact that an unsuccessful intervention will have on the probability of other interventions being taken up. Despite the origins in the field of addiction, stepped-care systems have not been the subject of much formal evaluation in the area.

A review by Bower and Gilbody (2005) of the evidence for the use of stepped care in the provision of psychological therapies generally was unable to identify a significant body of evidence. However, they set out three assumptions on which they argued a stepped-care framework should be built and which should be considered in any evaluation of stepped care. These assumptions concern the equivalence of clinical outcomes (between minimal and more intensive interventions, at least for some patients), the efficient use of resources (including healthcare resources outside the immediate provision of stepped care) and the acceptability of low-intensity interventions (to both patients and professionals). They reviewed the existing evidence for stepped care against these three assumptions and found some evidence to suggest that stepped care may be a clinically and cost-effective system for the delivery of psychological therapies, but no evidence that strongly supported the overall effectiveness of the model.

In the field of alcohol misuse there are well-developed brief interventions which are suitable for use in a stepped-care system (see NICE, 2010a, for a comprehensive review) such as brief motivational interventions, but other low-intensity interventions that are less dependent on the availability of professional staff and focus on patient-initiated approaches to treatment are also available and include self-help materials such as books and computer programmes (Bennet-Levey *et al.*, 2010). In addition, many alcohol treatment services already operate forms of stepped care and they are implicit in current national policy guidance (MoCAM; Department of Health, 2006a) but as yet there has been little formal evaluation or systematic review of the area.

Definition

For the purposes of this review, stepped care is defined as a system for the organisation and delivery of care to people with harmful or dependent drinking which:

a) provides to the majority, if not all harmful or dependent drinkers, the least restrictive and least costly brief interventions that will be effective for a person's presenting problems

b) has a system of built-in monitoring that ensures that those who have not benefited from the initial intervention will be identified

c) has the referral systems and capacity to ensure that more intensive interventions are provided to those who have not benefited from a low intensity intervention.

5.8.2 Clinical review protocol

Information about the databases searched and the inclusion/exclusion criteria used for this section of the guideline can be found in Table 11 (further information about the search for health economic evidence can be found in Chapter 3).

5.8.3 Studies considered[13]

The review team conducted a new systematic search for RCTs and systematic reviews that assessed the efficacy of stepped-care approaches.

Three trials relating to clinical evidence that potentially met the eligibility criteria set by the GDG were found, providing data on 496 participants. These trials

Table 11: Databases searched and inclusion/exclusion criteria for clinical evidence

Electronic databases	CINAHL, EMBASE, MEDLINE, PsycINFO, Cochrane Library
Date searched	Systematic reviews from 1993 to March 2010. All other searches from database inception to March 2010
Study design	Systematic reviews, RCTs
Patient population	Those with alcohol dependence or alcohol misuse
Interventions	Stepped-care approach versus TAU
Outcomes	Any drinking outcome; engagement or attendance in aftercare sessions or programmes

---

[13]Here and elsewhere in the guideline, each study considered for review is referred to by a study ID in capital letters (primary author and date of study publication, except where a study is in press or only submitted for publication, then a date is not used).

(Bischof *et al.*, 2008; Breslin *et al.*, 1999; Drummond *et al.*, 2009) were published in peer-reviewed journals between 1999 and 2009. The trials are listed below in Table 12 and the outcomes of the studies are described in the text below. The GDG considered these studies very carefully and concluded that, despite the claims of individual studies (for example, labelling the intervention as stepped care), none of these studies delivered a form of stepped care that was fully consistent with the definition of a stepped-care approach adopted for this guideline.

5.8.4 Evidence summary

Breslin and colleagues (1997) evaluated the contribution of pre- and within treatment predictors with 212 'problem drinkers' who initially completed a brief cognitive behavioural motivational outpatient intervention. The analyses revealed that in the absence of the ability to systematically monitor within treatment drinking outcomes and goals, therapist prognosis ratings can be used in making stepped-care treatment decisions. These prognosis ratings improve predictions of outcomes even after pre-treatment characteristics are controlled. In a later study, Breslin and colleagues (1999) evaluated a stepped-care model (but which the GDG considered might be more accurately described as an evaluation of sequenced as opposed to stepped care[14]) for harmful drinkers, with the initial treatment consisting of four sessions of motivationally-based outpatient treatment. The design split participants into treatment responders and non-responders, with treatment non-responders defined as those having consumed more than 12 drinks per week between assessment and the third session of the intervention. There was also a third group of non-responders who did not respond to initial treatment, but received a supplemental intervention consisting of post-treatment progress reports. A repeated measures ANOVA indicated a significant effect of time for percent days abstinent (PDA), F $(2,116) = 35.89$, p <0.0001, for all groups) and for DDD, F $(2,115) = 26.91$, p <0.0001. F results from follow-up contracts revealed that those who received a supplemental intervention showed no additional improvements on drinking outcome measures in comparison with those who did not receive a supplemental intervention (no significant differences on PDA or DDD). Furthermore, treatment responders and non-responders sought additional help at the same rate. It should be noted that this intervention was aimed at problem drinkers and not at severely dependent drinkers. Furthermore, it is possible that the lack of effect in this study was due to the 'intensity' of the 'stepped' intervention, as it only consisted of a progress report. It is possible that confidence in the effect could be increased if the supplemental intervention provided to treatment non-responders from the initial intervention was more intensive and alcohol-focused.

Bischof and colleagues (2008) compared two types of 'stepped-care' interventions (but which the GDG consider to be a comparison of two different models of

---

[14]'Stepped care' is a system for the organisation of care in which the least intrusive and most effective intervention is offered first. 'Sequenced care' refers to a process of care where intervention often of equivalent intensity is offered in sequence if there is no response to the first intervention.

Table 12: Characteristics of studies evaluating stepped-care approaches

Study	Study design	Comparisons	Outcomes	Baseline severity	Treatment characteristics	Results
Bischof *et al.*, 2008 (Germany)	RCT	Stepped care Full care Untreated control group	Grams of alcohol per day at follow-up	Grams of alcohol per day (mean [SD]): Control group: Overall: 41.0 (50.3) Stepped care: 46.9 (49.3) Full care: 49.0 (41.3)	Full care: (n = 131) Received computerised feedback. Received brief counselling sessions based on motivational interviewing and behavioural change counselling, each session 30 minutes. Stepped care: (n = 138) Computerised intervention and maximum of three brief counselling sessions at 1, 3 and 6 months after baseline. 30 to 40 minutes each. If a participant within the stepped-care group reported a reduction of alcohol consumption below the study criteria for at-risk drinking and binge drinking within the last 3 weeks, and also indicated a high self-efficacy to keep the acquired behavioural change up, the intervention was discontinued and no further contact made until 12-month follow-up. Control: (n = 139) Received a booklet on health behaviour.	No significant differences except when split by severity, where at-risk drinkers were significantly different from the control group on difference in grams alcohol per day baseline to follow-up (Mann–Whitney U test, p = 0.002) and binge criteria at follow-up, Mann–Whitney U test, p = 0.039) Ordinary least squares (OLS)-regression: no significant difference, overall, (R^2 change = 0.006, p = 0.124) A significant difference for people at risk/who misuse alcohol (R^2 change = 0.039, p = 0.036) but not for alcohol dependence (R^2 change = 0.002, p = 0.511) or heavy episodic driving (R^2 change = 0.000, p = 0.923)

Continued

Table 12: (*Continued*)

Study	Study design	Comparisons	Outcomes	Baseline severity	Treatment characteristics	Results
Breslin *et al.*, 1999 (Canada)	RCT	Stepped-care approach (treatment non-responders assigned to three groups based on whether they were heavily drinking or not)	PDA DDD	Alcohol Dependence Scale score: Range: 11.3–12.8	Initial treatment: Four sessions of motivationally-based outpatient treatment. Treatment non-responders who consumed more than 12 drinks per week between assessment and third session were considered to be 'drinking heavily during treatment' an additional 'step', which consisted of additional readings, written exercises and a personalised progress report. N = 67 responded to initial treatment N = 33 received supplemental intervention N = 36 did not respond to initial treatment	No significant differences between groups for PDA or DDD due to having a supplemental intervention. Multivariate analysis of variance (MANOVA) indicated a significant effect of time for PDA, F (2116 = 35.89, p <0.0001, for all groups) DDD F (2,115) = 26.91, p <0.0001.
Drummond *et al.*, 2009 (UK)	RCT	Stepped-care intervention Minimal intervention (Control)	Total alcohol consumed in 180 days DDD	Total alcohol consumed in 180 days (mean [SD])	Intervention: (n = 39) Sequential series of interventions according to need/response. Step 1: 40-minute session of behaviour-change counselling	Greater reduction in stepped-care group than control in total alcohol consumed (−408.6 g versus −238.8 g) and DDD (−2.4 versus −1.0), with an adjusted mean difference of 145.6 (95% CI -101.7 to 392.9) and

PDA Intervention: 1699.6 (194.8) Control: 1423 (113.3) DDD Intervention: 15.2 (1.1) Control: 12.9 (0.8) PDA intervention: 37.9 (3.8) Control: 36.6 (3.4)	from a nurse with follow-up 28 days after initial session. Patients consumed >21 units of alcohol in any 1 week or 10 units per day were referred to Step 2. Step2: Four 50-minute sessions of MET (trained alcohol counsellor); follow-up 28 days. If consumed same as in Step 1, referred to Step 3. Step 3: Referral to local community alcohol team for specialist intervention. No limit on duration/intensity of treatment; where necessary, assisted withdrawal, inpatient treatment, outpatient counselling, relapse prevention and drug therapy given. Control: (n = 52) 5-minute directive advice session from practice nurse addressing alcohol consumption reduction. Received self-help booklet.	1.1 (−0.9 to 3.1) but not significant.

brief interventions) with a control group. The 'stepped-care' group received a computerised feedback programme after assessment and a maximum of three brief counselling sessions delivered by telephone, lasting 30 to 40 minutes each. The counselling was delivered based on the success of the previous intervention, the computerised feedback programme. If a participant reported a reduction of alcohol consumption, the intervention was discontinued. Those in the full-care group received a fixed number of four telephone-based brief counselling sessions at 30 minutes each in addition to the computerised feedback system. The control group received a booklet on health behaviour. An OLS regression analysis indicated that there was no significant difference overall, in terms of efficacy of the intervention (R^2 change $= 0.006$, p $= 0.124$). A significant difference was found for at risk/alcohol misuse at 12-month follow-up (R^2 change $= 0.039$, p $= 0.036$), but not for alcohol dependence (R^2 change $= 0.002$, p $= 0.511$) or heavy episodic driving (R^2 change $= 0.000$, p $= 0.923$). Thus stepped-care and full-care groups did not differ on drinking outcomes, but when compared with the control group the intervention showed small to medium effect size for at-risk drinkers only. It should be noted that this intervention does not fit with the definition of stepped care used for this guideline because the approach employed in this study represents more intensive levels of the same interventions rather than 'stepped'-up care if the participant does not respond to the initial intervention.

More recently, Drummond and colleagues (2009) conducted an RCT pilot study to evaluate a stepped-care intervention in primary care primarily for hazardous and harmful drinkers (and, in the view of the GDG, not a stepped-care model with much relevance to the population which is the focus of this guideline), compared with a minimal intervention. Participants received either a three-stage stepped-care intervention or 5 minutes of brief advice delivered by a practice nurse. Participants in the stepped-care intervention received a single session of behaviour change counselling (delivered by a practice nurse), four 50-minute sessions of MET provided by an alcohol counsellor and, lastly, referral to a community alcohol treatment agency. At 6-month follow-up, there was a reduction on drinking outcome measures in both groups and a slight trend favouring the stepped-care intervention for total alcohol consumed (adjusted mean difference $= 145.6$, 95% CI, -101.7 to 392.9, effect size difference $= 0.23$) and drinks per drinking day (adjusted mean difference $= 1.1$, 95% CI, -0.9 to 3.1, effect size difference $= 0.27$). These differences were not significant.

5.8.5 Special populations

No studies evaluating the efficacy of a stepped-care approach for children and young people or older people which met inclusion criteria were identified.

5.8.6 Health economic evidence

The study by Drummond and colleagues (2009) included a cost-effectiveness analysis of a stepped-care alcohol intervention compared with minimal intervention in the primary care setting. The study population consisted of UK males with a diagnosis of an alcohol-use disorder and follow-up was 6 months post-randomisation. The primary outcome measure used in the economic analysis was the quality-adjusted life year (QALY), estimated from European Quality of Life – 5 Dimensions (EQ-5D) utility scores obtained from the study participants. A societal perspective was adopted for the analysis which included costs relating to staff training, specific psychological interventions, and other healthcare, social care and criminal justice services. In the intervention group, mean total treatment costs were £216 at baseline and total mean service costs were £2,534 at follow-up, compared with £20 and £12,637 in the control group. These differences in 6-month follow-up costs were largely explained by criminal justice services utilisation in the control group (£8,000 versus £0). At 6 months, the intervention group gained a mean 0.3849 QALYs compared with 0.3876 in the control group. Therefore the control group was both more costly and more effective in comparison with the intervention group, although the difference in both costs and QALYs were not statistically significant. The authors did not present the incremental cost-effectiveness ratio (ICER) for the control group versus the intervention group but calculated that, at a UK cost-effectiveness threshold range of between £20,000 to £30,000 per QALY, stepped care had a 98% probability of being the most cost-effective option. The results from this study are directly applicable to UK clinical practice and the primary outcome measure ensures comparability across healthcare interventions. However, potential limitations include the small sample size which limits the ability to detect statistically significant differences in costs and outcomes, and the short time horizon of the study. In addition, no sensitivity analyses were carried out to test the robustness of the cost-effectiveness results.

5.8.7   Health economics summary

Only one study was identified that considered the cost-effectiveness of a stepped-care approach to the management of alcohol-use disorders (Drummond *et al.*, 2009). The initial results of this short-term pilot study suggest that stepped care may offer significant cost savings without any significant impact on health outcomes over 6 months. However, the GDG expressed the opinion that the study described a stepped-care model that was not of much relevance to the population that is the focus of this guideline. In addition, longer term trial based evidence is required to confirm the cost-effectiveness of stepped care beyond 6 months.

5.9   CLINCIAL EVIDENCE SUMMARY

The five studies (three RCTs and two observational) reviewed for case management indicate that when case management is compared with standard treatment it is significantly better in reducing lapse and days using alcohol. All other outcomes assessing drinking frequency and measures of abstinence did not reach significance. The five studies reviewed narratively to support the results of the meta-analysis all found significant improvements in favour of case management on aftercare attendance, those attending intake sessions and completion of treatment. Only one of these additional studies (Stout *et al.*, 1999) reported a significant difference on any drinking outcome, lapse and relapse in favour of case management. The overall quality of the

111

evidence is *moderate*, therefore more studies would help increase confidence in the estimate of the effect of case management.

One observational study assessing ACT methods versus standard care found that ACT improved rates of completion and attendance in medically-assisted withdrawal and aftercare programmes.

Four studies assessing stepped-care methods found that there may be a small effect in favour of stepped care for hazardous drinkers. There were no significant differences found on alcohol outcomes for more harmful and dependent drinkers, which are the population covered by this guideline.

5.10   FROM EVIDENCE TO RECOMMENDATIONS

5.10.1   Case management

The GDG reviewed the evidence for the clinical efficacy of case management as an intervention to promote abstinence and reduce alcohol consumption, as well as improving client engagement, treatment adherence and use of aftercare services. Evidence from randomised trials and observational studies indicates that when case management is compared with standard treatment, case management had significant benefit over treatment as usual for certain drinking-related outcomes (for example, lapse and frequency/quantity of alcohol use), and outcomes evaluating engagement and completion of treatment and aftercare. It must be noted, however, that the overall quality of the evidence base was limited because the results of the meta-analysis had to be supported by additional evidence that could not be included in meta-analyses. In terms of aftercare, the components of aftercare and outcome measures vary widely across studies. There are many ways of motivating a patient to engage in aftercare programmes and of structuring an aftercare programme in an attempt to retain the patient. These include the use of incentives, having help to access aftercare sessions, being prompted and contacted by an aftercare therapist, and having structured aftercare programmes. The GDG considered case management to be an effective but relatively intensive intervention for people who misuse alcohol. The GDG felt, therefore, that case management should be targeted at those with moderate and severe dependence, and in particular those who have a history of difficulty in engaging with services. The GDG were also aware that care coordination is part of routine care (see the introduction to this chapter) in all specialist alcohol services, but were concerned that if the focus of case management were only on the severely alcohol dependent that, as a consequence, the coordination of care for harmful alcohol misuse and those with mild alcohol dependence would be at risk of being neglected. This was a particular concern, given the considerable number of agencies involved in the delivery of alcohol misuse services. To address this issue, the GDG made a recommendation for the delivery of care coordination for those with harmful alcohol misuse and mild dependence.

5.10.2   Assertive community treatment

Although assertive community interventions have been reviewed in another NICE guideline under development for the treatment of individuals with a diagnosis of psychosis and a history of substance misuse (NICE, 2011a), the narrative review of these studies in this guideline identified a very limited evidence base. In this review, one trial assessing ACT versus standard care suggested that assertive methods may be beneficial in improving rates of completion and attendance in medically-assisted withdrawal and aftercare programmes. On the basis of this single trial, there is insufficient evidence to support any clinical recommendation. However, the GDG did develop a research recommendation because it considered that the ACT might have value in ensuring more effective care and treatment for severely alcohol dependent people who have significant problems in engaging with services.

5.10.3 Stepped care

None of the studies reviewed directly addressed stepped care either as defined in the guideline or for the populations covered by this guideline. The GDG therefore has no recommendations that might suggest changes to or developments of the current, well-established system for stepped care that structures the provision of alcohol misuse services in the NHS and related services.

5.11 RECOMMENDATIONS

Care coordination and case management
5.11.1.1   Care coordination should be part of the routine care of all service users in specialist alcohol services and should:
- be provided throughout the whole period of care, including aftercare
- be delivered by appropriately trained and competent staff working in specialist alcohol services
- include the coordination of assessment, interventions and monitoring of progress, and coordination with other agencies.
5.11.1.2   Consider case management to increase engagement in treatment for people who have moderate to severe alcohol dependence and who are considered at risk of dropping out of treatment or who have a previous history of poor engagement. If case management is provided it should be throughout the whole period of care, including aftercare.
5.11.1.3   Case management should be delivered in the context of Tier 3 interventions[15] by staff who take responsibility for the overall coordination of care and should include:
- a comprehensive assessment of needs
- development of an individualised care plan in collaboration with the service user and relevant others (including families and carers and other staff involved in the service user's care)

---

[15]See Figure 4.

- coordination of the care plan to deliver a seamless multiagency and integrated care pathway and maximisation of engagement, including the use of motivational interviewing approaches
- monitoring of the impact of interventions and revision of the care plan when necessary.

5.12   RESEARCH RECOMMENDATION

5.12.1.1   For which service users who are moderately and severely dependent on alcohol is an assertive community treatment model a clinically- and cost-effective intervention compared with standard care?

This question should be answered using a randomised controlled design in which participants are stratified for severity and complexity of presenting problems. It should report short- and medium-term outcomes (including cost-effectiveness outcomes) of at least 18 months' duration. Particular attention should be paid to the reproducibility of the treatment model and training and supervision of those providing the intervention to ensure that the results are robust and generalisable. The outcomes chosen should reflect both observer and service user-rated assessments of improvement (including personal and social functioning) and the acceptability of the intervention. The study needs to be large enough to determine the presence or absence of clinically important effects, and mediators and moderators of response should be investigated.

Why this is important
Many people, in particular those with severe problems and complex comorbidities, do not benefit from treatment and/or lose contact with services. This leads to poor outcomes and is wasteful of resources. Assertive community treatment models have been shown to be effective in retaining people in treatment in those with serious mental illness who misuse alcohol and drugs, but the evidence for an impact on outcomes is not proven. A number of small pilot studies suggest that an assertive community approach can bring benefit in both service retention and clinical outcomes in alcohol misuse. Given the high morbidity and mortality associated with chronic severe alcohol dependence the results of this study will have important implications for the structure and provision of alcohol services in the NHS.

SECTION 3 – THE ASSESSMENT OF HARMFUL DRINKING AND ALCOHOL DEPENDENCE

5.13   INTRODUCTION

The purpose of this section is to identify best practice in the diagnosis and assessment of alcohol misuse across a range of clinical settings; NHS provided and funded services, including primary care and non-statutory alcohol services. Previous reviews of assessment procedures (for example, Allen & Wilson, 2003; Raistrick *et al.*, 2006) have outlined the role of clinical interview procedures, identification questionnaires and investigations in developing an assessment of needs. To obtain a comprehensive overview of the range and variety of assessment procedures, this chapter should be read in conjunction with the reviews and recommendations on identification and assessment contained in two other NICE guidelines on alcohol misuse (NICE, 2010a and 2010b).

A key aim of the assessment process should be to elicit information regarding the relevant characteristics of alcohol misuse as outlined in the current diagnostic systems for alcohol-use disorders; that is, the ICD–10 (WHO, 1992) and the DSM–IV (APA, 1994). Although diagnosis is an important aspect of most assessments, the focus of assessment should not only be on diagnosis and alcohol consumption but should also consider physical, psychological and social functioning. The range and comprehensiveness of any assessment will vary depending on the setting in which it is undertaken and the particular purpose of the assessment, but in all cases the central aim is to identify a client's need for treatment and care. The comprehensiveness of the assessment should be linked to the intended outcomes (for example, onward referral of an individual or offering treatment interventions). The range and depth of the components of assessment should reflect the complexity of tasks to be addressed and the expertise required to carry out the assessment. Crucial to the effective delivery of any assessment process is the competence of the staff who are delivering it, including the ability to conduct an assessment, interpret the findings of the assessment and use these finding to support the development of appropriate care plans and, where necessary, risk management plans.

Current practice in the assessment of alcohol misuse is very varied across England and Wales, including the range of assessments in specialist alcohol services (MoCAM; Department of Health, 2006a). To some extent this reflects the different aims and objectives of the services (including specialist alcohol services) in which assessments are undertaken, but it also reflects the lack of clear guidance and subsequent agreement on what constitutes the most appropriate assessment methods for particular settings (MoCAM; Department of Health, 2006a). Given the high prevalence of alcohol misuse and comorbidity with a wide range of other physical and mental disorders, effective diagnosis and assessment can have major implications for the nature of any treatment provided and the likely outcome of that treatment. In an attempt to address some of these concerns the National Treatment Agency (NTA) developed MoCAM, which outlined a four-tiered conceptual framework for treatment and describes three levels of assessment that should be considered in different clinical settings: a screening assessment, a triage assessment and a comprehensive assessment. However, the extent to which this framework has led to improvements in the nature and quality of assessments provided remains unclear (but it has been more influential in determining the structure of services). The importance of MoCAM for this chapter (and for the guideline in general) is that it provides a conceptual framework in which to place the recommendations on assessment and which also link with the recommendation on assessment in the other NICE guidelines on alcohol (NICE, 2010a and 2010b). With this in mind, the GDG decided to develop a set of recommendations for assessment that supported the development of clinical care pathways to promote access to effective care, where possible integrating with the existing service structure. Where this is not possible, the GDG has developed recommendations which suggest changes in existing service structures.

5.14   CLINICAL QUESTIONS

The clinical questions that the GDG addressed and from which the literature searches were developed were:
a) What are the most effective (i) diagnostic and (ii) assessment tools for alcohol dependence and harmful alcohol use?
b) What are the most effective ways of monitoring clinical progress in alcohol dependence and harmful alcohol use?
c) To answer these questions, what are the advantages, disadvantages and clinical utility of:
- The structure of the overall clinical assessment?
- Biological measures?
- Psychological/behavioural measures?
- Neuropsychiatric measures (including cognitive impairment)?
- Physical assessment?

5.15   AIM OF REVIEW OF DIAGNOSTIC AND ASSESSMENT TOOLS FOR ALCOHOL DEPENDENCE AND HARMFUL ALCOHOL USE

5.15.1   Introduction

This review aims to identify the most appropriate tools for assessing the presence of alcohol dependence or harmful drinking, the severity of dependence, alcohol consumption/frequency of use, motivation and readiness to change, alcohol withdrawal, and alcohol-related problems in adults. (The issue of assessment in special populations is dealt with in Sections 5.21 and 5.22.) The GDG were also tasked with identifying all the potential components of a clinical assessment (and their respective places in the care pathway) that would facilitate the most effective delivery of any assessment. This section sets out the criteria for a quantitative analysis of the assessment tools included in the review, and the subsequent synthesis of the characteristics and psychometric properties of the tools. Please note, the GDG was not tasked with evaluating assessment tools used for the screening of alcohol dependence and harmful alcohol use because this is outside the scope of the guideline. See the NICE public health guideline (NICE, 2010a) for a review of screening tools.

5.15.2   Clinical review protocol

Information about the databases searched and the inclusion/exclusion criteria used for this section of the guideline can be found in Table 13.

Table 13: Clinical review protocol for the evaluation of tools for assessing alcohol dependence and harmful alcohol use

Electronic databases Library	CINAHL, EMBASE, MEDLINE, PsycINFO, Cochrane Library
Date searched	Systematic reviews from 1993 to March 2010. All other searches from database inception to March 2010
Study design	Systematic reviews; RCTs
Patient population	Adults (over 18 years old)
	At least 80% of the sample meet the criteria for alcohol dependence or harmful alcohol use (clinical diagnosis or drinking >30 drinks per week)
Assessment domains	Dependence (and severity of dependence); consumption/frequency; alcohol withdrawal; motivation and readiness to change; physical, psychological and social problems; clinical interview; physical examination; blood, breath and urine testing
Outcomes	Critical outcomes for quantitative review: sensitivity, specificity, area under the curve, positive predictive value, negative predictive value
	For quantitative meta-analyses calculating the diagnostic accuracy of an assessment tool, raw data (true positive, true negative, false positive, false negative) is needed. See methods, Chapter 3, for a definition of these terms

5.16   QUANTITATIVE REVIEW OF ASSESSMENT TOOLS

5.16.1   Aim of a quantitative review of assessment tools

The initial aim of this review was to assess the pooled diagnostic accuracy of the assessment tools using meta-analytic receiver operating characteristic (ROC) curve analyses. ROC analyses would therefore provide the pooled sensitivity and specificity of each assessment tool, and give an indication of positive predictive value and negative predictive value. For a definition and explanation of these terms, see Chapter 3.

5.16.2 Evaluating assessment tools for use in a review to assess diagnostic accuracy

The review team conducted a systematic review of studies that assessed the psychometric properties of all alcohol-related assessment tools. From these, references were excluded by reading the title and/or abstract. At this stage of the sifting process, studies were excluded if they did not address the diagnostic accuracy of an assessment tools and hence were not relevant for this section of the review. Further, the focus of this review was on assessment and not screening or case identification (latter issues are covered in the NICE guideline on preventing hazardous and harmful drinking [NICE, 2010a]). Therefore, tools developed solely for those purposes were excluded from the review. The remaining references were assessed for eligibility for use in meta-analyses on the basis of the full text using certain inclusion criteria and papers excluded if they did not meet those criteria. The inclusion criteria were as follows:

● The study meets basic guideline inclusion criteria (see Chapter 3).
● The population being assessed in the study reflects the scope of this guideline (see Table 13).
● Extractable data is available to perform pooled sensitivity and specificity analyses (see methods Chapter 3).
● The assessment tool is tested against a validated gold-standard diagnostic instrument (for example, DSM–IV, ICD–10, CIDI) (APA, 1994; WHO, 1992).

5.16.3 Outcome of study search for quantitative review

Following the sifting process as outlined above, 33 studies assessing the diagnostic accuracy of a wide range of assessment tools were identified for possible inclusion in meta-analyses. Twenty-seven studies were excluded and could not be used for a quantitative review. The main reason for this was that the population being assessed were outside the scope of this guideline (for example, pregnant women, hazardous drinkers, or less than 80% of the sample were alcohol dependent or harmful drinkers). Studies were further excluded because they did not report sensitivity and specificity data in an extractable format.

After all exclusion criteria were applied, there were only six studies remaining which could have been used for a quantitative review. This number of studies was insufficient to perform an unbiased and comprehensive diagnostic accuracy meta-analyses of all the assessment tools identified in the review for alcohol misuse. Although there were a wide range of tools initially identified for the meta-analyses, most studies did not provide appropriate psychometric information and the majority of studies reported the results of their own sensitivity and specificity analyses. As outlined above, the actual number of participants identified as true positive, true negative, false positive, false negative (see Chapter 3 for definition) is needed to run pooled sensitivity and specificity analyses.

In view of the limitations of the data, it was decided by the GDG that a narrative synthesis of assessment tools should be undertaken. Therefore, all papers were reconsidered for use in a narrative review.

5.17   NARRATIVE SYNTHESIS OF ASSESSMENT TOOLS

5.17.1   Aim of narrative synthesis

The main aim of the narrative synthesis was to identify tools that could inform clinical decision-making and treatment planning in the following areas: the assessment of alcohol dependence; the severity of alcohol dependence and the associated harms; and motivation for change. This guideline did not aim to review assessment tools to aid in the measurement of alcohol withdrawal because these tools have already been reviewed in the accompanying NICE guideline on the management of alcohol-related physical complications (NICE, 2010b), which recommends the use of the Clinical Institute Withdrawal Assessment for Alcohol scale, revised, (CIWA-Ar) (Sullivan *et al.*, 1989). To facilitate understanding and use of the CIWA-Ar, its characteristics can be seen in Table 14 and Table 15.

5.17.2   Evaluating assessment tools for use in a narrative synthesis

The inclusion and exclusion criteria of the initial sifting process were reapplied to the available literature and involved identifying assessment tools that were applicable to the population of interest in this guideline. The literature was evaluated for a number of important study characteristics, and assessment tools/literature were excluded on this basis. First, the patient population was required to meet inclusion criteria for alcohol misuse, that is harmful or dependent drinkers. Further, the psychometric data for the study was required to adequately distinguish between alcohol misuse and substance misuse in an adult dual-diagnosed sample. The context in which the tool is used was also evaluated, that is, to ascertain if the tool is used for opportunistic screening in non-treatment seeking populations (see the NICE [2010a] guideline on preventing hazardous and harmful drinking) or can be used for assessment of dependence and outcome monitoring in a treatment-seeking population.

The second stage of the review was to identify tools for a narrative that could be recommended for use in assessing alcohol misuse in a clinical setting. In the absence of a formal quantitative review, the decision to include assessment tools in a narrative synthesis was made using the three criteria outlined below. These criteria were developed and agreed by the GDG, and informed by the NIAAA guide for assessing alcohol misuse (Allen & Wilson, 2003).

Clinical utility
This criterion required the primary use of the assessment tool to be feasible and implementable in a routine clinical care. The tool should contribute to the identification of treatment needs and therefore be useful for treatment planning.

Table 14: Assessment tools included in narrative review

Assessment instruments included in narrative review	Population		Assessment category				
	Adult	Young people (>10 years)	Dependence	Consumption and frequency	Alcohol withdrawal	Motivation and readiness to change	Harm and alcohol problems
Alcohol Problems Questionnaire (APQ)	●						●[1]
Alcohol Use Disorders Identification Test (AUDIT)	●	●	●[1]	●	●[1]		
Clinical Institute Withdrawal Assessment (CIWA-Ar)	●				●[1]		
Leeds Dependence Questionnaire (LDQ)	●	● (>16 years)	●[1]				
Severity of Alcohol Dependence Questionnaire (SADQ)	●		●[1]	●	●		
Readiness to Change Questionnaire – Treatment Version (RCQ-TV)	●	●				●[1]	

Note. ● = Tool used; [1] Primary use

Table 15: Characteristics of assessment tools included in narrative review

Assessment instrument	Number of items & format	Scale and cut-offs	Time taken to administer and by whom	Training required for administration	Time to score and by whom	Copyright and cost of test
Alcohol Problems Questionnaire (APQ)	44 items (eight subscales), pencil and paper self-administered	Maximum score = 23	3 to 5 minutes; respondent	No training	Minimal; minimally trained technician	No; free to use
Alcohol Use Disorders Identification Test (AUDIT)	Ten items (three subscales), pencil and paper or computer self-administered	Scale: 0 to 40. Cut-offs: 8 to 15 = hazardous; 16 to 19 = harmful, mild or moderate dependence; ≥20 = severe dependence	2 minutes; trained personnel	Minimal training	1 minute; trained personnel	Yes; test and training manual free to use, training costs $75
Clinical Institute Withdrawal Assessment (CIWA-Ar)	Eight items, observation format	Total score ranges from: 0 to 9 = minimal/absent withdrawal; withdrawal	2 minutes; trained personnel	Training required for administration	4 to 5 minutes; trained personnel	Yes; free to use
Leeds Dependence Questionnaire (LDQ)	Ten items, paper and pencil self-administered	Scale: 0 to 30. Cut-offs: 0 = no dependence; 1 to 10 = low/moderate dependence; 11 to 20 = moderate/high dependence; 21 to 30 = high dependence	2 to 5 minutes; respondent or personnel	No training	Half a minute; non-trained personnel	No; free to use
Readiness to Change Questionnaire – Treatment Version (RCQ-TV)	15 items (three subscales). Most up-to-date version has 12 items, pencil and paper self-administered	Original total score range: −10 to +10; current version total score range: −8 to +8	2 to 3 minutes; respondent	No training	1 minute; non-trained personnel	Yes; free to use
Severity of Alcohol Dependence Questionnaire (SADQ)	20 (five subscales), pencil and paper self-administered	Scale: 0 to 60; Cut-offs: <15 = mild dependence; 16 to 30 = moderate dependence; ≥31 = severe dependence	5 minutes; respondent	No training	1 minute; trained personnel or clinician	No; free to use

Psychometric data

Reported findings for sensitivity, specificity, area under the curve, positive predictive value, negative predictive value, reliability and validity of the assessment tools were considered. Although sensitivity and specificity are important outcomes in deciding on the usefulness of an assessment tool, particularly for diagnostic purposes, for other clinical purposes reliability and validity are also important. See Chapter 3 for a description of diagnostic test accuracy terms. The tool should be applicable to a UK population, for example by being validated in either a UK population or one that is similar to the UK population.

Tool characteristics and administrative properties

The assessment tool should have well-validated cut-offs in the patient population of interest. Furthermore, and dependent on the practitioner skill-set and the setting, tools were evaluated for the time needed to administer and score them as well as the nature of the training (if any) required for administration or scoring. Lastly, the cost of the tool and copyright issues were also considered.

5.17.3   Outcome of the narrative synthesis

The studies initially identified were the result of the original quantitative review search and sift. A total of 73 tools were identified and 34 were excluded from the review, leaving 39 assessment questionnaires and clinical interview tools that were considered for a narrative review.

The clinical interview tools identified did not form a part of the narrative review of assessment questionnaires. Most (n = 5) were excluded as being not feasible for routine use in a UK NHS setting (see criteria above).

The outcome of the initial sift and the exclusion criteria applied was discussed with the GDG, and the preliminary list of 39 assessment tools were put forward for possible inclusion in the narrative synthesis. Using the additional criteria (that is, clinical utility, psychometric data and characteristics of the tool), this discussion resulted in a subset of five questionnaires (excluding the CIWA-Ar) being included in the subsequent narrative synthesis. Of these included assessment tools, three measure the domain of alcohol dependence, one assesses alcohol-related problems and one assesses motivation. These assessment tools are described below accordingly. Table 14 displays information pertaining to the questionnaires which met criteria for a narrative review. Table 15 and Table 16 provide information of the domain the tool assesses (for example, dependence, problems and so on) and indicates if the tool is appropriate for the assessment of young people or adults (see Section 5.22 for a review of the assessment of children and young people). Additionally, Table 15 displays the characteristics of the assessment question- naires included in the narrative review. This table gives more extensive information, such as the scale and cut-offs, number of items, time to administer and score, whether training is required for use, copyright/cost of the tool, and the source reference.

Table 16 identifies the questionnaires and clinical interview tools identified in the original sift but excluded for the reasons outlined above.

Table 16: Assessment tools excluded from narrative review

Assessment tools excluded from narrative review	Population		Assessment category						Reference
	Adult	Young people (>10 years)	Dependence	Consumption and frequency	Alcohol withdrawal	Motivation and readiness to change	Harm and alcohol problems	Clinical interview tool	
Adolescent Alcohol Involvement Scale (AAIS)		●	●[1,2]	●[1]					Mayer and Filstead (1979)
Adolescent Drinking Index (ADI)		●	●[1,2]						Harrell and Wirtz (1990)
Alcohol Dependence Scale (ADS)	●		●[1]		●				Skinner and Horn (1984)
Alcohol Withdrawal Syndrome Scale (AWS)	●								Wetterling and colleagues (1997)
Clinical Institute Withdrawal Assessment (CIWA-AD)	●				●[1]				Sullivan and colleagues (1989)
Cognitive Lifetime Drinking History (CLDH)	●			●[1]					Russell and colleagues (1997)
Composite International Diagnostic Interview (CIDI) Version 2.1	●		●	●	●			●[1]	Robins and colleagues (1989)
Comprehensive Addiction Severity Inventory for Adolescents (CASI-A)[3]		● (>16 years)	●[1,2]					●[1]	Meyers and colleagues (1995)
Customary Drinking and Drug Use Record (CDDR)[3]		●	●[1,2]		●		●	●[1]	Brown and colleagues (1998)
Diagnostic Interview Schedule for DSM–IV (DIS–IV) – Alcohol Module	●		●					●[1]	No source reference
Drinker Inventory of Consequences (DrInC)	●								Miller and colleagues (1995)

Continued

123

Table 16: (Continued)

Assessment tools excluded from narrative review	Population		Assessment category						Reference
	Adult	Young people (>10 years)	Dependence	Consumption and frequency	Alcohol withdrawal	Motivation and readiness to change	Harm and alcohol problems	Clinical interview tool	
Drinking Problems Index (DPI)	●						●[1]		Finney and colleagues (1991)
Drinking Self-Monitoring Log (DSML)	●	●		●[1]					Sobell and colleagues (1993)
Ethanol Dependence Syndrome (EDS) Scale	●		●[1]		●				Babor (1996)
Form 90-AQ (Alcohol Questionnaire)	●	●		●[1]					Tonigan and colleagues (1997)
Global Appraisal of Individual Needs (GAIN)	●	●	●			●	●	●[1]	Dennis and colleagues (2002)
Lifetime Drinking History (LDH)	●			●[1]					Skinner and Sheu (1982)
Mini International Neuropsychiatric Interview – Clinician Rated (MINI-CR)	●		●			●[1]		●[1]	Sheehan and colleagues (1998)
Motivational Structure Questionnaire (MSQ)	●	●				●[1]			Cox and Klinger (2004)
Personal Experience Inventory (PEI)[3]		●	●[2]				●[1]		Winters and Henly (1989)
Psychiatric Research Interview for Substance and Mental Disorders (PRISM)	●		●		●		●	●[1]	Hasin and colleagues (1996)

degree of substance dependence and applicable to a population with severe mental health problems in an inpatient setting. The LDQ has also been found to have high internal consistency in a 'juvenile delinquent' sample (Lennings, 1999).

In a young adult population (18 to 25 years old) undergoing residential treatment for substance dependence, the LDQ was reported to have high internal consistency, acceptable (but lower than expected) concurrent validity when compared with DSM–IV dependence criteria and PDA (Kelly *et al.*, 2010). Additionally, in a young adult population (mean age 20.3 years), the LDQ had satisfactory test–retest reliability and internal consistency (Thomas & McCambridge, 2008).

The LDQ is an applicable diagnostic measure of severity of alcohol dependence and hence can be used for other purposes in a clinical setting, such as for setting treatment goals and outcome monitoring. Further, it is brief and does not require training for administration and scoring. It was developed and validated in the UK, and is free to use.

5.19 THE ASSESSMENT OF PROBLEMS ASSOCIATED WITH ALCOHOL MISUSE

5.19.1 Introduction

The causal relationship between alcohol consumption and alcohol-related problems such as adverse social consequences, physical disease and injury is well established (Drummond, 1990; Rehm *et al.*, 2009). The extent to which problems are attributable to alcohol means that those presenting for clinical interview may experience considerable problems that are diagnostically important in helping to establish if the patient is experiencing harmful alcohol use or alcohol dependence.

From the initial review, the GDG identified one measure for inclusion in the narrative review of tools for measuring problems associated with alcohol misuse; this is the APQ (Drummond, 1990). Several other questionnaires were identified that included alcohol related problem items, but these were mixed with other conceptual content (for example, dependence symptoms). Information on the characteristics of the APQ are summarised in Table 14 and Table 15.

5.19.2 Alcohol Problems Questionnaire

The APQ (Drummond, 1990) was developed for use as a clinical instrument and assesses problems associated with alcohol alone, independent of dependence. The APQ is a 44-item questionnaire (maximum possible score of 44) which assesses eight problem domains (friends, money, police, physical, affective, marital, children and work). The first five domains make up 23 items that are common to all individuals. The maximum score of 23 is derived from these items to arrive at a common score for all individuals.

In the original validation study of the APQ, Drummond (1990) reported that the APQ common score (based on the common items) was significantly highly correlated with total SADQ score ($R = 0.63$) and drinking quantity as indicated by the alcohol consumption items of the SADQ ($R = 0.53$). Partial correlations, however, (which control for each item included in the analyses) revealed that there was a highly significant relationship between alcohol-related problems and alcohol dependence that is independent of the quantity of alcohol consumed (Drummond, 1990). Williams and Drummond (1994) similarly reported a highly significant correlation between the APQ common score and the SADQ ($R = 0.51$), and a significant partial correlation between the APQ common score and SADQ (controlling for alcohol consumption) ($R = 0.37$). However, when controlling for dependence, the partial correlation between alcohol problems as measured by the APQ and alcohol consumption was low, which suggests that dependence may mediate the relationship between these two variables (Williams & Drummond, 1994). The results of these two studies indicate that the APQ has high reliability and validity for assessing alcohol-related problems in an alcohol-dependent population. The APQ is quick and easy to administer.

5.20   THE ASSESSMENT OF MOTIVATION

Self-awareness, with respect to the adverse consequences of drinking, levels of motivation and readiness to change drinking behaviour, vary enormously across the population presenting for alcohol treatment. The need to assess such issues is widely accepted. For example, Raistrick and colleagues (2006) noted that 'an understanding of the service user's motivation to change drinking behaviour is a key to effective treatment and can be used to decide on the specific treatment offered'. A number of methods have been developed to aid the assessment of motivational status; these are usually linked to the cycle of change developed by Prochaska and DiClemente (1983) and are designed to site drinkers at specific stages within the cycle. The key stages of change are pre-contemplation (seemingly unaware of any problem), contemplation (aware and considering change), preparation (decision to change taken, planning what to do), action (doing it) and maintenance (working to secure the change).

From the initial review the GDG identified two related measures for possible inclusion in the narrative synthesis of tools to measure motivation in people with alcohol misuse problems; these are the RCQ (Rollnick *et al.*, 1992) and the RCQ-TV (Heather *et al.*, 1999). The original RCQ is for a harmful and hazardous non-treatment seeking population and hence is not described in this narrative review.

5.20.1   Readiness to Change Questionnaire – treatment version

The RCQ-TV (Heather *et al.*, 1999) was developed from the original RCQ for use in a treatment-seeking alcohol misuse population. Both versions refer to drinking reduction. However, the treatment version also refers to abstinence from drinking.

The RCQ-TV has 15 items and three subscales (pre-contemplation, contemplation and action). The items are scored from -2 (strongly disagree) to $+2$ (strongly agree), with a maximum of $+10$ and minimum of -10.

Heather and colleagues (1999) found low item–total correlations for the pre-contemplation, contemplation and action scale of the RCQ-TV. Internal consistencies were low to moderate (Cronbach's α ranged from 0.60 to 0.77 across subscales). Test–retest reliability was adequate ($R = 0.69$ to 0.86 across subscales). With regard to concurrent validity, those in the contemplation group reported drinking more than those in the action group, had less desire to stop drinking and reported less confidence in being able to stop drinking. The various subscales on the RCQ-TV correlated significantly with their URICA equivalents (that is, pre-contemplation, contemplation and action), although correlations were small in magnitude (for example, $R = 0.39$ to 0.56).

Participants who had been in treatment for more than 6 months or who had had any treatment were more likely to be in the action group than those treated for less than 6 months or those who had had no treatment ($x^2 = 8.75$, p <0.005). Similarly, those initially assigned to the action group were more likely than those in the contemplation group to have a good outcome at follow-up. This result remained when re-classifying participants at follow-up.

Heather and Hönekopp (2008) examined the properties of the standard 15-item version as well as a new 12-item version of the RCQ-TV in the UKATT sample of participants. The authors reported that there was little difference between the two versions. For example, the internal consistency of the 15-item version ranged from $\alpha = 0.64$ to 0.84 across subscales and for the 12-item version $\alpha = 0.66$ to 0.85 across subscales. Both versions showed adequate consistency over time when assessed at 3- and 12-month follow-up. Heather and Hönekopp (2008) also assessed the construct validity of both versions of the RCQ-TV by analysing their correlation with other important variables, namely PDA, DDD and alcohol problems (using the APQ). Both versions showed a low correlation with these items at baseline but high correlations at 3- and 12-month follow-up, indicating that the RCQ-TV may have good predictive value. However, the shorter version was better able to predict outcome (unsigned predictive value of 12-item version varied between $R = 0.19$ to 0.43).

Because the RCQ-TV has seen specifically developed for a treatment-seeking population, it has value for both treatment planning and monitoring. Furthermore, it is short and requires no training for administration. Although it is copyrighted, it is available at no cost by contacting the original developers. However, the RCQ-TV adopts a very narrow focus on motivation and does not add much value to what could be obtained from a well-structured clinical interview.

5.20.2   Evidence summary

The above narrative review identifies a number of tools used in the assessment of several domains of alcohol misuse that met the criteria set out at the beginning of this section and which the GDG considered to be feasible and appropriate to use in an NHS or related setting. They are:

- *The Alcohol Use Disorders Inventory Test (AUDIT)* – for case identification and initial assessment of problem severity.
- *The Severity of Alcohol Dependence Questionnaire (SADQ)* – to assess the presence and severity of alcohol dependence.
- *The Leeds Dependence Questionnaire (LDQ)* – to assess the presence and severity of alcohol dependence.
- *The Alcohol Problems Questionnaire (APQ)* – to assess the nature and extent of the problems associated with of alcohol misuse.
- *The Readiness to Change Questionnaire – Treatment Version (RCQ-TV)* – to assess the motivation to change their drinking behaviour.

The assessment tools above can only be fully effective when they are used as part of a structured clinical assessment, the nature and purpose of which is clear to both staff and client. The nature and purpose of the assessment will vary according to what prompts the assessment (for example, a request for help from a person who is concerned that they are dependent on alcohol, or further inquiries following the diagnosis of liver disease which is suspected to be alcohol related).

The following section of the guideline aims to review the structures for the delivery of assessment services. The following review will then provide the context in which the recommendations for assessment are developed.

5.21 SPECIAL POPULATIONS – OLDER PEOPLE

No assessment tools specifically developed for treatment-seeking older people who misuse alcohol were identified. A number of assessment tools for screening in an older population have been developed. However, screening tools are outside the scope of this guideline. Please see the public health guideline (NICE, 2010a) for a review of screening tools.

5.22 SPECIAL POPULATIONS – CHILDREN AND YOUNG PEOPLE

5.22.1 Introduction

A number of instruments that aid in the identification and diagnosis of alcohol misuse in children and young people are available. In considering the development of the assessment tools for children and young people, the GDG considered the framework set out within the *Models of Care for Alcohol Misusers* (Department of Health, 2006a), but felt that the service structures for children and adolescent services, the nature of the problems presented by children, and the need for an integrated treatment approach with child and adolescent services meant that this service model needed significant modification. After consideration, the GDG decided to concentrate on two key areas for assessment tools:

1) Case identification/diagnostic assessment
2) Comprehensive assessment.

The remainder of this review is therefore structured around these two areas. The clinical questions set out below relate specifically to these two areas.

5.22.2   Clinical questions

The clinical questions which the GDG addressed, and from which the literature searches were developed were:

a) What are the most effective (i) diagnostic and (ii) assessment tools for alcohol dependence and harmful alcohol use in children and young people (aged 10 to 18 years)?

b) What are the most effective ways of monitoring clinical progress in alcohol dependence and harmful alcohol use in children and young people (aged 10 to 18 years)?

5.22.3   Definition and aim of review of diagnostic and assessment tools for alcohol dependence and harmful alcohol use

This section was developed in conjunction with the review of assessment tools, and the structure and format for the delivery assessment of alcohol services for adults. The strategy for identifying potential tools was the same as adopted for the adult review. See Section 5.15.2 for databases searched and clinical review protocol, and procedure for evaluating assessment tools for inclusion in diagnostic accuracy meta-analyses.

As was the case with the review of adult assessment tools, the original intention was to conduct a quantitative review assessing the sensitivity, specificity and positive predictive value of the instruments for case identification, diagnosis, assessment and alcohol-related problems in children and young people. However, the search failed to identify sufficient data to allow for a quantitative review. As a result, a narrative synthesis of the tools was undertaken and the conclusions are presented below. The identification and subsequent criteria necessary for inclusion in the narrative review of assessment tools were that:

● the tool assesses primarily alcohol and not drugs
● the tool has either been developed for use in children and young people or has been validated in this population
● the tool has established and satisfactory psychometric data (for example, validity/reliability and sensitivity/specificity)
● the tool assesses a wide range of problem domains (for example, dependence, quantity/frequency of alcohol consumed, alcohol-related problems and so on)
● the tool has favourable administrative properties (for example, copyright, cost, time to administer and so on).

5.22.4 Narrative synthesis of assessment tools for children and young people

Case identification/diagnosis

From the review of the literature, using the stipulated inclusion and exclusion criteria and properties outlined above, the GDG identified three tools for case identification in children and young people. These were the AAIS (Mayer & Filstead, 1979), the ADI (Harrell & Wirtz, 1985) and AUDIT (Babor *et al.*, 2001). Both the AAIS and ADI have both been developed for use in an adolescent population. However, the AAIS has not been adequately validated and the ADI, although claiming adequate reliability and validity data, is not routinely used in the UK. As was the case in the review of adult assessment tools, the AUDIT questionnaire was found to be the most appropriate and suitable for use as a case identification/diagnostic instrument. For a review of the psychometric properties and characteristics of the AUDIT, see Section 5.18.1. The need for a revised cut-off in young people using the AUDIT questionnaire was evaluated. Chung and colleagues (2000) recommended modification of the AUDIT so that it is more appropriate to young people. Two studies using representative populations suggest a cut off score of 4 or more (Chung *et al.*, 2000; Santis *et al.*, 2009).

Comprehensive assessment instruments

As part of the systematic review and associated search strategies, a number of clinical interview tools which provide a comprehensive assessment of alcohol misuse in children and young people specifically were identified. These are: the ADI (Winters & Henly, 1993); the CASI-A (Meyers *et al.*, 1995); the CDDR (Brown *et al.*, 1998); the Diagnostic Interview Schedule for Children (DISC; Piacentini *et al.*, 1993); the SCID SUDM (Martin *et al.*, 1995a); the SUDDS-IV (Hoffman & Harrison, 1995); and the Teen Addiction Severity Index (T-ASI; Kaminer *et al.*, 1991). Based on the criteria outlined above, the clinical interview tools that met inclusion criteria and are included in this narrative review are the ADI, DISC and T-ASI (see Table 17 below for characteristics of these tools). The GDG made a consensus-based decision to exclude the CASI-A, CDDR, SCID SUDM and SUDDS-IV from the narrative review because these tools have been developed for the use in an adolescent population over the age of 16 years old only, and hence may be inappropriate for use with children under that age. See Table 16 for characteristics of these excluded tools.

Adolescent Drinking Index

The ADI is a comprehensive assessment instrument which provides a DSM–III–R-based psychiatric diagnosis of alcohol abuse or dependence in 12- to 18-year-olds. As well as substance and alcohol 'abuse'/'dependence', the ADI also assesses a variety of other problems such as psychosocial stressors, cognitive impairment, and school and interpersonal functioning. The ADI as a clinical instrument has been reported to have good inter-rater reliability (alcohol 'abuse' = 0.86; alcohol 'dependence' = 0.53), test–retest reliability (0.83), significant concurrent validity among all variables (range = 0.58 to 0.75), adequate criterion validity assessed by agreement with a clinician rating (alcohol 'abuse' k = 0.71; alcohol dependence k = 0.82), and high sensitivity and specificity for alcohol 'abuse' (both 0.87) and dependence (0.90

134

and 0.95, respectively) (Winters & Henly, 1989; Winters *et al.*, 1993). The ADI takes 50 minutes to complete and can be obtained at a cost from the developer.

Diagnostic Interview Schedule for Children
The DISC provides a diagnosis of alcohol 'dependence' or 'abuse' based on DSM–IV criteria. It has been found to be highly sensitive in identifying young people who have previously been diagnosed as having a substance-use disorder (sensitivity = 75%) (Fisher *et al.*, 1993). However, although the DISC has been found to have acceptable reliability and validity data, this has been for non-substance specific psychiatric disorders (see Jensen *et al.*, 1995; Piacentini *et al.*, 1993; Schaffer *et al.*, 1996; Schwab-Stone *et al.*, 1996). It is also relatively lengthy (1 to 2 hours), and copyrighted.

Teen Addiction Severity Index
The T-ASI is a semi-structured clinical interview designed to provide a reliable and valid measure in the evaluation of substance misuse in adolescents. It has 126 items that provide severity ratings for psychoactive substance use, school or employment status, family function, peer-social relationships, legal status and psychiatric status. The T-ASI has satisfactory inter-rater reliability ($R = 0.78$) and has been found to

Table 17: Characteristics of clinical interview tools for children and adolescents included in the narrative review

Assessment instrument	Number of items and format	Time to administer and by whom
		Training required for administration; time to score; by whom
Adolescent Diagnostic Interview (ADI)	213 items (not all asked), structured interview	Approximately 50 minutes (depends on number of substances used), trained personnel
		Yes; 15 to 20 minutes; trained personnel
Diagnostic Interview Schedule for Children (DISC)	Variable depending on module assessed, structured interview	1 to 2 hours; trained personnel
	Scoring algorithms are provided by National Institute of Mental Health – DISC	No; immediate; computer program
Teen Addiction Severity Index (T-ASI)	154 items (seven subscales), structured interview	20 to 45 minutes; trained personnel
		Yes; 10 minutes; non-trained personnel

have utility in both the clinical identification of alcohol dependence or harmful alcohol use, as well as in the assessment of changes of severity over time as a response to treatment, and hence may be applicable as an outcome monitoring tool (Kaminer *et al.*, 1991). Kaminer and colleagues (1993) also established that the T-ASI could adequately distinguish between 12- to 17-year-olds with and without substance-use disorders as defined by the DSM–III-R. The T-ASI has an added benefit as it can be administered in less than 30 minutes, it is free to use and not copyrighted.

No measures of alcohol problems, such as the APQ for adults, was identified and nor was any specific instrument, such as the RCQ-TV for motivation, identified.

Use of biological markers
The review of adult alcohol misuse identified that no particular biological markers were of value in achieving a diagnosis of harmful or dependent drinking. Given that clinically significant changes in liver enzymes are rare in adults, even in those with established alcohol dependence (Clark *et al.*, 2001), it seems unlikely that the routine use of such biological markers is of value in children and young people. However, the use of urine analysis or breath testing to determine the presence during treatment and/or assessment of drug or alcohol misuse may be of value in assessing the veracity in the overall assessment, but should not be used as a diagnostic marker.

5.22.5   Evidence summary

The GDG identified that the AUDIT is appropriate for case identification of alcohol misuse in children and young people, but with the proviso that the cut-offs are adjusted downwards to a score of 4 or more. Also, modification of AUDIT items to make them relevant to adolescents should be considered. The advantages identified for adults (that it is brief, and easy to administer and score) remain the same.

The review of tools to aid a comprehensive assessment in children and young people identified three possible tools – the ADI, the DISC and the T-ASI. The review identified some problems with the DISC including population in which it was standardised, its duration and its cost. The other two instruments (the ADI and the T-ASI) met the criteria chosen by the GDG and therefore both could be used as part of a comprehensive assessment of alcohol misuse. However, although the T-ASI is free to use, the ADI can only be obtained at a monetary cost. Furthermore, the T-ASI has utility as an outcome monitoring tool and, although perhaps too long for routine use (30 minutes), it may have value as an outcome measure for periodic reviews. As with the adult assessment, these tools should be used and interpreted by trained staff. The comprehensive interview should not only assess the presence of an alcohol-use disorder, but also other comorbid and social problems, development needs, educational and social progress, motivation and self-efficacy, and risk. A child/young person may be competent to consent to a treatment; this depends on the age and capacity of the child and assessment of competence. Where appropriate, consent should be obtained from parents or those with parental responsibility. The aim of the assessment should be, wherever possible, to set a treatment goal of abstinence.

Other substances of misuse
The assessment of alcohol misuse is often complicated by the presence of co-occurring conditions; these, along with the implications for assessment, are outlined below.

Comorbid opioid and alcohol dependence
In treatment services for opioid dependency, about a quarter to a third of patients will have problems with alcohol (Department of Health, 2007). In addition, prognosis for this group can be poor with many showing limited changes in drinking behaviour. A recent systematic review about whether alcohol consumption is affected during the course of methadone maintenance treatment concluded that alcohol use is not likely to reduce by just entering such programmes, with most studies reporting no change (Srivastava *et al.*, 2008). In the UK National Treatment Outcome Research Study, 25% of people misusing opiates were drinking heavily (more than 10 units per day) at the start of the study and 4 to 5 years later about a quarter were continuing to do so (Gossop *et al.*, 2003).

Comorbid cocaine and alcohol dependence
Cocaine use is increasing in England (NHS Information Centre & National Statistics, 2009), and comorbid cocaine and alcohol dependence is commonly seen and can be challenging to treat. There is little known in the UK about the level of this comorbidity in alcohol treatment services. In the US Epidemiological Catchment Area study, 85% of cocaine-dependent patients were also alcohol dependent (Regier *et al.*, 1990). In a sample of 298 treatment-seeking cocaine users, 62% had a lifetime history of alcohol dependence (Carroll *et al.*, 1993). In a sample of people in contact with drug treatment agencies (mainly for opiate addiction and in the community abusing cocaine), heavy drinking was common. Those using cocaine powder were more likely to drink heavily than those using crack cocaine (Gossop *et al.*, 2006).

When taken together, cocaine and alcohol interact to produce cocaethylene, an active metabolite with a half-life three times that of cocaine. In addition alcohol inhibits some enzymes involved in cocaine metabolism, so can increase its concentration by about 30% (Pennings *et al.*, 2002). Due to the presence of cocaethylene, which has similar effects to cocaine and a longer half-life, this leads to enhanced effects. For instance, taken together cocaine and alcohol result in greater euphoria and increased heart rate compared with either drug alone (McCance-Katz *et al.*, 1993; see Pennings *et al.*, 2002).

Comorbid alcohol and benzodiazepine dependence
Benzodiazepine use is more common in patients with alcohol misuse than in the general population, with surveys reporting prevalence of around 10 to 20% (Ciraulo *et al.*, 1988; Busto *et al.*, 1983). In more complex patients it can be as high as 40%, which is similar to that seen in psychiatric patients. A proportion of alcohol misusers who take benzodiazepines will be benzodiazepine dependent. For some individuals, their growing dependence on benzodiazepines began when a prescription for withdrawal from alcohol was extended and then repeatedly renewed. For others the prescription may have been initiated as a treatment for anxiety or insomnia, but then was not discontinued in line with current guidelines.

141

Comorbid alcohol and nicotine dependence
Many patients with alcohol misuse smoke cigarettes, which leads to an extra burden of morbidity and mortality in addition to the alcohol misuse. The prevalence of smoking has been estimated at around 40% in population-based studies of alcohol-use disorder and as much as 80% in people with alcohol dependence who are seeking treatment (Grant *et al.*, 2004b; Hughes, 1995). Comorbidity is higher in men than women and in younger compared with older people (Falk *et al.*, 2006). Comorbid nicotine and alcohol dependence has been comprehensively reviewed recently by Kalman and colleagues (2010).

Motivation and self-efficacy
The assessment of an individual's willingness to engage in treatment can vary considerably and has been the subject of considerable debate. Assessment can be effective as an intervention in itself and has been shown to influence behaviour change (McCambridge & Day, 2008), increasing an individual's confidence towards change that may prompt reductions in alcohol consumption (Rollnick *et al.*, 1999). Being sensitive to the individual's needs, developing rapport and a therapeutic alliance have all been identified as important aspects in the effective engagement of an individual who drinks excessively (Najavits & Weiss, 1994; Raistrick *et al.*, 2006; Edwards *et al.*, 2003). Indeed, there is evidence to suggest that a premature focus on information gathering and completion of the assessment process may have a negative impact on the engagement of the patient (Miller & Rollnick, 2002). Where this approach is adopted, there is some evidence to suggest that initial low levels of motivation are not necessarily a barrier to an effective assessment and the future uptake of treatment (Miller & Rollnick, 2002).

An openness to discussion aimed at understanding a person's reasons for seeking help and the goals they wish to attain has also been positively associated with engagement in assessment and treatment (Miller, 1996). The individual's personal drinking goals can then be acknowledged and used as a basis for negotiation once the assessment is completed (Adamson *et al.*, 2010).

Alcohol-related problems present in a number of different settings, often concurrently (for example, a person may present as depressed in primary care subsequent to a brief admission for acute pancreatitis, both related to excessive alcohol intake). Therefore, effective assessment systems need to be linked to equally effective communication between those involved in the care and treatment of people with alcohol-related problems (Maisto *et al.*, 2003). Sharing of information between agencies should be encouraged to maximise safety and effectiveness of treatment (MoCAM; Department of Health, 2006a).

5.24   FRAMEWORK FOR ASSESSMENT OF ALCOHOL MISUSE

As noted above, the presentation of alcohol-related problems are rarely straightforward and can span a wide range of settings and organisations. This complexity of presentation is often matched by a need for comprehensive assessment and treatment responses. It is therefore important that clear structures are in place to identify and assess the presenting problems, to determine the most appropriate treatment option and, where necessary, to make an appropriate referral. This section reviews the evidence, albeit limited, for the organisation and delivery of assessment systems. In doing so it not only draws on the evidence that relates directly to the organisation and delivery of care (see Section 2 of this chapter) but also on the evidence reviewed in the two other NICE guidelines on prevention and early detection of hazardous and harmful drinking (NICE, 2010a) and on management of alcohol-related physical complications (NICE, 2010b). This section also draws on other parts of this guideline that consider evidence relevant to a framework for the assessment of alcohol misuse. It should be noted that the framework of assessment in this guideline is not specifically concerned with the opportunistic screening for hazardous and harmful drinking that is covered by the NICE (2010a) guideline on prevention and early detection. However, it is important that the assessment framework considers both those who seek treatment and those who do not respond to brief interventions.

In developing the framework for assessment, the evidence for the discussion of stepped-care systems in Section 2 of this chapter was particularly influential. The evidence review provided no convincing evidence to suggest a significant variation for the stepped-care framework set out in *Models of Care for Alcohol Misusers* (MoCAM; Department of Health, 2006a) developed by the National Treatment Agency. Building on the framework in MoCAM, a conceptualisation for the assessment (and management) of harmful drinking and alcohol dependence at four-levels emerges[16]:

1. Case identification/diagnosis
2. Withdrawal assessment
3. Triage assessment
4. Comprehensive assessment.

These four levels, which are defined below, take account of the broad approach to the delivery of assessment and interventions across different agencies and settings including primary healthcare, third sector providers, criminal justice settings, acute hospital settings and specialist alcohol service providers. It should be noted, however, that this does not follow a strictly stepped-care model because an assessment for withdrawal could follow from a triage and a comprehensive assessment. Withdrawal assessment was not included in the MoCAM assessment framework as a separate assessment algorithm, but was considered by the GDG to merit separate inclusion in these guidelines. Alcohol withdrawal assessment is an area of clinical management that often requires immediate intervention. This is particularly apparent where an alcohol dependent individual may experience acute alcohol withdrawal as a consequence of an admission to an acute hospital ward (NICE, 2010b) due to an acute health problem, or has been recently committed to prison.

The framework for assessment (see Figure 4) sits alongside the four-tiered conceptual framework described in MoCAM (Department of Health, 2006a) and

---

[16]The terms 'levels' and 'tiers' are adopted from MoCAM (Department of Health, 2006a) to facilitate ease of understanding and implementation.

Figure 4: Assessment levels

Level 1: Case identification/diagnosis	Trained and competent staff in all services providing Tier 1 to 4 interventions
Level 2: Withdrawal assessment	Trained and competent staff in all services providing Tier 1 to 4 interventions
Level 3: Triage assessment	Trained and competent staff in all services providing Tier 2 to 4 interventions
Level 4: Comprehensive assessment	Trained and competent staff in all services providing Tier 3 to 4 interventions (and some Tier 2 interventions)

assumes that only appropriately skilled staff will undertake the assessment elements. The Drug and Alcohol National Occupational Standards (DANOS) (Skills for Health, 2002, and Skills for Care[17]) set out the skills required to deliver assessment and interventions under the four-tiered framework. The different levels of assessment will require varying degrees of competence, specialist skills and expertise to undertake the more complex assessments.

5.25 THE FRAMEWORK FOR ASSESSMENT OF ALCOHOL MISUSE

5.25.1 Case identification and diagnosis

Aims

Case identification and, following on from that, diagnosis seek to identify individuals who are in need of intensive care-planned treatment because of possible alcohol dependence, those with harmful alcohol use who are in need of or have not responded to brief interventions and those experiencing comorbid problems which may complicate the treatment of the alcohol misuse. Given the overall stepped framework in which the assessment takes place it is anticipated that this level of care would have two main objectives:

a) To identify those individuals who need an intervention (see Chapters 6 and 7) for harmful or alcohol dependence

b) To identify those who may need referral for a comprehensive assessment and/or withdrawal assessment including those who:
   - have not responded to an extended brief intervention
   - have moderate to severe alcohol dependence or otherwise may need assisted alcohol withdrawal
   - those that show signs of clinically significant alcohol-related impairment (for example, liver disease or significant alcohol-related mental health problems).

---

[17]See www.skillsforcare.org.uk.

and acts as a useful guide for the quantity of medication to be prescribed during alcohol withdrawal.

5.25.3   Withdrawal assessment in children and young people

As has already been noted, the diagnosis and identification of withdrawal symptoms in children and young people is difficult. This means that the potential for harm through under-identification of alcohol withdrawal on young people is considerable. Unfortunately, there is little direct evidence to guide the process of withdrawal management, including both its identification and treatment in young people. In the development of this section the GDG drew extensively on the review of assisted withdrawal for adults, contained both in the NICE guideline for acute withdrawal (NICE, 2010b) and for planned withdrawal within this guideline. In essence, the data used to support much of this review is an extrapolation from a data set developed from the management of withdrawal in adults. The principle that the GDG approached this data with is one of considerable caution and a desire to, as far as possible, reduce any significant harm arising from withdrawal symptoms in young people.

Identification of need for assisted alcohol withdrawal
Identification of withdrawal should be based on careful assessment of the pattern, frequency and intensity of drinking. The limited data available for review, the evidence from adults and the greater vulnerability of young people to the harmful effects of alcohol led the GDG to conclude that there should be a significant reduction in the threshold for young people for initiating withdrawal management. The threshold that has been established for adults of an AUDIT score of more than 20, an SADQ score of more than 20 or the typical consumption of 15 units per day is not appropriate for adolescents. In adolescents, binge drinking is common (defined as more than five units of alcohol on any one occasion) and a pattern of frequent binge drinking (for example, a pattern of two or more episodes of binge drinking in a month) or an AUDIT score of 15 should alert the clinician to possible dependence and trigger a comprehensive assessment. The presence of any potential withdrawal symptoms should be taken seriously and a comprehensive assessment initiated. A range of factors including age, weight, previous history of alcohol misuse and the presence of co-occurring disorders will also influence the threshold for initiating a comprehensive assessment and withdrawal management. See Figure 6 for a summary of the care pathway for withdrawal assessment.

5.25.4   Level 3: brief triage assessment

Aims
A brief triage assessment should be undertaken when an individual first contacts a specialist alcohol service, and it has the aim of developing an initial plan of care (MoCAM; Department of Health, 2006a). Failure to identify clinical and/or social

149

Figure 6: Care pathway: withdrawal assessment

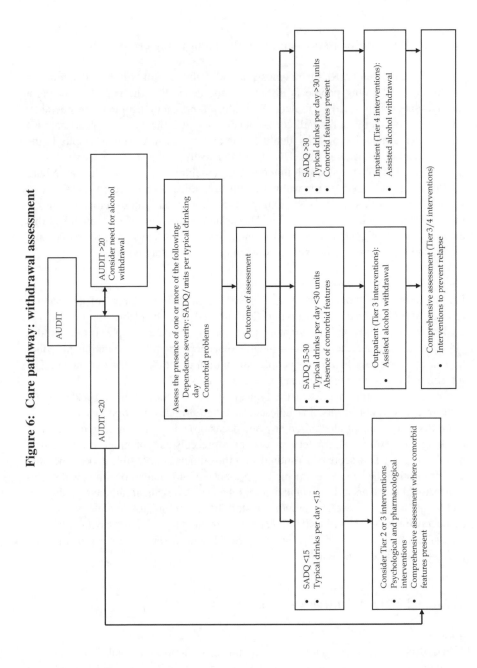

priorities may result in an individual being directed to inappropriate services or lost to any form of care. Typically, people presenting for a triage assessment may be harmful drinkers who have not benefitted from an extended brief intervention (see NICE, 2010a) and/or those with an AUDIT score of more than 20, or have been referred to or have self-referred to a specialist alcohol services.

A brief triage assessment is not simply a brief assessment of alcohol misuse only. The focus is equally on the management risk, identification of urgent clinical or social problems to be addressed and accessing the most appropriate pathways of care for alcohol misuse. The triage assessment therefore incorporates the common elements of assessment identified above with the aim of establishing the severity of the individual's problems, the urgency to action required and referral to the most appropriate treatment interventions and service provider.

Specifically the triage assessment should establish:

- the need for emergency or acute interventions, for example referral to accident and emergency for an acute medical problem or to a crisis team for a mental health emergency
- presence and degree of risk of harm to the person or others (including children) due to alcohol or substance misuse and related problems (medical, mental health, social and criminal)
- the appropriate alcohol treatment intervention(s) and setting(s) for the problems assessed
- an appropriate level of communication and liaison with all those involved in the direct care and management of the individual
- the need for a further comprehensive specialist assessment (see Section 5.25.5 below)
- the need to agree follow-up plans.

Settings

All specialist alcohol services (including those that provide combined drug and alcohol services) should operate a triage assessment according to agreed local procedures. This level of assessment is not intended to be a full assessment of an individual's needs on which to base a care plan. The triage assessment should identify immediate plans of care through the use of standardised procedures to ensure that all clinically significant information and risk factors are captured in one assessment. Incorporating tools and questionnaires as an adjunct to the clinical interview will help improve consistency of decision making.

Methods

The triage assessment should include:

- alcohol use history including:
  - typical drinking; setting, brand, and regularity
  - alcohol consumption using units of alcohol consumed on a typical drinking day
  - features of alcohol dependence
  - alcohol-related problems
  - adjunctive assessment tools (including the AUDIT and SADQ) to inform the assessment of risk and the immediate and future clinical management plan

- co-occurring problems (medical, mental health, substance misuse, social and criminal)
- risk assessment
- readiness and motivation to change.

Risk assessment

The increasing importance of risk assessment in the clinical decision-making process has led to a number of tools being developed to systematically screen for high-risk problems and behaviours which draw on a common framework for risk assessment systems in mental health (Department of Health, 2006a). In the NHS, it is expected that local protocols are agreed that specify the elements and tools for risk assessment to be applied (MoCAM; Department of Health, 2006a). Establishing these protocols and standards will also identify the competencies required for the collation and interpretation of risk to develop a risk management plan.

The risk assessment process should review all aspects of the information collected during the clinical interview and, where appropriate, consider results from investigations, questionnaire items, correspondence and records, and liaison with other professionals as well as family and carers, to formulate an assessment of risks to the individual, to others and to the wider community. The risk assessment should consider the interaction between comorbid features to arrive at an informed opinion of the severity of risk and the urgency to act.

MoCAM (Department of Health, 2006a) identifies that risk assessment should consider the following domains:

- risks associated with alcohol use or other substance misuse (such as physical damage or alcohol poisoning)
- risk of self-harm or suicide
- risk of harm to others (including risk of harm to children and other domestic violence, harm to treatment staff and risk of driving while intoxicated)
- risk of harm from others (including being a victim of domestic abuse)
- risk of self-neglect
- safeguarding-children procedures (must be included).

Where risks are identified, a risk management plan that considers monitoring arrangements, contingency plans and information sharing procedures needs to be developed and implemented (MoCAM; Department of Health, 2006a). Guidance developed for those working with patients with mental health problems indicates that the most effective risk assessments and risk management plans are developed by multidisciplinary teams and in collaboration between health and social care agencies (Department of Health, 2007).

Urgency to act

The urgency to act will be linked to the severity and level of risks identified from all the information gathered and should consider:

- The individual's intentions to carry out acts of self-harm or harm to others
- The state of distress being experienced by the individual

- The severity of comorbid medical or mental health conditions and the sudden deterioration of the individual's presentation
- The safeguarding needs of children/young people.

5.25.5   Level 4: comprehensive assessment

Aims

A comprehensive assessment should be undertaken where an individual experiences significant comorbidity, moderate or severe alcohol dependence or presents a high level of risk to themselves or others. This group will often require structured and/or intensive interventions and is often involved with multiple agencies. Those presenting with complex problems will require their care to be planned and co-ordinated.

The comprehensive assessment aims:
- to determine the exact nature of problems experienced by the individual across multiple domains
- to specify needs to inform development of a care plan
- to identify planned outcomes to be achieved and methods to assess these outcomes

Settings

Comprehensive assessment is undertaken by specialist alcohol services that provide Tier 3 and 4 interventions, although some Tier 2 services with sufficiently experienced staff may also offer comprehensive assessments as outlined by MoCAM (Department of Health, 2006a).

Methods

Comprehensive assessment should not be seen as a single event conducted by one member of the multidisciplinary team, although coordination of the assessment process may bring real benefit (see Section 5.3 for a review of care coordination and case management). The complex nature of the problems experienced by an individual with long-standing alcohol misuse or dependence suggests that the comprehensive assessment may need to be spread across a number of appointments and may typically involve more than one member of the multidisciplinary team. A range of expertise will often be necessary to assess the nature of problems. Comprehensive assessment may require specific professional groups to undertake tasks such as physical examination, prescribing needs, social care needs, psychiatric assessment and a formal assessment of cognitive functioning. Specialist alcohol services conducting comprehensive assessments therefore need to have access to: GPs and specialist physicians, addiction psychiatrists, nurses, psychologists and specialist social workers.

The comprehensive assessment should include an in-depth consideration and assessment of the following domains:
- alcohol use and related consequences
  - alcohol consumption
  - alcohol dependence
  - alcohol-related problems

- motivation
- self-efficacy
- co-occurring problems
  - substance misuse
  - physical health history and problems
  - mental health history and problems
  - social functioning and problems
- risk assessment
- treatment goals
- assessment of the service user's capacity to consent to treatment
- formulation a plan of care and risk management plan.

5.25.6   Methods of physical investigation

Breath/blood alcohol level
Alcohol is excreted in the breath and its concentration in the breath is correlated with blood alcohol concentration. On average it takes approximately 1 hour to eliminate one unit of alcohol from the body; however, the elimination rate varies between individuals and is more rapid in people who are alcohol dependent than those who are not (Allen *et al.*, 2003; Ugarte *et al.*, 1977). Breath alcometers reliably measure the breath alcohol concentration in a non-invasive way. Blood/breath alcohol concentration may be a useful part of the clinical assessment in the following areas:
- Although self report has been found to be a reliable indicator of levels of alcohol consumption in treatment-seeking populations, patients with alcohol in their system at the time of assessment are more likely to underestimate their levels of alcohol consumption (Sobell & Sobell, 2003).
- Clinicians have a responsibility to discuss drink-driving concerns with patients and their responsibilities in reporting this to the Driver and Vehicle Licensing Agency (DVLA, 2010). Service users who have driven on the way to an assessment and who are over the legal limit for driving (80 mg/100 ml) need to be advised not to drive until they are legally able to do so.

Blood investigations
There are a number of biomarkers suggested to be clinically useful in the assessment of alcohol-related physical harm (Allen *et al.*, 2003), monitoring of clinical outcome and as a motivational enhancement strategy (Miller *et al.*, 1992). However, in people who are seeking treatment for alcohol misuse, biomarkers do not offer any advantage over self-report measures in terms of accuracy of assessing alcohol consumption (Allen *et al.*, 2003; Sobell & Sobell, 2003*)*, and are less sensitive and specific than the AUDIT in screening for alcohol misuse (Drummond & Ghodse, 1999).

Gamma-glutamyl transferase (GGT) has a sensitivity of 50 to 70% in the detection of high levels of alcohol consumption in the last 1 to 2 months and a specificity of 75 to 85% (Drummond & Ghodse, 1999). Reasons for false positive results include hepatitis, cirrhosis, cholestatic jaundice, metastatic carcinoma, treatment with simvastatin and obesity.

Mean corpuscular volume has a sensitivity of 25 to 52% and specificity of 85 to 95% in the detection of alcohol misuse. It remains elevated for 1 to 3 months after abstinence. Reasons for false positives include vitamin B12 and folate deficiency, pernicious anaemia, pregnancy and phenytoin (Allen *et al.*, 2003; Drummond & Ghodse, 1999).

Carbohydrate-deficient transferrin (CDT) has greater specificity (80 to 98%) than other biomarkers for heavy alcohol consumption, and there are few causes of false positive results (severe liver disease, chronic active hepatitis) (Schwan *et al.*, 2004). However, routine CDT monitoring is not routinely available and there remains some debate about how best to measure it. Evidence suggests that the test is less sensitive in women (Anton & Moak, 1994). CDT increases and recovers more rapidly than GGT in response to a drinking binge, increasing within 1 week of onset of heavy drinking, and recovery typically occurs in 1 to 3 weeks compared with 1 to 2 months for GGT (Drummond & Ghodse, 1999).

Advantages of blood investigations as part of the initial assessment include:
- screening for alcohol-related physical conditions that may need further investigation and onward referral
- providing baseline measures of alcohol-related damage (in some patients) against which to measure improvement and act as motivational enhancement strategy
- objective measurement of outcome, particularly when combined (for example, CDT and GGT; Allen *et al.*, 2003) and in conjunction with other structured outcome measures (Drummond *et al.*, 2007).

Hair and sweat analysis
As alcohol is rapidly excreted from the body, there is currently no reliable or accurate way of measuring alcohol consumption in the recent past and the mainstay of outcome measurement is self-report (Sobell & Sobell, 2003). This is less useful for regulatory monitoring purposes and so there is a growing interest by manufacturers in the design of biomarkers for recent alcohol consumption. Studies to date focus on hair and skin sweat analysis, but there is currently a lack of evidence to recommend their use in routine clinical care (Pragst & Balikova, 2006).

Assessment of alcohol-related physical harm
The assessment of alcohol-related physical harm is an important component of a specialist service (Edwards *et al.*, 2003). The aims of such an assessment are to:
- identify physical health problems that require immediate attention and onward referral to appropriate acute medical care
- identify physical health problems that are a consequence of the alcohol misuse and require monitoring, and potential future referral

The relationship between alcohol-related physical health problems and level of alcohol consumption is complex (Morgan & Ritson, 2009), as is the presence of physical signs in relation to underlying pathology. Consequently, patients presenting with

155

longstanding, severe alcohol dependence may have few overt physical signs, but have significant underlying organ damage (for example, liver disease). Others may present with significant symptoms (for example, gastritis) or signs (for example, hypertension) that may resolve without active treatment once the service user abstains.

Liver/gastrointestinal problems
Alcohol-related liver disease often develops 'silently' over a 10 to 15 year period and blood tests of liver function (alanine amino transferase [ALT]) may only become abnormal at quite advanced stages of disease, so a test that is within the normal range does not exclude liver damage (Prati *et al.*, 2002). Equally, raised ALT may be the result of induction of liver enzymes by alcohol rather than an indication of liver pathology (Drummond & Ghodse, 1999). Other laboratory test results including GGT and serum aspartate amino transferase (AST) may be raised in people who misuse alcohol, but do not necessarily indicate the presence of significant organ damage as a result of enzyme induction (Bagrel *et al.*, 1979). Patients with signs of severe (decompensated) liver disease (for example, presenting with jaundice, fluid retention, spontaneous bruising or hepatic encephalopathy) will need urgent specialist medical care from a hepatology service. Symptoms of anorexia, nausea, vomiting and diarrhoea, and malabsorption syndromes are common in people who misuse alcohol. In many cases these symptoms resolve with treatment of the underlying alcohol misuse, but people with significant pain or evidence of gastrointestinal blood loss will need referral for further investigation.

Cardiovascular
Alcohol has a dose-related effect on blood pressure in addition to blood pressure being elevated during alcohol withdrawal (Xin *et al.*, 2001). Patients who present with hypertension or who are already prescribed anti-hypertensive medication will need to have this reviewed as treatment progresses.

Neurological
Wernicke's encephalopathy classically presents with a triad of symptoms (ataxia, confusion and ophthalmoplegia), but in practice this triad only occurs in a minority of cases (Thomson & Marshall, 2006). Given the severity of brain damage (Wernicke–Korsakoff syndrome [WKS]) that may occur if the condition is untreated, clinicians need to have a high index of suspicion particularly in those patients who are malnourished and have any of the following clinical signs: ataxia, ophthalmoplegia, nystagmus, acute confusional state, or (more rarely) hypotension or hypothermia. Patients presumed to have a diagnosis of WE will need immediate treatment or onward referral (NICE, 2010b).

Symptoms of peripheral neuropathy are common (30 to 70%) in people who misuse alcohol (Monteforte *et al.*, 1995). The symptoms are predominantly sensory (although muscle weakness is also seen) and include numbness, pain and hyperaesthesia in a 'glove and stocking' distribution, primarily in the legs. Symptoms should be monitored and will require referral if they do not improve with alcohol abstinence.

5.25.7 Mental health: comorbidity and cognitive functioning

Alcohol is strongly associated with a wide range of mental health problems, particularly depression, anxiety and self-harm (Weaver *et al.*, 2003). In addition, many patients have deficits in cognitive function that may not be identified without systematic investigation (Evert & Oscar-Berman, 1995). The presence of psychological distress and/or comorbid psychiatric diagnoses, particularly if undetected, may have a substantial impact on treatment engagement and progress, leading to suboptimal treatment outcomes (Weaver *et al.*, 2003).

There are significant challenges in the assessment and diagnosis of mental health comorbidity. Some symptoms may be the direct result of excessive alcohol consumption or withdrawal and these tend to reduce once abstinence has been achieved (Brown *et al.*, 1995). The same symptoms may, however, also be the result of a comorbidity that requires parallel treatment, but the presence of which may also worsen the alcohol misuse. Finally, there are comorbid conditions (for example, social anxiety and some forms of cognitive impairment) that are not apparent whilst the person is drinking, but which emerge following abstinence and may have an impact on retention in treatment.

Depression and anxiety

Although many symptoms of depression or anxiety may be directly attributable to alcohol misuse, many people still reach the threshold for a diagnosis of a psychiatric disorder. For instance, 85% of patients in UK alcohol treatment services had one or more comorbid psychiatric disorders including 81% with affective and/or anxiety disorders (34% severe depression; 47% mild depression; 32% anxiety) and 53% had a personality disorder (Weaver *et al.*, 2003). Such high levels of comorbidity are not surprising given that the underlying neurobiology of depression or anxiety and alcoholism have many similarities, particularly during withdrawal (Markou & Koob, 1991). In addition there are shared risk factors because twin studies reveal that the presence of one disorder increases the risk of the other disorder (Davis *et al.*, 2008).

There is a high prevalence of comorbidity between anxiety and alcohol misuse, both in the general and clinical populations. Anxiety disorders and alcohol dependence demonstrate a reciprocal causal relationship over time, with anxiety disorders leading to alcohol dependence and vice versa (Kushner *et al.*, 1990). Panic disorder and generalised anxiety disorder can emerge during periods of alcohol misuse; however, the association with obsessive-compulsive disorder is less robust.

Social phobia and agoraphobia often predate the onset of alcohol misuse. The prevalence of social anxiety ranges from 8 to 56% in people who misuse alcohol, which makes it the most prevalent psychiatric comorbidity. People who are alcohol dependent and have comorbid social anxiety disorder show significantly more symptoms of alcohol dependence, higher levels of reported depression, and greater problems and deficits in social support networks as compared with alcohol dependent patients without social anxiety (Thevos *et al.*, 1999).

The relationship between alcohol and depression is also reciprocal in that depression can increase consumption, but depression can also be caused or worsened by alcohol misuse (Merikangas *et al.*, 1996).

Sleep disorders
Sleep disorders (commonly insomnia) increase the risk of alcohol misuse and also contribute to relapse (Brower, 2003; Krystal *et al.*, 2008). Whilst many people believe that alcohol helps them sleep, this is not the case. Although onset of sleep may be reduced after drinking alcohol, disruption to sleep patterns occur later in the night such as rapid eye-movement rebound and increased dreaming, as well as sympathetic arousal (Krystal *et al.*, 2008). Abstinence may reveal a sleep disorder that the person has not been entirely aware of because they have always used alcohol to sleep. Insomnia is also a prominent feature of both acute and protracted alcohol withdrawal syndromes, the latter of which can last for 3 to 12 months.

Eating disorders
There is substantial evidence that alcohol misuse and eating disorders commonly co-occur (Sinha & O'Malley, 2000). In specialist alcohol inpatient treatment, the prevalence of eating disorders can be as high as 40%. Commonly, an eating disorder exists together with other psychiatric disorders such as depression. In people with an eating disorder, up to half have been reported to misuse alcohol (Dansky *et al.*, 2000). A number of studies have found the strongest relationship for bulimia nervosa, followed by patients suffering from binge eating disorder and eating disorder not otherwise specified (EDNOS) (Gadalla & Piran, 2007). No association has been reported between anorexia nervosa and alcohol misuse. In a study of European specialist eating-disorder services, alcohol consumption was higher in patients with EDNOS and bulimia nervosa than anorexia nervosa, but a greater lifetime prevalence of alcohol misuse was not found (Krug *et al.*, 2009).

Psychosis
Patients with psychotic disorders (including schizophrenia and bipolar disorder) are vulnerable to the effects of alcohol and at increased risk of alcohol misuse (Weaver *et al.*, 2003). Approximately 50% of patients requiring inpatient psychiatric treatment for these disorders will also misuse alcohol (Barnaby *et al.*, 2003; Sinclair *et al.*, 2008). However, a smaller proportion of patients will present without a diagnosis of an underlying psychotic or mood disorder, which will need to be identified as part of a comprehensive assessment. For a more thorough review of this area see the NICE guideline on psychosis and substance misuse (NICE, 2011a).

Self-harm and suicide
There is a significant but complex association between alcohol misuse and self-harm and suicide. Approximately 50% of all patients presenting to hospital following an episode of self-harm have consumed alcohol immediately before or as part of the act of self-harm (Hawton *et al.*, 2007). The mortality by suicide in patients who present following an episode of self-harm is significantly increased in the next 12 months (66 times that of the general population) (Zahl & Hawton, 2004) and this risk remains high after many years (Owens *et al.*, 2002). However, recent data from a long-term follow-up study suggests that the mortality of self-harm patients appears to be caused by alcohol-related conditions as much as suicide (Sinclair *et al.*, 2009). For people

whose self-harm occurs only when intoxicated, abstinence from alcohol was recognised as the effective intervention (Sinclair & Green, 2005). Alcohol dependence has been shown to increase the risk of suicide by five to 17 times, with the RR being greatest in women (Wilcox *et al.*, 2004).

Cognitive impairment

Prolonged cognitive deficits are seen in 50 to 80% of people with alcohol dependence who have undergone assisted alcohol withdrawal (Bates *et al.*, 2002). Cognitive impairments frequently improve significantly once abstinence has been achieved and so should be reassessed after 2 to 3 weeks of abstinence (Loeber *et al.*, 2009).

A number of assessment tools can be used to assess cognitive function in people who misuse alcohol have been identified. These include the Mini-Mental State Examination (MMSE; Folstein *et al.*, 1975); the Cognitive Capacity Screening Examination (CCSE; Jacobs *et al.*, 1977); the Neuropsychological Impairment Scale (NIS; O'Donnell & Reynolds, 1983); and the Cognitive Laterality Battery (CLB; Gordon, 1986).

The MMSE (Folstein *et al.*, 1975) is a cognitive screening instrument widely used in clinical practice and has been established as a valid and reliable test of cognitive function (Folstein *et al.*, 1975). It measures orientation, registration, short-term memory, attention and calculation, and language. A score of 17 or less is considered to be severe cognitive impairment, 18 to 24 to be mild to moderate impairment and 25 to 30 to be normal or borderline impairment. It has the advantage of being brief, requiring little training in administration and interpretation, free to use, and is designed to assess specific facets of cognitive function (Small *et al.*, 1997). The MMSE has been found to have high sensitivity for detecting moderate to severe cognitive impairment as well as satisfactory reliability and validity (see Nelson and colleagues [1986] for a review). The MMSE can be utilised as a brief screening tool as well as for assessing changes in cognitive function over time (Brayne *et al.*, 1997).

It must be noted, however, that the MMSE has been found to be sensitive to educational level in populations where educational levels are low (Escobar *et al.*, 1986; Liu *et al.*, 1994). Therefore, the cut-offs used to identify cognitive impairment may need to be adjusted for people who misuse alcohol with few years of formal education (Crum *et al.*, 1993; Cummings, 1993). Furthermore, the MMSE has been criticised for not being sensitive enough for those in various cultures where the education levels are low and participants may fail to respond correctly to specific items (Escobar *et al.*, 1986; Iype *et al.*, 2006; Katzman *et al.*, 1988; Liu *et al.*, 1994). Because of this, it is necessary (and often practised) to amend and adjust aspects of the MMSE to increase applicability to a particular cultural setting. For example, a Hindi version of the MMSE, the Hindi Mental State Examination (Ganguli *et al.*, 1995) was designed to address some of the cultural problems with the MMSE and to make it more applicable to an Indian cultural setting.

Most research evaluating the accuracy, reliability and validity of the MMSE has been in the assessment of age-related cognitive impairment and dementia, whereas research in the field of alcohol and substance misuse is limited. However, the MMSE has been utilised in substance-misuse research (Smith *et al.*, 2006). Additionally, it

159

has been highlighted that the MMSE mainly assesses verbal cognitive function and is limited in assessing non-dominant hemisphere skills and executive functions (Bak & Mioshi, 2007). This could lead to frontal-dysexecutive and visuospatial symptoms going undetected.

The CCSE (Jacobs *et al.*, 1977) was designed to screen for diffuse organic mental syndromes. The CCSE has 30 items that provide information on the areas of orientation, digit span, concentration, serial sevens, repetition, verbal concept formulation and short-term verbal memory. A score of less than 19 has been suggested as indicative of organic dysfunction (Haddad & Coffman, 1987; Hershey *et al.*, 1987; Jacobs *et al.*, 1977). As with most cognitive screening instruments, the CCSE has been studied extensively in people with dementia (Nelson *et al.*, 1986). It has been found to have adequate reliability and validity in detecting cognitive impairment (Foreman, 1987; Villardita & Lomeo, 1992). However, the CCSE has been found to be sensitive to age and education (Luxenberg & Feigenbaum, 1986; Omer *et al.*, 1983) and has been found to have a high false-negative rate and hence low sensitivity (Nelson *et al.*, 1986; Schwamm *et al.*, 1987). Furthermore, Gillen and colleagues (1991) and Anderson and Parker (1997) reported that the CCSE did not adequately distinguish between cognitively impaired and non-impaired people who misuse substances.

The NIS is a 50-item scale that has been designed to identify brain damage. The reliability and validity of the NIS has been previously reported in normal and neuropsychiatric populations (O'Donnell *et al.*, 1984a and 1984b), as well as having a sensitivity of between 68 and 91% and a specificity of between 43 and 86% (O'Donnell *et al.*, 1984b). Errico and colleagues (1990) further reported predictive validity, and test–retest reliability in a sample of people undergoing assisted alcohol withdrawal.

The CLB was developed to measure visuospatial and verbosequential functioning, with tests administered on a sound/sync projector, and takes 80 minutes for administration. However, the CLB has been reported to have limited clinical utility in the assessment of cognitive function in an alcohol-dependent population (Errico *et al.*, 1991).

Addenbrooke's Cognitive Evaluation (ACE; Mathuranath *et al.*, 2000) was developed as a brief test of key aspects of cognition which expanded on the MMSE by assessing memory, language and visuospatial abilities in greater depth, as well as including assessment of verbal fluency. ACE is designed to be sensitive to the early stages of dementia (Mioshi *et al.*, 2006) and was found to detect dementia earlier and discriminate more between different subtypes of dementia than the MMSE (Mathuranath, 2000). To comprehensively assess cognitive impairment, ACE can be used in a cognitive test battery along with tests which assess other cognitive domains (Lezak, 1995; Spreen & Strauss, 1998), such as the Trail-Making Test, Part B (Army Individual Test Battery, 1944) or the Block Design subtest of the revised Wechsler Adult Intelligence Scale (Wechsler, 1981). Mioshi and colleagues (2006) developed a revised version of the test, ACE-R, which addressed previously-identified weaknesses in the original test and made it easier to administer. Bak and colleagues (2007) found that ACE-R has a good specificity for the detection of dementia (94%) with a specificity of 89% (at a cut-off score of 88/100). The ACE-R is administered as a bedside test, takes approximately 16 minutes to complete and consists of five sections each designed to assess a specific cognitive domain (Mioshi *et al.*, 2006). Although the ACE-R takes longer to administer than some other tests for cognitive impairment, such as the MMSE, it has been found to have a high level of patient acceptability and can be administered without specialist training (Larner, 2007). The ACE and ACE-R tests are published in 19 languages, although no evidence was found regarding the effect of cultural or educational differences on testing outcomes.

The ACE has been used in screening for cognitive dysfunction in people who misuse alcohol (Gilchrist & Morrison, 2004), although no research in this field using ACE-R could be identified. Additionally, research into the efficacy and sensitivity of ACE-R in assessing substance induced cognitive impairment is negligible. It has been suggested, however, that it is possible to extrapolate the validity of the ACE as an instrument to assess age-related cognitive impairment and apply it in assessing cognitive impairment in people who misuse alcohol. The increased sensitivity of ACE in relation to the MMSE may mean that it is subtle enough to identify people who misuse alcohol that have mild cognitive impairment who are able to function successfully in the community but have a history of non-engagement with alcohol services (personal communication, Ken Wilson, October, 2010).

Childhood abuse
A history of physical and/or sexual abuse is common in patients seeking treatment for alcohol misuse, particularly women (Moncrieff *et al.*, 1996). Patients identified with childhood trauma who wish for further intervention should be referred to appropriate services once they have reached a degree of stability in terms of their alcohol use (guideline on PTSD; NCCMH, 2005).

Family and relationships
Relationships with partners, parents, children and significant others are often affected by alcohol misuse (Copello *et al.*, 2005). Families and carers also suffer significantly in their own right, with an increased incidence of mental disorder (Dawson *et al.*, 2007). Involvement of partners or family can help identify the needs of the help seeking individual. The prevalence of alcohol misuse in the victims and perpetrators of domestic violence provides an important rationale for the exploration of these issues.

Employment
The status of the individual's occupation is significant in terms of the individual's ability to remain economically active. Past employment history may indicate the individual's capacity to obtain and retain employment. Employment history might provide insights into factors that maintain the individuals drinking status that need to be explored. Those assessing employed individuals will need to consider potential risks to the person, colleagues and the public because of excessive drinking (for example, when the individual has responsibility for the safety of others).

Criminality and offending
Assessment of criminality and offending behaviour should encompass a number of factors including the presence and onset of criminal activity, the severity of offending

behaviour, the relationship between offending and alcohol consumption and/or alcohol withdrawal, and the presence of violence and aggressive behaviour, and hence risk to others. Liaison with criminal justice services is necessary to ensure that appropriate co-ordination of care, and effective communication and information-sharing protocols, are in place.

Fitness to drive

For people who misuse alcohol and continue to drive a motor vehicle, clinical staff have a duty to advise the individual that it is the duty of the license holder or license applicant to notify the DVLA of any medical condition that may affect safe driving. There are circumstances in which the license holder cannot or will not notify the DVLA. Clinicians will need to consult the national medical guidelines of fitness to drive in these circumstances (DVLA, 2010).

5.25.8   Goals for drinking behaviour

The information collated from the comprehensive assessment will identify the type and severity of the alcohol misuse experienced, and the presence and significance of comorbid problems. This information should be considered alongside the individual's preferred drinking goals as basis for a negotiated care plan with drinking goals specified. Previous reviews and studies (Adamson *et al.*, 2010; Heather *et al.*, 2010; Raistrick *et al.*, 2006) have identified that:

● Individuals seeking abstinence from alcohol should be supported in their aim regardless of their severity of problems.
● Individuals with comorbid problems for which continued drinking is clearly contraindicated should be strongly advised that abstinence should be considered.
● Individuals who seek non-abstinence goals (that is, moderation or controlled drinking) usually experience less severe problems and should be supported. However, where a practitioner identifies that abstinence should be promoted but the individual seeks non-abstinence as a goal, a negotiated approach should be supported where abstinence is considered if moderation goals prove unsuccessful.
● If the individual is uncertain as to which goal to pursue, further motivational interventions should be considered to arrive at a consensus approach.
● Treatment goals need to be regularly reviewed and changed where indicated. Staff should adopt a flexible approach to goal setting that recognises the above parameters.

5.25.9   Formulating a care plan and risk management plan

The intention of any assessment whether triage, withdrawal or comprehensive is to arrive at a care plan that takes into account the individual's views and preferences, and those of their family and carer's where indicated, as well as any safeguarding issues. The development of a care plan needs to address the presenting alcohol misuse and consider the impact of treatment on existing problems (MoCAM; Department of Health, 2006a). It should take account of the presence, severity and complexity of problem areas that in turn will influence the choice of treatment interventions, medications and/or settings that are offered.

The care plan should be developed in negotiation with the individual (National Treatment Agency for Substance Misuse, 2006). The care plan may include short-, intermediate- and long-term objectives in addition to any contingency planning needed where risk increases. Care plans need to be shared with those also involved in providing care to the individual as planned treatment interventions and medications may have significant interactions with existing or planned care for other problems or conditions.

5.25.10   Outcome monitoring

Outcome monitoring is important in assessing how treatment for alcohol misuse is progressing. The main aim of outcome evaluation should be to assess whether there has been a change in the targeted behaviour following treatment. Outcome monitoring aids in deciding whether treatment should be continued or if further evaluation and a change of the care plan is needed. There are three important areas of outcome monitoring: deciding what outcome to measure; how to measure outcomes (the appropriate tools); and when to measure outcomes. Routine outcome monitoring (including feedback to staff and patients) has been shown to be effective in improving outcomes (Lambert *et al.*, 2002). Routine session-by-session measurement provides a more accurate assessment of overall patient outcomes (Clark *et al.*, 2009).

What outcome should be measured?
Assessment of alcohol consumption (for example, intensity and frequency of drinking) is a basic component of outcome monitoring. For example, Emrick (1974) states that monitoring abstinence post-treatment is a significant predictor of psychosocial functioning. Alcohol-related problems or harm have also been suggested to be important in outcome monitoring. Longabaugh and colleagues (1994) state that outcome measurement should contain a range of assessment domains and include life functioning (such as physical health and social functioning). Alcohol problems are the only assessment domain significantly associated with drinking outcome measures (PDA, DDD, first drink) (Project MATCH Research Group, 1997 and 1998). This suggests that alcohol-related problem outcome measures should be assessed in addition to alcohol consumption.

How should outcome be measured?
When selecting a suitable tool for outcome monitoring there are a number of factors that need to be considered, as suggested in a review of by Raistrick and colleagues (2006). An outcome monitoring tool should be:
● universal and not constrained by any particular substance or social group
● have proven validity and reliability, and have published psychometric properties

- sensitive to change
- easily readable and in a neutral language
- either practitioner-completed, self completed, or a combination of both
- appropriate for the clinical population.

The outcome measure that is applicable to all tiers of services is assessing the level of alcohol consumption by interviewing the patient about their quantity and frequency of alcohol consumption, but the use of a formal measure will improve the reliability and validity of measurement (Sobell *et al.*, 1979). The most valid and reliable measures of alcohol consumption include a diary method to obtain drinking data (Sobell & Sobell, 2003). However, measures such as the Timeline Followback questionnaire (Sobell & Sobell, 2003) are more feasible to administer in the research setting rather than a routine clinical setting. Some clinical services in the UK use prospective weekly drinking diaries that are self-completed by service users, but their reliability and validity is unknown.

A number of assessment tools have been designed specifically for outcome measurement in addiction treatment. They all measure multiple domains of functioning, but their comprehensiveness, utility and specificity to alcohol treatment vary. The most widely used tools for outcome measurement are the Addiction Severity Index (ASI), AUDIT, the Maudsley Addiction Profile (MAP), the Christo Inventory for Substance Misuse Services (CISS), the Comprehensive Drinker Profile (CDP), the Routine Evaluation of the Substance-Use Ladder of Treatments (RESULT) and the Treatment Outcomes Profile (TOP). The GDG evaluated the clinical utility of these tools in alcohol treatment on the extent to which each tool has sufficient validity and reliability data in an alcohol dependent population and if the tool has high usability (that is, it is easy to read and understand, it does not require extensive training for use and it is brief). Table 19 describes the characteristics of the outcome measurement tools identified.

The GDG excluded the ASI because it was excluded in the earlier review of primary outcome tools and also is too lengthy for use as an outcome monitoring tool. The CISS, CDP, MAP and RESULT were also excluded because they have not been adequately validated in an alcohol-dependent clinical sample in the UK. Lastly, the TOP is primarily used in a drug misusing population with only limited psychometric data for alcohol-dependent clinical samples. The protocol for reporting TOP states explicitly that 'the reporting of the TOP for adult primary alcohol users is not required' (National Treatment Agency for Substance Misuse, 2010) and therefore the TOP is not being applied in routine practice.

Based on these criteria, a GDG consensus-based decision was made that the AUDIT has the greatest utility as a routine outcome monitoring tool to evaluate drinking-related outcomes. The AUDIT questionnaire is already widely used. It contains several relevant drinking domains in addition to alcohol consumption (problems and dependence). The time taken to complete the AUDIT (less than 2 minutes) also lends itself to use in routine practice. The AUDIT-C (Bush *et al.*, 1998) is a three-item version of the AUDIT which measures only alcohol consumption; that is, frequency of drinking, quantity consumed on a typical occasion and the frequency of heavy episodic drinking (six or more standard drinks on a single occasion). Bush and

Table 19: Characteristics of routine outcome monitoring tool

Outcome monitoring tool	Is there adequate psychometric data in primarily alcohol dependent population?	Does the tool have high usability (for example, readable, short time to administer, limited training required)?	Source study
Addiction Severity Index (ASI)	Yes (but validity and reliability are questionable)	No – requires a trained interviewer and takes 50 to 60 minutes	McLellan and colleagues (1980)
Alcohol Use Disorders Identification Test (AUDIT)	Yes – extensive data that supports validity and reliability	Yes – takes 2 minutes	Babor and colleagues (2001)
Maudsley Addiction Profile (MAP)	No	Yes – takes 20 minutes	Marsden and colleagues (1998)
Christo Inventory for Substance Misuse Services (CISS)	No	Yes – takes 10 minutes	Christo and colleagues (2000)
Comprehensive Drinker Profile (CDP)	No	No – requires a trained interviewer and takes 2 hours	Miller and Marlatt (1987)
Routine Evaluation of the Substance-Use Ladder of Treatments (RESULT)	No	Yes – takes 30 minutes	Raistrick and Tober (2003)
Treatment Outcomes Profile (TOP)	No – primarily in drug misuse population	Yes – one page, 20 items	Marsden and colleagues (2007)

colleagues (1998) reported that the AUDIT-C performed better than the full AUDIT in detecting heavy drinking and was just as effective as the full AUDIT in identifying active alcohol misuse or dependence. The study also found that using a cut-off of 3 out of a possible 12 points, the AUDIT-C correctly identified 90% of active alcohol 'abuse'/'dependence' and 98% of patients drinking heavily. However, other studies have reported that a cut-off of 5 or more for men and 4 or more for women results in the optimal sensitivity and specificity for detecting any alcohol-use disorders (Dawson *et al.*, 2005b; Gual *et al.*, 2002). In addition, the AUDIT-C has been found to be equally effective in detecting alcohol-use disorders across ethnic groups (Frank *et al.*, 2008). However, it should be noted that the AUDIT-C has been reported to have a high false positive rate when used as a screening tool (Nordqvist *et al.*, 2004).

Nevertheless, the ease of use and the already established relationship between frequency/quantity of drinking and alcohol misuse/dependence give the AUDIT-C credence for the use of outcome monitoring.

The APQ has been widely used in alcohol treatment outcome studies as a measure of alcohol-related problems in the UK (for example, Drummond, 1990; Drummond *et al.*, 2009; UKATT Research Team, 2005). Furthermore, it is quick and easy to administer. Therefore, the APQ can be used to measure alcohol-related problems in conjunction with a drinking-related outcome tool such as the AUDIT-C. However, the ten-item AUDIT still has the advantage of measuring a wider range of domains in one simple validated questionnaire and therefore more readily lends itself to routine clinical outcome monitoring.

When should outcome be measured?
Most changes in drinking behaviour and the largest reduction in severity of drinking occurs in the first 3 months of treatment (Babor *et al.*, 2003; Weisner *et al.*, 2003). Initial benefits in drinking-related outcomes may be more apparent at 3 months, but other non-drinking domains such as social functioning and global health may need longer to show improvements following treatment. Because there is a high attrition rate in many alcohol services this can result in poor response rates in routine outcome monitoring. This underlines the importance of routine session-by-session measurement and the utility of a brief measure such as the AUDIT or a prospective weekly drinking diary. The latter requires considerable cooperation of service users and is of unknown reliability and validity.

5.25.11   Special populations

A framework for assessment for children and young people with alcohol problems
As with the adult assessment, the use of any assessment tool needs to be set in context. The context here is that all children who are beyond initial identification should be offered an assessment within specialist CAMHS. Although recommendations are made below for the use of specific measures to assess the nature and extent of the alcohol misuse and related problems, it was also the view of the GDG that the assessment should take place in the context of a comprehensive overall assessment of the mental health, educational, and social care needs of the children and young people, in line with current best practice (Department for Education and Skills, 2007). In common with good assessment practice in CAMHS services, the involvement of parents, carers and others (for example, schools) is an essential part of any assessment. It should also be noted that parents not only have a key role as informants, advisors and participants in the process of assessment, but they also have a key role to play in the development of any future treatment plans. It is therefore important that wherever possible they are involved from the beginning.

The overall structure of assessment (at least for the assessment of alcohol misuse) is provided by the assessment tools reviewed above. However, whatever assessment tool is used from both the child and adult literature, (Harrington *et al.*, 1999, and see

Chapter 5) suggest that the following domains need to be considered as part of any assessment of alcohol related problems in children and young people:
- Alcohol use – consumption, dependence features and associated problems
- Comorbid substance misuse – consumption, dependence features and associated problems
- Motivation
- Self-efficacy
- Other problem domains
  - Physical history and problems
  - Mental health and problems
  - Social functioning
  - Educational attainment and attendance
  - Peer relationships
  - History of abuse and trauma
  - Family functioning and relationships
- Risk assessment
- Developmental needs of the young person
- Treatment goals
- Obtaining consent to treatment
- Formulation of a care plan and risk management plan.

An additional point to bear in mind is the use of further informants. For example, in terms of the assessment of consumption, the use of other informants such as parents, carers or schools may assist in detailing the history of consumption, and in clarifying the level and veracity of use.

As was identified in the introduction, the presentation of alcohol misuse or dependence does not typically follow the pattern seen in adults. More often, a pattern of binge drinking is observed that is often accompanied by drug misuse. It is important, therefore, to detail both the pattern of drinking and the comorbid drug misuse. It should also be noted that adolescents may have lower prevalence of withdrawal symptoms along with a lower tolerance. Both of these factors may contribute to continued high alcohol intake, particularly of binge drinking, with consequent serious implications for psychological and physical health but without the 'warning signs' of emerging withdrawal symptoms.

History of trauma and abuse
It has already been noted that comorbidity of substance misuse is significantly higher in adolescents who misuse alcohol. It is also important to note that alcohol misusing adolescents have a significant increased rate of physical abuse (by a factor of 6 to 12) and a significant increased rate of sexual abuse (by up to a factor of 20) (Clark *et al.*, 1997a). Given that it is possible that these histories may have a significant aetiological role in the development of alcohol misuse, it is important that these issues are part of assessment. It is also likely that a history of trauma has an impact for the likely comorbidity, for example the existence of PTSD (Clark *et al.*, 2003), and also that it may be associated with poor response to treatment and the need for more complex treatment interventions.

5.25.12   Evidence summary

Content of the clinical assessment
The literature review identified a number of components of a structured clinical interview. These included assessment of the current extent and history of drinking, associated potential for withdrawal, the likelihood of withdrawal, the need for review of associated physical health problems, the examination of mental health and the impact of alcohol on social, personal, occupational and educational functioning. It also identified that the impact of alcohol on the family would be an important issue also to be considered. Considerable emphasis on the literature reviewed was placed on the importance of engaging people with alcohol-related problems in treatment and negotiating appropriate goals. It is clear from the literature that for people who are moderately and severely dependent drinkers, the initial goal should be one of abstinence. For others who are harmful and mildly dependent drinkers, it may be possible to consider a reduction in drinking as a reasonable treatment goal. However, past history of unsuccessful attempts to moderate drinking should be born in mind when making these assessments.

There is little evidence that indicates the identification and assessment methods needed for assisted withdrawal in children and young people. Therefore, the GDG makes a consensus-based decision to extrapolate from the review of the adult literature and combine this with expert opinion. The group concluded that a comprehensive assessment and an assessment for assisted withdrawal should be offered to all children and young people with established binge drinking, an AUDIT score of more than 15 and those who consume more than five units per day, but this decision should also take into consideration other factors such as age, weight, previous history of alcohol misuse and the presence of co-occurring disorders.

The review of formal assessment measures also considered a number of measures of motivation (readiness to change). It was not felt by the group that the quality of these measures (in part because of impracticality of these measures which were designed primarily for use in research) warranted their use in standard clinical care. However, a consideration of a patient's readiness and/or motivation for change is a vital part of assessment.

Physical investigations
An awareness of and inquiry into the nature of commonly presenting physical health problems with alcohol misuse are important. This guideline, and other related NICE guidelines (NICE, 2010a and 2010b), considered the value of biomarkers; for example, liver function tests as indicators for diagnosis of alcohol-related disorders. From the reviews conducted for this and the other NICE guidelines it was concluded that these measures have insufficient sensitivity and specificity compared with validated assessment methods such as the AUDIT. However, for people with specific physical health problems, for those whom regular feedback on a particular biological marker may act as a motivational tool and those for whom pharmacological treatments may require liver function tests (for example, naltrexone and disulfiram), these measures may have an important part to play in the ongoing treatment and management of alcohol misuse. No evidence was identified in this or the other NICE guidelines (2010a

and 2010b) to support the use of other biomarkers (for example, hair analysis) for routine clinical use in assessment or outcome monitoring of alcohol misuse.

Assessment of comorbid substance misuse
It is recognised that smoking, drinking and drug taking behaviours cluster together (Farrell *et al.*, 2001) and that excessive drinkers with high AUDIT scores are more likely to have used drugs in the past (Coulthard *et al.*, 2002). Therefore, the evidence suggests that co-existing substance misuse should be assessed. Clinical assessment should include the type of drug and its route of administration, the quantity and the frequency with which it is used.

Assessment of comorbid mental health problems
Mental health problems which co-exist with alcohol misuse can have a significant impact, both on the treatment and long-term outcome of the alcohol-related problem. However, depression and anxiety can often develop as a consequence of alcohol misuse. At assessment there is no reliable way of determining whether a comorbid mental health problem is primary or secondary to alcohol misuse. This means that symptoms of comorbid mental disorders need to be monitored throughout the course of assessment and treatment. A common presentation in alcohol misuse is suicidal ideation. This needs to be assessed and actively managed as part of an overall risk management process. The GDG considered that as, a minimum, the re-assessment of common mental disorders should occur 3 to 4 weeks following abstinence from alcohol. At this point, consideration may be given to treatment. NICE guideline for the management of these disorders should be consulted.

Cognitive impairment
Cognitive impairment is present in most people who misuse alcohol presenting for treatment. These impairments, which may be transitory, are, however, often missed in the initial assessment. The evidence reviewed suggested that the MMSE has reasonable validity as an initial identification tool and should be supplemented with specific questions to detect duration extent or functional impairment. There is also evidence to suggest that the ACE-R has good sensitivity for diagnosing mild cognitive impairment. However, it does not assess all aspects of cognitive function and should be used as a part of a specialist comprehensive assessment test battery in conjunction with an executive test such as the Block Design subtest of the Wechsler Adult Intelligence Scale (WAIS-III) (Wechsler, 1945/1997) or the Trail-Making Test, Part B (Army Individual Test Battery, 1944). It is not possible to conduct an effective cognitive assessment in people who misuse alcohol who are actively drinking. Unless there is evidence of gross cognitive impairment that may require further and immediate investigation, the GDG took the view that adequate assessment of cognitive impairment is best left until 3 to 4 weeks following abstinence from alcohol. At this point if significant cognitive impairment persists, it should be subject to more formal assessment including conducting a more detailed history and neuropsychological testing. Those patients presenting acutely with a confused state and significant memory loss may be suffering from WE and should be assessed and treated accordingly (see NICE, 2010b).

Organisation and delivery of assessment

The evidence for the organisation and delivery of the range of assessment was reviewed. This included a review of the currently recommended assessment systems in England and, in particular, the MoCAM stepped-care framework. This approach begins with an initial case identification/diagnostic assessment. Here, the emphasis is on brief assessments that can be administered by staff in a range of services in health-care and related settings. There is good evidence from the assessment tools reviewed above that scores on measures such as the AUDIT and SADQ provide a useful indication of the appropriate level of intervention needed. There is also evidence that people who misuse alcohol can be assessed in a relatively brief triage assessment. The guideline also reviewed the evidence for the factors to be considered in a withdrawal assessment. Finally, the indications for and content of comprehensive assessment was reviewed. In summary the GDG felt that a stepped approach to assessment in line with that set out in MoCAM (Department of Health, 2006a) was appropriate.

Outcome monitoring

The GDG reviewed the evidence for the use of routine outcome monitoring. A range of assessment tools were considered as part of the overall view of assessment tools. Although these measures are effective at identifying the presence or severity of the disorder, most were felt unsuitable or impractical for routine outcome measurement. The evidence suggested that the AUDIT questionnaire provides a valid, reliable and feasible method to monitor outcome in routine clinical care. Prospective weekly drinking diaries, whilst widely used in clinical services, are of unknown reliability and validity. The routine use of breath alcohol concentration measurement was not supported by the evidence either in initial assessment or routine outcome monitoring, although it has a useful place in monitoring abstinence in the context of an assisted withdrawal programme. The GDG therefore favoured the AUDIT (specifically the first three questions from the questionnaire with subsequent questions only used for 6-month follow-up) as a routine measure, but recognised that in some services, especially Tier 3 and Tier 4 specialist services, an additional, more detailed assessment measure may also be used. The GDG also favoured the APQ as an outcome monitoring tool when assessing alcohol-related problems.

5.26   FROM EVIDENCE TO RECOMMENDATIONS

Assessment tools

The review of assessment tools identified a number of measures which had sufficiently robust psychometric properties to be used in routine clinical care. In addition to these factors, the GDG also used its expert knowledge to assess the benefit and feasibility of their use in routine care. As a case identification tool (that is, one that would indicate whether or not further treatment was required) the AUDIT questionnaire is the most appropriate instrument. On occasions where the AUDIT questionnaire was not available and/or not practical, then a simple typical daily alcohol consumption measure could also be used as an indicator of potential need for treatment. For people suspected of having alcohol dependence, the use of the SADQ or the LDQ were supported by the GDG as effective instruments to measure the severity of alcohol dependence in order to guide further management. For assessing the extent of problems associated with alcohol misuse, the APQ was identified as meeting all the necessary criteria. In addition, on the basis of the NICE guideline on the management of alcohol-related physical complications review (NICE, 2010b), the CIWA-Ar was judged to be the most appropriate instrument to measure alcohol withdrawal symptoms.

Content of the clinical assessment and the organisation and delivery of assessment systems
It is important to recognise that the use of individual assessment tools alone, such as those identified above, does not constitute a comprehensive assessment. The evidence suggested that, in addition to a historical and recent history of drinking, the associated physical and mental health problems, and the impact on health and social and economic problems, should also be assessed. This section also identified the importance of the impact on family (including, importantly, children). It is also important to recognise that a key aspect of effective assessment is the process of engaging people and identifying treatment goals. For example, determining whether abstinence, which is the initial preferred goal for moderately and severely dependent drinkers, or moderation of alcohol consumption is the preferred goal. The GDG therefore decided to provide detail on the content of the range of assessment domains. The GDG also reviewed the evidence for the organisation and delivery of assessment systems and supported the established system recommended within MoCAM (Department of Health, 2006a). This may require additional specialist assessment resources and systems to ensure that individuals have the capacity and competency to deliver these assessments.

Physical investigations
The review for this guideline (based in significant part on parallel work undertaken on other NICE guidelines; NICE, 2010b) established that physical investigations (in particular, blood tests including measures of liver function) are not sufficiently sensitive or specific measures for routine use in specialist alcohol services. However, biomarkers can have added benefit as motivational tools by providing feedback on progress and in assessing suitability for some pharmacological interventions (for example, naltrexone and disulfiram). The GDG also considered that the measurement of breath alcohol is a useful, objective part of the clinical monitoring in the management of assisted alcohol withdrawal.

Assessment of comorbid substance misuse
The presence of comorbid substance misuse is associated with poorer outcomes for those with alcohol misuse and the GDG reviewed evidence on this along with the recommendation in the NICE (2007a) guideline on psychosocial management of substance misuse. It was agreed that assessment of comorbid drug misuse should therefore be a part of routine assessment of alcohol misuse. Consideration should be

given to the use of biological testing (for example, of urine or saliva samples) as part of a comprehensive assessment of drug misuse, but clinicians should not rely on it as the sole method of diagnosis and assessment.

Assessment of comorbid mental health problems

Comorbid mental health problems are a common presentation in people who misuse alcohol. It is important that this is assessed at initial presentation. However, it should be noted that for many people, symptoms of, for example, depression and anxiety may remit following 3 to 4 weeks of abstinence from alcohol. It is therefore often not appropriate or necessary to instigate treatment for the disorder at the point of the initial assessment. Careful monitoring and reassessment of mental health symptoms following abstinence are an important part of the assessment procedure. Treatment of mental health disorders that persist beyond 3 to 4 weeks after abstinence should be considered.

Routine outcome monitoring

Routine outcome monitoring is an essential part of any effective healthcare system provision. The AUDIT questionnaire was identified as the most reliable and feasible measure for routine outcome monitoring. Prospective drinking diaries are of unknown reliability and validity. The APQ was also identified as beneficial for the assessment of alcohol-related problems when monitoring treatment outcome.

Competence of staff

It is essential that clinicians performing assessments of people who misuse alcohol should be fully competent to do so.

Children and young people

Due to the lack of sufficient evidence specifically for children and young people, the GDG decided to adopt a modified version of the assessment framework adopted for adults. As with the adult review the GDG favoured the use of the AUDIT tool as a case identification/screening tool and this is consistent with the approach adopted the NICE prevention and brief intervention guideline (NICE, 2010a) However, the GDG decided to adjust the threshold for AUDIT in light of evidence that this increased the sensitivity for adolescent alcohol misuse. For a more comprehensive assessment, the GDG recommended two possible assessment tools and the integration of any assessment of alcohol misuse into a comprehensive assessment of the needs of the child or young person.

5.26.1   Recommendations

Identification and assessment

General principles

5.26.1.1   Staff working in services provided and funded by the NHS who care for people who potentially misuse alcohol should be competent to identify harmful drinking and alcohol dependence. They should be competent to initially assess the need for an intervention or, if they are not competent, they should refer people who misuse alcohol to a service that can provide an assessment of need.

5.26.1.2 Make sure that assessment of risk is part of any assessment, that it informs the development of the overall care plan, and that it covers risk to self (including unplanned withdrawal, suicidality and neglect) and risk to others.

5.26.1.3 When conducting an initial assessment, as well as assessing alcohol misuse, the severity of dependence and risk, consider the:
  ● extent of any associated health and social problems
  ● need for assisted alcohol withdrawal.

5.26.1.4 Use formal assessment tools to assess the nature and severity of alcohol misuse, including the:
  ● AUDIT for identification and as a routine outcome measure
  ● SADQ or LDQ for severity of dependence
  ● Clinical Institute Withdrawal Assessment for Alcohol scale, revised (CIWA-Ar) for severity of withdrawal
  ● APQ for the nature and extent of the problems arising from alcohol misuse.

5.26.1.5 When assessing the severity of alcohol dependence and determining the need for assisted withdrawal, adjust the criteria for women, older people, children and young people[20], and people with established liver disease who may have problems with the metabolism of alcohol.

5.26.1.6 Staff responsible for assessing and managing assisted alcohol withdrawal (see Section 5.30.2) should be competent in the diagnosis and assessment of alcohol dependence and withdrawal symptoms and the use of drug regimens appropriate to the settings (for example, inpatient or community) in which the withdrawal is managed.

5.26.1.7 Staff treating people with alcohol dependence presenting with an acute unplanned alcohol withdrawal should refer to 'Alcohol-use disorders: diagnosis and clinical management of alcohol-related physical complications' (NICE clinical guideline 100).

Assessment in all specialist alcohol settings
Treatment goals
5.26.1.8 In the initial assessment in specialist alcohol services of all people who misuse alcohol, agree the goal of treatment with the service user. Abstinence is the appropriate goal for most people with alcohol dependence, and people who misuse alcohol and have significant psychiatric or physical comorbidity (for example, depression or alcohol-related liver disease). When a service user prefers a goal of moderation but there are considerable risks, advise strongly that abstinence is most appropriate, but do not refuse treatment to service users who do not agree to a goal of abstinence.

---

[20]See Section 5.22 for assessment of children and young people.

5.26.1.9   For harmful drinking or mild dependence, without significant comorbidity, and if there is adequate social support, consider a moderate level of drinking as the goal of treatment unless the service user prefers abstinence or there are other reasons for advising abstinence.

5.26.1.10   For people with severe alcohol dependence, or those who misuse alcohol and have significant psychiatric or physical comorbidity, but who are unwilling to consider a goal of abstinence or engage in structured treatment, consider a harm reduction programme of care. However, ultimately the service user should be encouraged to aim for a goal of abstinence.

5.26.1.11   When developing treatment goals, consider that some people who misuse alcohol may be required to abstain from alcohol as part of a court order or sentence.

Brief triage assessment

5.26.1.12   All adults who misuse alcohol who are referred to specialist alcohol services should have a brief triage assessment to assess:
- the pattern and severity of the alcohol misuse (using AUDIT) and severity of dependence (using SADQ)
- the need for urgent treatment including assisted withdrawal
- any associated risks to self or others
- the presence of any comorbidities or other factors that may need further specialist assessment or intervention.

Agree the initial treatment plan, taking into account the service user's preferences and outcomes of any previous treatment.

Comprehensive assessment

5.26.1.13   Consider a comprehensive assessment for all adults referred to specialist alcohol services who score more than 15 on the AUDIT. A comprehensive assessment should assess multiple areas of need, be structured in a clinical interview, use relevant and validated clinical tools (see Section 5.16), and cover the following areas:
- alcohol use, including:
  - consumption: historical and recent patterns of drinking (using, for example, a retrospective drinking diary), and if possible, additional information (for example, from a family member or carer)
  - dependence (using, for example, SADQ or LDQ)
  - alcohol-related problems (using, for example, APQ)
- other drug misuse, including over-the-counter medication
- physical health problems
- psychological and social problems
- cognitive function (using, for example, the Mini-Mental State Examination [MMSE][21])
- readiness and belief in ability to change.

---

[21]Folstein and colleagues (1975).

5.26.1.14 Assess comorbid mental health problems as part of any comprehensive assessment, and throughout care for the alcohol misuse, because many comorbid problems (though not all) will improve with treatment for alcohol misuse. Use the assessment of comorbid mental health problems to inform the development of the overall care plan.

5.26.1.15 For service users whose comorbid mental health problems do not significantly improve after abstinence from alcohol (typically after 3–4 weeks), consider providing or referring for specific treatment (see the relevant NICE guideline for the particular disorder).

5.26.1.16 Consider measuring breath alcohol as part of the management of assisted withdrawal. However, breath alcohol should not usually be measured for routine assessment and monitoring in alcohol treatment programmes.

5.26.1.17 Consider blood tests to help identify physical health needs, but do not use blood tests routinely for the identification and diagnosis of alcohol-use disorders.

5.26.1.18 Consider brief measures of cognitive functioning (for example, MMSE) to help with treatment planning. Formal measures of cognitive functioning should usually only be performed if impairment persists after a period of abstinence or a significant reduction in alcohol intake.

SECTION 4 – DETERMINING THE APPROPRIATE SETTING FOR THE DELIVERY OF EFFECTIVE CARE

5.27   INTRODUCTION

This section is concerned with identifying the settings in which to deliver clinical care for people who misuse alcohol. It begins with a review of planned assisted withdrawal, which is linked to and draws heavily on the review conducted for the NICE guideline on management of alcohol-related physical complications (NICE, 2010b). It then considers the range of settings in which assisted withdrawal and the interventions covered in Chapters 6 and 7 of this guideline may be best provided, including community, residential and inpatient settings.

The majority of services provide treatment for alcohol misuse in community or outpatient settings, whereby a patient is visited at home by a health or social care professional or attends a clinic or a day hospital. There are also approximately 200 voluntary or independent sector providers of residential rehabilitation treatment for drug or alcohol misuse in England (National Treatment Agency, 2009b). The services that they offer can be differentiated according to factors such as the principal aims of treatment, patient group and length of stay. Residential rehabilitation services may offer medically assisted withdrawal from alcohol, but usually only as a prelude to longer-term rehabilitation or aftercare. Finally, medically-managed inpatient facilities are usually run by the NHS, and a review of national provision in 2004 highlighted

77 NHS hospitals that admitted patients for drug or alcohol withdrawal, and a further 28 non-statutory or private providers (Day *et al.*, 2005).

Current practice in the management of assisted withdrawal, and the general provision of alcohol treatment services, tends to follow MoCAM (Department of Health, 2006a) guidance that suggested community settings were preferred for the treatment of the majority of people who misuse alcohol, as they are seen as more cost effective and more likely to promote change in their drinking behaviour in a normal social environment. However, it was noted that some people would require treatment in hospital or in supported residential accommodation, including those who are severely dependent, have a history of withdrawal complicated by seizures or DTs, are in poor physical or psychological health, are at risk of suicide, or misuse drugs. Homeless people, those who lack social support or stability, or those who have had previous unsuccessful attempts at withdrawal in the community may also require inpatient treatment. MoCAM also stipulated that inpatient assisted withdrawal should lead seamlessly into structured care-planned treatment and support, whether delivered in the community or in residential rehabilitation services. However, it should also be noted, as discussed at the beginning of this chapter, that there is considerable variation in practice (including in the settings) in which services are provided.

A number of authors have considered the possible benefits of treatment in a residential setting (Gossop, 2003; Mattick & Hall, 1996; McKay *et al.*, 1995; Weiss, 1999). In considering the potential benefits of any setting, it is useful to distinguish between the provision of withdrawal management and the provision of further treatment and rehabilitation. Residential settings provide a high level of medical supervision and safety for individuals who require intensive physical and/or psychiatric monitoring, and the possibility of more intensive treatment may also help patients who do not respond to interventions of lower intensity. Residential settings may also offer the patient respite from their usual social milieu (that is, the people and places associated with alcohol use) and improved continuity of care. However, the protectiveness of a residential unit may also be one of its main disadvantages – it may limit opportunities for the patient to develop new coping strategies (Annis, 1996). Time away from work or study, reduced family contact and the stigmatisation associated with some residential service settings may also be potential disadvantages of residential care (Strang *et al.*, 1997). Finally, residential settings are considerably more expensive than non-residential alternatives.

Previous reviews of studies of residential treatment for alcohol misuse conducted in the 1980s concluded that residential/inpatient treatment had no advantages over outpatient treatment (Annis, 1996; Miller & Hester, 1986). Furthermore, every controlled study of length of inpatient treatment found no advantage in longer over shorter stays, or in extended inpatient care over assisted withdrawal alone (Annis, 1996; Miller & Hester, 1986). However, the authors noted a variety of methodological problems with the studies, not least that the nature of the treated populations varied substantially, from general psychiatric patients assessed for alcohol misuse and outpatient problem drinkers to inpatient alcoholics (Miller & Hester, 1986). Miller and Hester also noted in their study that a course of outpatient treatment averaged less than 10% of the cost of inpatient treatment. Therefore, even if residential settings afforded a modest advantage in overall effectiveness, preference might still be given to non-residential treatment based on cost effectiveness.

Further research conducted since the mid-1980s has challenged some of these conclusions. In a review of the literature, Finney and colleagues (1996) found 14 studies in which setting effects might have been detected. Of these studies, seven found significant setting effects on one or more drinking-related outcomes, with five favouring inpatient over outpatient treatment and a further two favouring day hospital over inpatient treatment (Finney *et al.*, 1996). In all but one instance in which a significant effect emerged, patients in the more effective setting received more intensive treatment, and participants were not 'pre-selected' for their willingness to accept random assignment. Other potential methodological problems were also identified. As mentioned above, it is often thought that an inpatient or residential setting will benefit patients from social environments where heavy drinking is common and encouraged by allowing the patient a period of respite. However, some studies randomised participants to inpatient or outpatient treatment after an initial period of inpatient treatment for medically-assisted withdrawal. Finney and colleagues (1996) commented that this treatment setting contamination might bias studies toward no-difference findings.

5.28   REVIEW QUESTIONS

1. In adults in planned alcohol withdrawal, what is the clinical efficacy, cost effectiveness, safety of, and patient satisfaction associated with:
   ● preparatory work before withdrawal
   ● different drug regimens
   ● the setting (that is, community, residential or inpatient)?
2. In adults in planned alcohol withdrawal, what factors influence the choice of setting in terms of clinical and cost effectiveness including:
   ● severity of the alcohol disorder
   ● physical comorbidities
   ● psychological comorbidities
   ● social factors?
3. In adults with harmful or dependent alcohol use, what are the preferred structures for and components of community-based and residential specialist alcohol services to promote long-term clinical and cost-effective outcomes?

5.29   ASSISTED ALCOHOL WITHDRAWAL

5.29.1   Introduction

This section is concerned with planned assisted alcohol withdrawal. It should be read in conjunction with the NICE guideline on management of alcohol-related physical complications (NICE, 2010b); the reviews conducted for that guideline informed the decisions of the GDG. Previous research assessing the settings for assisted withdrawal from alcohol has yielded a considerable amount of debate about the safety, efficacy and cost effectiveness of the various options available. Settings for assisted withdrawal include the community (where assisted withdrawal may be delivered in a day hospital setting), in specialist community alcohol teams or in primary care, specialist inpatient and specialist residential settings. In addition, assisted withdrawal programmes are also provided in the prison healthcare system, police custody and a range of acute general medical settings. This section is also concerned with the indications for inpatient assisted withdrawal. Some further details about the settings in which assisted withdrawal can take place are given below. Special populations or patient groups who may be at risk of complications are considered separately in Sections 5.29.6 and 5.30.7.

Community settings

In a community setting, a person undergoing assisted withdrawal lives in their own accommodation throughout the treatment. A spectrum of treatment intensity is also possible. Day hospital treatment (sometimes known as 'partial hospitalisation'; see Mee-Lee *et al.*, 2001) may involve the patient attending a treatment facility for up to 40 hours per week during working hours, Monday to Friday, and returning home in the evening and weekends. This facility may be located within an inpatient or residential rehabilitation unit, or may be stand-alone. It is likely to be staffed by a multidisciplinary team, with input from medical and nursing staff, psychologists, occupational therapists, social workers, counsellors, and other staff specialising in debt, employment or housing issues. Other community assisted withdrawal programmes may invite the patient to attend for appointments with a similar range of multidisciplinary staff, but at a much lower frequency and intensity (for example, once or twice a week), or they may be provided by GPs often with a special interest in treating alcohol-related problems. Alternatively, staff may visit the patient in their own home to deliver interventions. Between these two options are most intensive community-based options, where an increased frequency of community visits and some limited use of office or team-based treatment may form part of an intensive community programme.

Inpatient and residential settings

In inpatient and residential settings, the service user is on-site for 24 hours a day for the duration of assisted withdrawal. Inpatient and residential settings encompass a spectrum of treatment intensity. At one end lie specialist units within either acute medical or psychiatric hospitals, dedicated to the treatment of alcohol or drug problems (known as 'inpatient units'). Such units have specialist medical and nursing input available 24 hours a day, and are staffed by a multidisciplinary team that may also include psychologists, occupational therapists, social workers, counsellors, and other staff specialising in debt, employment or housing issues. At the other end of the spectrum are facilities usually known as 'residential rehabilitation' units, which are usually provided by the non-statutory sector and not sited within hospital premises. Although the goal of such units is usually the provision of longer-term treatment

(3 to 12 months) aimed at enhancing the patient's ability to live without using alcohol, increasingly they also provide an initial period of assisted withdrawal. Such units may also have access to medical and nursing input over the full 24-hour period, but this is usually at a lower level of intensity and more likely to utilise non-specialist staff (for example, GPs). Such units are more likely to adopt a 'social model' rather than a 'medical model', and may be staffed by both professionals and individuals in recovery. In addition, a number of prisons may offer a high level of medical supervision including, where necessary, admission to the hospital wing of the prison.

5.29.2   Aim of review and review protocol

The initial aim of this review was to perform a systematic meta-analysis of RCT data that addressed the review question. However, only one well-designed RCT assessing the benefits and harms of different settings for assisted withdrawal has been published (Hayashida *et al.*, 1989). Therefore, the GDG decided to assess all available studies and provide a narrative review. The review team assessed the literature identified from the search conducted by the NICE guideline on management of alcohol-related physical complications (NICE, 2010b); full details of the search strategies can be found in that guideline. Studies were considered for inclusion in a narrative review for this guideline if they met the inclusion criteria (see Chapter 3) and if the population being assessed in the study reflected the scope of this guideline (see Appendix 1). Furthermore, studies were considered for inclusion in the narrative review using the clinical review protocol in Table 20. The key outcomes of interest were: the efficacy of the setting for assisted withdrawal (for example, the patient successfully completed the programme and remained abstinent during the period assisted withdrawal); the safety profile (for example, the development of complications, and hence the patient factors that indicate that a non-residential setting for assisted withdrawal is unsuitable or unsafe); and participation in consequent rehabilitation treatment. Other outcomes of interest are patient satisfaction and other patient and physician related factors.

5.29.3   Studies considered

Five studies comparing different settings for assisted withdrawal were identified. Of these, one was an RCT (Hayashida *et al.*, 1989), three were retrospective matching studies (Bartu & Saunders, 1994; Parrott *et al.*, 2006; Stockwell *et al.*, 1991) and one was a retrospective case study comparing patient characteristics in different settings (Allan *et al.*, 2000). In addition, five open prospective studies (Collins *et al.*, 1990; Drummond & Chalmers, 1986; Feldman *et al.*, 1975; Soyka & Horak, 2004; Stinnett, 1982) and an RCT assessing adding a brief psychological intervention to home-based assisted withdrawal (Alwyn *et al.*, 2004) were also identified. These additional studies did not compare different settings for assisted withdrawal but reported treatment outcomes for a community setting for assisted withdrawal.

Table 20: Clinical review protocol for the evaluation of different settings for assisted withdrawal from alcohol

Electronic databases	CINAHL, EMBASE, MEDLINE, PsycINFO, Cochrane Library; see the NICE guideline on management of alcohol-related physical complications (NICE, 2010b) for search strategies
Date searched	Systematic reviews from 1993 to March 2010. All other searches from database inception to March 2010
Study design	Systematic reviews, RCTs
Patient population	Adults (over 18 years old) Patients with alcohol withdrawal syndrome
Outcomes	Main outcomes: severity of withdrawal; completion rates; abstinence during assisted withdrawal; safety (development of complications); participation in further rehabilitation treatment after assisted withdrawal Other outcomes: patient and physician factors

The literature search also identified studies and systematic reviews evaluating circumstances in which inpatient admission for assisted withdrawal may be appropriate, as well as special populations and patient groups whom may require inpatient assisted withdrawal from alcohol. These studies are considered separately.

5.29.4   Narrative review of settings for assisted withdrawal

Studies comparing different settings for assisted withdrawal
Apart from the Hayashida and colleagues (1989) study, the studies discussed above were observational in design and participants were only matched for severity of alcohol dependence. Furthermore, although these studies indicated that it is feasible for assisted withdrawal to take place in a community setting for a severely dependent population, it is probable that a number of patients with significant comorbidities and previous history of seizures where excluded. As these patients form a significant proportion of those who are referred to and receive inpatient or residential assisted withdrawal, caution is needed when interpreting these results.

Only one randomised trial (Hayashida *et al.*, 1989), conducted in a US Department of Veterans Affairs (VA) medical centre, compared the effectiveness and safety of inpatient (n = 77) and outpatient (n = 87) assisted withdrawal. Patients with serious medical or psychiatric symptoms, predicted DTs and a very recent history of seizures were excluded from this study. The authors reported that more inpatients than outpatients completed assisted withdrawal. However, inpatient treatment was significantly longer and more costly than outpatient treatment. Additionally, both groups had similar reductions in problems post-treatment when assessed at 1- and 6-month follow-up. Although abstinence was statistically significantly higher for the inpatient group at 1-month follow-up, these differences were not observed at 6-month follow-up. The authors concluded that outpatient assisted withdrawal should be considered for people with mild-to-moderate symptoms of alcohol withdrawal.

Stockwell and colleagues (1991) compared a retrospective inpatient sample (n = 35) with a group receiving home-based assisted withdrawal (n = 41). The two samples were matched for age, sex and drinking severity. Patients undertaking home-based assisted withdrawal were severely dependent (SADQ score = 28.7; mean alcohol consumption 174.6 units per week) and had a high level of alcohol-related problems (APQ score = 4.6). The authors reported that home-based assisted withdrawal was as safe and effective for a severely dependent population as inpatient care. However, the matched inpatient sample did not include anyone with severe alcohol withdrawal syndrome or physical or psychiatric symptoms and, therefore, is not representative of an inpatient population.

Bartu and Saunders (1994) also compared people undertaking home-based assisted withdrawal (n = 20) with patients in an inpatient specialist unit (n = 20). Patients were matched for age, sex, presence of social support, absence of medical complications and severity of withdrawal symptoms. It was reported that home-based assisted withdrawal was as beneficial as inpatient assisted withdrawal. It should be noted, however, that the matched inpatient sample was not representative of a typical inpatient, who may be severely dependent and have several complications.

Parrott and colleagues (2006) compared alcohol-focused outcomes and cost of residential (n = 54) with any day (n = 49) settings for assisted withdrawal in the UK and reported similar alcohol-focused outcomes (PDA and DDD). This paper mainly discusses cost implications and is reviewed in the health economic section (Section 5.29.7).

In a comparison between home-based assisted withdrawal (n = 29) and day hospital services (n = 36) in severely dependent patients, Allan and colleagues (2000), in a UK-based study, evaluated the types of patients selected for home-based assisted withdrawal, its safety and efficacy, and patient satisfaction and involvement in further treatment. Participants in both groups were severely dependent (two thirds had a SADQ score of over 30), although the day hospital group drank significantly more at baseline (home-based group = 178 units, day hospital group = 194 units in the week before assisted withdrawal). Furthermore, although both groups had alcohol-related problems, as assessed by the APQ, the day hospital group had significantly more severe problems and social instability. The authors reported that there were no significant differences between the groups in the proportion of participants who completed assisted withdrawal, complication rates (which were low) and uptake of treatment post withdrawal. However, it should be noted that this study did not match participants in both settings but aimed to assess the characteristics of the patients who use home-based and day hospital assisted withdrawal.

Prospective studies evaluating outpatient assisted withdrawal
Further studies assessing the treatment outcomes and characteristics of patients in various settings were identified from the literature search. These studies were open prospective studies and aimed to evaluate the safety and efficacy of outpatient assisted withdrawal. Feldman and colleagues (1975) evaluated an outpatient treatment programme for alcohol withdrawal (n = 564). The authors reported that only 47% required outpatient assisted withdrawal and 19% required inpatient assisted withdrawal. Outpatient assisted withdrawal was successful and had a low dropout rate of 14%. However, the authors attributed this success to the early involvement of the family, the use of withdrawal medication and involvement in peer group therapeutic activity. The results of an earlier study reflected these findings (Alterman *et al.*, 1988). The investigators reported that ambulatory assisted withdrawal was relatively successful for mild-to-moderate alcohol withdrawal symptomatology.

Soyka and Horak (2004) assessed the efficacy and safety of outpatient assisted withdrawal in a German open prospective study. Alcohol dependent participants were excluded if they presented with severe alcohol-related disorders, such as seizures or psychosis, or major psychiatric and medical comorbidity. Some participants referred to the treatment clinic had to be admitted for inpatient care (n = 348), leaving 331 patients to be treated in an outpatient setting. The study reported very high completion rates (94%) for patients in an outpatient assisted withdrawal programme. Furthermore, outpatient assisted withdrawal was associated with increased participation in further treatment (91% of initial sample). Soyka and Horak (2004) additionally found that of those who completed assisted withdrawal successfully, all entered either motivationally- or psychotherapy-based treatment.

Stinnett (1982) evaluated the effectiveness and safety of 116 participants referred for outpatient assisted withdrawal in an alcoholism treatment centre. Fifty per cent completed treatment, and 89% of these completers went on to continue with follow-up rehabilitation treatment. Collins and colleagues (1990) assessed the efficacy of a UK-based outpatient alcohol withdrawal programme. Of those deemed suitable for outpatient assisted withdrawal (n = 76; 44% of all referrals), 79% successfully completed the treatment. These patients were severely alcohol dependent (91% had an SADQ score greater than 30). However, not all studies have reported such favourable completion rates. For example, in a severely dependent sample of 26 patients (77% with a SADQ score greater than 31), Drummond and Chalmers (1986) reported that only 23% of patients completed assisted withdrawal and 19% attended a follow-up 1 month later.

In a UK-based RCT, Alwyn and colleagues (2004) evaluated the addition of a brief psychological intervention to GP-managed home-based assisted withdrawal. The psychological intervention consisted of five 30-minute sessions with motivational, coping skills and social support approaches. The study reported that both the control and the psychological intervention group (total n = 91) showed significant improvements in drinking outcomes from baseline to follow-up (3- and 12-month) indicating that home-based assisted withdrawal was effective. In addition, the psychological intervention group showed significantly greater improvements than the control group at 12-month follow-up. These results suggest that there is benefit in adding a brief psychological intervention to assisted withdrawal.

From the patients' perspective, it has been suggested that gains made in inpatient assisted withdrawal may not be easily transferable to the patient's home and social environment (Bischof *et al.*, 2003). Undertaking assisted withdrawal in a home or outpatient setting enables the patient to retain important social contacts that may facilitate their attempts to achieve abstinence as well as subsequent rehabilitation. Patients can continue in employment (if appropriate) and be in a familiar environment with family support, which may help to minimise stress and anxiety and help to motivate them. It has also been suggested that the home environment is also less stigmatising than an inpatient setting for assisted withdrawal (Allen *et al.*, 2005). In a study assessing patients' perceptions and fears of alcohol withdrawal, Allen and colleagues (2005) found that patients were fearful and concerned about the psychiatric residential setting for assisted withdrawal and expressed feelings of stigmatisation associated with being in an 'institutional' setting. The authors also reported no difference in patient satisfaction between a home and outpatient setting for assisted withdrawal. Additionally, patient satisfaction with outpatient assisted withdrawal services have also been found to be high when administered in an intensive day programme (Strobbe *et al.*, 2004). Stockwell and colleagues (1990) found that three quarters of patients preferred their home as the setting for assisted withdrawal, and two fifths and one third were unwilling to undergo withdrawal in, respectively, a psychiatric hospital and a general hospital. The patients also emphasised the importance of support from the nurse supervising their assisted withdrawal, the breathalyser, medications, telephone support service and the involvement of supporters, familiar surroundings, privacy and confidentiality, and being able to stay with their family.

Another factor that may be relevant to the provision of home or outpatient assisted withdrawal is availability of treatment capacity. An early report (Stockwell *et al.*, 1986) revealed that in the Exeter Health Authority, GPs arranged as many home-based assisted withdrawals as hospital-based. However, of the home-based assisted withdrawals, two fifths were unsupervised. Approximately a third of GPs were reluctant to take medical responsibility for home-based assisted withdrawal, but of those who were happy to, they reported a preference for this setting. Winters and McGourty (1994) also surveyed GPs in Chester and Ellesmere Port. Approximately 60% reported that they provided home-based assisted withdrawal from their practices. However, 10% believed specialist help was required. Additionally, they reported that unsuccessful home-based assisted withdrawal was usually due to lack of support at weekends and lack of patient motivation. Over 20% of Northumberland GPs reported carrying out home-based assisted withdrawals in the last year (Kaner & Masterson, 1996). Similar to Winters and McGourty (1994), most GPs stressed the importance of having daily supervision as well as more information about the process of assessing patients for suitability for home-based assisted withdrawal.

5.29.5 Inappropriate admission for residential assisted withdrawal

In services with ready access to inpatient facilities for assisted withdrawal, there is evidence to suggest that given the likelihood of medical complications more patients are admitted than is necessary. Whitfield (1980) reported that only 5% of people who misuse alcohol require hospitalisation for withdrawal management. Booth and colleagues (1996) assessed appropriate and inappropriate utilisation of inpatient services for assisted withdrawal for alcohol in the US. The study, which randomly sampled a number of patients admitted into VA medical centres, found that only 16% of alcoholics undergoing inpatient assisted withdrawal were appropriately admitted, and that the majority of these had medical or neurological complications such as liver cirrhosis, chest pains, kidney failure, gastrointestinal bleeding and seizures, and therefore met admission criteria. However, 84% were admitted for the purpose of monitoring alone and did not meet Appropriateness Evaluation Protocol criteria for inpatient admission. Furthermore, the majority of inappropriately admitted patients did not develop any serious complications that could have justified inpatient care. These patients had lengthy admission length of 11 days on average, which has serious cost implications. An earlier study (Booth *et al.*, 1991) also reported similar findings, albeit with a higher percentage (55%) of appropriate admissions.

The implementation of a standardised policy that guides the decision about inpatient admission or outpatient assisted withdrawal in a small community hospital resulted in a significant reduction in the number of admissions (Asplund *et al.*, 2004). Furthermore, no patients needed hospitalisation for withdrawal complications, which indicates that outpatient assisted withdrawal is safe for the majority of patients without prior complications as identified by a thorough assessment. Outpatient assisted withdrawal may be more appropriate for a population with less severe problems. In a sample of male military veterans enrolled in outpatient withdrawal, Webb and Unwin (1988) reported that 54% successfully completed outpatient assisted withdrawal, 22% were admitted for inpatient care and 24% dropped out of the treatment. The group referred for inpatient care had a significantly higher level of dependence (measured by SADQ score) than those who successfully completed outpatient assisted withdrawal. This would suggest that inpatient assisted withdrawal may be more appropriate for patients with more severe alcohol dependence.

5.29.6 Special populations

Medical or psychiatric comorbidities
For the majority of people who misuse alcohol, outpatient or home-based assisted withdrawal appears to be safe, viable and effective (see above). However, for a minority of patients, a non-residential setting for assisted withdrawal may be inappropriate or unsafe. An inpatient setting may be more appropriate for the management of moderate to severe withdrawal symptoms such as DTs and seizures, comorbid medical, surgical and psychiatric problems (for example, suicidal ideation), pregnancy, or if the patient is not able to take medication by mouth (Bischof *et al.*, 2003; Blondell *et al.*, 2002; Blondell, 2005; Dukan *et al.*, 2002; Ferguson *et al.*, 1996; Kraemer *et al.*, 1997; Saitz & O'Malley, 1997). There is evidence to suggest that a

history of multiple prior episodes of assisted withdrawal may lead to an increased risk of seizures and withdrawal problems (Booth & Blow, 1993; Brown *et al.*, 1988; Lechtenberg & Worner, 1990), and so a number of previous unsuccessful attempts at outpatient assisted withdrawal may also suggest the need for referral to an inpatient setting. Dependence on drugs can increase the risks associated with withdrawal and also the duration and severity of withdrawal symptoms, therefore patients with comorbid drug misuse disorders may require treatment in an inpatient setting. In addition, Pettinati and colleagues (1993) found that those with high psychiatric comorbidity and/or poor social support benefited more from inpatient than outpatient treatment.

Children and young people
No evidence evaluating the safety and efficacy of different settings for withdrawal management in children and young people was identified. The GDG therefore drew from the adult literature with special consideration to the additional problems often associated with alcohol misuse in children and young people (for example, problems with school, family, crime and mental health). A significant concern of the GDG for children and young people was with the identification of potential dependence and subsequent withdrawal. In formulating recommendations about the appropriate setting for assisted withdrawal, the GDG considered that the safety issues concerning assisted withdrawal might differ for children (aged 10 to 15 years) and young people (aged 16 to 18 years).

Older people
The GDG did not identify any clinical evidence evaluating the efficacy and safety of different settings for assisted withdrawal specifically for older people. However, research suggests that older patients (aged 60 years and above) are more at risk of cognitive and functional impairment during withdrawal and hence should be considered for inpatient care (Kraemer *et al.*, 1997).

Homeless patients
Homeless patients requiring assisted withdrawal may also require inpatient care unless other shelter and accommodation can be arranged. For example, in a large study assessing the effectiveness of an ambulatory assisted withdrawal programme in the VA system in the US (Wiseman *et al.*, 1997), half of the patients were homeless. The study reported that 88% of patients successfully completed assisted withdrawal and 96% of these successful completers were referred for further treatment on either an inpatient or an outpatient basis. However, the programme provided supported housing for the homeless during the period of assisted withdrawal. Although low socioeconomic status and homelessness may make outpatient assisted withdrawal more challenging, they are not necessarily contraindications for treatment failure and hence should be assessed on a more detailed individual basis. O'Connor and colleagues (1991) reported that socially disadvantaged people were not at an increased risk of unsuccessful assisted withdrawal in an outpatient setting.

5.29.7   Health economics evidence

Systematic literature review

The literature search identified only one economic study that assessed the cost effectiveness and cost utility of different settings for assisted withdrawal (Parrott *et al.*, 2006). The study evaluated two UK-based withdrawal programmes for people dependent on alcohol. The first intervention was a 10-day assisted withdrawal in a 22-bed facility in Manchester staffed by mental health nurses with support from a local GP. The first part of the intervention involved managing withdrawal safely whilst the second part involved social care interventions. The second intervention was a brief hospitalisation programme based at a Newcastle NHS inpatient unit. This involved 3-day inpatient assisted withdrawal, if required, followed by attendance at a day programme. Patients in this programme were also given counselling based on cognitive-behavioural principles, including motivational intervention prior to structured interventions aimed at abstinence or moderate drinking. Both programmes were compared with no intervention rather than with each other because baseline data was compared with clinical and economic outcome data collected at 6 months after implementation. The economic analysis adopted a societal perspective. It included costs to the NHS, other alcohol treatment services, social services and the criminal justice system. The outcome measures used were QALYs for the cost-utility analysis and reduction in units of alcohol per day and reduction in percentage of drinking days in the cost-effectiveness analysis. QALYs were estimated using EQ-5D scores obtained from participants in the study.

In the cost-effectiveness analysis, the cost per unit reduction in alcohol consumption was £1.87 in the Manchester sample and £1.66 in the Newcastle sample. The cost per reduction of one drink per day was £92.75 in the Manchester sample and £22.56 in the Newcastle sample. The cost per percentage point reduction in drinking was £30.71 in the Manchester sample and £45.06 in the Newcastle sample. In the cost-utility analysis, the ICER per QALY gained, compared with no intervention, was £65,454 (£33,727 when considering treatment costs only) in the Manchester sample and £131,750 (£90,375 treatment costs only) in the Newcastle sample. Overall, the authors concluded that both alcohol withdrawal programmes improved clinical outcomes at a reasonable cost to society. However QALY differences were not significant over 6 months, with both ICERs well above current NICE thresholds for cost-effectiveness.

The validity of the study results is limited by the absence of a non-treatment group for both alcohol withdrawal programmes as changes in clinical outcomes may have occurred without the interventions. Also, the within-group before-and-after study design meant that time-dependent confounding variables could not be controlled for. Data for each programme were collected from single centres, which may limit generalisability of the study findings to other UK centres. The small patient sample-size in both centres and substantial loss to follow-up also limits the robustness of the analysis. It should be noted that patients in the two centres were different in terms of severity of dependence, the number and severity of alcohol-related problems, and socioeconomic status, and therefore direct comparison of costs and outcomes associated with each intervention is not appropriate. No sensitivity analyses were performed to test the robustness of the base case results.

Summary of existing economic evidence

The findings of Parrott and colleagues (2006) suggest that both programmes may be cost effective in terms of reduction in alcohol consumption rather than QALYs gained. The settings, costs reported and measure of benefit adopted in the study make this study directly applicable. However, the effectiveness evidence is not without limitations: the comparator of 'no treatment' may not be relevant and the robustness of the results was not fully explored in sensitivity analyses.

Cost analysis of assisted withdrawal in different settings

The cost effectiveness of assisted withdrawal across different settings was considered by the GDG as an area with potentially significant resource implications. As previously discussed, clinical evidence was derived from studies with different designs and therefore it was not possible to synthesise the clinical data in order to conduct a formal economic evaluation. Nevertheless, existing clinical evidence does not suggest that the effectiveness of home-based or outpatient assisted withdrawal attempted in outpatient/home settings differs significantly from that of assisted withdrawal provided in inpatient/residential settings. Therefore, a simple cost analysis was undertaken to estimate costs associated with assisted withdrawal that are specific to the setting in which assisted withdrawal is provided.

Three different assisted withdrawal settings were considered in the cost analysis: inpatient/residential, outpatient and home-based. The healthcare resource-use estimates for each setting were based on descriptions of resource use in studies included in the systematic literature review of clinical evidence. Information was mainly sought in studies conducted in the UK, as clinical practice and respective resource use described in these studies is directly relevant to the guideline context. After reviewing the relevant literature it was decided to utilise resource-use estimates reported in Alwyn and colleagues (2004), which were then adapted according to the expert opinion of the GDG to reflect current routine clinical practice within the NHS. The estimated resource use was subsequently combined with national unit costs to provide a total cost associated with provision of assisted withdrawal in the three settings assessed. Unit costs were derived from national sources (Curtis, 2009; Department of Health, 2010) and reflected 2009 prices. It should be noted that the cost estimates reported below do not include the cost of drugs administered to people undergoing assisted withdrawal. However, such a cost is expected to be similar across all assisted withdrawal settings and therefore its omission is unlikely to significantly affect the relative costs between different options assessed.

Inpatient/residential assisted withdrawal

According to Alwyn and colleagues (2004), inpatient/residential assisted withdrawal lasts for 2 weeks and requires an extra outpatient visit. The GDG estimated that inpatient assisted withdrawal may last longer, between 2 and 3 weeks. The unit cost of NHS adult acute mental health inpatient care is £290 per patient day (Department of Health, 2010). The unit cost of hospital outpatient consultant drug and alcohol services is £85 per face-to-face contact for a follow-up visit (Department of Health, 2010). By combining the above resource-use estimates with the respective unit costs, the total cost of inpatient/residential assisted withdrawal is estimated to range between £4,145 and £6,175 per person treated.

Outpatient assisted withdrawal
Outpatient assisted withdrawal is estimated to require six outpatient attendances (Alwyn *et al.*, 2004). The unit cost of a face-to-face contact with hospital outpatient consultant drug and alcohol services is £181 for the first visit and £85 for each follow-up visit (Department of Health, 2010). By combining these data, the total cost of outpatient assisted withdrawal is estimated at £606 per person treated.

Home-based assisted withdrawal
Alwyn and colleagues (2004) estimated that home-based assisted withdrawal requires six CPN home visits lasting 30 minutes each. The GDG were of the opinion that the first of these visits should be replaced by an outpatient visit to alcohol consultant services, so that appropriate assessment is carried out before starting assisted withdrawal. Moreover, the GDG advised that the travel time of the healthcare professional providing home-based assisted withdrawal should be taken into account. Considering that home visits often take place in remote areas, the GDG estimated that the travelling time of the healthcare professional staff was likely to range between 1 and 2 hours per home visit. The unit cost of a face-to-face contact with outpatient consultant drug and alcohol services is £181 for the first visit (Department of Health, 2010). The unit cost of a CPN is not available for 2009. The total cost of home-based assisted withdrawal was therefore based on the unit cost of community nurse specialists (Band 6), as this type of healthcare professional is expected to provide home-based assisted withdrawal. The unit cost for community nurse specialists is £35 per working hour and £88 per hour of patient contact (Curtis, 2009). This unit cost includes salary (based on the median full-time equivalent basic salary for Agenda for Change (AfC) Band 6 of the January to March 2009 NHS Staff Earnings estimates for qualified nurses), salary oncosts, capital and revenue overheads, as well as qualification costs. The unit cost per working hour was combined with the estimated travelling time, while the unit cost per hour of patient contact was combined with the estimated total duration of home visiting. A £4 travel cost was assumed for each visit. By combining all the above data, the total cost of home-based assisted withdrawal was estimated to range between £596 and £771.

Summary
The cost analysis indicates that, provided that the different assisted withdrawal settings have similar effectiveness, then outpatient and home-based assisted withdrawal are probably less costly (and thus potentially more cost effective) than

inpatient assisted withdrawal, resulting in an estimated cost saving of approximately £3,400 to £5,600 per person treated.

5.29.8 Clinical and health economic evidence summary

The evidence indicates that a community setting for assisted withdrawal is as effective and safe for the majority of patients as an inpatient or residential assisted withdrawal as long as the patient is without serious medical contraindications. It is also likely to be more cost effective as cost savings of between £3,400 to £5,600 per person may be generated The evidence reviewed is limited because there is only one RCT, but it should be noted that it is extremely difficult to undertake an RCT in this area given the clinicians concerns about the relative safety for more severely dependent patients. The GDG (drawing on the evidence in the reviews conducted for this guideline) therefore decided that it was important to consider the following factors when determining whether a community or residential/inpatient assisted withdrawal is the most appropriate:

- a history of epilepsy or withdrawal-related seizures or DTs during previous assisted withdrawal
- a significant psychiatric or physical comorbidity (for example, chronic severe depression, psychosis, malnutrition, congestive cardiac failure, unstable angina or chronic liver disease)
- a significant learning disability
- significant cognitive impairment
- homelessness
- pregnancy
- children and young people
- older people

5.30 EVALUATING DOSING REGIMES FOR ASSISTED WITHDRAWAL

5.30.1 Introduction

This section assesses the safety, efficacy, cost effectiveness and patient satisfaction associated with different medication regimens used in assisted withdrawal from alcohol. When undertaking assisted withdrawal, the patient is required to stop alcohol intake abruptly, and the ensuing withdrawal symptoms are treated with medication, usually benzodiazepines. Once the withdrawal symptoms are controlled, the medication can be gradually reduced and stopped at a rate that prevents withdrawal symptoms re-emerging but without creating over-sedation. Key elements of the process are to provide a large enough initial dose to prevent severe withdrawal symptoms including seizures, DTs, severe anxiety or autonomic instability, but to withdraw the medication at a rate which prevents re-emergence of symptoms or serious complications such as DTs or seizures. Special populations with indications for specific dosing regimens are discussed in Section 5.30.7.

5.30.2 Definitions of dosing regimen methods

Fixed-dose regimen

A fixed-dose (FD) regimen involves starting treatment with a standard dose determined by the recent severity of alcohol dependence and/or typical level of daily alcohol consumption, followed by reducing the dose to zero usually over 7 to 10 days according to a standard protocol.

Table 21 gives an example of a titrated FD regimen (Ghodse *et al.*, 1998; South West London and St George's Mental Health NHS Trust, 2010). Note that due to the gradual rate of reduction, with higher starting doses, the duration of treatment is longer than with lower starting doses. A common error in management of alcohol withdrawal is too rapid reduction of chlordiazepoxide, which can result in emergence or re-emergence of severe alcohol withdrawal symptoms. Another common error is too low a starting dose of chlordiazepoxide. This can be avoided by taking account of typical daily alcohol consumption and/or SADQ score in determining the starting dose. In addition, the response to FD withdrawal regimes should be monitored using a validated tool such as the CIWA-Ar (Sullivan *et al.*, 1989) and the dose of medication adjusted upwards or downwards accordingly in the early stages of withdrawal. In severe alcohol dependence the doses of chlordiazepoxide required may exceed the British National Formulary (BNF) prescribing range. It is more clinically effective to increase the dose of chlordiazepoxide to adequately control alcohol withdrawal symptoms than to add another type of medication (for example, haloperidol).

The first dose of medication should be given before withdrawal symptoms begin to emerge. Delay in initiating chlordiazepoxide treatment can result in withdrawal symptoms either becoming difficult to control or the emergence of complications such as DTs or seizures. Therefore, in people with severe alcohol dependence, the first dose should be given before the breath alcohol concentration falls to zero, as withdrawal will emerge during the falling phase of breath alcohol concentration. The more severe the alcohol dependence, the earlier withdrawal symptoms emerge after last alcohol intake. Some people who are severely alcohol dependent can experience withdrawal with a blood alcohol concentration of 100 mg per 100 ml or more.

Symptom-triggered regimen

A symptom-triggered (ST) approach involves tailoring the drug regimen according to the severity of withdrawal and complications the patient is displaying. The patient is monitored on a regular basis and pharmacotherapy is administered according to the patient's level of withdrawal symptoms. Pharmacotherapy only continues as long as the patient is displaying withdrawal symptoms and the administered dose is

Table 21: Titrated fixed-dose chlordiazepoxide protocol for treatment of alcohol withdrawal (Ghodse *et al.*, 1998; South West London and St George's Mental Health NHS Trust, 2010)

Typical recent daily consumption	15 to 25 units		30 to 49 units		50 to 60 units
Severity of alcohol dependence	MODERATE SADQ score 15 to 25		SEVERE SADQ score 30 to 40		VERY SEVERE SADQ score 40 to 60
Starting doses of chlordiazepoxide	15 to 25 mg q.d.s.[1]		30 to 40 mg q.d.s.		50 mg q.d.s.
Day 1 (starting dose)	15 q.d.s.	25 q.d.s.	30 q.d.s.	40 q.d.s.*	50 q.d.s.*
Day 2	10 q.d.s.	20 q.d.s.	25 q.d.s.	35 q.d.s.	45 q.d.s.
Day 3	10 t.d.s.[2]	15 q.d.s.	20 q.d.s.	30 q.d.s.	40 q.d.s.
Day 4	5 t.d.s.	10 q.d.s.	15 q.d.s.	25 q.d.s.	35 q.d.s.
Day 5	5 b.d.[3]	10 t.d.s.	10 q.d.s.	20 q.d.s.	30 q.d.s.
Day 6	5 nocte[4]	5 t.d.s.	10 t.d.s.	15 q.d.s.	25 q.d.s.
Day 7		5 b.d.	5 t.d.s.	10 q.d.s.	20 q.d.s.
Day 8		5 nocte	5 b.d.	10 t.d.s.	10 q.d.s.
Day 9			5 nocte	5 t.d.s.	10 q.d.s.
Day 10				5 b.d.	10 t.d.s.
Day 11				5 nocte	5 t.d.s.
Day 12					5 b.d.
Day 13					5 nocte

Note. * Doses of chlordiazepoxide in excess of 30 mg q.d.s. should only be prescribed in cases where severe withdrawal symptoms are expected and the patient's response to the treatment should always be regularly and closely monitored. Doses in excess of 40 mg q.d.s. should only be prescribed where there is clear evidence of very severe alcohol dependence. Such doses are rarely necessary in women and never in the elderly or where there is severe liver impairment.
[1] *Quater die sumendus* (four times a day); [2] *ter die sumendum* (three times a day); [3] *bis die* (twice daily); [4] At night.

dependent on the assessed level of alcohol withdrawal. Withdrawal symptoms are usually assessed by clinical assessment including observation and interview, and/or with the use of a validated withdrawal measurement tool such as the CIWA-Ar. See Table 22 for an example of an ST dosing regimen (NICE, 2010b).

Table 22: Examples of symptom-triggered and front-loaded dosing regimens for treating alcohol withdrawal with chlordiazepoxide

Dosing regimen	Day 1	Day 2	Day 3	Day 4
Symptom triggered	20 to 30 mg as needed up to hourly, based on symptoms[1]			
Front loaded[2]	100 mg every 2 to 4 hours until sedation is achieved; then 50 to 100 mg every 4 to 6 hours as needed	50 to 100 mg every 4 to 6 hours as needed	50 to 100 mg every 4 to 6 hours as needed	None

Note. [1] These symptoms include pulse rate greater than 90 beats per minute, diastolic blood pressure greater than 90 mm Hg or signs of withdrawal.
[2] Frequently, very little additional medication is necessary after initial loading.

Front-loading regimen
A front-loading regimen involves providing the patient with an initially high dose of medication and then using either an FD or ST dosing regimen for subsequent assisted withdrawal. See Table 22 for an example of a front-loading dosing regimen (NICE, 2010b).

5.30.3   Aim of review and review protocol

As stated above, this section is concerned with the safety, efficacy, cost effectiveness and patient satisfaction of different dosing regimens for assisted withdrawal and their appropriateness in various treatment settings. Furthermore, this section aims to evaluate medication for assisted withdrawal that is not appropriate or safe in a setting without 24-hour monitoring. The GDG identified that there would be insufficient RCT literature available to answer the review question, therefore it was decided by consensus to include all available studies in a systematic narrative review of the evidence. The review team assessed the literature identified from the search conducted by the NICE guideline on management of alcohol-related physical complications (NICE, 2010b); full details of the search strategies can be found in that guideline. Studies were considered for inclusion in the narrative synthesis if they met the inclusion criteria (see Chapter 3) and if the population being assessed in the study reflected the scope of this guideline (see Appendix 1). Furthermore, studies were considered for inclusion in the narrative synthesis using the clinical review protocol described in Table 23. The outcomes of interest were the efficacy (management of alcohol withdrawal syndrome, duration of treatment and amount of medication

Table 23: Clinical review protocol for the evaluation of different dosing regimens for assisted withdrawal from alcohol

Electronic databases	CINAHL, EMBASE, MEDLINE, PsycINFO, Cochrane Library; see the NICE guideline (NICE, 2010b) on management of alcohol-related physical complications for search strategies
Date searched	Systematic reviews from 1993 to March 2010. All other searches from database inception to March 2010
Study design	Systematic reviews; RCTs
Patient population	Adults (over 18 years old); patients with alcohol withdrawal syndrome
Outcomes	Main outcomes: severity of withdrawal; duration of treatment; total amount of medication; incidence of seizures and DTs or other complications Other outcomes: patient and physician satisfaction; completion rates

required), safety (development of complications), as well as patient and physician satisfaction of the dosing regimens.

In addition, the review team conducted a search for studies that evaluated patient indications for inpatient assisted withdrawal. The review team also reviewed the safety of using different types of medication for assisted withdrawal in a setting that does not have 24-hour clinical monitoring, which is the more typical situation in clinical practice. Due to the nature of the review question, the GDG identified that there would be a lack of RCT literature (confirmed by the original RCT search for this guideline) and hence a search was conducted for systematic reviews. The review team assessed the available literature identified from the search conducted by the NICE guideline on management of alcohol-related physical complications (NICE, 2010b).

5.30.4 Studies considered

Twelve studies evaluating the efficacy and safety of different regimens for assisted withdrawal were identified. Nine of these studies compared an ST regimen of administering alcohol withdrawal medication (with or without front-loading) with an FD regimen (Daeppen *et al.*, 2002; Day *et al.*, 2004; Hardern & Page, 2005; Lange-Asschenfeldt *et al.*, 2003; Manikant *et al.*, 1993; Saitz *et al.*, 1994; Sullivan *et al.*, 1991; Wasilewski *et al.*, 1996; Weaver *et al.*, 2006), and three studies compared usual non-protocol routine based hospital care to an ST regimen (DeCaroulis *et al.*, 2007; Jaeger *et al.*, 2001; Reoux & Miller, 2000). The characteristics and settings of the included studies can be found in Table 24.

Table 24: Characteristics of studies evaluating dosing regimen methods

Study	Study design	Setting	Comparison	Method of assessing alcohol withdrawal syndrome
Daeppen and colleagues (2002)	Placebo RCT	Inpatient alcohol treatment unit	1. ST (n = 56) 2. FD (n = 61)	CIWA-Ar administered 30 minutes after placebo dose
Day and colleagues (2004)	RCT	Inpatient alcohol treatment unit	1. ST front loading (n = 11) 2. FD (n = 12)	CIWA-Ar administered every 90 minutes
DeCarolis and colleagues (2007)	Retrospective audit	Inpatient intensive care unit (VA medical centre)	1. ST (n = 21) 2. Routine hospital FD (n = 16)	Minnesota Detoxification Scale (MIND)
Hardern and Page (2005)	Retrospective audit	General hospital inpatient ward	1. ST (n −23) 2. Regular dosing (n = 28)	CIWA-Ar (when administered not reported)
Jaeger and colleagues (2001)	Retrospective chart analyses	General hospital inpatient ward	1. ST (n = 84) 2. Usual care: FD or as needed at discretion of medical staff (n = 132)	CIWA-Ar administered every 1 to 2 hours
Lange-Asschenfeldt and colleagues (2003)	Retrospective chart analysis	General hospital inpatient ward	1. ST (n = 33) 2. FD (n = 32)	Modified German CIWA-Ar administered at: initial assessment; first day of admission and days 1 to 3 (every 2 hours); days 4 and 5 (every 4 hours); day 6 (4 times daily); day 7 (three times daily); days 8 and 9 (twice daily)

Study	Design	Setting	Groups (n)	CIWA-Ar administration
Manikant and colleagues (1993)	RCT	Psychiatric inpatient ward	1. ST front loading (n = 20) 2. FD (n = 21)	CIWA-Ar administered every 90 minutes
Reoux and Miller (2000)	Retrospective chart analysis	ST = inpatient specialist alcohol unit (VA medical centre) Routine care = general medical ward or inpatient psychiatry unit	1. ST (n = 26) 2. Routine hospital alcohol withdrawal practice (varied and non-protocol-based) (n = 14)	CIWA-Ar administered 1 hour after being medicated
Saitz and colleagues (1994)	Placebo RCT	Inpatient specialist alcohol unit (VA medical centre)	1. ST (n = 51) 2. FD (n = 50)	CIWA-Ar administered hourly
Sullivan and colleagues (1991)	Retrospective case series	General hospital inpatient ward	1. ST front loading (n = 133) 2. FD front loading (n = 117)	CIWA-Ar administered hourly and then as needed (clinical judgement)
Wasilewski and colleagues (1996)	Prospective cohort	Psychiatric inpatient ward	1. ST front loading (n = 51) 2 FD (n = 45)	CIWA-Ar administered every 1 to 2 hours
Weaver and colleagues (2006)	Quasi-randomised	General hospital inpatient ward	1. ST (n = 91) 2. FD (n = 92)	CIWA-Ar at initial assessment and then every 4 hours

Continued

Table 24: *(Continued)*

Study	Outcomes	Results
Daeppen and colleagues (2002)	Total amount of medication required	ST (95.4 [107.7] mg) significantly less than FD (231.4 [29.4] mg) (Mann-Whitney $U = 5.84$; $p <0.001$)
	Number using medication	ST (39.3%) significantly fewer patients than FD (100%) ($\chi^2 = 52.2$; $p <0.001$)
	Duration of treatment	Subgroup analyses (n = 19) with history of complications: ST (22.7 [26.68] hours) significantly shorter than FD (62.1 [6.18] hours) (Mann-Whitney $U = 2.87$, $p = 0.004$)
	Patient well-being	No significant difference between groups in health concerns, anxiety, energy or depression
	Incidence of complications	No significant difference in number of seizures, hallucinations or DTs
Day and colleagues (2004)	Total amount of medication required	ST (222 mg) significantly less than FD (700 mg) ($p <0.001$)
	Duration of treatment	ST (8 hours) significantly shorter than FD (242 hours) ($p <0.001$)
	Severity of alcohol withdrawal	No significant difference between groups
	Incidence of complications	No significant difference between groups
	Patient satisfaction	No significant difference in self-perceived adverse symptoms or patient satisfaction with regimens
DeCarolis and colleagues (2007)	Time to reach symptom control	ST (7.7 [4.9] hours) significantly shorter time than routine FD (19.4 [9.7] hours) ($p = 0.002$)
	Total amount of medication required	ST (1044 [534] mg) significantly less than routine FS (1677 [937] mg) ($p = 0.014$)
	Duration of treatment	No significant difference between groups
Hardern and Page (2005)	Total amount of medication required	No significant difference between groups
	Duration of treatment	No significant difference between groups
	Time from first to last administration	ST (48 hours) significantly shorter than regular dosing (110 hours) ($p = 0.086$)
Jaeger and colleagues (2001)	Duration of treatment	No significant difference between groups
	Total amount of medication required	No significant difference between groups
	Incidence of complications	No significant difference in incidence of complications overall; ST had significantly less incidence of DTs ($p = 0.04$) (ST = 20.5%; usual care = 6.9%)
Lange-Asschenfeldt and colleagues (2003)	Total amount of medication required	ST (median 4352 [4589] mg) significantly less than FD (median 9921 [6599]) ($p = 0.0004$)
	Duration of treatment	ST (median 4.2 [2.9] hours) significantly less than FD (median 7.5 [3.3]) ($p = 0.0003$)
	Incidence of complications	No significant difference between groups
	Use of co-medication	No significant difference between groups

Study	Outcome measure	Result
Manikant and colleagues (1993)	Total amount of medication required	No statistical data provided: ST = 67 mg; FD = 200 mg
	Severity of alcohol withdrawal	No significant difference between groups
Reoux and Miller (2000)	Total amount of medication required	ST (82.7 [153.6] mg) significantly less than routine practice (367.5 [98.2] mg) (p = 0.004)
	Number of doses required	ST (1.7 [3.1]) significantly less than routine practice (10.4 [7.9]) (p = 0.001)
	Duration of medication use	ST (10.7 [20.7] hours) significantly less than routine practice (64.3 [60.4]) (p = 0.006)
	Adverse effects	None present in both groups
Saitz and colleagues (1994)	Duration of treatment	ST (median = 9 hours) significantly shorter than FD (median 68 hours) (Wilcoxon z = 5.68; p <0.001)
	Total amount of medication required	ST (100 mg) significantly less than FD (425 mg) (Wilcoxon z = 5.30, p <0.001)
	Severity of alcohol withdrawal	No significant difference between groups (p = 0.73)
	Incidence of complications	No significant difference between groups in incidence of DTs (p = 0.36); hallucinations (p = 0.62); seizures (none); lethargy (p = 0.42); leaving the hospital against medical advice (p = 0.68); readmission within 30 days (p = 0.72)
	Participation in further rehabilitation treatment after assisted withdrawal	ST (69%) greater than FD (50%) (non-significant) (p = 0.06)
Sullivan and colleagues (1991)	Total amount of medication required	ST (50 mg) significantly less than FD (75 mg) (p = 0.04)
	Duration of treatment	No significant difference between groups
	Number of patients requiring <20 mg of medication	ST (33%) significantly more than FD (12.8%) (p = 0.05)
	Rate of discharge against medical advice	No significant difference between groups
	Rates of complication	No significant difference between groups
Wasilewski and colleagues (1996)	Total amount of medication required	SD (87 [47.2] mg) significantly less than FD (1784 [1800] mg) (p <0.00001)
	Duration of delirium	ST (6.9 [4.8]) significantly less than FD (33.8 [25.7] hours) (Mann-Whitney U = 265.0, p <0.001)
	Abnormalities and somatic disorders	No significant difference between groups
Weaver and colleagues (2006)	Total amount of medication required	ST (29 mg) significantly less than FD (100 mg) (p <0.0001)
	Severity of alcohol withdrawal	No significant difference between groups in first 2 days
	Protocol errors	ST (17.6%) significantly more than FD (7.6%) ($\chi 2$ = 4.14; p = 0.042)

5.30.5   Narrative summary of findings

Medication use and duration of treatment
The results of most studies favoured the use of ST over FD regimens for outcomes assessing medication use and duration of treatment. The ST approach resulted in lower medication needed (Daeppen *et al.*, 2002; Day *et al.*, 2004; DeCaroulis *et al.*, 2007; Lange-Asschenfeldt *et al.*, 2003; Reoux & Miller, 2000; Saitz *et al.*, 1994; Sullivan *et al.*, 1991; Wasilewski *et al.*, 1996; Weaver *et al.*, 2006), lower frequency of administration (Daeppen *et al.*, 2002; Reoux & Miller, 2000) and a shorter duration of treatment (Daeppen *et al.*, 2002; Day *et al.*, 2004; Lange-Asschenfeldt *et al.*, 2003; Reoux & Miller, 2000; Saitz *et al.*, 1994). However, not all studies assessing these outcomes reported results favouring an ST approach. Sullivan and colleagues (1991) and Jaeger and colleagues (2001) found no difference between ST front-loading and FD front-loading regimens in terms of length of stay, and Jaeger and colleagues (2001) reported no significant difference between groups in total dose of medication required. Hardern and Page (2005) found no difference in dose administered and length of stay between ST and regular FD regimens.

Severity of withdrawal symptoms
DeCaroulis and colleagues (2007) reported significantly less time to reach symptom control in the ST protocol group when compared with an FD regimen. Saitz and colleagues (1994) found no difference between an ST and FD regimen in time taken from admission to achieving a CIWA-Ar score of less than 8. Manikant and colleagues (1993) and Day and colleagues (2004) also found no significant difference in severity of withdrawal (using the CIWA-Ar) between an ST front loading and an FD regimen.

Rates of complications or adverse effects
Jaeger and colleagues (2001) reported significantly fewer episodes of DTs in the ST regimen group when compared with routine care but found no difference in overall complication rates. Other studies, however, reported no difference between ST and other FD regimens/routine care in rates of complications and adverse effects (for example, incidence of seizures, DTs and hallucinations) (Lange-Asschenfeldt *et al.*, 2003; Reoux & Miller, 2000; Saitz *et al.*, 1994; Sullivan *et al.*, 1991). In Wasilewski and colleagues' (1996) study, although patients in the ST front loading group had a significantly shorter duration of delirium than the FD group, no significant difference was observed in somatic disorders and abnormalities. Additionally, Day and colleagues (2004) did not find a significant difference between ST front loading and FD regimens in self-reported adverse symptoms.

Other outcomes
Other outcomes, including patient satisfaction, discharge against medication advice, use of co-medication and protocol errors, were reported in the reviewed studies.

Daeppen and colleagues (2002)[22] and Sullivan and colleagues (1991) reported that there were no significant differences in patient comfort level between groups, and Day and colleagues (2004) reported no significant difference between ST front loading and FD regimens in terms of patient satisfaction. Two studies (Saitz *et al.*, 1994; Sullivan *et al.*, 1991) reported no difference between ST and FD regimens in terms of rates of discharge against medical advice, and Lange-Asschenfeldt and colleagues (2003) found no difference in use of co-medication. Weaver and colleagues (2006) reported significantly more protocol errors in the ST group as opposed to the FD regimen group.

Symptom-triggered assisted withdrawal in a general medical setting
The studies reviewed above are not likely to be reflective of patients with complex problems who typically are admitted to a general hospital ward for medical treatment and present with withdrawal symptoms (that is, they are undergoing unplanned withdrawal) (Hecksel *et al.*, 2008). For example, although the Jaeger and colleagues' (2001) study found fewer episodes of DTs in the ST regimen group, patients were excluded from the study if they presented with medical comorbidities. In a general admissions unit, this in effect would exclude any post-surgical patients (Hecksel *et al.*, 2008). Additionally, Reoux and Miller (2000) excluded any patients with complex medical histories, and Sullivan and colleagues (1991) did not take into account medical comorbidity. Therefore, Hecksel and colleagues (2008) suggested that in these studies, which have assessed an ST approach in a non-specialist general medical setting, patients that are most likely to develop complications such as DTs have not been investigated using the CIWA-Ar tool and therefore some uncertainty about its value with this population remains (Ferguson *et al.*, 1996).

The majority of the ST studies were conducted in addiction specialist inpatient settings or psychiatric hospitals, which have highly trained specialist staff familiar with the ST dosing regimen and methods (Daeppen *et al.*, 2002; Day *et al.*, 2004; Lange-Asschenfeldt *et al.*, 2003; Manikant *et al.*, 1993; Reoux & Miller, 2000; Saitz *et al.*, 1994; Wasilewski *et al.*, 1996). When dosing regimens were compared in non-alcohol specialist settings (that is, in general hospital medical wards), extensive training was delivered to staff (Jaeger *et al.*, 2001; Sullivan *et al.*, 1991; Weaver *et al.*, 2006). For example, in the study by Sullivan and colleagues, training was delivered over a 6-month period with the assistance of clinical nurse specialist in alcohol and substance misuse. In the Hardern and Page (2005) study, a retrospective audit compared the use of an ST regime (which had been introduced in the medical admissions unit) with regular fixed dosing. However, nurses who were trained to use the scoring tool were frequently unavailable when the patient was admitted. This is reflective of the competing demands on staff in a non-addiction treatment setting. This variability can also be observed in different non-specialist departments such as emergency departments (Kahan *et al.*, 2005).

---

[22]In Daeppen and colleagues' (2002) study, 60.3% of patients did not require pharmacological assisted withdrawal.

Nurses, whether in a specialist unit, psychiatric ward, general medical ward or in the community, play a vital role in successful assisted withdrawal. Stockwell and colleagues (1990) found both patients and family members rated the support from community nurses as more important than medication for assisted withdrawal. Nursing staff in specialist addiction treatment centres are highly skilled and trained in all aspects of the medical management of alcohol withdrawal (Cooper, 1994), and have a working knowledge of current working practices and liaise with other staff and services (Choudry, 1990). This may well have an impact on the efficacy of the ST programmes in the studies above.

Most physicians and nurses working in general medical wards are not specialists in the management of alcohol dependence. This is a concern because the first point of contact for many alcohol-dependent people is not a specialist addiction unit, but more usually a general physician in a non-specialist treatment setting such as a general medical ward (O'Connor & Schottenfeld, 1998). Nurses in general medical practice may also lack specialised knowledge and education about addiction and assisted withdrawal (Coffey, 1996; Happell & Taylor, 1999; Ryan & Ottlinger, 1999). Even if training were provided, the obstacles to ensuring comprehensive training in a general medical setting also needs consideration (Moriarty *et al.*, 2010; Schumacher *et al.*, 2000).

Bostwick and Lapid (2004) reported on the use of an ST approach by psychiatrists at the Mayo Clinic in Rochester, Minnesota. A CIWA-Ar controlled protocol was not effective in managing alcohol withdrawal and patients deteriorated with use of an ST approach. In these specific cases reported by Bostwick and Lapid (2004), patients were assumed to be presenting with pure alcohol withdrawal syndrome. However, because no thorough clinical interview was utilised and the patients could not communicate effectively, medical staff did not ascertain whether the apparent presenting alcohol withdrawal symptoms were a result of other acute medical conditions such as sepsis, pain and shock. In another study of admissions in Mayo Clinics, Hecksel and colleagues (2008) found that half of patients receiving ST assisted withdrawal did not meet criteria using the CIWA-Ar. The investigators reported that 44% of patients given this protocol had not been drinking and 23% were unable to communicate effectively. Surprisingly, of those who could communicate, 64% were not currently drinking but were still receiving ST medication. Again, and reflective of Bostwick and Lapid's (2004) study, medical histories were overlooked by physicians with a slight hint at alcohol use in the patient's history informing a decision to use this approach. Physicians also regularly assumed that autonomic hyperactivity and psychological distress were a result of alcohol withdrawal and hence a high CIWA-Ar score was attained, resulting in unnecessary benzodiazepine treatment. The investigators concluded that in patients with a history of alcohol dependence who are likely to develop adverse effects (DTs and seizures), a CIWA-Ar-based ST approach is not appropriate and a more patient-centred, personalised approach to medication management that goes beyond the CIWA-Ar is needed. Furthermore, in medical and surgical patients with a history of drinking, the ST approach to medication management has not been proven. Bostwick and Lapid (2004) and Hecksel and colleagues (2008) also conclude that an ST approach is not appropriate for patients with complex medical and surgical comorbidities, and hence may not be suitable for many patients presenting with alcohol withdrawal syndrome in a general medical setting.

Medication not appropriate for use in a setting without 24-hour monitoring
The use of certain medications for assisted withdrawal may not be appropriate in non-residential settings such as an outpatient clinic or the patient's home. Outpatient medication should be administered orally, have low potential for misuse or overdose, and have few side effects (O'Connor *et al.*, 1994).

Contraindications for benzodiazepines and chlormethiazole in non-residential settings identified in the literature are set out below.

Benzodiazepines
Although long-acting benzodiazepines (such as chlordiazepoxide and diazepam) are preferred for patients with alcohol withdrawal syndrome, short-acting benzodiazepines (such as oxazepam) may be preferred in those for whom over-sedation must be avoided, in people with liver disease who may not be able to metabolise long-acting agents efficiently, and in people with chronic obstructive pulmonary disease (COPD) (Blondell, 2005; Mayo-Smith *et al.*, 2004). However, apart from patients with liver failure and those with COPD (who may well be managed as inpatients; see above), short-acting benzodiazepines may not be suitable for outpatient assisted withdrawal due to the risk of breakthrough seizures (Mayo-Smith, 1997). Furthermore, short-acting benzodiazepines (such as oxazepam and halazepam) may have a greater potential for misuse than benzodiazepines (such as diazepam, chlordiazepoxide, alprazolam and lorazepam) (Griffiths & Wolf, 1990; McKinley, 2005; Soyka & Horak, 2004).

Chlormethiazole
Chlormethiazole is used in inpatient care as it has a short half-life (Majumdar, 1990). However, it requires close medical supervision and is therefore not recommended for non-residential settings such as outpatient clinics, patients' homes and prisons. Furthermore, it is addictive (although this is unlikely to develop in the short time period of an assisted withdrawal) and, more importantly, it can have fatal consequences in overdose resulting from coma and respiratory depression, especially when taken with alcohol (Gregg & Akhter, 1979; Horder, 1978; McInnes *et al.*, 1980; McInnes, 1987; Stockwell *et al.*, 1986).

5.30.6   Assisted withdrawal in the prison setting

Research evaluating assisted withdrawal in custodial settings such as police custody and the prison setting is scarce. Individuals taken into police custody are often under the influence of alcohol and some of these individuals may be alcohol dependent (Naik & Lawton, 1996). Deaths in UK police custody have been associated with alcohol intake (Yoshida *et al.*, 1990) and 86% of fatalities in police custody are associated with recent alcohol consumption and alcohol dependence (Giles & Sandrin, 1990). However, there is little guidance on the assessment and management of alcohol withdrawal in police custody or prison settings but also evidence to suggest that any such guidance is not always followed (Ghodse *et al.*, 2006).

People received into prison carry a heightened risk of suicide in the early days of their custody; one third of all prison suicides happen within the first week of imprisonment (Shaw *et al.*, 2003). This phase coincides with alcohol withdrawal for around one in five prisoners, and the above study found an association between alcohol dependence and risk of suicide. Alcohol dependence is commonplace among people entering prison: the most recent national study of prisoners to be conducted found that 6% of all prisoners returned AUDIT scores of 32 and above (Singleton *et al.*, 1998). (It should be noted that screening with AUDIT now forms part of the assessment of alcohol misuse in the prison service). The break in consumption that begins with arrest means that many people with alcohol dependence arrive in prison in active states of withdrawal. This position is further complicated by the high levels of comorbid drug (including opiates, benzodiazepines and cocaine) misuse in the prison population (Ramsay, 2003). Due to the increased risk of suicide, severity of alcohol dependence and high risk of developing withdrawal effects, clinical management of alcohol withdrawal should begin on the day of reception into custody. The preferred agent of assisted withdrawal in the prison service is chlordiazepoxide (Department of Health, 2006c).

Following alcohol withdrawal, there is some evidence that alcohol treatment programmes addressing offending behaviour can reduce rates of re-offending (Hollis, 2007; McCulloch & McMurran, 2008), but these studies both lack a well-matched control group. A comparative study of a modified therapeutic community and a standard mental health intervention for the treatment of male prisoners with both mental health and substance misuse problems found evidence that the therapeutic community group re-offended at a significantly reduced rate (Sacks *et al.*, 2004). Because alcohol is prohibited in prison, the majority of people with alcohol dependence will remain alcohol-free prior to their release.

5.30.7 Assisted alcohol withdrawal dosing regimens for special populations

Children and young people
The use of the same drug regimens as for adults should be used, with doses appropriately adjusted for age and alcohol consumption. The evidence for favouring either ST or FD regimens with children and young people remains uncertain as there are no trials which have investigated this issue. Nevertheless whichever regimen is chosen there is a clear requirement for very close monitoring of withdrawal symptoms. Given the uncertainty identified in this guideline about the capacity of staff to manage symptom triggered withdrawal, where symptoms are easily identifiable it was suggested that a cautious approach to the management of symptoms in young people is a fixed dose regimen but with very close symptom monitoring using a validated rating scale such as the CIWA-Ar.

Older people
As noted earlier, older people can have higher levels of physical comorbidity, cognitive impairment, a lower capacity to metabolise alcohol and medications, and be in

receipt of a larger number of medications than younger people. In addition, older people can be more frail and prone to accidents and falls. Therefore it is prudent to have a lower threshold for admission for inpatient assisted alcohol withdrawal in older people who misuse alcohol. Further, doses of benzodiazepines may need to be reduced in older people compared with guidelines for younger adults.

5.30.8 Clinical evidence summary

There is some evidence to suggest that for assisted withdrawal, an ST regimen reduces medication use and duration of treatment and, therefore, is preferred in settings where 24-hour monitoring is available and the staff are highly trained in the use of this regimen. However, the evidence is not conclusive and some previous research has found no difference between ST and FD regimens in efficacy as well as for other outcomes such as rates of complication and patient experience. Furthermore, the studies that have evaluated this question were conducted in settings where 24-hour monitoring from trained staff is available and in the majority of cases these are specialist addiction units; where this was not the case, the staff involved in these studies were extensively trained (for periods up to 6 months) for the purpose of the study.

Due to the skill required to treat alcohol withdrawal with an ST regimen, there is a higher possibility of protocol errors where staff are not highly trained. This suggests that in a non-specialist inpatient setting the ST approach may not be feasible, because staff in general medical settings may not have the training, expertise and resources to conduct an ST regimen. Therefore, in non-specialist general settings, a tapered FD regimen may be more appropriate for assisted withdrawal.

There are currently no RCTs that assess the efficacy of an ST regimen for assisted withdrawal in an outpatient setting. This may be because the use of an inpatient or specialist ST dosing regimen in a community setting is unpractical as 24-hour is not possible, or ad hoc monitoring is not appropriate. The gradual tapering FD regimen is therefore more appropriate for outpatient assisted withdrawal as it involves providing medication in specified doses for a predetermined number of days. The medication dose is gradually reduced until cessation as in inpatient FD regimes. The evidence also indicates that chlormethiazole is not appropriate for use in outpatient assisted withdrawal because there is a high risk of misuse and overdose.

It is common for people with alcohol dependence who are taken into police custody to develop alcohol withdrawal syndrome. However, previous research suggests that the alcohol withdrawal syndrome is not always detected in this setting. Staff should be aware of the importance of identifying potential or possible alcohol withdrawal and be trained in the use of tools to detect alcohol dependence (for example, the AUDIT). Furthermore, due to the risk of suicide and medical complications that could develop as a consequence of alcohol withdrawal, the management of the alcohol withdrawal syndrome should be instituted immediately upon entry into custody.

There is no direct evidence that suggests added benefit of an ST regimen over an FD regimen for children and young people. However, as the GDG believe that all assisted withdrawal for children and young people should take place in an inpatient setting which should have 24-hour monitoring and care, and a tapered FD approach should be used.

There should be a lower threshold for admission for inpatient assisted withdrawal in older people. Further, doses of benzodiazepine medication for assisted withdrawal may need to be reduced compared with guidelines for younger adults.

5.31 FROM EVIDENCE TO RECOMMENDATIONS: ASSISTED WITHDRAWAL

This section draws on the preceding reviews of assisted withdrawal settings and drug regimens; the summaries of these reviews can be found in Sections 5.29 and 5.30.

The evidence indicated that a community setting for assisted withdrawal is as clinically effective and safe for the majority of patients as an inpatient or residential setting, and it is also likely to be more cost effective. The GDG agreed that both efficacy and safety outcomes were of critical importance for this review. The GDG therefore decided that community-based assisted withdrawal should be the first choice for most people. However, the GDG was aware that some of those with more severe alcohol dependence, often with complex comorbidities, were often excluded from the studies reviewed. Consequently, the severity and complexity of the population in these studies was not representative of those who would typically require inpatient withdrawal management. The GDG considered this, as well as other evidence presented that might inform this issue, and identified a number of factors that would indicate that a residential or inpatient setting may be preferred to a community setting. They also considered which of the factors would suggest that assisted withdrawal should be managed in an inpatient setting with access to 24-hour specialist doctors and nurses with expertise in managing alcohol withdrawal in the context of significant comorbidity. The factors the GDG considered important are as follows:

● a history of epilepsy or withdrawal-related seizures or DTs during previous assisted withdrawal
● significant psychiatric or physical comorbidity (for example, chronic severe depression, psychosis, malnutrition, congestive cardiac failure, unstable angina or chronic liver disease)
● significant learning disability
● significant cognitive impairment
● a history of poor adherence and previous failed attempts
● homelessness
● pregnancy
● children and young people
● older people.

The review of drug regimens for assisted withdrawal drew on the NICE guideline on management of alcohol-related physical complications (NICE, 2010b) for both the initial review of the medication regimens and to ensure that there was a comprehensive and coherent approach to assisted withdrawal across both guidelines. The GDG was, therefore, concerned to build on the other guideline and develop recommendations that were feasible for use in a range of settings, both specialist and non-specialist in inpatient, residential and community (including primary care) services. After carefully considering the evidence, the GDG came to the conclusion that symptom-triggered assisted withdrawal was only practical in those inpatient settings that contained 24-hour medical monitoring and high levels of specially trained staff. The GDG therefore took the view that the preferred method for assisted withdrawal was an FD regimen for community and residential settings. In addition, the GDG also considered how some of the complex comorbidities often encountered in specialist alcohol services may be best managed. In particular the GDG were concerned to provide advice on the management of comorbid alcohol and benzodiazepine misuse. This was of concern because the GDG recognised the need to go above recommended BNF dosages for people who were dually dependent to reduce the likelihood of seizures. In the absence of any evidence from the studies reviewed, the GDG reached agreement on this issue by consensus.

Given the uncertainty about the severity of withdrawal symptoms, and the potential negative consequences of withdrawal for children and young people, the GDG concluded that there should be a lower threshold in the admission criteria for children and young people who misuse alcohol than for adults, and that specialist advice should be made available to the healthcare professional. The GDG also felt that it was prudent that all assisted withdrawal for children aged 10 to 15 years take place in an acute inpatient or residential setting with significant medical and nursing staff availability on a 24-hour basis. For young people aged 16 to 18 years, if withdrawal management is conducted in a community setting (that is, a non-residential setting where the young person does not sleep in the unit), particular care needs to be taken in monitoring the young person.

The GDG did not identify any evidence evaluating different dosing regimens for children and young people. The GDG suggest an inpatient setting with 24-hour monitoring for 10- to 15-year-olds for assisted withdrawal. There is a lack of clinical evidence suggesting the appropriate dose of medication for assisted withdrawal for children and young people as well as older people. However the GDG felt that the dose should be lower than that provided for a working-age adult taking into consideration the age, size, and gender of the individual.

Dose regimes for older people undergoing assisted withdrawal may need to be reduced compared with guidelines for younger adults.

5.31.1   Recommendations

Assessment and interventions for assisted alcohol withdrawal
[Refer to 5.31.1.19–5.31.1.22 for assessment for assisted withdrawal in children and young people]
5.31.1.1   For service users who typically drink over 15 units of alcohol per day and/or who score 20 or more on the AUDIT, consider offering:

- an assessment for and delivery of a community-based assisted withdrawal, **or**
- assessment and management in specialist alcohol services if there are safety concerns (see 5.31.1.5) about a community-based assisted withdrawal.

205

5.31.1.2   Service users who need assisted withdrawal should usually be offered a community-based programme, which should vary in intensity according to the severity of the dependence, available social support and the presence of comorbidities.
- For people with mild to moderate dependence, offer an outpatient-based withdrawal programme in which contact between staff and the service user averages 2–4 meetings per week over the first week.
- For people with mild to moderate dependence and complex needs[23], or severe dependence, offer an intensive community programme following assisted withdrawal in which the service user may attend a day programme lasting between 4 and 7 days per week over a 3-week period.

5.31.1.3   Outpatient-based community assisted withdrawal programmes should consist of a drug regimen (see 5.31.1.7–5.31.1.18) and psychosocial support including motivational interviewing (see 6.23.1.1).

5.31.1.4   Intensive community programmes following assisted withdrawal should consist of a drug regimen (see 7.15.1.1–7.15.1.3) supported by psychological interventions including individual treatments (see 7.15.1.1–7.15.1.3), group treatments, psychoeducational interventions, help to attend self-help groups, family and carer support and involvement, and case management (see 5.11.1.2).

5.31.1.5   Consider inpatient or residential assisted withdrawal if a service user meets one or more of the following criteria. They:
- drink over 30 units of alcohol per day
- have a score of more than 30 on the SADQ
- have a history of epilepsy, or experience of withdrawal-related seizures or delirium tremens during previous assisted withdrawal programmes
- need concurrent withdrawal from alcohol and benzodiazepines
- regularly drink between 15 and 20 units of alcohol per day and have:
  - significant psychiatric or physical comorbidities (for example, chronic severe depression, psychosis, malnutrition, congestive cardiac failure, unstable angina, chronic liver disease) or
  - a significant learning disability or cognitive impairment.

5.31.1.6   Consider a lower threshold for inpatient or residential assisted withdrawal in vulnerable groups, for example, homeless and older people.

Drug regimens for assisted withdrawal

5.31.1.7   When conducting community-based assisted withdrawal programmes, use fixed-dose medication regimens[24].

5.31.1.8   Fixed-dose or symptom-triggered medication regimens[25] can be used in assisted withdrawal programmes in inpatient or residential settings. If a

---

[23]For example, psychiatric comorbidity, poor social support or homelessness.

[24]A fixed dose regimen involves starting treatment with a standard dose, not defined by the level of alcohol withdrawal, and reducing the dose to zero over 7 to 10 days according to a standard protocol.

[25]A symptom-triggered approach involves tailoring the drug regimen according to the severity of withdrawal and any complications. The service user is monitored on a regular basis and pharmacotherapy only continues as long as the service user is showing withdrawal symptoms.

symptom-triggered regimen is used, all staff should be competent in monitoring symptoms effectively and the unit should have sufficient resources to allow them to do so frequently and safely.

5.31.1.9   For service users having assisted withdrawal, particularly those who are more severely alcohol dependent or those undergoing a symptom-triggered regimen, consider using a formal measure of withdrawal symptoms such as the CIWA-Ar.

5.31.1.10 Prescribe and administer medication for assisted withdrawal within a standard clinical protocol. The preferred medication for assisted withdrawal is a benzodiazepine (chlordiazepoxide or diazepam).

5.31.1.11 In a fixed-dose regimen, titrate the initial dose of medication to the severity of alcohol dependence and/or regular daily level of alcohol consumption. In severe alcohol dependence higher doses will be required to adequately control withdrawal and should be prescribed according to the Summary of Product Characteristics (SPC). Make sure there is adequate supervision if high doses are administered. Gradually reduce the dose of the benzodiazepine over 7–10 days to avoid alcohol withdrawal recurring[26].

5.31.1.12 Be aware that benzodiazepine doses may need to be reduced for children and young people[27], older people, and people with liver impairment (see 5.31.1.13).

5.31.1.13 If benzodiazepines are used for people with liver impairment, consider one requiring limited liver metabolism (for example, lorazepam); start with a reduced dose and monitor liver function carefully. Avoid using benzodiazepines for people with severe liver impairment.

5.31.1.14 When managing withdrawal from co-existing benzodiazepine and alcohol dependence increase the dose of benzodiazepine medication used for withdrawal. Calculate the initial daily dose based on the requirements for alcohol withdrawal plus the equivalent regularly used daily dose of benzodiazepine[28]. This is best managed with one benzodiazepine (chlordiazepoxide or diazepam) rather than multiple benzodiazepines. Inpatient withdrawal regimens should last for 2–3 weeks or longer, depending on the severity of co-existing benzodiazepine dependence. When withdrawal is managed in the community, and/or where there is a high level of benzodiazepine dependence, the regimen should last for longer than 3 weeks, tailored to the service user's symptoms and discomfort.

---

[26]See Table 21.

[27]At the time of publication of the NICE guideline (February 2011), benzodiazepines did not have UK marketing authorisation for use in children and young people under 18. Informed consent should be obtained and documented.

[28]At the time of publication of the NICE guideline (February 2011), benzodiazepines did not have UK marketing authorisation for this indication or for use in children and young people under 18. Informed consent should be obtained and documented. This should be done in line with normal standards of care for patients who may lack capacity (see www.publicguardian.gov.uk or www.wales.nhs.uk/consent) or in line with normal standards in emergency care.

5.31.1.15 When managing alcohol withdrawal in the community, avoid giving people who misuse alcohol large quantities of medication to take home to prevent overdose or diversion[29]. Prescribe for installment dispensing, with no more than 2 days' medication supplied at any time.

5.31.1.16 In a community-based assisted withdrawal programme, monitor the service user every other day during assisted withdrawal. A family member or carer should preferably oversee the administration of medication. Adjust the dose if severe withdrawal symptoms or over-sedation occur.

5.31.1.17 Do not offer clomethiazole for community-based assisted withdrawal because of the risk of overdose and misuse.

5.31.1.18 For managing unplanned acute alcohol withdrawal and complications including delirium tremens and withdrawal-related seizures, refer to NICE clinical guideline 100.

Special considerations for children and young people who misuse alcohol –
assessment and referral

5.31.1.19 If alcohol misuse is identified as a potential problem, with potential physical, psychological, educational or social consequences, in children and young people aged 10–17 years, conduct an initial brief assessment to assess:
- the duration and severity of the alcohol misuse (the standard adult threshold on the AUDIT for referral and intervention should be lowered for young people aged 10–16 years because of the more harmful effects of a given level of alcohol consumption in this population)
- any associated health and social problems
- the potential need for assisted withdrawal.

5.31.1.20 Refer all children and young people aged 10–15 years to a specialist child and adolescent mental health service (CAMHS) for a comprehensive assessment of their needs, if their alcohol misuse is associated with physical, psychological, educational and social problems and/or comorbid drug misuse.

5.31.1.21 When considering referral to CAMHS for young people aged 16-17 years who misuse alcohol, use the same referral criteria as for adults (see 5.26.1.8–5.26.1.18).

5.31.1.22 A comprehensive assessment for children and young people (supported if possible by additional information from a parent or carer) should assess multiple areas of need, be structured around a clinical interview using a validated clinical tool (such as the Adolescent Diagnostic Interview [ADI] or the Teen Addiction Severity Index [T-ASI]), and cover the following areas:
- consumption, dependence features and patterns of drinking
- comorbid substance misuse (consumption and dependence features) and associated problems
- mental and physical health problems
- peer relationships and social and family functioning

---

[29]When the drug is being taken by someone other than for whom it was prescribed.

- developmental and cognitive needs, and educational attainment and attendance
- history of abuse and trauma
- risk to self and others
- readiness to change and belief in the ability to change
- obtaining consent to treatment
- developing a care plan and risk management plan.

5.31.2   Research recommendation

5.31.2.1   What methods are most effective for assessing and diagnosing the presence and severity of alcohol misuse in children and young people?

This question should be answered in a programme of research that uses a cross-sectional cohort design testing:

- the sensitivity and specificity of a purpose-designed suite of screening and case identification measures of alcohol misuse against a diagnostic gold standard (DSM–IV or ICD–10)
- the reliability and validity of a purpose-designed suite in characterising the nature and the severity of the alcohol misuse in children and young people and their predictive validity in identifying the most effective treatment when compared with current best practice.

Particular attention should be paid to the feasibility of the measures in routine care and the training required to obtain satisfactory levels of accuracy and predictive validity. The programme needs to be large enough to encompass the age range (10 to 17 years) and the comorbidity that often accompanies alcohol misuse in children and young people.

Why this is important

Alcohol misuse is an increasingly common problem in children and young people. However, diagnostic instruments are poorly developed or not available for children and young people. In adults there is a range of diagnostic and assessment tools (with reasonable sensitivity and specificity, and reliability and validity) that are recommended for routine use in the NHS to both assess the severity of the alcohol misuse and to guide treatment decisions. No similar well-developed measures exist for children and young people, with the result that problems are missed and/or inappropriate treatment is offered. The results of this study will have important implications for the identification and the provision of effective treatment in the NHS for children and young people with alcohol-related problems.

5.32   RESIDENTIAL AND COMMUNITY SETTINGS FOR THE DELIVERY OF INTERVENTIONS FOR ALCOHOL MISUSE

5.32.1   Introduction

This section assesses the settings that are most clinically and cost effective in the delivery of interventions to reduce alcohol consumption, promote abstinence and reduce relapse. In the UK most such interventions are provided in community settings, usually by a specialist alcohol team. However, some services are provided in residential settings, usually following a period of residential assisted withdrawal. There is considerable debate in the UK regarding the value of residential treatment and, specifically, for which alcohol-related problems a residential unit is most appropriate.

As with the previous reviews, caution is needed in the assessment and interpretation of the evidence as it is possible that some of the most severely dependent patients may have been excluded from the studies (for example, Pettinati *et al.*, 1993). In addition, as others have identified, it is possible to confuse the setting with treatment intensity and duration (for example, Finney *et al.*, 1996; Mosher *et al.*, 1975). Another problem arises when separating the benefits of a period of inpatient or residential assisted withdrawal from the effects of continued residential psychosocial treatment (see Walsh *et al.*, 1991). Also, as is the case when evaluating many complex interventions, it is difficult to identify which elements of the intervention are mutative; for example McKay and colleagues (1995) and Rychtarik and colleagues (2000a) evaluated the same treatment in both residential and non-residential settings and reported that the milieu (that is, living in the residential setting for 24 hours a day) added little to the likelihood of a positive outcome of treatment. Relatively few studies in the area report differential outcomes based on patient characteristics, but the picture that does emerge is reasonably consistent. The most commonly studied predictor variables in the treatment of alcohol dependence have been measures of alcohol problem severity and social stability. More severe and less socially stable patients who misuse alcohol seem to fare better in inpatient (or more intensive treatment), whereas among married patients with stable accommodation, fewer years of problem drinking, and less history of treatment, outpatient (and less intensive) treatment yields more favourable outcomes than inpatient treatment (Kissin *et al.*, 1970; McLellan *et al.*, 1983; Orford *et al.*, 1976; Smart *et al.*, 1977; Stinson, 1970; Willems *et al.*, 1973). Finally, some studies provide limited descriptions of the interventions (in particular the comparator interventions) and this, along with the different healthcare systems in which the studies took place, makes interpretation of the evidence challenging.

5.32.2 Clinical review protocol

Information about the databases searched and the inclusion/exclusion criteria used for this section of the guideline can be found in Table 25 (further information about the search for health economic evidence can be found in Chapter 3).

5.32.3 Studies considered[30]

The review team conducted a new systematic search for RCTs that assessed the beneficial and detrimental effects of different settings for the delivery of alcohol treatment

---

[30]Here and elsewhere in the guideline, each study considered for review is referred to by a study ID in capital letters (primary author and date of study publication, except where a study is in press or only submitted for publication, then a date is not used).

Table 25: Databases searched and inclusion/exclusion criteria for clinical evidence

Electronic databases	CINAHL, EMBASE, MEDLINE, PsycINFO, Cochrane Library
Date searched	Database inception to March 2010
Study design	Systematic reviews; RCTs. Systematic reviews from 1993 to March 2010. All other searches from database inception to March 2010
Patient population	Diagnosed with having an alcohol-use disorder (alcohol dependence or harmful alcohol use)
Interventions	Residential treatment settings versus community treatment settings; duration of residential treatment (long versus short)
Outcomes	Relapse; lapse (non-abstinence); number of participants consuming alcohol; PDA; drinking frequency measures (for example, mean number of drinking days, number of intoxicated days, number drinking daily); quantity of alcohol measures (for example, DDD)

interventions after an assisted withdrawal programme and related health economic evidence (see Section 5.29.7).

A variety of different treatment settings are described in the research literature. Services were designated as: inpatient units; residential units; day hospitals (also known as partial hospitalisation or day centres); or outpatient based interventions of differing intensity and duration (involving attendance at an outpatient clinic, home visits, a combination of both, or containing some limited elements of a day programme). These are in line with the definitions set out in Section 1 of this chapter).

It is also important to note that most of the studies included in this review are North American, with few studies conducted in the UK or Europe. They cover a diverse range of populations, including some very specific samples (that is, employment schemes, VA populations), which may limit generalisability to the UK treatment population.

Fourteen trials met the eligibility criteria set by the GDG, providing data on 2,679 participants. All of the studies were published in peer-reviewed journals between 1972 and 2005. Summary study characteristics of the included studies are presented in Table 26. (Further information about both included and excluded studies can be found in Appendix 16c).

A meta-analyses was conducted for an adult population only as there was not enough evidence to perform a meta-analysis for children and young people.

Residential units versus outpatient treatment
Of the 14 included trials, three involved a comparison of residential units versus outpatient treatment. RYCHTARIK2000A compared a residential unit versus an outpatient setting; CHAPMAN1988 compared a 6-week inpatient programme with a 6 week outpatient programme. WALSH1991 compared compulsory inpatient treatment versus compulsory attendance at AA; this study was atypical in that the sample

211

Table 26: Study characteristics table for residential settings

	Residential unit versus outpatient treatment	Residential unit versus day hospital	Day hospital versus outpatient treatment	Residential unit versus residential unit	Short duration versus longer duration inpatient
Total number of trials (total number of participants)	3 RCTs (N = 334)	7 RCTs (N = 1453)	1 RCT (N = 382)	1 RCT (N = 141)	3 RCTs (N = 493)
Study ID	(1) CHAPMAN1988 (2) RYCHTARIK2000A (3) WALSH1991	(1) BELL1994 (2) LONGABAUGH 1983 (3) MCKAY1995 (4) MCLACHLAN1982 (5) RYCHTARIK2000A (6) WEITHMANN2005 (7) WITBRODT2007	(1) MORGENSTERN 2003 (2) RYCHTARIK 2000A	KESO1998	(1) MOSHER1975 (2) PITTMAN1975 (3) STEIN1975
Baseline severity: mean (SD)	(1) Average daily absolute alcohol (g): Inpatient: 256.3 Outpatient: 202.2 Confrontational interview: 226.2 (2) DDD (mean [SD]) Inpatient (n = 62): 10.95 (8.14) Intensive outpatient (n = 69): 10.24 (6.62) Standard outpatient (n = 61): 10.66 (6.77)	(1) Not available (2) Mean number of days of abstinence in preceding 6 months Inpatient: 7.51 Day: 8.28 (3) Number of days of alcohol intoxication (in previous 30 days): (mean [SD]) Random assignment Day hospital: 16.79 (7.29)	(1) Baseline PDA (mean): Inpatient: 48.1 Intensive outpatient: 54.4 Outpatient: 61.8 (2) Not available	Consumption of alcohol 2-month average in grams per day (mean [SD]) Kalliola AA-type: (Hazelden/Minnesota model): 112.2 (80.3) Jarvenpaa traditional-type treatment: 98.3 (72.8)	(1) Not available (2) 92.3% intoxicated upon admission to treatment, all alcoholism diagnosis (3) Not available

Continued

	(3) Averaged 6.3 drinks a day and 19.8 drinking days in the month preceding interview; 21% had been drink daily and 45% weekly in previous month	Inpatient: 12.96 (7.64) (4) Consumed alcohol on an average of 295 of the previous 365 days Consumed an average of 18 × 1.5-fluid-ounce drinks (17 ml) of 40% ethanol per day (5) Not available (6) DDD (30 days prior to admission) (mean [SD]) Inpatient: 12.3 (6.9) Day hospital: 26.6 (32.2) PDA (mean [SD]) Inpatient: 26.6 (32.) Day hospital: 28.6 (28.9) (7) Not available			
Treatment length	(1) 6 weeks (2) 28 days (3) 3 weeks	(1) Range: 28 to 31 days (2) Range: 2 to 3 weeks (3)–(6) Range: 28 to 31 days (7) Day hospital range: 2 to 3 weeks Residential: up to 60 days	(1) Range: 22.77 days to 12 weeks (2) Range: 28 to 31 days	28 days	(1) 9 day versus 21 day (2) 7 to 20 days versus 3 to 6 weeks (3) 9 day versus 21 day

Table 26: (*Continued*)

	Residential unit versus outpatient treatment	Residential unit versus day hospital	Day hospital versus outpatient treatment	Residential unit versus residential unit	Short duration versus longer duration inpatient
Length of follow-up (if available)	(1) 6 and 18 months (2) 6, 9, 12, 15 and 18 months (3) 1, 3, 6, 12, 18 and 24 months post-treatment	(1) Not available (2) 6, 12, 18 and 24 months (3) 3, 6 and 12 months (4) 12 months (5) 6, 9, 12, 15 and 18 months (6) 3, 6, 9 and 12 months (7) 6 and 12 months	(1) 3, 6 and 9 months (2) 6, 9, 12, 15 and 18 months	12 months	(1) 3 and 6 months (2) 3 and 12 months (3) 2, 4, 7, 10 and 13 months
Abstinent or non-abstinent prior to trial		(1)–(2) Not available (3) Non-abstinent (4)–(5) Not available (6) Combined with initial inpatient assisted withdrawal (7) Not available			
Country	(1) New Zealand (2)–(3) US	(1)–(3) US (4) Canada (5) US (6) Germany (7) US	(1)–(2) US	Finland	(1)–(3) US

consisted of workers at an industrial plant in the US who were part of an employee assistance programme and whose jobs were at risk should they fail to attend treatment. A 3-week period of residential treatment was followed by a year of job probation, during which attendance at AA meetings at least three times per week, sobriety at work and weekly checks with the programme staff were compulsory if the person wanted to keep their job. The outpatient treatment group were referred and offered an escort to a local AA meeting, which they were advised to continue attending at least three times a week for a year. They were treated in the same way as participants in the residential group for the following year.

Residential units versus day hospital
Of the 14 included trials, seven (BELL1994; LONGABAUGH1983; MCKAY1995; MCLACHLAN1982; RYCHTARIK2000A; WEITHMANN2005; WITBRODT2007) involved a comparison of residential rehabilitation units versus day hospital. All seven trials had a 28-day length of stay in treatment. Both MCKAY1995 and WITBRODT2007 looked at day hospital versus residential rehabilitation treatment, with the populations being split into a self-selected arm and a randomised arm.

Day hospital versus outpatient treatment
Two trials out of the 14 involved a comparison of day hospital versus outpatient treatment (MORGENSTERN2003; RYCHTARIK2000A).

Residential unit versus residential unit
Of the 14 included trials, one (KESO1990) involved a comparison of two different types of residential treatment, assessing the efficacy of two different therapeutic approaches. The Kalliola programme was based on the Hazelden or Minnesota model, with a focus on AA 12-step principles with abstinence as the designated treatment goal, whereas the Jarvenpaa programme was a more traditional approach to residential rehabilitation without the focus on AA 12-step principles.

Short versus long duration inpatient treatment
Three of the 14 trials involved a comparison of different lengths of admission to inpatient treatment. MOSHER1975 compared a 9-day versus a 30-day inpatient stay. STEIN1975 compared a 9-day residential inpatient stay with a 9-day stay with an additional 25 days of residential rehabilitative care. PITTMAN1972 compared a group receiving 7 to 10 days of inpatient care only with 3 to 6 weeks of inpatient care with an additional option of further outpatient aftercare.

5.32.4 Clinical evidence for residential and community settings for the delivery of alcohol treatment interventions

Evidence from the important outcomes and overall quality of evidence are presented in Table 27, Table 28, Table 29, Table 30 and Table 31. The associated forest plots are in Appendix 17b.

Table 27: Residential unit versus outpatient treatment

Outcome or subgroup	k	Total N	Statistics	Effect (95% CI)	Quality of the evidence (GRADE)
Abstinence					
PDA at 3-month follow-up	1	119	SMD (IV, Random, 95% CI)	0.22 (-0.14, 0.58)	⊕⊕⊕⊖ MODERATE
DDD at 3-month follow-up	1	119	SMD (IV, Random, 95% CI)	0.02 (-0.34, 0.38)	⊕⊕⊕⊕ HIGH
Lapse (number of participants non-abstinent)					
Lapse at 6-month follow-up	1	46	RR (M-H, Random, 95% CI)	0.92 (0.64, 1.32)	⊕⊕⊕⊖ MODERATE
Lapse at 18-month follow-up	1	48	RR (M-H, Random, 95% CI)	1.30 (0.87, 1.95)	⊕⊕⊕⊖ MODERATE
Lapse (number of participants non-abstinent) at 2-year follow-up	1	156	RR (M-H, Random, 95% CI)	0.76 (0.61, 0.94)	⊕⊕⊕⊕ HIGH
Number drinking <60 g absolute alcohol on a drinking day at 6-month follow-up	1	46	RR (M-H, Random, 95% CI)	0.66 (0.26,1.66)	⊕⊕⊕⊖ MODERATE
Number drinking <60 g absolute alcohol on a drinking day at 18-month follow-up	1	48	RR (M-H, Random, 95% CI)	0.66 (0.29, 1.48)	⊕⊕⊕⊖ MODERATE

Table 28: Residential unit versus day hospital

Outcome or subgroup	k	Total N	Statistics	Effect (95% CI)	Quality of the evidence (GRADE)
Abstinence					
PDA at 3-month follow-up	1	121	SMD (IV, Random, 95% CI)	0.23 (−0.13, 0.59)	⊕⊕⊕⊖ MODERATE
Alcohol consumption outcomes	2	169	SMD (IV, Random, 95% CI)	Subtotals only	
Drinks per drinking day at 3-month follow-up	1	121	SMD (IV, Random, 95% CI)	0.01 (−0.34, 0.37)	⊕⊕⊕⊕ HIGH
Mean number of drinking days at 3-month follow-up	1	48	SMD (IV, Random, 95% CI)	0.33 (−0.24, 0.90)	⊕⊕⊕⊖ MODERATE
Mean number of drinking days at 6-month follow-up	1	48	SMD (IV, Random, 95% CI)	0.76 (0.17, 1.35)	⊕⊕⊕⊕ HIGH
Mean number of drinking days at 12-month follow-up	1	48	SMD (IV, Random, 95% CI)	0.51 (−0.06, 1.09)	⊕⊕⊕⊖ MODERATE
Relapse	2	209	RR (M-H, Random, 95% CI)	Total events	
Post-treatment	1	109	RR (M-H, Random, 95% CI)	0.51 (0.16, 1.59)	⊕⊕⊕⊖ MODERATE
At 12-month follow-up	1	100	RR (M-H, Random, 95% CI)	1.20 (0.69, 3.68)	⊕⊕⊕⊖ MODERATE

Continued

Table 28: (*Continued*)

Outcome or subgroup	k	Total N	Statistics	Effect (95% CI)	Quality of the evidence (GRADE)
Lapse (non-abstinence)	5	722	RR (M-H, Random, 95% CI)	Subtotals only	
Number of participants non-abstinent at 6-month follow-up	2	467	RR (M-H, Random, 95% CI)	1.05 (0.82, 1.34)	⊕⊕⊕○ MODERATE
Number of participants non-abstinent at 12-month follow-up	2	393	RR (M-H, Random, 95% CI)	1.05 (0.88, 1.25)	⊕⊕⊕○ MODERATE
Number of participants non-abstinent throughout 12-month follow-up	1	109	RR (M-H, Random, 95% CI)	1.04 (0.86, 1.26)	⊕⊕⊕○ MODERATE
Drinking frequency	3	260	RR (M-H, Random, 95% CI)	Subtotals only	⊕⊕⊕○ MODERATE
Number of participants drinking daily at 6-month follow-up	1	174	RR (M-H, Random, 95% CI)	0.24 (0.03, 1.85)	⊕⊕⊕○ MODERATE
Number not retained in treatment	1	646	RR (M-H, Random, 95% CI)	0.67 (0.52, 0.85)	⊕⊕⊕○ MODERATE

Table 29: Day hospital versus outpatient treatment

Outcome or subgroup	k	Total N	Statistics	Effect (95% CI)	Quality of the evidence (GRADE)
Abstinence	2	376	SMD (IV, Random, 95% CI)	Subtotals only	
PDA	2	376	SMD (IV, Random, 95% CI)	-0.05 (-0.26, 0.15)	⊕⊕⊕⊕ HIGH
DDD at 3-month follow-up	1	124	SMD (IV, Random, 95% CI)	0.01 (-0.34, 0.36)	⊕⊕⊕⊕ HIGH

Table 30: Residential unit versus residential unit (two different models of treatment)

Outcome or subgroup	k	Total N	Statistics	Effect (95% CI)	Quality of the evidence (GRADE)
Relapse	1	109	RR (M-H, Random, 95% CI)	Subtotals only	
Number relapsed at 4- to 8-month follow-up	1	109	RR (M-H, Random, 95% CI)	0.79 (0.58, 1.08)	⊕⊕⊕○ MODERATE
Number relapsed at 8- to 12-month follow-up	1	109	RR (M-H, Random, 95% CI)	0.87 (0.67, 1.13)	⊕⊕⊕○ MODERATE

Table 31: Short versus longer duration inpatient treatment

Outcome or subgroup	k	Total N	Statistics	Effect (95% CI)	Quality of the evidence (GRADE)
Lapse (non-abstinence)	3	513	RR (M-H, Random, 95% CI)	Subtotals only	
Post-treatment	3	513	RR (M-H, Random, 95% CI)	0.94 (0.84, 1.05)	⊕⊕⊕○ MODERATE
At 6-month follow-up	1	200	RR (M-H, Random, 95% CI)	1.05 (0.91, 1.21)	⊕⊕⊕○ MODERATE
At 7-month follow-up	1	58	RR (M-H, Random, 95% CI)	0.86 (0.60, 1.23)	⊕⊕⊕○ MODERATE
At 10-month follow-up	1	58	RR (M-H, Random, 95% CI)	0.82 (0.58, 1.16)	⊕⊕⊕○ MODERATE
At 13-month follow-up	1	58	RR (M-H, Random, 95% CI)	0.95 (0.64, 1.40)	⊕⊕⊕○ MODERATE
Number consuming alcohol 60% to 90% of the time at 3-month follow-up	1	200	RR (M-H, Random, 95% CI)	0.95 (0.78, 1.14)	⊕⊕⊕○ MODERATE
Number consuming alcohol 60% to 90% of time at 6-month follow-up	1	200	RR (M-H, Random, 95% CI)	1.09 (0.91, 1.30)	⊕⊕⊕○ MODERATE
Number consuming alcohol less than 60% of time at 3-month follow-up	1	200	RR (M-H, Random, 95% CI)	1.01 (0.82, 1.24)	⊕⊕⊕○ MODERATE
Number consuming alcohol less than 60% of time at 6-month follow-up	1	200	RR (M-H, Random, 95% CI)	0.82 (0.61, 1.09)	⊕⊕⊕○ MODERATE

5.32.5　Clinical evidence summary

Residential unit versus outpatient treatment

Residential unit treatment was no more effective than an outpatient treatment in maintaining abstinence or in reducing the number of DDD at 3-month follow-up (RYCHTARIK2000A). Furthermore, there was no significant difference observed between treatment in a residential unit and a day hospital in reducing the number of participants drinking more than 60 g of alcohol per drinking day at 6-month follow-up (CHAPMAN1988).

A residential unit setting was significantly more effective than an outpatient setting in increasing the number of participants abstinent at 2-year follow-up in only one study (WALSH1991). This study population was atypical and is unlikely to be representative of patients attending UK alcohol treatment services, and the study included treatment elements that would be difficult to replicate in the UK.

Based on the GRADE method outlined in Chapter 3, the quality of this evidence is *moderate* and further research is likely to have an important impact on the confidence in the estimate of the effect and may change the estimate (for further information, see Table 27).

Residential unit versus day hospital

On measures of alcohol consumption, there was no significant difference between a residential unit and a day hospital on DDD day at 3-month follow-up. At 6-month follow-up, there was a significant difference between the two groups favouring day hospital treatment on mean number of drinking days, based on the results of the MCKAY1995 study. This effect did not remain at 12-month follow-up, however there was a trend (p = 0.08) slightly favouring day hospital treatment. It should be noted that this study had both a randomised and self-selected sample, and, because inclusion into this analysis was restricted to RCTs, only the randomised population was used. However, the results from the self-selected sample parallel the results from the randomised arm. The self-selected participants did not do any better on drinking outcomes than those who were randomly assigned at 6- or 12-month follow-up. Any differences that did emerge from the self-selected group, tended to favour the partial hospitalisation group (day hospital), as found in the randomised sample.

On rates of relapse or lapse to alcohol at 6 and 12 months post-treatment, there were no significant differences between residential unit and day hospital treatment. Additionally, there were no significant differences in the number of participants drinking daily at 6-month follow-up (LONGABAUGH1983), or in the PDA at 3-month follow-up (RYCHTARIK2000A).

One study found that more participants were retained in treatment in the residential setting than the day hospital setting (BELL1994). However, this study included a mixture of participants with primary drug and alcohol misuse problems, and so the results may not be representative of individuals presenting to an alcohol treatment service.

Based on the GRADE methodology outlined in Chapter 3, the quality of this evidence is *moderate* and further research is likely to have an important impact on the confidence in the estimate of the effect and may change the estimate (for further information see Table 28).

Day hospital versus outpatient treatment
A day hospital was not found to be any more effective than a less intensive outpatient setting in terms of PDA or DDD at 3-month follow-up. However, it is important to consider that the MORGENSTERN2003 study contained a mixture of both primary drug and alcohol users, so these results may not be generalisable to the wider population presenting for treatment of alcohol problems.

Based on the GRADE methodology outlined in Chapter 3, the quality of this evidence is *moderate* to *high* and further research is likely to have an important impact on the confidence in the estimate of the effect and may change the estimate (for further information, see Table 29).

Residential unit versus residential unit
When analysing two different therapeutic approaches to residential treatment, no difference was found between the two different residential treatment models (Kalliola and Jarvenpaa) on reducing the number of participants who relapsed between 4- and 12-month follow-up.

Based on the GRADE methodology outlined in Chapter 3, the quality of this evidence is *moderate* and further research is likely to have an important impact on the confidence in the estimate of the effect and may change the estimate (for further information, see Table 30).

Short duration versus longer duration level (inpatient)
There was no significant difference between a 21-day inpatient stay and an extended 9-day inpatient stay at reducing the number of participants consuming alcohol post-treatment, or at 3- or 6-month follow-up (MOSHER1975). A longer duration in an inpatient setting was no more effective in preventing lapse (non-abstinence) than a shorter duration in an inpatient setting. No effect remained at 6-, 7-, 10- and 13-month follow-up.

Based on the GRADE methodology outlined in Chapter 3, the quality of this evidence is *moderate* and further research is likely to have an important impact on the confidence in the estimate of the effect and may change the estimate (for further information, see Table 31).

5.32.6 Additional trials assessing different treatment settings

Randomised controlled trials
There are several additional studies that were well-conducted trials but could not be included in meta-analyses and did not evaluate the treatment settings as defined above. These studies nevertheless found similar results that support this meta-analysis. Chick (1988) compared simple advice with amplified advice (simple advice plus one session of motivational interviewing) with extended treatment,

which included the offer of further outpatient appointments, inpatient, or day treatment. There were no differences between the advice groups or the extended treatment on abstinence outcomes at 2-year follow-up, nor on drinking frequency outcomes. There were no significant differences found on alcohol consumed in 7 days prior to follow-up, frequency of drinking over 200 g per day in the past year, period of abstinence in the past year, or on other measures such as employment or marital situation. Edwards and Guthrie (1966) assigned participants to an average of 9 weeks of inpatient or outpatient treatment, and found no significant differences on measures of drinking at 6- and 12-month follow-up. Lastly, Eriksen (1986a) assigned 17 'alcoholics' who were post-assisted withdrawal to either immediate inpatient treatment or a 4-week waitlist control. Results indicated no significant differences between groups on outcomes of days drinking, or on other outcomes such as sick leave or institutionalisation.

Predictor studies
Even in the absence of overall differences in treatment outcomes between residential and outpatient settings, it is possible that certain types of patients derive differential benefits or harms from being treated in these alternative settings. This is the central issue in matching patients to optimal treatment approaches. Relatively few of the above studies report differential outcome based on patient characteristics, but a reasonably consistent picture does emerge – although it should be pointed out this is often based on *post hoc* analysis of non-randomised populations and so should be treated with caution. The GDG considered this issue, the main evidence points of which are summarised below; in doing so the GDG drew on the existing systematic review developed by the Specialist Clinical Addiction Network (Specialist Clinical Addiction Network, 2006) for the consensus statement on in-patient treatment.

The most commonly studied predictor variables in the treatment of alcohol dependence have been measures of problem severity and social stability. More severe and less socially stable patients who misuse alcohol seem to fare better in inpatient or more intensive treatment (possibly outpatient based), whereas among married patients with stable accommodation, fewer years of problem drinking and less history of treatment, outpatient (and less intensive) treatment yields more favourable outcomes than inpatient treatment (Kissin *et al.*, 1970; McLellan *et al.*, 1983; Orford *et al.*, 1976; Smart, 1977; Stinson, 1979; Willems, 1973). When heterogeneous populations of people who misuse alcohol are averaged together, the consistent finding is of comparable (or better) outcomes from outpatient as opposed to residential treatment (McLellan *et al.*, 1983). Moos and colleagues (1999) found in an effectiveness trial of inpatient treatment of different theoretical orientations within the VA treatment system that longer lengths of stay were associated with better outcomes. Likewise, in Project MATCH, patients who received inpatient treatment prior to 12 weeks of outpatient care had better drinking outcomes than those who went directly into outpatient care (Project MATCH Research Group, 1997).

5.32.7   Special populations

No clinical evidence evaluating the efficacy of different settings for the treatment of alcohol misuse were identified for children, young people or older populations.

5.32.8   Health economic evidence

Systematic literature review

One study was identified in the systematic search of the economic literature that considered the cost effectiveness of different settings for rehabilitation treatment for people with an alcohol-use disorder (alcohol dependence or harmful alcohol use) (Pettinati *et al.*, 1999). Details of the methods used for the systematic search of the economic literature are described in Chapter 3.

The study by Pettinati and colleagues (1999) assessed the cost-effectiveness of inpatient versus outpatient treatment of people with alcohol dependence. Both inpatient and outpatient treatment programmes followed the same multi-modal clinical approach based on the traditional 12-step programme of AA. This involved individual, marital, family and group counselling provided in the intensive treatment period, including 4 weeks of inpatient and 6 weeks of outpatient treatment. The primary difference between the inpatient and outpatient programmes was the amount of treatment hours and attendance at support groups. Inpatients attended educational and therapy sessions from 9 a.m. to 5 p.m., and attended an AA meeting in the evening, whilst outpatients were expected to attend individual and/or group sessions approximately one to two evenings a week, and AA meetings on the evenings that they did not attend therapy sessions as well as a family educational programme at the weekends. The study population consisted of 173 patients with a formal diagnosis of alcohol dependence but no other substance dependence. The primary outcome measure used in the study was the probability of returning to significant drinking over 12 months. This was defined as three or more alcoholic drinks in one sitting, admission to an inpatient or detoxification centre or incarceration due to alcohol-related disorders. A US healthcare payer perspective was adopted for the analysis. Resource use and cost items included the total number of treatment service hours attended during the intensive treatment programme each week via interviews with the subject. A weighted cost-to-charge ratio was applied to the billing charges for services to adjust for geographic- or institution-specific charges.

Rather than calculate ICERs, the authors presented cost-effectiveness ratios by dividing treatment costs by the probability of returning to significant drinking. For treatment responders, the inpatient:outpatient cost-effectiveness ratio was calculated for the 3-month follow-up as 4.5:1, at the 6-month follow-up as 5.3:1 and at the 12-month follow-up as 5.6:1. For treatment responders, the mean (SD) cost of successfully completing inpatient treatment was \$9,014 (\$2,986) versus \$1,420 (\$619), (p <0.01); a ratio of 6.5:1. The validity of the study findings are limited it was based on a non-randomised study design within the US healthcare system which may not be generalisable to the UK setting. Only the costs of treatment were included in the cost analysis, with no consideration of any subsequent healthcare and very little detail was given by the authors on resource use and cost estimation. Finally, health outcomes, which were not formally combined with cost differences to compute ICERs.

Cost analysis of rehabilitation treatment in different settings
The cost effectiveness of rehabilitation treatment for people with an alcohol-use disorder in different settings was considered by the GDG as an area with potentially significant resource implications. A formal economic evaluation comparing different rehabilitation settings was not attempted due to time constraints and problems in synthesising relevant clinical evidence. Nevertheless, a cost analysis was undertaken to estimate costs associated with rehabilitation treatment of people who misuse alcohol in different settings in the UK. The results of this analysis were considered by the GDG alongside the findings of the clinical effectiveness review, to make a judgement regarding the cost effectiveness of different settings for rehabilitation treatment.

Two different settings for rehabilitation treatment were considered in the analysis: residential settings and day hospital (partial hospitalisation) settings. The healthcare resource-use estimates for each setting were based on descriptions of resource use in studies included in the systematic literature review of clinical evidence. Studies conducted in the UK were limited in this review. Therefore, resource-use estimates from studies conducted outside the UK were refined using the expert opinion of the GDG to reflect current routine clinical practice within the NHS. The estimated resource use was subsequently combined with national unit costs to provide a total cost associated with rehabilitation treatment in the three settings assessed. Unit costs were derived from national sources (Curtis, 2009; Department of Health, 2010) and reflected 2009 prices.

Residential treatment unit
The duration of treatment in this setting has been reported to vary from 4 weeks (Sannibale *et al.*, 2003) to 60 days (Zemore & Kaskutas, 2008). Both studies were conducted outside the UK. The GDG estimated that residential treatment typically lasts 12 weeks (3 months) in the UK setting. No unit costs for residential treatment for people with an alcohol-use disorder provided within the NHS are available. Residential units for people who misuse drugs/alcohol provided by the voluntary sector cost £808 per resident week (Curtis, 2009). By combining estimated duration of residential treatment with the respective unit cost, the total cost of residential rehabilitation treatment is estimated at £9,696.

Day hospital treatment
According to Zemore and Kaskutas (2008) and McKay and colleagues (1995), the duration of rehabilitation treatment taking place in day hospitals ranges between 2 and 4 weeks. The GDG considered 4 weeks to be a reasonable duration of day hospital rehabilitation in the UK. McKay and colleagues (1995) reported that participants in their study attended a day hospital 5 days per week. The GDG estimated that

frequency of attendance in day hospital rehabilitation should be between 5 and 7 days per week. UK unit costs of such services are not available. The NHS unit cost of mental health day care is £102 per attendance (Department of Health, 2010). However, this facility is likely to provide, on average, non-specialist services and therefore this unit cost is expected to be somewhat lower than the cost of a day hospital rehabilitation service. On the other hand, Parrott and colleagues (2006) reported a local unit cost of a day hospital assisted withdrawal and rehabilitation service for people who are alcohol dependent of £129 per day (uplifted from the originally reported cost of £109 per day in 2004 prices, using the Hospital and Community Health Services pay and prices inflation indices provided in Curtis, 2009). Using the range of these two unit costs and combining them with the estimated resource use, the total cost of a day hospital rehabilitation treatment for people who misuse alcohol is estimated to range from £2,040 (for a 5-day per week programme, using the lower unit cost) to £3,612 (for a 7-day per week programme, using the higher unit cost).

Summary
The cost analysis indicates that, as expected, day hospital treatment is less costly than residential rehabilitation.

5.32.9   Clinical and health economic evidence summary

A range of treatment settings were reviewed for treatment taking place after an assisted withdrawal programme. These included: inpatient facilities, residential units, outpatient treatment, and day hospital treatment. For all the treatment settings, the evidence in support of them was assessed to be of a high or moderate quality using GRADE profiles.

Overall, inpatient settings were not seen as any more effective than outpatient, or day hospital settings. The exception to this was that day hospital settings were favoured over inpatient settings in one study on improving drinking outcomes at 6- and 12-month follow-up. Additional time in an inpatient setting did not improve outcomes and a standard, shorter inpatient stay seemed to be equally as effective.

Furthermore, three studies (BELL1994; MORGENSTERN2003; WITBRODT2007) included people who misused both drugs and alcohol, and it can be difficult to disentangle the effects for those with a primary alcohol-misuse problem. However, alcohol data were reported separately from other substances and it was possible to use these data in this review.

The studies also include a wide range of different programmes. For example, the nature of the outpatient programmes in these studies varied considerably in content, duration and intensity. However, the results of the meta-analysis are in line with the findings of previous reviews assessing the effectiveness of residential versus non-residential treatment (for example, Finney *et al.*, 1996). A cost analysis undertaken for this guideline indicated that day hospital treatment incurs considerably lower costs than residential treatment.

Taking both cost and clinical effectiveness evidence into account, these results suggest that once an assisted withdrawal programme has been completed a psychosocial treatment package delivered in a non-residential day hospital or community treatment programme[31] is likely to be the more cost-effective option.

5.32.10   From evidence to recommendations

The GDG conducted a systematic review evaluating the efficacy of residential and community settings for the delivery of interventions for alcohol misuse. A meta-analysis was conducted evaluating drinking related critical outcomes identified by the GDG such as relapse, lapse, drinking frequency and drinking quantity. The evidence from this review suggests that community settings are at least as effective as residential units and less costly in providing effective treatment alcohol misuse. The evidence did not show any additional benefit of residential-based interventions. The GDG therefore recommend a community setting as the preferred setting for delivering effective treatment. For some of the more severely dependent patients there is some evidence to suggest that more intensive programme are more effective, but the GDG took the view that these intensive programme can also be provided in the community in the form of day hospital or similarly intensive community-based programmes. The GDG took the view that a small number of people who are alcohol dependent may benefit from residential treatment after assisted withdrawal and identified the homelessness as such a group. It should be noted that the evidence base is this topic areas is limited for a number of reasons. Firstly, the clinical studies use varied descriptions of the settings evaluated. Secondly, outcomes assessed across studies were also heterogeneous, which meant that not all studies could be included in the meta-analysis. Thirdly, the majority of studies included in the review are based in the US, covering a diverse range of populations (for example, employment schemes, VA populations), thus limiting the generalisability to a UK setting. The GDG considered these limitations in the interpretation of the results of the systematic review and when making recommendations.

5.32.11   Recommendations

Interventions to promote abstinence and relapse prevention
5.32.11.1 For people with alcohol dependence who are homeless, consider offering residential rehabilitation for a maximum of 3 months. Help the service user find stable accommodation before discharge.
5.32.11.2 For all children and young people aged 10–17 years who misuse alcohol, the goal of treatment should usually be abstinence in the first instance.

---

[31]The costs of such a programme are likely to be lower than a day hospital programme given its reduced intensity.

5.32.12 Research recommendations

5.32.12.1 For people with moderate and severe alcohol dependence who have significant comorbid problems, is an intensive residential rehabilitation programme clinically and cost effective when compared with intensive community-based care?

This question should be answered using a prospective cohort study of all people who have moderate and severe dependence on alcohol entering residential and intensive community rehabilitation programmes in a purposive sample of alcohol treatment services in the UK. It should report short- and medium-term outcomes (including cost-effectiveness outcomes) of at least 18 months' duration. Particular attention should be paid to the characterisation of the treatment environment and the nature of the interventions provided to inform the analysis of moderators and mediators of treatment effect. The outcomes chosen should reflect both observer and service user-rated assessments of improvement (including personal and social functioning) and the acceptability of the intervention. The study needs to be large enough to determine the presence or absence of clinically important effects, and mediators and moderators of response should be investigated. A cohort study has been chosen as the most appropriate design as previous studies in this area that have attempted to randomise participants to residential or community care have been unable to recruit clinically representative populations.

Why this is important
Many people, in particular those with severe problems and complex comorbidities, do not benefit from treatment and/or lose contact with services. One common approach is to offer intensive residential rehabilitation and current policy favours this. However, the research on the effectiveness of residential rehabilitation is uncertain with a suggestion that intensive community services may be as effective. The interpretation of this research is limited by the fact that many of the more severely ill people are not entered into the clinical trials because some clinicians are unsure of the safety of the community setting. However, clinical opinion is divided on the benefits of residential rehabilitation, with some suggesting that those who benefit are a motivated and self-selected group who may do just as well with intensive community treatment, which is currently limited in availability. Given the costs associated with residential treatment and the uncertainty about outcomes, the results of this study will have important implications for the cost effectiveness and provision of alcohol services in the NHS.

6   PSYCHOLOGICAL AND PSYCHOSOCIAL INTERVENTIONS

6.1   INTRODUCTION

This chapter is concerned with structured psychological interventions used to help people who experience alcohol dependence or harmful alcohol use. These approaches have been the focus of much research and debate over the years.

Psychological interventions for people experiencing alcohol misuse or dependence have traditionally made use of the interaction between the service user and a therapist, worker, helper or counsellor (the latter terminologies may vary depending on services and settings). In addition, more recently, there has been some growth and expansion in the use of self-help-based interventions that involve the use of DVDs, books, computer programmes or self-help manuals.

Psychological approaches vary depending on the theoretical models underpinning them. Broadly, psychological interventions can be classified into behavioural, cognitive, psychodynamic, humanistic, systemic, motivational, disease, and social and environmental. The emphasis of each therapy is different, depending on the theoretical underpinning of the approach. Behavioural approaches, for example, are based on the premise that excessive drinking is a learned habit and therefore influenced by principles of behaviour. The latter can hence be used to teach the individual a different behavioural pattern that will reduce the harm emerging from excessive drinking. Cognitive approaches, on the other hand, emphasise the role of thinking and cognition either prior to engaging in drinking behaviour or to prevent or avoid lapse or relapse. Social approaches focus the work on the social environment, for example families or wider social networks. In some instances, a combination of approaches is used and described under the term of 'multimodal' treatment, guided by the rationale that a combination of approaches is more powerful than each individual component. Each category of intervention is discussed in more detail later in this chapter within subsections describing the studies reviewed that are relevant to each type of approach.

Whilst the rationale and theoretical frameworks for treatments have been clearly articulated in the various research studies, the evidence for the superiority of one form of treatment over another in the field of alcohol has been difficult to find (Miller & Wilbourne, 2002). This has led to the general view in the field that whilst psychological interventions are better than no intervention, no single approach is superior to another. In this chapter, where available, the evidence for each psychological intervention is assessed in relation to three comparators: (i) is the intervention superior to treatment as usual or a control condition? (ii) is the intervention superior to other interventions? and (iii) is the intervention superior to other variants of the same type of approach (for example, behavioural cue exposure [BCE] versus behavioural self-control training [BSCT])?

The review of this literature is of significant importance, given the potential wide use of psychological interventions in NHS and non-statutory services as well as the need to provide an evidence base to inform and guide the implementation and use of these approaches. It is important to note that previous influential reviews of alcohol treatment (for example, 'Mesa Grande', Miller & Wilbourne, 2002) have combined findings from a large number of trials that included a wide range of populations (for example, opportunistic versus help-seeking, mild versus severe dependence). In the current review, only studies that involved treatment-seeking populations experiencing harmful drinking or alcohol dependence were included and therefore the number of trials meeting these criteria was reduced to make them relevant to the population addressed in this guideline.

Finally, psychological treatments can also be used to help people experiencing harmful alcohol use or dependence to address coexisting problems such as anxiety and depression. These approaches are not covered within this review and the reader is referred to the separate NICE guidelines that address psychological interventions for specific mental health problems. Healthcare professionals should note that, although the presence of alcohol misuse may impact, for example, on the duration of a formal psychological treatment, there is no evidence supporting the view that psychological treatments for common mental health disorders are ineffective for people who misuse alcohol. A number of NICE mental health guidelines have specifically considered the interaction between common mental health problems and drug and alcohol use. For example, NICE guidelines, such as for anxiety (NICE, 2004) or obsessive-compulsive disorder (NICE, 2006a), provide advice on assessment and the impact that drug and alcohol misuse may have on the effectiveness or duration of treatment. There is also some evidence to suggest that the active treatment of comorbid mental health problems may improve drug and alcohol substance misuse outcomes (Charney *et al.*, 2001; Hesse, 2004; Watkins *et al.*, 2006). This may be particularly important for service users who have achieved abstinence (note that symptoms of depression and anxiety may remit following successful treatment of the alcohol problem), but whose alcohol use is at risk of returning or escalating due to inadequately treated anxiety or depression.

6.1.1　Current practice

Services for people who are alcohol dependent and harmful drinkers are commonly delivered by statutory and non-statutory providers. The field is undergoing rapid change across different areas of the country due to the impact of the commissioning process. Traditionally, services have been provided by teams where the detoxification and counselling aspects of treatment have been fairly clearly separated. Within the NHS, teams tend to consist of different disciplines including nurses, counsellors, medical practitioners and, less often, other professions such as psychologists and occupational therapists. Teams are commonly under-resourced with practitioners having high caseloads and limited access to supervision. Most practice involves an eclectic approach that combines strategies from various psychological approaches. A more recent development involves contracts between commissioners and providers that may determine, for example the number of sessions to be delivered, yet this is rarely informed by the evidence and tends to be driven by pragmatic or resource issues (Drummond *et al.*, 2005).

Whilst the research literature to date has concentrated mostly on the comparison of well-defined treatment interventions commonly incorporated into treatment manuals, this stands in contrast to what is normally delivered in routine practice. Despite the research on psychological treatments, current UK practice is not underpinned by a strong evidence base and there is wide variation in the uptake and implementation of psychological approaches to treatment across services (Drummond *et al.*, 2005).

A number of factors may contribute to the low implementation of evidence-based psychological interventions. First, there is a lack of availability of reviews of the current evidence in a clear and practical format that can be accessible to practitioners, managers and commissioners. This has led to a weak dissemination of the evidence base concerning psychological interventions for alcohol misuse within routine service provision. Second, there is the varied composition of the workforce with a range of training experiences, not all of which include training in the delivery of psychological interventions. Furthermore, as noted by Tober and colleagues (2005), training programmes for the management of substance misuse vary widely in content with no consensus on methods to provide and evaluate such training or to maintain its effects. Supervision of psychological interventions is equally varied and not always available. Finally, there is a tendency in the field to eclecticism fuelled by the perception that all approaches are either equally valid or equally ineffective.

6.2 THERAPIST FACTORS

Several therapist factors that could potentially affect treatment have been considered, including demographics, professional background, training, use of supervision and competence. Two related aspects are dealt with below, namely the therapeutic alliance and therapist competence.

6.2.1 The therapeutic alliance

There are various definitions of the therapeutic alliance, but in general terms it is viewed as a constructive relationship between therapist and client, characterised by a positive and mutually respectful stance in which both parties work on the joint enterprise of change. Bordin (1979) conceptualised the alliance as having three elements: agreement on the relevance of the tasks (or techniques) employed in therapy; agreement about the goals or outcomes the therapy aims to achieve; and the quality of the bond between therapist and patient.

There has been considerable debate about the importance of the alliance as a factor in promoting change, with some commentators arguing that technique is inappropriately privileged over the alliance, a position reflected in many humanistic models where the therapeutic relationship itself is seen as integral to the change process, with technique relegated to a secondary role (for example, Rogers, 1951). The failure of some comparative trials to demonstrate differences in outcome between active psychological therapies (for example, Elkin, 1994; Miller & Wilbourne, 2002) is often cited in support of this argument and is usually referred to as 'the dodo-bird hypothesis' (Luborsky *et al.*, 1975). However, apart from the fact that dodo-bird findings may not be as ubiquitous as is sometimes claimed, this does not logically imply that therapy technique is irrelevant to outcome. Identifying and interpreting equivalence of benefit across therapies remains a live debate (for example, Ahn & Wampold, 2001; Stiles *et al.*, 2006) but should also include a consideration of cost effectiveness as well as clinical efficacy (NICE, 2008a).

Meta-analytic reviews report consistent evidence of a positive association of the alliance with better outcomes with a correlation of around 0.25 (for example, Horvath & Symonds, 1991; Martin *et al.*, 2000), a finding that applies across a heterogeneous group of trials (in terms of variables such as type of therapy, nature of the disorder, client presentation, type of measures applied and the stage of therapy at which measures are applied). However, it is the consistency rather than the size of this correlation that is most striking because a correlation of 0.25 would suggest it could account for only 6% of the variance in the outcome. Specific studies of the role of the alliance in drug and alcohol treatment programmes have been conducted. Luborsky and colleagues (1985), Connors and colleagues (1997) and Ilgen and colleagues, (2006) reported a relationship between treatment outcomes, but others (for example, Ojehagen *et al.,* 1997) have not. Ojehagen and colleagues (1997) suggest that this discrepancy between the various studies may have arisen from methodological differences between the studies; in contrast to Luborsky and colleagues (1985), Connors and colleagues (1997) and Ilgen and colleagues (2006), in Ojehagen and colleagues' (1997) study ratings of the alliance were made by an independent rater from video tapes as opposed to ratings made by the therapist early in treatment. This is consistent with other studies; for example, Feeley and colleagues (1999) reported that alliance quality was related to early symptom change. Therefore, it seems reasonable to debate the extent to which a good alliance is necessary for a positive outcome of an intervention, but it is unlikely to be sufficient to account for the majority of the variance in outcome.

6.2.2   Therapist competence

Studies of the relationship between therapist competence and outcome suggest that all therapists have variable outcomes, although some therapists produce consistently better outcomes (for example, Okiishi *et al.*, 2003). There is evidence that more competent therapists produce better outcomes (Barber *et al.*, 1996 and 2006; Kuyken & Tsivrikos, 2009). This is also the case for psychological interventions in the alcohol field; the Project MATCH Research Group (1998) reported therapist differences that impact on outcome. A number of studies have also sought to examine more precisely therapist competence and its relation to outcomes; that is, what is it that therapists do to achieve good outcomes? A number of studies are briefly reviewed here.

This section draws on a more extensive review of the area by Roth and Pilling (2011), which focused on CBT because this area had the most extensive research. In an early study, Shaw and colleagues (1999) examined competence in the treatment of 36 patients treated by eight therapists offering CBT as part of the National Institute of Mental Health trial of depression (Elkin *et al.*, 1989). Ratings of competence were made on the Cognitive Therapy Scale (CTS). Although the simple correlation of the CTS with outcome suggested that it contributed little to outcome variance, regression analyses indicated a more specific set of associations; specifically, when controlling for pre-therapy depression scores, adherence and the alliance, the overall CTS score accounted for 15% of the variance in outcome. However, a subset of items on the CTS accounted for most of this association.

Some understanding of what may account for this association emerges from three studies by DeRubeis's research group (Feeley *et al.*, 1999; Brotman *et al.*, 2009). All of the studies made use of the Collaborative Study Psychotherapy Rating Scale (CSPRS: Hollon *et al.*, 1988), subscales of which contained items specific to CBT. On the basis of factor analysis, the CBT items were separated into two subscales labelled 'cognitive therapy – concrete' and 'cognitive therapy – abstract'. Concrete techniques can be thought of as pragmatic aspects of therapy (such as establishing the session agenda, setting homework tasks or helping clients identify and modify negative automatic thoughts). Both DeRubeis and Feeley (1990) and Feeley and colleagues (1999) found some evidence for a significant association between the use of 'concrete' CBT techniques and better outcomes. The benefits of high levels of competence over and above levels required for basic practice has been studied in most detail in the literature on CBT for depression. In general, high severity and comorbidity, especially with Axis II pathology, have been associated with poorer outcomes in therapies, but the detrimental impact of these factors is lessened for highly competent therapists. DeRubeis and colleagues (2005) found that the most competent therapists had good outcomes even for patients with the most severe levels of depression. Kuyken and Tsivrikos (2009) found that therapists who are more competent have better patient outcomes regardless of the degree of patient comorbidity. In patients with neurotic disorders (Kingdon *et al.*, 1996) and personality disorders (Davidson *et al.*, 2004), higher levels of competence were associated with greater improvements in depressive symptoms. Although competence in psychological therapies is hard to measure in routine practice, degrees of formal training (Brosan *et al.,* 2007) and experience in that modality (James *et al.*, 2001) are associated with competence and are independently associated with better outcomes (Burns & Nolen-Hoeksema, 1992). All therapists should have levels of training and experience that are adequate to ensure a basic level of competence in the therapy they are practicing, and the highest possible levels of training and experience are desirable for those therapists treating patients with severe, enduring or complex presentations. In routine practice in services providing psychological therapies for depression, therapists should receive regular supervision and monitoring of outcomes. Roth and colleagues (2010) reviewed the training programmes associated with clinical trials as part of a programme exploring therapist competence (Roth & Pilling, 2008). They showed that clinical trials are associated with high levels of training, supervision and monitoring–factors that are not always found in routine practice. This is partly due to the inadequate description of training programmes in the trial reports. However, there is an increasing emphasis on describing the process of training in clinical trials, the report by Tober and colleagues (2005) being a notable recent publication describing the training programme for UKATT.

Trepka and colleagues (2004) examined the impact of competence by analysing outcomes in Cahill and colleagues' (2003) study. Six clinical psychologists (with between 1 and 6 years' post-qualification experience) treated 30 clients with depression using CBT, with ratings of competence made on the CTS. In a completer sample (N = 21) better outcomes were associated with overall competence on the CTS ($r = 0.47$); in the full sample this association was only found with the 'specific CBT skills' subscale of the CTS. Using a stringent measure of recovery (a Beck Depression Inventory score no more than one SD from the non-distressed mean), nine of the ten completer patients treated by the more competent therapists recovered, compared with four of the 11 clients treated by the less competent therapists. These results remained even when analysis controlled for levels of the therapeutic alliance.

Miller and colleagues (1993) looked at therapist behaviours in a brief (two-session) 'motivational check-up'; they identified one therapist behaviour (a confrontational approach) that was associated with increased alcohol intake. Agreeing and monitoring homework is one of the set of 'concrete' CBT skills identified above. All forms of CBT place an emphasis on the role of homework because it provides a powerful opportunity for clients to test their expectations. A small number of studies have explored whether compliance with homework is related to better outcomes, although rather fewer have examined the therapist behaviours associated with better client 'compliance' with homework itself. Kazantzis and colleagues (2000) report a meta-analysis of 27 trials of cognitive and/or behavioural interventions that contained data relevant to the link between homework assignment, compliance and outcome. In 19 trials, clients were being treated for depression or anxiety; the remainder were seen for a range of other problems. Of these, 11 reported on the effects of assigning homework in therapy and 16 on the impact of compliance. The type of homework varied, as did the way in which compliance was monitored, although this was usually by therapist report. Overall there was a significant, although modest, association between outcome and assigning homework tasks ($r = 0.36$), and between outcome and homework compliance ($r = 0.22$). While Kazantzis and colleagues (2000) indicate that homework has greater impact for clients with depression than anxiety disorders, the number of trials on which this comparison is made is small and any conclusions must therefore be tentative.

Bryant and colleagues (1999) examined factors leading to homework compliance in 26 clients with depression receiving CBT from four therapists. As in other studies, greater compliance with homework was associated with better outcome. In terms of therapist behaviours, it was not so much therapists' CBT-specific skills (such as skilfully assigning homework or providing a rationale for homework) that were associated with compliance, but ratings of their general therapeutic skills and particularly whether they explicitly reviewed the homework assigned in the previous session. There was also some evidence that compliance was increased if therapists checked how the client felt about the task being set and identified potential difficulties in carrying it out.

6.3   MATCHING EFFECTS/SEVERITY

One of the main challenges in providing services for alcohol treatment is to increase the effectiveness of the interventions offered. The concept of tailoring treatments to particular types of clients to increase effectiveness has been appealing to researchers both in terms of its logical plausibility and as a possible explanation for the reason why no one intervention has universal effectiveness. However, despite this, there is limited evidence to date that matching people with alcohol misuse or dependence to treatment approaches demonstrates effectiveness.

In 1989 the NIAAA began the largest national multisite RCT of alcoholism treatment matching, entitled Matching Alcoholism Treatments to Client Heterogeneity (Project MATCH). This study outlined matching hypotheses that were investigated across both 'outpatient' and 'aftercare' settings following inpatient or day hospital treatment. Clients were randomly allocated to one of three manual-guided treatment approaches individually offered, namely cognitive behavioural coping-skills therapy, MET or TSF therapy (Project MATCH Research Group, 1997). However, tests of the primary matching hypotheses over the 4- to 15-month follow-up period revealed few matching effects. Of the variables considered, psychiatric severity was considered an attribute worthy of further consideration because this alone appeared to influence drinking at 1-year follow-up. A UK trial later explored client treatment-matching in the treatment of alcohol misuse comparing MET with SBNT (UKATT Research Team, 2007), the findings of which strongly supported those of Project MATCH in that none of the five matching hypotheses was supported at either follow-up point on any outcome measure.

Despite the limited findings from these major trials, other studies have detected more positive conclusions that have highlighted methodological considerations associated with matching. Several studies have acknowledged the usefulness of matching treatment approaches for individuals who are experiencing severe psychiatric co-morbidity. In a trial comparing people with alcohol dependence with a range of psychiatric impairments, more structured coping-skills training yielded lower relapse rates at 6-month follow-up (Kadden *et al.*, 1989). Studies that looked specifically at matching in the context of psychiatric disturbance have acknowledged that the severity of the psychiatric presentation has a negative impact upon the relapse rates (Brown *et al.*, 2002), although matching appears to have assisted in retaining individuals in treatment (McLellan *et al.*, 1997). Although in some cases no significant differences have been detected between overall relapse rates when matching treatments at 2 years' follow-up, relapse to alcohol was found to have occurred more slowly where high psychiatric co-morbidity is matched with more structured coping-skills training (Cooney *et al.*, 1991).

The importance of service user choice in relation to self-matching treatments has been associated with more positive outcomes in two studies (Brown *et al.*, 2002;

UKATT Research Group, 2007), whilst other trials have emphasised the negative consequences of 'mismatching' including earlier relapse (Cooney *et al.*, 1991), poorer outcomes (Karno & Longabaugh, 2007) and increased need of support services (Conrod *et al.*, 2000).

Treatment providers are now required to consider not only treatment efficacy but also cost effectiveness, and for this reason treatment matching has remained an appealing option (Moyer *et al.*, 2000). However, for the findings of matching trials to be meaningful, one must consider a variety of methodological issues. Many of the recent studies considered have involved small samples, comparing a diverse range of variables both in terms of sample characteristics and treatment process factors (McLellan & Alterman, 1991). It has been suggested that for trials to provide more meaningful findings, there is a need for a clearer focus on matching questions which then focus upon well-specified treatments that have clear goals with specific patient populations. In this way, such designs may be more likely to provide interpretable results as well as a clearer understanding of the processes likely to be responsible for such findings.

Despite the steady development of patient-treatment matching studies in relation to alcohol dependence, the outcomes to date indicate that there is no single treatment that is effective for all clients. There continue to be many obstacles to matching clients to specific treatment programmes in real world settings and for many organisations patient–treatment matching remains impractical. Research would appear to indicate that the nature and severity of co-morbid and complex presentations such as psychiatric disturbance have a negative impact upon treatments for addiction, and this is arguably an area for further research (McLellan *et al.*, 1997). It has been suggested that, given the diversity of presentations and the large number of variables implicated in such research, the development of reliable and generalisable measures will be important for both the effective training and evaluation of treatment-matching efficacy (McLellan & Alterman, 1991).

6.4 SETTING THE CONTEXT FOR 12-STEP FACILITATION AND ALCOHOLICS ANONYMOUS

The 12-step principles were first set out in a publication by AA in the 1950s. AA describes itself as a 'Fellowship' and AA groups are widely available in the UK as support networks for people with alcohol dependence. AA is a self-help movement with the 12-step principles at the core. The 12 steps lay out a process that individuals are recommended to follow, based on an assumption that dependence on alcohol is a disease and therefore a goal of lifelong abstinence should be promoted. Membership is entirely voluntary and free of charge, there is a spiritual element to participation and life-long membership is encouraged. Attendance has been associated with successful abstinence from alcohol in a number of studies (see Ferri and colleagues [2006] for a systematic review).

Most 12-step treatment is predicated on the understanding that the treatment would fail without subsequent attendance at 12-step fellowship meetings. However, a common problem in the treatment of alcohol dependence with AA or 12-step groups is that people who misuse alcohol frequently discontinue AA involvement at the end of their designated treatment period and usually do not continue with aftercare treatment (Kaskutas *et al.*, 2005; Kelly *et al.*, 2003; Moos *et al.*, 2001; Tonigan *et al.*, 2003). As a result, manual-guided TSF has been developed as an active standalone or adjunctive intervention which involves: introducing the person who misuses alcohol to the principles of AA and the 12 steps of treatment (for example, Project MATCH Research Group, 1993), providing information on AA facilitates in the geographical area, and engaging with the client in setting goals for attendance and participation in the meetings. The aim of TSF is to maintain abstinence whilst in treatment and to sustain gains made after treatment concludes. This guideline is concerned with the use of TSF as an active intervention in the treatment of alcohol dependence and harmful alcohol use. An evaluation of the classic AA approach is outside the scope of this guideline.

6.5   REVIEW OF PSYCHOLOGICAL THERAPIES

6.5.1   Aim of review

This section aims to review the evidence for psychological interventions without pharmacological interventions for the treatment of alcohol dependence and harmful alcohol use. The literature reviewed in this section is focused on a reduction or cessation of drinking and hence assesses any outcomes pertaining to this. Most of the literature in the field is focused on adults over the age of 18 years. However, for young people under the age of 18 years old, literature assessing the clinical efficacy of psychological therapies for alcohol misuse alone (without comorbid drug misuse) is limited. The psychological evidence below is for an adult population only and a review of the evidence for the treatment of young people is described in Section 6.22.

Psychological interventions were considered for inclusion in the review if they were:
- Planned treatment
- For treatment-seeking participants only (of particular importance for the brief interventions because the scope did not cover opportunistic brief interventions – see scope, Appendix 1)
- Manual-based or, in the absence of a formal manual, the intervention should be well-defined and structured
- Ethical and safe

The following psychological therapies used in the treatment of alcohol misuse were considered for inclusion in this guideline:
- Brief interventions (planned only)
  - for example, psychoeducational and motivational techniques
- Self-help based treatments
  - brief self-help interventions (including guided self-help/bibliotherapy)
- TSF

- Cognitive behavioural-based therapies
  - standard cognitive behavioural therapy
  - coping skills
  - social skills training
  - relapse prevention
- Behavioural therapies
  - cue exposure
  - BSCT
  - contingency management
  - aversion therapy
- MET
- Social network and environment-based therapies
  - social behaviour and network therapy (SBNT)
  - the community reinforcement approach
- Counselling
  - couples therapy (including behavioural couples therapy and other variants of couples therapy)
- Family-based interventions
  - functional family therapy
  - brief strategic family therapy
  - multisystematic therapy
  - five-step family interventions
  - multidimensional family therapy
  - community reinforcement and family training
- Psychodynamic therapy
  - short-term psychodynamic intervention
  - supportive expressive psychotherapy.

In addition, physical therapies such as meditation and acupuncture are also covered in this review.

Good quality RCT evidence for the clinical efficacy of some of the psychological therapies listed was not always available. Therefore, the evidence summaries in this chapter describe the psychological therapies for which evidence of sufficient quality (see Chapter 3 for methodological criteria) was available. There are a number of useful studies that add value to the RCT data presented and they are included in this review. For the purpose of this guideline, and to obtain an overview of the available literature, studies that have met other methodological criteria are described in the evidence summaries of the individual therapies.

Full characteristics of included studies, forest plots and GRADE profiles can be found in Appendix 16d, 17c and 18c, respectively, because they were too extensive to place within this chapter.

6.5.2   Review questions

Primary review questions addressed in this chapter:

1. For people with alcohol dependence or who are harmful drinkers, is psychological *treatment x*, when compared with *y*, more clinically and cost effective and does this depend on:
   ● presence of comorbidities
   ● subtypes (matching effects)
   ● therapist-related factors (quality, therapeutic alliance, competence, training and so on).

6.6   OUTCOMES

There were no consistent critical outcomes across studies and outcomes were mainly continuous in nature. This variability in outcomes poses some difficulties in pooling data from different studies. Therefore, continuous outcomes were grouped into three categories:
● Abstinence, for example,
  – percentage/proportion of days abstinent
  – abstinent days per week/month
  – longest duration abstinent
● Rates of consumption, for example,
  – percentage/proportion of days heavy drinking
  – drinking days per month
  – days drinking greater than *X* drinks per week
● Amount of alcohol consumed, for example,
  – DDD
  – mean number of drinks per week
  – grams of alcohol per drinking day
  – number of drinks per drinking episode.
  Dichotomous outcomes included:
● abstinence (number of participants abstinent)
● lapse (number of participants who have drank at all)
● relapse (number of participants who have drank more than *X* number of drinks)
● attrition (the number of participants leaving the study for any reason).
     Studies varied in their definition of these dichotomous terms. For example, the number of drinks defined as constituting a relapse varied.

6.7   MOTIVATIONAL TECHNIQUES

6.7.1   Definition

Motivational enhancement therapy (MET) is the most structured and intensive motivational-based intervention. It is based on the methods and principles of motivational interviewing (Miller *et al.*, 1992). It is patient centred and aims to result in rapid internally-motivated changes by exploring and resolving ambivalence towards behaviour.

The treatment strategy of motivational interviewing is not to guide the client through recovery step-by-step, but to use motivational methods and strategies to utilise the patient's resources. A more specific manualised and structured form of motivational interviewing based on the work of Project MATCH is usually utilised (Project MATCH Research Group, 1993).

Brief motivational interventions include the computerised Drinker's Check-Up (DCU), which assesses symptoms of dependence, alcohol-related problems and motivation for change, and 'feedback, responsibility, advice, menu, empathy, self-efficacy' (FRAMES; Bien *et al.*, 1993[32]).

6.7.2   Clinical review protocol (motivational techniques)

Information about the databases searched and the inclusion/exclusion criteria used for this section of the guideline can be found in Chapter 3 (further information about the

Table 32: Clinical review protocol for the review of motivational techniques

Electronic databases	CINAHL, EMBASE, MEDLINE, PsycINFO, Cochrane Library
Date searched	Database inception to March 2010
Study design	RCT (at least ten participants per arm)
Population	Adults (over 18 years old) At least 80% of the sample meet the criteria for alcohol dependence or harmful alcohol use (clinical diagnosis or drinking more than 30 drinks per week)
Excluded populations	Hazardous drinkers and those drinking fewer than 30 drinks per week Pregnant women
Interventions	Motivational techniques
Comparator	Control or other active intervention
Outcomes	Abstinence Amount of alcohol consumed Rates of consumption Relapse (>X number of drinks or number of participants who have relapsed) Lapse (time to first drink or number of participants who have lapsed) Attrition (leaving the study early for any reason)

---

[32]www.drinkerscheckup.com.

search for health economic evidence can be found in Section 6.21 of this chapter). See Table 32 below for a summary of the clinical review protocol for the review of motivational techniques.

6.7.3   Studies considered for review[33]

The review team conducted a systematic review of RCTs that assessed the beneficial or detrimental effects of motivational techniques in the treatment of alcohol dependence or harmful alcohol use. See Table 33 for a summary of the study characteristics. It should be noted that some trials included in analyses were three- or four-arm trials. To avoid double counting, the number of participants in treatment conditions used in more than one comparison was divided (by half in a three-arm trial and by three in a four-arm trial).

Eight trials relating to clinical evidence met the eligibility criteria set by the GDG, providing data on 4,209 participants. All eight studies were published in peer-reviewed journals between 1997 and 2007. A number of studies identified in the search were initially excluded because they were not relevant to this guideline. Studies were excluded because they did not meet methodological criteria (see Chapter 3). When studies did meet basic methodological inclusion criteria, the main reason for exclusion was not meeting the drinking quantity/diagnostic criteria; that is, participants were not drinking enough to be categorised as harmful or dependent drinkers, or less than 80% of the sample met criteria for alcohol dependence or harmful alcohol use. Other reasons were that treatment was opportunistic as opposed to planned, the study was not directly relevant to the review questions, or no relevant alcohol-focused outcomes were available. A list of excluded studies can be found in Appendix 16d.

Motivational techniques versus minimal intervention control
Of the eight included trials, three that involved a comparison of motivational techniques versus control met the criteria for inclusion. HESTER2005 assessed the drinker's check-up versus waitlist control; ROSENBLUM2005b investigated MET plus relapse prevention versus information and referral only; and SELLMAN2001 assessed MET versus feedback only. The included studies were conducted between 2001 and 2005. The 5-year follow-up outcomes were obtained from Adamson and Sellman (2008).

Motivational techniques versus other active intervention
Of the eight included trials, six assessed motivational techniques versus another active intervention met criteria for inclusion. DAVIDSON2007 investigated MET versus cognitive behavioural broad spectrum therapy; MATCH1997 assessed MET versus both CBT and TSF; SELLMAN2001 compared MET with non-directive reflective listening

---

[33]Here and elsewhere in the guideline, each study considered for review is referred to by a study ID in capital letters (primary author and date of study publication, except where a study is in press or only submitted for publication, then a date is not used).

Table 33: Summary of study characteristics for motivational techniques

	Motivational versus minimal intervention control	Motivational versus other active intervention
K (total N)	3 RCTs (N = 433)	6 RCTs (N = 3818)
Study ID	(1) HESTER2005 (2) ROSENBLUM2005b (3) SELLMAN2001	(1) DAVIDSON2007 (2) MATCH1997 (3) SELLMAN2001 (4) SHAKESHAFT2002 (5) SOBELL2002 (6) UKATT2005
Diagnosis	(1) AUDIT score 8+ (2) DSM alcohol dependent/abuse (3) DSM alcohol dependent	(1) DSM alcohol dependent (2) DSM alcohol dependent/abuse (3) DSM alcohol dependent (4)–(5) Not reported (6) DSM alcohol dependent/abuse
Baseline severity	(1) DDD: approximately 7 (2) Not reported (3) Mild/moderate dependence Unequivocal heavy drinking more than six times (in 6 months prior to treatment): 90.2%	(1) PDA: approximately 30%, percent days heavy drinking: approximately 63% (2) PDA: approximately 30%, DDD: approximately 16 (3) Unequivocal heavy drinking six or more times in 6 months prior to treatment: 90.2% (4) Weekly Australian units per week: approximately 32 units (5) Number of drinking days per week: approximately 5.5 days, DDD: approximately 5 (6) PDA: 29.5%, number of DDD: 26.8 drinks
Number of sessions	Range: 1 to 12 sessions	Range: 1 to 12 sessions
Length of treatment	Range: 1 to 6 weeks	Range: 1 to 12 weeks
Length of follow-up	Range: 1 month to 5 years	Range: 6 months to 5 years
Setting	(1) Computer-based intervention (2) Homeless soup-kitchen (3) Outpatient treatment centre	(1) Outpatient treatment centre (2) Clinical research unit (3)–(4) Outpatient treatment centre (5) Mail information (6) Outpatient treatment centre
Treatment goal	(1) Abstinence or drinking reduction/moderation (2) Drinking reduction/moderation (3) Not explicitly stated	(1)–(2) Abstinence or drinking reduction/moderation (3)–(5) Not explicitly stated (6) Abstinence or drinking reduction/moderation
Country	(1)–(2) US (3) New Zealand	(1)–(2) US (3) New Zealand (4) Australia (5) US (6) UK

(counselling); SHAKESHAFT2002 assessed FRAMES with CBT; SOBELL2002 compared motivational enhancement/personalised feedback with psychoeducational bibliotherapy/drinking guidelines; and, lastly, UKATT2005 investigated MET versus SBNT. The included studies were conducted between 1997 and 2007.

6.7.4 Evidence summary[34]

The GRADE profiles and associated forest plots for the comparisons can be found in Appendix 18c and Appendix 17c, respectively.

Motivational techniques versus minimal intervention control
One computerised session of MET (drinker's check up) was significantly better than control in reducing average drinks per day at 1-month follow-up (moderate effect size). However, this finding was based on the results of a single study. Furthermore, no significant difference in average drinks per day and DDD was observed between the drinker's check up and control at 2- and 12-month follow-up.

MET (with relapse prevention) (ROSENBLUM2005b) was significantly more effective than control at reducing heavy alcohol use when assessed at 5-month follow-up (moderate effect size). This was further supported by the SELLMAN2001 study, which favoured MET over control in the number of people who drank excessively and frequently (ten or more drinks, six or more times) at 6-month follow-up (large effect size). However, this effect was not observed at long follow-up assessment (5 years). Although no significant difference was observed between groups in reducing the days on which *any* alcohol was consumed, the analyses showed a trend favouring MET with relapse prevention over control (p = 0.07). No significant difference in attrition rates were observed between MET and control groups across studies.

The quality of this evidence is *moderate* and further research is likely to have an important impact on confidence in the estimate of the effect. An evidence summary of the results of the meta-analyses can be seen in Table 34.

Motivational techniques versus other active intervention
The clinical evidence showed that no significant difference could be found between motivational techniques and other active interventions in maintaining abstinence at up to 15-month follow-up. Furthermore, no difference between groups was observed in reducing the number of participants who had lapsed or reducing heavy drinking at all follow-up points.

Other therapies (namely CBT and TSF) were more effective than motivational techniques in reducing the quantity of alcohol consumed when assessed post-treatment. However, the effect size was small (0.1) and was no longer seen at longer follow-up points of 3 to 15 months.

---

[34]Sensitivity analyses were conducted to assess the effect of combining studies investigating brief motivational techniques with structured MET studies. The findings were found to be robust in sensitivity analysis and the effects found were not determined by the intensity and duration the motivational intervention.

Table 34: Motivational techniques versus control evidence summary

Outcome or subgroup	N	Statistical method	Effect estimate (SMD, 95% CI)
Lapse or relapse			
Lapsed up until 6-month follow-up			
At 6 months	82	RR (M-H, Random, 95% CI)	0.90 (0.77, 1.06)
Lapsed >12-month follow-up			
At 5-year follow-up	56	RR (M-H, Random, 95% CI)	1.03 (0.77, 1.37)
Amount of alcohol consumed			
Amount of alcohol consumed up to 6-month follow-up			
Average drinks per day (log transformed) over entire assessment period at 1-month follow-up	61	SMD (IV, Random, 95% CI)	-0.67 (-1.20, -0.15)
Average drinks per day (log transformed) over entire assessment period at 2-month follow-up	61	SMD (IV, Random, 95% CI)	-0.46 (-0.97, 0.06)
DDD (log transformed) at 1-month follow-up	61	SMD (IV, Random, 95% CI)	-0.17 (-0.68, 0.34)
DDD (log transformed) at 2-month follow-up	61	SMD (IV, Random, 95% CI)	0.21 (-0.30, 0.72)
Amount of alcohol consumed 7- to 12-month follow-up			
Average drinks per day (log transformed) over entire assessment period at 12-month follow-up	61	SMD (IV, Random, 95% CI)	-0.20 (-0.71, 0.31)
DDD (log transformed) at 12-month follow-up	61	SMD (IV, Random, 95% CI)	0.36 (-0.15, 0.88)
Rates of consumption			
Rates of consumption up to 6-month follow-up			
Days any alcohol use at 5-month follow-up	139	SMD (IV, Random, 95% CI)	-0.31 (-0.64, 0.03)
Days heavy alcohol use (more than four drinks) at 5-month follow-up	46	SMD (IV, Random, 95% CI)	-0.70 (-1.30, -0.11)

Continued

Table 34: (*Continued*)

Outcome or subgroup	N	Statistical method	Effect estimate (SMD, 95% CI)
Rate of consumption up to 6-month follow-up			
Exceeded national drinking guidelines at least once at 6-month follow-up	82	RR (M-H, Random, 95% CI)	0.89 (0.66, 1.19)
Exceeded national drinking guidelines six or more times at 6-month follow-up	82	RR (M-H, Random, 95% CI)	0.89 (0.66, 1.19)
Drank at least ten standard drinks at least once at 6-month follow-up	82	RR (M-H, Random, 95% CI)	0.77 (0.58, 1.03)
Drank at least ten drinks six or more times at 6-month follow-up	82	RR (M-H, Random, 95% CI)	0.66 (0.43, 1.00)
Rates of consumption >12-month follow-up			
Exceeded national drinking guidelines at least once at 5-year follow-up	56	RR (M-H, Random, 95% CI)	0.90 (0.60, 1.36)
Exceeded national drinking guidelines six or more times at 5-year follow-up	56	RR (M-H, Random, 95% CI)	0.92 (0.52, 1.62)
Drank at least ten standard drinks at least once at 5-year follow-up	56	RR (M-H, Random, 95% CI)	0.64 (0.34, 1.22)
Drank at least ten drinks six or more times at 5-year follow-up	56	RR (M-H, Random, 95% CI)	0.72 (0.29, 1.74)
Attrition (dropout)			
Attrition (dropout) post-treatment	290	RR (M-H, Random, 95% CI)	1.09 (0.76, 1.57)
Attrition (dropout) up to 6-month follow-up	82	RR (M-H, Random, 95% CI)	Not estimable
At 6-month follow-up	82	RR (M-H, Random, 95% CI)	Not estimable
Attrition (dropout) at 7- to 12-month follow-up	61		
At 12 months	61	RR (M-H, Random, 95% CI)	0.89 (0.30, 2.61)
Attrition (dropout) >12-month follow-up	82	RR (M-H, Random, 95% CI)	1.30 (0.68, 2.48)
At 5-year follow-up	82	RR (M-H, Random, 95% CI)	1.30 (0.68, 2.48)

No significant difference was observed between groups in attrition rates post-treatment or at 3-month follow-up. However, other therapies were more effective at retaining participants at 6-month follow-up (low effect size). Follow-up periods longer than 6 months did not indicate any significant difference between groups.

The quality of this evidence is *moderate*, therefore further research is likely to have an important impact on confidence in the estimate of the effect. An evidence summary of the results of the meta-analyses can be seen in Table 35.

6.8   12-STEP FACILITATION

6.8.1   Definition

TSF is based on the 12-step or AA concept that alcohol misuse is a spiritual and medical disease (see Section 6.4 for a discussion of AA). As well as a goal of abstinence, this intervention aims to actively encourage commitment to and participation in AA meeting. Participants are asked to keep a journal of AA attendance and participation, and are given AA literature relevant to the 'step' of the programme that they have reached. TSF is highly structured and manualised (Nowinski *et al.*, 1992) and involves a weekly session in which the patient is asked about their drinking, AA attendance and participation, given an explanation of the themes of the current sessions, and goals for AA attendance are set.

6.8.2   Clinical review protocol (12-step facilitation)

Information about the databases searched and the inclusion/exclusion criteria used for this section of the guideline can be found in Chapter 3 (further information about the search for health economic evidence can be found in Section 6.21). See Table 36 below for a summary of the clinical review protocol for the review of TSF.

6.8.3   Studies considered for review

The review team conducted a systematic review of RCTs that assessed the beneficial or detrimental effects of TSF in the treatment of alcohol dependence or harmful alcohol use. See Table 37 for a summary of the study characteristics. It should be noted that some trials included in analyses were three- or four-arm trials. To avoid double counting, the number of participants in treatment conditions used in more than one comparison was divided (by half in a three-arm trial, and by three in a four-arm trial).

Six trials relating to clinical evidence met the eligibility criteria set by the GDG, providing data on 2,556 participants. All six studies were published in peer-reviewed journals between 1997 and 2009. A number of studies identified in the search were initially excluded because they were not relevant to this guideline. Studies were

Table 35: Motivational techniques versus other intervention evidence summary

Outcome or subgroup	N	Statistical method	Effect estimate (SMD, 95% CI)
Abstinence			
Abstinent post-treatment	1801	SMD (IV, Random, 95% CI)	0.08 (−0.02, 0.18)
Abstinence up to 6-month follow-up	2476	SMD (IV, Random, 95% CI)	0.02 (−0.06, 0.10)
At 3-month follow-up	835	SMD (IV, Random, 95% CI)	0.09 (−0.12, 0.30)
At 6-month follow-up	1641	SMD (IV, Random, 95% CI)	−0.01 (−0.11, 0.10)
Abstinence – 7- to 12-month follow-up			
At 9-month follow-up	1616	SMD (IV, Random, 95% CI)	0.05 (−0.06, 0.15)
At 12-month follow-up	1672	SMD (IV, Random, 95% CI)	0.04 (−0.07, 0.15)
Abstinence >12-month follow-up			
At 15-month follow-up	1573	SMD (IV, Random, 95% CI)	0.06 (−0.05, 0.16)
Lapse or relapse			
Lapsed up to 6-month follow-up			
At 6 months	82	RR (M-H, Random, 95% CI)	0.93 (0.78, 1.10)
Lapsed >12-month follow-up			
At 5 year follow-up	48	RR (M-H, Random, 95% CI)	1.02 (0.75, 1.40)
Rates of consumption			
Rate of consumption post-treatment			
Percent heavy drinking days	149	SMD (IV, Random, 95% CI)	0.05 (−0.27, 0.37)
Rate of consumption up to 6-month follow-up	115	SMD (IV, Random, 95% CI)	0.02 (−0.35, 0.38)
Binge consumption (occasions in prior 30 days where at least seven (males) or five (females) drinks consumed at 6 months	115	SMD (IV, Random, 95% CI)	0.02 (−0.35, 0.38)
Rate of consumption up to 6-month follow-up			
Exceeded national drinking guidelines at least once at 6-month follow-up	82	RR (M-H, Random, 95% CI)	0.83 (0.63, 1.10)
Exceeded national drinking guidelines six or more times at 6-month follow-up	82	RR (M-H, Random, 95% CI)	0.83 (0.63, 1.10)
Drank at least ten standard drinks at least once at 6-month follow-up	82	RR (M-H, Random, 95% CI)	0.80 (0.60, 1.07)

Continued

Table 35: (*Continued*)

Outcome or subgroup	N	Statistical method	Effect estimate (SMD, 95% CI)
Drank at least ten or more drinks six or more times at 6-month follow-up	82	RR (M-H, Random, 95% CI)	0.69 (0.45, 1.05)
Rate of consumption –7- to 12-month follow-up			
Number of days drinking per week at 12-month follow-up	657	SMD (IV, Random, 95% CI)	0.00 (−0.15, 0.15)
Days with more than five drinks at 12 months	657	SMD (IV, Random, 95% CI)	−0.08 (−0.23, 0.08)
Rates of consumption >12-month follow-up			
Exceeded national drinking guidelines at least once at 5-year follow-up	48	RR (M-H, Random, 95% CI)	0.96 (0.61, 1.51)
Exceeded national drinking guidelines 6 or more times at 5-year follow-up	48	RR (M-H, Random, 95% CI)	0.85 (0.47, 1.53)
Drank at least ten standard drinks at least once at 5-year follow-up	48	RR (M-H, Random, 95% CI)	0.88 (0.41, 1.88)
Drank at least ten or more drinks six or more times at 5-year follow-up	48	RR (M-H, Random, 95% CI)	1.17 (0.38, 3.61)
Amount of alcohol consumed			
Amount of alcohol consumed post-treatment			
DDD	1652	SMD (IV, Random, 95% CI)	0.10 (−0.00, 0.20)
Amount of alcohol consumed up to 6-month follow-up	2380	SMD (IV, Random, 95% CI)	0.05 (−0.04, 0.13)
DDD at 3-month follow-up	624	SMD (IV, Random, 95% CI)	−0.04 (−0.20, 0.12)
DDD at 6-month follow-up	1641	SMD (IV, Random, 95% CI)	0.08 (−0.02, 0.18)
Drinks per week at 6 months	115	SMD (IV, Random, 95% CI)	0.09 (−0.27, 0.46)
Amount of alcohol consumed –7- to 12-month follow-up			
DDD at 9-month follow-up			
DDD at 12-month follow-up	2771	SMD (IV, Random, 95% CI)	0.01 (−0.07, 0.08)
Drinks per week at 12 months	657	SMD (IV, Random, 95% CI)	−0.01 (−0.16, 0.14)

Continued

Table 35: *(Continued)*

Outcome or subgroup	N	Statistical method	Effect estimate (SMD, 95% CI)
Amount of alcohol consumed >12-month follow-up			
DDD at 15-month follow-up	1573	SMD (IV, Random, 95% CI)	0.05 (−0.05, 0.16)
Attrition (dropout)			
Attrition (dropout) post-treatment	2022	RR (M-H, Random, 95% CI)	0.70 (0.31, 1.59)
Attrition (dropout) up to 6 months follow-up	2719	RR (M-H, Random, 95% CI)	1.37 (1.05, 1.80)
At 3-month follow-up	762	RR (M-H, Random, 95% CI)	1.36 (0.84, 2.18)
At 6-month follow-up	1957	RR (M-H, Random, 95% CI)	1.38 (1.00, 1.92)
Attrition (dropout) at 7- to 12-month follow-up			
At 9-month follow-up	1641	RR (M-H, Random, 95% CI)	1.85 (0.83, 4.11)
At 12-month follow-up	3130	RR (M-H, Random, 95% CI)	1.15 (0.87, 1.52)
Attrition (dropout) >12-month follow-up	1676	RR (M-H, Random, 95% CI)	0.86 (0.55, 1.35)
At 15-month follow-up	1594	RR (M-H, Random, 95% CI)	1.27 (0.52, 3.08)
At 5-year follow-up	82	RR (M-H, Random, 95% CI)	0.75 (0.45, 1.27)

Table 36: Clinical review protocol for the review of 12-step facilitation

Electronic databases	CINAHL, EMBASE, MEDLINE, PsycINFO, Cochrane Library
Date searched	Database inception to March 2010
Study design	RCT (at least ten participants per arm)
Population	Adults (over 18 years old) At least 80% of the sample meet the criteria for alcohol dependence or harmful alcohol use (clinical diagnosis or drinking more than 30 drinks per week)
Excluded populations	Hazardous drinkers and those drinking fewer than 30 drinks per week Pregnant women
Interventions	TSF
Comparator	Control or other active intervention
Outcomes	Abstinence Amount of alcohol consumed Rates of consumption Relapse (>X number of drinks or number of participants who have relapsed) Lapse (time to first drink or number of participants who have lapsed) Attrition (leaving the study early for any reason)

excluded because they did not meet methodological criteria (see Chapter 3). When studies did meet basic methodological inclusion criteria, the main reason for exclusion was that the studies were assessing the efficacy of 12-step groups (that is, AA) directly (not TSF) and hence were also naturalistic studies. Other reasons included a drug and not alcohol focus, secondary analysis and not being directly relevant to the current guideline. A list of excluded studies can be found in Appendix 16d.

12-step facilitation versus other active intervention
Of the six included trials, five compared TSF with another active intervention. The comparator against TSF was CBT (EASTON2007), couples therapy and psychoeducational intervention (FALSSTEWART2005; FALSSTWEART2006), MET and CBT (MATCH1997), and coping skills (WALITZER2009).

Comparing different formats of 12-step facilitation
Two included studies assessed one form of TSF versus another. TIMKO2007 evaluated intensive TSF versus standard TSF. In the standard TSF condition, people who misuse alcohol were given an AA schedule and encouraged to attend sessions. Counsellors and patients reviewed relapse prevention, but treatment was more focused on psychoeducation. In the intensive TSF condition, standard treatment was provided and counsellors actively arranged AA meeting attendance. Participants were encouraged to keep an AA attendance journal. WALITZER2009 assessed a directive approach to TSF versus a motivational approach to TSF in addition to treatment-as-usual (coping skills).

6.8.4   Evidence summary

The GRADE profiles and associated forest plots for the comparisons can be found in Appendix 18c and Appendix 17c, respectively.

12-step facilitation versus other active interventions
The clinical evidence revealed no significant difference between TSF and other active interventions in maintaining abstinence, reducing heavy drinking episodes when assessed post-treatment and at various follow-up points up to 12 months. TSF was significantly better than other active interventions in reducing the amount of alcohol consumed when assessed at 6-month follow-up. However, the effect size was small (SMD = -0.09) and no significant difference between groups was observed for any other follow-up points.

No significant difference in attrition rates was observed between TSF and other active interventions in attrition post-treatment and up to 6-month follow-up. However, those receiving TSF were more likely to be retained at 9-month follow-up, although his difference was not observed at 12- and 15-month follow-up.

The quality of this evidence is *high*, therefore further research is unlikely to change confidence in the estimate of the effect. An evidence summary of the results of the meta-analyses can be seen in Table 38.

Table 37: Summary of study characteristics for 12-step facilitation

	TSF versus other active intervention	Different formats of TSF
K (total N)	5 RCTs (N = 1221)	2 RCTs (N = 456)
Study ID	(1) EASTON2007 (2) FALSSTEWART2005 (3) FALSSTWEART2006 (4) MATCH1997 (5) WALITZER2009	(1) TIMKO2007 (2) WALITZER2009
Diagnosis	(1)–(2) DSM alcohol dependent (3)–(4) DSM IV alcohol dependent/abuse (5) Not reported	(1)–(2) Not reported
Baseline severity	(1) Approximately 19 years of alcohol use, alcohol use in past 28 days: approximately 6 days (2) Percent days heavy drinking: 56 to 59% across treatment groups (3) PDA: 40 to 44% across treatment groups (4) PDA: approximately 30, DDD: approximately 16 drinks (5) PDA: 35.4%, percent days heavy drinking: 32.7%	(1) ASI alcohol score: approximately 0.28 (2) PDA: 35.4%, percent days heavy drinking: 32.7%
Number of sessions	Range: 12 to 32 sessions	(1) 1 session (2) 12 sessions in which TSF was in addition to other treatment
Length of treatment	12 weeks	Unclear
Length of follow-up	Range: 3 to 15 months	Range: 3 to 12 months
Setting	(1)–(3) Outpatient treatment centre (4) Clinical research unit (5) Outpatient treatment centre	(1)–(2) Outpatient treatment centre
Treatment goal	(1) Drinking reduction/moderation (2) Not explicitly stated (3) Abstinence (4) Abstinence or drinking reduction/moderation (5) Not explicitly stated	(1)–(2) Not explicitly stated
Country	(1)–(5) US	(1)–(2) US

Comparing different formats of 12-step facilitation
Directive TSF was more effective at maintaining abstinence than motivational TSF up to 12-month follow-up (RR = −0.41 to −0.81 across follow-up points). However, no difference between groups was observed in reducing heavy drinking episodes.

Table 38: 12-Step Facilitation versus other intervention evidence summary

Outcome or subgroup	N	Statistical method	Effect estimate (SMD, 95% CI)
Abstinence			
Abstinence post-treatment	1860	SMD (IV, Random, 95% CI)	0.04 (−0.10, 0.18)
Abstinence up to 6-month follow-up			
PDA at 3-month follow-up	340	SMD (IV, Random, 95% CI)	−0.05 (−0.41, 0.31)
PDA at 6-month follow-up	1975	SMD (IV, Random, 95% CI)	−0.03 (−0.23, 0.16)
Abstinence 7- to 12-month follow-up			
PDA at 9-month follow-up	1942	SMD (IV, Random, 95% CI)	0.00 (−0.18, 0.18)
PDA at 12-month follow-up	1911	SMD (IV, Random, 95% CI)	−0.01 (−0.21, 0.19)
Abstinence >12-month follow-up			
At 15-month follow-up	1573	SMD (IV, Random, 95% CI)	−0.01 (−0.12, 0.09)
Rates of consumption			
Rate of alcohol consumption post-treatment			
Percentage days heavy drinking at post-treatment	99	SMD (IV, Random, 95% CI)	−0.01 (−0.47, 0.45)
Rate of alcohol consumption up to 6-month follow-up			
Percentage days heavy drinking at 3-month follow-up	301	SMD (IV, Random, 95% CI)	−0.13 (−0.43, 0.17)
Percentage days heavy drinking at 6-month follow-up	296	SMD (IV, Random, 95% CI)	−0.08 (−0.42, 0.26)
Rate of alcohol consumption −7- to 12-month follow-up			
Percentage days heavy drinking at 9-month follow-up	288	SMD (IV, Random, 95% CI)	0.13 (−0.14, 0.40)
Percentage days heavy drinking at 12-month follow-up	282	SMD (IV, Random, 95% CI)	0.15 (−0.28, 0.58)
Amount of alcohol consumed			
Amount of alcohol consumed post-treatment	1651	SMD (IV, Random, 95% CI)	0.01 (−0.13, 0.15)
Amount of alcohol consumed up to 6-month follow-up			
At 6-month follow-up	2194	SMD (IV, Random, 95% CI)	−0.09 (−0.17, −0.00)
Amount of alcohol consumed 7- to 12-month follow-up			

Continued

Table 38: (*Continued*)

Outcome or subgroup	N	Statistical method	Effect estimate (SMD, 95% CI)
At 9-month follow-up	1615	SMD (IV, Random, 95% CI)	−0.04 (−0.15, 0.06)
At 12-month follow-up	1594	SMD (IV, Random, 95% CI)	−0.09 (−0.20, 0.01)
At 6-month follow-up	1640	SMD (IV, Random, 95% CI)	−0.09 (−0.19, 0.01)
Amount of alcohol consumed >12-month follow-up			
At 15-month follow-up	1573	SMD (IV, Random, 95% CI)	−0.04 (−0.14, 0.07)
Attrition (dropout)			
Attrition (dropout) post-treatment	1864	RR (M-H, Random, 95% CI)	1.11 (0.73, 1.70)
Attrition (dropout) up to 6-month follow-up			
At 3-month follow-up	227	RR (M-H, Random, 95% CI)	0.57 (0.19, 1.73)
At 6-month follow-up	1853	RR (M-H, Random, 95% CI)	1.21 (0.29, 5.11)
Attrition (dropout) 7- to 12-month follow-up			
At 9-month follow-up	1837	RR (M-H, Random, 95% CI)	0.37 (0.15, 0.88)
At 12-month follow-up	1930	RR (M-H, Random, 95% CI)	1.21 (0.55, 2.65)
Attrition (dropout) >12-month follow-up			
At 15-month follow-up	1594	RR (M-H, Random, 95% CI)	0.46 (0.16, 1.37)

In addition, intensive TSF was significantly more effective than standard TSF in maintaining abstinence at 12-month follow-up (RR = 0.81).

No significant difference between TSF methods was observed in attrition post-treatment or at various follow-up points up to 12 months.

Additionally, KAHLER2004 was identified as assessing brief advice to facilitate AA involvement versus a motivational enhancement approach to facilitate AA involvement. This study could not be included in analyses because data could not be extracted. However, the study reported that although AA attendance was associated with better drinking outcomes, the more intensive motivational enhancement format of facilitating involvement did not improve involvement in AA and hence did not result in better alcohol outcomes.

The quality of this evidence is *moderate*, therefore further research is likely to have an important impact on confidence in the estimate of the effect and may change the estimate (see Appendix 18c). An evidence summary of the results of the meta-analyses can be seen in Table 39.

Table 39: Comparing different formats of 12-step facilitation evidence summary

Outcome or subgroup	N	Statistical method	Effect estimate (SMD, 95% CI)
Abstinence			
PDA up to 6 months follow-up			
At 3-month follow-up	102	SMD (IV, Random, 95% CI)	−0.40 (−0.79, −0.00)
At 6-month follow-up	97	SMD (IV, Random, 95% CI)	−0.41 (−0.81, −0.01)
PDA 7- to 12-month follow-up			
At 9-month follow-up	95	SMD (IV, Random, 95% CI)	−0.57 (−0.98, −0.16)
At 12-month follow-up	95	SMD (IV, Random, 95% CI)	−0.58 (−0.99, −0.17)
Lapse or relapse			
Number of participants lapsed 7- to 12-month follow-up			
At 12-month follow-up	307	RR (M-H, Random, 95% CI)	0.81 (0.66, 1.00)
Rates of consumption			
Percentage of days heavy drinking up to 6-month follow-up			
At 3-month follow-up	102	SMD (IV, Random, 95% CI)	−0.20 (−0.59, 0.19)
At 6-month follow-up	97	SMD (IV, Random, 95% CI)	−0.07 (−0.47, 0.33)
Percentage of days heavy drinking at 7- to 12-month follow-up			
At 9-month follow-up	95	SMD (IV, Random, 95% CI)	−0.20 (−0.60, 0.20)
At 12-month follow-up	95	SMD (IV, Random, 95% CI)	−0.09 (−0.50, 0.31)
Attrition (dropout)			
Attrition (dropout) post-treatment	345	RR (M-H, Random, 95% CI)	1.01 (0.55, 1.84)
Attrition (dropout) up to 6-month follow-up			
At 3-month follow-up	111	OR (M-H, Fixed, 95% CI)	0.29 (0.06, 1.44)
At 6-month follow-up	102	OR (M-H, Fixed, 95% CI)	1.53 (0.24, 9.57)
Attrition (dropout) 7- to 12-month follow-up			
At 9-month follow-up	97	RR (M-H, Random, 95% CI)	1.02 (0.07, 15.86)
At 12-month follow-up	440	RR (M-H, Random, 95% CI)	1.04 (0.52, 2.06)

6.9 COGNITIVE BEHAVIOURAL THERAPY

6.9.1 Definition

CBT encompasses a range of therapies, in part derived from the cognitive behavioural model of affective disorders in which the patient works collaboratively with a therapist using a shared formulation to achieve specific treatment goals. Such goals may include recognising the impact of behavioural and/or thinking patterns on feeling states and encouraging alternative cognitive and/or behavioural coping skills to reduce the severity of target symptoms and problems. Cognitive behavioural therapies include standard CBT, relapse prevention, coping skills and social skills training.

Standard cognitive behavioural therapy
Standard CBT is a discrete, time-limited, structured psychological intervention, derived from a cognitive model of drug misuse (Beck *et al.*, 1993). There is an emphasis on identifying and modifying irrational thoughts, managing negative mood and intervening after a lapse to prevent a full-blown relapse.

Relapse prevention
A CBT adaptation based on the work of Marlatt and Gordon (1985), this incorporates a range of cognitive and behavioural therapeutic techniques to identify high-risk situations, alter expectancies and increase self-efficacy. This differs from standard CBT in the emphasis on training people who misuse alcohol to develop skills to identify situations or states where they are most vulnerable to alcohol use, to avoid high-risk situations, and to use a range of cognitive and behavioural strategies to cope effectively with these situations (Annis, 1986; Marlatt & Gordon, 1985).

Coping and social skills training
Coping and social skills training is a variety of CBT that is based on social learning theory of addiction and the relationship between drinking behaviour and life problems (Kadden *et al.*, 1992; Marlatt & Gordon, 1985). Treatment is manual-based (Marlatt & Gordon, 1985) and involves increasing the individual's ability to cope with high-risk social situations and interpersonal difficulties.

6.9.2 Clinical review protocol (cognitive behavioural therapies)

Information about the databases searched and the inclusion/exclusion criteria used for this Section of the guideline can be found in Chapter 3 (further information about the search for health economic evidence can be found in Section 6.21). See Table 40 below for a summary of the clinical review protocol for the review of cognitive behavioural therapies.

**Table 40: Clinical review protocol for the review of cognitive
behavioural therapies**

Electronic databases	CINAHL, EMBASE, MEDLINE, PsycINFO, Cochrane Library
Date searched	Database inception to March 2010
Study design	RCT (at least participants per arm)
Population	Adults (over 18 years old) At least 80% of the sample meet the criteria for alcohol dependence or harmful alcohol use (clinical diagnosis or drinking more than 30 drinks per week)
Excluded populations	Hazardous drinkers and those drinking fewer than 30 drinks per week Pregnant women
Interventions	Cognitive behavioural therapies
Comparator	Control or other active intervention
Outcomes	Abstinence Amount of alcohol consumed Rates of consumption Relapse (>X number of drinks or number of participants who have relapsed) Lapse (time to first drink or number of participants who have lapsed) Attrition (leaving the study early for any reason)

6.9.3   Studies considered for review

The review team conducted a systematic review of RCTs that assessed the beneficial or detrimental effects of cognitive behavioural therapies in the treatment of alcohol dependence or harmful alcohol use. See Table 41 for a summary of the study characteristics. It should be noted that some trials included in analyses were three- or four-arm trials. To avoid double counting, the number of participants in treatment conditions used in more than one comparison was divided (by half in a three-arm trial, and by three in a four-arm trial).

Twenty RCT trials relating to clinical evidence met the eligibility criteria set by the GDG, providing data on 3,970 participants. All 20 studies were published in peer-reviewed journals between 1986 and 2009. A number of studies identified in the search were initially excluded because they were not relevant to this guideline. Studies were excluded because they did not meet methodological criteria (see Chapter 3). When studies did meet basic methodological inclusion criteria, the main reasons for exclusion were not having alcohol-focused outcomes that could be used for analysis and not meeting drinking quantity/diagnosis criteria (that is, participants were not drinking enough to be categorised as harmful or dependent drinkers, or less than 80% of the sample met criteria for alcohol dependence or harmful alcohol use). Other reasons were that the study was outside the scope of this guideline, presented secondary analyses, and was drug-focused or did not differentiate between drugs and alcohol, and was focused on aftercare. A list of excluded studies can be found in Appendix 16d.

Cognitive behavioural therapies versus treatment as usual or control[35]
Three studies compared CBT with treatment as usual or control. BURTSCHEIDT2002 assessed CBT versus coping skills versus treatment as usual (unstructured, non-specific support and therapy). MONTI1993 investigated cue exposure with coping skills against control (unspecified treatment as usual and daily cravings monitoring). ROSENBLUM2005B assessed relapse prevention with MET versus control (information and referral only).

Cognitive behavioural therapies versus other active intervention
Thirteen studies assessed CBT versus another active intervention. CONNORS2001 was complex in design and investigated alcohol-focused coping skills with or without the addition of life coping skills and with or without the addition of psychoeducational interventions at different intensities. Additionally, the study investigated the difference between low- and high-intensity treatment of these conditions. The results of the 30-month follow-up were obtained from Walitzer and Connors (2007). The other studies included in this analyses were DAVIDSON2007 (broad-spectrum treatment versus MET), EASTON2007 (CBT versus TSF), ERIKSEN1986B and LITT2003 (both assessed coping skills versus group counselling), LAM2009 (coping skills versus BCT with/without parental skills training), MATCH1997 (CBT versus both MET and TSF), MORGENSTERN2007 (coping skills with MET versus MET alone), SANDAHL1998 (relapse prevention versus psychodynamic therapy), SHAKESHAFT2002 (CBT versus FRAMES), SITHARTHAN1997 (CBT versus cue exposure), VEDEL2008 (CBT versus BCT) and WALITZER2009 (coping skills versus TSF).

Comparing different formats of cognitive behavioural therapy
Six studies investigated one form of CBT versus another form of CBT. BURTSCHEIDT2001 investigated CBT versus coping skills; MARQUES2001 assessed group versus individual CBT); CONNORS2001 investigated different intensities of alcohol-focused coping skills; LITT2009 assessed a packaged CBT program versus an individual assessment treatment program, which was cognitive behavioural in nature; MONTI1990 investigated communication skills training (both with and without family therapy) as well as cognitive behavioural mood management training; and ROSENBLUM2005A investigated relapse prevention versus relapse prevention with motivational enhancements.

---

[35]Treatment as usual and control were analysed together because treatment as usual was unstructured, unspecified and brief, and similar to what would be classified as control in other studies.

Table 41: Summary of study characteristics for cognitive behavioural therapies

	Cognitive behavioural therapies versus TAU or control	Cognitive behavioural therapies versus other active intervention	Different formats of cognitive behavioural therapies
K (total N)	3 RCTs (N = 450)	13 RCTs (N = 2956)	6 RCTs (N = 771)
Study ID	(1) BURTSCHEIDT2001 (2) MONTI1993 (3) ROSENBLUM2005B	(1) CONNORS2001 (2) DAVIDSON2007 (3) EASTON2007 (4) ERIKSEN1986B (5) LAM2009 (6) LITT2003 (7) MATCH1997 (8) MORGENSTERN2007 (9) SANDAHL1998 (10) SHAKESHAFT2002 (11) SITHARTHAN1997 (12) VEDEL2008 (13) WALITZER2009	(1) BURTSCHEIDT2001 (2) MARQUES2001 (3) CONNORS2001 (4) LITT2009 (5) MONTI1990 (6) ROSENBLUM2005A
Diagnosis	(1)–(2) DSM alcohol dependent (3) Not reported	(1)–(3) DSM alcohol dependent (4) Not reported (5)–(8) DSM alcohol dependent/abuse (9) DSM alcohol dependent (10) Not reported (11) Not reported (12) DSM alcohol dependent/abuse (13) Not reported	(1)–(3) DSM/ICD alcohol dependent (4) DSM alcohol dependent/abuse (5) DSM/ICD alcohol dependent (6) DSM alcohol dependent/abuse

| Baseline severity | (1) Not reported
(2) ADS score: 20.7
SMAST* score: 9.97
DDD: 12.1 drinks, PDA: 47%
Percentage days heavy drinking: 45%
(3) Not reported | (1) Percentage of sample severe dependence: 8.3%
Percentage of sample moderate dependence: 66%
Percentage of sample mild dependence: 18.1%
(2) PDA: approximately 30%
Percentage days heavy drinking: approximately 63%
(3) Approximately 19 years of alcohol use
Alcohol use in past 28 days: approximately 6 days
(4) Previous alcoholism inpatient status: 66.7%
(5) PDA: approximately 37%
(6) Drinking days 6 months prior to intake: 72%
(7) PDA: approximately 30%
DDD: approximately 16 drinks
(8) DDD: 9.5 drinks
ADS core: 12.2
(9) Duration of alcohol dependence: 11 years
Reported morning drinking: 75.5%
(10) Weekly Australian units per week: approximately 32 units | (1) Not reported
(2) Number of drinking days in last 90 days: 49
Number of heavy drinking days in last 90 days : 34.5
Number of problem drinking days in last 90 days: 16.5
Mean weekly consumption: 36.5 drinks
SADD** score abstinence/moderate rates: 17
(3) Percentage of sample severe dependence: 8.3%
Percentage of sample moderate dependence: 66%
Percentage of sample mild dependence: 18.1%
Average monthly abstinent days: 10.1 days
Average monthly light days: 6.1 days
Average monthly moderate days: 8 days
Average monthly heavy days: 5.7 days
(4) Proportion days abstinence: 0.19 days
Proportion days heavy drinking: approximately 0.59 days
(5) Percentage of possible drinking days abstinent: approximately 43% |

Continued

Table 41: *(Continued)*

	Cognitive behavioural therapies versus TAU or control	Cognitive behavioural therapies versus other active intervention	Different formats of cognitive behavioural therapies
		(11) SADQ-C score: 18.81 Impaired Control Questionnaire (ICQ) score: 13.05 CDSES score: 35.93 Drinking days per month: 20.2 days Consumption per occasion: 8.82 drinks (12) 62% alcohol dependent 50% drank seven or more units 57% drank daily or nearly daily (13) PDA: 35.4% Percentage of days heavy drinking: 32.7%	Number of possible DDD: 11 drinks Number of actual DDD: 17 drinks Percentage possible drinking days in which heavy drinking: 45% (6) Number of days abstinent in past 30 days: 14 days ASI alcohol score: approximately 0.47
Number of sessions	Range: 6 to 26 sessions	Range: 6 to 26 sessions	Range: 12 to 23 sessions
Length of treatment	Range: 2 weeks to 6 months	Range: 10 weeks to 6 months	Range: 6 to 10 weeks
Length of follow-up	Range: 0 to 6 months	Range: 3 to 18 months	Range: 3 to 18 months
Setting	(1) Outpatient treatment centre (2) Inpatient (3) Homeless soup-kitchen	(1)–(3) Not reported (4) Inpatient (5) Not reported	(1)–(2) Outpatient treatment centre (3) Outpatient research unit (4) Outpatient treatment centre

		(6) Outpatient research unit (7)–(12) Not reported (13) Outpatient treatment centre	(5) Inpatient (6) Outpatient research unit
Treatment goal	(1)–(3) Not explicitly stated	(1) Drinking reduction/moderation (2) Abstinence or drinking reduction/moderation (3) Drinking reduction/moderation (4) Abstinence or drinking reduction/moderation (5)–(6) Not explicitly stated (7) Abstinence or drinking reduction/moderation (8) Drinking reduction/moderation (9) Drinking reduction/moderation (10) Not explicitly stated (11) Drinking reduction/moderation (12) Abstinence or drinking reduction/moderation[1] (13) Not explicitly stated	(1)–(2) Not explicitly stated (3) Drinking reduction/moderation (4)–(6) Not explicitly stated
Country	(1) Germany (2)–(3) US	(1)–(3) US (4) Norway (5)–(8) US (9) Sweden (10)–(11) Australia (12) Netherlands (13) US	(1) Germany (2) Brazil (3)–(6) US

*SMAST = Short Michigan Alcohol Screening Test; **SADD = Short Alcohol Dependence Data; [1]Guidelines were stipulated for controlled drinking.

6.9.4 Evidence summary

The GRADE profiles and associated forest plots for the comparisons can be found in Appendix 18c and Appendix 17c, respectively.

Cognitive behavioural therapies versus treatment as usual or control
Cognitive behavioural therapies were significantly better than control at reducing heavy drinking episodes but no significant difference between groups was observed for a reduction in days any alcohol is used (assessed post-treatment) or the number of participants who have lapsed and relapsed (assessed at 3-month follow-up) when compared with treatment as usual. However, resulting in a moderate effect size, cognitive behavioural therapies were significantly better than treatment as usual in reducing the number of participants who lapsed and relapsed when assessed at 6-month follow-up. No difference between groups was observed in attrition rates post-treatment or at 6-month follow-up.

The quality of this evidence is *moderate*, therefore further research is likely to have an important impact on confidence in the estimate of the effect and may change the estimate (see Appendix 18c for full GRADE profile).

One study assessing cognitive behavioural therapies versus control could not be added to the meta-analyses. Källmén and colleagues 2003 could not be included because the data was presented in an unusable format. The study reported that the control group (unstructured discussion) drank significantly less alcohol at 18-month follow-up than the group receiving coping skills. An evidence summary of the results of the meta-analyses can be seen in Table 42.

Cognitive behavioural therapies versus other active intervention
Meta-analyses results revealed no significant difference between cognitive behavioural therapies and other therapies in maintaining abstinence both post-treatment and up to 15-month follow-up. A single study, however, did favour coping skills over counselling in the number of sober days at 12-month follow-up, and another single study favouring relapse prevention over psychotherapy at 15-month follow-up. However, these single outcomes do not reflect the meta-analyses results described above. In addition, cognitive behavioural therapies were found to be more effective at maintaining abstinence/light days when assessed up to 18-month follow-up (based on data by CONNORS2001). No significant difference was observed between groups in reducing heavy drinking episodes and the amount of alcohol consumed both post-treatment and up to 18-month follow-up. A single study outcome (ERIKSEN1986B) favoured coping skills over counselling in reducing the amount of alcohol consumed, but, again, this single study was not reflective of other analyses with similar variables.

The VEDEL2008 study assessed severity of relapse in their sample. The results indicated that other active intervention (namely CBT) was more effective than couples therapy (namely BCT) in reducing occasions in which participants lapsed (drank over six drinks on one occasion) or relapsed (drank more than six drinks most

Table 42: Cognitive behavioural therapies versus TAU or control evidence summary

Outcome or subgroup	N	Statistical method	Effect estimate (SMD, 95% CI)
Rates of consumption			
Rates of consumption post-treatment			
Number of days any alcohol use	139	SMD (IV, Random, 95% CI)	−0.31 (−0.64, 0.03)
Number of days heavy alcohol use (more than 4 drinks)	46	SMD (IV, Random, 95% CI)	−0.70 (−1.30, −0.11)
Lapse or relapse			
Lapse up to 6 months follow-up			
At 3-month follow-up	34	RR (M-H, Random, 95% CI)	1.27 (0.64, 2.54)
At 6-month follow-up	137	RR (M-H, Random, 95% CI)	0.75 (0.57, 0.99)
Relapse up to 6-month follow-up			
At 3-month follow-up	30	RR (M-H, Random, 95% CI)	1.57 (0.69, 3.59)
At 6-month follow-up	133	RR (M-H, Random, 95% CI)	0.55 (0.38, 0.80)
Attrition (dropout)			
Attrition (dropout) post-treatment	324	RR (M-H, Random, 95% CI)	1.07 (0.74, 1.53)
Attrition (dropout) up to 6-month follow-up			
At 3-month follow-up	32	RR (M-H, Random, 95% CI)	Not estimable
At 6-month follow-up	135	RR (M-H, Random, 95% CI)	0.53 (0.18, 1.54)

days of the week), but no significant difference was observed in the number of participants who relapsed on a regular basis (a few times a month). It must be noted that effect sizes were small and the results of a single study cannot be generalised.

No significant difference was observed between CBT and other active therapies in attrition rates.

The quality of this evidence is *high*, therefore further research is unlikely to change confidence in the estimate of the effect. An evidence summary of the results of the meta-analyses can be seen in Table 43 and Table 44.

Comparing different formats of cognitive behavioural therapies
For maintaining abstinence, an individual assessment treatment programme was significantly more effective than a packaged CBT program when assessed post-treatment (moderate effect size, based on a single study). However, for the same comparison, no significant difference was observed between groups in reducing heavy drinking episodes. The addition of motivational enhancement to relapse prevention

Table 43: Cognitive behavioural therapies versus other interventions evidence summary (1)

Outcome or subgroup	N	Statistical method	Effect estimate (SMD, 95% CI)
Abstinence			
Abstinence post-treatment			
Days abstinent	1901	SMD (IV, Random, 95% CI)	−0.09 (−0.21, 0.03)
Abstinence up to 6-month follow-up			
PDA at 3-month follow-up	280	SMD (IV, Random, 95% CI)	0.14 (−0.23, 0.51)
PDA at 6-month follow-up	1946	SMD (IV, Random, 95% CI)	0.02 (−0.12, 0.17)
Abstinence from 7- to 12-month follow-up			
PDA at 9 months	1886	SMD (IV, Random, 95% CI)	−0.01 (−0.14, 0.13)
PDA at 12 months	1887	SMD (IV, Random, 95% CI)	0.01 (−0.12, 0.15)
Number of sober days at 12-month follow-up	23	SMD (IV, Random, 95% CI)	−1.67 (−2.65, −0.70)
Abstinence >12-month follow-up			
PDA at 15-month follow-up	1702	SMD (IV, Random, 95% CI)	−0.06 (−0.16, 0.04)
Number of days abstinent at 15-month follow-up	44	SMD (IV, Random, 95% CI)	0.64 (0.03, 1.24)
PDA at 18-month follow-up	128	SMD (IV, Random, 95% CI)	−0.22 (−0.57, 0.13)
Abstinent/light (one to three standard drinks) up to 6-month follow-up			
At 6-month follow-up	61	SMD (IV, Random, 95% CI)	−0.94 (−1.48, −0.40)
Abstinent/light (one to three standard drinks) 7 to 12-month follow-up			
At 12-month follow-up	61	SMD (IV, Random, 95% CI)	−0.84 (−1.40, −0.27)
Abstinent/light (one to three standard drinks) >12-month follow-up			
At 18-month follow-up	61	SMD (IV, Random, 95% CI)	−0.74 (−1.26, −0.21)
Lapse or relapse			
Days to first drink at 18-month follow-up	128	SMD (IV, Random, 95% CI)	0.15 (−0.20, 0.50)
Days to first heavy drinking day at 18-month follow-up	128	SMD (IV, Random, 95% CI)	−0.09 (−0.44, 0.26)
Relapse (more than six units most days of the week) post-treatment	48	RR (M-H, Random, 95% CI)	0.39 (0.18, 0.86)

Continued

Table 43: (*Continued*)

Outcome or subgroup	N	Statistical method	Effect estimate (SMD, 95% CI)
Regular relapse (more than six units a few times a month) post-treatment	48	RR (M-H, Random, 95% CI)	1.56 (0.44, 5.50)
Severe lapse (more than six units on one occasion) post-treatment	48	RR (M-H, Random, 95% CI)	2.33 (1.01, 5.38)
Rates of consumption			
Rates of consumption post-treatment			
Percentage of heavy drinking days	149	SMD (IV, Random, 95% CI)	−0.05 (−0.37, 0.27)
Rate of consumption up to 6-month follow-up			
Proportion days heavy drinking at 3-month follow-up	280	SMD (IV, Random, 95% CI)	0.18 (−0.21, 0.57)
Proportion days heavy drinking at 6-month follow-up	275	SMD (IV, Random, 95% CI)	0.15 (−0.26, 0.55)
Drinking days per month at 6-month follow-up	42	SMD (IV, Random, 95% CI)	0.61 (−0.01, 1.23)
Binge consumption (occasions in prior 30 days where at least 7 (males) or 5 (females) drinks consumed at 6-month follow-up	115	SMD (IV, Random, 95% CI)	−0.02 (−0.38, 0.35)
Rate of consumption −7- to 12-month follow-up			
Proportion days heavy drinking at 9-month follow-up	271	SMD (IV, Random, 95% CI)	−0.04 (−0.29, 0.20)
Proportion days heavy drinking at 12-month follow-up	267	SMD (IV, Random, 95% CI)	0.03 (−0.25, 0.30)
Rate of consumption at >12-month follow-up			
Days >80 g of absolute alcohol at 15-month follow-up	44	SMD (IV, Random, 95% CI)	0.06 (−0.53, 0.65)
Proportion days heavy drinking at 15 months	128	SMD (IV, Random, 95% CI)	−0.07 (−0.42, 0.27)
Proportion days heavy drinking at 18 months	190	SMD (IV, Random, 95% CI)	−0.20 (−0.50, 0.10)

Table 44: Cognitive behavioural therapies versus other interventions evidence summary (2)

Outcome or subgroup	N	Statistical method	Effect estimate (SMD, 95% CI)
Amount of alcohol consumed			
Amount of alcohol consumed post-treatment	1788	SMD (IV, Random, 95% CI)	0.02 (−0.19, 0.22)
Amount of alcohol consumed up to 6-month follow-up			
Number of participants consuming at hazardous/harmful levels weekly – at 6-month follow-up	295	RR (M-H, Random, 95% CI)	1.09 (0.80, 1.49)
Number of participants binge drinking had at least 12 binge episodes in previous 30 days – at 6-month follow-up	295	RR (M-H, Random, 95% CI)	1.12 (0.84, 1.49)
Number of participants binge drinking at all (at least one binge episode in previous 30 days) at 6-month follow-up	295	RR (M-H, Random, 95% CI)	0.95 (0.87, 1.05)
Units of alcohol per week at 5-month follow-up	48	SMD (IV, Random, 95% CI)	0.20 (−0.37, 0.77)
Units of alcohol per week at 6-month follow-up	45	SMD (IV, Random, 95% CI)	0.16 (−0.42, 0.75)
Drinks per occasion/drinking day at 6 months	1683	SMD (IV, Random, 95% CI)	0.07 (−0.13, 0.26)
Drinks per week at 6 months	115	SMD (IV, Random, 95% CI)	−0.09 (−0.46, 0.27)
Amount of alcohol consumed – 7- to 12-month follow-up			
Alcohol consumption (centilitres pure alcohol) at 12-month follow-up	24	SMD (IV, Random, 95% CI)	−1.15 (−2.02, −0.27)
DDD at 9-month follow-up	1615	SMD (IV, Random, 95% CI)	−0.03 (−0.13, 0.08)
DDD at 12-month follow-up	1683	SMD (IV, Random, 95% CI)	0.07 (−0.04, 0.17)
Amount of alcohol consumed >12-month follow-up	1618	SMD (IV, Random, 95% CI)	−0.02 (−0.12, 0.08)
Grams absolute alcohol per drinking day at 15-month follow-up	44	SMD (IV, Random, 95% CI)	−0.07 (−0.66, 0.53)
DDD at 15-month follow-up	1574	SMD (IV, Random, 95% CI)	−0.02 (−0.12, 0.09)
Attrition (dropout)			
Attrition (dropout) post-treatment	2267	RR (M-H, Random, 95% CI)	1.05 (0.61, 1.80)

Continued

Table 44: (*Continued*)

Outcome or subgroup	N	Statistical method	Effect estimate (SMD, 95% CI)
Attrition (dropout) – up to 6-month follow-up			
At 3-month follow-up	200	RR (M-H, Random, 95% CI)	1.29 (0.60, 2.78)
At 6-month follow-up	2296	RR (M-H, Random, 95% CI)	0.93 (0.59, 1.48)
Attrition (dropout) – 7- 12-month follow-up			
At 9-month follow-up	1788	RR (M-H, Random, 95% CI)	1.61 (0.76, 3.40)
At 12-month follow-up	1988	RR (M-H, Random, 95% CI)	1.27 (0.47, 3.41)
Attrition (dropout) – >12-month follow-up	1773	RR (M-H, Random, 95% CI)	1.75 (0.84, 3.64)
At 15-month follow-up	1643	RR (M-H, Random, 95% CI)	1.65 (0.77, 3.52)
At 18-month follow-up	130	RR (M-H, Random, 95% CI)	4.29 (0.21, 85.82)

did not reduce the number of possible drinking days (at 6-month follow-up) and analyses favoured standard relapse prevention (moderate effect size). Furthermore, the addition of family therapy to coping skills did not show any significant benefit. Also, no significant difference in various drinking outcomes was observed between coping skills and other types of cognitive behavioural therapies (for example, cognitive behavioural mood-management training [CBMMT] when assessed at 6-month follow-up. No difference between CBT and coping skills were observed in the number of participants who had lapsed or relapsed at 6-month follow-up. No difference in attrition rates was observed between the various types of CBT.

More intensive coping skills was significantly better than standard coping skills at maintaining abstinent/light drinking at 12-month follow-up (moderate effect size) but this benefit was no longer significant at 18-month follow-up. Individual CBT was significantly more effective than group CBT in reducing the number of heavy drinkers at 15-month follow-up.

The quality of this evidence is *moderate*, therefore further research is likely to have an important impact on confidence in the estimate of the effect. An evidence summary of the results of the meta-analyses can be seen in Table 45 and Table 46.

Table 45: Comparing different formats of CBT evidence summary

Outcome or subgroup	N	Statistical method	Effect estimate (SMD, 95% CI)
Abstinence			
Abstinence post-treatment	110	SMD (IV, Random, 95% CI)	0.39 (0.01, 0.77)
Abstinence up to 6-month follow-up			
At 15-week follow-up	186	SMD (IV, Random, 95% CI)	-0.31 $(-0.60, -0.02)$
Percentage of possible drinking days (any day not in inpatient treatment or jail) abstinent at 6-month follow-up	94	SMD (IV, Random, 95% CI)	-0.10 $(-0.52, 0.32)$
Abstinent/light (one to three standard drinks) drinking days up to 6-month follow-up			
At 6-month follow-up	61	SMD (IV, Random, 95% CI)	-0.39 $(-0.90, 0.12)$
Abstinent/light (one to three standard drinks) drinking days 7- to 12-month follow-up			
At 12-month follow-up	61	SMD (IV, Random, 95% CI)	-0.65 $(-1.21, -0.09)$
Abstinent/light (one to three standard drinks) drinking days >12-month follow-up			
At 18-month follow-up	61	SMD (IV, Random, 95% CI)	-0.38 $(-0.96, 0.20)$
Rates of consumption			
Rates of consumption post-treatment			
Proportion of heavy drinking days (men more than six and women more than four drinks)	110	SMD (IV, Random, 95% CI)	0.34 $(-0.04, 0.72)$
Rates of consumption up to 6-month follow-up			
Percentage of possible days (any day not in inpatient treatment or jail) heavy (more than six) drinking at 6-month follow-up	94	SMD (IV, Random, 95% CI)	-0.22 $(-0.65, 0.20)$
Rates of consumption >12-month follow-up			
Number of drinking days at 15-month follow-up	106	SMD (IV, Random, 95% CI)	-0.03 $(-0.41, 0.35)$
Number of problem drinking days at 15-month follow-up	106	SMD (IV, Random, 95% CI)	0.24 $(-0.14, 0.62)$
Number of heavy drinking days at 15-month follow-up	106	SMD (IV, Random, 95% CI)	0.37 $(-0.01, 0.75)$
Amount of alcohol consumed			
Amount of alcohol consumed up until 6-month follow-up			
Number of drinks per possible drinking day (any day not in inpatient treatment or jail) at 6-month follow-up	94	SMD (IV, Random, 95% CI)	-0.30 $(-0.73, 0.13)$
Number of actual DDD at 6-month follow-up	94	SMD (IV, Random, 95% CI)	-0.49 $(-1.44, 0.47)$

Table 46: Comparing different formats of CBT evidence summary

Outcome or subgroup	N	Statistical method	Effect estimate (SMD, 95% CI)
Lapse or relapse/ other outcomes			
Number of participants lapsed – up to 6-month follow-up	63	RR (M-H, Random, 95% CI)	1.09 (0.70, 1.70)
At 6 months	63	RR (M-H, Random, 95% CI)	1.09 (0.70, 1.70)
Number of participants relapse – up to 6-month follow-up	63	RR (M-H, Random, 95% CI)	1.03 (0.53, 2.03)
At 6 months	63	RR (M-H, Random, 95% CI)	1.03 (0.53, 2.03)
Number of days to first drink (lapse) up until 6-month follow-up	94	SMD (IV, Random, 95% CI)	0.19 (-0.23, 0.61)
At 6-month follow-up	94	SMD (IV, Random, 95% CI)	0.19 (-0.23, 0.61)
Number of days to first heavy drink (relapse) up until 6-month follow-up	94	SMD (IV, Random, 95% CI)	0.11 (-0.31, 0.53)
At 6-month follow-up	94	SMD (IV, Random, 95% CI)	0.11 (-0.31, 0.53)
Number heavy drinkers more than 20 drinks per week and more than 10% heavy days (five or more drinks per occasion) at 15-month follow-up	100	RR (M-H, Random, 95% CI)	2.86 (1.26, 6.48)
Attrition (dropout)			
Attrition (dropout) post-treatment	204	RR (M-H, Random, 95% CI)	0.87 (0.44, 1.71)
Attrition (dropout) up to 6-month follow-up	515	RR (M-H, Random, 95% CI)	1.07 (0.69, 1.68)
At 15-week follow-up	230	RR (M-H, Random, 95% CI)	1.11 (0.65, 1.90)
At 6 months	285	RR (M-H, Random, 95% CI)	0.99 (0.44, 2.23)
Attrition (dropout) 7- to 12-month follow-up	132	RR (M-H, Random, 95% CI)	0.89 (0.06, 13.57)
At 12-month follow-up	132	RR (M-H, Random, 95% CI)	0.89 (0.06, 13.57)
Attrition (dropout) >12-month follow-up	285	RR (M-H, Random, 95% CI)	0.99 (0.42, 2.35)
At 15-month follow-up	155	RR (M-H, Random, 95% CI)	0.87 (0.55, 1.39)
At 18-month follow-up	130	RR (M-H, Random, 95% CI)	4.43 (0.22, 88.74)

6.10   BEHAVIOURAL THERAPIES (EXCLUDING CONTINGENCY MANAGEMENT)[36]

6.10.1   Definition

Behavioural interventions use behavioural theories of conditioning to help achieve abstinence from drinking by creating negative experiences/events in the presence of

---

[36]See Section 6.11 for a review of contingency management.

alcohol, and positive experiences/events in alcohol's absence. Behavioural therapies considered for review included cue exposure, behavioural self-control training, aversion therapy and contingency management. Variants of two therapies (cue exposure and behavioural self-control training) which were based on a similar theoretical understanding of the nature of alcohol misuse, were considered as a single entity for the purposes of the review. Contingency management, although a behavioural intervention, was analysed separately because it is based on the classic reinforcement model and has no alcohol specific formulation (see Section 6.11 for evidence review). Aversion therapy was excluded because it is no longer routinely used in alcohol-misuse treatment in the UK.

Cue exposure

Cue-exposure treatment for alcohol misuse is based on both learning theory and social learning theory models and suggests that environmental cues associated with drinking can elicit conditioned responses, which can in turn lead to a relapse (Niaura *et al.*, 1988). The first case study using cue exposure treatment for excessive alcohol consumption was reported by Hodgson and Rankin (1976). Treatment is designed to reduce cravings for alcohol by repeatedly exposing the service user to alcohol-related cues until they 'habituate' to the cues and can hence maintain self-control in a real-life situation where these cues are present.

Behavioural self-control training

Behavioural self-control training is also referred to as 'behavioural self-management training' and is based on the techniques described by Miller and Munóz (1976). Patients are taught to set limits for drinking and self-monitor drinking episodes, undergo refusal-skills training and training for coping with behaviours in high-risk relapse situations. Behavioural self-control training is focused on a moderation goal rather than abstinence.

6.10.2   Clinical review protocol (behavioural therapies)

Information about the databases searched and the inclusion/exclusion criteria used for this section of the guideline can be found in Appendix 16d (further information about the search for health economic evidence can be found in Section 6.21). See Table 47, below, for a summary of the clinical review protocol for the review of behavioural therapies.

6.10.3   Studies considered for review

The review team conducted a systematic review of RCTs that assessed the beneficial or detrimental effects of behavioural therapies in the treatment of alcohol dependence or harmful alcohol use. See Table 48 for a summary of the study characteristics. It should be noted that some trials included in analyses were three- or four-arm trials.

Table 47: Clinical review protocol for the review of behavioural therapies

Electronic databases	CINAHL, EMBASE, MEDLINE, PsycINFO, Cochrane Library
Date searched	Database inception to March 2010
Study design	RCT (at least ten participants per arm)
Population	Adults (over 18 years old) At least 80% of the sample meet the criteria for alcohol dependence or harmful alcohol use (clinical diagnosis or drinking more than 30 drinks per week)
Excluded populations	Hazardous drinkers and those drinking fewer than 30 drinks per week Pregnant women
Interventions	Behavioural self-management, behavioural self-management training, behavioural self-control training, cue exposure (alone or with CBT or coping skills), moderation-oriented cue exposure
Comparator	Control or other active intervention
Outcomes	Abstinence Amount of alcohol consumed Rates of consumption Relapse (>X number of drinks or number of participants who have relapsed) Lapse (time to first drink or number of participants who have lapsed) Attrition (leaving the study early for any reason)

To avoid double counting, the number of participants in treatment conditions used in more than one comparison was divided (by half in a three-arm trial, and by three in a four-arm trial).

Six RCT trials relating to clinical evidence met the eligibility criteria set by the GDG, providing data on 527 participants. All six studies were published in peer-reviewed journals between 1988 and 2006. A number of studies identified in the search were initially excluded because they were not relevant to this guideline. Studies were excluded because they did not meet the methodological criteria (see Chapter 3). When studies did meet basic methodological inclusion criteria, the main reasons for exclusion were not having alcohol-focused outcomes that could be used for analysis, and not meeting drinking quantity/diagnosis criteria, that is, participants were not drinking enough to be categorised as harmful or dependent drinkers or less than 80% of the sample meet criteria for alcohol dependence or harmful alcohol use. A list of excluded studies can be found in Appendix 16d.

Table 48: Summary of study characteristics for behavioural therapies

	Behavioural therapies versus control/TAU	Behavioural therapies versus other active intervention	Different formats of behavioural therapy
K (total N)	2 RCTs (N = 134)	4 RCTs (N = 3420)	2 RCTs (N = 199)
Study ID	(1) ALDEN1988 (2) MONTI1993	(1) ALDEN1988 (2) KAVANAGH2006 (3) SITHARTHAN1997 (4) WALITZER2004	(1) HEATHER2000 (2) KAVANAGH2006
Diagnosis	(1) Not reported (2) DSM alcohol dependent	(1) Not reported (2) DSM alcohol dependent (3) Not reported (4) 85% had low level alcohol dependence and 15% had moderate levels	(1) Not reported (2) DSM alcohol dependent
Baseline severity	(1) Consuming >84 standard ethanol units per week (2) ADS score: 20.7 SMAST score: 9.97 DDD: 12.1; abstinent days: 47%; heavy drinking days: 45%	(1) Consuming >84 standard ethanol units per week (2) SADQ-C score: approximately 13.7 AUDIT score: approximately 28 Weekly alcohol consumption: approximately 37 (3) SADQ-C score: 18.81 ICQ score: 13.05 CDSES* score: 35.93 Drinking days per month: 20.2; consumption per occasion: 8.82 (4) ADS score: 8.4 Abstinent days/month: 11.0; Frequency of more than six drinks per drinking period per month: 5.1	(1) SADQ-C score: 18.7 APQ score: 10.1 DDD: 19.96; abstinent days: 19.14% (2) SADQ-C score: approximately 13.7 AUDIT score: approximately 28 Weekly alcohol consumption: approximately 37
Number of sessions	Range: 6 to 12	Range: 6 to 12	8 sessions
Length of treatment	Range: 6 to 12 weeks	Range: 6 to 12 weeks	8 weeks
Length of follow-up	Range: 6 to 24 months	Range: 3 to 12 months	Range: 3 to 12 months
Setting	(1) Outpatient clinical research unit (2) Inpatient VA medical centre	(1)–(4) Outpatient clinical research unit	(1)–(2) Outpatient clinical research unit
Treatment goal	(1) Drinking reduction/moderation (2) Not explicitly stated	(1)–(4) Drinking reduction/moderation	(1)–(2) Drinking reduction/moderation
Country	(1) Canada (2) US	(1)–(3) Australia (4) US	(1) UK (2) Australia

Note. *CDSES = Controlled Drinking Self-Efficacy Scale.

Behavioural therapies versus control
Of the six included trials, there were two involving a comparison of behavioural therapies versus control which met criteria for inclusion. ALDEN1988 assessed behavioural self-management training versus waitlist control and MONTI1993 assessed cue exposure with coping skills versus control (treatment as usual and daily cravings monitoring). The included studies were conducted between 1988 and 1993.

Behavioural therapies versus other active interventions
Of the six included trials, four trials that evaluated behavioural therapies versus other active interventions met criteria for inclusion. Behavioural and other active therapies were as follows: ALDEN1988 (behavioural self-management versus developmental counselling); KAVANAGH2006 (cue exposure plus CBT versus emotional cue exposure plus CBT); SITHARTHAN1997 (cue exposure versus CBT); WALITZER2004 (behavioural self management versus BCT with alcohol-focused spousal involvement and alcohol-focused spousal involvement alone). The included studies were conducted between 1988 and 2006.

Comparing different formats of behavioural therapy
Of the six included trials, two trials that assessed one type of behavioural therapy versus another met criteria for inclusion. The behavioural therapies in the HEATHER2000 study were moderation-oriented cue exposure and behavioural self-control training. In the KAVANAGH2006 study, they were cue exposure (plus CBT) and emotional cue exposure (plus CBT). The included studies were conducted between 2000 and 2006.

6.10.4   Evidence summary

The GRADE profiles and associated forest plots for the comparisons can be found in Appendix 18c and Appendix 17c, respectively.

Behavioural therapies versus control/treatment as usual
The review evidence indicated that behavioural therapies were more effective than control in reducing the amount of alcohol consumed (SMD = −0.97, large effect size) and maintaining controlled drinking (SMD = −0.60, medium effect size) when assessed post-treatment. However, it must be noted that this was based on a single study.

No significant difference was observed between behavioural therapies and control in maintaining abstinence when assessed post-treatment. Furthermore, no significant difference could be found between behavioural therapies and control in the number of participants who lapsed or relapsed up to 6-month follow-up. In addition, there was no significant difference between behavioural therapies and control in attrition rates.

The quality of this evidence is *moderate*, therefore further research is likely to have an important impact on confidence in the estimate of the effect. An evidence summary of the results of the meta-analyses can be seen in Table 49.

Table 49: Behavioural therapy versus TAU or control evidence summary

Outcome or subgroup	N	Statistical method	Effect estimate (SMD, 95% CI)
Abstinence			
Abstinent days per week post-treatment	94	SMD (IV, Random, 95% CI)	−0.37 (−0.79, 0.04)
Amount of alcohol consumed			
Total weekly consumption post-treatment	94	SMD (IV, Random, 95% CI)	−0.97 (−1.40, −0.54)
Lapse or relapse			
Lapse up to 6-month follow-up			
At 0 to 3 months	34	RR (M-H, Random, 95% CI)	1.27 (0.64, 2.54)
At 3 to 6 months	34	RR (M-H, Random, 95% CI)	0.57 (0.29, 1.10)
Relapse up to 6-month follow-up			
At 0 to 3 months	34	RR (M-H, Random, 95% CI)	1.60 (0.68, 3.79)
At 3 to 6 months	34	RR (M-H, Random, 95% CI)	0.63 (0.25, 1.61)
Rates of consumption			
Controlled (three or more standard drinks) per week at post-treatment	94	SMD (IV, Random, 95% CI)	−0.60 (−1.02, −0.18)
Attrition (dropout)			
Attrition (dropout) post-treatment	34	RR (M-H, Random, 95% CI)	0.44 (0.04, 4.45)
Attrition (dropout) up to 6-month follow-up			
At 3 months	32	RR (M-H, Random, 95% CI)	Not estimable
At 6 months	32	RR (M-H, Random, 95% CI)	3.95 (0.20, 76.17)

Behavioural therapy versus other active intervention

The review evidence indicated that behavioural therapies were not as effective as other interventions (in this case, couples-based therapies) in maintaining abstinent/light drinking days up to 12-month follow-up. In addition, there was no significant difference between behavioural therapies and counselling in maintaining abstinence both post-treatment and up to 24-month follow-up.

No difference was observed between behavioural therapies and other active interventions (for example, CBT) in reducing the amount of alcohol consumed up to 24-month follow-up. However, one study (SITHARTHAN1997) showed a medium effect size favouring cue exposure over CBT in reducing drinks per occasion at 6-month follow-up.

Behavioural therapies were not as effective as other active interventions (namely couples therapies) in reducing heavy drinking days. Medium to high effects favouring couples therapy were found at all assessment points up to 12-month follow-up.

The review results revealed that other therapies (that is, CBT and counselling) had significantly less post-treatment attrition than behavioural therapies. However, no significant difference was observed between treatments at follow-up (3 to 24 months).

The quality of this evidence is *moderate,* therefore further research is likely to have an important impact on confidence in the estimate of the effect. An evidence summary of the results of the meta-analyses can be seen in Table 50.

Comparing different formats of behavioural therapy
The clinical evidence indicates that there was no significant difference between cue exposure and BSCT in maintaining abstinence post-treatment or at 6-month follow-up. Furthermore, no significant difference was observed between cue exposure and emotional cue exposure in reducing the amount of alcohol consumed at 6- to 12-month follow-up. In line with this, no significant difference was observed between moderation-oriented cue exposure and behaviour self-control training in reducing alcohol consumption when assessed at 6-month follow-up.

No difference was observed between behavioural therapies in attrition both at post-treatment and 6-month follow-up.

The quality of this evidence is *moderate,* therefore further research is likely to have an important impact on confidence in the estimate of the effect. An evidence summary of the results of the meta-analyses can be seen in Table 51.

6.11 CONTINGENCY MANAGEMENT

6.11.1 Definition

Contingency management provides a system of reinforcement designed to make continual alcohol use less attractive and abstinence more attractive. There are four main methods of providing incentives:

- *Voucher-based reinforcement*: people who misuse alcohol receive vouchers with various monetary values (usually increasing in value after successive periods of abstinence) for providing biological samples (usually urine) that are negative for alcohol. These vouchers are withheld when the biological sample indicates recent alcohol use. Once earned, vouchers are exchanged for goods or services that are compatible with an alcohol-free lifestyle.
- *Prize-based reinforcement*: This is more formally referred to as the 'variable magnitude of reinforcement procedure' (Prendergast *et al.*, 2006). Participants receive draws, often from a number of slips of paper kept in a fishbowl, for providing a negative biological specimen. Provision of a specimen indicating recent alcohol use results in the withholding of draws. Each draw has a chance of winning a 'prize', and the value of which varies. Typically, about half the draws say 'Good job!'. The other half results in the earning of a prize, which may range in value from £1 to £100 (Prendergast *et al.*, 2006).

Table 50: Behavioural therapy versus other intervention evidence summary

Outcome or subgroup	N	Statistical method	Effect estimate (SMD, 95% CI)
Abstinence			
Abstinence post-treatment			
PDA per week	73	SMD (IV, Random, 95% CI)	0.11 (−0.35, 0.57)
Controlled (three or more standard drinks) per week post-treatment	73	SMD (IV, Random, 95% CI)	0.00 (−0.46, 0.47)
Abstinence up to 6-month follow-up			
PDA/light per month at 3-month follow-up	63	SMD (IV, Random, 95% CI)	0.77 (0.23, 1.31)
PDA/light per month at 6-month follow-up	83	SMD (IV, Random, 95% CI)	0.49 (0.06, 0.93)
Abstinence 7- to 12-month follow-up			
PDA/light per month at 9-month follow-up	61	SMD (IV, Random, 95% CI)	0.60 (0.05, 1.15)
PDA/light per month at 12-month follow-up	61	SMD (IV, Random, 95% CI)	0.54 (−0.01, 1.09)
Abstinent days per week at 12-month follow-up	105	SMD (IV, Random, 95% CI)	0.22 (−0.17, 0.60)
Controlled (three or more standard drinks) per week at 12-month follow-up	105	SMD (IV, Random, 95% CI)	0.19 (−0.19, 0.57)
Abstinence >12-month follow-up			
Abstinent days per week at 24-month follow-up	93	SMD (IV, Random, 95% CI)	0.14 (−0.26, 0.55)
Controlled (three or more standard drinks) per week at 24-month follow-up	93	SMD (IV, Random, 95% CI)	0.28 (−0.13, 0.69)
Amount of alcohol consumed			
Amount of alcohol consumed post-treatment	73	SMD (IV, Random, 95% CI)	−0.12 (−0.59, 0.34)
Total weekly alcohol consumption (standard drinks) post-assessment	73	SMD (IV, Random, 95% CI)	−0.12 (−0.59, 0.34)
Amount of alcohol consumed up to 6-month follow-up			
Total weekly alcohol consumption at 3-month follow-up	164	SMD (IV, Random, 95% CI)	0.12 (−0.21, 0.44)
Drinks per occasion at 6-month follow-up	42	SMD (IV, Random, 95% CI)	−0.66 (−1.29, −0.04)
Total weekly alcohol consumption at 6-month follow-up	164	SMD (IV, Random, 95% CI)	0.14 (−0.19, 0.46)
Amount of alcohol consumed per week 7- to 12-month follow-up			

Continued

Table 50: (*Continued*)

Outcome or subgroup	N	Statistical method	Effect estimate (SMD, 95% CI)
Total weekly alcohol consumption at 9-month follow-up	164	SMD (IV, Random, 95% CI)	0.05 (−0.28, 0.37)
Total weekly alcohol consumption at 12-month follow-up	269	SMD (IV, Random, 95% CI)	0.18 (−0.07, 0.42)
Amount of alcohol consumed per week >12-month follow-up	105	SMD (IV, Random, 95% CI)	0.08 (−0.31, 0.46)
Total weekly alcohol consumption at 24 months follow-up	105	SMD (IV, Random, 95% CI)	0.08 (−0.31, 0.46)
Rates of consumption			
Rates of consumption up to 6-month follow-up			
Percentage of days heavy drinking (more than six drinks per day) at 3-month follow-up	64	SMD (IV, Random, 95% CI)	0.96 (0.42, 1.51)
Percentage of days heavy drinking (more than six drinks per day) at 6-month follow-up	63	SMD (IV, Random, 95% CI)	0.59 (0.06, 1.13)
Drinking days per month at 6-month follow-up	42	SMD (IV, Random, 95% CI)	−0.61 (−1.23, 0.01)
Rates of consumption up to 7- to 12-month follow-up			
Percentage of days heavy drinking (more than six drinks per day) at 9-month follow-up	62	SMD (IV, Random, 95% CI)	0.85 (0.30, 1.41)
Percentage of days heavy drinking (more than six drinks per day) at 12-month follow-up	62	SMD (IV, Random, 95% CI)	0.66 (0.12, 1.21)
Attrition (dropout) post-treatment	306	RR (M-H, Random, 95% CI)	1.73 (1.13, 2.63)
Attrition (dropout) up to 6-month follow-up			
At 3 months	64	RR (M-H, Random, 95% CI)	0.61 (0.03, 13.87)
At 6 month	110	RR (M-H, Random, 95% CI)	1.55 (0.35, 6.82)
Attrition (dropout) – 7- to 12-month follow-up	251	RR (M-H, Random, 95% CI)	1.49 (0.72, 3.07)
At 9 months	63	RR (M-H, Random, 95% CI)	3.10 (0.41, 23.61)
At 12 months	188	RR (M-H, Random, 95% CI)	1.34 (0.61, 2.90)
Attrition (dropout) – >12-month follow-up	105	RR (M-H, Random, 95% CI)	0.98 (0.34, 2.85)
At 24 months	105	RR (M-H, Random, 95% CI)	0.98 (0.34, 2.85)

Table 51: Comparing various formats of behavioural therapy evidence summary

Outcome or subgroup	N	Statistical method	Effect estimate (SMD, 95% CI)
Abstinence			
Abstinent post-treatment (MOCE versus BSCT)	77	SMD (IV, Random, 95% CI)	−0.23 (−0.68, 0.22)
Abstinence up to 6-month follow-up			
At 6-month follow-up (MOCE versus BSCT)	91	RR (M-H, Random, 95% CI)	0.90 (0.19, 4.21)
Amount of alcohol consumed			
Amount of alcohol consumed up to 6-month follow-up			
At 3-month follow-up (CE versus ECE)	108	SMD (IV, Random, 95% CI)	−0.02 (−0.40, 0.36)
At 6-month follow-up (CE versus ECE)	108	SMD (IV, Random, 95% CI)	−0.05 (−0.43, 0.33)
Amount of alcohol consumed 7- to 12-month follow-up			
DDD at 6-month follow-up (MOCE versus BSCT)	77	SMD (IV, Random, 95% CI)	0.41 (−0.04, 0.86)
Amount of alcohol consumed at 9 months (CE versus ECE)	108	SMD (IV, Random, 95% CI)	−0.01 (−0.39, 0.37)
Amount of alcohol consumed at 12-month follow-up (CE versus ECE)	108	SMD (IV, Random, 95% CI)	−0.02 (−0.40, 0.36)
Attrition (dropout)			
Attrition (dropout) post-treatment (CE versus ECE)	108	RR (M-H, Random, 95% CI)	0.75 (0.50, 1.14)
Attrition (dropout) up to 6-month follow-up			
At 6-month follow-up (MOCE versus BSCT)	91	RR (M-H, Random, 95% CI)	1.61 (0.59, 4.44)

Note. ECE = emotional cue exposure; MOCE = moderation-oriented cue exposure.

- *Cash incentives*: people who misuse alcohol receive cash (usually of a relatively low value, for example, £1.50 to £10) for performing the target behaviour, such as submitting a urine sample negative for alcohol or compliance with particular interventions. Cash incentives are withheld when the target behaviour is not performed.
- *Clinic privileges*: participants receive clinic privileges for performing the target behaviour, for example providing a negative biological sample. But these privileges are withheld when the target behaviour is not performed. An example of a clinic privilege is a take-home methadone dose (for example, Stitzer *et al.*, 1992).

This incentive is appropriate for drug treatment for substances such as heroin but is not applicable to alcohol treatment.

6.11.2 Clinical review protocol (contingency management)

Information about the databases searched and the inclusion/exclusion criteria used for this section of the guideline can be found in Chapter 3 (further information about the search for health economic evidence can be found in Section 6.21). See Table 52 below for a summary of the clinical review protocol for the review of contingency management).

6.11.3 Studies considered for review

The review team conducted a systematic review of RCTs that assessed the beneficial or detrimental effects of contingency management in the treatment of alcohol

Table 52: Clinical review protocol for the review of contingency management

Electronic databases	CINAHL, EMBASE, MEDLINE, PsycINFO, Cochrane Library
Date searched	Database inception to March 2010
Study design	RCT (at least ten participants per arm)
Population	Adults (over 18 years old) At least 80% of the sample meet the criteria for alcohol dependence or harmful alcohol use (clinical diagnosis or drinking more than 30 drinks per week)
Excluded populations	Hazardous drinkers and those drinking fewer than 30 drinks per week Pregnant women
Interventions	Contingency management
Comparator	Control or other active intervention
Outcomes	Abstinence Amount of alcohol consumed Rates of consumption Relapse (>X number of drinks or number of participants who have relapsed) Lapse (time to first drink or number of participants who have lapsed) Attrition (leaving the study early for any reason)

dependence or harmful alcohol use. See Table 53 for a summary of the study characteristics.

Three trials relating to clinical evidence met the eligibility criteria set by the GDG, providing data on 355 participants. All three studies were published in peer-reviewed journals between 2000 and 2007. A number of studies identified in the search were initially excluded because they were not relevant to this guideline. Studies were excluded because they did not meet methodological criteria (see Chapter 3). When studies did meet basic methodological inclusion criteria, the main reason for exclusion was that the participants in the study did not meet drinking quantity/diagnosis criteria (that is, participants were not drinking enough to be categorised as harmful or dependent drinkers, or less than 80% of the sample meet criteria for alcohol dependence or harmful alcohol use). Another reason was that the study was drug-focused or did not differentiate between drugs and alcohol. A list of excluded studies can be found in Appendix 16d.

Table 53: Summary of study characteristics for contingency management

	Contingency management versus control	Contingency management versus TAU	Contingency management versus other active intervention
K (total N)	1 RCTs (N = 139)	2 RCTs (N = 145)	1 RCTs (N = 141)
Study ID	LITT2007	(1) ALESSI2007 (2) PETRY2000	LITT2007
Diagnosis	DSM alcohol dependent/abuse	(1) DSM alcohol dependent/abuse (2) DSM alcohol dependent	DSM alcohol dependent/abuse
Baseline severity	Drinking days in past 3 months: 72%	(2) Years of alcohol dependence: 23.5 years	Drinking days in past 3 months: 72%
Number of sessions	12 sessions	(1) Rewards for negative sample and attendance (2) Rewards for negative sample	12 sessions
Length of treatment	12 weeks	(1)–(2) Not applicable	12 weeks
Length of follow-up	27 months	Range: Post-treatment only	27 months
Setting	Outpatient treatment centre	(1)–(2) Outpatient treatment centre	Outpatient treatment centre
Treatment goal	Not explicitly stated	(1)–(2) Abstinence	Not explicitly stated
Country	US	(1)–(2) US	US

Contingency management versus control
Of the three included trials, there was only one involving a comparison between contingency management and control that met the criteria for inclusion. LITT2007 assessed contingency management with network support versus case management (an active control).

Contingency management versus treatment as usual
Of the three included trials, two trials evaluating contingency management versus treatment as usual (standard care) met criteria for inclusion. Both ALESSI2007 and PETRY2000 assessed contingency management with standard care versus standard care alone. The included studies were conducted between 2000 and 2007.

Contingency management versus other active intervention
Of the three included trials, one trial that assessed contingency management versus another active intervention met criteria for inclusion. The treatment conditions in LITT2007 were contingency management with network support versus network support alone.

6.11.4   Evidence summary

The GRADE profiles and associated forest plots for the comparisons can be found in Appendix 18c and Appendix 17c, respectively.

Contingency management versus control
The review evidence indicated that contingency management (with network support) was more effective at maintaining abstinence than control post-treatment (large effect size) and up to 15-month follow-up (medium effect size). However, no significant differences were observed between contingency management with network support and control for follow-up periods greater than 15 months. It should be noted that this analyses was based on the LITT2007 study only.

Contingency management (with network support) was more effective than control (low to medium effect size) at reducing drinking quantity when assessed at 6-, 9- and 21-month follow-up. However, no significant difference was found between treatment conditions post-treatment at 12-, 15-, 18-, 24- and 27-month follow-up.

No significant difference was observed between conditions in attrition post-treatment and at all follow-up points up to 27 months.

The quality of this evidence is *moderate*, therefore further research is likely to have an important impact on confidence in the estimate of the effect. An evidence summary of the results of the meta-analyses can be seen in Table 54.

Contingency management versus treatment as usual (standard care)
The clinical review revealed no significant beneficial effect of adding contingency management to standard care in maintaining abstinence when assessed post-treatment. However, the addition of contingency management to standard care was

Table 54: Contingency management versus control evidence summary

Outcome or subgroup	N	Statistical method	Effect estimate (SMD, 95% CI)
Abstinence			
Abstinence post-treatment			
PDA post-treatment	114	SMD (IV, Random, 95% CI)	−0.80 (−1.18, −0.42)
Abstinence up to 6-month follow-up			
At 6-month follow-up	114	SMD (IV, Random, 95% CI)	−0.68 (−1.06, −0.31)
Abstinence 7- to 12-month follow-up			
At 9-month follow-up	114	SMD (IV, Random, 95% CI)	−0.58 (−0.96, −0.21)
At 12-month follow-up	114	SMD (IV, Random, 95% CI)	−0.39 (−0.76, −0.02)
Abstinence >12-month follow-up			
At 15-month follow-up	114	SMD (IV, Random, 95% CI)	−0.50 (−0.87, −0.12)
At 18-month follow-up	114	SMD (IV, Random, 95% CI)	0.10 (−0.27, 0.47)
At 21-month follow-up	114	SMD (IV, Random, 95% CI)	−0.15 (−0.52, 0.22)
At 24-month follow-up	114	SMD (IV, Random, 95% CI)	−0.24 (−0.61, 0.12)
At 27-month follow-up	114	SMD (IV, Random, 95% CI)	0.09 (−0.27, 0.46)
Amount of alcohol consumed			
Amount of alcohol consumed (DDD) post-treatment	114	SMD (IV, Random, 95% CI)	−0.25 (−0.61, 0.12)
Amount of alcohol consumed (DDD) up to 6-month follow-up	114		
At 6-month follow-up	114	SMD (IV, Random, 95% CI)	−0.66 (−1.04, −0.28)
Amount of alcohol consumed (DDD) 7- to 12-month follow-up			
At 9-month follow-up	114	SMD (IV, Random, 95% CI)	−0.38 (−0.75, −0.01)
At 12-month follow-up	114	SMD (IV, Random, 95% CI)	−0.10 (−0.47, 0.26)
Amount of alcohol consumed (DDD) >12-month follow-up			
At 15-month follow-up	114	SMD (IV, Random, 95% CI)	−0.11 (−0.48, 0.26)
At 18-month follow-up	114	SMD (IV, Random, 95% CI)	−0.26 (−0.63, 0.11)
At 21-month follow-up	114	SMD (IV, Random, 95% CI)	−0.53 (−0.90, −0.16)
At 24-month follow-up	114	SMD (IV, Random, 95% CI)	−0.10 (-0.47, 0.27)
At 27-month follow-up	114	SMD (IV, Random, 95% CI)	0.13 (−0.23, 0.50)
Attrition (dropout)			
Attrition (dropout) post-treatment	139	RR (M-H, Random, 95% CI)	1.23 (0.35, 4.40)

Continued

Table 54: (*Continued*)

Outcome or subgroup	N	Statistical method	Effect estimate (SMD, 95% CI)
Attrition (dropout) up to 6-month follow-up			
At 6-month follow-up	130	RR (M-H, Random, 95% CI)	2.00 (0.19, 21.52)
Attrition (dropout) 7- to 12-month follow-up			
At 9-month follow-up	127	RR (M-H, Random, 95% CI)	7.11 (0.37, 134.89)
At 12-month follow-up	124	RR (M-H, Random, 95% CI)	Not estimable
Attrition (dropout) >12-month follow-up			
At 18-month follow-up	123	RR (M-H, Random, 95% CI)	1.08 (0.07, 16.95)
At 27-month follow-up	117	RR (M-H, Random, 95% CI)	2.18 (0.20, 23.37)

beneficial in reducing the number of participants who relapsed to heavy drinking. Furthermore, the addition of contingency management to standard care was beneficial in reducing attrition rates.

The quality of this evidence is *moderate*, therefore further research is likely to have an important impact on confidence in the estimate of the effect. An evidence summary of the results of the meta-analyses can be seen in Table 55.

Table 55: Contingency management versus standard care (TAU) evidence summary

Outcome or subgroup	N	Statistical method	Effect estimate (SMD, 95% CI)
Abstinence			
Abstinence post-treatment			
Longest duration abstinent (weeks) post-treatment	103	SMD (IV, Random, 95% CI)	-0.27 (-0.66, 0.12)
Lapse or relapse			
Number relapsed to heavy drinking at end of treatment	42	RR (M-H, Random, 95% CI)	0.43 (0.19, 0.98)
Number lapsed (non-abstinent) at the end of treatment	42	RR (M-H, Random, 95% CI)	0.52 (0.25, 1.09)
Attrition (dropout)			
Attrition (dropout) abstinence post-treatment	145	RR (M-H, Random, 95% CI)	0.19 (0.07, 0.52)

Contingency management versus other active interventions
The addition of contingency management to network support was not beneficial in maintaining abstinence both post-treatment and up to 9-month follow-up. However, network support without contingency management was more effective at maintaining abstinence at 12- to 24-month follow-up.

The quality of this evidence is *moderate*, therefore further research is likely to have an important impact on confidence in the estimate of the effect. An evidence summary of the results of the meta-analyses can be seen in Table 56.

Table 56: Contingency management versus other intervention evidence summary

Outcome or subgroup	N	Statistical method	Effect estimate (SMD, 95% CI)
Abstinence			
Abstinence post-treatment			
PDA post-treatment	112	SMD (IV, Random, 95% CI)	−0.12 (−0.49, 0.25)
Abstinence up to 6-month follow-up			
At 6-month follow-up	112	SMD (IV, Random, 95% CI)	0.13 (−0.24, 0.50)
Abstinence 7- to 12-month follow-up			
At 9-month follow-up	112	SMD (IV, Random, 95% CI)	0.19 (−0.18, 0.56)
At 12-month follow-up	112	SMD (IV, Random, 95% CI)	0.37 (−0.00, 0.75)
Abstinence >12-month follow-up			
At 15-month follow-up	112	SMD (IV, Random, 95% CI)	0.35 (−0.02, 0.72)
At 18-month follow-up	112	SMD (IV, Random, 95% CI)	0.70 (0.32, 1.08)
At 21-month follow-up	112	SMD (IV, Random, 95% CI)	0.37 (−0.01, 0.74)
At 24-month follow-up	112	SMD (IV, Random, 95% CI)	0.48 (0.11, 0.86)
At 27-month follow-up	112	SMD (IV, Random, 95% CI)	0.84 (0.45, 1.22)
Amount of alcohol consumed			
Amount of alcohol consumed (DDD) post-treatment	114	SMD (IV, Random, 95% CI)	−0.36 (−0.73, 0.01)
Amount of alcohol consumed (DDD) up to 6-month follow-up			
At 6-month follow-up	114	SMD (IV, Random, 95% CI)	−0.25 (−0.62, 0.12)
Amount of alcohol consumed (DDD) 7- to 12-month follow-up			
At 9-month follow-up	114	SMD (IV, Random, 95% CI)	−0.05 (−0.42, 0.31)
At 12-month follow-up	114	SMD (IV, Random, 95% CI)	0.32 (−0.05, 0.69)

Continued

Table 56: (*Continued*)

Outcome or subgroup	N	Statistical method	Effect estimate (SMD, 95% CI)
Amount of alcohol consumed (DDD) >12-month follow-up			
At 15-month follow-up	114	SMD (IV, Random, 95% CI)	0.49 (0.12, 0.87)
At 18-month follow-up	114	SMD (IV, Random, 95% CI)	0.17 (−0.20, 0.54)
At 21-month follow-up	114	SMD (IV, Random, 95% CI)	−0.21 (−0.57, 0.16)
At 24-month follow-up	114	SMD (IV, Random, 95% CI)	0.03 (−0.34, 0.40)
At 27-month follow-up	114	SMD (IV, Random, 95% CI)	0.15 (−0.22, 0.52)
Attrition			
Attrition (dropout) post-treatment	141	RR (M-H, Random, 95% CI)	0.85 (0.27, 2.64)
Attrition (dropout) up to 6-month follow-up			
At 6 months	130	RR (M-H, Random, 95% CI)	5.00 (0.24, 102.16)
Attrition (dropout) 7- to 12-month follow-up			
At 9 months	128	RR (M-H, Random, 95% CI)	3.10 (0.33, 28.97)
At 12 months	124	RR (M-H, Random, 95% CI)	Not estimable
Attrition (dropout) >12-month follow-up			
At 18 months	122	RR (M-H, Random, 95% CI)	3.20 (0.13, 77.04)
At 27 months	117	RR (M-H, Random, 95% CI)	0.73 (0.13, 4.19)

6.12   SOCIAL NETWORK AND ENVIRONMENT-BASED THERAPIES

6.12.1   Definition

Social network and environment-based therapies use the individual's social environment as a way to help achieve abstinence or controlled drinking. These therapies include SBNT and the community reinforcement approach.

Social behaviour and network therapy
SBNT comprises a range of cognitive and behavioural strategies to help clients build social networks supportive of change which involve the patient and members of the patient's networks (for example, friends and family) (Copello *et al.*, 2002). The integration of these strategies has the aim of helping the patient to build 'positive social support for a change in drinking'.

285

Psychological and psychosocial interventions

The community reinforcement approach
In the community reinforcement approach (Hunt & Azrin, 1973; Meyers & Miller, 2001; Sisson & Azrin, 1989), emphasis is placed on maintaining abstinence through the development of activities that do not promote alcohol use, for example recreational and social activities, employment and family involvement.

6.12.2   Clinical review protocol (social network and environment-based therapies)

Information about the databases searched and the inclusion/exclusion criteria used for this section of the guideline can be found in Chapter 3 (further information about the search for health economic evidence can be found in Section 6.21). See Table 57 below for a summary of the clinical review protocol for the review of social network and environment-based therapies.

Table 57: Clinical review protocol for the review of social network and environment-based therapies

Electronic databases	CINAHL, EMBASE, MEDLINE, PsycINFO, Cochrane Library
Date searched	Database inception to March 2010
Study design	RCT (at least ten participants per arm)
Population	Adults (over 18 years old) At least 80% of the sample meet the criteria for alcohol dependence or harmful alcohol use (clinical diagnosis or drinking more than 30 drinks per week)
Excluded populations	Hazardous drinkers and those drinking fewer than 30 drinks per week Pregnant women
Interventions	Social network and environment-based therapies
Comparator	Control or other active intervention
Outcomes	Abstinence Amount of alcohol consumed Rates of consumption Relapse (>X number of drinks or number of participants who have relapsed) Lapse (time to first drink or number of participants who have lapsed) Attrition (leaving the study early for any reason)

6.12.3   Studies considered for review

The review team conducted a systematic review of RCTs that assessed the beneficial or detrimental effects of social network and environment-based therapies in the treatment of alcohol dependence or harmful alcohol use. See Table 58 for a summary of the study characteristics. It should be noted that some trials included in analyses were three- or four-arm trials. To avoid double counting, the number of participants in treatment conditions used in more than one comparison was divided (by half in a three-arm trial, and by three in a four-arm trial).

Three trials relating to clinical evidence met the eligibility criteria set by the GDG, providing data on 1,058 participants. All three studies were published in peer-reviewed journals between 1999 and 2007. A number of studies identified in the search were initially excluded because they were not relevant to this guideline. Studies were excluded because they did not meet methodological criteria (see Chapter

Table 58: Summary of study characteristics for social network and environment-based therapies

	Social network and environment-based therapies versus control	Social network and environment-based therapies versus other active intervention
K (total N)	1 RCT (N = 210)	2 RCTs (N = 989)
Study ID	LITT2007	(1) LEIGH2009 (2) UKATT2005
Diagnosis	DSM alcohol dependent/ abuse	(1) Not reported (2) DSM alcohol dependent/abuse
Baseline severity	Drinking days in past 3 months: 72% Prior treatment for alcohol dependence: 1.3	(1) Outpatient alcoholics drinking 5.5 days per week Drinks per week: Range 73 to 89 (2) Days abstinent: 29.5% per month Number of drinks per drinking day: 26.8
Number of sessions	12 sessions	8 sessions
Length of treatment	12 weeks	Range: 8 to 16 weeks
Length of follow-up	6- to 27-month	Range: 1- to 12-month
Setting	Outpatient treatment centre	(1)–(2) Outpatient treatment centre
Treatment goal	Not explicitly stated	(1)–(2) Abstinence or drinking reduction/moderation
Country	US	(1) Canada (2) UK

3). When studies did meet basic methodological inclusion criteria, the main reason for exclusion was not having alcohol-focused outcomes that could be used for analysis. A list of excluded studies can be found in Appendix 16d.

Social network and environment-based therapies versus control
Of the three included trials, there was only one involving a comparison of social network and environment-based therapies versus control that met the criteria for inclusion. LITT2007 assessed network support (both with and without contingency management) versus a case management active control. In this study, network support involved encouraging the participant to change their social network from one that promotes drinking to one that encourages abstinence as well as encouraging the use of established social support networks such as AA.

Social network and environment-based therapies versus other active intervention
Two of the three included trials that met criteria for inclusion assessed social network and environment-based therapies versus another active intervention. LEIGH1999 investigated a volunteer support condition (a volunteer was part of most treatment sessions and spent a substantial amount of time with the participant whilst in the community) versus an unspecified office-based individual intervention. UKATT2005 investigated SBNT (see Section 6.12.1 for definition) versus MET.

6.12.4   Evidence summary

The GRADE profiles and associated forest plots for the comparisons can be found in Appendix 18c and Appendix 17c, respectively.

Social network and environment-based therapies versus control
The clinical evidence showed that social network and environment-based therapies were significantly better than control at maintaining abstinence (moderate effect size) when assessed post-treatment and at 6-, 9-, 12-, 15- and 24-month follow-up. However, no significant difference was observed at 18-, 21- and 27-month follow-up.

Social network and environment-based therapies were not significantly better than control in reducing drinking post-treatment or at 12-, 15-, 24- and 27-month follow-up. However, a significant benefit (low to moderate effect size) was observed for social network and environment-based therapies over control in reducing the quantity of alcohol consumed when assessed at 6-, 9-, 18- and 21-month follow-up.

No significant difference was observed between treatment conditions in attrition either post-treatment or at all follow-up points. It must be noted that the comparison between social network and environment-based therapies versus control was based on a single study.

The quality of this evidence is *moderate*, therefore further research is likely to have an important impact on confidence in the estimate of the effect. An evidence summary of the results of the meta-analyses can be seen in Table 59.

**Table 59: Social network and environment-based therapies versus control
evidence summary**

Outcome or subgroup	N	Statistical method	Effect estimate (SMD, 95% CI)
Abstinence			
Abstinence post-treatment			
PDA post-treatment	172	SMD (IV, Random, 95% CI)	−0.76 (−1.08, −0.43)
Abstinence up to 6-month follow-up			
At 6-month follow-up	172	SMD (IV, Random, 95% CI)	−0.75 (−1.08, −0.43)
Abstinence 7- to 12-month follow-up			
At 9-month follow-up	172	SMD (IV, Random, 95% CI)	−0.70 (−1.03, −0.38)
At 12-month follow-up	172	SMD (IV, Random, 95% CI)	−0.59 (−0.99, −0.19)
Abstinence >12-month follow-up			
At 15-month follow-up	172	SMD (IV, Random, 95% CI)	−0.68 (−1.03, −0.32)
At 18-month follow-up	172	SMD (IV, Random, 95% CI)	−0.28 (−1.02, 0.46)
At 21-month follow-up	172	SMD (IV, Random, 95% CI)	−0.35 (−0.74, 0.05)
At 24-month follow-up	172	SMD (IV, Random, 95% CI)	−0.49 (−0.96, −0.01)
At 27-month follow-up	172	SMD (IV, Random, 95% CI)	−0.31 (−1.12, 0.49)
Amount of alcohol consumed			
DDD post-treatment	172	SMD (IV, Random, 95% CI)	−0.07 (−0.41, 0.28)
DDD up to 6-month follow-up			
At 6-month follow-up	172	SMD (IV, Random, 95% CI)	−0.54 (−0.86, −0.22)
DDD 7- to 12-month follow-up			
At 9 months	172	SMD (IV, Random, 95% CI)	−0.37 (−0.68, −0.05)
At 12-month follow-up	172	SMD (IV, Random, 95% CI)	−0.25 (−0.57, 0.06)
DDD >12-month follow-up			
At 15-month follow-up	172	SMD (IV, Random, 95% CI)	−0.35 (−0.83, 0.12)
At 18-month follow-up	172	SMD (IV, Random, 95% CI)	−0.34 (−0.66, −0.03)
At 21-month follow-up	172	SMD (IV, Random, 95% CI)	−0.43 (-0.75, -0.11)
At 24-month follow-up	172	SMD (IV, Random, 95% CI)	−0.11 (−0.43, 0.20)
At 27-month follow-up	172	SMD (IV, Random, 95% CI)	0.06 (−0.26, 0.37)
Attrition (dropout)			
Attrition (dropout) post-treatment	211	RR (M-H, Random, 95% CI)	1.36 (0.45, 4.13)

Continued

Table 59: (*Continued*)

Outcome or subgroup	N	Statistical method	Effect estimate (SMD, 95% CI)
Attrition (dropout) up to 6-month follow-up			
At 6 months	196	RR (M-H, Random, 95% CI)	0.54 (0.08, 3.59)
Attrition (dropout) 7- to 12-month follow-up			
At 9-month follow-up	192	RR (M-H, Random, 95% CI)	2.41 (0.28, 20.76)
At 12-month follow-up	188	RR (M-H, Random, 95% CI)	Not estimable
Attrition (dropout) >12-month follow-up	365	RR (M-H, Random, 95% CI)	0.78 (0.22, 2.79)
At 18-month follow-up	186	RR (M-H, Random, 95% CI)	0.33 (0.04, 2.64)
At 27-month follow-up	179	RR (M-H, Random, 95% CI)	1.31 (0.26, 6.61)

Social network and environment-based therapies versus other active intervention
The clinical evidence did not reveal any significant difference between social network and environment-based therapies and other active interventions in maintaining abstinence, reducing the quantity of alcohol consumed, reducing the number of drinking days and attrition.

The quality of this evidence is *moderate* therefore further research is likely to have an important impact on confidence in the estimate of the effect. An evidence summary of the results of the meta-analyses can be seen in Table 60.

6.13   COUPLES THERAPY

6.13.1   Definition

The content and definition of couples therapy can vary and reflect different approaches, for example cognitive behavioural or psychodynamic. Couples-based interventions (including behavioural couples therapy [BCT]) involve the spouse or partner expressing active support for the person who misuses alcohol in reducing alcohol use, including support via the use of behavioural contracts. Couples are helped to improve their relationship through more effective communication skills, and encouraged to increase positive behavioural exchanges through acknowledgement of pleasing behaviours and engagement in shared recreational activities (Fals-Stewart *et al.*, 2005). Standard BCT is manual-based and structured (Fals-Stewart *et al.*, 2004), and combines cognitive-behavioural treatment strategies with methods that address relationship issues arising from alcohol misuse as well as more general relationship problems with the aim of reducing distress.

Table 60: Social network and environment-based therapies versus other intervention evidence summary

Outcome or subgroup	N	Statistical method	Effect estimate (SMD, 95% CI)
Abstinence			
Abstinence up to 6-month follow-up			
PDA at 3-month follow-up	686	SMD (IV, Random, 95% CI)	−0.02 (−0.17, 0.13)
Abstinence at 7- to 12-month follow-up			
PDA at 12-month follow-up	612	SMD (IV, Random, 95% CI)	−0.02 (−0.18, 0.14)
Rates of consumption			
Rate of consumption up to 6-month follow-up			
Number drinking days at 1-month follow-up	79	SMD (IV, Random, 95% CI)	−0.03 (−0.47, 0.41)
Number of drinking days at 6-month follow-up	79	SMD (IV, Random, 95% CI)	0.09 (−0.35, 0.54)
Rate of consumption at 7- to 12-month follow-up			
Number of drinking days at 12-month follow-up	79	SMD (IV, Random, 95% CI)	0.15 (−0.29, 0.60)
Amount of alcohol consumed			
Amount of alcohol consumed up to 6-month follow-up			
Mean quantity per day at 1-month follow-up	79	SMD (IV, Random, 95% CI)	0.02 (−0.42, 0.46)
Mean quantity per day at 6 months follow-up	79	SMD (IV, Random, 95% CI)	0.43 (−0.02, 0.87)
Number DDD at 3-month follow-up	624	SMD (IV, Random, 95% CI)	0.04 (−0.12, 0.20)
Amount of alcohol consumed 7- to 12-month at follow-up	599	SMD (IV, Random, 95% CI)	0.07 (−0.09, 0.23)
Mean quantity per day at 12-month follow-up	79	SMD (IV, Random, 95% CI)	0.13 (−0.31, 0.57)
Number of DDD at 12-month follow-up	520	SMD (IV, Random, 95% CI)	0.06 (−0.11, 0.23)
Attrition (dropout)			
Attrition (dropout) post-treatment	193	RR (M-H, Random, 95% CI)	0.93 (0.68, 1.28)
Attrition (dropout) up to 6-month follow-up			
At 3-month follow-up	762	RR (M-H, Random, 95% CI)	0.68 (0.42, 1.08)
Attrition (dropout) 7- to 12-month follow-up			
At 12-month follow-up	689	RR (M-H, Random, 95% CI)	1.00 (0.65, 1.56)

Psychological and psychosocial interventions

6.13.2 Clinical review protocol (couples therapy)

Information about the databases searched and the inclusion/exclusion criteria used for this section of the guideline can be found in Chapter 3 (further information about the search for health economic evidence can be found in Section 6.21). See Table 61 below for a summary of the clinical review protocol for the review of couples therapy.

6.13.3 Studies considered for review

The review team conducted a systematic review of RCTs that assessed the beneficial or detrimental effects of couples therapies in the treatment of alcohol dependence or harmful alcohol use. See Table 62 for a summary of the study characteristics. It should be noted that some trials included in analyses were three- or four-arm trials. To avoid double counting, the number of participants in treatment conditions used in more than one comparison was divided (by half in a three-arm trial, and by three in a four-arm trial).

Table 61: Clinical review protocol for the review of couples therapy

Electronic databases	CINAHL, EMBASE, MEDLINE, PsycINFO, Cochrane Library
Date searched	Database inception to March 2010
Study design	RCT (at least ten participants per arm)
Population	Adults (over 18 years old) At least 80% of the sample meet the criteria for alcohol dependence or harmful alcohol use (clinical diagnosis or drinking more than 30 drinks per week)
Excluded populations	Hazardous drinkers and those drinking fewer than 30 drinks per week Pregnant women
Interventions	Couples therapy
Comparator	Control or other active intervention
Outcomes	Abstinence Amount of alcohol consumed Rates of consumption Relapse (>X number of drinks or number of participants who have relapsed) Lapse (time to first drink or number of participants who have lapsed) Attrition (leaving the study early for any reason)

292

Eight trials relating to clinical evidence met the eligibility criteria set by the GDG, providing data on 602 participants. All eight studies were published in peer-reviewed journals between 1988 and 2009. A number of studies identified in the search were initially excluded because they were not relevant to this guideline. Studies were excluded because they did not meet methodological criteria (see Chapter 3). When studies did meet basic methodological inclusion criteria, the main reason for exclusion was not having alcohol-focused outcomes that could be used for analysis. Other reasons were not meeting drinking quantity/diagnosis criteria, that is, participants were not drinking enough to be categorised as harmful or dependent drinkers, or less than 80% of the sample meet criteria for alcohol dependence or harmful alcohol use, the study was outside the scope of this guideline, or the study was drug-focused or did not differentiate between drugs and alcohol. A list of excluded studies can be found in Appendix 16d.

Couples therapy versus other active intervention
Of the eight included RCT trials, seven compared couples therapy with another active intervention met criteria for inclusion. In the FALSSTEWART2005 study, participants received one of two methods of couples therapy (BCT and brief relationship counselling) or individually-based TSF or psychoeducational intervention. All groups also had group counselling as standard. FALSSTEWART2006 assessed BCT (with individual TSF) versus individual TSF or psychoeducational intervention alone. LAM2009 investigated BCT (both with and without parental skills training) versus individually-based coping skills. OFARRELL1992 assessed two methods of couples therapy (interactional couples therapy and behavioural marital therapy) versus counselling. SOBELL2000 compared couples therapy in the form of direct social support with natural social support. VEDEL2008 compared BCT with CBT. WALITZER2004 investigated BCT with and without alcohol-focused spousal involvement with behavioural self-management.

Behavioural couples therapy versus other couples therapy
Three studies assessed BCT versus other methods of couples therapy. Studies that could be included in these analyses compared BCT with the following; brief relationship therapy (FALSSTEWART2005), interactional couples therapy (OFARRELL1992) and alcohol-focused spousal involvement (WALITZER2004).

Intensive behavioural couples therapy versus brief couples therapy
Two studies were included to assess the possible difference in outcome between more intensive and less intensive couples therapy. FALSSTEWART2005 assessed BCT (plus counselling) versus brief relationship therapy plus counselling (brief BCT). ZWEBEN1988 assessed eight sessions of conjoint therapy versus one session of couples advice counselling.

Parental skills and behavioural couples therapy versus behavioural couples therapy alone
This analysis involved a single study (LAM2009), which assessed BCT with and without the addition of parental skills training.

Table 62: Summary of study characteristics for couples therapy

	Couples therapy versus other active intervention	BCT versus other couples therapy	Intensive versus BCT	Parental skills and BCT versus BCT alone
K (total N)	7 RCTs (N = 486)	3 RCTs (N = 114)	2 RCTs (N = 216)	1 RCT (N = 20)
Study ID	(1) FALSSTEWART2005 (2) FALSSTEWART2006 (3) LAM2009 (4) OFARRELL1992 (5) SOBELL2000 (6) VEDEL2008 (7) WALITZER2004	(1) FALSSTEWART2005 (2) OFARRELL1992 (3) WALITZER2004	(1) FALSSTEWART2005 (2) ZWEBEN1988	LAM2009
Diagnosis	(1) DSM alcohol dependent (2)–(3) DSM dependent/abuse (4)–(5) Not reported (6) DSM dependent/abuse	(1) DSM alcohol dependent (2)–(3) Not reported	(1) DSM alcohol dependent (2) Not reported	DSM dependent/ abuse
Baseline severity	(1) Percentage of days heavy drinking: 56 to 59% across groups (2) Percent days abstinent: 40 to 44% across groups (3) Percent days abstinent: approximately 37% (4) MAST score: >7 Years of problem drinking: 15.79 years Previous alcohol hospitalisations: 2.09 (5) ADS score: 12.6 Proportion of days abstinent: approximately 0.22 Proportion of days consuming one to four drinks: approximately 0.35 Proportion of days consuming five	(1) Percent days heavy drinking: 56 to 59% across groups (2) MAST score: >7 Years of problem drinking: 15.79 years Previous alcohol hospitalisations: 2.09 (3) Abstinent days per month: 11 Frequency of drinking at least six drinks per drinking period, per month: 5.1 ADS score: 8.4 85% low dependence; 15% moderate dependence	(1) Percent days heavy drinking: 56 to 59% across groups (2) ADS core: 8.4 MAST score: approximately 20 44% heavy drinking in past year 36.5% abstinent in the past year	Percent days abstinent: approximately 37%

	to nine drinks: approximately 0.32 Proportion of days consuming ten or more drinks: approximately 0.12 Mean number of drinks per drinking day: approximately 6 drinks (6) 62% alcohol dependent 50% when drinking drank at least seven units 57% drank daily or nearly daily (7) Abstinent days per month: 11 days Frequency of drinking at least six drinks per drinking period per month: 5.1 ADS score: 8.4 85% low dependence; 15% moderate dependence			
Number of sessions	Range: 4 to 18 sessions	Range: 10 to 12 sessions	Range: 1 to 12 sessions	12 sessions
Length of treatment	Range: 4 to 12 weeks	Range: 10 to 12 weeks	Range: 1 to 12 weeks	12 weeks
Length of follow-up	Range: 2 to 24 months	Range: 2 to 24 months	Range: 2 to 24 months	6 and 12 month
Setting	(1)–(4) Outpatient treatment centre (5) Outpatient research unit (6)–(7) Outpatient treatment centre	(1)–(3) Outpatient treatment centre	(1)–(2) Outpatient treatment centre	Outpatient treatment centre
Treatment goal	(1) Not explicitly stated (2) Abstinence (3) Not explicitly stated (4) Abstinence (5) Drinking reduction/moderation (6) Abstinence or controlled drinking (7) Drinking reduction/moderation	(1) Not explicitly stated (2) Abstinence (3) Drinking reduction/moderation	(1) Not explicitly stated (2) Abstinence or drinking reduction/moderation	Not explicitly stated
Country	(1)–(4) US (5) Canada (6) Netherlands (7) US	(1)–(3) US	(1) US (2) Canada	US

6.13.4 Evidence summary

The GRADE profiles and associated forest plots for the comparisons can be found in Appendix 18c and Appendix 17c, respectively.

Couples therapy versus other active intervention
Not significant difference was observed between couples therapy (all types) and other active interventions in maintaining abstinence at post-treatment and 2-month follow-up assessment. However, over longer periods, couples therapy was significantly more effective than other therapies in maintaining abstinence and/or light drinking (moderate effect size) when assessed up to 12-month follow-up. This difference was not observed in follow-up periods longer than 12 months. An additional randomised study (MCCRADY2009) could not be included in these analyses as no extractable data was provided. The study reported that BCT was more effective than individual coping-skills treatment in maintaining abstinence and reducing heavy drinking days.

Couples therapy was significantly more effective than other active interventions in reducing heavy drinking episodes when assessed up to 12-month follow-up. However, there was no difference between couples therapy and other active interventions post-treatment.

The VEDEL2008 study assessed severity of relapse in their sample. The results indicated that other active intervention (namely CBT) was more effective than couples therapy (namely BCT) in reducing occasions in which participants lapsed (drank over six drinks on one occasion) or relapsed (drank more than six drinks most days of the week), but no significant difference was observed in the number of participants who relapsed on a regular basis (a few times a month). It must be noted that effect sizes were small and from a single study.

No difference in attrition rates was observed between groups post-treatment and at 3-month follow-up. Couples therapy had less attrition than other therapies at 6-month follow-up (large effect size), and other therapies had less attrition than couples therapy at 12-month follow-up (large effect size).

The quality of this evidence is *moderate*, therefore further research is likely to have an important impact on the confidence in the estimate of the effect. An evidence summary of the results of the meta-analyses can be seen in Table 63.

Behavioural couples therapy versus other couples therapy
No significant difference was observed between BCT and other forms of couples therapy in maintaining abstinence when assessed post-treatment and up to 24-month follow-up. Similarly, no difference between these groups was observed in reducing heavy drinking and attrition rates post-treatment, and up to 12-month follow-up.

The quality of this evidence is *moderate*, therefore further research is likely to have an important impact on the confidence in the estimate of the effect. An evidence summary of the results of the meta-analyses can be seen in Table 64.

Table 63: Couples therapy versus other intervention evidence summary

Outcome or subgroup	N	Statistical method	Effect estimate (SMD, 95% CI)
Abstinence			
Abstinence (percentage or proportion) post-treatment	214	SMD (IV, Random, 95% CI)	−0.16 (−0.44, 0.13)
Abstinence (percentage or proportion) up to 6-month follow-up			
PDA at 2-month follow-up	34	SMD (IV, Random, 95% CI)	−0.42 (−1.14, 0.29)
PDA at 3-month follow-up	138	SMD (IV, Random, 95% CI)	−0.37 (−0.72, −0.01)
PDA/light (no alcohol or one to three drinks) at 3-month follow-up	63	SMD (IV, Random, 95% CI)	−0.77 (−1.31, −0.23)
PDA at 6-month follow-up	202	SMD (IV, Random, 95% CI)	−0.47 (−0.77, −0.18)
PDA/light (no alcohol or one to three drinks) at 6-month follow-up	63	SMD (IV, Random, 95% CI)	−0.52 (−1.04, 0.01)
Abstinence (percentage or proportion) 7- to 12-month follow-up			
PDA abstinent at 9-month follow-up	138	SMD (IV, Random, 95% CI)	−0.60 (−0.96, −0.24)
PDA/light (no alcohol or one to three drinks) at 9-month follow-up	61	SMD (IV, Random, 95% CI)	−0.60 (-1.15, −0.05)
PDA at 12-month follow-up	245	SMD (IV, Random, 95% CI)	−0.54 (−0.81, −0.27)
PDA/light (no alcohol or one to three drinks) at 12-month follow-up	61	SMD (IV, Random, 95% CI)	−0.54 (−1.09, 0.01)
Abstinence (percentage or proportion) >12-month follow-up			
At 18 months	34	SMD (IV, Random, 95% CI)	−0.26 (−0.97, 0.45)
At 24 months	34	SMD (IV, Random, 95% CI)	−0.34 (−1.05, 0.37)
Lapse or relapse			
Relapse (more than six units most days of the week) post-treatment	48	RR (M-H, Random, 95% CI)	2.57 (1.16, 5.71)
Regular relapse (more than six units a few times a month) post-treatment	48	RR (M-H, Random, 95% CI)	0.64 (0.18, 2.27)
Severe lapse (more than six units on one occasion) post-treatment	48	RR (M-H, Random, 95% CI)	1.71 (1.06, 2.78)
Rates of consumption			
Rates of consumption post-treatment			
Percentage of days heavy drinking post-treatment	152	SMD (IV, Random, 95% CI)	0.01 (−0.33, 0.35)
Rates of consumption up to 6-month follow-up			

Continued

Table 63: (*Continued*)

Outcome or subgroup	N	Statistical method	Effect estimate (SMD, 95% CI)
Percentage of days heavy drinking (more than drinks per day) at 3-month follow-up	215	SMD (IV, Random, 95% CI)	−0.50 (−0.79, −0.22)
Percentage of days heavy drinking (more than drinks per day) at 6-month follow-up	215	SMD (IV, Random, 95% CI)	−0.57 (−0.86, −0.29)
Rates of consumption 7- to 12-month follow-up			
Days light drinking (proportion) at 12-month follow-up	43	SMD (IV, Random, 95% CI)	−0.08 (−0.68, 0.52)
Percentage of days heavy drinking (more than drinks per day) at 9-month follow-up	213	SMD (IV, Random, 95% CI)	−0.70 (−0.99, −0.41)
Percentage of days heavy drinking (more than drinks per day) at 12-month follow-up	213	SMD (IV, Random, 95% CI)	−0.71 (−1.01, −0.42)
Days drinking five to nine drinks (proportion) at 12-month follow-up	43	SMD (IV, Random, 95% CI)	0.05 (−0.56, 0.65)
Days drinking at least ten drinks (proportion) at 12-month follow-up	43	SMD (IV, Random, 95% CI)	−0.25 (−0.86, 0.35)
Amount of alcohol consumed			
Amount of alcohol consumed post-treatment			
Units per week	48	SMD (IV, Random, 95% CI)	−0.38 (−0.95, 0.20)
Amount of alcohol consumed up to 6-month follow-up			
Units per week at 6-month follow-up	45	SMD (IV, Random, 95% CI)	−0.16 (−0.75, 0.42)
Amount of alcohol consumed at 7- to 12-month follow-up			
Mean DDD at 12-month follow-up	43	SMD (IV, Random, 95% CI)	−0.11 (−0.71, 0.49)
Attrition (dropout)			
Attrition (dropout) post-treatment	313	RR (M-H, Random, 95% CI)	1.22 (0.74, 2.02)
Attrition (dropout) up to 6-month follow-up			
At 3-month follow-up	64	RR (M-H, Random, 95% CI)	1.64 (0.07, 37.15)
At 6-month follow-up	111	RR (M-H, Random, 95% CI)	0.05 (0.00, 0.75)
Attrition (dropout) 7- to 12-month follow-up			
At 9-month follow-up	63	RR (M-H, Random, 95% CI)	0.19 (0.03, 1.17)
At 12-month follow-up	242	RR (M-H, Random, 95% CI)	2.26 (1.33, 3.84)

Table 64: Behavioural couples therapy versus other couples therapy evidence summary

Outcome or subgroup	N	Statistical method	Effect estimate (SMD, 95% CI)
Abstinence			
Abstinence (percentage or proportion) post-treatment	22	SMD (IV, Random, 95% CI)	−0.67 (−1.54, 0.20)
Abstinence (percentage or proportion) up to 6-month follow-up			
At 2-month follow-up	22	SMD (IV, Random, 95% CI)	−0.17 (−1.01, 0.67)
PDA/light (no alcohol or one to three drinks) at 3-month follow-up	41	SMD (IV, Random, 95% CI)	−0.13 (−0.74, 0.48)
At 6-month follow-up	22	SMD (IV, Random, 95% CI)	0.11 (−0.73, 0.95)
PDA/light (no alcohol or one to three drinks) at 6-month follow-up	41	SMD (IV, Random, 95% CI)	−0.05 (−0.67, 0.56)
Abstinence (percentage or proportion) 7- to 12-month follow-up			
PDA or light (no alcohol or one to three drinks) at 9-month follow-up	41	SMD (IV, Random, 95% CI)	−0.17 (−0.78, 0.44)
PDA at 12-month follow-up	22	SMD (IV, Random, 95% CI)	0.11 (−0.73, 0.95)
PDA or light (no alcohol or one to three drinks) at 12-month follow-up	41	SMD (IV, Random, 95% CI)	−0.40 (−1.02, 0.22)
PDA (or proportion) >12-month follow-up			
At 18 months follow-up	22	SMD (IV, Random, 95% CI)	0.10 (−0.74, 0.94)
At 24-month follow-up	22	SMD (IV, Random, 95% CI)	0.26 (−0.58, 1.10)
Rates of consumption			
Rates of consumption post-treatment			
Percentage of days heavy drinking	50	SMD (IV, Random, 95% CI)	0.02 (−0.54, 0.57)
Rates of consumption up to 6-month follow-up			
Percentage of days heavy drinking (more than six drinks per day) at 3-month follow-up	91	SMD (IV, Random, 95% CI)	−0.07 (−0.48, 0.34)
Percentage of days heavy drinking (more than six drinks per day) at 6-month follow-up	91	SMD (IV, Random, 95% CI)	0.08 (−0.33, 0.49)
Rates of consumption 7 - 12-month follow-up			
Percentage of days heavy drinking (more than six drinks per day) at 9-month follow-up	91	SMD (IV, Random, 95% CI)	−0.02 (−0.43, 0.39)

Continued

Table 64: (*Continued*)

Outcome or subgroup	N	Statistical method	Effect estimate (SMD, 95% CI)
Percentage of days heavy drinking (more than six drinks per day) at 12-month follow-up	91	SMD (IV, Random, 95% CI)	0.07 (−0.34, 0.49)
Attrition (dropout)			
Attrition (dropout) post-treatment	22	RR (M-H, Random, 95% CI)	Not estimable
Attrition (dropout) up to 6-month follow-up			
At 3-month follow-up	42	RR (M-H, Random, 95% CI)	3.00 (0.13, 69.70)
At 6-month follow-up	41	RR (M-H, Random, 95% CI)	Not estimable
At 9-month follow-up	42	RR (M-H, Random, 95% CI)	1.00 (0.07, 14.95)
Attrition (dropout) 7- to 12-month follow-up	41	RR (M-H, Random, 95% CI)	Not estimable
At 12-month follow-up	41	RR (M-H, Random, 95% CI)	Not estimable

Intensive versus standard couples therapy

At 1-month follow-up, brief couples therapy was more effective than more intensive couples therapy in maintaining abstinence (moderate effect size). However, this difference was not maintained up to 18-month follow-up. Furthermore, no significant benefit of more intensive couples therapy over brief couples therapy in reducing heavy drinking was observed up to 18-month follow-up. Those who received more intensive couples therapy were more likely to be retained for follow-up assessment at 12 months than brief couples therapy (small effect size).

The quality of this evidence is *moderate*, therefore further research is likely to have an important impact on the confidence in the estimate of the effect. An evidence summary of the results of the meta-analyses can be seen in Table 65.

Parental skills and behavioural couples therapy versus behavioural couples therapy alone

The addition of parental skills training to BCT did not significant improve abstinence rates both post-treatment and up to 12-month follow-up.

The quality of this evidence is *moderate*, therefore further research is likely to have an important impact on the confidence in the estimate of the effect. An evidence summary of the results of the meta-analyses can be seen in Table 66.

Table 65: Intensive couples therapy versus brief couples therapy evidence summary

Outcome or subgroup	N	Statistical method	Effect estimate (SMD, 95% CI)
Abstinence			
Abstinence (percentage or proportion) up to 6-month follow-up			
At 1-month follow-up	116	SMD (IV, Random, 95% CI)	0.64 (0.26, 1.02)
At 2-month follow-up	116	SMD (IV, Random, 95% CI)	0.22 (−0.15, 0.60)
At 6-month follow-up	116	SMD (IV, Random, 95% CI)	0.17 (−0.21, 0.54)
Abstinence (percentage or proportion) 7- to 12-month follow-up			
At 12-month follow-up	116	SMD (IV, Random, 95% CI)	0.26 (−0.11, 0.63)
Abstinence (percentage or proportion) >12-month follow-up			
At 18-month follow-up	116	SMD (IV, Random, 95% CI)	0.15 (−0.22, 0.52)
Rates of consumption			
Rates of consumption post-treatment			
Percentage of days heavy drinking	50	SMD (IV, Random, 95% CI)	0.02 (−0.54, 0.57)
Rates of consumption up to 6-month follow-up			
Percentage of days heavy drinking (more than six drinks per day) at 1-month follow-up	116	SMD (IV, Random, 95% CI)	0.36 (−0.02, 0.73)
Percentage of days heavy drinking (more than six drinks per day) at 2-month follow-up	116	SMD (IV, Random, 95% CI)	−0.14 (−0.51, 0.23)
Percentage of days heavy drinking (more than six drinks per day) at 3-month follow-up	50	SMD (IV, Random, 95% CI)	−0.01 (−0.57, 0.54)
Percentage of days heavy drinking (at least five drinks per day) at 6-month follow-up	166	SMD (IV, Random, 95% CI)	0.02 (−0.29, 0.32)
Percentage of moderate drinking days (one to four drinks per day) at 1-month follow-up	116	SMD (IV, Random, 95% CI)	−0.57 (−0.95, −0.20)
Percentage of moderate drinking days (one to four drinks per day) at 2-month follow-up	116	SMD (IV, Random, 95% CI)	−0.34 (−0.71, 0.04)

Continued

Table 65: (*Continued*)

Outcome or subgroup	N	Statistical method	Effect estimate (SMD, 95% CI)
Percentage of moderate drinking days (one to four drinks per day) at 6-month follow-up	116	SMD (IV, Random, 95% CI)	−0.15 (−0.52, 0.22)
Rates of consumption 7- to 12-month follow-up			
Percentage of moderate drinking days (one to four drinks per day) at 12-month follow-up	116	SMD (IV, Random, 95% CI)	−0.30 (−0.67, 0.07)
Percentage of days heavy drinking (more than six drinks per day) at 9-month follow-up	50	SMD (IV, Random, 95% CI)	−0.01 (−0.57, 0.54)
Percentage of days heavy drinking (at least five drinks per day) at 12-month follow-up	166	SMD (IV, Random, 95% CI)	−0.03 (−0.34, 0.27)
Rates of consumption >12-month follow-up			
Percentage of moderate drinking days (one to four drinks per day) at 18-month follow-up	116	SMD (IV, Random, 95% CI)	−0.23 (−0.60, 0.14)
Percentage of days heavy drinking (at least five drinks per day) at 18-month follow-up	116	SMD (IV, Random, 95% CI)	−0.04 (−0.42, 0.33)
Attrition (dropout)			
Attrition (dropout) post-treatment	218	RR (M-H, Random, 95% CI)	63.43 (3.97, 1012.92)
Attrition (dropout) >12-month follow-up			
At 1- to 18-month follow-up	163	RR (M-H, Random, 95% CI)	0.40 (0.23, 0.69)

Table 66: Parental skills and behavioural couples therapy versus behavioural couples therapy alone evidence summary

Outcome or subgroup	N	Statistical method	Effect estimate
Abstinence			
PDA post-treatment	20	SMD (IV, Random, 95% CI)	0.12 (−0.75, 1.00)
PDA at 6-month follow-up	20	SMD (IV, Random, 95% CI)	0.04 (−0.84, 0.91)
PDA abstinent at 12-month follow-up	20	SMD (IV, Random, 95% CI)	−0.04 (−0.92, 0.84)

6.14   COUNSELLING

6.14.1   Definition

The British Association for Counselling and Psychotherapy defines counselling as 'a systematic process which gives individuals an opportunity to explore, discover and clarify ways of living more resourcefully, with a greater sense of well-being' (British Association of Counselling, 1992). This definition, which has been used in other NICE guidelines, was adopted for this review, but in the included studies counselling for alcohol treatment was not often well-defined or manual-based making decisions about inclusion difficult; where there was uncertainty this was resolved in discussion with the GDG.

6.14.2   Clinical review protocol (counselling)

Information about the databases searched and the inclusion/exclusion criteria used for this section of the guideline can be found in Chapter 3 (further information about the search for health economic evidence can be found in Section 6.21). See Table 67, below, for a summary of the clinical review protocol for the review of counselling.

Table 67: Clinical review protocol for the review of counselling

Electronic databases	CINAHL, EMBASE, MEDLINE, PsycINFO, Cochrane Library
Date searched	Database inception to March 2010
Study design	RCT (at least ten participants per arm)
Population	Adults (over 18 years old) At least 80% of the sample meet the criteria for alcohol dependence or harmful alcohol use (clinical diagnosis or drinking more than 30 drinks per week)
Excluded populations	Hazardous drinkers and those drinking fewer than 30 drinks per week Pregnant women
Interventions	Counselling
Comparator	Control or other active intervention
Outcomes	Abstinence Amount of alcohol consumed Rates of consumption Relapse (>X number of drinks or number of participants who have relapsed) Lapse (time to first drink or number of participants who have lapsed) Attrition (leaving the study early for any reason)

6.14.3   Studies considered for review

The review team conducted a systematic review of RCTs that assessed the beneficial or detrimental effects of counselling in the treatment of alcohol dependence or harmful alcohol use. See Table 68 for a summary of the study characteristics. It should be noted

Table 68: Summary of study characteristics for counselling

	Counselling versus control	Counselling versus other active intervention
K (total N)	1 RCT (N = 80)	5 RCT (N = 590)
Study ID	(1) SELLMAN2001	(1) ERIKSEN1986B (2) JOHN2003 (3) LITT2003 (4) OFARRELL1992 (5) SELLMAN2001
Diagnosis	(1) DSM alcohol dependent	(1) Not reported (2) ICD–10 alcohol dependent (3) DSM alcohol dependent/abuse (4) Not reported (5) DSM alcohol dependent
Baseline severity	(1) Unequivocal heavy drinking six or more times in 6-month follow-up period: 90.2%	(1) Previous alcoholism inpatient status: 66.7% (3) Drinking days 6 months prior to intake: 72% (4) MAST score: >7 (5) Unequivocal heavy drinking 6+ times in 6-month follow-up period: 90.2%
Number of sessions	4 sessions	Range: 8 to 26 sessions
Length of treatment	6 weeks	Range: 3 to 26 weeks
Length of follow-up (only including papers reporting follow-up measures)	6 months and 5 years	Range: 2 months to 5 years
Setting	(1) Outpatient treatment centre	(1)–(2) Inpatient (3) Outpatient research unit (4)–(5) Outpatient treatment centre
Treatment goal	(1) Not explicitly stated	(1) Drinking reduction/moderation (2) Abstinence (3) Not explicitly stated (4) Abstinence (5) Not explicitly stated
Country	(1) New Zealand	(1) Norway (2) Germany (3)–(4) US (5) New Zealand

that some trials included in analyses were three- or four-arm trials. To avoid double counting, the number of participants in treatment conditions used in more than one comparison was divided (by half in a three-arm trial, and by three in a four-arm trial).

Five trials relating to clinical evidence met the eligibility criteria set by the GDG, providing data on 630 participants. All five studies were published in peer-reviewed journals between 1986 and 2003. A number of studies identified in the search were initially excluded because they were not relevant to this guideline. Counselling studies were mainly excluded for not being randomised trials. When studies did meet basic methodological inclusion criteria, the main reason for exclusion were that treatment was opportunistic as opposed to planned, the study was not directly relevant to the review questions, or no relevant alcohol-focused outcomes were available. A list of excluded studies can be found in Appendix 16d.

Counselling versus control
Of the five included trials, there was only one involving a comparison of counselling versus control that met criteria for inclusion. SELLMAN2001 assessed counselling (non-directive reflective listening) versus control (no further treatment – feedback only).

Counselling versus other active intervention
All five included trials assessed counselling versus another active intervention and met criteria for inclusion. ERIKSEN1986B assessed counselling (group) versus social skills training (coping skills), JOHN2003 assessed counselling (individual) versus multi-modal standard intervention (see Appendix 16d for more information), LITT2003 assessed counselling (group) versus coping skills, OFARRELL1992 assessed counselling (individual) versus both interactional couples therapy and behavioural marital therapy, and SELLMAN2001 assessed counselling (non-directive reflective listening) versus MET. The included studies were conducted between 1986 and 2003.

6.14.4   Evidence summary

The GRADE profiles and associated forest plots for the comparisons can be found in Appendix 18c and Appendix 17c, respectively.

Counselling versus Control
Based on the SELLMAN2001 study, no significant difference was observed between treatment groups, hence the clinical evidence does not support the benefits of counselling over control in maintaining abstinence or reducing heavy drinking.

The quality of this evidence is *moderate*, therefore further research is likely to have an important impact on confidence in the estimate of the effect. An evidence summary of the results of the meta-analyses can be seen in Table 69.

Counselling versus other active intervention
In maintaining abstinence, no significant difference was observed between counselling and other therapies when assessed up to 6-month follow-up. However, bar the 6-month follow-up, these results are based on a single study (OFARRELL1992)

Table 69: Counselling versus control evidence summary

Outcome or subgroup	Number of participants	Statistical method	Effect estimate
Rates of consumption			
Rates of consumption up to 6-month follow-up			
Exceeded national guidelines at least once (at 6 months)	80	RR (M-H, Random, 95% CI)	1.07 (0.83, 1.38)
Exceeded national guideline at least six times (at 6 months)	80	RR (M-H, Random, 95% CI)	1.07 (0.83, 1.38)
Drank at least ten standard drinks at least once (at 6 months)	80	RR (M-H, Random, 95% CI)	0.97 (0.77, 1.22)
Drank at least ten standard drinks at least six times (at 6 months)	80	RR (M-H, Random, 95% CI)	0.96 (0.69, 1.34)
Rates of consumption >12-month follow-up			
Exceeded national guidelines at least once (at 5 years)	50	RR (M-H, Random, 95% CI)	0.94 (0.62, 1.45)
Exceeded national guidelines at least six times (at 5 years)	50	RR (M-H, Random, 95% CI)	1.09 (0.62, 1.89)
Drank at least ten standard drinks at least once (at 5 years)	50	RR (M-H, Random, 95% CI)	0.74 (0.38, 1.41)
Drank at least ten standard drinks at least six times (at 5 years)	50	RR (M-H, Random, 95% CI)	0.61 (0.22, 1.73)
Lapse or relapse			
Lapse up to 6-month follow-up		RR (M-H, Random,	
Broke abstinence (lapse) at 6 months	80	95% CI)	0.97 (0.85, 1.11)
Lapse >12-month follow-up			
Broke abstinence (lapse) at 5 years	50	RR (M-H, Random, 95% CI)	1.00 (0.73, 1.38)
Attrition (dropout)			
Attrition (dropout) post-treatment	80	RR (M-H, Random, 95% CI)	Not estimable
Attrition (dropout) >12-month follow-up			
At 5-year follow-up	80	RR (M-H, Random, 95% CI)	1.73 (0.95, 3.15)

whereas in the analyses assessing couples therapies versus other active therapies, more studies were included in the analyses for this outcome. Other therapies (namely couples therapies and coping skills) showed significant benefits over counselling in maintaining abstinence at longer follow-up periods of up to 18 months.

Overall, no significant difference was observed between counselling and other therapies up to 18-month follow-up in time to first drink (lapse), time to first heavy drink (relapse) and reducing heavy drinking episodes. These analyses were based on data from a single study (LITT2003). However, other therapies (coping skills) were more effective than counselling in reducing amount of alcohol consumed when assessed at 12-month follow-up. Again, this result was based on a single study (ERIKSEN1986B) limiting the ability to generalise the findings.

Lastly, no significant difference was observed between counselling and other therapies in attrition rates.

The quality of this evidence is *moderate*, therefore further research is likely to have an important impact on confidence in the estimate of the effect. An evidence summary of the results of the meta-analyses can be seen in Table 70.

Table 70: Counselling versus other intervention evidence summary

Outcome or subgroup	N	Statistical method	Effect estimate
Abstinence			
Abstinence (percentage) post-treatment	34	SMD (IV, Random, 95% CI)	0.31 (−0.86, 1.47)
Abstinence (percentage or proportion) up to 6 months			
PDA at 2-month follow-up	34	SMD (IV, Random, 95% CI)	0.42 (−0.29, 1.14)
PDA at 3-month follow-up	128	SMD (IV, Random, 95% CI)	0.12 (−0.23, 0.47)
PDA at 6-month follow-up	162	SMD (IV, Random, 95% CI)	0.25 (−0.06, 0.56)
Abstinence (percentage or proportion) at 7- to 12-month follow-up			
Sober days at 12-month follow-up	23	SMD (IV, Random, 95% CI)	1.67 (0.70, 2.65)
PDA at 9-month follow-up	128	SMD (IV, Random, 95% CI)	0.24 (−0.11, 0.58)
PDA at 12-month follow-up	162	SMD (IV, Random, 95% CI)	0.28 (−0.03, 0.59)
Abstinence (percentage or proportion) >12-month follow-up			
PDA at 15-month follow-up	128	SMD (IV, Random, 95% CI)	0.28 (−0.07, 0.63)
PDA at 18-month follow-up	162	SMD (IV, Random, 95% CI)	0.30 (−0.01, 0.61)
PDA at 24-month follow-up	34	SMD (IV, Random, 95% CI)	0.34 (−0.37, 1.05)
Lapse or relapse			
Lapse up to 6-month follow-up			
Broke abstinence (lapse) at 6-month follow-up	404	RR (M-H, Random, 95% CI)	1.15 (1.01, 1.32)
Lapsed – 7- to 12-month follow-up			
At 12-month follow-up	322	RR (M-H, Random, 95% CI)	0.92 (0.81, 1.05)

Continued

Table 70: (*Continued*)

At >12-month follow-up			
Broke abstinence (lapse) at 5-year follow-up	48	RR (M-H, Random, 95% CI)	0.98 (0.72, 1.34)
Rates of consumption			
Rates of consumption up to 6-month follow-up			
Proportion days heavy drinking (at least six men, four women) at 3-month follow-up	128	SMD (IV, Random, 95% CI)	0.14 (-0.21, 0.49)
Proportion days heavy drinking at least six men, four women) at 6-month follow-up	128	SMD (IV, Random, 95% CI)	0.20 (-0.15, 0.55)
Rates of consumption 7- to 12-month follow-up			
Proportion days heavy drinking (at least six men, four women) at 9-month follow-up	128	SMD (IV, Random, 95% CI)	0.10 (-0.24, 0.45)
Proportion days heavy drinking (at least six men, four women) at 12-month follow-up	128	SMD (IV, Random, 95% CI)	0.17 (-0.18, 0.52)
Rates of consumption >12-month follow-up			
Proportion days heavy drinking (at least six men, four women) at 15-month follow-up	128	SMD (IV, Random, 95% CI)	0.07 (-0.27, 0.42)
Proportion days heavy drinking (at least six men, four women) at 18-month follow-up	128	SMD (IV, Random, 95% CI)	0.20 (-0.15, 0.55)
Rates of consumption up to 6-month follow-up			
Exceeded national guidelines at least once (at 6 months)	82	RR (M-H, Random, 95% CI)	1.21 (0.91, 1.60)
Exceeded national guideline at least six times (at 6 months)	82	RR (M-H, Random, 95% CI)	1.21 (0.91, 1.60)
Drank at least ten standard drinks at least once (at 6 months)	82	RR (M-H, Random, 95% CI)	1.25 (0.94, 1.67)
Drank at least ten standard drinks at) least six times (at 6 months	82	RR (M-H, Random, 95% CI)	1.46 (0.95, 2.23)
Rates of consumption >12 months follow-up			
Exceeded national guidelines at) least once (at 5 years	48	RR (M-H, Random, 95% CI)	1.04 (0.66, 1.65)

Exceeded national guidelines at least six times (at 5 years)	48	RR (M-H, Random, 95% CI)	1.18 (0.66, 2.12)
Drank at least ten standard drinks at least once (at 5 years)	48	RR (M-H, Random, 95% CI)	1.14 (0.53, 2.45)
Drank at least ten standard drinks) at least six times (at 5 years	48	RR (M-H, Random, 95% CI)	0.86 (0.28, 2.65)
Amount of alcohol consumed			
Amount of alcohol consumed at 7- to 12-month follow-up			
Centilitres of pure alcohol at 12-month follow-up	23	SMD (IV, Random, 95% CI)	1.15 (0.26, 2.05)
Time to first drink assessed at 18-month follow-up	128	SMD (IV, Random, 95% CI)	0.15 (−0.20, 0.50)
Time to first heavy drink assessed at 18-month follow-up	128	SMD (IV, Random, 95% CI)	0.09 (−0.26, 0.44)
Attrition (dropout)			
Attrition (dropout) post-treatment	128	RR (M-H, Random, 95% CI)	Not estimable
Attrition (dropout) up to 6-month follow-up			
At 3- to 6-month follow-up	322	RR (M-H, Random, 95% CI)	1.02 (0.74, 1.42)
Attrition (dropout) 7- to 12-month follow-up			
At 12-month follow-up	247	RR (M-H, Random, 95% CI)	0.85 (0.67, 1.08)
Attrition (dropout) >12-month follow-up			
At 5-year follow-up	82	RR (M-H, Random, 95% CI)	1.33 (0.79, 2.24)

6.15   SHORT-TERM PSYCHODYNAMIC THERAPY

6.15.1   Definition

Short-term psychodynamic therapy is a derived from a psychodynamic/psychoanalytic model in which: (a) therapist and patient explore and gain insight into conflicts, and how these are represented in current situations and relationships, including the therapeutic relationship; (b) service users are given an opportunity to explore feelings, and conscious and unconscious conflicts originating in the past, with the technical focus on interpreting and working through conflicts; and (c) therapy is non-directive and service users are not taught specific skills such as thought monitoring, re-evaluation or problem solving. Treatment typically consists of 16 to 30 sessions (Leichsenring *et al.*, 2004), but there are interventions that offer more or less than this range.

6.15.2   Clinical review protocol (short-term psychodynamic therapy)

Information about the databases searched and the inclusion/exclusion criteria used for this section of the guideline can be found in Chapter 3 (further information about the search for health economic evidence can be found in Section 6.21). See Table 71 for a summary of the clinical review protocol for the review of short-term psychodynamic therapy).

6.15.3   Studies considered for review

The review team conducted a systematic review of RCTs that assessed the beneficial or detrimental effects of psychodynamic therapies in the treatment of alcohol

Table 71:   Clinical review protocol for the review of short-term psychodynamic therapy

Electronic databases	CINAHL, EMBASE, MEDLINE, PsycINFO, Cochrane Library
Date searched	Database inception to March 2010
Study design	RCT (at least ten participants per arm)
Population	Adults (over 18 years old) At least 80% of the sample meet the criteria for alcohol dependence or harmful alcohol use (clinical diagnosis or drinking more than 30 drinks per week)
Excluded populations	Hazardous drinkers and those drinking fewer than 30 drinks per week Pregnant women
Interventions	Short-term psychodynamic therapy
Comparator	Control or other active intervention
Outcomes	Abstinence Amount of alcohol consumed Rates of consumption Relapse (>X number of drinks or number of participants who have relapsed) Lapse (time to first drink or number of participants who have lapsed) Attrition (leaving the study early for any reason)

dependence or harmful alcohol use. See Table 72 for a summary of the study characteristics.

One trial relating to clinical evidence met the eligibility criteria set by the GDG, providing data on 49 participants. The study was published in a peer-reviewed journal in 1998. A number of studies identified in the search were initially excluded because they were not relevant to this guideline. Studies were further excluded because they did not meet methodological criteria (see Chapter 3). When studies did meet basic methodological inclusion criteria, the main reasons for exclusion were that the study was not directly relevant to the review questions, or no relevant alcohol-focused outcomes were available. A list of excluded studies can be found in Appendix 16d.

Short-term psychodynamic therapy versus other active intervention
The only trial suitable for inclusion was SANDAHL1998, which investigated group-based time-limited group psychotherapy (or a short-term psychodynamic therapy, as described above) versus another active intervention, which in this case was relapse prevention.

6.15.4 Evidence summary

The GRADE profiles and associated forest plots for the comparisons can be found in Appendix 18c and Appendix 17c, respectively.

Table 72: Summary of study characteristics for short-term psychodynamic therapy

	Short-term psychodynamic therapy versus other active intervention
K (total N)	1 RCT(N = 49)
Study ID	SANDAHL1998
Diagnosis	DSM–III–R alcohol dependence
Baseline severity	Duration of alcohol misuse: 11 years Reported morning drinking: 75.5%
Number of sessions	15 sessions
Length of treatment	15 weeks
Length of follow-up	15 months
Setting	Outpatient treatment centre
Treatment goal	Drinking reduction/moderation
Country	Sweden

Table 73: Short-term psychodynamic therapy versus other intervention evidence summary

Outcome or subgroup	N	Statistical method	Effect estimate
Abstinence			
Days abstinent at 15-month follow-up	44	SMD (IV, Random, 95% CI)	−0.64 (−1.24, −0.03)
Rates of consumption			
Days >80 g absolute alcohol (heavy drinking) at 15-month follow-up	44	SMD (IV, Random, 95% CI)	−0.06 (−0.65, 0.53)
Amount of alcohol consumed			
Grams absolute alcohol per drinking day at 15-month follow-up	44	SMD (IV, Random, 95% CI)	0.07 (−0.53, 0.66)
Attrition (dropout)			
At 15-month follow-up	49	RR (M-H, Random, 95% CI)	0.64 (0.12, 3.50)

Short-term psychodynamic therapy versus other active intervention
At 15-month follow-up, short-term psychodynamic therapy was significantly more effective than other therapies (in this case, cognitive behavioural relapse prevention) in maintaining abstinence, although the effect size was moderate. However, no significant difference was observed between short-term psychodynamic therapy and other therapies in reducing the quantity of alcohol consumed, heavy drinking rate or attrition. It must be noted that this analysis was based on a single study.

The quality of this evidence is *moderate*, therefore further research is likely to have an important impact on the confidence in the estimate of the effect. An evidence summary of the results of the meta-analyses can be seen in Table 73.

6.16   MULTI-MODAL TREATMENT

6.16.1   Definition

Multi-modal treatment for alcohol misuse involves a combination of a number of interventions that have been developed and evaluated as stand-alone interventions for alcohol misuse. Components of a multi-modal treatment could include motivational aspects (such as MET), TSF, AA or self-help group participation, group counselling, CBT-based relapse-prevention training and psychoeducational sessions. The intention is that by combining a number of effective interventions the combined treatment will be greater than any one individual treatment.

6.16.2   Clinical review protocol (multi-modal treatment)

Information about the databases searched and the inclusion/exclusion criteria used for this section of the guideline can be found in Chapter 3 (further information about the search for health economic evidence can be found in Section 6.21).

6.16.3   Studies considered for review

The review team conducted a systematic review of RCTs that assessed the beneficial or detrimental effects of multi-modal therapies in the treatment of alcohol dependence or harmful alcohol use. See Table 75 for a summary of the study characteristics.

Table 74: Clinical review protocol for the review of multi-modal treatment

Electronic databases	CINAHL, EMBASE, MEDLINE, PsycINFO, Cochrane Library
Date searched	Database inception to March 2010
Study design	RCT (at least ten participants per arm)
Population	Adults (over 18 years old) At least 80% of the sample meet the criteria for alcohol dependence or harmful alcohol use (clinical diagnosis or drinking more than 30 drinks per week)
Excluded populations	Hazardous drinkers and those drinking fewer than 30 drinks per week Pregnant women
Interventions	Multi-modal treatment
Comparator	Control or other active intervention
Outcomes	Abstinence Amount of alcohol consumed Rates of consumption Relapse (>X number of drinks or number of participants who have relapsed) Lapse (time to first drink or number of participants who have lapsed) Attrition (leaving the study early for any reason)

Table 75: Summary of study characteristics for multi-modal treatment

	Multi-modal treatment versus other active intervention
K (total N)	2 RCTs (N = 427)
Study ID	(1) DAVIS2002 (2) JOHN2003
Diagnosis	(1) DSM treatment-seeking alcohol abuse or dependent (2) ICD–10 alcohol dependent
Baseline severity	(1) Days drinking in last 6 months: approximately 110 days (2) Not reported
Number of sessions	Variable (see description of treatment modalities)
Length of treatment	(1) 14 days inpatient (2) 6 months inpatient and outpatient
Length of follow-up	Range: 6- to 12-month
Setting	(1) Outpatient treatment centre (2) Inpatient
Treatment goal	(1) Drinking reduction/moderation (2) Abstinence
Country	(1) US (2) Germany

Two trials relating to clinical evidence met the eligibility criteria set by the GDG, providing data on 427 participants. Both studies were published in peer-reviewed journals between 2002 and 2003. A number of studies identified in the search were initially excluded because they were not relevant to this guideline. Studies were excluded because they did not meet methodological criteria (see Chapter 3). When studies did meet basic methodological inclusion criteria, the main reason for exclusion was that no relevant alcohol-focused outcomes were available. A list of excluded studies can be found in Appendix 16d.

Multi-modal treatment versus other active intervention
Both included trials assessed multi-modal treatment versus another active intervention. DAVIS2002 assessed standard multi-modal outpatient treatment versus a psychoeducational intervention. Standard multi-modal treatment included a 3-week orientation period, which consisted of six group therapy sessions, three alcohol

education and three leisure education films, three community meetings and a minimum of six AA meetings. After orientation, participants were assigned to a permanent therapist for a mixture of individual and group therapy sessions tailored to the needs of the participant. JOHN2003 assessed multi-modal standard inpatient and outpatient treatment versus individual counselling. Standard treatment was based on the principles of motivational interviewing, relapse prevention and psychoeducational films, with a focus to support the motivation to seek help for substance-misuse problems.

6.16.4   Evidence summary

The GRADE profiles and associated forest plots for the comparisons can be found in Appendix 18c and Appendix 17c, respectively.

Multi-modal versus other active intervention
A small effect was observed favouring other therapies (that is, psychoeducational) over multi-modal treatment in maintaining abstinence when assessed post-treatment. In addition, other therapies (that is, counselling) were significantly better than multi-modal treatment in reducing the number of participants who had lapsed (small effect size). However, this was not the case at 12-month follow-up because no difference between groups was observed. Furthermore, no difference was observed between multi-modal treatment and other therapies in reducing the number of days drinking, the quantity of alcohol consumed and attrition up to 12-month follow-up.

The quality of this evidence is *low*, therefore further research is very likely to have an important impact on the confidence in the estimate of the effect and is likely to change the estimate. An evidence summary of the results of the meta-analyses can be seen in Table 76.

6.17   SELF-HELP-BASED TREATMENT

6.17.1   Definition

A self-help intervention is where a healthcare professional (or para-professional) would facilitate the use of the self-help material by introducing, monitoring and reviewing the outcome of such treatment. The intervention is limited in nature–usually no more than three to five sessions, some of which may be delivered by telephone. Self-administered interventions are designed to modify drinking behaviour and make use of a range of books, web pages, CD-ROMs or a self-help manual that is based on an evidence-based intervention and designed specifically for the purpose. An example is guided self-change (Sobell & Sobell, 1993). This treatment is manual-based and uses the principles of CBT and MET. The patient has an initial assessment followed by four treatment sessions and two follow-up telephone calls.

Table 76: Multimodal intervention versus other intervention evidence summary

Outcome or subgroup	N	Statistical method	Effect estimate
Abstinence			
Length of sobriety (in months) post-treatment	77	SMD (IV, Random, 95% CI)	0.48 (0.02, 0.93)
Lapse or relapse			
Lapsed post-treatment	84	RR (M-H, Random, 95% CI)	0.79 (0.60, 1.03)
Lapsed up to 6-month follow-up			
At 6 months	322	RR (M-H, Random, 95% CI)	1.23 (1.04, 1.45)
Lapsed - 7- to 12-month follow-up			
At 12-month follow-up	322	RR (M-H, Random, 95% CI)	0.92 (0.81, 1.05)
Rates of consumption			
Days drinking post-treatment	80	SMD (IV, Random, 95% CI)	−0.41 (−0.85, 0.04)
Amount of alcohol consumed			
Fluid ounces per day post-treatment	75	SMD (IV, Random, 95% CI)	−0.25 (−0.71, 0.21)
Attrition (dropout)			
Attrition (dropout) post-treatment	89	RR (M-H, Random, 95% CI)	1.05 (0.43, 2.57)
Attrition (dropout) up to 6 months follow-up			
At 6-month follow-up	322	RR (M-H, Random, 95% CI)	1.02 (0.74, 1.42)
Attrition (dropout) at 7- to 12-month follow-up			
At 12-month follow-up	223	RR (M-H, Random, 95% CI)	0.86 (0.67, 1.09)

6.17.2   Clinical review protocol (self-help-based treatment)

Information about the databases searched and the inclusion/exclusion criteria used for this section of the guideline can be found in Chapter 3 (further information about the search for health economic evidence can be found in Section 6.21). See Table 77 for a summary of the clinical review protocol for the review of self-help-based treatment.

6.17.3   Studies considered for review

The review team conducted a systematic review of RCTs that assessed the beneficial or detrimental effects of self-help-based treatment in the treatment of alcohol dependence or harmful alcohol use. See Table 78 for a summary of the study characteristics.

Table 77: Clinical review protocol for the review of self-help-based treatment

Electronic databases	CINAHL, EMBASE, MEDLINE, PsycINFO, Cochrane Library
Date searched	Database inception to March 2010
Study design	RCT (at least ten participants per arm)
Population	Adults (over 18 years old) At least 80% of the sample meet the criteria for alcohol dependence or harmful alcohol use (clinical diagnosis or drinking more than 30 drinks per week)
Excluded populations	Hazardous drinkers and those drinking fewer than 30 drinks per week Pregnant women
Interventions	Self-help-based treatment
Comparator	Control or other active intervention
Outcomes	Abstinence Amount of alcohol consumed Rates of consumption Relapse (>X number of drinks or number of participants who have relapsed) Lapse (time to first drink or number of participants who have lapsed) Attrition (leaving the study early for any reason)

One trial relating to clinical evidence met the eligibility criteria set by the GDG, providing data on 93 participants. The included study was published in a peer-reviewed journal in 2002. A number of studies identified in the search were initially excluded because they were not relevant to this guideline. Studies were excluded because they did not meet methodological criteria (see Chapter 3). A particular problem for self-help-based treatments is that they usually fall under the grouping of 'brief interventions'. Therefore, the main reasons for exclusions were the population assessed were hazardous drinkers (outside the scope of this guideline), the population were not treatment seeking, or no relevant alcohol-focused outcomes were available. A list of excluded studies can be found in Appendix 16d.

Guided self-help-based treatment (guided) versus non-guided self-help-based treatment
The single trial included in this analyses involved a comparison of guided self-help-based treatment versus non-guided self-help-based treatment. ANDREASSON2002 assessed guided self change versus self-help manual and advice only (non-guided).

Table 78: Summary of study characteristics for self-help-based treatment

	Self-help-based treatment (guided) versus self-help-based treatment (non-guided)
K (total N)	1 RCT (N = 93)
Study ID	ANDREASSON2002
Diagnosis	SADD score of 12.1, indicating a medium level of alcohol dependence
Baseline severity	Number of drinks per week: 24.3 drinks Number of DDD: 5.7
Number of sessions	Guided self-help: Assessment = one session Treatment = four sessions Follow-up = two telephone calls Non-guided self-help: Assessment = one session Treatment = one session
Length of treatment	N/A
Length of follow-up	9- and 23-month
Setting	Outpatient treatment centre
Treatment goal	Not explicitly stated
Country	Sweden

6.17.4 Evidence summary

The GRADE profiles and associated forest plots for the comparisons can be found in Appendix 18c and Appendix 17c, respectively.

Guided self-help-based treatment (guided) versus non-guided self-help-based treatment
Guided self-help was significantly more effective than non-guided self-help in reducing the quantity of drinks consumed per week when assessed at 9-month follow-up. However, no significant difference was observed between groups for the same variable at 23-month follow-up, or for the number of DDD (at 9- and 23-month follow-up) or attrition at 23-month follow-up.

The quality of this evidence is *moderate*, therefore further research is likely to have an important impact on the confidence in the estimate of the effect. An evidence summary of the results of the meta-analyses can be seen in Table 79.

Table 79: Comparing different formats of self-help-based treatment evidence summary

Outcome or subgroup	N	Statistical method	Effect estimate
Amount of alcohol consumed			
Amount of alcohol consumed at 7- to 12-month follow-up			
Number standard drinks per week at 9-month follow-up	59	SMD (IV, Random, 95% CI)	−0.54 (−1.06, −0.02)
Number of DDD at 9-month follow-up	59	SMD (IV, Random, 95% CI)	−0.19 (−0.70, 0.32)
Amount of alcohol consumed >12-month follow-up			
Number of standard drinks per week at 23-month follow-up	59	SMD (IV, Random, 95% CI)	−0.45 (−0.97, 0.07)
Number of DDD at 23-month follow-up	59	SMD (IV, Random, 95% CI)	−0.10 (−0.61, 0.41)
Attrition (dropout)			
Attrition at 23-month follow-up	93	RR (M-H, Random, 95% CI)	0.91 (0.53, 1.55)

6.18   PSYCHOEDUCATIONAL INTERVENTIONS

6.18.1   Definition

A psychoeducational intervention involves an interaction between an information provider and service user. It has the primary aim of offering information about the condition, as well as providing support and management strategies. Psychoeducational intervention for alcohol misuse involves the use of education videos, literature and lectures that highlight the health and lifestyle risks of excessive alcohol consumption. It is not usually used as a formal method of treatment, but an adjunct to conventional treatment methods. Psychoeducational attention control treatment (PACT) is a form of manual-based psychoeducational therapy developed by Fals-Stewart and Klostermann (2004) and used in some alcohol treatment trials.

6.18.2   Clinical review protocol (psychoeducational interventions)

Information about the databases searched and the inclusion/exclusion criteria used for this section of the guideline can be found in Chapter 3 (further information about the search for health economic evidence can be found in Section 6.21). See Table 80 for a summary of the clinical review protocol for the review of psychoeducational interventions.

Table 80: Clinical review protocol for the review of psychoeducational interventions

Electronic databases	CINAHL, EMBASE, MEDLINE, PsycINFO, Cochrane Library
Date searched	Database inception to March 2010
Study design	RCT (at least ten participants per arm)
Population	Adults (over 18 years old) At least 80% of the sample meet the criteria for alcohol dependence or harmful alcohol use (clinical diagnosis or drinking more than 30 drinks per week)
Excluded populations	Hazardous drinkers and those drinking fewer than 30 drinks per week Pregnant women
Interventions	Psychoeducational intervention
Comparator	Control or other active intervention
Outcomes	Abstinence Amount of alcohol consumed Rates of consumption Relapse (>X number of drinks or number of participants who have relapsed) Lapse (time to first drink or number of participants who have lapsed) Attrition (leaving the study early for any reason)

6.18.3 Studies considered for review

The review team conducted a systematic review of RCTs that assessed the beneficial or detrimental effects of behavioural therapies in the treatment of alcohol dependence or harmful alcohol use. See Table 50 (above, in Section 6.11) for a summary of the study characteristics. It should be noted that some trials included in analyses were three- or four-arm trials. To avoid double counting, the number of participants in treatment conditions used in more than one comparison was divided (by half in a three-arm trial, and by three in a four-arm trial).

Five trials relating to clinical evidence met the eligibility criteria set by the GDG, providing data on 1,312 participants. All five studies were published in peer-reviewed journals between 2001 and 2006. A number of studies identified in the search were initially excluded because they were not relevant to this guideline. Studies were excluded because they did not meet methodological criteria (see Chapter 3). When studies did meet basic methodological inclusion criteria, the main reason for exclusion was not meeting drinking quantity/diagnosis criteria, that is, participants were not drinking enough to be categorised as harmful or dependent or less than 80% of the sample meet criteria for alcohol dependence or harmful alcohol use. A list of excluded studies can be found in Appendix 16d.

Psychoeducational interventions versus other active intervention
All five included trials assessed psychoeducational interventions versus another active intervention. CONNORS2001 was complex in design and investigated a psychoeducational intervention plus alcohol-focused coping skills versus life skills plus alcohol-focused coping skills. Additionally, the study investigated the difference between low- and high-intensity treatment of these conditions. The results of the 30-month follow-up were obtained from Walitzer and Connors (2007). DAVIS2002 assessed a psychoeducational intervention versus standard multi-modal treatment. FALSSTEW-ART2005 investigated a psychoeducational intervention (used as an attentional control) versus BCT (plus group counselling), brief relationship therapy (plus group counselling) and individually-based TSF (plus group counselling). FALSSTEW-ART2006 investigated a psychoeducational intervention (as an attentional control) versus BCT (plus individually-based TSF) as well as individually-based TSF alone. SOBELL2002 investigated psychoeducational (bibliotherapy/drinking guidelines) versus motivational enhancement/personalised feedback. See Table 81 for a summary of the study characteristics.

6.18.4   Evidence summary

The GRADE profiles and associated forest plots for the comparisons can be found in Appendix 18c and Appendix 17c, respectively.

Table 81: Summary of study characteristics for psychoeducational intervention

	Psychoeducational versus other active intervention
K (total N)	5 RCTs (N = 1312)
Study ID	(1) CONNORS2001 (2) DAVIS2002 (3) FALSSTEWART2005 (4) FALSSTEWART2006 (5) SOBELL2002
Diagnosis	(1) DSM alcohol dependent (2) DSM alcohol dependent/abuse (3)–(4) DSM alcohol dependent (5) Not reported

Continued

Table 81: *(Continued)*

Baseline severity	(1) Percentage of sample severe dependence: 8.3% Percentage of sample moderate dependence: 66% Percentage of sample mild dependence: 18.1% Average monthly abstinent days: 10.1 Average monthly light days: 6.1 Average monthly moderate days: 8 Average monthly heavy days: 5.7 (2) Days drinking over 6 months: 110 (3) Percent day heavy drinking: 56 to 59% across treatment groups (4) PDA: 40 to 44% across treatment groups (5) Drinking days per week: 5.5 DDD: five drinks
Number of sessions	Range: 1 to 26 sessions
Length of treatment	Range: 1 to 26 weeks
Length of follow-up	Range: 3 to 18 months
Setting	(1) Outpatient clinical research unit (2)−(4) Outpatient treatment centre (5) Community level mail intervention
Treatment goal	(1)–(2) Drinking reduction/moderation (3) Not explicitly stated (4) Abstinence (5) Not explicitly stated
Country	(1)–(5) US

Psychoeducational versus other active intervention
The clinical findings for this comparison are mixed whether in favour of other active intervention over a psychoeducational intervention or finding no clinically significant difference between psychoeducational and other interventions. Other interventions were significantly better than psychoeducational interventions in increasing length of sobriety (post-treatment), and the percentage of abstinent/light drink days at 6- and 12-month follow-up.

No significant difference was observed between a psychoeducational intervention and other active interventions in attrition rates and other drinking-related variables.

The quality of this evidence is *moderate*, therefore further research is likely to have an important impact on the confidence in the estimate of the effect. An evidence summary of the results of the meta-analyses can be seen in Table 82.

Table 82: Psychoeducational intervention versus other intervention evidence summary

Outcome or subgroup	N	Statistical method	Effect estimate
Abstinence			
Length of sobriety post-treatment (months)	77	SMD (IV, Random, 95% CI)	0.48 (0.02, 0.93)
Abstinence post-treatment			
Percentage of days abstinent post-treatment	138	SMD (IV, Random, 95% CI)	0.03 (-0.32, 0.38)
Abstinence up to 6-month follow-up			
At 3-month follow-up	138	SMD (IV, Random, 95% CI)	0.12 (-0.26, 0.50)
At 6-month follow-up	138	SMD (IV, Random, 95% CI)	0.30 (-0.23, 0.84)
Abstinence 7- to 12-month follow-up			
At 9-month follow-up	138	SMD (IV, Random, 95% CI)	0.28 (-0.35, 0.92)
At 12-month follow-up	138	SMD (IV, Random, 95% CI)	0.26 (-0.43, 0.96)
Abstinent/light (one to three standard drinks) up to 6-month follow-up			
At 6-month follow-up	61	SMD (IV, Random, 95% CI)	0.94 (0.40, 1.48)
Abstinent/light (one to three standard drinks) 7- to 12-month follow-up			
At 12-month follow-up	61	SMD (IV, Random, 95% CI)	0.84 (0.27, 1.40)
Abstinent/light (one to three standard drinks) >12-month follow-up			
At 18-month follow-up	61	SMD (IV, Random, 95% CI)	0.74 (0.21, 1.26)
Number lapsed (non-abstinent) post-treatment			
At 6-month follow-up	84	RR (M-H, Random, 95% CI)	1.27 (0.97, 1.66)
Rates of consumption			
Rate of alcohol consumption post-treatment	179	SMD (IV, Random, 95% CI)	0.21 (-0.11, 0.53)
Percentage days heavy drinking at post-treatment	99	SMD (IV, Random, 95% CI)	-0.00 (-0.46, 0.46)
Days drinking (over last 6 months) post-treatment	80	SMD (IV, Random, 95% CI)	0.41 (-0.04, 0.85)

Continued

Table 82: (*Continued*)

Rate of alcohol consumption up to 6-month follow-up			
Percentage days heavy drinking at 3-month follow-up	99	SMD (IV, Random, 95% CI)	0.19 (−0.27, 0.65)
Percentage days heavy drinking at 6-month follow-up	99	SMD (IV, Random, 95% CI)	0.37 (−0.10, 0.83)
Rate of alcohol consumption − 7- to 12-month follow-up			
Days drinking per week at 12-month follow-up	657	SMD (IV, Random, 95% CI)	0.00 (−0.15, 0.15)
Days drinking five or more drinks at 12-month follow-up	657	SMD (IV, Random, 95% CI)	0.08 (−0.08, 0.23)
Percentage days heavy drinking at 9-month follow-up	99	SMD (IV, Random, 95% CI)	0.38 (−0.09, 0.84)
Percentage days heavy drinking at 12-month follow-up	99	SMD (IV, Random, 95% CI)	0.50 (−0.04, 1.04)
Amount of alcohol consumed			
Amount of alcohol consumed post-treatment			
Fluid ounces per day	75	SMD (IV, Random, 95% CI)	0.25 (−0.21, 0.71)
Amount of alcohol consumed 7- to 12-month follow-up			
DDD at 12-month follow-up	657	SMD (IV, Random, 95% CI)	0.00 (−0.15, 0.15)
Drinks per week at 12-month follow-up	657	SMD (IV, Random, 95% CI)	0.01 (−0.14, 0.16)
Attrition (dropout)			
Attrition (dropout) post-treatment	227	RR (M-H, Random, 95% CI)	0.93 (0.46, 1.87)
Attrition up to 6-month follow-up			
At 6-month follow-up	144	RR (M-H, Random, 95% CI)	1.01 (0.32, 3.19)
Attrition (dropout) 7- to 12-month follow-up			
At 12-month follow-up	1082	RR (M-H, Random, 95% CI)	0.83 (0.64, 1.07)
Attrition (dropout) >12-month follow-up			
At 18-month follow-up	130	RR (M-H, Random, 95% CI)	0.23 (0.01, 4.67)

6.19   MINDFULNESS MEDITATION

6.19.1   Definition

Mindfulness meditation is rooted in the principles of Buddhism and is characterised by having a non-judgemental approach to experiences that result in the practitioner acting reflectively rather than impulsively on these experiences (Chiesa, 2010). Mindfulness meditation has a goal of developing a non-judgemental attitude and relationship to thoughts, feelings and actions as they are experienced by the practitioner, and not necessarily to change the content of thoughts as in CBT for example (Teasdale *et al.*, 1995).

Mindfulness-based meditation has been suggested as a method of improving physical and mental health (for a review, see Allen *et al.*, 2006). However, the quality of this research is generally poor, not focused on alcohol as the substance of misuse, and few in number.

6.19.2   Clinical review protocol (mindfulness meditation)

In the current review, the role of meditation in maintaining abstinence and drinking reduction was investigated. Its application to other aspects usually associated with alternative therapies in this topic area (such as craving and withdrawal symptoms) was beyond the scope of this guideline and hence was not investigated. Information about the databases searched and the inclusion/exclusion criteria used for this section of the guideline can be found in Chapter 3. See Table 83 for a summary of the clinical review protocol for the review of meditation.

6.19.3   Studies considered for review

The review team conducted a systematic search of RCTs and systematic reviews that assessed the beneficial or detrimental effects of meditation in the treatment of alcohol dependence or harmful alcohol use. Following the literature search, there was an insufficient number of studies remaining to perform an unbiased and comprehensive meta-analysis of meditation for the treatment of alcohol misuse. Therefore, the GDG consensus was that a narrative summary of these studies would be conducted and observational studies would be included in the review. See Table 84 for a summary of the study characteristics.

Two trials (BOWEN2006[37]; ZGIERSKA2008) providing data on 320 participants were identified by the search. Both studies were published in peer-reviewed journals between 2006 and 2008. To the GDG's knowledge, no other studies that evaluated meditation for a population with alcohol misuse with alcohol-focused outcomes have been published.

---

[37]A secondary analysis of this sample was conducted by Bowen and colleagues (2007).

Table 83: Clinical review protocol for the review of meditation

Electronic databases	AMED, CINAHL, EMBASE, MEDLINE, PsycINFO, Cochrane Library
Date searched	Systematic reviews from 1993 to March 2010. All other searches from database inception to March 2010
Study design	RCTs (at least ten participants per arm); systematic reviews
Population	Adults (over 18 years old) At least 80% of the sample meet the criteria for alcohol dependence or harmful alcohol use (clinical diagnosis or drinking more than 30 drinks per week)
Excluded populations	Hazardous drinkers and those drinking fewer than 30 drinks per week Pregnant women
Interventions	Meditation
Comparator	Control or other active intervention
Outcomes	Abstinence Amount of alcohol consumed Rates of consumption Relapse (>X number of drinks or number of participants who have relapsed) Lapse (time to first drink or number of participants who have lapsed) Attrition (leaving the study early for any reason)

6.19.4   Evidence summary

Bowen and colleagues (2006) investigated the effectiveness of mindfulness meditation on substance-use outcomes in an incarcerated population. The study compared mindfulness meditation with treatment as usual (a chemical dependency programme and psychoeducational intervention). The authors reported that mindfulness meditation was significantly more effective than treatment as usual in the amount of alcohol consumed at 3-month follow-up (p <0.005). However, adherence to the therapy was not assessed and therefore the authors were unclear whether participants correctly followed the principles of mindfulness meditation. Furthermore, the level of alcohol dependence in this sample was unclear.

In a feasibility pilot prospective case series study, Zgierska and colleagues (2008) evaluated the efficacy of mindfulness meditation in increasing abstinence and reducing the quantity of alcohol consumed. Alcohol-dependent participants who had recently completed an intensive outpatient treatment programme were recruited. The study found

Table 84: Summary of study characteristics for mindfulness meditation

Study (country)	Treatment conditions and number of participants	Baseline severity and diagnosis	Setting, treatment characteristics and assessment points
BOWEN2006 (US)	1. Mindfulness meditation (n = 63)	No indication of level of dependence	Setting: prison
	2. Treatment as usual (n = 242)	Baseline drinks per week: Meditation = 64.83 (SD = 73.01) TAU = 43.98 (SD = 55.61)	Treatment characteristics Meditation: 10-day course, TAU: chemical dependency treatment, psychoeducational intervention
			Assessment point: 3 months after release from prison
ZGIERSKA2008 (US)	Mindfulness meditation (n = 19). Participants continued usual outpatient treatment	DSM–IV alcohol-dependent graduates from an intensive outpatient treatment programme	Setting: alcohol treatment centre
			Treatment characteristics: 8-week course, 2-hour weekly sessions; course involved both meditation training and relapse prevention using cognitive behavioural techniques.
			Assessment points: 4, 8, 12 and 16 weeks post-baseline

that participants reported significantly fewer heavy drinking days at 4-, 8- and 12-week follow-up (all p <0.005), but not at 16-week follow-up. Furthermore, participants were drinking substantially less when assessed at 4- and 8-week follow-up (p <0.005), but no significant difference was observed at 12- and 16-week follow-up. No significant difference over time was observed in increasing PDA. It must be noted, however, that meditation in this study was not used as an active intervention but as a post-treatment intervention. Furthermore, the sample size was small and the study had no control group.

These studies reported a significant effect of mindfulness meditation on alcohol consumption. Overall, there is limited and poor-quality evidence that does not support the use of mindfulness-based meditation for treating alcohol dependence and harmful alcohol use.

6.20   CLINICAL EVIDENCE SUMMARY

A range of psychological interventions to prevent relapse or promote abstinence in harmful and dependent alcohol misuse were reviewed. The participant populations of the studies included in this review were either harmful drinkers or mildly dependent on alcohol. Evidence for efficacy showed an advantage for BCT both over treatment as usual, active controls and other active interventions. In the cases of the other psychological interventions there was evidence that CBT, SBNT, and behavioural therapies were better than treatment as usual or control. The evidence for the efficacy of the addition of contingency management to standard care was limited and contradictory overall, which was further complicated because contingency management was not a stand-alone intervention and was added to standard care or network support. In the case of TSF and motivational techniques, although there was evidence of equivalence to other interventions, there was no evidence to show that these interventions were, for harmful and dependent alcohol use, more effective than the other interventions. Importantly, there was a lack of evidence for their effectiveness compared with treatment as usual or control. For all of the above interventions the evidence was judged to be of a high or moderate quality on the GRADE profiles.

The duration of treatment and number of sessions across the treatment trials included in the review was also considered. The duration of treatment for motivational techniques was 1 to 6 weeks, TSF was 12 weeks, cognitive behavioural therapies was 2 weeks to 6 months (with most ending at 12 weeks), behavioural therapies was 6 to 12 weeks, social network and environment-based therapies ranged from 8 to 16 weeks, and couples therapies ranged from 4 to 12 weeks. Taking into consideration the intensity of the treatments in these trials, for those with a high-intensity intervention, the duration of treatment was on average 12 weeks.

In addition, the GDG felt that both motivational techniques and TSF were best seen as components of any effective psychosocial intervention delivered in alcohol services, with the assessment and enhancing of motivation forming a key element of the assessment process. It should also be noted that facilitation of uptake of community support (for example, AA) is seen as a key element of care coordination and case management (see Chapter 5) and that the individual psychological interventions form a required component part of any pharmacological intervention. In developing the recommendations, this was also borne in mind.

There was very limited evidence of low-to-moderate quality to support the efficacy of counselling, short-term psychodynamic therapy, multi-modal treatment, self-help-based treatment, psychoeducational interventions and mindfulness meditation.

6.21   HEALTH ECONOMIC EVIDENCE

6.21.1   Review overview

The literature search identified six studies that assessed the cost effectiveness of psychological interventions for the treatment of alcohol dependence or harmful alcohol use (Alwyn *et al.*, 2004; Fals-Stewart *et al.*, 2005; Holder *et al.*, 2000; Mortimer & Segal 2005; Slattery *et al.*, 2003; UKATT Research Team, 2005). Full references, characteristics and results of all studies included in the economic review are presented in the form of evidence tables in Appendix 19.

The study by Alwyn and colleagues (2004) considered the cost effectiveness of adding a psychological intervention to a conventional home detoxification programme for the treatment of 'problem drinkers'. The home detoxification programme comprised five home visits of 30 minutes duration delivered by CPNs. The study population consisted of 91 heavy drinkers in the UK who fulfilled inclusion criteria for home detoxification. A number of outcome measures were assessed in the study including: number of DDD; total number of days abstinent; total number of alcohol units consumed; abstinence or moderate drinking; and severity of dependence. The NNT to produce one extra non-drinker was also calculated. An NHS perspective was used for the economic analysis. Resource-use data included inpatient days, outpatient care (including CPN visits) and medications. Because clinical outcomes were left disaggregated and no summary outcome measure was used in the economic analysis, a cost-consequences analysis was used.

The authors made no formal attempt to compare the total costs of a psychological intervention in addition to home detoxification with home detoxification alone. Instead the authors calculated total costs per person of inpatient treatment (£2,186 to £3,901), outpatient treatment (£581 to £768) and home detoxification plus psychological intervention (£231). Therefore, the extra cost of a psychological intervention programme was substantially lower than the cost of inpatient treatment and outpatient visits. In terms of clinical outcomes, significantly better results were observed in people treated with home detoxification plus a psychological intervention. The authors concluded that, due to the low NNT to obtain an extra non-drinker, it is likely that the implementation of a psychological intervention would lead to cost savings to the NHS. Although the results of this study are highly relevant to the UK context, there are a number of methodological limitations. Firstly, no attempt was made to combine costs and effectiveness with an array of effectiveness measures used in the study. The measures of effectiveness used are of limited usefulness to policy makers when assessing the comparative cost effectiveness of healthcare interventions. The clinical-effectiveness study compared psychological intervention and home detoxification with home detoxification alone. However, in the cost-analysis, home detoxification was compared with other detoxification programmes, such as inpatient and outpatient programmes. Therefore, the study did not directly assess the cost-effectiveness of adding psychological intervention to home detoxification.

The study by Fals-Stewart and colleagues (2005) considered the cost-effectiveness of brief relationship therapy (BRT) compared with standard BCT (S-BCT), individual-based treatment (IBT) and PACT for alcohol-dependent males and their non-substance-misusing female partners. BRT, IBT and PACT consisted of 18 therapy sessions over 12 weeks whilst S-BCT consisted of 24 sessions over 12 weeks with participants randomised to one of the four groups and followed up for 12 months. A societal perspective was taken for the analysis with costs including those associated with the four treatment programmes and costs of participants' and their partners' travel time. The primary measure of effectiveness for the economic analysis was the change in percentage days of heavy drinking from baseline to 12 months. Rather than calculating ICERs, the authors calculated mean change in PDHD over 12 months divided by mean cost of treatment delivery (in US$100 units), with higher ratios indicating greater cost effectiveness. Overall, BRT had the highest mean ratio (4.61) of the four treatment programmes considered, suggesting this was the most cost-effective treatment. The findings of this study have limited applicability to this guideline as it is based within the US health system, outcomes were not expressed as QALYs and a societal perspective was taken for the cost analysis (both outside the NICE reference case). Furthermore, no formal attempt at an incremental analysis, in terms of differences in costs and outcomes, was attempted by the authors.

The study by Holder and colleagues (2000) compared the healthcare costs of three treatment modalities (12-session CBT, 4-session MET and 12-session TSF) over 3 years' follow-up. The study participants were a sample (65%) of individuals with alcohol dependency symptoms taken from the US Project MATCH study (Project MATCH Research Group, 1998). The perspective of the cost analysis was from US healthcare providers. Resource-use data included the three treatments and any subsequent inpatient or outpatient care over 3 years. The authors calculated mean monthly costs for the three treatments rather than total costs over 3 years and no incremental or statistical analyses were presented. Overall, mean monthly costs were US$186 for CBT, US$176 for MET and US$225 for TSF, suggesting that MET had the largest potential healthcare savings over 3 years. The major limitations of this analysis were the lack of descriptive detail on the resource use and costs considered whilst no incremental analysis was presented. The findings have limited applicability to this guideline as it was based on the US healthcare system and no formal attempt was made by the authors to combine cost and clinical-outcomes data, which were collected in the study and reported elsewhere (Project MATCH Research Group, 1998).

The study by Mortimer and Segal (2005) conducted separate, mutually exclusive, model-based economic analyses of interventions for 'problem drinking' and alcohol dependence. A lifetime horizon was used for all of the analyses considered. The first analysis compared three brief motivational interventions with different levels of intensity (simple was 5 minutes, brief was 20 minutes and extended was four sessions of 120 to 150 minutes) with no active treatment in a population of heavy drinkers within the Australian healthcare setting. The outcome measure used in the analysis was QALYs calculated from disability weights derived from a single published source (Stouthard *et al.*, 1997). Clinical effectiveness data were taken from published studies evaluating interventions that were targeting heavy drinkers at lower severity levels. These data were used to estimate how patients would progress between specific drinking states (problem, moderate or dependent) within the model. The authors did not specify the resource use and cost components included in the model, although a health service perspective was adopted for the analysis. The results of the analysis suggested that brief motivational interventions were cost effective compared with no active treatment. The ICERs ranged from under AUS$82 (£61) per QALY for the simple intervention to under AUS$282 (£179) per QALY for the extended intervention.

The second analysis compared psychotherapies for mild to moderate alcohol dependence. The comparators were moderation-oriented cue exposure (MOCE) versus BSCT and MET or non-directive reflective listening versus no further counselling after initial assessment, also within the Australian healthcare setting. Again, the outcome measure used in the analysis was the QALY calculated from disability weights derived from a single published source (Stouthard *et al.*, 1997). Clinical effectiveness data were taken from published studies evaluating interventions for mild to severe dependence. These data were used to estimate how patients would progress between specific drinking states (problem, moderate or dependent) within the model. No resource use and cost components were specified within the article. The results of the analysis suggested that MOCE was cost effective in comparison with BSCT, resulting in an ICER of AUS\$2,145 (£1,589) per QALY. Non-directive reflective listening was dominated by no further counselling after initial assessment, resulting in higher costs but lower QALYs. However, the results of the analysis suggested that MET was cost effective compared with no further counselling after initial assessment, resulting in an ICER of AUS\$3366 (£2,493) per QALY.

There are several limitations of the results of the study by Mortimer and Segal (2005) that reduce their applicability to any UK-based recommendations. In the second analysis of interventions for mild to moderate alcohol dependence, a common baseline comparator was not used in the analyses of MOCE, MET and non-directive reflective listening, limiting their comparability in terms of cost effectiveness. Ideally, indirect comparisons of the three interventions would have provided additional information about their relative effectiveness. Little explanation was given in the article as to how the clinical effectiveness data, which were taken from various sources, were used to inform the health states used in the economic models. The article did not specify the resource use and costs that were included in the analyses although a health perspective was used. The analyses all used QALYs as the primary outcome measure, which allows for comparison across interventions, although again there was insufficient description of the utility weights that were applied to the health states within the model.

The study by Slattery and colleagues (2003) developed an economic model to assess the cost effectiveness of four psychological interventions in comparison with standard care within the Scottish health service: coping/social skills training; BSCT; MET and marital/family therapy. The populations examined were 45-year-old men and women with a diagnosis of alcohol dependence. The outcome measures used in the economic model were the number of people who have abstained and number of deaths averted. The clinical effectiveness data were based on a methodologically diverse selection of trials which were not described within the study. Most studies included a treatment arm in which the intervention was thought likely to have little or no effect and this was used as the comparator arm when available. Resource use involved in the delivery of psychological interventions was estimated from expert clinical opinion and included the number and duration of sessions, staff and educational materials. Unit costs were taken from Scottish health service estimates. Other healthcare costs included in the model were those associated with alcohol-related disease endpoints such as stroke, cancer, cirrhosis and alcohol-related psychoses. Costs were applied according to inpatient length of stay taken from Scottish medical records.

For each intervention, the costs of psychological treatment and any disease endpoints for a hypothetical cohort of 1000 patients were compared with standard care over a 20-year time horizon, to determine any net healthcare cost savings. All four therapies demonstrated net savings ranging from £274,008 (coping/social skills training) to £80,452 (BSCT) in comparison with standard care. All four interventions resulted in lower costs per additional abstinent person and lower costs per death averted in comparison with standard care. Whilst the results of the study, based on a hypothetical cohort of patients within the Scottish health service, may be applicable

331

to a UK setting, there are several problematic methodological issues with the study. First, the sources of the effectiveness data used in the model were not explicitly described by the authors, who suggested that the data were taken from a methodologically diverse selection of trials, thus suggesting a high level of heterogeneity. Second, no attempt was made to translate intermediate clinical endpoints such as abstinence rates into QALYs, which are useful to decision makers when assessing the comparative cost effectiveness of healthcare interventions.

The UKATT study (2005) evaluated the cost effectiveness of MET versus SBNT amongst a population comprising people who would normally seek treatment for alcohol misuse at UK treatment sites. The outcome measure used in the economic analysis was the QALY, which was estimated by using the EQ-5D questionnaire completed by patients at baseline, 3 and 12 months. The primary measures of clinical effectiveness were changes in alcohol consumption, alcohol dependence and alcohol-related problems over the 12-month period. A societal perspective was taken for the analysis. Resource-use data that were collected during the study included training and supervision, and materials related to treatment, hospitalisation, outpatient visits, GP and CPN visits, rehabilitation and consultation in alcohol agencies, social service contacts and court attendances. Unit-cost estimates were derived from a variety of UK published sources.

At 12 months, the total mean costs were higher in the MET group, resulting in a mean difference of £206 per patient (95% CI, −£454 to £818) versus SBNT. After adjusting for baseline differences, the MET group achieved slightly higher QALYs than SBNT, resulting in a mean difference of 0.0113 QALYs (95% CI, −0.0532 to 0.0235). Combining costs and QALYs, the MET group had an ICER of £18,230 in comparison with SBNT. CEACs showed that, at a cost-effectiveness threshold of £30,000 per QALY, MET had a 57.6% probability of being more cost effective than SBNT. The results of the study are applicable to a UK setting and the outcome measure used enables comparison across healthcare interventions. However, as the authors note, the analysis had a short time horizon and the longer-term effects of a reduction in drinking were not taken into consideration.

6.21.2 Health economic summary

The systematic search of the health economic literature did not identify evidence on the cost effectiveness of all of the psychological interventions considered in this guideline. Three of the studies identified were UK-based (Alwyn *et al.*, 2004; Slattery *et al.*, 2003; UKATT Research Team, 2005), two were US-based (Fals-Stewart *et al.*, 2005; Holder *et al.*, 2000) and one was Australian (Mortimer & Segal, 2005). The study by Alwyn and colleagues (2004) suggested that adding a psychological intervention to a home detoxification programme may offer the NHS cost savings in 'problem drinkers'. The study by Slattery and colleagues (2003) showed that four psychological interventions, including coping/social skills training, BSCT, MET and marital/family therapy, offered significant healthcare cost savings compared with standard care for alcohol-dependent patients. The UKATT Research Team (2005) suggested that MET was cost effective in people who misuse alcohol, at current UK thresholds, in comparison with SBNT (but note that it was not identified as a clinically effective intervention in this guideline). Fals-Stewart and colleagues (2005) concluded that brief relationship therapy was significantly more cost effective compared with standard BCT, IBT and psychoeducational control treatment. Holder and colleagues (2000) suggested that MET offered the largest potential healthcare cost savings over 3 years when compared with CBT or TSF. Mortimer and Segal (2005) concluded that brief motivational interventions were cost effective compared with no active treatment among 'problem drinkers' whilst MOCE and MET were cost-effective treatments for alcohol dependency, although no common comparators were used in either analysis.

Providing an adequate summary of the health economic evidence presented here is difficult due to the differences across the studies in terms of the interventions and comparators considered, study populations, costs and outcomes considered, and other methodological differences. Overall, the health economic review does not provide evidence of superior cost effectiveness for any particular psychological intervention.

6.21.3   Economic considerations

Of all the psychological interventions included in the systematic effectiveness review and then found suitable for recommendation in the NHS, only a few of these have supporting economic evidence.

A potential solution to this problem would be to undertake economic modelling to determine the most cost-effective psychological intervention. However, certain aspects of the effectiveness evidence made it difficult to do so (that is, there was a lack of common comparators and interventions were usually compared with other active interventions, a 'no treatment/usual care/placebo' arm was rarely identified).

Furthermore, the meta-analyses showed that there were small if any differences in effect between active treatments, and only a few of these, for example BCT, showed much evidence of a consistent positive effect, particularly against other therapies.

Therefore, the following costing exercise was undertaken for the possible recommended psychological interventions.

Behavioural couples therapy
The clinical effective studies in the guideline systematic literature review described this intervention being delivered in a variety of ways. The GDG were of the opinion that the number of sessions and duration of these sessions as described by Lam and colleagues (2009) that is, 12 weekly sessions of 60 minutes' duration under the supervision of a competent practitioner, were considered to be reflective of what should be delivered in the UK NHS.

It is very likely that these sessions would be conducted by a clinical psychologist. The unit cost of a clinical psychologist is £75 per hour of patient contact in 2008/09 prices (Curtis, 2009). This cost includes salary, salary on-costs, overheads and capital overheads plus any qualification costs.

Based on these estimates the average cost of a BCT intervention would be £900 per couple.

Psychological and psychosocial interventions

Cognitive behavioural therapy
No evidence on the cost effectiveness of CBT in this population was identified by the systematic search of the health economic literature.

The clinical evidence in the guideline systematic literature review described CBT interventions being delivered in a variety of sessions and durations either individually or in structured groups under the supervision of a competent practitioner. The clinical evidence was taken in consideration and the GDG agreed that a CBT programme would typically involve weekly sessions of 1 hour's duration over a 12-week period.

These sessions would be conducted by a clinical psychologist. The unit cost of a clinical psychologist is £75 per hour of patient contact in 2008/09 prices (Curtis, 2009). This cost includes salary, salary oncosts, overheads and capital overheads plus any qualification costs.

Based on these estimates the average cost of an individual-based CBT intervention would be £900 per patient.

The GDG were of the opinion that group interventions, although likely to be more cost effective per patient, were unlikely to be delivered successfully in an outpatient setting because of the expected high attrition/low retention rates. They were also of the opinion that group interventions would potentially be more suitable to inpatient/residential settings as the likelihood of patients attending all treatment sessions would be higher. It was unclear from the literature what the optimal number of patients per group would be. Obviously, if the number and duration of sessions as well as the number of staff delivering the service remained the same, the total costs per person would be expected to decrease significantly.

Social network and environment-based therapies
The UKATT Research Team described SBNT as comprising up to eight 50-minute sessions (UKATT2005). This particular intervention can be delivered by a range of mental health professionals. The GDG highlighted that it is likely that the sessions would be supervised by a nurse (or an NHS professional who is trained to deliver this intervention). It was assumed that such workers would be on AfC salary scale 6, which is likely to be comparable with the salary scales of a community nurse. The unit cost of an AfC Band 6 community nurse is £70 per hour of patient contact in 2008/09 prices (Curtis, 2009). This cost includes salary, salary oncosts, overheads and capital overheads plus any qualification costs. Based on these estimates the average cost of such a therapy would be £467 per patient.

Behavioural therapies
The clinical evidence in the guideline systematic literature review described a variety of interventions that were considered to be behavioural therapies. They were delivered in a variety of sessions and durations either individually or in structured groups under the supervision of a competent practitioner. The clinical evidence was taken in consideration and the GDG agreed that behavioural therapies would typically involve weekly sessions of 1 hour's duration over a 12-week period.

Behavioural therapies can also be delivered by a range of mental health professionals. The GDG highlighted the following professionals: a clinical psychologist, a

334

nurse, or an NHS professional who is trained to deliver this intervention. It was assumed that such workers would be on AfC salary scale 6, which would be likely to be comparable with the salary scales of a community nurse. The unit cost of an AfC Band 6 community nurse is £70 per hour of patient contact and the unit cost of a clinical psychologist is £75 per hour of patient contact in 2007/08 prices (Curtis, 2009). These costs include salary, salary oncosts, overheads and capital overheads plus any qualification costs. Based on these estimates the average cost of a behavioural intervention would be £900 per patient if delivered by a clinical psychologist and £840 per patient if delivered by a mental health professional described above.

A summary of the estimated resource use and costs involved in delivering these psychological interventions is presented in Table 85.

Table 85: Summary of resource use and costs associated with psychological interventions

BCT	**£900 per couple**	
12 weekly sessions, 60 minutes long	This estimate is based on Lam and colleagues' (2009) study, included in the clinical evidence review	
Clinical psychologist	£75 per hour of client contact (Curtis, 2009)	
CBT	**£900 per patient**	
12 weekly sessions, 60 minutes long	GDG expert opinion and clinical evidence	
Clinical psychologist	£75 per hour of client contact (Curtis, 2009)	
Social network and environment-based therapies		
8 sessions, 50 minutes long	UKATT2005	
Nurse (community)	AfC Band 6. £70 per hour spent with patient (£1.17 per minute)	£467 per patient
Behavioural therapies		
12 weekly sessions, 60 minutes long	GDG expert opinion and clinical evidence	
Clinical psychologist	£75 per hour of client contact (Curtis, 2009)	£900 per patient
Nurse (community)	AfC Band 6. £68 per hour spent with patient (£1.13 per minute)	£816 per patient

6.22 SPECIAL POPULATIONS – CHILDREN AND YOUNG PEOPLE

6.22.1 Introduction

In the development of the adult treatment sections of this guideline it was accepted that for some people who misuse alcohol (in particular those with harmful use or mild dependence) the reduction in alcohol consumption might be an option. However, given the potential long-term harm experienced by children and young people who are alcohol dependent or harmful drinkers, and the frequent presence of comorbid substance misuse and other psychiatric disorders, it was felt that the appropriate goal for children and young people should be achieving abstinence. However, it was recognised by the GDG that considerable difficulties are faced by some young people in trying to achieve abstinence, particularly if the support they receive from their families, carers and others is limited or non-existent or they experience considerable peer pressure to drink alcohol. Therefore, for some young people the GDG accepted that that an initial reduction in alcohol misuse may be the only achievable short-term objective. Nevertheless, the GDG's view was that, given the considerable problems that young people face, abstinence remained the preferred goal.

A further important difference between the treatment of adults and young people concerns the presence of comorbidities. Although comorbid depressive and anxiety symptoms are common in adults with harmful drinking and alcohol misuse (Weaver *et al.*, 2006), the extent and severity of the comorbidities often found in children is greater (Perepletchikova *et al.*, 2008). Comorbid disorders such as conduct disorder and ADHD significantly complicate the management of alcohol misuse, and concurrent treatment of them is to be considered. This problem is well known (Perepletchikova *et al.*, 2008) and a number of treatments (for example, multisystemic therapy [Henggeler *et al.*, 1999], brief strategic family therapy [Szapocznik *et al.*, 2003] or multidimensional family therapy [Liddle, 1992]) have been developed for conduct disorder explicitly to deal with the complexity of problems faced by children and young people, including drug and alcohol misuse. The latter two interventions have a very explicit focus on substance misuse. At the heart of all these interventions lies the recognition of the considerable complexity of problems presented by young people who misuse alcohol and drugs, and the need often to develop a multisystem, multi-level approach to deliver integrated care.

6.22.2 Aim of review

This section aims to review the evidence for psychological interventions for the treatment of alcohol dependence and harmful alcohol use in children and young people. However, although there are several published reviews on the efficacy of psychological interventions for adults and for the prevention of adolescent substance misuse, there are only a limited number of trials assessing the clinical efficacy of psychological interventions for alcohol misuse alone (without comorbid drug misuse) for children and young people under the age of 18 years. In addition, the patient populations assessed in these trials more often than not have comorbid substance misuse. Therefore, a GDG consensus-based decision was agreed that the literature search would be for alcohol-specific primary studies as well as published systematic reviews to guide the overall strategy of a narrative synthesis of the evidence.

Psychological therapies were considered for inclusion in the review if they were:
- alcohol-focused only
- planned treatment (especially for brief interventions)
- for treatment-seeking participants only (of particular importance for the brief interventions because the scope did not cover opportunistic brief interventions – see Appendix 1)
- manual-based or, in the absence of a formal manual, the intervention should be well-defined and structured
- ethical and safe.

6.22.3 Review questions

The primary review question addressed in this section is:

For children and young people who are alcohol dependent or harmful drinkers, is *treatment x* when compared with *y* more clinically- and cost-effective, and does this depend on the presence of comorbidities?

6.22.4 Clinical review protocol

As part of the overall search for effective individual, group and multicomponent psychological and psychosocial interventions for children and young people, the review team conducted a systematic review of published systematic reviews (in part, to take account of the complex comorbidity) of interventions for young people who misuse drugs and alcohol, and also RCTs of interventions for children and young people for alcohol misuse specifically. The literature search identified a number of primary studies investigating the efficacy of psychological interventions for children and young people. However, the participant population in the majority of these studies did not reach inclusion criteria for drinking severity and could not be classified as dependent/harmful. See Table 86 for a summary of the clinical review protocol for the review of psychological interventions for children and young people.

6.22.5 Narrative review

This review of psychological and psychosocial interventions for children and young people should be read in conjunction with the review of brief interventions contained in the NICE public health guidance (NICE, 2010a), and the review of psychological interventions for adults contained within this guideline. A limited number of studies,

337

Table 86: Clinical review protocol for the review of psychological interventions for children and young people

Electronic databases	CENTRAL, CINAHL, EMBASE, MEDLINE, PsycINFO
Date searched	Database inception to March 2010
Study design	Systematic reviews; RCT (at least ten participants per arm)
Population	Children and young people (10 to 18 years)
	At least 80% of the sample meet the criteria for alcohol dependence or harmful alcohol use (clinical diagnosis)
Excluded populations	Hazardous drinkers and those drinking fewer than 30 drinks per week
Interventions	Individual or group interventions; multicomponent interventions
Comparator	Control or other active intervention
Outcomes	Abstinence
	Amount of alcohol consumed
	Rates of consumption
	Relapse (>X number of drinks or number of participants who have relapsed)
	Lapse (time to first drink or number of participants who have lapsed)
	Attrition (leaving the study early for any reason)

specifically on alcohol-focused interventions, have been undertaken for children and young people. However, a number of studies have considered the treatment of conduct disorder in the presence of drug or alcohol misuse. In light of this significant comorbidity, in addition to the two guidelines referred to above, the GDG also drew on other recent NICE guidelines, specifically the review of conduct disorders in young people contained within the NICE guideline on antisocial personality disorder (NICE, 2008a) and three other systematic reviews (Perepletchikova *et al.*, 2008; Tripodi *et al.*, 2010; Waldron & Kaminer, 2004). Individual- and group-based therapies and multicomponent interventions used in the treatment of alcohol dependence and harmful alcohol use in children and young people were considered in the review of the evidence.

Individual and group psychological interventions

The public health guidance on the prevention of alcohol-related problems in adults and young people (NICE, 2010a), and also on community interventions for vulnerable young adults (NICE, 2007b), recognise the value of individual and/or group CBT. A number of studies that assess the use of individual- or group-based psychological interventions have been identified and reviewed (Perepletchikova *et al.,* 2008; Tripodi *et al.,* 2010; Waldron & Kaminer, 2004).

In a recent systematic review, Tripodi and colleagues (2010) conducted a meta-analysis of experimental studies (including RCTs) evaluating both individual- and group-based interventions collectively (brief interventions, MET and CBT) as well as family-based interventions with a focus on reducing alcohol misuse. However, of these studies only a limited number of trials evaluated the use of CBT (with an emphasis on relapse prevention) and MET in a sample of children or young people identified with harmful or dependent drinking. The review consisted of 16 studies (14 RCTs, two of which were quasi-experimental) assessing both individual and group treatment, and multicomponent therapies. Ten of these included studies assessing individual/group treatment. However the studies included in the meta-analysis were concerned with individuals who did not meet criteria for harmful drinking or alcohol dependence (n = 1), had a participant population that had a significant comorbid psychiatric disorder (n = 2), and in the majority of cases the focus was not specifically on alcohol misuse, but rather on substance misuse more generally (n = 7). The results of the meta-analyses showed a significantly large effect in drinking reduction for individual interventions (effect size −0.75; 95% CI, −1.10 to −0.40). However, the meta-analyses did not distinguish between different types of individual interventions in pooled analyses; therefore, other reviews that focused on specific interventions were considered.

Brief interventions and motivational interviewing

The NICE guidance on prevention of alcohol-related problems in adults and young people (NICE, 2010a) and on community interventions for vulnerable young adults (NICE, 2007b) both consider the evidence for brief motivational techniques (motivational interviewing and MET). Motivational interviewing and other brief interventions may serve to heighten motivation, increase self-efficacy, and provide personalised feedback and education tailored to specific substances and comorbid problems such as psychiatric disorders. The evidence for this is mainly from the adult literature although there is an emerging, albeit still limited, literature for young people where modifications of motivational interviewing or MET for young people have shown promise for both evaluation and treatment (Colby *et al.,* 1998; Monti *et al.,* 1999). However, a more recent review by Perepletchikova and colleagues (2008) reported uncertain outcomes for MET when used alone for alcohol misuse (this is consistent with the approach to harmful and dependent alcohol misuse identified for adults in this guideline). There is some evidence to suggest that motivational techniques when combined with CBT may be effective, for example in the Cannabis Youth Trial (CYT; Dennis *et al.,* 2004), although this population was predominately diagnosed as dependent on cannabis.

Cognitive behavioural therapy

Waldron and Kaminer (2004), in a review of CBT approaches to substance-use disorders (which is broader than alcohol misuse alone), concluded that individual CBT treatment may be effective in reducing substance misuse as well as other related problems. They also made a number of suggestions about the adaptation of CBT approaches to young people, addressing developmental stages and levels of maturity. This review reported that CBT in group format was as effective as individual therapy. CBT has been applied both in individual and group modalities, in combination with family approaches and MET. Interventions with the young person alone (for example, CBT or CBT plus MET) have been reported as effective (Dennis *et al.,* 2004; Kaminer & Burleson, 1999; Kaminer *et al.,* 1998). However, much of the evidence base is from approaches dealing with comorbidity such as conduct disorders, and anxiety and affective disorders where information on the extent and severity of alcohol misuse specifically is lacking. Perepletchikova and colleagues (2008) in a subsequent review considered five studies looking at the effectiveness of CBT in the reduction of alcohol misuse, three of which were of CBT alone, one evaluated an integrated family- and group-CBT approach and one looked at the efficacy of CBT on the reduction of substance use in those with comorbid conduct disorder. Again it appears that the data is primarily concerned with children and young people who did not have a high severity of alcohol misuse.

Kaminer and colleagues (2002), in one of the few studies that had a more substantial proportion of participants with alcohol dependence, randomised participants to CBT or a psychoeducational intervention. Of 88 included participants, 12.5% (n = 11) had an alcohol-use disorder only and 60% (n = 53) had an alcohol-use disorder as well as marijuana-use disorder. Of these 64 participants with an alcohol-use disorder, 58% met criteria for abuse and 42% for dependence (DSM III-R; APA, 1987). The authors reported reductions across both therapies in alcohol use. At 3 months alcohol use had improved significantly, and up to 9 months showed continued improvement. Substance use also showed a positive trend towards improvement. Kaminer and colleagues (2008) only included participants who met DSM–IV criteria for alcohol dependence, although 81.8% of the sample also used marijuana. However, all participants received CBT and the focus on the study was on aftercare.

Although the primary focus of studies of comorbidity has been on individuals with conduct disorder, a few studies have also examined the problems presented by co-occurring common mental health disorders such as depression and anxiety. One study evaluated the efficacy of an integrated 20-week programme of CBT with case management in a population of substance-misusing young people (aged between 15 and 25 years). Sixty-three per cent of the sample met criteria for alcohol dependence. Treatment resulted in a significant improvement in abstinence rates as well as a reduction in the number or participants meeting diagnostic thresholds for dependence. These positive effects were also observed at 44-week follow-up. This study (like others) evaluates the effectiveness of psychological interventions for young people including participants whom are over the age of 18 years. However, this age-range makes interpretation of datasets such as this difficult.

12-step facilitation
The development of TSF, which grew out of the initial work of AA, has been developed into a treatment intervention for adults (Project MATCH Research Group, 1993 and 1997) but has not been tested as an individual treatment in young people with harmful and dependent drinking. There have been no programmes for young people built around the 12-step model and, as far as the GDG was aware (or was able to identify), no evaluation of the effectiveness of a 12-step model for children and young people. It should be noted that some residential treatment centres for young people have refined the TSF, resulting in the development of residential treatment models (for example, the Minnesota model [Winters *et al.*, 2000]). However, no formal evaluations in alcohol-dependent young people were identified.

6.22.6   Evidence summary

The evidence reviewed using these systematic reviews and primary studies suggests that, although there has been recent progress in the development of individual or group psychological treatment of alcohol dependence and harmful alcohol use in children and young people, no individual treatment has a convincing evidence base for harmful alcohol use or dependence. In some respects this is in line with the adult literature and findings of the guideline meta-analyses where a number of structured treatments (including CBT, behavioural therapies and SBNT) had some benefits for harmful and mildly dependent use, but it was not possible to distinguish between them on the basis of the current available evidence. The issue is further complicated by the fact that many of the trials that evaluate the efficacy of these interventions, and that are representative of this population, involved participants with comorbid drug misuse.

6.22.7   Multicomponent psychological interventions

Components of a multicomponent intervention
The need to involve family members, particularly parents, has been recommended in policy guidance, for example *Every Parent Matters* (DfES, 2007) and in *Supporting and Involving Carers* (National Treatment Agency, 2008). Family involvement has been shown to be positively associated with improved outcomes on domains and level of engagement of the young person (Dakof *et al.*, 2001). This involvement is multifold and aims:
- to obtain (depending on consent of the child and capacity) any necessary consent to treatment
- to engage the support of the family in the treatment process
- to obtain more information on the assessment of the child's alcohol use and general functioning
- to ascertain possible family involvement in parent training, coping skills and problem-solving approaches to parenting, and more formal involvement in specific family programmes.

Common elements identified for review in these programmes include:
● comprehensive assessment and monitoring
● a focus on engagement of individuals (and usually their families) in treatment
● an explicit linking of goals and interventions at all levels of the system
● a goal-focused approach to treatment of family substance misuse
● the involvement of the family aimed at improving family communication, problem solving and parenting skills
● the provision of individual interventions, again often focused on coping skills identified for the child or young person.

The programmes also require staff who are experienced and highly trained clinicians (all were graduates; most had masters or doctoral degrees).

Although there are many approaches to family intervention for substance-misuse treatment, they have common goals: providing education about alcohol and drug misuse; improving motivation and engagement; assisting in achieving and maintaining abstinence; setting consistent boundaries and structure; improving communication; and providing support. Family interventions are the most evaluated modality in the treatment of young people with substance-use disorders. Among the forms of family-based interventions are functional family therapy (Alexander *et al.*, 1990), brief strategic family therapy (Szapocznik *et al.*, 1988), multisystemic therapy (Henggeler *et al.*, 1992) and multidimensional family therapy (Liddle, 1992). An integrated behavioural- and family-therapy model that combines a family systems model and CBT has also been developed (Waldron *et al.*, 2001). These interventions fall broadly under what would be called a systemic approach. They do not focus explicitly on the provision of specified individual interventions, but rather it is for the therapist, in conjunction with their supervisor, to develop the specific therapeutic approach in light of the identified needs of the young person. Some trials, such as the large trial of cannabis misuse and dependence (Dennis *et al.*, 2004), have focused on the provision of a systemic approach (in this case, multi-dimensional family therapy), but have also provided a specified range of psychological interventions such as MET, the development of a family support network including parental education, and the development of conditioning models from children in the community.

Definitions of interventions
Functional family therapy is a psychological intervention that is behavioural in focus. The main elements of the intervention include engagement and motivation of the family in treatment, problem solving and behaviour change through parent training and communication training, and seeking to generalise change from specific behaviours to have an impact on interactions both within the family and with community agencies such as schools (see, for example, Gordon *et al.*, 1995).

Brief strategic family therapy is a psychological intervention that is systemic in focus and is influenced by other approaches such as structural family therapy. The main elements of this intervention include engaging and supporting the family, identifying maladaptive family interactions, and seeking to promote new and more adaptive family interactions (see for example, Szapocznik *et al.*, 1989).

Multisystemic therapy involved using strategies from family therapy and behavioural therapy to intervene directly in systems and processes related to antisocial behaviour (for example, parental discipline, family affective relations, peer associations and school performances) for children or young people (Henggeler *et al.*, 1992).

Effectiveness of multicomponent interventions

The GDG used the NICE antisocial personality disorder guideline (NICE, 2008a) review of family interventions and multisystemic therapies for the treatment of conduct disorder in evaluating the effectiveness of multicomponent interventions for children and adolescents. The primary focus of the review in the antisocial personality disorder guideline was on a reduction in offending behaviour, but all the interventions, in particular brief strategic family therapy and multi-dimensional family therapy, had an explicit focus on substance misuse. The current guideline utilises the definitions from the antisocial personality disorder guideline.

In the antisocial personality disorder guideline, the meta-analysis of 11 trials assessed the effectiveness of family interventions. The results of the meta-analysis showed that family interventions are more effective than control for reducing both behavioural problems (SMD -0.75; -1.19 to -0.30) and offending (RR -0.67; 0.42 to 1.07). Furthermore, 10 trials on multisystemic therapy that met the inclusion criteria for the review were analysed. There was significant heterogeneity for most outcomes; however, there was consistent evidence of a medium effect on reduction in offending outcomes including number of arrests (SMD -0.44; -0.82 to -0.06) and being arrested (RR 0.65; 0.42 to 1.00).

In a recent meta-analysis, Tripodi and colleagues (2010) evaluated six trials of multicomponent and family-based interventions. However, none was focused specifically on alcohol misuse and, in two of the trials, only approximately 50% of the sample met criteria for alcohol dependence and harmful alcohol use. The overall findings were in line with the NICE antisocial personality disorder guideline (NICE, 2008a). The review did, however, report that multicomponent family therapies were effective in reducing drinking in young people (Hedges $g = -0.46$; 95% CI, -0.66 to -0.26). Perepletchikova and colleagues (2008) reviewed the evidence of family interventions specifically on alcohol use, although some included substance-use disorders. The types of family therapies evaluated included: multisystemic therapy, multidimensional therapy, brief family therapy, functional family therapy and strength-oriented family therapy. The review reported that multi-component therapy again showed some benefits over standard group therapy for substance misuse and criminal activity outcomes.

6.22.8   Evidence summary

The evidence for the use of multicomponent interventions demonstrates clear benefits on offending behaviour and promising results for the reduction of alcohol and drug misuse. As was found with the individual- or group-based interventions, much

343

of the research focuses on children and young people with substance-use disorders and who are more likely have comorbid psychiatric disorders. Although not specifically focused on alcohol, this does not significantly detract from their applicability to this guideline because comorbidity with conduct disorder and polydrug use is a common feature among young people with significant alcohol misuse. The research to date does not, however, favour one particular multicomponent intervention over another for the treatment of alcohol misuse.

6.23   FROM EVIDENCE TO RECOMMENDATIONS

The GDG reviewed the evidence for the clinical and cost effectiveness of various psychological interventions for the treatment of alcohol misuse. The GDG discussed and agreed that the main outcomes of interest related to drinking-focused outcomes. When considering the evidence presented, it should be noted that due to the lack of consistent critical outcomes assessed across studies, the number of studies evaluating the same outcomes within the included reviews was generally low. Outcomes had to be grouped according to more general outcomes that would indicate efficacy of treatment (for example, outcomes relating to abstinence, the amount of alcohol consumed and the frequency or intensity of consumption). The GDG took the view that to be recommended, an active psychological intervention should show evidence of effectiveness against no treatment control/waitlist in the first instance, then against treatment as usual, and preferably should be more effective than other active interventions. However, the evidence evaluating the effectiveness of an intervention against no treatment control/waitlist or standard care was not always available because most studies compared two or more active interventions with each other. The GDG considered this limitation of the evidence as well as individual treatment comparisons and the patient population evaluated in the trials during the process of making recommendations about the relative efficacy of the interventions. The overall quality of the evidence was *moderate* and any limitations of the data addressed in the GRADE profiles were considered before making recommendations.

As can be seen from the above evidence summary, the strongest evidence for effectiveness in harmful and dependent drinking was for BCT. The GDG therefore agreed that BCT should be considered as an effective stand-alone intervention for individuals with harmful and mildly-dependent alcohol misuse who have a partner and who are willing to engage in treatment. Consideration should also be given to giving BCT in combination with a pharmacological intervention for those individuals who meet the above criteria and have moderate or severe alcohol dependence (see Chapter 7).

The evidence for individual psychological interventions for harmful and mildly dependent use was limited but stronger for cognitive behavioural therapies, social network and environment-based therapies, and behavioural therapies than other individual therapies reviewed, and are therefore recommended. The GDG considered the costings of the various psychological interventions (indications from these costings were that SBNT was less costly than either CBT or behavioural therapy) but came to the conclusion that, given the uncertainty about the relative cost effectiveness of the interventions and the need to have available a range of interventions to meet the complexity of presenting problems, all three interventions should be recommended as stand-alone therapies. One of the three interventions should also used in combination with the drug treatments reviewed in Chapter 7.

As can be seen from the clinical summary, the GDG considered that appropriate elements of TSF and motivational-based interventions should be provided as a component of an assessment and subsequent intervention because the evidence, particularly against treatment as usual or similar controls, was not strong enough to support their use as a stand-alone intervention for harmful and mildly dependent use.

Children and young people
The evidence base is limited for the treatment of alcohol misuse in children and young people. As a consequence, the GDG was required to extrapolate from a number of datasets and sources that did not directly address the treatment of alcohol misuse in children and young people. This included data on adults with alcohol misuse, as well as children and young people with substance misuse, conduct disorder and anti-social personality disorder. The GDG considered this to be a justified approach because there is an urgent need to provide recommendations for the treatment of the increasing problem of alcohol misuse in children and young people. In extrapolating from these datasets the GDG was cautious, recognising that as new evidence emerges the recommendations in this guideline will need revision.

Despite limited evidence a reasonably clear picture emerged about the effectiveness of interventions to promote abstinence and prevent relapse in children and young people. There was some evidence for individual interventions such as CBT and less so for MET. There was stronger evidence for the use of multicomponent interventions such as multisystemic therapy, functional family therapy, brief strategic family therapy, and multi-dimensional family therapy, but little evidence to determine whether one of the interventions had any advantage over the others. This evidence also mirrored the evidence for effectiveness in adults. The GDG therefore decided that both types of intervention should be made available with CBT reserved for cases where comorbidity is either not present or of little significance; where comorbidity is present, multicomponent interventions should be offered.

6.24   RECOMMENDATIONS

6.24.1.1   For all people who misuse alcohol, carry out a motivational intervention as part of the initial assessment. The intervention should contain the key elements of motivational interviewing including:

- helping people to recognise problems or potential problems related to their drinking
- helping to resolve ambivalence and encourage positive change and belief in the ability to change
- adopting a persuasive and supportive rather than an argumentative and confrontational position.

345

6.24.1.2 For all people who misuse alcohol, offer interventions to promote abstinence or moderate drinking as appropriate (see 5.26.1.8–5.26.1.11) and
prevent relapse, in community-based settings.

6.24.1.3 Consider offering interventions to promote abstinence and prevent relapse
as part of an intensive structured community-based intervention for people
with moderate and severe alcohol dependence who have:

- very limited social support (for example, they are living alone or have
  very little contact with family or friends) **or**
- complex physical or psychiatric comorbidities **or**
- not responded to initial community-based interventions (see 6.23.1.2).

6.24.1.4 All interventions for people who misuse alcohol should be delivered by
appropriately trained and competent staff. Pharmacological interventions
should be administered by specialist and competent staff[38]. Psychological
interventions should be based on a relevant evidence-based treatment
manual, which should guide the structure and duration of the intervention.
Staff should consider using competence frameworks developed from the
relevant treatment manuals and for all interventions should:

- receive regular supervision from individuals competent in both the
  intervention and supervision
- routinely use outcome measurements to make sure that the person who
  misuses alcohol is involved in reviewing the effectiveness of treatment
- engage in monitoring and evaluation of treatment adherence and practice competence, for example, by using video and audio tapes and
  external audit and scrutiny if appropriate.

6.24.1.5 All interventions for people who misuse alcohol should be the subject of
routine outcome monitoring. This should be used to inform decisions about
continuation of both psychological and pharmacological treatments. If
there are signs of deterioration or no indications of improvement, consider
stopping the current treatment and review the care plan.

6.24.1.6 For all people seeking help for alcohol misuse:

- give information on the value and availability of community support
  networks and self-help groups (for example, Alcoholics Anonymous or
  SMART Recovery) **and**
- help them to participate in community support networks and self-help
  groups by encouraging them to go to meetings and arranging support
  so that they can attend.

6.24.1.7 For children and young people aged 10–17 years who misuse alcohol offer:

- individual cognitive behavioural therapy for those with limited comorbidities and good social support
- multicomponent programmes (such as multidimensional family
  therapy, brief strategic family therapy, functional family therapy or

---

[38]If a drug is used at a dose or for an application that does not have UK marketing authorisation, informed
consent should be obtained and documented.

multisystemic therapy) for those with significant comorbidities and/or limited social support.

Delivering psychological and psychosocial interventions for children and young people

6.24.1.8 Multidimensional family therapy should usually consist of 12–15 family-focused structured treatment sessions over 12 weeks. There should be a strong emphasis on care coordination and, if necessary, crisis management. As well as family sessions, individual interventions may be provided for both the child or young person and the parents. The intervention should aim to improve:
- alcohol and drug misuse
- the child or young person's educational and social behaviour
- parental well-being and parenting skills
- relationships with the wider social system.

6.24.1.9 Brief strategic family therapy should usually consist of fortnightly meetings over 3 months. It should focus on:
- engaging and supporting the family
- using the support of the wider social and educational system
- identifying maladaptive family interactions
- promoting new and more adaptive family interactions.

6.24.1.10 Functional family therapy should be conducted over 3 months by health or social care staff. It should focus on improving interactions within the family, including:
- engaging and motivating the family in treatment (enhancing perception that change is possible, positive reframing and establishing a positive alliance)
- problem solving and behaviour change through parent training and communication training
- promoting generalisation of change in specific behaviours to broader contexts, both within the family and the community (such as schools).

6.24.1.11 Multisystemic therapy should be provided over 3–6 months by a dedicated member of staff with a low caseload (typically between three and six cases). It should:
- focus specifically on problem-solving approaches with the family
- use the resources of peer groups, schools and the wider community.

Interventions for harmful drinking and mild alcohol dependence

6.24.1.12 For harmful drinkers and people with mild alcohol dependence, offer a psychological intervention (such as cognitive behavioural therapies, behavioural therapies or social network and environment-based therapies) focused specifically on alcohol-related cognitions, behaviour, problems and social networks.

6.24.1.13 For harmful drinkers and people with mild alcohol dependence who have a regular partner who is willing to participate in treatment, offer behavioural couples therapy.

Psychological and psychosocial interventions

6.24.1.14 For harmful drinkers and people with mild alcohol dependence who have not responded to psychological interventions alone, or who have specifically requested a pharmacological intervention, consider offering acamprosate[39] or oral naltrexone[40] in combination with an individual psychological intervention (cognitive behavioural therapies, behavioural therapies or social network and environment-based therapies) or behavioural couples therapy (see Chapter 7 for pharmacological interventions).

Delivering psychological interventions

6.24.1.15 Cognitive behavioural therapies focused on alcohol-related problems should usually consist of one 60-minute session per week for 12 weeks.

6.24.1.16 Behavioural therapies focused on alcohol-related problems should usually consist of one 60-minute session per week for 12 weeks.

6.24.1.17 Social network and environment-based therapies focused on alcohol-related problems should usually consist of eight 50-minute sessions over 12 weeks.

6.24.1.18 Behavioural couples therapy should be focused on alcohol-related problems and their impact on relationships. It should aim for abstinence, or a level of drinking predetermined and agreed by the therapist and the service user to be reasonable and safe. It should usually consist of one 60-minute session per week for 12 weeks.

6.24.2 Research recommendation

6.24.2.1 Is contingency management effective in reducing alcohol consumption in people who misuse alcohol compared with standard care?

This question should be answered using a randomised controlled design that reports short-and medium-term outcomes (including cost-effectiveness outcomes) of at least 18 months' duration. Particular attention should be paid to the reproducibility of the treatment model and training and supervision of those providing the intervention to ensure that the results are robust and generalisable. The outcomes chosen should reflect both observer and service user-rated assessments of improvement and the acceptability of the intervention. The study needs to be large enough to determine the presence or absence of clinically important effects, and mediators and moderators of response should be investigated.

Why this is important

Psychological interventions are an important therapeutic option for people with alcohol-related problems. However, even with the most effective current treatment (for

---

[39]Note that the evidence for acamprosate in the treatment of harmful drinkers and people who are mildly alcohol dependent is less robust than that for naltrexone. At the time of publication of the NICE guideline (February 2011), acamprosate did not have UK marketing authorisation for this indication. Informed consent should be obtained and documented.

[40]At the time of publication of the NICE guideline (February 2011), oral naltrexone did not have UK marketing authorisation for this indication. Informed consent should be obtained and documented.

example, cognitive behavioural therapies and social network and environment-based therapies), the effects are modest at best and the treatments are not effective for everyone. Contingency management has a considerable and compelling evidence base in the treatment of substance misuse (for example, opioid misuse) but there is only a limited, if promising, evidence base for contingency management in the treatment of alcohol-related problems. The results of this research will have important implications for the provision of psychological treatment for alcohol misuse in the NHS.

6.25   ACUPUNCTURE

Introduction

Acupuncture is a form of Chinese medicine that has been practiced for over 3,000 years (Jordan, 2006). It involves inserting fine needles at selected points on the skin to balance the body's energy (*chi*), with the aim of treating and preventing disease. Acupuncture was introduced specifically for use in the treatment of substance-related disorders approximately 30 years ago (Kao, 1974; Leung, 1977; Sacks, 1975; Wen, 1973). However, research has predominantly been for drug misuse, for example opioid dependence (Jordan, 2006) and cocaine dependence (Gates *et al.*, 2006; Mills *et al.*, 2005), as well as nicotine dependence (White *et al.*, 2006). Research for the use of acupuncture in alcohol misuse is rather more limited and to date there are only two systematic reviews of acupuncture for alcohol dependence (Cho & Whang, 2009; Kunz *et al.*, 2007). Addiction-specific auricular acupuncture involves inserting five small needles on each ear at points regarded to be specific to chemical dependence (known as '*shen men*', 'sympathetic', 'kidney', 'liver' and 'lung') (Smith & Khan, 1988; Wen, 1979).

6.25.1   Clinical review protocol

In the current review, the role of acupuncture in maintaining abstinence and drinking reduction was investigated. Its application to other aspects usually associated with alternative therapies in this topic area (such as craving and withdrawal symptoms) was beyond the scope of this guideline and hence was not considered. Information about the databases searched and the inclusion/exclusion criteria used for this section of the guideline can be found in Chapter 3. The GDG was of the opinion that a search for RCT studies alone may result in an insufficient number of studies to perform a review, therefore a consensus-based decision was made to also search for systematic reviews. See Table 87 for a summary of the clinical review protocol for the review of acupuncture.

6.25.2   Studies considered for review

The review team conducted a systematic search of RCTs and published systematic reviews that assessed the beneficial or detrimental effects of acupuncture in the treatment of alcohol dependence or harmful alcohol use. Following the literature search, 11 primary studies were identified. Of these, four investigated the effects of

Table 87: Clinical review protocol for the review of acupuncture

Electronic databases	AMED, CINAHL, EMBASE, MEDLINE, PsycINFO, Cochrane Library
Date searched	Systematic reviews from 1993 to March 2010. All other searches from database inception to March 2010
Study design	RCTs (at least ten participants per arm); systematic reviews
Population	Adults (over 18 years old) At least 80% of the sample meet the criteria for alcohol dependence or harmful alcohol use (clinical diagnosis or drinking more than 30 drinks per week)
Excluded populations	Hazardous drinkers and those drinking fewer than 30 drinks per week Pregnant women
Interventions	Acupuncture (all types)
Comparator	Control or other active intervention
Outcomes	Abstinence Amount of alcohol consumed Rates of consumption Relapse (>X number of drinks or number of participants who have relapsed) Lapse (time to first drink or number of participants who have lapsed) Attrition (leaving the study early for any reason)

acupuncture on withdrawal symptoms and two assessed its use for the management of cravings. These six studies were excluded because the outcomes are outside the scope of this guideline. Therefore, five studies (four RCTs and one observational study) were identified for inclusion in the review. However, the review team could not perform an unbiased and comprehensive meta-analysis because there were inconsistent outcome measures across studies. Therefore, the GDG consensus was that a narrative summary of these studies would be conducted. The studies included for review were Bullock and colleagues (1987) (addiction-specific versus non-specific acupuncture); Bullock and colleagues (1989) (addiction-specific versus non-specific acupuncture); Bullock and colleagues (2002) (addiction-specific acupuncture versus symptom-based acupuncture versus non-specific acupuncture versus standard care); Rampes and colleagues (1997) (addiction-specific versus non-specific acupuncture versus no treatment control); and Worner and colleagues (1992) (addiction specific acupuncture versus sham transdermal stimulations versus standard care control).

These studies were conducted between 1987 and 2002, and provided data on 752 participants. See Table 88 for characteristics of these studies. All included studies were RCTs except Bullock and colleagues (1989).

6.25.3   Evidence summary

Bullock and colleagues (1987) investigated acupuncture at addiction-specific points versus non-specific points for reducing craving and maintaining abstinence. The authors reported that the treatment group had significantly fewer drinking episodes than the control group (p = 0.007) after the second (28 days) and third (45 days) phase of treatment, but not after the first phase (5 days).

Bullock and colleagues (1989) also investigated acupuncture at addiction-specific points versus non-specific points for craving reduction, maintaining abstinence and drinking reduction in people with chronic alcohol misuse. The study found that there was no significant difference between the treatment group and control group at 1-month follow-up in the number of drinking episodes (consumption of more than three drinks in one period). However, at both 3- and 6-month follow-up, the treatment group reported significantly fewer drinking episodes than the control group (p <0.001). Furthermore, the treatment group was significantly more effective than control at maintaining abstinence and controlled drinking goals when assessed at 1-month (p <0.01), and at 3- and 6-month follow-up (both p <0.05). This study was not randomised, therefore the results must be viewed with caution.

Worner and colleagues (1992) evaluated acupuncture at addiction-specific points versus needleless transdermal stimulation as well as a standard care group that received no acupuncture. This study found no significant difference between groups in the number of participants who relapsed or needed further withdrawal management at 3-month follow-up.

Rampes and colleagues (1997) assessed addiction-specific electro-acupuncture versus non-specific electro-acupuncture and no treatment (control). The main outcome of interest was craving reduction, which is outside the scope of this guideline. However, the authors also reported no significant difference between groups in amount of alcohol consumed at 2- and 6-month follow-up.

Bullock and colleagues (2002) investigated addiction-specific and non-specific acupuncture as well as symptom-based acupuncture and standard care (based on the Minnesota model). The authors found no significant difference in alcohol consumption at 3-, 6- and 12-month follow-up. Overall, the evidence suggests that acupuncture is not effective in drinking reduction and maintaining abstinence.

The results of these studies are conflicting and show both a benefit of addiction-specific acupuncture as well as no difference between addiction-specific acupuncture and other control conditions. Additionally, the treatments across studies are not comparable because the studies used different body parts for acupuncture treatment, different types of control group, had different length of treatment and follow-up, and varied significantly in sample size. Although the quality of these trials are acceptable in the most part, the number of studies are limited and there is not enough evidence to confirm the benefit of acupuncture in maintaining abstinence or reducing the

Table 88: Summary of study characteristics for acupuncture

Study (country)	Treatment conditions and number of participants	Baseline severity and diagnosis	Setting, treatment characteristics and assessment points
Bullock and colleagues, 1987 (US)	1. Addiction specific acupuncture (n = 27)	98.1% of sample indicated alcohol as single substance of misuse	Setting: alcohol treatment centre
	2. Non-addiction specific acupuncture (control) (n = 27) Auricular and hand acupuncture	Mean years of alcohol misuse: Treatment group = 21.6; Control group = 18.5 68.5% of sample drink daily; 27.7% binge drink	Treatment characteristics: 45-day standard acupuncture treatment Assessment points: no follow-up, assessing during different phases of treatment
Bullock and colleagues, 1989 (US)	1. Addiction specific acupuncture (n = 40)	Alcohol dependent participants	Setting: alcohol treatment centre
	2. Non-addiction specific acupuncture (control) (n = 40) Auricular and hand acupuncture	Mean years of alcohol misuse: Treatment group = 23.2; Control = 20.8 71% of the sample drink daily; 21% binge drink	Treatment characteristics: patients received treatment after 3- to 5-day withdrawal management Assessment points: 1-, 3- and 6-month follow-up
Worner and colleagues, 1992 (US)	1. Addiction specific acupuncture (n = 19)	Alcohol dependent participants	Setting: alcohol treatment centre
	2. Needleless transdermal stimulation (control) (n = 21)	Daily intake approximately 253.6 g per day	Treatment characteristics: 3-month treatment; all participants received standard care (individual and group counselling, AA, task-oriented group activities)
	3. Standard care control (n = 16) Acupuncture at various body parts		Assessment points: 3-month follow-up

Study	Groups	Population/Diagnosis	Setting/Treatment
Rampes and colleagues, 1997 (UK)	1. Addiction specific electro auricular acupuncture (n = 23) 2. Non-addiction specific electro auricular acupuncture (control) (n = 20) 3. No treatment control (n = 16) Auricular acupuncture	DSM–III–R alcohol dependence or abuse SADQ score approximately 32 across groups	Setting: alcohol treatment centre Treatment characteristics: 30 minutes per week for 6 weeks Assessment points: 2- and 6-month follow-up
Bullock and colleagues, 2002 (US)	1. Addiction specific auricular acupuncture (n = 132) 2. Symptom-based auricular acupuncture (n = 104) 3. Non-addiction specific acupuncture (control) (n = 133) 4. Standard care only – Minnesota model (control) (n = 134) Auricular acupuncture	Alcohol dependent participants in a residential treatment facility	Setting: alcohol treatment centre Treatment characteristics: three cycles of six treatments for 3 weeks Assessment points: 3-, 6- and 12-month follow-up

amount of alcohol consumed. Therefore no clinical recommendations are made but the GDG has developed a recommendation for further research.

6.25.4   Research recommendation

6.25.4.1   Is acupuncture effective in reducing alcohol consumption compared with usual care?
This question should be answered using a randomised controlled design that reports short- and medium-term outcomes (including cost-effectiveness outcomes) of at least 12 months' duration. Particular attention should be paid to the reproducibility of the treatment model and training and supervision of those providing the intervention to ensure that the results are robust and generalisable. The outcomes chosen should reflect both observer and service user-rated assessments of improvement and the acceptability of the treatment. The study needs to be large enough to determine the presence or absence of clinically important effects, and mediators and moderators of response should be investigated.

Why this is important
Non-pharmacological treatments are an important therapeutic option for people with alcohol-related problems. There is an evidence base for acupuncture in reducing craving but not alcohol consumption in a number of small trials. The evidence for pharmacological treatments (for example, acamprosate or naltrexone) and psychological treatments (for example, cognitive behavioural therapies and social network and environment-based therapies) is modest at best and the treatments are not effective for everyone. Anecdotal evidence suggests that acupuncture, like psychological treatment, is valued by service users both in alcohol misuse and substance misuse services (although the evidence base for effectiveness is weak). The results of this study will have important implications for increased treatment choice in the NHS for people who misuse alcohol.

6.26   PSYCHOLOGICAL INTERVENTIONS FOR CARERS

6.26.1   Introduction

There is an increasing recognition that alcohol misuse affects the entire family and the communities in which these families live but what constitutes best practice in the area is not well understood (Copello *et al.*, 2006). What is not in doubt is the considerable suffering and hardship experienced by many families where a family member has a significant alcohol misuse problem (Orford *et al.*, 2005).

In developing this guideline the GDG drew on a previous review of psychological interventions for carers that had been undertaken for the NICE guideline on psychosocial interventions for drug misuse (NCCMH, 2008). This was a pragmatic decision because the previous review had drawn on literature covering both drug misuse and alcohol misuse, and searches conducted for this current guideline had failed to find any substantial new evidence for interventions to support family members and carers. The outcome of the NCCMH (2008) review is summarised below in narrative form.

The NCCMH (2008) guideline identified a number of interventions in the drug and alcohol field that had been developed and tested in formal trials. They are listed below.

Five-step intervention
The five-step intervention seeks to help families and carers in their own right, independent of relatives who misuse drugs or alcohol. It focuses on three key areas: stress experienced by relatives; their coping responses; and the social support available to them. Step 1 consists of listening to and reassuring the carer, step 2 involves providing relevant information, step 3 is counselling about coping, step 4 is counselling about social support and step 5 is discussion of the need for other sources of specialist help. This intervention consists of up to five sessions.

Community reinforcement and family training
Community reinforcement and family training is a manualised treatment programme that includes training in domestic violence precautions, motivational strategies, positive reinforcement training for carers and their significant other, and communication training. However, the primary aim of the treatment appears to be encouraging the person who misuses drugs or alcohol to enter treatment. This intervention again consists of up to five sessions.

Self-help support groups
A group of families and carers of people who misuse drugs meets regularly to provide help and support for one another.

Guided self-help
A professional offers a self-help manual (for example, based on the five-step intervention), provides a brief introduction to the main sections of the manual and encourages the families and/or carers of people who misuse drugs to work through it in their own time at home.

6.26.2   Summary of the NCCMH 2008 review

The review identified a total of three RCTs including two trials (Kirby *et al.*, 1999; Meyers *et al.*, 2002) for community reinforcement and family training compared with 12-step self-help groups and one trial (Copello *et al.*, 2009[41]) of the five-step intervention in which five-step interventions of various intensities were compared.

Neither Kirby and colleagues (1999), or Meyers and colleagues (2002) found any significant different between community reinforcement and family training and 12-step self-help groups for reported levels of drug or alcohol use[42]. However, Kirby and colleagues (1999) found statistically significant changes from baseline for both groups in relation to carer problems and psychological functioning. In contrast, Meyers and

---

[41]This trial was identified prior to publication in 2008, but the reference to the published trial is used here.
[42]For family members' reports of a person misusing alcohol or drugs and self-report measures.

colleagues (2002) found no statistically significant differences (after Bonferroni correcttions for multiple testing) in changes from baseline at 12-month follow-up. In the case of the five-step intervention Copello and colleagues (2009) on two primary outcomes related to physical and psychological health and coping, found no statistically significant differences between the full intervention and the guided self-help conditions for both physical and psychological health (WMD -0.23; 95% CI, -4.11 to 3.65) and coping (WMD -0.12; 95% CI, -5.42 to 5.19).

6.26.3   Clinical summary

For both community reinforcement and family training and five-step intervention, there were no statistically significant differences found between these more intensive interventions and self-help (that is, 12-step self-help groups and guided self-help). It appears that self-help interventions are as effective as more intensive psychological interventions in reducing stress and improving psychological functioning for families and carers of people who misuse drugs and alcohol.

6.26.4   From evidence to recommendations

In developing the recommendations for this section of the guideline the GDG also took into account the reviews of family members' experience in Chapter 4 of this guideline which confirmed the view that families typically have considerable unmet needs. This meant that despite the limited evidence the GDG felt that the provision of information and the use of a range of self-help interventions (with relatively low cost) should be offered to families. The GDG also felt that where families could not make use of or have not benefitted from the use of the self-help materials that an offer of a structured intervention as set out in the five-step intervention should be made.

6.26.5   Recommendations

6.26.5.1   When the needs of families and carers of people who misuse alcohol have been identified:
- offer guided self-help, usually consisting of a single session, with the provision of written materials
- provide information about, and facilitate contact with, support groups (such as self-help groups specifically focused on addressing the needs of families and carers).

6.26.5.2   If the families and carers of people who misuse alcohol have not benefited, or are not likely to benefit, from guided self-help and/or support groups and continue to have significant problems, consider offering family meetings. These should:
- provide information and education about alcohol misuse
- help to identify sources of stress related to alcohol misuse
- explore and promote effective coping behaviours
- usually consist of at least five weekly sessions.

7   PHARMACOLOGICAL INTERVENTIONS

7.1   INTRODUCTION

Pharmacological interventions can be involved in different stages of treating alcohol misuse and its consequences. Medication is recognised as an adjunct to psychosocial treatment to provide an optimum treatment package to improve physical and mental health (Casswell & Thamarangsi, 2009). Prescribed medications are not a stand-alone treatment option and are only recommended as part of care-planned treatment (Berglund, 2005; Department of Health, 2006a; Raistrick *et al.*, 2006; Woody, 2003). This chapter aims to detail the utility and efficacy of pharmacological interventions in the treatment of alcohol misuse. It focuses on the use of pharmacological interventions in the promotion of abstinence and the reduction in alcohol consumption, and the treatment of comorbid disorders. For the use of pharmacological interventions in a planned withdrawal programme see Chapter 5 and for the use of pharmacological interventions in an unplanned withdrawal programme see the NICE guideline on the management of alcohol-related physical complications (NICE, 2010b).

7.1.1   Current practice

Pharmacotherapy is most frequently used to facilitate withdrawal from alcohol in people who are dependent; many fewer individuals receive medication for relapse prevention such as acamprosate, disulfiram or naltrexone. Indeed, some people may be reluctant to take medication and traditionally many residential rehabilitation units have not been prepared to accept or support people taking such medication, although this is slowly changing. A US survey revealed that only about 9% of people needing treatment for alcohol dependence received medication for relapse prevention; prescriptions of disulfiram declined by 3% between 2003 and 2007, while prescriptions for naltrexone rose by 3% and for acamprosate by 10% (Mark *et al.*, 2009). The level of prescribing is likely to be similar or even lower in the UK. One estimate from data on prescriptions shows in 2008 that there were almost 135,000 prescriptions for acamprosate or disulfiram from primary care or NHS settings, with the majority (62%) for acamprosate (The NHS Information Centre, Lifestyles Statistics, 2009). In NHS hospitals, the use of disulfiram has increased with slightly more (54%) prescriptions issued than for acamprosate. There are regional variations with London issuing 104 prescriptions per 100,000 population and the North East issuing 417 per 100,000. Some doctors can be reluctant to prescribe pharmacological interventions such as acamprosate, naltrexone and disulfiram, due to lack of knowledge or familiarity (Mark *et al.*, 2003). Barriers to prescribing naltrexone in the US have been described as including a 'lack of awareness, a lack of evidence of efficacy in practice, side effects, time for patient management, a reluctance to take medications,

357

medication addiction concerns, AA philosophy, and price' (Mark *et al.*, 2003). Nevertheless, there are a variety of medications with proven effectiveness and others with emerging efficacy that deserve due consideration as part of any individual treatment package.

For relapse prevention, both acamprosate and disulfiram are licensed for relapse prevention in the UK, much of Europe, Australasia and North America. Naltrexone is used in the UK but licensed elsewhere (for example, in the US).

In this guideline, some pharmacotherapies described do not have a UK licence for the indication discussed. It is important to realise that in this area of medicine the absence of a licence can mean that one has not been applied for, rather than that the pharmacotherapy is not safe or appropriate. The terms 'unlicensed' and 'off-label' should not necessarily be taken to automatically imply disapproval, nor incorrect or improper use. There is no contraindication to prescribing a drug off-licence provided there is a body of evidence that supports its efficacy and safety (Healy & Nutt, 1998; Royal College of Psychiatrists, 2007), and often evidence of safety may come from its use in other disorders where a licence may have been granted. In particular, many drugs will not have a licence for use in young people, children or in older people, but this does not mean they necessarily lack efficacy or are unsafe. Nevertheless, when prescribing in these populations, due care must be taken in terms of dosage and monitoring of side effects, as well as potential interactions with other medications or physical morbidity.

7.1.2 The effects of alcohol on brain chemistry and how this relates to medication

As described in Chapter 2, alcohol affects many of the brain's chemical systems. The pharmacology of most of the medications commonly used, such as benzodiazepines for alcohol withdrawal and disulfiram, acamprosate and naltrexone for relapse prevention, is well characterised and provides a potential neurobiological rationale for their effectiveness. Understanding more about how alcohol interacts with the brain has revealed many potential targets of interest, for example to reduce drinking or craving. In many cases, medication already exists with the desired pharmacology but is used for another indication, for example baclofen for muscle spasm. Most new medication is being developed to prevent relapse rather than for use in alcohol withdrawal, or to improve cognition or prevent toxicity.

7.1.3 Brain chemistry and medication for relapse prevention

Dopamine
The pleasurable effects of alcohol are principally mediated by an increase in activity in the mesolimbic dopaminergic system. This dopaminergic system is regarded as the 'reward' pathway and is involved in 'natural' pleasures and motivations or drives such as food, sex and also responses to stress (Koob & Volkow, 2010).

As substance dependence develops, this dopaminergic system is involved in responding to significant or salient cues and motivation to take more (Schultz, 2007). Therefore, increases in dopaminergic activity arise for people with harmful and dependent drinking when a 'cue' such as a pub or glass of a favourite drink is seen, which encourages the person to seek alcohol. Some individuals may describe this as craving, although many may not be consciously aware of it. Therefore, the role of dopamine switches from signalling pleasure to 'alcohol-seeking or motivation' in response to a cue. In addition, over time, activity is reduced in the dopaminergic system in alcohol dependence and is associated with greater risk of relapse as well as symptoms of dysphoria (Heinz, 2002).

Because increases in dopamine mediate reward or motivation, blocking or antagonising the dopaminergic system, for example with antipsychotics, has been attempted as a strategy to reduce drinking. However, these drugs have not shown clinical widespread effectiveness. Alternatively, because dependence is associated with reduced dopaminergic activity, boosting the dopamine system would be a reasonable strategy. Bromocriptine, a dopamine agonist, has shown promise in a clinical trial associated with a particular polymorphism of one of the dopamine receptors (Lawford *et al.*, 1995) but not in all studies (Naranjo *et al.*, 1997). It is possible for a drug to act like an agonist when there is low activity in the tissue and act like an antagonist when there is high activity – these are called partial agonists (for example aripiprazole, which is an antipsychotic). Preliminary studies have shown limited promise in relapse prevention (Anton *et al.*, 2008a; Martinotti *et al.*, 2009).

Disulfiram may be one medication that has some effects through the dopaminergic system in the brain. The effect of disulfiram is to block an enzyme (aldehyde dehydrogenase) in the liver that is involved in metabolising or getting rid of alcohol. Blocking this enzyme causes an unpleasant reaction involving flushing, nausea, palpitations and so on. However, the enzyme in the brain that turns dopamine into noradrenaline is from the same family as the liver enzyme and so is also blocked by disulfiram, leading to an increase in dopamine (Gaval-Cruz & Weinshenker, 2009). Whether this increase is linked to disulfiram's effectiveness remains unproven.

Opioid system

Alcohol increases levels of endorphins or opiates in the brain, which in turn increase dopaminergic activity. The main opioid receptor involved in 'alcohol-liking' is mu, but the other opioid receptors, kappa and delta, also appear to have some role in alcohol liking and dependence (Herz, 1997).

Consequently opioid antagonists or blockers, such as naltrexone or nalmefene, have been used to try and treat alcohol misuse. Naltrexone is a non-specific opioid antagonist, blocking mu, kappa and delta receptors, whilst nalmefene is a mu antagonist and possibly a kappa partial agonist (Bart *et al.*, 2005). Both of these medications can reduce the pleasurable effects of alcohol, although naltrexone is more widely used (Drobes *et al.*, 2004). A polymorphism of the mu opioid receptor has been reported to be predictive of treatment response to naltrexone in some studies (Anton *et al.*, 2008b).

Pharmacological interventions

Gamma-aminobutyric acid – glutamate systems

The GABA system is the brain's inhibitory or calming chemical system. Stimulation of one of its receptors, the GABA-B, reduces dopaminergic activity in the so-called reward pathway, and therefore drugs that boost this system have been shown to reduce drug-liking and seeking (Cousins *et al.*, 2002). Baclofen is a medication that has long been used to treat muscle spasms and acts as a GABA-B agonist, for example it will boost activity. This mechanism is proposed to underlie baclofen's recently reported efficacy in relapse prevention for alcohol dependence (Addolorato *et al.*, 2007).

The glutamatergic system is the brain's excitatory system and is involved in modulating the dopaminergic reward pathway. Acamprosate is a drug used for maintaining abstinence and has been shown to primarily reduce glutamatergic activity in the brain with some effect on increasing GABA-ergic activity. Because alcohol dependence is associated with hyperactivity in the glutamatergic system and reduced GABA-ergic activity, acamprosate may also improve abstinence rates by 'normalising' this imbalance (Littleton, 2000). It is also suggested that in abstinence, conditioned withdrawal (a withdrawal-like state such as anxiety induced by an object or place previously associated with drinking) is associated with a similar GABA-glutamatergic imbalance. Such conditioned withdrawal may be experienced as craving and acamprosate is proposed to also 'correct' this imbalance (Littleton, 2000). More recently roles in relapse prevention for other glutamatergic receptor subtypes, for example mGLuR2/3 and mGLuR5, have begun to be characterised (Olive, 2009). To reduce glutamatergic activity, memantine, a blocker or antagonist of one of glutamate's receptors, NMDA, has been investigated but has not shown efficacy in preventing relapse (Evans et al., 2007).

Anticonvulsants such as topiramate can also reduce glutamatergic activity and boost GABA activity. In addition, they can alter ion (calcium, sodium, potassium) channel activity thus further reducing brain activity. Several anticonvulsants are being studied for efficacy in treating alcohol misuse with the most evidence currently being for topiramate (Johnson *et al.*, 2007). Of the newer anticonvulsants, gabapentin and its analogue pregabalin have received some attention because they appear to have some efficacy in treating a variety of disorders commonly seen in those with alcohol misuse, such as depression, anxiety or insomnia. Both medications are licensed for use in epilepsy and neuropathic pain, and pregabalin for generalised anxiety disorder. Despite their names they have not been shown to have any effect on the GABA system, although there is some limited and inconsistent evidence that pregabalin may interact with the GABA-B receptor (Landmark, 2007). Both gabapentin and pregabalin interact with the alpha2delta voltage-activated calcium channel subunits resulting in inhibition of excitatory neurotransmitter release, mostly glutamate (Landmark, 2007).

Gamma-hydroxybutyric acid (GHB) is a short-chain fatty acid that naturally occurs in the brain, and GABA is its precursor. It has been used as an anaesthetic drug and to treat narcolepsy. Together with its pro-drug, gamma-butyrolactone (GBL), however, it is also a drug of misuse and is used as a club drug or by bodybuilders. The exact mechanisms of action in the brain are not clear, particularly around how it modulates reward pathways, but it has been suggested that it mimics alcohol.

360

Serotonergic system

The acute and chronic effects of alcohol on the serotonin system are complex and not fully understood. One consistent demonstration has been of reduced serotonergic activity in so-called 'early onset alcoholism', which describes individuals who become dependent before the age of 25 years, have impulsive or antisocial personality traits, have a family history of alcoholism and are often male (Cloninger *et al.*, 1981). In addition, many disorders commonly seen in individuals with alcohol misuse are also proposed to have serotonergic dysfunction, for example bulimia, depression, anxiety and obsessive-compulsive disorder.

Because a dysfunctional serotonergic system is implicated in alcohol misuse, drugs that can modulate this system have been studied as treatments for preventing relapse. These include selective serotonin reuptake inhibitor (SSRI) antidepressants and the anxiolytic, buspirone, a 5-hydroxytryptamine subtype (5HT1A) partial agonist. Such an approach is separate from any effect these drugs might have in treating any comorbid depression or anxiety for which they are licensed. Both SSRIs and buspirone have been found to reduce alcohol consumption in animal models (Johnson, 2008). However, for both SSRIs and buspirone, clinical efficacy in preventing relapse has been hard to demonstrate.

One particular serotonin receptor subtype, 5HT3, modulates the dopaminergic reward pathway. Blockers or antagonists of 5HT3 receptors reduce dopaminergic activity, which results in reduced alcohol drinking in animal models. Therefore, ondansetron, a 5HT3 antagonist used to treat nausea, has been studied and clinical efficacy has been shown for some doses, more so in early-onset alcoholism (Johnson *et al.*, 2000). Critical roles for the other serotonin receptors in alcohol use and dependence have not been demonstrated.

7.1.4 Brain chemistry and medication for alcohol withdrawal

A significant number of alcohol's effects on the brain involve interacting with the inhibitory GABA system. In addition to the GABA-B system described above, there is a GABA-A or GABA-benzodiazepine system that plays several important roles in mediating effects of alcohol on the brain.

The GABA-A receptor is made of different subunits on which there are various binding sites for benzodiazepines, barbiturates, neurosteroids and some anaesthetics, as well as for GABA. Alcohol interacts with the GABA-benzodiazepine receptor and increases its inhibitory activity, resulting in reduced anxiety and sedation, and can contribute to ataxia, slurred speech and respiratory depression. Thus alcohol has a similar effect to benzodiazepines such as diazepam. Alcohol is often used for its anxiolytic or sedative effects rather than pleasurable effects and anxiety and sleep disorders are associated with vulnerability to alcohol misuse.

Tolerance is the need to drink more alcohol to obtain the same or desired effect, and it develops in those drinking more heavily and regularly. A reduced sensitivity of the GABA system to alcohol underlies tolerance. It is thought that changes in the subunit profile of the GABA-A receptor complex are involved (Krystal *et al.*, 2006). In alcohol withdrawal, benzodiazepines such as chlordiazepoxide (Librium) or diazepam (Valium) will boost this reduced GABA-ergic function to increase the inhibitory activity in the brain. This is important to control symptoms such as anxiety and tremor, and to reduce the risk of complications such as seizures and delirium tremens.

In addition to boosting the inhibitory GABA system, alcohol antagonises the excitatory neurotransmitter system, glutamate and particularly the NMDA receptor. To overcome this blockade, the number of NMDA receptors increase in response to continued drinking. This increase has been associated with memory impairment in animal models and may therefore underlie amnesia or blackouts, which can be experienced by people who drink heavily (Krystal *et al.*, 2003). In alcohol withdrawal, therefore, the increased glutamatergic activity significantly contributes to the associated symptoms and risks such as tremor and seizures. Anticonvulsants, which reduce glutamatergic activity as well as increasing GABA-ergic activity, can therefore be used to treat alcohol withdrawal. In addition to this GABA-glutamate activity, anticonvulsants will also inhibit voltage-activated sodium channels and, consequently, further excitatory activity.

Another consequence of increased glutamatergic and calcium channel activity is cell death. Therefore a potential advantage of antagonising this increased activity in withdrawal is neuroprotection or preventing cell death. In animal models, acamprosate has been shown to reduce increased glutamatergic activity in withdrawal but robust clinical evidence is lacking. Whether it occurs with anticonvulsants has not been systematically studied.

7.2   REVIEW OF PHARMACOLOGICAL INTERVENTIONS

7.2.1   Aim of review

The focus of this chapter is the effectiveness and cost-effectiveness of pharmacological interventions to prevent relapse or reduce alcohol consumption. The use of drugs alone or in combination with a range of other psychosocial interventions were considered. The drugs considered for inclusion in the review are set out in Table 89.

The review aimed to evaluate all available pharmacological interventions for relapse prevention. This was conducted for adults and, where evidence was available, separately for special populations such as children and young people or older people. The GDG decided to conduct a meta-analysis only on the drugs that were licensed for alcohol use in the UK or drugs that are in common usage with a large amount of clinical evidence of efficacy. From these criteria, the drugs identified for review were acamprosate, naltrexone and disulfiram. For naltrexone and disulfiram, only the oral delivery preparations of these drugs was considered for meta-analysis due to the lack of available evidence and the uncommon usage of the extended-release and subcutaneous implantation preparations of these drugs. These drugs are evaluated in the first instance for both adults and for special populations (children and young people). The narrative review of the available literature for the use of pharmacological interventions for special populations can be found in Section 7.12. For other pharmacological interventions that are not licensed for used in the UK for the treatment of alcohol misuse, meta-analyses were not

Table 89: Pharmacology of medications for the treatment of alcohol misuse

Medication	Main target – system and action	Other relevant targets	Use
Acamprosate	Antagonises glutamatergic function (NMDA, mGLuR5)	Increases GABA-ergic function	Relapse prevention
Naltrexone	Opioid antagonist	–	Relapse prevention
Disulfiram	Blocks aldehyde dehydrogenase in liver, increasing acetaldehyde	Blocks dopamine-B-hydroxylase in brain, increasing dopamine	Relapse prevention
Antipsychotics – variety of 'first or second generation'	Dopamine receptor D2 antagonists (for example, olanzapine and quetiapine); partial agonist (for example, aripiprazole)	–	Relapse prevention Antipsychotic
Benzodiazepines	Increases GABA-benzodiazepine function	–	Medically assisted withdrawal, possible role in relapse prevention
Baclofen	GABA-B agonist	–	Relapse prevention
Gabapentin	Ca channel antagonist	–	Relapse prevention and withdrawal
Pregabalin	Ca channel antagonist	–	Relapse prevention
Topiramate	Increases GABA-ergic function and antagonises some glutamate	Reduces excitatory ion channel activity	Relapse prevention
Memantine	NMDA antagonist	–	Relapse prevention
Odansetron	5HT3 antagonist	–	Relapse prevention
Antidepressants – SSRIs, for example sertraline	5HT reuptake inhibitor	–	Relapse prevention Antidepressant Anxiolytic
Buspirone	5HT1A partial agonist	–	Relapse prevention Anxiolytic

conducted. The reasons for this and the narrative synthesis of the evidence can be found in Section 7.14.

Literature evaluating pharmacological interventions for less severely dependent and non-dependent drinkers is limited and a meta-analysis could not be conducted. A narrative synthesis of the available literature is provided in Section 7.16. Similarly, trials where the participant sample included a very high prevalence of comorbid mental health disorders were excluded from the meta-analysis and are reviewed separately in Section 7.17. See Chapter 3 for a further discussion of the review methods used in this chapter. Lastly, a review of the long-term management of WKS can be found in Section 7.18.

7.2.2   Review questions

The review question that the GDG addressed, and from which the literature searches were developed, is:
1. For people with alcohol dependence or harmful alcohol use, what pharmacological interventions are more clinically and cost-effective?
In addition:
(a) What are the impacts of severity and comorbidities on outcomes?
(b) When should pharmacological treatments be initiated and for what duration should they be prescribed?

7.3   CLINICAL REVIEW PROTOCOL FOR PHARMACOLOGICAL INTERVENTIONS FOR RELAPSE PREVENTION

The drugs identified for this review have been listed in Table 89. Information about the databases searched and the inclusion/exclusion criteria used for this section of the guideline can be found in Appendix 16e (further information about the search for health economic evidence can be found in Chapter 3). See Table 90 for the clinical review protocol followed for this review. The clinical and health economic reviews of the pharmacological interventions licensed for use for alcohol in the UK (acamprosate, naltrexone and disulfiram) can be found in Section 7.4 to 7.12. The pharmacological interventions not licensed for use in the UK are reviewed in Section 7.14.

7.4   ACAMPROSATE

7.4.1   Studies considered for review[43]

The review team conducted a systematic search for RCTs that assessed the benefits and disadvantages of acamprosate for relapse prevention. The clinical review protocol for this section can be found in Section 7.3. Study characteristics are summarised in Table 91. For the related health economic evidence see Section 7.10.

---

[43]Here and elsewhere in the guideline, each study considered for review is referred to by a study ID in capital letters (primary author and date of study publication, except where a study is in press or only submitted for publication, then a date is not used).

Table 90: Clinical review protocol for pharmacological interventions for relapse prevention

Electronic databases	CINAHL, EMBASE, MEDLINE, PsycINFO, Cochrane Library
Date searched	Database inception to March 2010
Study design	RCTs
Population	At least 80% of the sample meet the criteria for alcohol dependence or harmful alcohol use (clinical diagnosis or drinking more than 30 drinks per week)
Excluded populations	Hazardous drinkers and those drinking less than 30 drinks per week Pregnant women
Interventions	Any pharmacological intervention
Comparator	Any other intervention
Outcomes	Discontinuing treatment for any reason Discontinuing treatment due to adverse events Lapsing (returning to a drinking state) Relapsing (returning to a heavy drinking state) PDA Cumulative abstinence duration DDD Total drinks consumed during treatment period Total days of heavy drinking during treatment Time to first drink Time to heavy drinking day

There were a total of 19 trials (including one study still awaiting translation) comparing acamprosate with placebo. These were typically large, high-quality studies, of which ten were sponsored by the drug company. A number of psychosocial interventions were used in addition to the trial medication, in line with the drug licensing agreement, which included alcohol counselling, medication management and relapse prevention as well as high-intensity alcohol treatment programmes. Data on participants lapsing to alcohol consumption was acquired from the authors of two meta-analyses (Mann, 2004; Rosner *et al.*, 2008), who had access to unpublished data and therefore allowed for the development of a more complete dataset. Both the PAILLE1995 and PELC1997 studies were three-armed trials where two different doses of acamprosate (1.3 g and 2 g) were compared with placebo. To avoid the double counting of the control data, only data for the groups

Table 91: Summary of study characteristics for acamprosate versus placebo

	Acamprosate versus placebo
Total number of trials (total number of participants)	19 RCTs (N = 4629)
Study ID	(1) ANTON2006 (2) BALTIERI2003 (3) BARRIAS1997 (4) BESSON1998 (5) CHICK2000A (6) GEERLINGS1997 (7) GUAL2001 (8) KIEFER2003 (9) LADEWIG1993 (10) MORLEY2006 (11) NAMKOONG2003 (12) PAILLE1995 (13) PELC1992 (14) PELC1997 (15) POLDRUGO1997 (16) ROUSSAUX1996 (17) SASS1996 (18) TEMPESTA2000 (19) WHITWORTH1996
Diagnosis	DSM or ICD diagnosis of alcohol dependence
Baseline severity	Units consumed per week Mean: 145.15 Range: 90 to 314.37
Mean dosage	1998 mg per day
Length of treatment	Range: 8 weeks to 52 weeks
Length of follow-up	(1) Up to 12 months (2)–(3) Not reported (4) Up to 12 months (5) Not reported (6) Up to 12 months (7)–(11) Not reported (12) Up to 12 months and up to 18 months (13)–(14) Not reported (15) Up to 12 months (16) Not reported

Continued

Table 91: (*Continued*)

	Acamprosate versus placebo
	(17) Up to 12 months (18) Not reported (19) Up to 12 months and up to 24 months
Setting	(1)–(2) Outpatient (3) Not reported (4)–(7) Outpatient (8)–(9) Inpatient/outpatient (10)–(12) Outpatient (13) Not reported (14)–(18) Outpatient (19) Inpatient/outpatient
Treatment goal	(1)–(6) Not reported (7)–(8) Abstinence (9)–(14) Not reported (15) Abstinence (16)–(19) Not reported

taking 2 g of acamprosate were used, because this is the dose recommended by the BNF. Reasons for exclusion of studies from this review included not providing an acceptable diagnosis of alcohol dependence, not being an RCT, having fewer than ten participants per group, not being double blind and not reporting any relevant outcomes. Further information about both included and excluded studies can be found in Appendix 16e.

The populations within these trials were typically presenting with moderate to severe alcohol dependence, either indicated through alcohol consumption or dependency scale shown at baseline. These studies were mainly conducted in Europe, with only one (CHICK2000A) conducted in the UK. Acamprosate was started after the participant completed assisted withdrawal (if required) in all trials except one, GUAL2001, when it was started during assisted withdrawal.

7.4.2   Evidence summary

Evidence from the important outcomes and overall quality of evidence are presented in Table 92. The full evidence profiles and associated forest plots can be found in Appendix 18d and Appendix 17d, respectively.

There was a significant but small effect of acamprosate in promoting abstinence in participants when compared with placebo (RR = 0.83; 95% CI = 0.77 to 0.88). The effect was most pronounced at 6 months, but remained significant up to 12

Table 92: Evidence summary table for trials of acamprosate versus placebo

	Acamprosate versus placebo
Total number of studies (number of participants)	19 RCTs (N = 4629)
Study ID	(1) ANTON2006 (2) BALTIERI2003 (3) BARRIAS1997 (4) BESSON1998 (5) CHICK2000A (6) GEERLINGS1997 (7) GUAL2001 (8) KIEFER2003 (9) LADEWIG1993 (10) MORLEY2006 (11) NAMKOONG2003 (12) PAILLE1995 (13) PELC1992 (14) PELC1997 (15) POLDRUGO1997 (16) ROUSSAUX1996 (17) SASS1996 (18) TEMPESTA2000 (19) WHITWORTH1996
Benefits	
Lapsed (participants returning to any drinking)	At 2 months: RR = 1.19 (0.76, 1.88) K = 1, N = 142 At 3 months: RR = 0.88 (0.75, 1.04) K = 1, N = 350 At 6 months: RR = 0.83 (0.77, 0.88) K = 17, N = 3964 At 12 months: RR = 0.88 (0.80, 0.96) K = 4, N = 1332 At 18 months: RR = 0.94 (0.87, 1.02) K = 1, N = 350

Continued

Table 92: (*Continued*)

	Acamprosate versus placebo
	At 24 months: RR = 0.92 (0.87, 0.98) K = 1, N = 448
Relapsed to heavy drinking	At 3 months: RR = 0.95 (0.86, 1.05) K = 1, N = 612 At 6 months: RR = 0.81 (0.72, 0.92) K = 10, N = 2654 At 12 months: RR = 0.96 (0.89, 1.04) K = 1, N = 612
PDA	At 2 months: SMD = −0.10 (−0.43, 0.23) K = 1, N = 142 At 3 months: SMD = 0.00 (−0.16, 0.15) K = 1, N = 612 At 12 months: SMD = 0.00 (−0.20, 0.20) K = 1, N = 612
Cumulative abstinence duration	At 3 months: SMD = −2.75 (−7.51, 2.01) K = 2, N = 241 At 6 months: SMD = −0.29 (−0.41, −0.17) K = 4, N = 1134 At 9 months: SMD = −0.24 (-0.46, −0.03) K = 1, N = 330 At 12 months: SMD = −0.35 (−0.46, −0.24) K = 4, N = 1316

Continued

Table 92: (*Continued*)

	Acamprosate versus placebo
	At 24 months: SMD = −0.34 (−0.66, −0.03) K = 2, N = 720
Time to first drink	SMD = −0.26 (−0.45, −0.06) K = 3, N = 738
DDD	SMD = −0.05 (−0.29, 0.20) K = 2, N = 258
Percentage of days without heavy drinking	SMD = −0.06 (−0.38, 0.27) K = 1, N = 142
Harms	
Discontinuation for any reason	RR = 0.90 (0.81, 0.99) K = 15, N = 4037
Discontinuation due to adverse events	RR = 1.36 (0.99, 1.88) K = 12, N = 3774

months. In the one trial that continued up to 2 years (WHITWORTH1996) this small effect continued for up to 12 months after the termination of treatment. The number of individuals relapsing to heavy drinking was also significantly less in the acamprosate group. This effect was also small (RR = 0.90; 95% CI = 0.81 to 0.99) but suggests participants were more likely to stay in treatment if randomised to acamprosate instead of placebo. However, more participants left the trials due to adverse events in the acamprosate group, although this was not statistically significant.

The quality of the evidence for acamprosate is *high*, therefore further research is unlikely to have an important impact on confidence in the estimate of the effect. An evidence summary of the results of the meta-analyses can be seen in Table 92.

7.5 NALTREXONE

7.5.1 Studies considered

The review team conducted a systematic review of RCTs that assessed the beneficial or detrimental effects of naltrexone for relapse prevention. See Section 7.2 for the aim of the review and the review questions. The clinical review protocol for this section can be found in Section 7.3. See Table 93 for a summary of the study characteristics of the included studies.

A total of 27 trials compared oral naltrexone with placebo and four trials compared naltrexone with acamprosate. In addition, there were two studies comparing naltrexone with naltrexone plus sertraline and one trial comparing naltrexone with topiramate. The majority of the trials were large, high-quality studies with five trials sponsored by drug companies. Twenty-six of the trials (LATT2002 being the exception) included one of a number of different psychosocial interventions in addition to either naltrexone or placebo, including alcohol counselling, coping skills or relapse prevention as well as high-intensity alcohol treatment programmes. Unpublished data on individuals relapsing to heavy drinking was acquired from the authors of a meta-analysis (Rosner *et al.*, 2008), who had access to unpublished data. Reasons for exclusion of studies from this review included not providing an acceptable diagnosis of alcohol dependence, not being an RCT, having fewer than ten participants per group, not being double blind and not reporting any relevant outcomes. Further information about both included and excluded studies can be found in Appendix 16e.

One additional study including naltrexone by Petrakis and colleagues (2005), although a high-quality trial, was excluded because the whole participant sample was comorbid with a range of Axis I disorders, with many participants having multiple co-existing disorders. This was unusual when compared with the included trials, where comorbidity was usually grounds for exclusion. This study is described more fully in the comorbidity in Section 7.17.

The participant population included in these trials ranged from mild to severe dependence based on baseline alcohol consumption and dependency scale scores. (This is in contrast to the studies included in the acamprosate review where participants generally presented with more severe dependence.) The majority of these trials were conducted in North America, and recruitment was most commonly through advertisements or referrals. If assisted withdrawal was required, then naltrexone was started after this was completed in these trials.

7.5.2 Evidence summary

Evidence on the important outcomes and overall quality of evidence are presented in Table 94. The full evidence profiles and associated forest plots can be found in Appendix 18d and Appendix 17d, respectively.

The comparison of oral naltrexone versus placebo showed a small but significant effect favouring naltrexone on rates of relapse to heavy drinking (RR = 0.83; 95% CI, 0.75 to 0.91). The mean DDD within the trial duration was less in the naltrexone group when compared with placebo, with a small but significant effect (SMD = −0.28; 95% CI, −0.44 to −0.11). A significant but small effect favouring naltrexone was also found on days of heavy drinking during the trial (SMD = −0.43; 95% CI, −0.82 to −0.03). Although overall discontinuation rates favoured naltrexone over placebo, there was no significant difference between the two groups.

Table 93: Summary of study characteristics for naltrexone

	Oral naltrexone versus placebo	Oral naltrexone versus acamprosate oral naltrexone	Oral naltrexone + sertraline versus oral naltrexone	Oral naltrexone versus topiramate
Total number of trials (total number of participants)	27 RCTs (N = 4296)	4 RCTs (N = 957)	2 RCTs (N = 178)	1 RCT (N = 101)
Study ID	(1) AHMADI2002 (2) ANTON1999 (3) ANTON2005 (4) ANTON2006 (5) BALLDIN2003 (6) BALTIERI2008 (7) CHICK2000B (8) GASTPAR2002 (9) GUARDIA2002 (10) HEINALA2001 (11) HUANG2005 (12) KIEFER2003 (13) KILLEEN2004 (14) KRANZLER2000 (15) KRYSTAL2001 (16) LATT2002 (17) LEE2001 (18) MONTI2001 (19) MORLEY2006 (20) MORRIS2001 (21) OMALLEY1992	(1) ANTON2006 (2) KIEFER2003 (3) MORLEY2006 (4) RUBIO2001	(1) FARREN2009 (2) OMALLEY2008	(1) BALTIERI2008

	(22) OMALLEY2003 (23) OMALLEY2008 (24) OSLIN1997 (25) OSLIN2008 (26) VOLPICELLI1992 (27) VOLPICELLI1997			
Diagnosis	DSM or ICD diagnosis of alcohol dependence	DSM or ICD diagnosis of alcohol dependence	DSM or ICD diagnosis of alcohol dependence	DSM or ICD diagnosis of alcohol dependence
Baseline severity – units consumed per week	Mean: 98.6 Range: 70.56 to 223	Mean: 128.1 Range: 74.3 to 223	Mean: 83.75 Range: 60 to 107.5	Mean: 263.64
Mean dosage	Naltrexone: 50 mg daily	Naltrexone: 50 mg daily Acamprosate: 1998 mg daily	Naltrexone: 50 mg daily Sertraline: 100 mg daily	Naltrexone: 50 mg daily Topiramate: 300 mg daily
Length of treatment	Range: 12 to 24 weeks	Range: 12 to 52 weeks	Range: 12 to 16 weeks	12 weeks
Length of follow-up	(1) Not reported (2) Up to 6 months (3) Not reported (4) Up to 12 months (5)–(11) Not reported (12) Up to 6 months (13)–(20) Not reported (21) Up to 6 months (22)–(27) Not reported	(1)–(3) Not reported (4) Up to 12 months	(1)–(2) Not reported	(1) Not reported

Continued

373

Table 93: (*Continued*)

	Oral naltrexone versus placebo	Oral naltrexone versus acamprosate oral naltrexone	Oral naltrexone + sertraline versus	Oral naltrexone versus topiramate
Setting	(1)–(7) Outpatient (8) Inpatient/outpatient (9)–(11) Outpatient (12) Inpatient/outpatient (13)–(16) Outpatient (17) Inpatient/outpatient (18)–(27) Outpatient	(1) Outpatient (2) Inpatient/outpatient (3)–(4) Outpatient	(1)–(2) Outpatient	(1) Outpatient
Treatment goal	(1)–(3) Not reported (4) Abstinence (5)–(8) Not reported (9) Abstinence (10) Abstinence and drinking reduction/moderation (11)–(13) Not reported (14)–(15) Abstinence (16) Not reported (17) Abstinence (18)–(20) Not reported (21) Abstinence (22)–(23) Not reported (24) Abstinence (25)–(27) Not reported	(1) Abstinence (2)–(3) Not reported (4) Abstinence	(1)–(2) Not reported	(1) Not reported

Table 94: Evidence summary table for trials of naltrexone

	Oral naltrexone versus placebo	Oral naltrexone versus acamprosate	Oral naltrexone + sertraline versus oral naltrexone	Oral naltrexone versus topiramate
Total number of studies (number of participants)	27 RCTs (N = 4164)	4 RCTs (N = 957)	2 RCTs (N = 178)	1 RCT (N = 101)
Study ID	(1) AHMADI2002 (2) ANTON1999 (3) ANTON2005 (4) ANTON2006 (5) BALLDIN2003 (6) BALTIERI2008 (7) CHICK2000B (8) GASTPAR2002 (9) GUARDIA2002 (10) HEINALA2001 (11) HUANG2005 (12) KIEFER2003 (13) KILLEEN2004 (14) KRANZLER2000 (15) KRYSTAL2001 (16) LATT2002 (17) LEE2001 (18) MONTI2001 (19) MORLEY2006	(1) ANTON2006 (2) KIEFER2003 (3) MORLEY2006 (4) RUBIO2001	(1) FARREN2009 (2) OMALLEY2008	(1) BALTIERI2008

Continued

375

Table 94: *(Continued)*

	Oral naltrexone versus placebo	Oral naltrexone versus acamprosate	Oral naltrexone + sertraline versus oral naltrexone	Oral naltrexone versus topiramate
	(20) MORRIS2001 (21) OMALLEY1992 (22) OMALLEY2003 (23) OMALLEY2008 (24) OSLIN1997 (25) OSLIN2008 (26) VOLPICELLI1992 (27) VOLPICELLI1997			
Benefits				
Lapsed (participants returning to any drinking)	At 3 months: RR = 0.92 (0.86, 1.00) K = 17, N = 1893 At 6 months (maintenance treatment): RR = 0.79 (0.60, 1.05) K = 1, N = 113 At 6 months (follow-up) RR = 0.90 (0.69, 1.17) K = 1, N = 84	At 12 months: RR = 0.71 (0.57, 0.88) K = 1, N = 157	At 3 months: RR = 1.08 (0.77, 1.51) K = 1, N = 67	At 1 month: RR = 1.44 (0.88, 2.35) K = 1, N = 101 At 2 months: RR = 1.54 (1.02, 2.33) K = 1, N = 101 At 3 months: RR = 1.48 (1.11, 1.97) K = 1, N = 101

			Not reported
Relapsed to heavy drinking	At 3 months: RR = 0.83 (0.76, 0.91) K = 22, N = 3320 At 6 months (endpoint): RR = 0.96 (0.79, 1.17) K = 1, N = 240 At 6 months (follow-up): RR = 0.74 (0.60, 0.90) K = 3, N = 284 At 6 months (maintenance treatment): RR = 0.46 (0.24, 0.89) K = 1, N = 113 At 9 months (endpoint): RR = 0.74 (0.56, 0.98) K = 1, N = 116 At 12 months (follow-up): RR = 0.95 (0.88, 1.03) K = 1, N = 618	At 3 months: RR = 0.96 (0.87, 1.06) K = 3, N = 800 At 6 months: RR = 0.95 (0.64, 1.43) K = 1, N = 80 At 12 months: RR = 0.99 (0.91, 1.08) K = 1, N = 612	At 3 months: RR = 1.03 (0.73, 1.46) K = 1, N = 67
PDA	At 3 months: SMD = −0.22 (−0.37, −0.07) K = 9, N = 1607	At 3 months: SMD = 0.04 (−0.21, 0.29) K = 2, N = 720	At 3 months: SMD = −0.12 (−0.79, 0.56) K = 2, N = 178

Continued

377

Table 94: (*Continued*)

	Oral naltrexone versus placebo	Oral naltrexone versus acamprosate	Oral naltrexone + sertraline versus oral naltrexone	Oral naltrexone versus topiramate
	At 6 months: SMD = −0.25 (−0.51, 0.00) K = 1, N = 240 At 12 months: SMD = −0.11 (−0.42, 0.20) K = 1, N = 618	At 12 months: SMD = −0.11 (−0.27, 0.04) K = 1, N = 612		
Time to first drink	SMD = −0.07 (−0.21, 0.08) K = 5, N = 730	SMD = −0.09 (−0.34, 0.15) K = 2, N = 265	Not reported	Not reported
Time to first heavy drinking episode	SMD = −0.32 (−0.68, 0.03) K = 8, N = 1513	SMD = −0.39 (−081, 0.03) K = 2, N = 265	Not reported	SMD = 0.43 (0.04, 0.83) K = 1, N = 101
Cumulative abstinence duration	SMD = −0.12 (−0.39, 0.15) K = 2, N = 217	Not reported	Not reported	SMD = 0.34 (−0.06, 0.73) K = 1, N = 101

DDD during study period	SMD = −0.28 (−0.44, −0.11) K = 10, N = 1639	SMD = −0.76 (−1.09, −0.44) K = 1, N = 157	SMD = −0.95 (−2.94, 1.04) K = 2, N = 178	Not reported
Heavy drinking episodes during study period	SMD = −0.43 (−0.82, −0.03) K = 7, N = 797	Not reported	SMD = −0.23 (−0.71, 0.25) K = 1, N = 67	SMD = 0.33 (−0.064, 0.72) K = 1, N = 101
Total drinks consumed during study period	SMD = −0.32 (−0.70, 0.06) K = 2, N = 257	Not reported	Not reported	Not reported
Harms				
Discontinuation for any reason	RR = 0.94 (0.84, 1.05) K = 25, N = 3926	RR = 0.85 (0.72, 1.01) K = 4, N = 957	RR = 1.55 (1.00, 2.42) K = 2, N = 178	RR = 1.12 (0.68, 1.83) K = 1, N = 101
Discontinuation due to adverse events	RR = 1.79 (1.15, 2.77) K = 12, N = 1933	RR = 1.44 (0.63, 3.29) K = 2, N = 769	RR = 2.92 (0.82, 10.44) K = 2, N = 178	Not reported

However, participants were significantly more likely to leave treatment due to adverse events in the naltrexone group, with significantly fewer adverse events reported in the placebo group.

When comparing oral naltrexone with acamprosate, the four trials reviewed showed no significant difference in discontinuation for any reason or due to adverse events between the two interventions. On critical outcomes, there were no significant differences between naltrexone and acamprosate except for number of individuals returning to any drinking (RR = 0.71; 95% CI, 0.57 to 0.88) and DDD (SMD = −0.76; 95% CI, −1.09 to −0.44). However, these findings were based on only one study (RUBIO2001), which found that participants in the naltrexone group were significantly less likely to return to any drinking and consumed significantly less DDD during the trial period. When comparing naltrexone with topiramate, the analysis showed no significant differences between the groups on any outcomes except number of participants continuously abstinent and weeks until first relapse, both outcomes favouring naltrexone. The analysis of naltrexone versus naltrexone plus sertraline showed no significant differences between the groups on any outcomes. However, discontinuation rates were less in the combination group.

The quality of the evidence reviewed for oral naltrexone versus placebo was *high*, therefore further research is unlikely to have an important impact on confidence in the estimate of the effect. The quality of the evidence for naltrexone versus acamprosate was also *high*. However, the quality for the evidence for the naltrexone plus sertraline combination intervention versus naltrexone alone and for naltrexone versus topiramate was *moderate*, therefore further research is likely to have an important impact on confidence in the estimate of these effects.

7.6 ACAMPROSATE + NALTREXONE (COMBINED INTERVENTION)

7.6.1 Studies considered

The review team conducted a systematic review of RCTs that assessed the beneficial or detrimental effects of acamprosate plus naltrexone for relapse prevention. See Section 7.2 for the aim of the review and the review questions. The clinical review protocol for this section can be found in Section 7.3. See Table 95 for a summary of the study characteristics of included studies.

There were two trials comparing the combination of acamprosate and naltrexone with placebo, acamprosate alone and naltrexone alone. Both were large multiple-armed trials designed specifically to test the effects of the drugs in isolation and together. The KIEFER2003 trial included a population of people with severe dependence recruited from inpatient facilities; their mean pre-admission consumption of alcohol was 223 units per week. Each participant received a relapse prevention intervention in addition to pharmacological therapy. The ANTON2006 study included a less severe population of people with dependence who were recruited through advertisements or clinical referrals; their mean pre-admission consumption of alcohol was

Table 95: Summary of study characteristics for naltrexone + acamprosate

	Naltrexone + acamprosate versus placebo	Naltrexone + acamprosate versus acamprosate	Naltrexone + acamprosate versus naltrexone
Total number of trials (total number of participants)	2 RCTs (N = 694)	2 RCTs (N = 688)	2 RCTs (N = 694)
Study ID	(1) ANTON2006 (2) KIEFER2003	(1) ANTON2006 (2) KIEFER2003	(1) ANTON2006 (2) KIEFER2003
Diagnosis	DSM or ICD diagnosis of alcohol dependence	DSM or ICD diagnosis of alcohol dependence	DSM or ICD diagnosis of alcohol dependence
Baseline severity – units comsumed per week	Mean: 160.05 Range: 97.1 to 223	Mean: 160.05 Range: 97.1 to 223	Mean: 160.05 Range: 97.1 to 223
Mean dosage	(1) Acamprosate: 3 g per day Naltrexone: 100 mg per day (2) Acamprosate: 1998 mg per day Naltrexone: 50 mg per day	(1) Acamprosate: 3 g per day Naltrexone: 100 mg per day (2) Acamprosate: 1998 mg per day Naltrexone: 50 mg per day	(1) Acamprosate: 3 g per day Naltrexone: 100 mg per day (2) Acamprosate: 1998 mg per day Naltrexone: 50 mg per day
Length of treatment	12 weeks	12 weeks	12 weeks
Length of follow-up	(1) Up to 12 months (2) Up to 6 months	(1) Up to 12 months (2) Up to 6 months	(1) Up to 12 months (2) Up to 6 months
Setting	(1) Outpatient (2) Inpatient/ outpatient	(1) Outpatient (2) Inpatient/ outpatient	(1) Outpatient (2) Inpatient/ outpatient
Treatment goal	(1) Abstinence (2) Not reported	(1) Abstinence (2) Not reported	(1) Abstinence (2) Not reporte

97 units per week. In addition to being randomised to one of four pharmacological interventions, participants were also randomised to a cognitive-behavioural intervention with medication management or medication management alone. Reasons for exclusion of studies from this review included not providing an acceptable diagnosis of alcohol dependence, not being an RCT, having fewer than ten participants per

group, not being double blind and not reporting any relevant outcomes. Further information about both included and excluded studies can be found in Appendix 16e.

7.6.2 Evidence summary

Evidence from the important outcomes and overall quality of evidence are presented in Table 96. The full evidence profiles and associated forest plots can be found in Appendix 18d and Appendix 17d, respectively.

There was no significant difference between the combination of acamprosate and naltrexone and either drug alone on reducing the likelihood of returning to heavy drinking at 3 months (combination versus acamprosate: RR = 0.93; 95% CI, 0.74 to 1.17; combination versus naltrexone: RR = 1.03 [0.90 to 1.17]), and the one trial continuing up to 12 months showed no effect. In addition, there were no significant differences on any other outcomes between the combination group and either drug. The combined drug group was also equivalent to the placebo group on discontinuation rates and PDA. Relapse rates at 6 months were significantly different with a moderate effect in favour of the combined intervention group (RR = 0.44; 95% CI, 0.28 to 0.69); however, there was no difference between the groups on relapse rates at 3 months or 12 months.

The quality of the evidence was *high*, therefore further research is unlikely to have an important impact on confidence in the estimate of the effect. It was also noted that there was significant heterogeneity between comparisons of the KIEFER2003 and the ANTON2006 studies, which is very likely to be due to the differences in the populations, baseline drinking level and from where they were recruited (inpatient facility versus advertisement or referral).

7.7 ORAL DISULFIRAM

7.7.1 Studies considered

The review team conducted a systematic review of RCTs that assessed the beneficial or detrimental effects of disulfiram for relapse prevention. See Section 7.2 for the aim of the review and the review questions. The clinical review protocol for this section can be found in Section 7.3. See Table 97 for the characteristics of the included studies. Unlike the reviews of acamprosate and naltrexone, there was much less high-quality evidence available on the efficacy and effectiveness of disulfiram, and for this reason the GDG decided to use open-label trials in the meta-analysis of disulfiram.

The reason for this was that due to the disulfiram–ethanol reaction, a number of the studies had to be open-label for ethical reasons so that participants were aware that they were taking a substance that can cause potentially dangerous side effects when taken with alcohol. This also contributes to the psychological effect of disulfiram, where the fear of the chemical reaction is believed to be as important as the pharmacological

Table 96: Evidence summary table for trials of acamprosate + naltrexone

	Acamprosate + naltrexone versus placebo	Acamprosate + naltrexone versus acamprosate	Acamprosate + naltrexone versus naltrexone
Total number of studies (number of participants)	2 RCTs (N = 694)	2 RCTs (N = 688)	2 RCTs (N = 694)
Study ID	(1) ANTON2006 (2) KIEFER2003	(1) ANTON2006 (2) KIEFER2003	(1) ANTON2006 (2) KIEFER2003
Benefits			
Relapsed to heavy drinking	At 3 months: RR = 0.78 (0.56, 1.09) K = 2, N = 694	At 3 months: RR = 0.93 (0.74, 1.17) K = 2, N = 688	At 3 months: RR = 1.03 (0.90, 1.17) K = 2, N = 694
	At 6 months: RR = 0.44 (0.28, 0.69) K = 1, N = 80	At 6 months: RR = 0.64 (0.38, 1.06) K = 1, N = 80	At 6 months: RR = 0.67 (0.40, 1.12) K = 2, N = 80
	At 12 months: RR = 0.97 (0.90, 1.05) K = 1, N = 614	At 12 months: RR = 1.02 (0.94, 1.10) K = 1, N = 608	At 12 months: RR = 1.02 (0.94, 1.10) K = 1, N = 612
PDA	At 3 months: SMD = −0.09 (−0.42, 0.25) K = 1, N = 614	At 3 months: SMD = −0.08 (−0.29, 0.13) K = 1, N = 608	At 3 months: SMD = −0.04 (−0.20, 0.12) K = 1, N = 614
	At 12 months: SMD = −0.09 (−0.25, 0.06) K = 1, N = 614	At 12 months: SMD = −0.11 (−0.27, 0.05) K = 1, N = 608	At 12 months: SMD = 0.02 (−0.18, 0.21) K = 1, N = 614
Harms			
Discontinuation for any reason	RR = 1.00 (0.53, 1.90) K = 2, N = 694	RR = 0.92 (0.65, 1.32) K = 2, N = 687	RR = 1.09 (0.87, 1.37) K = 2, N = 694
Discontinuation due to adverse events	RR = 3.16 (1.03, 9.76) K = 1, N = 614	RR = 1.39 (0.34, 5.71) K = 1, N = 608	RR = 1.10 (0.50, 2.40) K = 1, N = 614

Table 97: Summary of study characteristics for oral disulfiram

	Oral disulfiram versus placebo	Oral disulfiram versus acamprosate	Oral disulfiram versus naltrexone	Oral disulfiram versus topiramate	Oral disulfiram + counselling versus counselling
Total number of trials (total number of participants)	3 RCTs (N = 859)	1 RCT (N = 243)	2 RCTs (N = 343)	1 RCT (N = 100)	1 RCT (N = 26)
Study ID	(1) CHICK1992 (2) FULLER1979 (3) FULLER1986	(1) LAAKSONEN2008	(1) DESOUSA2004 (2) LAAKSONEN2008	(1) DESOUSA2008	(1) GERREIN1973
Diagnosis	National Council on alcoholism diagnostic criteria or by an undefined diagnosis tool	ICD diagnosis of alcohol dependence	DSM or ICD diagnosis of alcohol dependence	DSM diagnosis of alcohol dependence	Undefined diagnosis tool
Baseline severity – units consumed per week	Mean: 198.5 Range: 190 to 207	Mean: 136.25	Mean: 111.35 Range: 86.45 to 136.25	Mean: 70	Not reported

	Disulfiram: 250 mg daily	Disulfiram: 150 mg daily Acamprosate: 1998 mg daily	Disulfiram: 200 mg daily Naltrexone: 50 mg daily	Disulfiram: 250 mg daily Topiramate: 150 mg daily	Disulfiram: 250 mg daily
Mean dosage					
Length of treatment	Range: 24 weeks – 52 weeks.	52 weeks	52 weeks	36 weeks	8 weeks
Length of follow-up	(1)–(3) No follow-up data recorded	(1) No follow-up data recorded	(1)–(2) No follow-up data recorded	(1) No follow-up data recorded	(1) No follow-up data recorded
Setting	(1)–(2) Outpatient (3) Inpatient/outpatient	(1) Outpatient	(1)–(2) Outpatient	(1) Inpatient/ outpatient	(1) Outpatient
Treatment goal (if mentioned)	(3) Abstinence	(1) Abstinence	(1)–(2) Abstinence	(1) Abstinence	Not mentioned

effects of the drug in determining the efficacy of the intervention. The FULLER1979 and FULLER1986 trials adapted their trials for this purpose and randomised participants to either the full dose of disulfiram (250 mg per day) or to 1 mg of disulfiram with a placebo agent that has been judged to have no clinical effect.

Due to the age of some of the trials, inclusion criteria for diagnosis was also relaxed to include papers that did not explicitly mention the diagnosis tool used to determine eligibility to the trial. The Petrakis and colleagues (2005) trial was also excluded from the meta-analysis as many participants had a range of Axis I disorders.

There were a total of three trials comparing oral disulfiram with placebo (FULLER1979; FULLER1986; CHICK1992), one trial comparing oral disulfiram with acamprosate (LAAKSONEN2008), two trials comparing oral disulfiram with naltrexone (DESOUSA2004; LAAKSONEN2008) and one trial comparing oral disulfiram with topiramate (DESOUSA2008). In addition, there was one trial comparing disulfiram and counselling with counselling alone (GERREIN1973).

The severity of dependence of the participants included in these trials was not reported for the older trials; however, in the more recent studies, dependency indicated through baseline consumption and dependency scales suggested that these participants were of moderate to severe dependency. The trials varied in terms of the country in which they were conducted, with CHICK1992 being the only trial conducted in the UK. Three studies were conducted in the US (FULLER1979; FULLER1986; GERREIN1973), two were conducted in India (DESOUSA2004; DESOUSA2008) and one was conducted in Finland (LAAKSONEN2008).

7.7.2 Evidence summary

Evidence on the important outcomes and the overall quality of evidence are presented in Table 98. The full evidence profiles and associated forest plots can be found in Appendix 18d and Appendix 17d, respectively.

Oral disulfiram was not significantly different from placebo in preventing participants lapsing to alcohol consumption (RR = 1.05; 95% CI, 0.96 to 1.15). There was also no difference in rates of discontinuation between the two groups. However, LAAKSONEN2008 showed that, in comparison with acamprosate, disulfiram was significantly more likely to increase the time until participants first drank any alcohol (SMD = -0.84; 95% CI, -1.28 to -0.40) and drank heavily (SMD = -1.17; 95% CI, -1.66 to -0.68), and also decreased the amount of alcohol consumed and the number of drinking days. In comparison with naltrexone, disulfiram was also significantly more likely to increase the time to first heavy drinking day and the number of abstinent days. Participants in the naltrexone group were significantly more likely to return to any drinking (RR = 0.18; 95% CI, 0.08 to 0.42) or relapse to heavy drinking (RR = 0.28; 95% CI, 0.13 to 0.59) when compared with the oral disulfiram group, although this was based on two open-label studies (DESOUSA2004; LAAKSONEN2008).

Table 98: Evidence summary table for trials of oral disulfiram

	Oral disulfiram versus placebo/1 mg disulfiram	Oral disulfiram versus acamprosate	Oral disulfiram versus naltrexone	Oral disulfiram versus topiramate	Oral disulfiram + counselling versus counselling
Total number of studies (number of participants)	3 RCTs (N = 859)	1 RCT (N = 243)	2 RCTs (N = 343)	1 RCT (N = 100)	1 RCT (N = 26)
Study ID	(1) CHICK1992 (2) FULLER1979 (3) FULLER1986	(1) LAAKSONEN2008	(1) DESOUSA2004 (2) LAAKSONEN2008	(1) DESOUSA2008	(1) GERREIN1973
Benefits					
Lapsed (participants returning to any drinking)	At 12 months: RR = 1.05 (0.96, 1.15) K = 2, N = 492	Not reported	At 12 months: RR = 0.18 (0.08, 0.42) K = 1, N = 100	Not reported	At 2 months: RR = 0.86 (0.55, 1.34) K = 1, N = 49
Relapsed to heavy drinking	Not reported	Not reported	At 12 months: RR = 0.28 (0.13, 0.59) K = 1, N = 100	At 12 months: RR = 0.23 (0.09, 0.55) K = 1, N = 100	Not reported
Abstinent days (per week or total days)	Total days change score: SMD = −0.45 (−0.86, −0.04) K = 1, N = 93	Abstinent days per week up to week 12: SMD = −1.11 (−1.52, −0.70) K = 1, N = 106	Total days: SMD = −0.41 (−0.81, −0.02) K = 1, N = 100	Total days: SMD = −0.30 (−0.70, 0.09) K = 1, N = 100	Not reported

Continued

Table 98: *(Continued)*

		Abstinent days per week from week 12 to 52: SMD = −0.74 (−1.17, −0.31) K = 1, N = 91	Abstinent days per week up to week 12: SMD = −1.09 (−1.50, −0.68) K = 1, N = 107 Abstinent days per week from week 12 to 52: SMD = −0.74 (−1.17, −0.31) K = 1, N = 91		
Time to first drink	Not reported	SMD = −0.84 (−1.28, −0.40) K = 1, N = 89	SMD = −1.22 (−2.47, 0.02) K = 2, N = 189	SMD = −3.16 (−3.75, −2.56) K = 1, N = 100	Not reported
Time to first heavy drinking episode	Not reported	SMD = −1.17 (−1.66, −0.68) K = 1, N = 77	SMD = −1.50 (−2.49, −0.51) K = 2, N = 180	SMD = −2.74 (−3.29, −2.19) K = 1, N = 100	Not reported
DDD during study period	Not reported	Not reported	SMD = −0.11 (−0.50, 0.28) K = 1, N = 100	Not reported	Not reported
Alcohol consumed during study period	Units consumed in last 4 weeks of trial – change score: SMD = −0.16 (−0.58, 0.25) K = 1, N = 90	Grams per week up to week 12: SMD = −1.06 (−1.44, −0.67) K = 1, N = 118	Grams per week up to week 12: SMD = −0.93 (−1.31, −0.56) K = 1, N = 124	Not reported	Not reported

Units consumed per week in last 6 months of trial – change score: SMD = −0.35 (−0.75, 0.05) K = 1, N = 97 Total units consumed in last 6 months of trial – change score: SMD = −0.49 (−0.91, −0.07) K = 1, N = 118	Grams per week from week 12 to 52: SMD = −0.66 (−1.12, −0.20) K = 1, N = 76	Grams per week from week 12 to 52: SMD = −0.74 (−1.20, −0.28) K = 1, N = 78			
Harms					
Discontinuation for any reason	RR = 1.15 (0.43, 3.12) K = 1, N = 406	RR = 1.24 (0.71, 2.16) K = 1, N = 162	RR = 1.27 (0.73, 2.19) K = 2, N = 262	RR = 1.00 (0.26, 3.78) K = 1, N = 100	RR = 0.46 (0.08, 2.56) K = 1, N = 49
Discontinuation due to adverse events	Not reported	Not reported	RR = 3.00 (0.13, 71.92) K = 1, N = 100	RR = 0.20 (0.01, 4.06) K = 1, N = 100	Not reported

The comparison of disulfiram and topiramate also showed a significant difference in the number of participants relapsing to heavy drinking (RR = 0.23; 95% CI, 0.09 to 0.55), time to first drink and time to first relapse in favour of disulfiram, but this was based on just one open-label study (DESOUSA2008). It may be that the psychological effects of knowing they were taking disulfiram may have contributed significantly to the results. The comparison of disulfiram with counselling versus counselling alone showed no significant differences between the groups on numbers of participants returning to drinking (RR = 0.86; 95% CI, 0.55 to 1.34).

The quality of the evidence was *moderate*, therefore further research is likely to have an important impact on confidence in the estimate of the effect. The main reason for the lower quality of the evidence was that the studies reviewed were generally not conducted in a double-blind trial.

7.8   META-REGRESSION ON BASELINE ALCOHOL CONSUMPTION AND EFFECTIVENESS

Whilst effectiveness has been established for acamprosate and naltrexone for adults, and to some extent for disulfiram, not everyone benefits from these medications. In order to give medication to those most likely to benefit as well as reducing inappropriate prescribing, studies have been examined for predictors of outcome. No trials have been explicitly set up to define predictors; rather, post-hoc analyses have been performed looking for relationships between outcome and clinical variables.

Concerning acamprosate and naltrexone, it has been suggested that severity of dependence may influence outcome based on the type of participants in the US (recruited by advert and do not generally require medication for assisted withdrawal) compared with European (recruited from treatment services and require medication for withdrawal) trials (Garbutt *et al.*, 2009).

A number of researchers have reported on the potential relationship between severity of alcohol dependence at baseline and effectiveness of both acamprosate and naltrexone (Monterosso *et al.*, 2001; Richardson *et al.*, 2008). The GDG decided to investigate whether baseline severity was associated with the effectiveness of either of these drugs. Craving has often been used as a measure of severity, but within the trials included in the meta-analyses the amount of alcohol consumed was much more frequently reported in the baseline demographics, and therefore baseline severity was used in the analysis measured as the number of alcohol units consumed per week by the study sample. An alcohol unit was defined as 8 g or 10 ml of alcohol, as per UK classification. In studies published outside the UK, the number of baseline 'drinks' was converted into UK alcohol units.

A random-effects meta-regression was performed in Stata Version 9.2 (StataCorp, 2007) using the revised meta-regression command with restricted maximum likelihood estimation and the improved variance estimator of Knapp and Hartung (2003). Covariates that were examined included: baseline severity (measured as the mean baseline consumption of alcohol in units per week); the setting of the trial (inpatient or outpatient); the year the study was published; the recruitment strategy of the trial;

and whether the trial was conducted in the US or elsewhere in the world. The regression coefficients are the estimated increase in the effect size (log RR) per unit increase in the covariate(s). Negative effect sizes indicate that the intervention had a better outcome than the control group. A random effects model (DerSimonian & Laird, 1986) was used in the analyses to incorporate the assumption that the different studies are estimating different yet related treatment effects, and to incorporate heterogeneity beyond that explained by the covariate(s) included in the model.

Figure 7 shows the association between baseline alcohol consumption and effectiveness for the 20 trials of naltrexone versus placebo that included extractable information on baseline drinking. There is a statistically significant association between baseline alcohol consumption and effectiveness (regression coefficient −0.004; 95% CI, −0.007 to −0.0002), with 54.43% of the between-study variance explained by baseline severity (p = 0.04) (see Table 95). To control for variables that may act as confounders, the following variables were entered into a multivariate model: setting, recruitment, country and year. The results suggest that baseline severity remains a significant covariate (regression coefficient −0.004; 95% CI, −0.007 to −0.001), with 97.61% of the between-study variance explained (see Table 96).

Figure 8 shows the association between baseline alcohol consumption and effectiveness in the 11 trials of acamprosate versus placebo that included extractable information on baseline drinking. The results suggest that there is no important association between baseline severity and effectiveness (regression coefficient −0.0001; 95% CI, −0.0017 to 0.0015), with 0% of the between-study variance explained by

Figure 7: Association between baseline severity and effect size in naltrexone versus placebo trials (logRR)

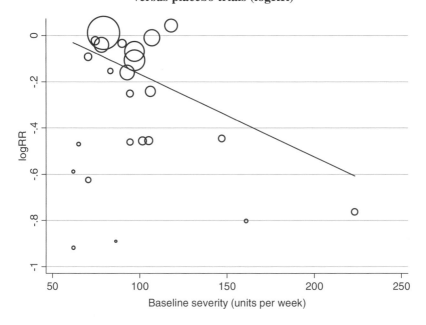

Table 95: Results of univariate meta-regression in naltrexone versus placebo trials

Variables	k (n)	Coefficient (standard error)	95% CI	Adjusted P[a]
Baseline drinking	20 (3338)	−0.003 (0.002)	−0.007 to −0.001	0.04
Constant		−0.19 (0.16)	−0.15 to 0.53	0.25
Note. k = number of studies; *n* = number of participants. [a]Calculated using the Higgins and Thompson Monte Carlo permutation test (10,000 permutations).				

Table 96: Results of multiple covariate meta-regression in naltrexone versus placebo trials

Variables	k (n)	Coefficient (standard error)	95% CI	Adjusted P[a]
Baseline drinking	20 (3338)	−0.004 (.002)	−0.007 to −0.001	0.02
Setting (inpatient/ outpatient)	20 (3338)	−0.16 (.17)	−0.51 to 0.19	0.35
Recruitment strategy	20 (3338)	0.05 (.13)	−0.22 to 0.31	0.73
Country trial conducted	20 (3338)	0.11 (.12)	−0.14 to 0.37	0.37
Year published	20 (3338)	0.021 (.011)	−0.001 to 0.043	0.07
Constant		−41.64 (21.51)	−86.82 to 3.55	0.07
Note. k = number of studies; *n* = number of participants. [a]Calculated using the Higgins and Thompson Monte Carlo permutation test (10,000 permutations).				

Figure 8: Association between baseline severity and effect size in acamprosate versus placebo trials (logRR)

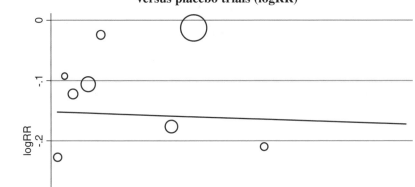

baseline severity ($p = 0.90$) (see Table 97). Baseline drinking was also found to have no association when controlling for the setting of the trial or the year the study was published (see Table 98). Recruitment strategy and the country where the trial was conducted could not be tested as covariates because there was not enough variation on these areas in the studies to use them as covariates.

Table 97: Results of univariate meta-regression in acamprosate versus placebo trials

Variables	k (n)	Coefficient (standard error)	95% CI	Adjusted pa
Baseline drinking	11 (3476)	−0.0001 (0.0007)	−0.002 to −0.001	0.9
Constant		−0.14 (.11)	−0.38 to 0.09	0.2
Abbreviations: *k*, number of studies; *n*, number of participants. [a]Calculated using the Higgins and Thompson Monte Carlo permutation test (10000 permutations).				

Table 98: Results of multiple covariate meta-regression in acamprosate versus placebo trials

Variables	k (n)	Coefficient (Standard error)	95% CI	Adjusted P[a]
Baseline drinking	11 (3476)	−0.002 (0.0008)	−0.002 to −0.001	0.82
Setting (inpatient/ outpatient)	11 (3476)	−0.03 (0.09)	−0.18 to 0.25	0.72
Year published	11 (3476)	0.01 (0.013)	−0.02 to 0.04	0.47
Constant		−19.3 (25.32)	−79.18 to 40.58	0.47

Note. k = number of studies; n = number of participants.
[a]Calculated using the Higgins and Thompson Monte Carlo permutation test (10,000 permutations).

7.9   PREDICTORS OF EFFICACY

Acamprosate

Lesch and Walter (1996) reviewed outcomes in their trial with reference to their four typologies: type I (social drinking develops into dependence; craving; relief drinking; family history); type II (alcohol consumed to medicate sleep or anxiety; consumption varies with context, behaviour changes with alcohol); type III (alcohol used to self-medicate a psychiatric disorder such as depression; family history positive for alcoholism or psychiatric disorder; impaired behaviours not always related to alcohol); and type IV (brain damage and psychiatric disorders before 14 years; seizures not related to alcohol; mild withdrawal symptoms). they reported that types I and II, but not III and IV, responded to acamprosate.

In the UK trial, Chick and colleagues (2000a) speculated whether the continuous rather than episodic drinker would be more likely to respond because their negative study had more participants with episodic drinking patterns. Kiefer and colleagues (2005) examined predictors in their original trial of acamprosate alone and with naltrexone, and reported that acamprosate was mainly efficacious in patients with low baseline somatic distress (mainly effective in type I) and that craving showed no predictive value.

Mason and Lehert (2010) explored the first US acamprosate trial (Mason *et al.*, 2006) and suggested that acamprosate may reduce the negative impact of subsyndromal anxiety or a past psychiatric history.

In contrast, Verheul and colleagues (2005) examined pooled data from seven RCTs that included 1,485 patients with alcohol dependence. Whilst 'cumulative abstinence duration', or continuous abstinence, was predicted by higher levels of craving or anxiety at baseline, this was for all patients and acamprosate showed no differentially efficacy. Other variables that were investigated and showed no significant relationship with outcomes, including severity of dependence (which was non-linearly associated with cumulative abstinence duration), family history, age of onset and gender. Therefore, they concluded that acamprosate is potentially effective for anyone with alcohol dependence.

Naltrexone

Monterosso and colleagues (2001) reported that those with a family history of alcoholism and high levels of craving were more likely to benefit from naltrexone. Rubio and colleagues (2005) similarly reported from their naltrexone trial that those with a family history of 'alcoholism' benefited more, as well as those whose onset of alcohol misuse was before the age of 25 years or those who had history of other substance misuse. Kiefer and colleagues (2005) reported that naltrexone was effective especially in patients with high baseline depression and in types III and IV (Lesch & Walter, 1996).

Several studies have investigated whether genetic variants of the opioid receptors, mu, kappa and delta, are related to naltrexone's efficacy. Several studies have reported an association between greater treatment response and A118G (OPRM1), a functional polymorphism of the μ-opioid receptor gene (Oslin *et al.*, 2003; Anton *et al.*, 2008a; Oroszi *et al.*, 2009; Kim *et al.*, 2009), but not all (Gelernter *et al.*, 2007). In a relatively small sample, Ooteman and colleagues (2009) explored other genotypes and reported effects of GABRA6, GABRA2, OPRM1 and dopamine D2 receptor genes moderated treatment response from acamprosate or naltrexone and subjective and physiological cue reactivity.

It is not clear whether gender influences treatment outcome, with studies of naltrexone in alcohol misuse reporting no gender differences (Anton *et al.*, 2006). Pettinati and colleagues (2008b) reported that in comorbid cocaine/alcohol dependence, men taking naltrexone (150 mg per day) reduced their cocaine and alcohol use whereas women did not; indeed, their cocaine use increased. However, most studies have limited power to detect gender by treatment outcome.

Disulfiram

There is no systematic review and little indication from trials of disulfiram about which type of person might be more likely to benefit from treatment.

7.9.1   Compliance and adherence

Compliance and adherence are related to predictors of efficacy because if a person is not taking their medication as prescribed, then its effectiveness is likely to be reduced. Because acamprosate and naltrexone are generally well-tolerated medications, problematic side effects are unlikely to contribute significantly to reduced compliance.

This issue has only been studied with naltrexone where Rohsenow and colleagues (2000) found that compliance was better in those who believed that the medication would help them stay sober and was not predicted by demographic or pre-treatment alcohol-use variables, commitment to abstinence or self-efficacy about abstinence.

For disulfiram, witnessing or supervision has been shown to be an important component of its effectiveness (Chick *et al.*, 1992; Sereny *et al.*, 1986). People who might do better with unsupervised disulfiram are older (Baekeland *et al.*, 1971; Fuller *et al.*, 1986); more socially stable (Fuller *et al.*, 1986); impulsive (Banys, 1988); and higher in motivation (Baekeland *et al.*, 1971).

7.9.2   When to start pharmacological treatment

People should be abstinent from alcohol at the time of starting medication for relapse prevention. All medications should be used as an adjunct to psychosocial treatment and not prescribed in isolation.

Acamprosate
The SPC recommends that 'treatment with acamprosate should be initiated as soon as possible after the withdrawal period and should be maintained if the patient relapses'. Advice to start as soon as possible was made because studies that allowed more than 2 to 3 weeks after assisted withdrawal resulted in more people drinking again before initiating acamprosate, with consequent reduced efficacy. Given that individuals are at particularly high risk of relapse in the first few days, and given that it takes about 5 days for acamprosate to achieve steady state levels, starting it as soon as possible is advised (Mason *et al.*, 2002).

In addition there is evidence from pre-clinical models that acamprosate can reduce glutamatergic hyperactivity associated with alcohol withdrawal, leading to reduced cellular damage (Qatari *et al.*, 2001; Spanagel *et al.*, 1996). Preliminary data from human studies suggest that acamprosate during withdrawal may also reduce hyperactivity and improve sleep (Boeijinga *et al.*, 2004; Staner *et al.*, 2006). Consequently, some practitioners start acamprosate for relapse prevention during or even before assisted withdrawal. Acamprosate has been started with assisted withdrawal with no reports of adverse events (Gual *et al.*, 2001; Kampman *et al.*, 2009). Acamprosate did not alter the course of alcohol withdrawal including CIWA-Ar score and amount of benzodiazepines taken. Unlike Gual and colleagues (2001), Kampman and colleagues (2009) found that acamprosate started during assisted withdrawal was associated with poorer drinking outcomes compared with those who had placebo. However, Gual and colleagues (2001) compared acamprosate with placebo for the entire treatment period whereas in Kampman and colleagues (2009) acamprosate was open label and without placebo in the relapse prevention phase.

Naltrexone
When using naltrexone for relapse prevention, people should be abstinent. However, there is no information on the optimal time to start medication. Like acamprosate, it is safe to start naltrexone while people are still drinking or during medically-assisted withdrawal.

Disulfiram
Given the reaction between alcohol and disulfiram, treatment should only be started at least 24 hours after the last alcoholic drink (SPC).

7.9.3 How long to continue with pharmacological treatment

Most trials of medication are between 3 and 6 months long and show efficacy. However, many patients relapse within months to years, but there is very limited evidence to guide how long medication should be continued. People who are doing well may be best advised to remain on medication for at least 6 months. However, some of these people may feel confident enough to stop medication earlier. Alternatively, some may prefer to stay on medication for longer, but continuation beyond 1 year would need to be justified. If a person is not engaging with other aspects of treatment (for example, psychosocial) and is drinking heavily, stopping the medication is appropriate until they engage with treatment. However, if a person is engaged but still drinking, a review of all of their treatment is indicated to assess whether this is optimal, including medication.

There is no evidence currently that long-term use of any of the relapse prevention pharmacotherapy incurs additional adverse consequences, particularly when relapse to heavy drinking will be associated with morbidity and mortality. However, medication is ideally used as an adjunct to support engagement with psychosocial approaches to alter behaviour and attitudes to alcohol.

For acamprosate, Mann (2004) reported from their meta-analysis that the effect sizes increased with time (the effect sizes on abstinence at 3, 6 and 12 months were 1.33, 1.50 and 1.95, respectively). This suggests that a clinically relevant benefit of treatment may be observed as early as 3 months, which gradually increases up to 1 year and possibly beyond. For naltrexone, there is evidence that its effects do not persist when it is stopped (O'Malley *et al.*, 1996).

7.10 HEALTH ECONOMIC EVIDENCE

7.10.1 Systematic review

The literature search identified seven studies that assessed the cost-effectiveness of pharmacological agents for the maintenance phase of treatment of alcohol dependence (Annemans *et al.*, 2000; Mortimer & Segal, 2005; Palmer *et al.*, 2000; Rychlik *et al.*, 2003; Schadlich & Brecht, 1998; Slattery *et al.*, 2003; Zarkin *et al.*, 2008). Full references, characteristics and results of all studies included in the economic review are presented in the form of evidence tables in Appendix 19.

Annemans and colleagues (2000) modelled the healthcare costs of acamprosate compared with no treatment in the prevention of alcoholic relapse over a 24-month time horizon. The patient population started the model following assisted withdrawal in an ambulatory state. Effectiveness data used to populate the model was sourced from several published and unpublished studies. A Belgian health payers' perspective was taken for the analysis. Therefore, only direct medical costs, relating to hospitalisations, psychiatric and GP consultations, and medications, were included in the model. The total expected cost of the acamprosate strategy was €5,255 over the 2-year time horizon compared with €5,783 in the no treatment arm. Therefore, despite the higher drug acquisition costs, acamprosate was shown to be a cost-saving intervention in terms of reduced hospitalisations due to alcohol-related complications. The major limitation of the study was that it was a cost-analysis and did not consider the impact of the interventions on overall clinical effectiveness and patient quality of life. Furthermore the study was from the Belgian health payer's perspective, which may have limited applicability to the UK context.

The study by Mortimer and Segal (2005) conducted a model-based economic analysis of naltrexone plus counselling versus counselling alone amongst detoxified patients with a history of severe alcohol dependence. A lifetime horizon was used for all of the analysis. Clinical effectiveness was measured using QALYs, which were calculated from disability weights derived from a single published source (Stouthard *et al.*, 1997). Clinical-effectiveness data were taken from published studies evaluating interventions targeting heavy drinkers at lower severity levels. These data were used to estimate how people would progress between specific drinking states (problem, moderate or dependent) within the model. The authors did not specify the resource use and cost components included in the model although an Australian health service perspective was adopted for the analysis. The results of the analysis suggested that naltrexone was cost effective in comparison with standard care resulting in an ICER of AUS$12,966.

There are several limitations with the results of the study that reduce their applicability to any UK-based recommendations. Little explanation was given in the article as to how the clinical effectiveness data, which was taken from various sources, was used to inform the health states used in the economic models. The article did not specify the resource use and costs that were included in the analyses although a health perspective was used. The analysis used QALYs as the primary outcome measure, which allows for comparison across interventions, although again there was insufficient description of the utility weights that were applied to the health states within the model.

Palmer and colleagues (2000) modelled the lifetime cost effectiveness of adjunctive acamprosate therapy in conjunction with standard counselling therapy, compared with standard counselling alone, in people with alcohol dependence. The study population comprised men of an average age of 41 years who had been withdrawn from alcohol and had a mixture of alcohol-related complications. The model allowed people to progress through various health states associated with important alcohol-related complications including liver disease, gastrointestinal disease, alcoholic cardiomyopathy and other complications. Clinical effectiveness data was sourced from 28 published studies that were not formally meta-analysed and authors' assumptions. The outcome measure used for the economic analysis was the number of life years gained with adjunctive acamprosate over standard therapy. The perspective of the cost analysis was from German third-party payers. Costs, again reported in Deutschmarks (DMs), included those associated with drug acquisition and treatment of alcohol-related complications.

The results of the cost-effectiveness analysis showed that adjunctive acamprosate therapy was the dominant treatment strategy, resulting in lower costs (DM48,245 versus DM49,907) and greater benefits (15.9 versus 14.6 life years gained) in comparison with standard therapy. Interpretation of the study results is subject to a number of methodological limitations. First, a formal literature review was not undertaken in order to derive effectiveness estimates and no formal meta-analysis of summary data was performed, with the authors using data from studies selectively. Second, cost items used in the analysis were not reported adequately and unit costs and resources were not reported separately. Finally, as noted by the authors, no consideration was given to quality of life in measuring the relative effectiveness of the treatments considered.

The objective of the study by Rychlik and colleagues (2003) was to compare the healthcare costs over 1 year of psychosocial rehabilitation support either alone or with adjunctive acamprosate treatment. The cost-effectiveness analysis was conducted alongside a prospective cohort study across 480 centres in the German primary care setting. Patients who fulfilled DSM–IV criteria for alcohol dependence were included in the study. The primary measure of clinical effectiveness in the study was abstinence rates after 1 year. The perspective of the study was from German health insurance. Direct healthcare costs included medications, hospitalisations, outpatient care and diagnostic and laboratory tests. Total 1-year costs were analysed according to both per-protocol and intention-to-treat analysis due to the expected patient attrition. Within both analyses, the adjunctive acamprosate treatment resulted in lower costs (€1225 to €1254 versus €1543 to €1592) and higher rates of abstinence (32 to 23% versus 20 to 21%) in comparison with no adjunctive treatment. The results of the economic analysis may be of limited applicability to the UK setting due to the cohort study design, the study setting and the short time horizon, as well as the effectiveness measure used.

The study by Schadlich and Brecht (1998) was a model-based cost-effectiveness analysis comparing adjunctive acamprosate therapy (in addition to standard care) with standard care (placebo and counselling or psychotherapy) for alcohol dependence. The population was defined as being alcohol dependent and abstinent from alcohol for up to 28 days prior to entering the study. Data were derived from a single double-blind RCT across 12 outpatient centres in Germany. The primary health outcome measure was the percentage of people remaining abstinent at the end of 48 weeks of medication-free follow-up. Transition probabilities to target events within the model were elicited from clinical expert opinion. The outcome measures used in the cost-effectiveness analysis were cases of target events avoided including cases of alcoholic psychoses, alcohol dependence syndrome, acute alcoholic hepatitis and alcoholic liver cirrhosis. A German healthcare-system perspective was taken for the cost analysis. Costs (reported in Deutschmarks) included in the model related to hospital treatment, acamprosate acquisition and patient rehabilitation for target events.

The ICER of acamprosate versus standard care was –DM2,602 (range: –DM406 to DM8,830) per additional abstinent patient, thus resulting in a net saving in terms of direct medical costs. The results of the study, based on a single RCT in Germany, are of limited relevance to the UK setting. No attempt was made to translate the intermediate outcome of abstinence into final outcomes such as QALYs, which are of greater relevance to decision makers. Another limitation of the study was that resource use quantities were not reported separately from the costs. Costing was also performed retrospectively and was not based on the same patient sample used in the effectiveness analysis, thus limiting the study's internal validity.

The study by Slattery and colleagues (2003) developed an economic model to assess the cost effectiveness of acamprosate, naltrexone and disulfiram compared with standard care within the Scottish health service setting. The populations examined were 45-year-old men and women with a diagnosis of alcohol dependence. The outcome measures used in the economic model were the number of patients who have abstained and number of deaths averted. The clinical effectiveness data was based on a methodologically diverse selection of trials that were not described within the study. Resource use involved in the pharmacological interventions included drug acquisition as well as outpatient and GP consultations. Costs were applied from Scottish health service estimates. Other healthcare costs included in the model were those associated with alcohol-related disease endpoints such as stroke, cancer, cirrhosis and alcohol-related psychoses. Costs were applied according to inpatient length of stay taken from Scottish medical records.

The total costs of pharmacological treatments and any disease endpoints for a hypothetical cohort of 1000 patients were compared with standard care over a 20-year time horizon, to determine any net healthcare cost savings. Acamprosate resulted in net savings of £68,928 whilst naltrexone and disulfiram resulted in net economic costs of £83,432 and £153,189, respectively, in comparison with standard care amongst a hypothetical cohort of 1000 patients. Whilst the results of the study, based on a hypothetical cohort of patients within the Scottish health service, may be applicable to a UK setting there are several problematic methodological issues with the study. First, the sources of the effectiveness data used in the model were not explicitly described by the authors, who suggested that the data was taken from a methodologically diverse selection of trials, thus suggesting a high level of heterogeneity. Second, no attempt was made to translate intermediate clinical endpoints such as abstinence rates into QALYs, which are useful to decision makers when assessing the comparative cost effectiveness of healthcare interventions.

Zarkin and colleagues (2008) evaluated the cost effectiveness of the COMBINE study (Anton *et al.*, 2006) interventions after 16 weeks of treatment. In the study, people with a primary diagnosis of alcohol dependence from across 11 US study sites were randomised to nine intervention groups. In eight groups all participants received medical management and were randomised to receive naltrexone, acamprosate, combination drugs (naltrexone and acamprosate) or placebo or a combined behavioural intervention in addition to naltrexone, acamprosate, combination drugs or placebo. The ninth treatment group received combined behavioural intervention only (without medical management). Three clinical measures were used in the economic analysis: PDA, avoidance of heavy drinking and achieving a good clinical outcome (abstinent, or moderate drinking without problems). Costs were analysed from the treatment provider perspective. Resource use included medication, staff time and laboratory tests.

Each intervention was ranked in increasing order of mean total cost for each of the three effectiveness measures. Only three interventions – medical management and placebo, medical management and naltrexone and naltrexone and acamprosate – were included in the final comparative analysis. This is because the other six interventions were dominated (resulting in higher mean costs but lower effectiveness) by the aforementioned interventions. The ICERs for the comparison of medical management and naltrexone versus medical management and placebo were US$42 per percentage increase in days abstinent, U$2,847 per person avoiding heavy drinking and US$1,690 per person achieving a good clinical outcome. The ICERs for the comparison of naltrexone and acamprosate versus medical management and naltrexone were US$664 per percentage point increase in days abstinent, US$8,095 per person avoiding heavy drinking and US$7,543 per person achieving a good clinical outcome.

This study is the only cost-effectiveness study reviewed that considered combinations of pharmacological and psychosocial interventions. However, there are a number of limitations when interpreting the results of the study. The cost analysis relied on the trial investigators' judgement of best clinical practice, which specifically relates to the US healthcare system and may not be generalisable to the UK health service. Interpretation of the results is further reduced by the short time horizon and the choice of outcome measures used in the analysis. Translation of intermediate outcomes such as rates of abstinence or moderate drinking into final outcomes such as QALYs would also be more helpful to decision makers.

7.10.2 Summary of existing health economic evidence

Of the seven cost-effectiveness studies identified in the literature, four compared acamprosate with standard care (Annemans *et al.*, 2000; Palmer *et al.*, 2000; Rychlik *et al.*, 2003; Schadlich & Brecht, 1998), one compared naltrexone with standard care (Mortimer & Segal, 2005) and one study compared naltrexone, acamprosate and disulfiram with standard care (Slattery *et al.*, 2003). The remaining study compared nine possible treatment combinations including naltrexone, acamprosate, combination drugs (naltrexone and acamprosate) or placebo either alone or in combination with a combined behavioural intervention. Only one study was UK-based (Zarkin *et al.*, 2008) whilst the other studies were based in Belgian, German or US populations. Nearly all of the studies were model-based economic analyses except for Rychlik and colleagues (2003), which was a cohort-based study, and Zarkin and colleagues (2008), which was based on the COMBINE RCT (ANTON2006). Within nearly all of the studies, pharmacological treatments were provided as adjunctive treatments to standard care, which differed across the studies considered.

In summary, the results suggested that acamprosate was either cost saving or the dominant treatment strategy (offering better outcomes at lower costs) in comparison with standard care. Naltrexone plus counselling was cost effective compared with counselling alone in people with a history of severe alcohol dependence (Mortimer & Segal, 2005). The one UK study showed that acamprosate resulted in significant healthcare cost savings whilst naltrexone and disulfiram resulted in significant net economic costs in comparison with standard care (Slattery *et al.*, 2003). Zarkin and colleagues (2008) showed that naltrexone in addition to medical management and combination therapy (naltrexone plus acamprosate) were cost effective over a 16-week period.

Providing an adequate summary of the health economic evidence presented here is difficult, due to the differences across the studies in terms of the comparator treatments considered (that is, definitions of 'standard care' differed across studies), study populations, costs and outcomes considered, and other methodological differences. Overall, the evidence reviewed is insufficient to support a single pharmacological treatment over any other.

7.11   ECONOMIC MODEL

This section considers the cost effectiveness of pharmacological interventions as an adjunctive treatment for the prevention of relapse in people who are in recovery from alcohol dependence.

7.11.1   Introduction

The systematic search of the economic literature identified a number of studies assessing the relative cost effectiveness of pharmacological treatments, either alone or as an adjunct to psychological therapy, in the prevention of relapse in people who are in recovery from alcohol dependence. The studies varied in terms of both methodological quality and applicability to the UK context. The results overall were inconsistent and did not support one pharmacological therapy over another. Therefore, an economic model was developed to answer this question. The objective of the economic model was to explore the relative cost effectiveness of pharmacological treatments for the prevention of relapse in people who are in recovery from alcohol dependence. The aim of the analysis was to reflect current UK clinical practice, using the most relevant and up-to-date information on costs and clinical outcomes. Details on the guideline systematic review of the economic literature on pharmacological interventions for relapse prevention are provided in Section 7.10.1.

7.11.2   Methods

Interventions assessed
The choice of interventions assessed in the economic analysis was determined by the clinical data that was analysed within the guideline systematic literature review. Only pharmacological interventions licensed in the UK as first-line adjunctive treatments in the prevention of relapse in people in recovery from alcohol dependence were considered. As a result, both naltrexone and acamprosate were considered in the economic analysis. Disulfiram was not included in the economic analysis due to the scarcity of available clinical data: only one open-label trial, comparing disulfiram with naltrexone, considered relapse to alcohol dependence as an outcome measure (De Sousa *et al.*, 2004). Trials comparing disulfiram with other treatments were also open-label, which also limited their comparability with trials of naltrexone and acamprosate, which were double blinded. The GDG acknowledged that this was a limitation of the analysis, in terms of providing a comprehensive consideration of the

relative cost effectiveness of all available pharmacological interventions that currently exist within the UK. The GDG decided that combination treatment (naltrexone and acamprosate) would also be excluded from the economic model due to uncertainty about the data, in particular the uncertainty about the risk of combined use of these drugs, one of which is not licensed for use in the UK. The pair-wise meta-analyses showed no benefit of combination treatment versus naltrexone or acamprosate alone, in terms of relapse to heavy drinking, at 3-, 6- or 12-month follow-up.

Model structure

A pragmatic decision model was constructed using Microsoft Excel (2007). Within the model a hypothetical cohort of 1000 patients who are in recovery from alcohol dependence can either relapse to heavy drinking (defined as at least five drinks for males; at least four drinks for females) or remain in recovery during a 12-month period. The structure of the decision tree is presented in Figure 9. The time horizon was chosen to reflect current UK guidance and recommendations, which recommend that patients should be maintained on pharmacological therapy for up to 12 months if patients are responding successfully to treatment. Three treatment groups were considered in the model: (1) acamprosate and standard care; (2) naltrexone and standard care; and (3) standard care alone. Standard care was defined as psychological therapy that patients would receive to prevent relapse to heavy drinking. The psychological therapy would be delivered by a community nurse over the 12-month period.

Costs and outcomes

The analysis adopted the perspective of the NHS and personal social services, as currently recommended by NICE. Costs relating to drug acquisition, blood tests, psychological interventions, outpatient secondary care and primary care were considered in the analysis. The outcome measured was the QALY.

Clinical input parameters and overview of methods of evidence synthesis

Clinical input parameters consisted of relapse rates associated with each intervention assessed: that is, naltrexone, acamprosate, or placebo. The economic analysis considered all relevant data reported in the studies included in the respective guideline systematic clinical review. To take all trial information into consideration, network (mixed treatment comparison [MTC]) meta-analytic techniques were employed. Network meta-analysis is a generalisation of standard pair-wise meta-analysis for A versus B trials to data structures that include, for example, A versus B, B versus C and

Figure 9: Schematic of model structure

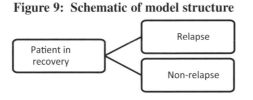

A versus C trials (Lu & Ades, 2004). A basic assumption of network meta-analysis is that direct and indirect evidence estimate the same parameter; in other words, the relative effect between A and B measured directly from an A versus B trial, is the same with the relative effect between A and B estimated indirectly from A versus C and B versus C trials. Network meta-analytic techniques strengthen inference concerning the relative effect of two treatments by including both direct and indirect comparisons between treatments and, at the same time, allow simultaneous inference on all treatments examined in the pair-wise trial comparisons while respecting randomisation (Caldwell *et al.*, 2005; Lu & Ades, 2004). Simultaneous inference on the relative effect of a number of treatments is possible, provided that treatments participate in a single 'network of evidence' (that is, every treatment is linked to at least one of the other treatments under assessment through direct or indirect comparisons).

Details on the methods and relapse data utilised in the network meta-analysis that was undertaken to estimate clinical input parameters for the economic analysis are presented in Appendix 15. Table 99 provides the mean probability of relapse (as well as the respective 95% credible intervals) at 1 year of treatment for naltrexone, acamprosate and placebo, as estimated by network meta-analysis. Overall, the results of the network meta-analysis are comparable with those obtained in the pair-wise comparisons, reported as the RR of relapse to heavy drinking at 3, 6 and 12 months. These comparisons showed small but significant differences favouring naltrexone and acamprosate versus placebo, but no significant differences between naltrexone and acamprosate over 12 months. The results of the network meta-analysis suggest that acamprosate had the highest probability (63%) of being the best treatment at reducing the probability of relapse over 12 months. However, the wide credible intervals around the mean estimates are indicative of the uncertainty surrounding these mean estimates.

Relapse data
Data on rates of relapse to alcohol dependency were taken from 32 RCTs included in the guideline systematic review of pharmacological treatments for the prevention of relapse in people in recovery from alcohol dependence. All trials included pharmacological treatments as an adjunct to psychological treatment. Data on combination

Table 99: Results of network meta-analysis – probability of relapse at 12 months

Treatment	Mean	Lower credible interval	Upper credible interval	Probability that treatment is best at reducing relapse over 12 months
Placebo	0.8956	0.5509	1.0000	0.000
Naltrexone	0.8253	0.4095	0.9997	0.369
Acamprosate	0.8176	0.3894	0.9996	0.631

treatment (acamprosate and naltrexone) or disulfiram were excluded because they did not strengthen inference between the three comparators included in the economic model. The RCTs reported rates of relapse at three different time-points: 3 months (n = 20), 6 months (n = 9) and 12 months (n = 3). Data were extracted from the guideline systematic review, which adopted an intention-to-treat analysis. Therefore, it was assumed that study participants who discontinued treatment early were likely to have an unfavourable outcome (that is, relapse to alcohol dependence). The RCTs included in the MTC meta-analysis used different definitions of relapse and different baseline psychological therapies, a factor that may limit the generalisability of relapse rates across the studies considered. For studies that reported relapse rates at multiple timepoints, for example 3 and 6 months, relapse from the final endpoint, in this case 6 months, was used in the network meta-analysis.

Within the economic model, it was assumed that an equal proportion of patients within each treatment group would relapse at any monthly time interval (from 1 to 12 months). Monthly probabilities were calculated using the following formula (Miller & Homan, 1994):

$$\text{Probability in month n} = 1 - (1 - \text{Probablility}_{12\text{ months}})^{\frac{\pi}{2}}$$

Where n = 1, 2, ..., 11

Utility data and estimation of quality-adjusted life years
To express outcomes in the form of QALYs, the health states of the economic model were linked to appropriate utility scores. Utility scores represent the health-related quality of life associated with specific health states on a scale from 0 (death) to 1 (perfect health). They are estimated using preference-based measures that capture people's preferences for the health states under consideration. The systematic search of the literature identified one study that reported utility scores for specific health states associated with alcohol-related disorders (Kraemer *et al.*, 2005).

The study by Kraemer and colleagues (2005) directly measured utility scores for a spectrum of alcohol-related health states using different methods of utility measurement including visual analogue scale, time trade-off (TTO) and standard gamble (SG) techniques. The study was based on a cross-sectional interview of 200 adults recruited from one clinic (n = 100) and one community (n = 100) sample in the US. Study subjects completed computerised versions of the utility rating exercises for their current health and six hypothetical alcohol-related health state scenarios presented in random order. Utility ratings were scaled from 0 to 1 and anchored by death (0) and perfect health (1). Table 100 summarises the mean utility scores for the six alcohol-related health states for the three techniques used. As the results in the table show, for each of the techniques used, utility scores decreased as the severity of alcohol use increased.

NICE recommends the EQ-5D as the preferred measure of health-related quality of life in adults for use in cost-utility analyses. NICE also suggests that the measurement of changes in health-related quality of life should be reported directly from people with the condition examined, and the valuation of health states should be based on public preferences elicited using a choice-based method, such as TTO or SG, in a representative

Table 100: Mean utility scores for alcohol-related health states and utility measurement technique (adapted from Kraemer *et al.*, 2005)

Alcohol-related health state scenario	Visual analogue scale mean (SD)	TTO mean (SD)	SG mean (SD)
Non-drinking	0.94 (0.09)	0.97 (0.13)	0.93 (0.15)
Safe drinking	0.85 (0.17)	0.94 (0.20)	0.88 (0.22)
At-risk drinking	0.72 (0.24)	0.84 (0.30)	0.82 (0.27)
Alcohol 'abuse'	0.52 (0.23)	0.72 (0.35)	0.75 (0.29)
Alcohol dependence	0.36 (0.22)	0.54 (0.37)	0.67 (0.29)
Alcohol dependence, in recovery	0.71 (0.24)	0.86 (0.25)	0.83 (0.24)

sample of the UK population. At the same time, it is recognised that EQ-5D utility scores may not be available or may be inappropriate for the condition or effects of treatment (NICE, 2008a). The study by Kraemer and colleagues (2005) did not use the EQ-5D questionnaire to estimate utility scores and was based on a US population sample who did not experience the alcohol-related health states they were asked to rate. Furthermore, the patient sample was not randomly selected but conveniently recruited either from clinic waiting rooms or self-selected within the community after responding to an advertisement. The low sample size (n = 200) also limits the results of the study, contributing to the uncertainty around the mean utility score estimates. However, this was the only study identified in the literature review that applied utility scores to specific alcohol-related health states using appropriate measurement techniques (SG or TTO) as recommended by NICE.

The two health states of interest in the economic model were: (a) in recovery from alcohol dependence; and (b) relapse to alcohol dependence. For these health states, the utility scores for the 'alcohol dependence' and 'alcohol dependence, in recovery' health states were chosen from Kraemer and colleagues (2005). In the base-case analysis the TTO utility scores were used whilst the SG utility scores were used in the sensitivity analysis.

Resource use and cost data
Costs associated with pharmacological interventions for relapse prevention in people in recovery from alcohol dependence were calculated by combining resource-use estimates with appropriate UK national unit costs. Costs relating to the interventions consisted of the relevant drug acquisition costs, psychological treatment, outpatient and primary care. People who relapsed to alcohol dependency were assumed to discontinue pharmacological and psychological treatment and incur other healthcare costs, as described below. Where necessary, costs were uplifted to 2009 prices using

the Hospital and Community Health Services pay and prices index (Curtis, 2009). Discounting was not required because the time horizon of the analysis was 12 months.

Drug acquisition costs
Drug acquisition costs were taken from the latest edition of the BNF (British Medical Association & The Royal Pharmaceutical Society of Great Britain, 2010). The recommended daily dosage for acamprosate was 1,998 mg per day and for naltrexone was 50 mg per day. The drug acquisition costs and monthly costs for both drugs included in the analysis are presented in Table 101.

Other costs of patient management
Estimates on resource use associated with the psychological intervention, outpatient and primary care and blood laboratory tests were based on the expert opinion of the GDG. It was assumed that patients in all three treatment arms would receive the same individual psychological intervention focused specifically on alcohol misuse (for example, CBT, behavioural therapy or social network and environment-based therapy) delivered by a practice nurse. It was assumed that each patient would receive one session per month or 12 sessions over the entire 12-month period if they did not relapse. It was assumed that patients in the three treatment groups would all require one initial 30-minute outpatient consultation with a consultant psychiatrist prior to starting treatment. Patients receiving adjunctive pharmacological interventions would require an additional two visits as part of their medical supervision. The second visit would be a 15-minute outpatient visit with a consultant psychiatrist and the third would be a GP consultation at the end of the 12-month period. At all three visits, it was assumed that patients would require blood tests (liver function test, and urea and electrolytes) to monitor for any potential hepatotoxic effects. It was assumed that patients receiving standard care would not require any further monitoring. Further details of resource use and costs associated with patient management are provided in Table 102.

Monthly cost of relapse to alcohol dependence
The monthly cost of relapse to alcohol dependence was based on estimates of the annual cost of alcohol misuse to the NHS in England by the Department of Health for 2007 (Department of Health, 2008a). Cost components included hospital inpatient and day visits, outpatient visits, A&E and ambulance visits, primary care consultations and prescribed medications. The report estimated the total annual cost of alcohol harm to be £2.7 billion in 2006/07 prices. These costs were based on the estimated number of

Table 101: Drug acquisition costs and estimated monthly costs of pharmacological interventions included in the economic model

Drug	Daily dosage	Unit cost (BNF 59, March 2010)	Monthly cost
Acamprosate	1998 mg	Campral 333 mg, 168-tab = £24	£26.10
Naltrexone	50 mg	Nalorex 50 mg, 28-tab = £22.79	£24.76

Table 102: Resource use over 12 months and unit costs associated with patient management for people in recovery from alcohol dependence

Service	Usage per person		Unit cost	Source of unit costs;
	Pharmacological intervention	Standard care	(2008/09 prices)	comments
Psychological treatment	12	12	£88	Curtis (2009); nurse specialist (community): £88 per hour of patient contact
Outpatient visit	2 (1 × 30 minutes; 1 × 15 minutes)	1 (1 × 30 minutes)	30 minutes: £161 15 minutes: £81	Curtis (2009); consultant psychiatrist: £322 per hour of patient contact
GP visits	1	0	£35	Curtis (2009); GP per surgery consultation lasting 11.7 minutes: £35
Laboratory blood tests (liver function; urea and electrolytes)	3	0	Liver function: £5.70 Urea and electrolytes: £4.63	Newcastle-upon-Tyne Hospitals NHS Foundation Trust – personal communication

higher-risk drinkers in England taken from mid-2006 estimates published by the Office for National Statistics (Goddard, 2006). 'Higher-risk drinkers' were defined as men who consumed 50 or more drinks per week and women who consumed 35 or more drinks per week. The total number of higher-risk drinkers in England in 2006 was estimated to be 2,653,545. To attribute a proportion of these NHS costs to people with alcohol dependence required calculating the ratio of the estimated prevalence of alcohol dependence (5.9%) to the prevalence of hazardous drinking (24.2%), which were taken from the recent survey for adult psychiatric morbidity in England for 2007 (McManus *et al.*, 2009). Hazardous drinking was defined in the survey as a score of 8 or more on the AUDIT scale. It was assumed that this definition of hazardous drinking was equivalent to the definition of higher-risk drinkers in the Department of Health report (Department of Health, 2008a). Multiplying this ratio by the total number of higher-risk drinkers produced an estimate of 646,939 people with alcohol dependence in England in 2006.

The survey also estimated the proportion of healthcare service use by people identified as dependent or hazardous drinkers (McManus *et al.*, 2009). It was estimated that 10% of hazardous drinkers (but not dependent) and 21% of people with alcohol dependence used healthcare services in England during 2007. Assuming a ratio of 2:1, it was possible to estimate the total annual and monthly NHS costs attributable to people who relapse to alcohol dependency. The costs were inflated from 2006/07 prices using the Hospital and Community Health Services pay and prices index (Curtis, 2009). Total annual costs attributable to alcohol dependency were estimated at £1,800, giving a monthly cost of £150.

Data analysis and presentation of the results

Two methods were used to analyse the input parameter data and present the results of the economic analysis.

Firstly, a deterministic analysis was undertaken, where data are analysed as mean estimates and results are presented as mean total costs and QALYs associated with each treatment under consideration. Relative cost effectiveness between alternative treatment options is estimated using incremental analysis: all options are first ranked from the most to the least effective; any options that are more costly than options that are more highly ranked are dominated (because they are also less effective) and excluded from further analysis. Subsequently, ICERs are calculated for all pairs of consecutive treatment options. ICERs express the additional cost per additional unit of benefit associated with one treatment option relative to its comparator. Estimation of such a ratio allows for consideration of whether the additional benefit is worth the additional cost when choosing one treatment option over another. If the ICER for a given treatment option is higher than the ICER calculated for the previous intervention in the ranking of all interventions, this strategy is then excluded from further analysis on the basis of extended dominance. After excluding cases of extended dominance, ICERs are recalculated. The treatment option with the highest ICER below the cost-effectiveness threshold is the most cost-effective option.

Several sensitivity analyses were conducted to explore the impact of the uncertainty characterising model input parameters on the results of the deterministic analysis. The following scenarios were explored:

- Using utility scores from Kraemer and colleagues (2005) obtained from the SG technique rather than TTO. These mean utility scores were 0.67 for 'alcohol dependence' and 0.83 for 'alcohol dependence, in recovery'.
- Increasing the level and intensity of patient monitoring whilst on pharmacological treatment so that people in recovery receive six outpatient visits (five with a consultant psychiatrist; one with a GP) over the 12 month period.
- Varying the monthly cost of relapse, from £0 to £300.

In addition to a deterministic analysis, a probabilistic analysis was also conducted. For this, model input parameters were assigned probability distributions (rather than expressed as point estimates), to reflect the uncertainty characterising the available clinical and cost data. Subsequently, 10,000 iterations were performed, each drawing random values from the distributions fitted to each model input parameter.

The probabilistic distribution of data on the probability of relapse over 12 months was based on the results of the MTC analysis with random values recorded for each of the 10,000 MTC iterations performed in WinBUGS (Lunn *et al.*, 2000). To maintain the correlation between the posterior estimates for the probability of relapse over 12 months, data from each of the common MTC simulations for this parameter were exported jointly and fitted into the Excel file of the economic model where the probabilistic analysis was carried out.

To account for likely high skewness and variability, all monthly cost inputs, including the monthly cost of relapse, were assigned a gamma distribution based on an assumed standard error of 30% of the mean value used in the deterministic analysis.

Utility estimates were assigned beta distributions, based on the standard errors around the mean values reported in the study by Kraemer and colleagues (2005).

Results of the probabilistic analysis are presented in the form of cost-effectiveness acceptability curves, which demonstrate the probability of each treatment option being the most cost effective among the strategies assessed at different levels of will-ingness-to-pay per unit of effectiveness (interpreted as different cost-effectiveness thresholds set by the decision maker).

In addition, the cost-effectiveness acceptability frontier is provided alongside cost-effectiveness acceptability curves, showing which treatment option among those examined offers the highest average net monetary benefit (NMB) at each level of willingness-to-pay (Fenwick *et al.*, 2001). The NMB of a treatment option at different levels of willingness-to-pay is defined by the following formula:

$$NMB = E \cdot \lambda - C$$

Where E and C are the effectiveness (number of QALYs) and costs associated with each treatment option, respectively, and λ is the level of the willingness-to-pay per unit of effectiveness.

7.11.3   Results of economic modelling

Deterministic analysis

Table 103 provides mean costs and QALYs per 1000 people for the interventions under consideration as well as the results of the incremental analyses. The interventions were ranked from highest to lowest in terms of the number of QALYs gained over 12 months. Acamprosate was associated with the highest costs and the highest number of QALYs whilst standard care was associated with the lowest costs and the lowest number of QALYs. The ICER of acamprosate was £5,043 per QALY versus standard care and £1,899 per QALY versus naltrexone. The ICER of naltrexone versus standard care was £5,395 per QALY, meaning that naltrexone was extendedly dominated. All ICERs lie well below the cost-effectiveness threshold of £20,000 to £30,000 per QALY currently set by NICE (NICE, 2008b).

Table 103: 12-month mean costs and QALYs per 1000 patients and ICERs for pharmacological interventions used for relapse prevention in people in recovery from alcohol dependency

Treatment	QALYs	Costs		ICERs
Acamprosate	683	£1,802,982	£1,899	£5,043 (versus standard care)
Naltrexone	680	£1,797,737	£5,395	Extendedly dominated
Standard care	656	£1,664,382	–	–

Table 104 shows that the cost-effectiveness results were fairly robust under the scenarios explored in the sensitivity analysis. The ICER of acamprosate versus standard care reached £10,000 per QALY, while naltrexone was extendedly dominated when utility scores estimated from the SG technique were used. The ICER of naltrexone versus standard care was approximately £11,000 per QALY. When the intensity of patient monitoring was increased, the ICER of acamprosate versus naltrexone was £13,323 per QALY and of naltrexone versus standard care was £10,789 per QALY. When the monthly cost of relapse was £0, the ICER of acamprosate compared with standard care increased to approximately £10,000, and naltrexone was extendedly dominated (with an ICER versus standard care of £11,000 per QALY). However, when the monthly cost of relapse was doubled to £300, both pharmacological interventions dominated standard care, resulting in lower costs and higher QALYs over 12 months; acamprosate dominated naltrexone under this scenario. It must be noted that under all scenarios explored in one-way sensitivity analysis, the ICERs of both drugs versus standard care were below the NICE lower cost-effectiveness threshold of £20,000 per QALY.

Probabilistic analysis
Results of the probabilistic analysis were very similar to those of the deterministic analysis – acamprosate was associated with the highest costs and QALYs and standard care was associated with the lowest costs and QALYs. ICERs were very similar to those calculated in the deterministic analysis. Probabilistic analysis demonstrated that standard care had the highest probability of being cost effective, as well as the highest NMB up to a willingness-to-pay level of £6,000 per QALY. Above this figure, acamprosate had the highest probability of being the most cost-effective treatment option

Table 104: Results of deterministic sensitivity analyses

Scenario tested	ICERs
Utility scores estimated from an SG instrument	Acamprosate versus standard care: £10,087 Naltrexone extendedly dominated
Increased intensity of patient monitoring over a 12-month period	Acamprosate versus naltrexone: £13,323 Naltrexone versus standard care: £10,789
Monthly cost of relapse is (a) £0; (b) £300	(a) Acamprosate versus standard care: £10,668 Naltrexone extendedly dominated (b) Acamprosate is dominant Standard care is dominated by both other options

and the highest NMB. Using the current threshold of £20,000 to £30,000 per QALY set by NICE, the probability of acamprosate or naltrexone being the most cost-effective treatment option were approximately 52 to 53% and 44 to 45%, respectively.

Figure 10 shows the cost-effectiveness acceptability curves generated for the three interventions considered whilst Table 105 shows the NMB and probability of each intervention being cost effective at various levels of WTP per QALY gained. Figure 11 shows the CEAF for the three options assessed. It can be seen that acamprosate provides the highest average NMB at any WTP above £10,000 per QALY.

7.11.4   Discussion of economic model

The results of the economic analysis suggest that acamprosate is potentially the most cost-effective pharmacological treatment, when used as an adjunct to a psychological intervention, for relapse prevention in people in recovery from alcohol dependence. Given the uncertainty characterising the model input parameters, in particular the 12-month probability of relapse, the probability of either acamprosate or naltrexone being the most cost-effective option at the NICE cost-effectiveness threshold of £20,000 was 52% and 44%, respectively.

A major limitation of the analysis was the exclusion of disulfiram, a pharmacological intervention that is currently licensed in the UK for the treatment of relapse prevention in people in recovery from alcohol dependence. Only one open-label RCT was identified in the systematic review that compared disulfiram with naltrexone, which used relapse to alcohol dependence as an outcome measure (De Sousa *et al.*, 2004). The GDG decided it would be inappropriate to include the results of an open-label study in the network meta-analysis. Another limitation was that the RCTs

Figure 10: CEACs for three treatment options over 12 months

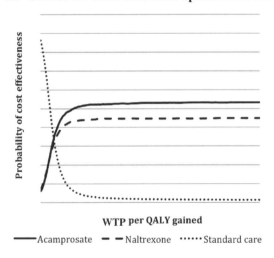

Table 105: Net monetary benefit and probability of each intervention being cost effective at various levels of WTP per QALY gained

Willingness to pay	Acamprosate		Naltrexone		Standard care	
	NMB	Probability	NMB	Probability	NMB	Probability
£0	−£1,803	0.062	−£1,798	0.071	−£1,664	0.867
£10,000	£5,027	0.457	£5,002	0.399	£4,896	0.144
£20,000	£11,857	0.519	£11,802	0.440	£11,456	0.041
£30,000	£18,687	0.527	£18,602	0.449	£18,016	0.024
£40,000	£25,517	0.532	£25,402	0.449	£24,576	0.019
£50,000	£32,347	0.533	£32,202	0.449	£31,136	0.018

included in the MTC meta-analysis used different definitions of relapse and different baseline psychological therapies, a factor that may undermine the pooled relapse rates considered in both the pair-wise and network meta-analyses.

Another possible limitation of the analysis is the relatively short time horizon of the economic model, although this reflected the time horizon of the RCTs that were included in the systematic review and meta-analyses. Indeed, the majority of the trials included in the network meta-analysis measured rates of relapse up to 3 and 6 months with only three studies actually measuring rates of relapse up to 12 months' follow-up. Ideally, a more comprehensive economic analysis would attempt to model the long-term cost-effectiveness of the three interventions, in terms of exploring the longer-term impact of relapse prevention on future alcohol-related complications and survival. Earlier economic models have attempted to explore the longer-term cost-effectiveness

Figure 11: CEAF for three treatment options over 12 months

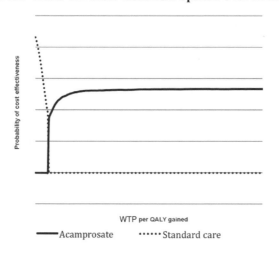

WTP per QALY gained

——Acamprosate   ••••••Standard care

of adjunctive pharmacological therapies over the patients' lifetime, by translating relapse to alcohol dependency into alcohol-related diseases including liver disease, cardiomyopathy, pancreatitis and alcoholic psychoses as well as alcohol-related mortality (Schadlich & Brecht, 1998; Palmer *et al.*, 2000). However, these models required assumptions, often based on limited clinical evidence, about the longer-term prognosis of patients who relapsed to alcohol dependence.

The results of the network meta-analysis are undermined by the heterogeneity between studies in terms of the range of underlying psychological interventions and the study time horizons. All studies included in the analysis were RCTs of pharmacological treatment or placebo as an adjunct to psychological interventions for the prevention of relapse. The RCTs included a wide range of psychological interventions including coping skills, counselling, brief combined behavioural intervention, MET and group therapies. The results of the meta-analyses presented here, including the network meta-analysis, assume that any differences in effectiveness are entirely explained by the adjunctive pharmacological interventions as opposed to the underlying psychological interventions. Whilst the economic model adopted a 12-month time horizon, the majority of the RCTs included in the network meta-analysis, were either of 3 months' (n = 20) or 6 months' (n = 9) duration. The analysis attempted to extrapolate the majority of this data over a 12-month period. If the effectiveness of pharmacological interventions for relapse prevention actually declines over 12 months, the analysis may have over-estimated the cost effectiveness of acamprosate or naltrexone as an adjunct to psychological interventions.

The analysis was based on the perspective of the NHS and personal social services, as recommended by NICE. Costs associated with the interventions considered were estimated from national sources and GDG expert opinion. The results suggested that drug acquisition costs did not determine the relative cost effectiveness of the three interventions. However, the results of the sensitivity analyses suggest that results may be sensitive to the intensity of patient monitoring (for example, specialist visits and blood tests), which were estimated from GDG expert opinion and also the monthly costs of relapse to heavy drinking. However, within both sensitivity analyses, the ICERs for acamprosate and naltrexone were still well below the current NICE cost-effectiveness threshold.

7.11.5   Conclusions

The economic analysis undertaken for this guideline showed that both acamprosate and naltrexone may be potentially cost-effective pharmacological interventions for the prevention of relapse among people in recovery from alcohol dependence. The probability of either drug being the most cost-effective option at the NICE cost-effectiveness threshold of £20,000 was 52% and 44% respectively. However, further research is necessary to establish whether these pharmacological interventions are clinically and cost effective in the longer term, in terms of preventing future alcohol-related diseases. Further clinical data, preferably based on appropriately controlled trials, is also needed to establish the clinical efficacy of disulfiram for relapse prevention.

7.12   CHILDREN AND YOUNG PEOPLE

7.12.1   Clinical review protocol

A systematic search of the literature was conducted to evaluate pharmacological interventions for relapse prevention for children and young people. See Section 7.2 for the aim of the review and the review questions. The clinical review protocol for this section can be found in Section 7.3.

7.12.2   Studies considered

Unlike the adult literature, the GDG was able to identify only three small pilot RCTs in this area for children and young people (Niederhofer & Staffen, 2003a; Niederhofer & Staffen, 2003b; Niederhofer *et al.*, 2003). Due to the limited number of studies and the heterogeneous nature of the outcomes, a narrative synthesis of the available literature was conducted by the review team in order to assess the efficacy of pharmacological interventions for children and young people.

7.12.3   Evidence summary

Niederhofer and Staffen (2003a) conducted a double-blind, placebo-controlled study with 26 participants with a DSM–IV diagnosis of chronic or episodic alcohol dependence. Participants ranged in age from 16 to 19 years. The participants were randomly allocated to treatment with acamprosate (1,332 mg daily) or placebo for 90 days. Participants were assessed at start of treatment, and at 30 and 90 days. Results revealed that the acamprosate group had a significantly higher proportion of days abstinent throughout the 90 days of treatment ($p < 0.001$), as well as a higher duration of mean cumulative abstinence ($p < 0.01$). There were no significant differences between the two groups with regards to side effects, and diarrhoea was the only reported side effect.

Niederhofer and colleagues (2003) assessed naltrexone compared with placebo in a double-blind, placebo-controlled study with 30 participants with a DSM–IV diagnosis of chronic or episodic alcohol dependence. Participants ranged in age from 15 to 19 years. All participants received 50 mg of naltrexone daily and were assessed at the start of treatment, and then at 30 and 90 days. At the 90-day assessment point, 60 of the 90 participants completed treatment. Results revealed that the naltrexone group remained abstinent longer during 90 days of treatment ($p < 0.01$) and had a longer duration of mean cumulative abstinence (69.8 days) than the placebo arm (22.8 days) ($p < 0.01$). It must be noted that it is not clear from the paper how many participants were randomised to each group; therefore, the findings should be interpreted with caution.

Lastly, Niederhofer and Staffen (2003b) compared disulfiram and placebo in a double-blind, placebo-controlled trial with 26 adolescent participants with DSM–IV chronic or episodic alcohol dependence. Participants ranged in age from 16 to 19 years. Participants received 200 mg of disulfiram daily and were assessed at the start of treatment, and then at 30 and 90 days. Twenty-six of the 49 participants recruited completed the 90 days of double-blind treatment. Results indicated that on day 90 of treatment, two of the placebo-treated patients compared with seven disulfiram-treated patients had been continuously abstinent (p = 0.0063). Additionally, the duration of mean cumulative abstinence was significantly higher in the disulfiram group (68.5 days) than in the placebo group (29.7 days) (p = 0.012).

7.12.4   Clinical evidence summary

Taken together, there is little evidence based on the results of three small pilot RCTs to assess the efficacy of pharmacological interventions in young people. The three studies do, however, provide some preliminary data indicating positive responses in young people to pharmacological interventions when compared with placebo. Due to the poor methodological quality of these studies, however, results should be interpreted with very considerable caution. As a result, recommendations for young people have to rely on extrapolations from the dataset for adults.

7.13   ASSESSMENT, MONITORING AND SIDE-EFFECT PROFILE

When medication is being considered, all patients require medical review and assessment of their general fitness and their renal and liver function. Medication should be used as an adjunct to psychosocial treatment, so their engagement in psychological and psychosocial treatment should also be monitored. For a full description of the side effects, contraindications and cautions, or interactions with other medications, prescribers must refer to the SPC or BNF.

Acamprosate
Acamprosate is a well-tolerated medication with minimal side effects, contraindications or cautions associated with its use. The most common side effect is diarrhoea with abdominal pain, nausea, vomiting and pruritus also described. Its contraindications include pregnancy and breastfeeding, renal insufficiency (serum creatinine >120 micromoles per litre) and severe hepatic failure (Childs-Pugh Classification C). There appear to be no interactions of clinical significance with alcohol.

Naltrexone
Naltrexone is also generally a well-tolerated medication with most trials reporting side effects similar to those reported with placebo or other drugs such as disulfiram or acamprosate. The most common side effects reported for naltrexone included nausea, headache, abdominal pain, reduced appetite and tiredness. However, in some of these studies, 100 mg per day rather than 50 mg per day was used. Nausea has been

reported more commonly at the start, particularly in female and lighter drinkers, which can be minimised by starting at 25 mg per day.

Because it is an opioid antagonist, naltrexone cannot be used in people using opioid agonist drugs for analgesia. In addition, if analgesia is required in an emergency, non-opioid medication will be required because naltrexone blockade will last for 48 to 72 hours after taking the last tablet. It is therefore helpful if people carry a card stating that they are taking naltrexone in case of such an emergency. If future analgesia is likely, for example in planned surgery, naltrexone is also therefore not ideal.

Hepatotoxicity was reported in association with use of naltrexone to treat obesity when high doses (>300 mg per day) were used. Reviews of available data suggest and current US guidelines recommend that hepatic toxicity is very unlikely to occur with doses of 50 mg per day and that continued alcohol use is more likely than naltrexone to cause liver damage (O'Malley *et al.*, 1993). Nevertheless, naltrexone should not be used in those with acute liver failure and caution is suggested when serum amino-transferases are four to five times above normal (Anton *et al.*, 2006; Kleber, 1985). However, naltrexone has been used in people with chronic hepatitis B and/or hepatitis C and no significant difference in liver function test results with naltrexone at the recommended doses has been reported (Lozano Polo *et al.*, 1997).

There is no consistent advice or evidence about monitoring of liver function tests for adverse effects on hepatic function. It is therefore important that the patient understands about the risk of hepatotoxicity and to stop taking naltrexone and promptly seek medical attention if they have any concerns about side effects or start to feel unwell. Deterioration in liver function tests or signs of liver failure have not been widely reported and increases generally normalise on stopping naltrexone. Before ascribing any increases to naltrexone, review other possible contributors such as other medications (prescribed and over-the-counter), complementary treatments and resumption of drinking.

Disulfiram

Given the potential seriousness of the disulfiram–alcohol interaction in addition to the potential adverse effects of disulfiram alone, prescribing needs due care and consideration. Patients must be warned about and have capacity to understand the disulfiram-alcohol reaction and be made aware of the presence of alcohol in foodstuffs, perfumes, aerosols and so on. In addition, they should not have consumed alcohol for at least 24 hours before starting disulfiram and should also be warned that a reaction with alcohol may be experienced for up to 7 days after their last tablet. The alcohol challenge test is no longer recommended (see the SPC and BNF). Fatal disulfiram–alcohol reactions have occurred with high doses of the drug (more than 1 g per day) and were associated with cardiovascular complications such as hypotension or corrected QT interval on the electrocardiograph (Chick, 1999; Kristenson, 1995). With the lower doses now prescribed, more severe reactions after consuming alcohol are less likely to be seen (Malcolm *et al.*, 2008). Indeed, a survey of people taking disulfiram found that for some an interaction only occurred when taking 800 to 1500 mg per day (Brewer, 1984).

The SPC or BNF lists several significant medical and psychiatric contraindications to its use, including cardiovascular problems, severe personality disorder, suicidal risk or psychosis, and contraindications to pregnancy and breast feeding. Caution is also advised in the presence of renal failure, hepatic or respiratory disease, diabetes mellitus and epilepsy. Nevertheless, against this background there is some evidence of its prescribing in a broad range of conditions including possible contraindications such as psychotic disorders or cocaine dependence or people taking methadone with no reports of significant adverse effects (Pani *et al.*, 2010; Petrakis *et al.*, 2005; Petrakis *et al.*, 2000).

Concerning the side effects of disulfiram alone, there have been many fewer trials compared with acamprosate or naltrexone and some are older, hence descriptions may be less comprehensive. Where reported, side effects and adverse events or reactions experienced include drowsiness, fatigue, abdominal pain, nausea and diarrhoea. Psychiatric problems such as dysphoria or psychosis were reported in some studies but the incidence was low. In newer trials comparing disulfiram with acamprosate or naltrexone, the reporting of side effects or adverse events is not dramatically different between the active drugs or placebo. Neuropathy has been reported by some but not all studies, with onset commonly described over months to a year, although onset within days has also been described (see Chick, 1999). From the Danish database, the estimated rate of neuropathy was 1 in 15,000 patient years (Poulsen *et al.*, 1992), although De Sousa and colleagues (2005) reported that three of the 50 (6%) people taking disulfiram in their trial dropped out due to neuropathy.

Use of disulfiram may be associated with the development of an acute hepatitis, which can be fatal. The nature and exact incidence or prevalence of hepatotoxicity is unclear; however, it appears rare with, for example, 30 reports of hepatitis in the previous 40 years (Chick, 1999) and 11 fatal liver reactions in 22 years (1968 to 1991). Based on estimates of number of people taking disulfiram, the estimated the risk of dying from hepatotoxicity caused by disulfiram was 1:30,000 people per year. However, some people received disulfiram for nickel sensitivity, for which they were reportedly at greater risk of hepatitis than those receiving disulfiram for alcohol dependence. Hepatotoxicity at 250 mg per day after 13 days has been described, although a review found disulfiram-related hepatitis starting 16 to 120 days later; however, in one case jaundice appeared within 5 days after taking 1.5 to 2 g per day (that is, up to ten times above the recommended dose) (Chick, 1999). Given the seriousness of hepatitis, a role for monitoring of liver function has been suggested but there is limited evidence to inform guidance. It is therefore important that the patient understands about the risk of hepatotoxicity, and to stop taking disulfiram and promptly seek medical attention if they have any concerns about side effects or start to feel unwell.

Psychiatric complications such as psychosis or confusional states are potentially serious side effects or adverse events and are more likely at higher doses (more than 500 mg per day; Chick, 1999). The Danish and WHO databases report that 4% and 13%, respectively, of all adverse effects of disulfiram were psychiatric (Poulsen *et al.*, 1992). One clinical trial reported over 1 year in over 600 people reported no difference in psychiatric complications between those treated with disulfiram 250 mg per day, or disulfiram 1 mg per day or placebo with the incidence in disulfiram groups at 2.4% (Branchey *et al.*, 1987). Nevertheless, in recent trials disulfiram has been used in people with a variety of psychiatric comorbidities including depression, psychosis or schizophrenia without apparent psychiatric adverse events (see Chick, 1999; Petrakis *et al.*, 2005 and 2006). The rate and quality of adverse events with cocaine and disulfiram are similar to those seen in studies of alcohol dependence (Pettinati, 2005; Carroll *et al.*, 1998). Disulfiram has also been used in people maintained on methadone without reported serious adverse reactions (Ling *et al.*, 1983).

The reader is directed to two comprehensive reviews regarding the safety of disulfiram by Chick (1999) and Malcolm and colleagues (2008).

7.14 REVIEW OF OTHER PHARMACOLOGICAL INTERVENTIONS NOT LICENSED IN THE UK FOR RELAPSE PREVENTION

7.14.1 Aim of review

The aim of this review was to assess the effectiveness of pharmacological interventions not licensed in the UK for the treatment of alcohol misuse. The GDG advised the review team that a large range of pharmacological interventions have been evaluated, often in single trials, with heterogeneous outcomes. Therefore, a narrative synthesis of RCTs was conducted, with no attempt to use meta-analysis. Information about the databases searched and the inclusion/exclusion criteria used for this section of the guideline can be found in Appendix 16e.

7.14.2 Studies considered

A total of nine trials met inclusion criteria for this section of the guideline. There were two trials of extended release injectable naltrexone, two trials of nalmefene, three trials of SSRIs, one current trial of baclofen (which has indicated preliminary findings), and six trials of anticonvulsants (two of topiramate, three of gabapentin and one of pregabalin).

7.14.3 Extended release injectable naltrexone

In addition to oral naltrexone an injectable formulation is available, which has an extended half-life and can overcome poor compliance.

In the US, naltrexone is also available in a once-monthly extended-release injectable formulation (380 mg) and has been used by some in the UK. Two RCTs have been published regarding its efficacy and safety. Kranzler and colleagues (2004) studied a depot formulation in patients who were still drinking but wanted to stop and showed no efficacy on the primary outcome of reduced heavy drinking days. A longer time until first drink and a higher rate of abstinence were reported. The second study compared the 380 mg injectable formulation with one containing 190 mg over 6 months in people still drinking and found reduced heavy drinking in all groups, with the greatest reduction in the higher dose of naltrexone (Garbutt *et al.*, 2005). In addition, greater efficacy was seen in males and in those who had been sober for a week before their injection. A post-hoc analysis revealed that naltrexone reduced alcohol consumption during holiday periods in the US, generally a time of great risk of relapse (Lapham *et al.*, 2009).

Side effects or adverse effects of the extended injectable formulation are reported as similar to oral naltrexone and include abdominal pain, nausea, anorexia and dizziness, although the hepatic safety profile appears similar to placebo (Lucey *et al.*, 2008). However, a greater number of injection site reactions with naltrexone have been reported, which may need medical attention and be due to poor injection technique (Garbutt *et al.*, 2009).

7.14.4   Nalmefene

Like naltrexone, nalmefene is an opioid antagonist but with some kappa partial agonist activity or inverse agonist activity. It was initially proposed as a treatment for alcohol dependence because it has a longer half-life and was thought to have less risk of hepatotoxicity then naltrexone. The first RCT in alcohol dependence reported significantly fewer relapses with nalmefene (20 mg or 80 mg per day; Mason *et al.*, 1999). However, a second multisite RCT comparing 5 mg per day, 20 mg per day with 40 mg per day and placebo reported no efficacy for nalmefene (Anton *et al.*, 2004).

7.14.5   Selective serotonin reuptake inhibitors

The efficacy of SSRIs in treating alcohol misuse without comorbid depression has been studied in three RCTs. They reported that SSRIs may have limited efficacy but importantly may also reduce the impact of psychosocial treatments in improving alcohol misuse in early-onset alcohol dependence. Kranzler and colleagues (1996) reported worse drinking outcomes in early-onset or type B alcohol dependence on fluoxetine compared with placebo. Pettinati and colleagues (2000) found that sertraline had no effect in type B alcohol dependence, whilst improving outcomes in type A. Chick and colleagues (2000a) reported that people with type II alcohol dependence, as defined by Cloninger's Tridimensional Personality Questionnaire, had worse outcomes compared with those on placebo and type I alcohol dependence. Therefore, these three studies suggest that in the absence of a depressive disorder, SSRIs may weaken improvements in alcohol misuse.

One RCT has investigated whether combining naltrexone with sertraline is effective in improving drinking behaviour in native and non-native Alaskan Americans by randomising people to daily naltrexone (50 mg), sertraline (100 mg), naltrexone plus sertraline, or placebo (O'Malley & Nanson, 2002). Naltrexone significantly improved abstinence rates rather than reducing the risk of heavy drinking whilst sertraline had no further benefit.

Overall, given the difficulties in making a diagnosis of depression in such a population and the limited efficacy shown when comorbid depression is present, an SSRI may not be the most appropriate first-line antidepressant to use in alcohol misuse.

7.14.6   Baclofen

According to one trial, baclofen, a GABA-B agonist, increases abstinence rates in people with alcohol-related cirrhosis compared with placebo (Addolorato *et al.*, 2008; 30 mg per day; 12 weeks). It was well tolerated with little contribution to dropouts due to side effects; there were no adverse events reported. There is a large RCT being conducted in the US whose results are yet to be formally published but some of the data have been reported and suggest no efficacy for baclofen (Leggio *et al.*, 2010). Key differences between the studies that may increase the likelihood of efficacy are: goal of abstinence, alcohol dependence requiring assisted withdrawal, and higher anxiety levels.

7.14.7   Anticonvulsants

Topiramate
Topiramate, an anticonvulsant with a rich pharmacology, including increasing GABA and reducing glutamatergic activity, has been shown to reduce heavy drinking to promote abstinence (Johnson *et al.*, 2003 and 2007). Unlike other trials of medication, the drug was started whilst people were still drinking but aiming for abstinence. Baltieri and colleagues (2008) reported that people receiving topiramate (up to 300 mg per day) showed significantly better drinking outcomes early in the 12-week trial but not at 12 weeks compared with placebo. In addition, there were no significant differences in drinking outcomes between topiramate and naltrexone (50 mg per day), although there were trends suggesting topiramate was more effective. An issue for topiramate has been its side-effect profile, such as paresthesia (up to 50%), dizziness, taste perversion, anorexia leading to weight loss, and difficulty with memory or concentration. In the largest multisite trial (Johnson *et al.*, 2007), 67 of 183 did not complete the study, of which 34 (almost 20%) had a limited adverse event. The dose was 25 mg increasing to 300 mg per day. Side effects are more pronounced and likely at higher doses and with more rapid titration.

Gabapentin and pregabalin
There is interest in both gabapentin and pregabalin for treating alcohol dependence because they have anticonvulsant and anxiolytic properties. They bind to calcium channels and reduce calcium currents resulting in reduced activity. In relapse prevention, gabapentin has been shown to increase time to heavy drinking and reduce alcohol craving (Brower *et al.*, 2008; Furieri & Nakamura-Palacios, 2007; Mason *et al.*, 2009). A small open study showed people who misused alcohol and were given pregabalin remained abstinent longer than those given naltrexone (Martinotti *et al.*, 2008).

7.14.8   Clinical summary

A number of pharmacological interventions not licensed for use in the treatment of moderate and severe alcohol dependence were also considered in the review. The evidence indicates that SSRIs do not improve drinking behaviour in non-depressed alcoholics and may worsen drinking-related outcome as well as reduce the efficacy of psychosocial interventions. The initial evidence for the efficacy of injectable naltrexone is encouraging, particularly in those who may not be as compliant with oral naltrexone. However, at the current time there is not enough evidence to support its routine use. The evidence for nalmefene is limited and inconclusive, with only two RCTs with contradictory reported efficacy. There is limited evidence of the efficacy of baclofen as a pharmacological intervention for alcohol dependence. There is limited and contradictory evidence for the efficacy of anticonvulsants in the treatment of alcohol dependence. Gabapentin and pregabalin were found to have some efficacy for reducing drinking. However, for topiramate the evidence was limited and this beneficial effect was not always found after 12 weeks of treatment. Furthermore, the side effects caused by the use of topiramate mean that when it is used the individual most be closely monitored and other pharmacological interventions need to be considered. Overall, there is evidence from a number of trials that some of these pharmacological interventions can reduce drinking and craving and may reduce associated problems with anxiety and insomnia. However, the evidence is limited and there are trials currently underway that will inform their potential role as an adjunct to psychosocial approaches.

7.15 FROM EVIDENCE TO RECOMMENDATIONS

The GDG reviewed the evidence for the clinical and cost effectiveness of naltrexone and acamprosate for relapse prevention in individuals with alcohol dependence. A review was also carried out on the clinical effectiveness of disulfiram for relapse prevention in individuals with alcohol dependence; however, because the evidence was much weaker and the potential for harm was greater, the GDG did not consider disulfiram as a suitable first-line pharmacological treatment for relapse prevention in individuals with alcohol dependence. Therefore, disulfiram was not considered in the guideline economic analysis.

The clinical evidence for acamprosate suggested that individuals were likely to benefit from an increased probability of remaining completely abstinent from alcohol within the treatment and follow-up periods. The amount of baseline drinking did not seem to have an impact on the effectiveness of acamprosate in preventing a lapse to drinking, but the studies included in the review on acamprosate were limited to trials where the participants were classed as at least moderately dependent. There was little evidence to show the effectiveness of acamprosate on harmful or mildly dependent drinking. The studies reviewed mainly included a psychological treatment in addition to acamprosate. From the clinical evidence, the GDG decided to recommend acamprosate for relapse prevention in moderate to severe dependence combined with a psychological intervention as indicated in the licence agreement.

The review of naltrexone for relapse prevention suggested a reduced likelihood of relapsing to heavy drinking in participants randomised to naltrexone instead of placebo. Further analysis also found that individuals drinking more at baseline were more likely to benefit from naltrexone in preventing relapse than individuals drinking at lower baseline levels. The main evidence for naltrexone effectiveness was in reducing rates of relapse and reducing the amount of alcohol consumed, but the evidence for an effect on abstinence was more limited. The studies reviewed almost always included a psychological intervention in addition to naltrexone.

For both acamprosate and naltrexone the GDG took the view that the psychological intervention provided in combination with either of the drugs should be one of those identified as effective in Chapter 6 (that is, cognitive behavioural therapies, behavioural therapies, social network and environment-based therapies or behavioural couples therapy) because this was likely to bring the most benefit.

There was limited evidence comparing acamprosate with naltrexone for relapse prevention, and there was little evidence to suggest a benefit of one drug over the other. In studies comparing acamprosate plus naltrexone compared with acamprosate alone, naltrexone alone or placebo, there were no significant differences in outcomes in favour of the combination.

The network meta-analysis that was undertaken to inform the guideline economic analysis demonstrated that acamprosate had a lower probability of relapse over 12 months' follow-up, compared with naltrexone, when used as an adjunct to psychological therapy[44]. The guideline economic analysis also demonstrated that acamprosate had the highest probability of being the most cost-effective adjunctive pharmacological treatment for relapse prevention (52% at a WTP threshold of £20,000 per QALY). However, the network meta-analysis and economic analysis considered only relapse prevention as an outcome and not the greater impact of naltrexone relative to acamprosate on the severity of drinking. Because of this limitation of the analysis, the GDG did not feel that acamprosate should be the drug of choice for the treatment of alcohol-related problems.

From the clinical and cost-effectiveness evidence, the GDG decided to recommend naltrexone for relapse prevention in moderate to severe dependence and, as with acamprosate, in combination with a psychological intervention.

The clinical evidence for disulfiram in relapse prevention was weaker than for acamprosate and naltrexone, with the trials versus other active interventions being open label. The double-blind evidence for disulfiram versus placebo suggested little benefit for disulfiram in maintaining abstinence or reducing drinking; however, open-label studies showed a large effect in favour of disulfiram on these outcomes when comparing disulfiram with other pharmacological agents.

Due to the weaker available evidence for disulfiram for relapse prevention and higher potential risks requiring monitoring, the GDG decided to recommend disulfiram as a second-line treatment option for moderate to severe alcohol dependence for people for whom acamprosate or naltrexone are not suitable, or who have specified a preference for disulfiram, and who aim to abstain from alcohol. The GDG consensus was that if people were seen taking their disulfiram by a family member or carer, their adherence to treatment would improve.

There is limited and inconclusive evidence for the use of SSRIs, injectable naltrexone, nalmefene, baclofen and anticonvulsants in the treatment of moderate to severe

---

[44]Note that the use of combined acamprosate and naltraxone was not included in the economic model due to uncertainty about the data, including concerns about the safety of the combined option.

alcohol dependence. In addition to the lack of evidence, some of these non-licensed drugs also have side-effect profiles that are detrimental to effectiveness of treatment. For example, topiramate (an anticonvulsant) has a number of adverse side effects and, when used, requires careful titration and monitoring. For others, there is evidence of potential harm due to their misuse liability (for example, GHB) and hence these interventions should not be used in the treatment of alcohol dependence. Although there is some evidence of efficacy for nalmefene, baclofen and some anticonvulsants, the evidence does not indicate any clear advantage of these interventions over other pharmacological interventions licensed for use in the treatment of alcohol dependence. Therefore, in the absence of a clear advantage over safer medications the GDG decided that these pharmacological interventions should not be used in routine clinical practice.

In the absence of any significant high-quality evidence on pharmacological interventions for children and young people as well as older people the GDG decided to extrapolate from the adult evidence-base.

7.15.1   Recommendations

Interventions for moderate and severe alcohol dependence after
successful withdrawal
7.15.1.1   After a successful withdrawal for people with moderate and severe alcohol dependence, consider offering acamprosate or oral naltrexone[45] in combination with an individual psychological intervention (cognitive behavioural therapies, behavioural therapies or social network and environment-based therapies) focused specifically on alcohol misuse (see 6.23.1.15–6.23.1.17).
7.15.1.2   After a successful withdrawal for people with moderate and severe alcohol dependence, consider offering acamprosate or oral naltrexone[44] in combination with behavioural couples therapy to service users who have a regular partner and whose partner is willing to participate in treatment (see 6.23.1.18).
7.15.1.3   After a successful withdrawal for people with moderate and severe alcohol dependence, consider offering disulfiram[46] in combination with a psychological intervention to service users who:
   ● have a goal of abstinence but for whom acamprosate and oral naltrexone are not suitable, **or**
   ● prefer disulfiram and understand the relative risks of taking the drug (see 7.15.1.18).

Drugs not to be routinely used for the treatment of alcohol misuse
7.15.1.4   Do not use antidepressants (including selective serotonin reuptake inhibitors [SSRIs]) routinely for the treatment of alcohol misuse alone.

---

[45]At the time of publication of the NICE guideline (February 2011), oral naltrexone did not have UK marketing authorisation for this indication. Informed consent should be obtained and documented.
[46]All prescribers should consult the SPC for a full description of the contraindications and the special considerations of the use of disulfiram.

7.15.1.5   Do not use gammahydroxybutyrate (GHB) for the treatment of alcohol misuse.

7.15.1.6   Benzodiazepines should only be used for managing alcohol withdrawal and not as ongoing treatment for alcohol dependence.

Assisted withdrawal in children and young people

7.15.1.7   Offer inpatient care to children and young people aged 10-17 years who need assisted withdrawal.

7.15.1.8   Base assisted withdrawal for children and young people aged 10–17 years on the recommendations for adults (see 5.31.1.7–5.31.1.18) and in NICE Clinical Guideline 100. Consult the SPC and adjust drug regimens to take account of age, height and body mass, and stage of development of the child or young person[47].

Delivering pharmacological interventions

7.15.1.9   Before starting treatment with acamprosate, oral naltrexone[48] or disulfiram, conduct a comprehensive medical assessment (baseline urea and electrolytes and liver function tests including gamma glutamyl transferase [GGT]). In particular, consider any contraindications or cautions (see the SPC), and discuss these with the service user.

7.15.1.10 After a careful review of the risks and benefits, specialists may consider offering acamprosate[49] or oral naltrexone[50] in combination with cognitive behavioural therapy to young people aged 16 and 17 years who have not engaged with or benefited from a multicomponent treatment programme.

Acamprosate

7.15.1.11 If using acamprosate, start treatment as soon as possible after assisted withdrawal. Usually prescribe at a dose of 1,998 mg (666 mg three times a day) unless the service user weighs less than 60 kg, and then a maximum of 1,332 mg should be prescribed per day. Acamprosate should:

● usually be prescribed for up to 6 months, or longer for those benefiting from the drug who want to continue with it[51]

● be stopped if drinking persists 4–6 weeks after starting the drug.

---

[47]If a drug does not have UK marketing authorisation for use in children and young people under 18, informed consent should be obtained and documented.

[48]At the time of publication of the NICE guideline (February 2011), oral naltrexone did not have UK marketing authorisation for this indication. Informed consent should be obtained and documented.

[49]At the time of publication of the NICE guideline (February 2011), acamprosate did not have UK marketing authorisation for this indication or for use in children and young people under 18. Informed consent should be obtained and documented.

[50]At the time of publication of the NICE guideline (February 2011), oral naltrexone did not have UK marketing authorisation for this indication or for use in children and young people under 18. Informed consent should be obtained and documented.

[51]At the time of publication of the NICE guideline (February 2011), acamprosate did not have UK marketing authorisation for use longer than 12 months. Informed consent should be obtained and documented.

Pharmacological interventions
Pharmacological interventions

7.15.1.12 Service users taking acamprosate should stay under supervision, at least monthly, for 6 months, and at reduced but regular intervals if the drug is continued after 6 months. Do not use blood tests routinely, but consider them to monitor for recovery of liver function and as a motivational aid for service users to show improvement.

Naltrexone

7.15.1.13 If using oral naltrexone[52], start treatment after assisted withdrawal. Start prescribing at a dose of 25 mg per day and aim for a maintenance dose of 50 mg per day. Draw the service user's attention to the information card that is issued with oral naltrexone about its impact on opioid-based analgesics. Oral naltrexone should:
- usually be prescribed for up to 6 months, or longer for those benefiting from the drug who want to continue with it
- be stopped if drinking persists 4–6 weeks after starting the drug.

7.15.1.14 Service users taking oral naltrexone[50] should stay under supervision, at least monthly, for 6 months, and at reduced but regular intervals if the drug is continued after 6 months. Do not use blood tests routinely, but consider them for older people, for people with obesity, for monitoring recovery of liver function and as a motivational aid for service users to show improvement. If the service user feels unwell advise them to stop the oral naltrexone immediately.

Disulfiram

7.15.1.15 If using disulfiram, start treatment at least 24 hours after the last alcoholic drink consumed. Usually prescribe at a dose of 200 mg per day. For service users who continue to drink, if a dose of 200 mg (taken regularly for at least 1 week) does not cause a sufficiently unpleasant reaction to deter drinking, consider increasing the dose in consultation with the service user.

7.15.1.16 Before starting treatment with disulfiram, test liver function, urea and electrolytes to assess for liver or renal impairment. Check the SPC for warnings and contraindications in pregnancy and in the following conditions: a history of severe mental illness, stroke, heart disease or hypertension.

7.15.1.17 Make sure that service users taking disulfiram:
- stay under supervision, at least every 2 weeks for the first 2 months, then monthly for the following 4 months
- if possible, have a family member or carer, who is properly informed about the use of disulfiram, oversee the administration of the drug
- are medically monitored at least every 6 months after the initial 6 months of treatment and monitoring.

---

[52]At the time of publication of the NICE guideline (February 2011), oral naltrexone did not have UK marketing authorisation for this indication. Informed consent should be obtained and documented.

7.15.1.18 Warn service users taking disulfiram, and their families and carers, about:

- the interaction between disulfiram and alcohol (which may also be found in food, perfume, aerosol sprays and so on), the symptoms of which may include flushing, nausea, palpitations and, more seriously, arrhythmias, hypotension and collapse

- the rapid and unpredictable onset of the rare complication of hepatotoxicity; advise service users that if they feel unwell or develop a fever or jaundice that they should stop taking disulfiram and seek urgent medical attention.

7.16 PHARMACOTHERAPY FOR LESS SEVERE DEPENDENNCE AND NON-DEPENDENT DRINKING

7.16.1 Clinical review protocol

A review of pharmacological interventions for individuals who are less severely dependent or non-dependent was conducted. Due to limited literature in this population, a meta-analysis of RCTs could not be conducted. Therefore, a narrative synthesis of the available evidence is presented. Information about the databases searched and the inclusion/exclusion criteria used for this section of the guideline can be found in Appendix 16e. See Table 106 for the clinical review protocol followed for this review.

7.16.2 Evidence summary

In general, psychosocial approaches should be offered to all individuals who misuse alcohol. For those for whom such approaches have not worked or who are mildly dependent, medication may be a treatment option. However the only medication that has been studied in this population is naltrexone. Whilst the majority of participants included in the trials in the meta-analyses were abstinent prior to starting naltrexone, in some of these studies people were still drinking with the aim that naltrexone would help to reduce consumption.

Heinala and colleagues (2001) investigated naltrexone (50 mg) started without assisted withdrawal in people who were dependent and treatment-seeking. They showed that in combination with coping skills but not supportive therapy, naltrexone reduced risk of relapse to heavy drinking but did not improve abstinence or time to first drink. In this study, abstinence was not emphasised as part of coping skills, but was in supportive therapy.

In those less severely dependent and non-dependent, naltrexone (50 mg per day) has been shown to reduce the likelihood of any drinking (Kranzler *et al.*, 2003). Interestingly, if they were taking medication (naltrexone or placebo) in a targeted manner (that is, when anticipating a high-risk situation), greater reductions in heavy drinking days were seen compared with taking medication daily. A follow-up trial confirmed 'targeted' naltrexone reduced drinks per day, but only in men (Kranzler *et al.*, 2009). Notably both trials excluded people who had an unsuccessful attempt to reduce their drinking.

**Table 106: Clinical review protocol for less severely dependent
or non-dependent populations**

Electronic databases	MEDLINE, EMBASE, CINAHL, PsycINFO, Cochrane Library
Date searched	Database inception to March 2010
Study design	RCTs
Population	At least 80% of the sample meet the criteria for mild alcohol dependence (50 to 70 drinks per week) or harmful alcohol use (30 to 50 drinks per week)
Excluded populations	Those drinking more than 70 drinks per week (moderate and severe dependence); hazardous drinkers Pregnant women
Interventions	Any pharmacological intervention
Comparator	Any other intervention
Outcomes	Discontinuing treatment for any reason Discontinuing treatment due to adverse events Lapsing (returning to a drinking state) Relapsing (returning to a heavy drinking state) PDA Cumulative abstinence duration DDD Total drinks consumed during treatment period Total days of heavy drinking during treatment Time to first drink Time to heavy drinking day

Leeman and colleagues (2008) reported in a pilot open study of heavy-drinking young adults (18 to 25 years old) that targeted naltrexone as an adjunct to counselling was well tolerated and reduced drinking, suggesting that this might be a way forward to improve outcomes beyond counselling alone.

Karhuvaara and colleagues (2007) reported that in harmful drinkers experiencing problems controlling their drinking (some may have been dependent), nalmefene (20 mg per day) similarly reduced the number of heavy drinking days.

7.16.3 Clinical summary

The evidence is limited but does support the use of medication (naltrexone) to reduce drinking in non-dependence or mild dependence and does not demonstrate equivalence with psychological interventions for this group. There was no direct evidence for the use of acamprosate in this group.

7.16.4   From evidence to recommendations

The GDG considered that given the limited evidence to support the use of naltrexone to reduce drinking in non-dependence or mild dependence that it should only be used where psychological interventions alone have not been effective. It should be prescribed in conjunction with a psychological intervention.

Although no direct evidence was identified for acamprosate, the GDG considered the equivalence of acamprosate and naltrexone in moderate and severe dependence and decided that it was reasonable to extrapolate from this data and also recommend acamprosate for use in this group.

7.16.5   Recommendation

7.16.5.1   For harmful drinkers and people with mild alcohol dependence who have not responded to psychological interventions alone, or who have specifically requested a pharmacological intervention, consider offering acamprosate[53] or oral naltrexone[54] in combination with an individual psychological intervention (cognitive behavioural therapies, behavioural therapies or social network and environment-based therapies) or behavioural couples therapy.[55]

7.17   COMORBIDITIES

7.17.1   Introduction

Individuals presenting for treatment with alcohol misuse may also present with features of other psychiatric disorders, most commonly anxiety or depression. For many, these symptoms will be closely linked to their alcohol misuse and lessen when drinking is reduced or stopped. For this reason, it is important target their alcohol misuse rather than just starting treatment for a comorbid psychiatric disorder. Such comorbidity is associated with a poorer prognosis (Bradizza *et al.*, 2006; Mason & Lehert, 2010; Verheul *et al.*, 1998), increased rates of relapse (Driessen *et al.*, 2001), poorer medication compliance, lower treatment attendance rates and higher rates of self-harm and suicidal behaviours (Martinez-Raga *et al.*, 2000).

There are a variety of treatment approaches for people with comorbid alcohol dependence and a psychiatric disorder but they all emphasise integrated treatment for

---

[53]Note that the evidence for acamprosate in the treatment of harmful drinkers and people who are mildly alcohol dependent is less robust than that for naltrexone. At the time of publication of the NICE guideline (February 2011), acamprosate did not have UK marketing authorisation for this indication. Informed consent should be obtained and documented.
[54]At the time of publication of the NICE guideline (February 2011), oral naltrexone did not have UK marketing authorisation for this indication. Informed consent should be obtained and documented.
[55]This recommendation also appears in Chapter 6.

both disorders. However, this is not always easy to achieve with thresholds for referral to 'addiction services' and 'psychiatric services' differing and a lack of dedicated dual-disorder services. In addition, addiction services vary in their psychiatric expertise. Provision varies considerably across the UK despite initiatives (Mental Health Policy-DH, 2002). A NICE guideline covers psychosis and co-existing substance misuse (NICE, 2011a).

Psychological treatment approaches aimed at addressing Axis 1 and Axis 2 disorders have been increasingly developed, but in many cases alcohol dependence remains a diagnosis of exclusion even though for many the comorbid psychopathology has preceded the diagnosis of alcohol dependence. On the basis of this, one might question whether or not relapse rates could be influenced were treatment for comorbid disorders provided at the same time as treatments for alcohol dependence.

7.17.2   Clinical review protocol

The review of pharmacological interventions where there is significant comorbidity is considered in this section. A systematic search and the expertise of the GDG were used to identify RCTs or meta-analyses of medication in non-psychotic psychiatric disorders. A further synthesis of the data was not undertaken because, apart from in depression, the number, nature and quality of the studies did not permit this. Two meta-analyses of treating comorbidity of alcohol dependence and depression were drawn on. The expertise of the GDG was used to focus on key trials of relevance to current practice in the UK. Information about the databases searched and the inclusion/exclusion criteria used for this section of the guideline can be found in Appendix 16e. A summary of the available evidence is described below.

7.17.3   Alcohol misuse comorbid with a psychiatric disorder

This section considers two approaches for using pharmacotherapy and psychological interventions. First, its use for treating the alcohol misuse in the context of a non-psychotic psychiatric disorder, and second, for treating the comorbid psychiatric disorder.

Pharmacological interventions
There are limited studies of disulfiram, acamprosate or naltrexone in people with a psychiatric disorder and alcohol dependence. The largest RCT assessed the efficacy and safety of disulfiram and naltrexone in 254 people who misused alcohol and had an Axis I psychiatric disorder (Petrakis *et al.*, 2005). It was a heterogenous group with some individuals having more than one diagnosis. Individuals were randomised to naltrexone (50 mg per day) or placebo (double blind), but openly randomised to disulfiram (250 mg per day) or nothing, resulting in four groups: naltrexone alone, placebo alone, naltrexone and disulfiram, placebo and disulfiram. There was no overall advantage of one medication over the other and no advantage of the combination of both medications over placebo. However, the abstinence rate is very high at 77%.

A series of secondary analyses were then conducted to compare people with and without particular Axis 1 disorders within the group. In those with PTSD (37%)

Table 107: Clinical review protocol for pharmacological interventions in the present of comorbidities

Electronic databases	MEDLINE, EMBASE, CINAHL, PsycINFO, Cochrane Library
Date searched	Database inception to March 2010
Study design	RCTs
Population	At least 80% of the sample meet the criteria for alcohol dependence or harmful alcohol use (clinical diagnosis or drinking more than 30 drinks per week); diagnosed comorbidities
Excluded populations	Hazardous drinkers and those drinking fewer than 30 drinks per week Pregnant women
Interventions	Any pharmacological intervention (excluding acamprosate, naltrexone and disulfiram)
Comparator	Any other intervention
Outcomes	Discontinuing treatment for any reason Discontinuing treatment due to adverse events Lapsing (returning to a drinking state) Relapsing (returning to a heavy drinking state) PDA Cumulative abstinence duration DDD Total drinks consumed during treatment period Total days of heavy drinking during treatment Time to first drink Time to heavy drinking day

compared with those without (63%), either naltrexone or disulfiram alone or together improved alcohol outcomes (Petrakis *et al.*, 2006). PTSD symptoms also improved, with those in the disulfiram group showing the greatest improvement. Those with PTSD were more likely to report gastrointestinal, emotional or neurological side effects. By comparison, the presence or absence of current depression did not influence outcomes (Petrakis *et al.*, 2007).

In people with depression and alcohol dependence, Pettinati and colleagues (2010) reported that the combination of sertraline and naltrexone resulted in better abstinence rates than with use of either medication alone or placebo (23.8%; c2 = 12.9, degrees of freedom = 1, p = 0.001). Notably, there was no difference between the groups in improvements in depressive symptoms, although a trend was reported favouring the combination (83% versus 58%; c2 = 6.1, degrees of freedom = 1, p = 0.014).

Psychological interventions
Standard CBT was applied in four of the trials to treat alcohol dependence in addition to anxiety symptoms, panic disorder, insomnia and bipolar disorder. CBT failed to demonstrate any significant improvement in relapse rates or PDA with regard to alcohol use, but did provide evidence of significant reduction in anxiety and avoidance symptoms (Schadé *et al.*, 2005), improved sleep (Currie *et al.*, 2004) and improved mood, medication compliance and attendance rates (Schmitz *et al.*, 2002). One trial failed to provide any evidence that CBT reduced either anxiety symptoms or PDA when compared with treatment as usual (Bowen *et al.*, 2000), although this was attributed, in part, to systemic resistance to introducing CBT into the setting and the subsequent poor planning associated with providing the intervention.

Integrated CBT, offered in two trials, also appeared to demonstrate limited effectiveness when applied to a population diagnosed with alcohol dependence and major depressive disorder when compared with TSF. One study (Glasner-Edwards *et al.*, 2007) failed to demonstrate any improvement in mood or PDA amongst participants receiving integrated CBT compared with those receiving TSF.

A psychodynamic approach using dynamic deconstructive psychotherapy (Gregory *et al.*, 2008) was applied in one of the trials to treat alcohol dependence or misuse with coexisting bipolar disorder. In this trial, dynamic deconstructive psychotherapy was compared with treatment as usual and results demonstrated a statistically significant improvement over time on each of the measures, including parasuicide behaviours, a reduction in alcohol and drug use, and fewer admissions to hospital. Integrated group therapy (Weiss *et al.*, 2007) was applied in one trial where it was compared with group drug counselling. Analysis indicated that participants undertaking the integrated group therapy revealed significantly fewer days of substance use during treatment and at follow-up with decreased alcohol use accounting for most of the differences between the groups.

7.17.4   Treatment of the comorbid psychiatric disorder

This section focuses on the pharmacological and combined pharmacological and psychological treatment of comorbid disorders. The issue of psychological interventions alone for harmful or dependent alcohol misuse has been considered in Chapter 6.

Depression
Several studies and trials have been performed to assess the efficacy of antidepressants in comorbid alcohol and depression, issues concerning methodology such as small numbers, unclear diagnoses, short treatment times, limit interpretation and translation to routine clinical practice. Two meta-analyses were undertaken of antidepressants in comorbid depression, one with substance misuse which included eight studies with alcohol dependence (Nunes & Levin, 2004) and a second that looked at the same studies in addition to one by another group, and also examined SSRIs and 'other' antidepressants separately (Torrens *et al.*, 2005).

In their review, Nunes and Levin (2004) included trials where participants met standard diagnostic criteria for current alcohol or other drug use and a current unipolar depressive disorder. The principal measure of effect size was the SMD on the Hamilton

Depression Rating Scale (HDRS). Their meta-analysis reported that antidepressant medication exerts a modest (SMD 0.38; 95% CI, 0.18 to 0.58) beneficial effect in reducing HDRS score for people with combined depressive and substance-use disorders. Those with lower placebo response rates had larger effect sizes. In such studies, the depression was diagnosed after at least a week of abstinence. On the other hand, where studies included people whose depression was transient and/or directly related to their substance misuse, the placebo response rate was high. This supports the widely-held clinical practice of waiting to start an antidepressant once an individual is abstinent, but suggests that 1 week rather than 2 to 3 weeks may be acceptable. In addition, psychosocial interventions also contributed to reduced effect sizes which may have acted via improving mood directly or through reducing substance misuse. The overall effect size for improvements in substance misuse were small (SMD 0.25; 95% CI, 0.08 to 0.42) with improvements observed in studies where the effect size in improving depression was more than 0.5. Although it was noted that abstinence was rarely sustained, they concluded that an antidepressant 'is not a standalone treatment, and concurrent therapy directly targeting the addiction is also indicated'.

Torrens and colleagues (2005) included studies of alcohol dependence and depression where explicit diagnostic criteria and methods for assessing the presence of comorbid depression (major depression or dysthymia) were used. This meta-analysis also failed to find an overall effect of antidepressants on depressive symptoms. However there was a significant effect pooling the three studies using 'other antidepressants' (imipramine, desipramine, nefazodone; OR = 4.15; 95% CI, 1.35 to 12.75), whereas no significant effect was seen for SSRIs (OR = 1.85; 95% CI, 0.73 to 4.68). However, the meta-analysis revealed no significant effect on reduction in alcohol consumption. Torrens and colleagues (2005) also note that cocaine misuse in addition to comorbid alcohol and depression misuse can result in greater levels of depression and poorer prognosis, as reported in Cornelius and colleagues (1998).

Therefore, these two meta-analyses are in broad agreement that antidepressants do not reduce alcohol misuse. Whilst antidepressant effect is modest at best, waiting even for a week of abstinence to establish the diagnosis improves outcomes for depression. This is likely due to any transient depression due directly to their alcohol misuse or withdrawal period improving.

Nevertheless, if an antidepressant is indicated, in view of several trials showing no or limited efficacy with SSRIs as opposed to more positive results with mixed noradrenergic-serotonergic antidepressants, choosing antidepressants with similar pharmacology is worth considering. Such antidepressants include tricyclics, but these may not be appropriate due to the risk of cardiotoxicity with alcohol, particularly in overdose. Newer mixed noradrenergic-serotonergic antidepressant drugs include mirtazapine. Unfortunately, there are only two preliminary studies investigating mirtazapine in comorbid alcohol dependence and depression. An open-label naturalistic study showed that mirtazapine (dose ranged on average from 17 mg to 23 mg per day) was associated with improved mood and craving for alcohol (Yoon *et al.*, 2006). A double-blind RCT comparing mirtazapine (average dose 45 mg per day) with amitriptyline (average dose 125 mg per day) found that both drugs improved mood and alcohol craving with no difference between them (Altintoprak *et al.*, 2008).

Anxiety

Despite how often alcohol dependence and anxiety are linked, few studies have investigated how to manage this challenging comorbidity. A comprehensive assessment is required to define how alcohol and anxiety are related. An assisted withdrawal is often required and a longer 'tail' of a benzodiazepine may be given to manage anxiety initially. It is reported that anxiety may take up to 6 to 8 weeks to reduce after stopping drinking. Benzodiazepines are also indicated for treating anxiety, but due to concerns about vulnerability to dependence (see Section 7.17.5), their use needs careful consideration.

A series of studies from the same group have shown that an SSRI, paroxetine, is safe and well-tolerated in people with harmful alcohol use or dependence who may be still drinking and that it can significantly reduce social phobia compared with placebo (Book *et al.*, 2008; Randall *et al.*, 2001; Thomas & McCambridge, 2008). However, improvements in alcohol outcomes were either not reported or were no different to those in the placebo group and nonsignificant during the study. For instance, Thomas and McCambridge (2008) found that although paroxetine successfully treated comorbid social anxiety, their drinking overall did not improve although their drinking to cope with anxiety reduced. This emphasises that improving a comorbid disorder does not necessarily lead to improved drinking and, as for depression, alcohol-focused treatment must be delivered.

In another study, Randall and colleagues (2001) investigated how simultaneous CBT treatment of alcohol misuse and social anxiety disorder compared with CBT treatment of alcoholism alone. Although drinking outcomes improved in both groups, those who received simultaneous treatment showed less improvement. Notably, social anxiety showed equal improvement in both groups. Similarly, an RCT in abstinent alcohol-dependent individuals with either social phobia or agoraphobia who received either intensive relapse prevention for alcoholism with or without a CBT anxiety programme, plus an SSRI (fluvoxamine) that was available if wanted, resulted in reduced anxiety symptoms but had no impact on alcohol outcomes (Schadé *et al.*, 2005).

A meta-analysis of five studies of buspirone in alcoholism and anxiety concluded that anxiety improved with buspirone, but not alcohol consumption (Malec *et al.*, 2007).

Benzodiazepines are used in the treatment of anxiety; however, their use in people with alcohol misuse is generally regarded as inappropriate. Clearly any such prescribing should be done with due consideration and monitoring. However, their use may be the best option if their anxiety improves without adverse consequences on their drinking. Mueller and colleagues (2005) monitored the clinical course of people in their anxiety research programme over 12 years and reported little misuse of benzodiazepines in those who had coexisting anxiety disorders and alcohol-use disorders.

Post-traumatic stress disorder

PTSD is commonly associated with alcohol misuse (see NCCMH, 2005). Longitudinal studies have shown that PTSD often predates alcohol misuse. Treatment for an individual's PTSD can improve their substance misuse, but once dependent this will need to be treated before they can benefit from trauma-focused psychological treatments.

In a placebo-controlled trial of sertraline treatment of PTSD in people with comorbid alcohol dependence, sertraline improved symptoms of PTSD but decreased alcohol use in only a small subset of the study population (Brady *et al.*, 2002). A more recent, placebo-controlled trial compared sertraline with placebo in the treatment of PTSD with co-occurring alcohol dependence (Brady *et al.*, 2005). Both groups demonstrated a significant decrease in alcohol use. Cluster analysis revealed that sertraline was better in those less severely dependent with early onset PTSD, whilst those more severely dependent with later onset PTSD improved more with placebo. Closer examination of this trial revealed that alcohol consumption tended to start improving before or together with improvements in PTSD symptoms (Back *et al.*, 2006). They concluded that PTSD symptoms could have a strong impact on alcohol consumption and that PTSD treatment may be important to optimise outcomes for those comorbid for PTSD and alcohol dependence.

Attention deficit hyperactivity disorder
The prevalence of alcohol misuse is higher in adults with ADHD than those in the general population (Upadhyaya, 2007). Some features of ADHD are similar to those seen in fetal alcohol syndrome or spectrum disorders and a comprehensive history should be taken to establish whether fetal alcohol syndrome or spectrum disorders is implicated. There are treatment and prognostic implications because those with fetal alcohol syndrome or spectrum disorders may respond differently to psychostimulants (O'Malley & Nanson, 2002).

Whilst psychostimulants are the first-line treatment for ADHD, their use in people with comorbid substance misuse is complex and either medication must be adequately supervised or an alternative found (see the guideline on ADHD [NCCMH, 2009]).

A 3-month, double-blind, placebo-controlled RCT in adults with ADHD and alcohol-use disorders reported improved ADHD symptoms from atomoxetine compared with placebo (Wilens *et al.*, 2008). However, there were inconsistent effects on alcohol with reduced cumulative number of heavy drinking days but not increased time to relapse of heavy drinking.

7.17.5 Comorbid alcohol and drug misuse

This section covers pharmacotherapy of comorbidities where it either plays a significant role in management, for example opioid dependence, or where pharmacotherapy has not been shown to be generally efficacious (for example, cocaine). It does not cover comorbidity with drugs of misuse where psychosocial approaches are preferable and pharmacotherapy does not play a significant role (for example, cannabis, ecstasy and ketamine).

Comorbid opioid and alcohol dependence
Alcohol dependence is a common comorbidity in opioid dependence. People with both alcohol and opioid dependence are at particularly high risk of drug-related death due to the combined sedative effects of alcohol and opioids in overdose. Staff managing people who are opioid dependent should therefore routinely identify alcohol

dependence in people presenting for treatment of primary opioid dependence, and either treat the alcohol dependence or refer to appropriate specialist alcohol services.

The reader is referred to the NICE guidelines (2007a and 2007b) and 'Orange Guideline' (National Treatment Agency for Substance Misuse, 2007)) for guidance about managing opioid dependence and alcohol misuse. Optimisation of their substitute pharmacotherapy is important, although it does not seem to influence drinking whether this is with buprenorphine or methadone. However, it is recommended that people misusing drugs who are also misusing alcohol should be offered standard alcohol treatments such as assisted withdrawal and alcohol-focused psychosocial interventions as appropriate.

Concerning pharmacotherapy for relapse prevention, naltrexone is not an option unless the individual is also abstinent from opioids. There is a small study of disulfiram in people maintained on methadone who are opioid dependent and have a drink problem (Ling *et al.*, 1983). No benefit of disulfiram was shown, but also no adverse events were reported.

There are no published studies of acamprosate in opioid dependent populations. Given its good tolerability and safety, there is no reason why acamprosate cannot be used to support abstinence from alcohol after the appropriate medical assessment.

The paucity of trials investigating pharmacotherapeutic options to reduce alcohol misuse in opioid dependence is notable.

Comorbid cocaine and alcohol misuse

If cocaine is taken with alcohol, cocaethylene is produced, which has a longer half-life than cocaine, leading to enhanced effects. For instance, taken together, cocaine and alcohol can result in greater euphoria and increased heart rate compared with either substance alone (McCance-Katz *et al.*, 1993; Pennings *et al.*, 2002).

The reader is directed to NICE guidance (NICE, 2007a) regarding psychosocial management of cocaine because there is limited evidence for efficacy of a broad range of pharmacotherapeutic approaches for cocaine misuse alone. There have been several trials of naltrexone and disulfiram in comorbid alcohol and cocaine misuse, but none with acamprosate.

Naltrexone does not appear to significantly improve outcomes when added to psychosocial approaches for cocaine or alcohol in comorbid dependence (Schmitz *et al.*, 2004 and 2009; Pettinati *et al.*, 2008a). A series of studies have reported that disulfiram in comorbid cocaine and alcohol dependence results in better retention in treatment and longer abstinence from cocaine or alcohol (Carroll *et al.*, 1998 and 2000). Although the initial rationale was that by reducing alcohol consumption, cocaine use would also reduce, effects on cocaine now appear somewhat independent of changes in alcohol consumption (Carroll *et al.*, 2004).

Comorbid nicotine and alcohol dependence

It is fair to say that conventional wisdom has been to 'give up one vice at a time'. The idea of stopping smoking and drinking alcohol concurrently has often not been encouraged. In addition, it is the clinical impression of the GDG that most people do not want to consider quitting smoking until they have achieved some sobriety. However, it is likely that since the smoking bans came into place and support to stop smoking has become more available, more alcoholics will be interested in stopping smoking.

Those who have achieved long-term abstinence from alcohol have similar quit rates to people who do not misuse alcohol (Hughes & Kalman, 2006; Kalman *et al.*, 2010). However, the length of abstinence does influence outcome, with quitting smoking less likely in those who are in the early months of sobriety. Two RCTs comparing concurrent with sequential treatment for alcohol and nicotine have been conducted. Joseph and colleagues (2004) compared giving smoking cessation treatment concurrently with an intensive programme for alcohol versus delaying the smoking cessation programme for 6 months. Whilst there was no difference in smoking cessation (~16%) between the groups, those who received the delayed intervention had higher rates of alcohol abstinence. However, there were no group differences in time to first relapse or number of days drinking in previous 6 months. Kalman and colleagues (2001) showed higher (19% versus 8%), but non-significant, smoking quit rates in people with alcohol dependence receiving concurrent smoking cessation interventions compared with those who received this intervention at 6 weeks. Regarding drinking outcomes, those who had the later smoking cessation interventions had greater relapse rates.

A meta-analysis of RCTs of smoking cessation interventions for people in treatment for or recovery from an addiction, five of which were primarily alcohol, concluded that there was no detrimental effect on substance-use outcomes from combined treatment (Prochaska *et al.*, 2004). Indeed, smoking cessation interventions during substance-misuse treatment seemed to improve rather than compromise long-term sobriety. Regarding smoking cessation, short-term abstinence looked promising but this was not sustained in the longer-term.

Therefore, evidence does not strongly support a particular approach or time for quitting smoking, but it is very important that it is considered as part of the person's care plan. Some suggest that whilst it is difficult to know conclusively that concurrent treatment should be avoided, this is a possibility and therefore only offered if the person requests it (Kodl *et al.*, 2006). Others cite that there is a wealth of evidence to suggest that treatment for smoking does not interfere with recovery in substance misuse (Fiore *et al.*, 2008).

Concerning pharmacotherapeutic strategies, Kalman and colleagues (2010) reviewed all studies which included those both abstinent from alcohol and still drinking. They suggest that more intensive treatment is needed because standard (weekly counselling plus 21-mg patch for 8 to 12 weeks) treatment does not produce good results for those still drinking or recently sober. In the absence of trials, standard protocols can be followed; however, a comprehensive medical assessment of any individual is needed given the contraindications/cautions for some pharmacotherapies that might be relevant in alcohol misuse, for example bupropion (history of seizures) and varenicline (close monitoring in those with psychiatric disorders) (see BNF, SPC).

A full assessment of smoking, and an individual's attitudes to changing their smoking behaviour and cessation, should be explored at initiation and throughout treatment. For management of smoking cessation, refer to the relevant NICE guidance about services, pharmacotherapeutic treatment and behavioural/psychological approaches (NICE, 2006b).

7.17.6   Clinical evidence summary

Whilst comorbidity with a psychiatric disorder or another substance is common, there were few studies investigating pharmacological treatments for these problems. Some studies were identified but were and therefore diagnostic criteria differed from those undertaken more recently; a significant proportion were of poor quality with small numbers.

In the RCTs that included people with alcohol dependence and a variety of psychiatric disorders, no benefit of medication (naltrexone, disulfiram or combination) on improving alcohol consumption was found. However, the abstinence rate was much higher than would normally be seen in routine clinical practice. Secondary analyses reported no advantage of medication in improving alcohol consumption when comparing those currently depressed versus non-depressed, but did show a beneficial effect in those with PTSD compared with those without. This emphasises the importance of treatment targeted at alcohol misuse rather than hoping an antidepressant will reduce drinking by improving mood. Whilst there were no adverse effects on their psychiatric disorder, no significant benefits were apparent either. A more recent trial in comorbid alcohol dependence and depression found that naltrexone but not sertraline improved alcohol outcomes, with mood similarly improving in all groups. There are no studies of acamprosate in comorbidity; however, it could be considered given its good safety profile. There is little consistent evidence for the use of psychological interventions for the treatment of alcohol dependence in people with comorbid psychiatric disorders. Where evidence of benefit from some psychological interventions was identified, it was often from mixed drug and alcohol populations from small single studies and was not judged sufficient evidence on which to base a recommendation.

The two meta-analyses of treatment of comorbid depression broadly came to the same conclusion that antidepressants had a modest to no effect on improving depressive symptoms in those who are not at least 1 week abstinent. The effect of the antidepressant on alcohol use was also of limited benefit, and where there was some abstinence was not sustained. In those with severe depression, antidepressants may improve mood, but alcohol-focused treatment is still required. There is little evidence to suggest which antidepressant is best, although one meta-analysis suggested that SSRIs were less effective than those with a mixed serotonergic-noradrenergic pharmacology. However, some of these medications also carry adverse safety profiles with alcohol and there is insufficient evidence about the newer antidepressants. In the few studies in those with an anxiety disorder, whilst antidepressant medication may improve anxiety symptoms this was not associated with a beneficial effect on alcohol consumption. The evidence for those with either comorbid depression or anxiety suggests that focusing on managing their alcohol misuse at the start is key because whilst medication may help their anxiety or depression, improvements in their alcohol misuse will not necessarily follow.

There were only a few studies about the role of pharmacotherapy in those with alcohol and illicit drug misuse. Treatment of illicit drug misuse must be optimised using psychosocial and/or pharmacological approaches as appropriate, whilst monitoring the effect this has on alcohol consumption to ensure alcohol does not substitute for reducing illicit drug misuse. Alcohol misuse must also be specifically addressed. Many individuals with alcohol misuse smoke heavily and should be offered support to stop. There is limited evidence to suggest whether alcohol and nicotine should be given up simultaneously or sequentially, therefore patient preference should guide the decision.

7.17.7 From evidence to recommendations

The GDG noted that symptoms of anxiety and depression are common in people with harmful alcohol-use or alcohol dependence. However, for many people the symptoms remit once abstinence or a significant reduction in alcohol consumption has been achieved. In addition, treatment for comorbid disorders (in particular depression and anxiety) whilst people are consuming significant levels of alcohol does not appear to be effective. However, a number of patients have comorbid disorders that do not remit when alcohol consumption is reduced. The GDG therefore recommend that the first step in treating people presenting with alcohol misuse and comorbid depression/anxiety is to treat the alcohol misuse. Given that the presence of a comorbid disorder following a reduction in alcohol consumption is associated with a poorer long-term prognosis, an assessment of the presence and need for treatment for any comorbid depression or anxiety should be considered 3 to 4 weeks after abstinence is achieved. Some people with depressive disorders will require immediate treatment (for example, those at significant risk of suicide) and the recommendations below should not on any way stand in the way of immediate treatment being provided in such a situation. In reviewing the evidence for comorbid disorders, the GDG did not find any treatment strategies or adjustments that should be made because of the comorbid problem and, in view of this, decided to refer to the relevant NICE guidelines (see also the NICE guideline on common mental health problems; NICE, 2011b). Given the high prevalence of smoking in people with alcohol-related problems, the GDG considered it to be important to emphasise the need for effective treatment in this population. For people with comorbid drug and alcohol misuse and psychotic disorders, see the relevant NICE guideline (NICE, 2011a).

7.17.8 Recommendations

7.17.8.1 For people who misuse alcohol and have comorbid depression or anxiety disorders, treat the alcohol misuse first as this may lead to significant improvement in the depression and anxiety. If depression or anxiety continues after 3 to 4 weeks of abstinence from alcohol, assess the depression or anxiety and consider referral and treatment in line with the relevant NICE guideline for the particular disorder[56].

7.17.8.2 Refer people who misuse alcohol and have a significant comorbid mental health disorder, and those assessed to be at high risk of suicide, to a psychiatrist to make sure that effective assessment, treatment and risk-management plans are in place.

---

[56]See NICE (2009b) and NICE (2011c).

7.17.8.3   For the treatment of comorbid mental health disorders refer to the relevant
NICE guideline for the particular disorder, and:

- for alcohol misuse comorbid with opioid misuse actively treat both
  conditions; take into account the increased risk of mortality with taking
  alcohol and opioids together[57]
- for alcohol misuse comorbid with stimulant, cannabis[58] or benzodiazepine misuse actively treat both conditions.

Service users who have been dependent on alcohol will need to be abstinent, or have very significantly reduced their drinking, to benefit from
psychological interventions for comorbid mental health disorders.

7.17.8.4   For comorbid alcohol and nicotine dependence, encourage service users to
stop smoking and refer to *Brief Interventions and Referral for Smoking
Cessation in Primary Care and Other Settings* (NICE Public Health
Guidance No. 1, 2006).

7.17.9   Research recommendation

7.17.9.1   For people with alcohol dependence which medication is most likely to
improve concordance and thereby promote abstinence and prevent relapse?
This question should be answered by: (a) an initial development phase in which a
series of qualitative and quantitative reasons for non-adherence/discontinuing drugs
used in the treatment of alcohol are explored; (b) a series of pilot trials of novel interventions developed to address the problems identified in (a) undertaken to support the
design of a series of definitive trials; (c) a (series of) definitive trial(s) of the interventions that were successfully piloted in (b) using a randomised controlled design that
reports short-term (for example, 3 months) and longer-term (for example, 18 months)
outcomes. The outcomes chosen should reflect both observer and service user-rated
assessments of improvement and the acceptability of the intervention. Each individual study needs to be large enough to determine the presence or absence of clinically
important effects, and mediators and moderators of response should be investigated.

Why this is important
Rates of attrition in trials of drugs to promote abstinence and prevent relapse in alcohol dependence are high (often over 65%), yet despite this the interventions are still
clinically and cost effective. Retaining more service users in treatment could further
significantly improve outcomes for people who misuse alcohol and ensure increased
effectiveness in the use of health service resources. The outcome of these studies may
also help improve clinical confidence in the use of effective medications (such as

---

[57]See NICE (2007a) and NICE (2007b).
[58]See NICE (2007b).

acamprosate and naltrexone), which, despite their cost effectiveness, are currently offered to only a minority of eligible NHS service users. Overall, the results of these studies will have important implications for the provision of pharmacological treatment in the NHS for alcohol misuse.

7.18   WERNICKE-KORSAKOFF SYNDROME

7.18.1   Aim of review

The following section draws on the review of Wernicke-Korsakoff syndrome (WKS) and is developed as part of the NICE (2010b) guideline on the management of alcohol-related physical complications including the management of acute withdrawal. The GDG failed to identify any evidence for specific interventions in WKS beyond prevention strategies using thiamine – these are covered in the guideline mentioned above (NICE, 2010b). The GDG therefore adopted a consensus-based approach to the review of the literature, synthesising previously published narrative reviews to assist in development of the recommendations for this guideline.

7.18.2   Narrative summary

Wernicke's encephalopathy (WE) is traditionally thought of as a disorder of acute onset characterised by nystagmus, abducent and conjugate gaze palsies, ataxia of gait, and a global confusional state, occurring together or in various combinations (Victor *et al.*, 1989). Wernicke first described the disorder in 1881 and the symptoms he recorded included disturbances of eye movement, ataxia of gait, polyneuropathy and mental changes including apathy, decreased attention span, and disorientation in time and space. Work by Alexander (1940) and then Jolliffe and colleagues (1941) established that a deficiency in thiamine (vitamin B1) was central to causation and potential treatment of the disorder (Lishman, 1998). Korsakoff gave the first comprehensive account of the amnestic syndrome now known as Korsakoff's psychosis (KP) in 1887, which includes features such as delirium characterised by recent memory loss with confabulation but with relative preservation of other intellectual functions. More recent work has highlighted a retrograde memory impairment with a 'temporal gradient', such that earlier memories are recalled better than more recent ones (Kopelman *et al.*, 2009). The two disorders were brought together by Victor and colleagues in 1971 (Victor *et al.*, 1971), and WKS is now considered to be a unitary disorder comprising acute WE, which proceeds in a proportion of cases to KP. A major complicating factor is that the pathology of WE may not be associated with the classical clinical triad (see above) in up to 90% of patients (Harper *et al.*, 1986). Therefore, it has been suggested that a presumptive diagnosis of WE should be made for any patient with a history of alcohol dependence who may be at risk. This includes anyone showing evidence of ophthalmoplegia, ataxia, acute confusion, memory disturbance, unexplained hypotension, hypothermia, coma or unconsciousness (Cook, 2000).

Untreated, WE leads to death in up to 20% of cases (Harper, 1979; Harper *et al.*, 1986), or KP in up to 85% of the survivors. A quarter of the latter group may then require long-term institutionalisation (Victor *et al.*, 1989). Furthermore, the incidence of KP has been reported to be rising in some parts of the UK (Ramayya & Jauhar, 1997). For the reasons mentioned above it is probable that WE is under-diagnosed and inadequately treated in hospital, let alone in the community (Thomson & Marshall, 2006). It is therefore not known how often people with alcohol dependence in the community unnecessarily suffer brain damage.

Cognitive impairment is common in people with chronic alcohol-use disorders, with between 50 and 80% experiencing mild to severe cognitive deficits (Bates *et al.*, 2002). The clinical and neuropsychological features of alcohol-related brain damage are well described, and the deficits appear to centre on visuospatial coordination, memory, abstract thinking and learning new information, with general knowledge, over-rehearsed information and verbal skills largely spared (Lishman, 1998). Attempts have been made to describe the unique features of 'alcoholic dementia' (Oslin & Cary, 2003), but there is a lack of evidence linking any specific neuropathology with heavy alcohol intake (Joyce, 1994). A range of potential factors have been implicated in the causation of alcohol-related brain damage, including direct alcohol neurotoxicity, thiamine deficiency, traumatic brain injury, familial alcoholism, childhood psychopathology, age and education (Bates *et al.*, 2002). Studies in people with features suggestive of WE have shown that their memory and general intellectual function are roughly equivalent (Bowden, 1990). Therefore, the effects of thiamine deficiency on cognition are more widespread than amnesia, with effects on visuospatial and abstracting functions being indicated (Jacobson *et al.*, 1990).

The mechanism by which chronic, heavy alcohol consumption causes thiamine deficiency is by increasing metabolic demand, decreasing dietary intake and reducing hepatic storage capacity due to liver damage (Cook *et al.*, 1998, Thomson *et al.*, 1987). Brain cells require three thiamine-dependent enzymes to metabolise glucose (transketolase, pyruvate dehydrogenase complex and α-ketoglutarate dehydrogenase) (Butterworth, 1989), and a deficiency of thiamine reduces the activity of these enzymes leading to brain cell death and reduced cognitive function (Butterworth, 1989). Cognitive impairment due to subclinical WKS in alcohol dependence may therefore be responsive to thiamine therapy. Abstinence can also improve cognition and therefore it remains the mainstay of any effective prevention programme. This is important because apart from thiamine there are no established pharmacotherapeutic strategies to specifically prevent impairment of or improve cognition once a deficit has been established.

For those with established WKS, appropriate rehabilitation, usually in supported accommodation for those with moderate and severe impairment, is the correct approach because there is some evidence to suggest that people with WKS are capable of new learning, particularly if they live in a calm and well-structured environment, and if new information is cued (Kopelman *et al.*, 2009). There have been a few case reports of using medications to treat dementia in WKS with mixed results (Cochrane *et al.*, 2005; Luykx *et al.*, 2008). In an open study, the noradrenergic antidepressant reboxetine appeared to improve cognitive performance in those who had

had WKS for less than 1 year (Reuster *et al.*, 2003). Fluvoxamine has been shown to improve memory consolidation and/or retrieval in patients with WKS (Martin *et al.*, 1995b).

The NICE (2010b) guideline on the management of alcohol-related physical complications made recommendations about people who did not have clinical features of WE, but were at high risk of developing it. They identified a high-risk group who may be characterised by the following features:

- alcohol-related liver disease
- medically-assisted withdrawal from alcohol (planned or unplanned)
- acute alcohol withdrawal
- malnourishment or risk of malnourishment; this may include:
  - weight loss in past year
  - reduced BMI
  - loss of appetite
  - nausea and vomiting
  - a general impression of malnourishment
- homelessness
- hospitalised for acute illness
- hospitalised for comorbidity or another alcohol issue.

From the perspective of acute inpatient care, the NICE guideline on alcohol-related physical complications (NICE, 2010b) also recommended the use of intramuscular thiamine because there were concerns about the absorption of oral thiamine in a group undergoing assisted withdrawal. There is also a problem of lack of compliance with oral preparations in people drinking heavily in the community, and so some authors advocate a choice between intravenous and intramuscular thiamine therapy (Thomson & Marshall, 2006). Intramuscular Pabrinex has a lower incidence of anaphylactic reactions than the intravenous preparation at 1 per 5 million pairs of Pabrinex ampoules, which is far lower than many frequently used drugs that carry no special warning in the BNF (Thompson & Cook, 1997; Thompson & Marshall, 2006).

Relatively little is also known about the outcomes of the treatment of alcoholic Korsakoff syndrome. The large case study by Victor and colleagues (1971) reported that 25% recovered, 50% showed improvement over time and 25% remained largely unchanged. Other authors also believe that some improvement does occur in approximately 75% of patients over a number of years if they remain abstinent from alcohol (Kopelman *et al.*, 2009). There is little evidence from research studies to design and inform effective rehabilitation specifically in WKS (Smith & Hillman, 1999) although strategies developed in cognitive rehabilitation for a range of cognitive impairments may be of value (Cicerone *et al.*, 2005).

7.18.3   From evidence to recommendations

The GDG accepted the evidence that thiamine has a key preventative role in WKS, and adapted the recommendations from the NICE guideline on alcohol-related physical complications (NICE, 2010b) to take account of the use of thiamine in a community-based population. Due to the high risk of long-term brain injury and the potentially serious consequences of WE, a high index of suspicion for WE should be adopted and thiamine prescribed accordingly. A number of at-risk groups are specified in the recommendation. The GDG also considered the care of people with established WKS and subsequent cognitive impairment. The limited data available suggested that continued abstinence from alcohol and a supportive and structured environment may have some beneficial effects for people with WKS and, given the high morbidity and mortality in this group, the GDG concluded that supported independent living for those with mild impairment and 24-hour care for those with severe impairment should be made available.

7.18.4 Recommendations

7.18.4.1 Follow the recommendations in NICE clinical guideline 100[59] on thiamine for people at high risk of developing, or with suspected, Wernicke's encephalopathy. In addition, offer parenteral thiamine followed by oral thiamine to prevent Wernicke-Korsakoff syndrome in people who are entering planned assisted alcohol withdrawal in specialist inpatient alcohol services or prison settings and who are malnourished or at risk of malnourishment (for example, people who are homeless) or have decompensated liver disease.

7.18.4.2 For people with Wernicke-Korsakoff syndrome, offer long-term placement in:
- supported independent living for those with mild cognitive impairment
- supported 24-hour care for those with moderate or severe cognitive impairment.

In both settings the environment should be adapted for people with cognitive impairment and support should be provided to help service users maintain abstinence from alcohol.

---

[59]See NICE (2010b).

8   SUMMARY OF RECOMMENDATIONS

8.1   PRINCIPLES OF CARE

8.1.1   Building a trusting relationship and providing information

8.1.1.1   When working with people who misuse alcohol:
- build a trusting relationship and work in a supportive, empathic and non-judgmental manner
- take into account that stigma and discrimination are often associated with alcohol misuse and that minimising the problem may be part of the service user's presentation
- make sure that discussions take place in settings in which confidentiality, privacy and dignity are respected.

8.1.1.2   When working with people who misuse alcohol:
- provide information appropriate to their level of understanding about the nature and treatment of alcohol misuse to support choice from a range of evidence-based treatments
- avoid clinical language without explanation
- make sure that comprehensive written information is available in an appropriate language or, for those who cannot use written text, in an accessible format
- provide independent interpreters (that is, someone who is not known to the service user) if needed.

8.1.2   Working with and supporting families and carers

8.1.2.1   Encourage families and carers to be involved in the treatment and care of people who misuse alcohol to help support and maintain positive change.

8.1.2.2   When families and carers are involved in supporting a person who misuses alcohol, discuss concerns about the impact of alcohol misuse on themselves and other family members, and:
- provide written and verbal information on alcohol misuse and its management, including how families and carers can support the service user
- offer a carer's assessment where necessary
- negotiate with the service user and their family or carer about the family or carer's involvement in their care and the sharing of information; make sure the service user's, family's and carer's right to confidentiality is respected.

8.1.2.3   When the needs of families and carers of people who misuse alcohol have been identified:
- offer guided self-help, usually consisting of a single session, with the provision of written materials
- provide information about, and facilitate contact with, support groups (such as self-help groups specifically focused on addressing the needs of families and carers).

8.1.2.4   If the families and carers of people who misuse alcohol have not benefited, or are not likely to benefit, from guided self-help and/or support groups and continue to have significant problems, consider offering family meetings. These should:
- provide information and education about alcohol misuse
- help to identify sources of stress related to alcohol misuse
- explore and promote effective coping behaviours
- usually consist of at least five weekly sessions.

8.1.2.5   All staff in contact with parents who misuse alcohol and who have care of or regular contact with their children, should:
- take account of the impact of the parent's drinking on the parent–child relationship and the child's development, education, mental and physical health, own alcohol use, safety, and social network
- be aware of and comply with the requirements of the Children Act (2004).

8.2   IDENTIFICATION AND ASSESSMENT

8.2.1   General principles

8.2.1.1   Make sure that assessment of risk is part of any assessment, that it informs the development of the overall care plan, and that it covers risk to self (including unplanned withdrawal, suicidality and neglect) and risk to others.

8.2.1.2   Staff working in services provided and funded by the NHS who care for people who potentially misuse alcohol should be competent to identify harmful drinking and alcohol dependence. They should be competent to initially assess the need for an intervention or, if they are not competent, they should refer people who misuse alcohol to a service that can provide an assessment of need.

8.2.1.3   When conducting an initial assessment, as well as assessing alcohol misuse, the severity of dependence and risk, consider the:
- extent of any associated health and social problems
- need for assisted alcohol withdrawal.

8.2.1.4   Use formal assessment tools to assess the nature and severity of alcohol misuse, including the:
- AUDIT for identification and as a routine outcome measure
- SADQ or LDQ for severity of dependence

- CIWA-Ar for severity of withdrawal
- APQ for the nature and extent of the problems arising from alcohol misuse.

8.2.1.5   When assessing the severity of alcohol dependence and determining the need for assisted withdrawal, adjust the criteria for women, older people, children and young people[60], and people with established liver disease who may have problems with the metabolism of alcohol.

8.2.1.6   Staff responsible for assessing and managing assisted alcohol withdrawal (see Section 8.3.4) should be competent in the diagnosis and assessment of alcohol dependence and withdrawal symptoms and the use of drug regimens appropriate to the settings (for example, inpatient or community) in which the withdrawal is managed.

8.2.1.7   Staff treating people with alcohol dependence presenting with an acute unplanned alcohol withdrawal should refer to *Alcohol-Use Disorders: Diagnosis and Clinical Management of Alcohol-Related Physical Complications* (NICE Clinical Guideline 100)[61].

8.2.2   Assessment in specialist alcohol services

Treatment goals

8.2.2.1   In the initial assessment in specialist alcohol services of all people who misuse alcohol, agree the goal of treatment with the service user. Abstinence is the appropriate goal for most people with alcohol dependence, and people who misuse alcohol and have significant psychiatric or physical comorbidity (for example, depression or alcohol-related liver disease). When a service user prefers a goal of moderation but there are considerable risks, advise strongly that abstinence is most appropriate, but do not refuse treatment to service users who do not agree to a goal of abstinence.

8.2.2.2   For harmful drinking or mild dependence, without significant comorbidity, and if there is adequate social support, consider a moderate level of drinking as the goal of treatment unless the service user prefers abstinence or there are other reasons for advising abstinence.

8.2.2.3   For people with severe alcohol dependence, or those who misuse alcohol and have significant psychiatric or physical comorbidity, but who are unwilling to consider a goal of abstinence or engage in structured treatment, consider a harm reduction programme of care. However, ultimately the service user should be encouraged to aim for a goal of abstinence.

8.2.2.4   When developing treatment goals, consider that some people who misuse alcohol may be required to abstain from alcohol as part of a court order or sentence.

---

[60]See Section 8.3.7 for assessment of children and young people.
[61]See NICE (2010b).

Brief triage assessment

8.2.2.5   All adults who misuse alcohol who are referred to specialist alcohol services should have a brief triage assessment to assess:
- the pattern and severity of the alcohol misuse (using AUDIT) and severity of dependence (using SADQ)
- the need for urgent treatment including assisted withdrawal
- any associated risks to self or others
- the presence of any comorbidities or other factors that may need further specialist assessment or intervention.

Agree the initial treatment plan, taking into account the service user's preferences and outcomes of any previous treatment.

Comprehensive assessment

8.2.2.6   Consider a comprehensive assessment for all adults referred to specialist alcohol services who score more than 15 on the AUDIT. A comprehensive assessment should assess multiple areas of need, be structured in a clinical interview, use relevant and validated clinical tools (see 8.2.1.4), and cover the following areas:
- alcohol use, including:
  - consumption: historical and recent patterns of drinking (using, for example, a retrospective drinking diary), and if possible, additional information (for example, from a family member or carer)
  - dependence (using, for example, SADQ or LDQ)
  - alcohol-related problems (using, for example, APQ)
- other drug misuse, including over-the-counter medication
- physical health problems
- psychological and social problems
- cognitive function (using, for example, the MMSE)
- readiness and belief in ability to change.

8.2.2.7   Assess comorbid mental health problems as part of any comprehensive assessment, and throughout care for the alcohol misuse, because many comorbid problems (though not all) will improve with treatment for alcohol misuse. Use the assessment of comorbid mental health problems to inform the development of the overall care plan.

8.2.2.8   For service users whose comorbid mental health problems do not significantly improve after abstinence from alcohol (typically after 3–4 weeks), consider providing or referring for specific treatment (see the relevant NICE guideline for the particular disorder).

8.2.2.9   Consider measuring breath alcohol as part of the management of assisted withdrawal. However, breath alcohol should not usually be measured for routine assessment and monitoring in alcohol treatment programmes.

8.2.2.10   Consider blood tests to help identify physical health needs, but do not use blood tests routinely for the identification and diagnosis of alcohol-use disorders.

8.2.2.11 Consider brief measures of cognitive functioning (for example, MMSE) to help with treatment planning. Formal measures of cognitive functioning should usually only be performed if impairment persists after a period of abstinence or a significant reduction in alcohol intake.

8.3 INTERVENTIONS FOR ALCOHOL MISUSE

8.3.1 General principles for all interventions

8.3.1.1 For all people who misuse alcohol, carry out a motivational intervention as part of the initial assessment. The intervention should contain the key elements of motivational interviewing including:
- helping people to recognise problems or potential problems related to their drinking
- helping to resolve ambivalence and encourage positive change and belief in the ability to change
- adopting a persuasive and supportive rather than an argumentative and confrontational position.

8.3.1.2 For all people who misuse alcohol, offer interventions to promote abstinence or moderate drinking as appropriate (see 8.2.2.1–8.2.2.4) and prevent relapse, in community-based settings.

8.3.1.3 Consider offering interventions to promote abstinence and prevent relapse as part of an intensive structured community-based intervention for people with moderate and severe alcohol dependence who have:
- very limited social support (for example, they are living alone or have very little contact with family or friends) **or**
- complex physical or psychiatric comorbidities **or**
- not responded to initial community-based interventions (see 8.3.1.2).

8.3.1.4 For people with alcohol dependence who are homeless, consider offering residential rehabilitation for a maximum of 3 months. Help the service user find stable accommodation before discharge.

8.3.1.5 All interventions for people who misuse alcohol should be delivered by appropriately trained and competent staff. Pharmacological interventions should be administered by specialist and competent staff[62]. Psychological interventions should be based on a relevant evidence-based treatment manual, which should guide the structure and duration of the intervention. Staff should consider using competence frameworks developed from the relevant treatment manuals and for all interventions should:
- receive regular supervision from individuals competent in both the intervention and supervision

---

[62]If a drug is used at a dose or for an application that does not have UK marketing authorisation, informed consent should be obtained and documented.

- routinely use outcome measurements to make sure that the person who misuses alcohol is involved in reviewing the effectiveness of treatment
- engage in monitoring and evaluation of treatment adherence and practice competence, for example, by using video and audio tapes and external audit and scrutiny if appropriate.

8.3.1.6   All interventions for people who misuse alcohol should be the subject of routine outcome monitoring. This should be used to inform decisions about continuation of both psychological and pharmacological treatments. If there are signs of deterioration or no indications of improvement, consider stopping the current treatment and review the care plan.

8.3.1.7   For all people seeking help for alcohol misuse:
- give information on the value and availability of community support networks and self-help groups (for example, Alcoholics Anonymous or SMART Recovery) **and**
- help them to participate in community support networks and self-help groups by encouraging them to go to meetings and arranging support so that they can attend.

8.3.2   Care coordination and case management

Care coordination is the routine coordination by any staff involved in the care and treatment of a person who misuses alcohol. Case management is a more intensive process concerned with delivering all aspects of care, including assessment, treatment, monitoring and follow-up.

8.3.2.1   Care coordination should be part of the routine care of all service users in specialist alcohol services and should:
- be provided throughout the whole period of care, including aftercare
- be delivered by appropriately trained and competent staff working in specialist alcohol services
- include the coordination of assessment, interventions and monitoring of progress, and coordination with other agencies.

8.3.2.2   Consider case management to increase engagement in treatment for people who have moderate to severe alcohol dependence and who are considered at risk of dropping out of treatment or who have a previous history of poor engagement. If case management is provided it should be throughout the whole period of care, including aftercare.

8.3.2.3   Case management should be delivered in the context of Tier 3 interventions by staff who take responsibility for the overall coordination of care and should include:
- a comprehensive assessment of needs
- development of an individualised care plan in collaboration with the service user and relevant others (including families and carers and other staff involved in the service user's care)

- coordination of the care plan to deliver a seamless multiagency and integrated care pathway and maximisation of engagement, including the use of motivational interviewing approaches
- monitoring of the impact of interventions and revision of the care plan when necessary.

8.3.3 Interventions for harmful drinking and mild alcohol dependence

8.3.3.1 For harmful drinkers and people with mild alcohol dependence, offer a psychological intervention (such as cognitive behavioural therapies, behavioural therapies or social network and environment-based therapies) focused specifically on alcohol-related cognitions, behaviour, problems and social networks.

8.3.3.2 For harmful drinkers and people with mild alcohol dependence who have a regular partner who is willing to participate in treatment, offer behavioural couples therapy.

8.3.3.3 For harmful drinkers and people with mild alcohol dependence who have not responded to psychological interventions alone, or who have specifically requested a pharmacological intervention, consider offering acamprosate[63] or oral naltrexone[64] in combination with an individual psychological intervention (cognitive behavioural therapies, behavioural therapies or social network and environment-based therapies) or behavioural couples therapy (see Section 8.3.6 for pharmacological interventions).

Delivering psychological interventions

8.3.3.4 Cognitive behavioural therapies focused on alcohol-related problems should usually consist of one 60-minute session per week for 12 weeks.

8.3.3.5 Behavioural therapies focused on alcohol-related problems should usually consist of one 60-minute session per week for 12 weeks.

8.3.3.6 Social network and environment-based therapies focused on alcohol-related problems should usually consist of eight 50-minute sessions over 12 weeks.

8.3.3.7 Behavioural couples therapy should be focused on alcohol-related problems and their impact on relationships. It should aim for abstinence, or a level of drinking predetermined and agreed by the therapist and the service user to be reasonable and safe. It should usually consist of one 60-minute session per week for 12 weeks.

---

[63]Note that the evidence for acamprosate in the treatment of harmful drinkers and people who are mildly alcohol dependent is less robust than that for naltrexone. At the time of publication of the NICE guideline (February 2011), acamprosate did not have UK marketing authorisation for this indication. Informed consent should be obtained and documented.

[64]At the time of publication of the NICE guideline (February 2011), oral naltrexone did not have UK marketing authorisation for this indication. Informed consent should be obtained and documented.

8.3.4   Assessment and interventions for assisted alcohol withdrawal

See Section 8.3.7 for assessment for assisted withdrawal in children and young people.

8.3.4.1   For service users who typically drink over 15 units of alcohol per day and/or who score 20 or more on the AUDIT, consider offering:

- an assessment for and delivery of a community-based assisted withdrawal, **or**
- assessment and management in specialist alcohol services if there are safety concerns (see 8.3.4.5) about a community-based assisted withdrawal.

8.3.4.2   Service users who need assisted withdrawal should usually be offered a community-based programme, which should vary in intensity according to the severity of the dependence, available social support and the presence of comorbidities.

- For people with mild to moderate dependence, offer an outpatient-based assisted withdrawal programme in which contact between staff and the service user averages 2–4 meetings per week over the first week.
- For people with mild to moderate dependence and complex needs[65], or severe dependence, offer an intensive community programme following assisted withdrawal in which the service user may attend a day programme lasting between 4 and 7 days per week over a 3-week period.

8.3.4.3   Outpatient-based community assisted withdrawal programmes should consist of a drug regimen (see Section 8.3.5) and psychosocial support including motivational interviewing (see 8.3.1.1).

8.3.4.4   Intensive community programmes following assisted withdrawal should consist of a drug regimen (see Section 8.3.6) supported by psychological interventions including individual treatments (see Section 8.3.6), group treatments, psychoeducational interventions, help to attend self-help groups, family and carer support and involvement, and case management (see 8.3.2.2).

8.3.4.5   Consider inpatient or residential assisted withdrawal if a service user meets one or more of the following criteria. They:

- drink over 30 units of alcohol per day
- have a score of more than 30 on the SADQ
- have a history of epilepsy, or experience of withdrawal-related seizures or delirium tremens during previous assisted withdrawal programmes
- need concurrent withdrawal from alcohol and benzodiazepines
- regularly drink between 15 and 20 units of alcohol per day and have:
  - significant psychiatric or physical comorbidities (for example, chronic severe depression, psychosis, malnutrition, congestive cardiac failure, unstable angina, chronic liver disease) **or**
  - a significant learning disability or cognitive impairment.

---

[65]For example, psychiatric comorbidity, poor social support or homelessness.

8.3.4.6   Consider a lower threshold for inpatient or residential assisted withdrawal in vulnerable groups, for example, homeless and older people.

8.3.5   Drug regimens for assisted withdrawal

8.3.5.1   When conducting community-based assisted withdrawal programmes, use fixed-dose medication regimens[66].

8.3.5.2   Fixed-dose or symptom-triggered medication regimens[67] can be used in assisted withdrawal programmes in inpatient or residential settings. If a symptom-triggered regimen is used, all staff should be competent in monitoring symptoms effectively and the unit should have sufficient resources to allow them to do so frequently and safely.

8.3.5.3   Prescribe and administer medication for assisted withdrawal within a standard clinical protocol. The preferred medication for assisted withdrawal is a benzodiazepine (chlordiazepoxide or diazepam).

8.3.5.4   In a fixed-dose regimen, titrate the initial dose of medication to the severity of alcohol dependence and/or regular daily level of alcohol consumption. In severe alcohol dependence higher doses will be required to adequately control withdrawal and should be prescribed according to the SPC. Make sure there is adequate supervision if high doses are administered. Gradually reduce the dose of the benzodiazepine over 7–10 days to avoid alcohol withdrawal recurring.

8.3.5.5   When managing alcohol withdrawal in the community, avoid giving people who misuse alcohol large quantities of medication to take home to prevent overdose or diversion[68]. Prescribe for installment dispensing, with no more than 2 days' medication supplied at any time.

8.3.5.6   In a community-based assisted withdrawal programme, monitor the service user every other day during assisted withdrawal. A family member or carer should preferably oversee the administration of medication. Adjust the dose if severe withdrawal symptoms or over-sedation occur.

8.3.5.7   Do not offer clomethiazole for community-based assisted withdrawal because of the risk of overdose and misuse.

8.3.5.8   For service users having assisted withdrawal, particularly those who are more severely alcohol dependent or those undergoing a symptom-triggered regimen, consider using a formal measure of withdrawal symptoms such as the CIWA-Ar.

---

[66]A fixed-dose regimen involves starting treatment with a standard dose, not defined by the level of alcohol withdrawal, and reducing the dose to zero over 7–10 days according to a standard protocol.

[67]A symptom-triggered approach involves tailoring the drug regimen according to the severity of withdrawal and any complications. The service user is monitored on a regular basis and pharmacotherapy only continues as long as the service user is showing withdrawal symptoms.

[68]When the drug is being taken by someone other than for whom it was prescribed.

8.3.5.9   Be aware that benzodiazepine doses may need to be reduced for children and young people[69], older people, and people with liver impairment (see 8.3.5.10).

8.3.5.10   If benzodiazepines are used for people with liver impairment, consider one requiring limited liver metabolism (for example, lorazepam); start with a reduced dose and monitor liver function carefully. Avoid using benzodiazepines for people with severe liver impairment.

8.3.5.11   When managing withdrawal from co-existing benzodiazepine and alcohol dependence increase the dose of benzodiazepine medication used for withdrawal. Calculate the initial daily dose based on the requirements for alcohol withdrawal plus the equivalent regularly used daily dose of benzodiazepine[70]. This is best managed with one benzodiazepine (chlordiazepoxide or diazepam) rather than multiple benzodiazepines. Inpatient withdrawal regimens should last for 2–3 weeks or longer, depending on the severity of co-existing benzodiazepine dependence. When withdrawal is managed in the community, and/or where there is a high level of benzodiazepine dependence, the regimen should last for longer than 3 weeks, tailored to the service user's symptoms and discomfort.

8.3.5.12   For managing unplanned acute alcohol withdrawal and complications including delirium tremens and withdrawal-related seizures, refer to NICE Clinical Guideline 100.

8.3.6   Interventions for moderate and severe alcohol dependence after successful withdrawal

8.3.6.1   After a successful withdrawal for people with moderate and severe alcohol dependence, consider offering acamprosate or oral naltrexone[71] in combination with an individual psychological intervention (cognitive behavioural therapies, behavioural therapies or social network and environment-based therapies) focused specifically on alcohol misuse (see Section 8.3.3).

8.3.6.2   After a successful withdrawal for people with moderate and severe alcohol dependence, consider offering acamprosate or oral naltrexone in combination with behavioural couples therapy to service users who have a regular partner and whose partner is willing to participate in treatment (see Section 8.3.3).

---

[69]At the time of publication of the NICE guideline (February 2011), benzodiazepines did not have UK marketing authorisation for use in children and young people under 18. Informed consent should be obtained and documented.

[70]At the time of publication of the NICE guideline (February 2011), benzodiazepines did not have UK marketing authorisation for this indication or for use in children and young people under 18. Informed consent should be obtained and documented. This should be done in line with normal standards of care for patients who may lack capacity (see www.publicguardian.gov.uk or www.wales.nhs.uk/consent) or in line with normal standards in emergency care.

[71]At the time of publication of the NICE guideline (February 2011), oral naltrexone did not have UK marketing authorisation for this indication. Informed consent should be obtained and documented.

8.3.6.3   After a successful withdrawal for people with moderate and severe alcohol dependence, consider offering disulfiram[72] in combination with a psychological intervention to service users who:

- have a goal of abstinence but for whom acamprosate and oral naltrexone are not suitable, **or**
- prefer disulfiram and understand the relative risks of taking the drug (see 8.3.6.12).

Delivering pharmacological interventions

8.3.6.4   Before starting treatment with acamprosate, oral naltrexone[73] or disulfiram, conduct a comprehensive medical assessment (baseline urea and electrolytes and liver function tests including gamma glutamyl transferase [GGT]). In particular, consider any contraindications or cautions (see the SPC), and discuss these with the service user.

Acamprosate

8.3.6.5   If using acamprosate, start treatment as soon as possible after assisted withdrawal. Usually prescribe at a dose of 1,998 mg (666 mg three times a day) unless the service user weighs less than 60 kg, and then a maximum of 1,332 mg should be prescribed per day. Acamprosate should:

- usually be prescribed for up to 6 months, or longer for those benefiting from the drug who want to continue with it[74]
- be stopped if drinking persists 4–6 weeks after starting the drug.

8.3.6.6   Service users taking acamprosate should stay under supervision, at least monthly, for 6 months, and at reduced but regular intervals if the drug is continued after 6 months. Do not use blood tests routinely, but consider them to monitor for recovery of liver function and as a motivational aid for service users to show improvement.

Naltrexone

8.3.6.7   If using oral naltrexone[75], start treatment after assisted withdrawal. Start prescribing at a dose of 25 mg per day and aim for a maintenance dose of 50 mg per day. Draw the service user's attention to the information card that is issued with oral naltrexone about its impact on opioid-based analgesics. Oral naltrexone should:

- usually be prescribed for up to 6 months, or longer for those benefiting from the drug who want to continue with it
- be stopped if drinking persists 4–6 weeks after starting the drug.

---

[72]All prescribers should consult the SPC for a full description of the contraindications and the special considerations of the use of disulfiram.

[73]At the time of publication of the NICE guideline (February 2011), oral naltrexone did not have UK marketing authorisation for this indication. Informed consent should be obtained and documented.

[74]At the time of publication of the NICE guideline (February 2011), acamprosate did not have UK marketing authorisation for use longer than 12 months. Informed consent should be obtained and documented.

[75]At the time of publication of the NICE guideline (February 2011), oral naltrexone did not have UK marketing authorisation for this indication. Informed consent should be obtained and documented.

8.3.6.8 Service users taking oral naltrexone[75] should stay under supervision, at least monthly, for 6 months, and at reduced but regular intervals if the drug is continued after 6 months. Do not use blood tests routinely, but consider them for older people, for people with obesity, for monitoring recovery of liver function and as a motivational aid for service users to show improvement. If the service user feels unwell advise them to stop the oral naltrexone immediately.

Disulfiram

8.3.6.9 If using disulfiram, start treatment at least 24 hours after the last alcoholic drink consumed. Usually prescribe at a dose of 200 mg per day. For service users who continue to drink, if a dose of 200 mg (taken regularly for at least 1 week) does not cause a sufficiently unpleasant reaction to deter drinking, consider increasing the dose in consultation with the service user.

8.3.6.10 Before starting treatment with disulfiram, test liver function, urea and electrolytes to assess for liver or renal impairment. Check the SPC for warnings and contraindications in pregnancy and in the following conditions: a history of severe mental illness, stroke, heart disease or hypertension.

8.3.6.11 Make sure that service users taking disulfiram:
- stay under supervision, at least every 2 weeks for the first 2 months, then monthly for the following 4 months
- if possible, have a family member or carer, who is properly informed about the use of disulfiram, oversee the administration of the drug
- are medically monitored at least every 6 months after the initial 6 months of treatment and monitoring.

8.3.6.12 Warn service users taking disulfiram, and their families and carers, about:
- the interaction between disulfiram and alcohol (which may also be found in food, perfume, aerosol sprays and so on), the symptoms of which may include flushing, nausea, palpitations and, more seriously, arrhythmias, hypotension and collapse
- the rapid and unpredictable onset of the rare complication of hepatotoxicity; advise service users that if they feel unwell or develop a fever or jaundice that they should stop taking disulfiram and seek urgent medical attention.

Drugs not to be routinely used for the treatment of alcohol misuse

8.3.6.13 Do not use antidepressants (including selective serotonin reuptake inhibitors [SSRIs]) routinely for the treatment of alcohol misuse alone.

8.3.6.14 Do not use gamma-hydroxybutyrate (GHB) for the treatment of alcohol misuse.

8.3.6.15 Benzodiazepines should only be used for managing alcohol withdrawal and not as ongoing treatment for alcohol dependence.

**8.3.7   Special considerations for children and young people
who misuse alcohol**

Assessment and referral of children and young people

8.3.7.1   If alcohol misuse is identified as a potential problem, with potential physical, psychological, educational or social consequences, in children and
young people aged 10–17 years, conduct an initial brief assessment to assess:
- the duration and severity of the alcohol misuse (the standard adult
threshold on the AUDIT for referral and intervention should be lowered
for young people aged 10–16 years because of the more harmful effects
of a given level of alcohol consumption in this population)
- any associated health and social problems
- the potential need for assisted withdrawal.

8.3.7.2   Refer all children and young people aged 10–15 years to a specialist child
and adolescent mental health service (CAMHS) for a comprehensive
assessment of their needs, if their alcohol misuse is associated with physical, psychological, educational and social problems and/or comorbid drug
misuse.

8.3.7.3   When considering referral to CAMHS for young people aged 16–17 years
who misuse alcohol, use the same referral criteria as for adults (see
Section 8.2.2).

8.3.7.4   A comprehensive assessment for children and young people (supported if
possible by additional information from a parent or carer) should assess
multiple areas of need, be structured around a clinical interview using a validated clinical tool (such as the Adolescent Diagnostic Interview [ADI] or the
Teen Addiction Severity Index [T-ASI]), and cover the following areas:
- consumption, dependence features and patterns of drinking
- comorbid substance misuse (consumption and dependence features)
and associated problems
- mental and physical health problems
- peer relationships and social and family functioning
- developmental and cognitive needs, and educational attainment and
attendance
- history of abuse and trauma
- risk to self and others
- readiness to change and belief in the ability to change
- obtaining consent to treatment
- developing a care plan and risk management plan.

Assisted withdrawal in children and young people

8.3.7.5   Offer inpatient care to children and young people aged 10–17 years who
need assisted withdrawal.

8.3.7.6   Base assisted withdrawal for children and young people aged 10–17 years
on the recommendations for adults (see Section 8.3.5) and in NICE

Clinical Guideline 100[76]. Consult the SPC and adjust drug regimens to take account of age, height and body mass, and stage of development of the child or young person[77].

Promoting abstinence and preventing relapse in children and young people

8.3.7.7 For all children and young people aged 10–17 years who misuse alcohol, the goal of treatment should usually be abstinence in the first instance.

8.3.7.8 For children and young people aged 10–17 years who misuse alcohol, offer:
- individual cognitive behavioural therapy for those with limited comorbidities and good social support
- multicomponent programmes (such as multidimensional family therapy, brief strategic family therapy, functional family therapy or multisystemic therapy) for those with significant comorbidities and/or limited social support.

8.3.7.9 After a careful review of the risks and benefits, specialists may consider offering acamprosate[78] or oral naltrexone[79] in combination with cognitive behavioural therapy to young people aged 16 and 17 years who have not engaged with or benefited from a multicomponent treatment programme.

Delivering psychological and psychosocial interventions for children and young people

8.3.7.10 Multidimensional family therapy should usually consist of 12–15 family-focused structured treatment sessions over 12 weeks. There should be a strong emphasis on care coordination and, if necessary, crisis management. As well as family sessions, individual interventions may be provided for both the child or young person and the parents. The intervention should aim to improve:
- alcohol and drug misuse
- the child or young person's educational and social behaviour
- parental well-being and parenting skills
- relationships with the wider social system.

8.3.7.11 Brief strategic family therapy should usually consist of fortnightly meetings over 3 months. It should focus on:
- engaging and supporting the family
- using the support of the wider social and educational system
- identifying maladaptive family interactions
- promoting new and more adaptive family interactions.

---

[76]See NICE (2010b).

[77]If a drug does not have UK marketing authorisation for use in children and young people under 18, informed consent should be obtained and documented.

[78]At the time of publication of the NICE guideline (February 2011), acamprosate did not have UK marketing authorisation for this indication or for use in children and young people under 18. Informed consent should be obtained and documented.

[79]At the time of publication of the NICE guideline (February 2011), oral naltrexone did not have UK marketing authorisation for this indication or for use in children and young people under 18. Informed consent should be obtained and documented.

8.3.7.12   Functional family therapy should be conducted over 3 months by health or social care staff. It should focus on improving interactions within the family, including:

● engaging and motivating the family in treatment (enhancing perception that change is possible, positive reframing and establishing a positive alliance)
● problem solving and behaviour change through parent training and communication training
● promoting generalisation of change in specific behaviours to broader contexts, both within the family and the community (such as schools).

8.3.7.13   Multisystemic therapy should be provided over 3–6 months by a dedicated member of staff with a low caseload (typically between three and six cases). It should:

● focus specifically on problem-solving approaches with the family
● use the resources of peer groups, schools and the wider community.

8.3.8   Interventions for conditions comorbid with alcohol misuse

8.3.8.1   For people who misuse alcohol and have comorbid depression or anxiety disorders, treat the alcohol misuse first as this may lead to significant improvement in the depression and anxiety. If depression or anxiety continues after 3 to 4 weeks of abstinence from alcohol, assess the depression or anxiety and consider referral and treatment in line with the relevant NICE guideline for the particular disorder[80].

8.3.8.2   Refer people who misuse alcohol and have a significant comorbid mental health disorder, and those assessed to be at high risk of suicide, to a psychiatrist to make sure that effective assessment, treatment and risk-management plans are in place.

8.3.8.3   For the treatment of comorbid mental health disorders refer to the relevant NICE guideline for the particular disorder, and:

● for alcohol misuse comorbid with opioid misuse actively treat both conditions; take into account the increased risk of mortality with taking alcohol and opioids together[81]
● for alcohol misuse comorbid with stimulant, cannabis[82] or benzodiazepine misuse actively treat both conditions.

Service users who have been dependent on alcohol will need to be abstinent, or have very significantly reduced their drinking, to benefit from psychological interventions for comorbid mental health disorders.

8.3.8.4   For comorbid alcohol and nicotine dependence, encourage service users to stop smoking and refer to 'Brief interventions and referral for smoking cessation in primary care and other settings' (NICE Public Health Guidance 1).

---

[80]See NICE (2009b) and NICE (2011c).
[81]See NICE (2007a) and NICE (2007b).
[82]See NICE (2007a).

Wernicke-Korsakoff syndrome

8.3.8.5 Follow the recommendations in NICE Clinical Guideline 100[83] on thiamine for people at high risk of developing, or with suspected, Wernicke's encephalopathy. In addition, offer parenteral thiamine followed by oral thiamine to prevent Wernicke-Korsakoff syndrome in people who are entering planned assisted alcohol withdrawal in specialist inpatient alcohol services or prison settings and who are malnourished or at risk of malnourishment (for example, people who are homeless) or have decompensated liver disease.

8.3.8.6 For people with Wernicke-Korsakoff syndrome, offer long-term placement in:
- supported independent living for those with mild cognitive impairment
- supported 24-hour care for those with moderate or severe cognitive impairment.

In both settings the environment should be adapted for people with cognitive impairment and support should be provided to help service users maintain abstinence from alcohol.

8.4   RESEARCH RECOMMENDATIONS

8.4.1.1 For which service users who are moderately and severely dependent on alcohol is an assertive community treatment model a clinically and cost-effective intervention compared with standard care?

This question should be answered using a randomised controlled design in which participants are stratified for severity and complexity of presenting problems. It should report short- and medium-term outcomes (including cost-effectiveness outcomes) of at least 18 months' duration. Particular attention should be paid to the reproducibility of the treatment model and training and supervision of those providing the intervention to ensure that the results are robust and generalisable. The outcomes chosen should reflect both observer and service user-rated assessments of improvement (including personal and social functioning) and the acceptability of the intervention. The study needs to be large enough to determine the presence or absence of clinically important effects, and mediators and moderators of response should be investigated.

Why this is important

Many people, in particular those with severe problems and complex comorbidities, do not benefit from treatment and/or lose contact with services. This leads to poor outcomes and wastes resources. Assertive community treatment models have been shown to be effective in retaining people in treatment in those with serious mental illness who misuse alcohol and drugs but the evidence for an impact on outcomes is not proven. A number of small pilot studies suggest that an assertive community approach can bring benefit in both service retention and clinical outcomes in alcohol misuse. Given the high morbidity and mortality associated with chronic severe

---

[83]See NICE (2010b).

alcohol dependence the results of this study will have important implications for the structure and provision of alcohol services in the NHS.

8.4.1.2   What methods are most effective for assessing and diagnosing the presence and severity of alcohol misuse in children and young people?

This question should be answered in a programme of research that uses a cross-sectional cohort design testing:

- the sensitivity and specificity of a purpose-designed suite of screening and case identification measures of alcohol misuse against a diagnostic gold standard (DSM–IV or ICD–10)
- the reliability and validity of a purpose-designed suite in characterising the nature and the severity of the alcohol misuse in children and young people and their predictive validity in identifying the most effective treatment when compared with current best practice.

Particular attention should be paid to the feasibility of the measures in routine care and the training required to obtain satisfactory levels of accuracy and predictive validity. The programme needs to be large enough to encompass the age range (10 to 17 years) and the comorbidity that often accompanies alcohol misuse in children and young people.

Why this is important

Alcohol misuse is an increasingly common problem in children and young people. However, diagnostic instruments are poorly developed or not available for children and young people. In adults there is a range of diagnostic and assessment tools (with reasonable sensitivity and specificity, and reliability and validity) that are recommended for routine use in the NHS to both assess the severity of the alcohol misuse and to guide treatment decisions. No similar well-developed measures exist for children and young people, with the result that problems are missed and/or inappropriate treatment is offered. The results of this study will have important implications for the identification and the provision of effective treatment in the NHS for children and young people with alcohol-related problems.

8.4.1.3   For people with moderate and severe alcohol dependence who have significant comorbid problems, is an intensive residential rehabilitation programme clinically and cost effective when compared with intensive community-based care?

This question should be answered using a prospective cohort study of all people who have moderate and severe alcohol dependence entering residential and intensive community rehabilitation programmes in a purposive sample of alcohol treatment services in the UK. It should report short- and medium-term outcomes (including cost-effectiveness outcomes) of at least 18 months' duration. Particular attention should be paid to the characterisation of the treatment environment and the nature of the interventions provided to inform the analysis of moderators and mediators of treatment effect. The outcomes chosen should reflect both observer and service user-rated assessments of improvement (including personal and social functioning) and the acceptability of the intervention. The study needs to be large enough to determine the presence or absence of clinically important effects, and mediators and moderators of response should be investigated. A cohort study has been chosen as the most appropriate design because as previous studies in this area that have attempted to randomise participants to residential or community care have been unable to recruit clinically representative populations.

Why this is important
Many people, in particular those with severe problems and complex comorbidities, do not benefit from treatment and/or lose contact with services. One common approach is to offer intensive residential rehabilitation and current policy favours this. However, the research on the effectiveness of residential rehabilitation is uncertain with a suggestion that intensive community services may be as effective. The interpretation of this research is limited by the fact that many of the more severely ill people are not entered into the clinical trials because some clinicians are unsure of the community setting. However, clinical opinion is divided on the benefits of residential rehabilitation, with some suggesting that those who benefit are a motivated and self-selected group who may do just as well with intensive community treatment, which is currently limited in availability. Given the costs associated with residential treatment and the uncertainty about outcomes, the results of this study will have important implications for the cost effectiveness and provision of alcohol services in the NHS.

8.4.1.4   Is contingency management effective in reducing alcohol consumption in people who misuse alcohol compared with standard care?
This question should be answered using a randomised controlled design that reports short-and medium-term outcomes (including cost-effectiveness outcomes) of at least 18 months' duration. Particular attention should be paid to the reproducibility of the treatment model and the training and supervision of those providing the intervention to ensure that the results are robust and generalisable. The outcomes chosen should reflect both observer and service user-rated assessments of improvement and the acceptability of the intervention. The study needs to be large enough to determine the presence or absence of clinically important effects, and mediators and moderators of response should be investigated.

Why this is important
Psychological interventions are an important therapeutic option for people with alcohol related problems. However, even with the most effective current treatment (for example, cognitive behavioural therapies and social network and environment-based therapies), the effects are modest at best and the treatments are not effective for everyone. Contingency management has a considerable and compelling evidence base in the treatment of substance misuse (for example, opioid misuse), but there is only a limited, if promising, evidence base for contingency management in the treatment of alcohol-related problems. The results of this research will have important implications for the provision of psychological treatment for alcohol misuse in the NHS.

8.4.1.5   Is acupuncture effective in reducing alcohol consumption compared with standard care?

This question should be answered using a randomised controlled design that reports short- and medium-term outcomes (including cost-effectiveness outcomes) of at least 12 months' duration. Particular attention should be paid to the reproducibility of the treatment model and training and supervision of those providing the intervention to ensure that the results are robust and generalisable. The outcomes chosen should reflect both observer and service user-rated assessments of improvement and the acceptability of the treatment. The study needs to be large enough to determine the presence or absence of clinically important effects, and mediators and moderators of response should be investigated.

Why this is important
Non-pharmacological treatments are an important therapeutic option for people with alcohol-related problems. There is an evidence base for acupuncture in reducing craving but not alcohol consumption in a number of small trials. The evidence for pharmacological treatments (for example, acamprosate or naltrexone) and psychological treatments (for example, cognitive behavioural therapies and social network and environment-based therapies) is modest at best and the treatments are not effective for everyone. Anecdotal evidence suggests that acupuncture, like psychological treatment, is valued by service users both in alcohol misuse and substance misuse services (although the evidence base for effectiveness is weak). The results of this study will have important implications for increased treatment choice in the NHS for people who misuse alcohol.

8.4.1.6   For people with alcohol dependence, which medication is most likely to improve adherence and thereby promote abstinence and prevent relapse?
This question should be answered by: (a) an initial development phase in which a series of qualitative and quantitative reasons for non-adherence/discontinuing drugs used in the treatment of alcohol are explored; (b) a series of pilot trials of novel interventions developed to address the problems identified in (a) undertaken to support the design of a series of definitive trials; (c) a (series of) definitive trial(s) of the interventions that were successfully piloted in (b) using a randomised controlled design that reports short-term (for example, 3 months) and longer-term (for example, 18 months) outcomes. The outcomes chosen should reflect both observer and service user-rated assessments of improvement and the acceptability of the intervention. Each individual study needs to be large enough to determine the presence or absence of clinically important effects, and mediators and moderators of response should be investigated.

Why this is important
Rates of attrition in trials of drugs to promote abstinence and prevent relapse in alcohol dependence are high (often over 65%), yet despite this the interventions are still clinically and cost effective. Retaining more service users in treatment could further significantly improve outcomes for people who misuse alcohol and ensure increased effectiveness in the use of health service resources. The outcome of these studies may also help improve clinical confidence in the use of effective medications (such as acamprosate and naltrexone), which despite their cost effectiveness are currently offered to only a minority of eligible NHS service users. Overall, the results of these studies will have important implications for the provision of pharmacological treatment in the NHS for alcohol misuse.

9   APPENDICES

- 16d: Psychological interventions study characteristics table
- 16e: Pharmacological interventions study characteristics table

Appendix 17: Clinical evidence forest plots   On CD

- 17a: Organisation of care forest plots
- 17b: Rehabilitation forest plots
- 17c: Psychological interventions forest plots
- 17d: Pharmacological interventions forest plots

Appendix 18: GRADE evidence profiles   On CD

- 18a: Organisation of care GRADE tables
- 18b: Rehabilitation GRADE tables
- 18c: Psychological interventions GRADE tables
- 18d: Pharmacological interventions GRADE tables

Appendix 19: Evidence tables for economic studies   On CD

APPENDIX 1:
SCOPE FOR THE DEVELOPMENT OF THE
CLINICAL GUIDELINE

1   GUIDELINE TITLE

Alcohol dependence and harmful use: diagnosis, assessment and management of harmful drinking and alcohol dependence[84]

1.1   SHORT TITLE

Alcohol dependence and harmful alcohol use

2   BACKGROUND

a) The National Institute for Health and Clinical Excellence ('NICE' or 'the Institute') has commissioned the National Collaborating Centre for Mental Health to develop a clinical guideline on alcohol dependence and harmful alcohol use for use in the NHS in England and Wales. This follows referral of the topic by the Department of Health. The guideline will provide recommendations for good practice that are based on the best available evidence of clinical and cost effectiveness.

b) NICE clinical guidelines support the implementation of National Service Frameworks (NSFs) in those aspects of care where a Framework has been published. The statements in each NSF reflect the evidence that was used at the time the Framework was prepared. The clinical guidelines and technology appraisals published by NICE after an NSF has been issued have the effect of updating the Framework.

c) NICE clinical guidelines support the role of healthcare professionals in providing care in partnership with patients, taking account of their individual needs and preferences, and ensuring that patients (and their carers and families, if appropriate) can make informed decisions about their care and treatment.

---

[84]The guideline title changed to 'Alcohol-use disorders: diagnosis, assessment and management of harmful drinking and alcohol dependence' during the course of development.

3   **CLINICAL NEED FOR THE GUIDELINE**

a) There are two main sets of diagnostic criteria in current use, the *International Classification of Mental and Behavioural Disorders* tenth Revision (ICD–10) and the *Diagnostic and Statistical Manual of Mental Disorders* fourth edition (DSM–IV). The ICD–10 definition of alcohol dependence (alcohol dependence syndrome) makes reference to a cluster of physiological, behavioural, and cognitive phenomena in which the use of alcohol takes a much higher priority than other behaviours. The DSM–IV defines a person with alcohol dependence as someone who continues the use of alcohol despite significant alcohol-related problems. In terms of harmful alcohol use, the ICD–10 defines 'harmful use' as a pattern of drinking that causes damage to physical and mental health.
b) Psychiatric disorders and problems associated with alcohol dependence and harmful alcohol use include: depression, anxiety, personality disorders, post-traumatic stress disorder, drug misuse, self-harm, suicide and brain damage. Alcohol use disorders are also associated with a wide range of physical problems, including liver disease, various cancers, heart disease and stroke.
c) The Alcohol Needs Assessment Research Project estimated that 38% of men and 16% of women aged between 16 and 64 have an alcohol-use disorder, and that 6% of men and 2% of women have alcohol dependence. There is a lack of reliable UK data on prevalence rates of alcohol use disorders in children.

4   **THE GUIDELINE**

a) The guideline development process is described in detail in two publications that are available from the NICE website (see 'Further information'). 'The guideline development process: an overview for stakeholders, the public and the NHS' describes how organisations can become involved in the development of a guideline. 'The guidelines manual' provides advice on the technical aspects of guideline development.
d) This scope defines what this guideline will (and will not) examine, and what the guideline developers will consider. The scope is based on a referral from the Department of Health.
e) The areas that will be addressed by the guideline are described in the following sections.

4.1   **POPULATION**

4.1.1   **Groups that will be covered**

a) Young people (10 years and older) and adults with a diagnosis of alcohol dependence or harmful alcohol use.

4.1.2   Groups that will not be covered

a) Children younger than 10 years.
b) Pregnant women.

4.2   HEALTHCARE SETTING

a) Care provided by primary, community and secondary healthcare and social care
    professionals who have direct contact with, and make decisions concerning, the
    care of young people and adults with alcohol dependence or harmful alcohol use.
    This will include:
    ● care in general practice
    ● community- and residential-based care, including inpatient treatment and
      rehabilitation
    ● the primary/secondary care interface
    ● transition through the range of healthcare services from childhood to older
      adulthood
    ● the criminal justice system, including prison healthcare.
b) This is a guideline for alcohol services funded by or provided for the NHS. It will
    make recommendations for services provided within the NHS, social services, the
    independent sector and non-statutory services.

4.3   CLINICAL MANAGEMENT

4.3.1   Areas that will be covered by the guideline

b) Definitions of alcohol dependence and harmful alcohol use according to the main
    diagnostic classification systems (ICD–10 and DSM–IV).
c) Early identification of alcohol dependence or harmful alcohol use in people in at-
    risk populations, in particular treatment-seeking populations, and identification of
    factors that should lead to investigation into the possibility of alcohol dependence
    or harmful alcohol use (please refer also to the prevention and clinical manage-
    ment guidance currently under development, see section 5).
d) Identifying people with alcohol dependence and harmful alcohol use in clinical
    practice, including the sensitivity and specificity of different methods, and thresh-
    olds.
e) Assessment, including identification and management of risk, and assessment of
    severity of alcohol-related problems, dependence and alcohol withdrawal.
f) Development of appropriate care pathways that support the integration of other
    NICE guidance on the management, treatment and aftercare of alcohol misuse.
g) The range of care routinely available in the NHS.

h) Pharmacological interventions, for example, initiation and duration of treatment, management of side effects and discontinuation. Specific pharmacological treatments considered will include:
- opioid antagonists (naltrexone and nalmefene)
- acamprosate
- disulfiram
- topiramate
- baclofen
- chlordiazepoxide
- serotogenic agents (selective serotonin reuptake inhibitors and serotonin-3 receptor antagonist, ondansetron).

i) Note that guideline recommendations will normally fall within licensed indications; exceptionally, and only if clearly supported by evidence, use outside a licensed indication may be recommended. The guideline will assume that prescribers will use a drug's SPC to inform their decisions for individual patients.

j) Common psychological and psychosocial interventions currently provided, for example, 12-step programmes, cognitive behavioural therapy, motivational enhancement therapy, relapse prevention, contingency management and community reinforcement approach.

k) Low-intensity psychological interventions, for example, referral to Alcoholics Anonymous and guided self-help.

l) Combined pharmacological and psychological/psychosocial treatments.

m) Management of alcohol withdrawal in community and residential settings.

n) Management of common mental health problems and drug misuse in the context of alcohol dependence, if this differs from their management alone.

o) Prevention and management of neuropsychiatric complications of alcohol dependence or harmful alcohol use including:
- alcohol-related brain damage
- Wernicke–Korsakoff syndrome.

p) Sensitivity to different beliefs and attitudes of people of different genders, races and cultures, and issues of social exclusion.

q) The role of family and carers in the treatment and support of people with alcohol dependence and harmful alcohol use (with consideration of choice, consent and help), and support that may be needed by family and carers (such as conjoint marital therapy and family therapy).

r) The Guideline Development Group will consider making recommendations on complementary interventions or approaches to care relevant to alcohol dependence and harmful alcohol use.

s) The Guideline Development Group will take reasonable steps to identify ineffective interventions and approaches to care. If robust and credible recommendations for re-positioning the intervention for optimal use, or changing the approach to care to make more efficient use of resources, can be made, they will be clearly stated. If the resources released are substantial, consideration will be given to listing such recommendations in the 'Key priorities for implementation' section of the guideline.

4.3.2   Areas that will not be covered by the guideline

a) Treatments not normally made available by the NHS.
b) The separate management of comorbid conditions.
c) The management of acute alcohol withdrawal in the emergency department and general medical and surgical settings. This will be covered in 'Alcohol-use disorders in adults and young people: clinical management' (publication expected May 2010)[85].
d) The prevention and management of Wernicke's encephalopathy. This will be covered in 'Alcohol-use disorders in adults and young people: clinical management' (publication expected May 2010)[85].

4.4   STATUS

4.4.1   Scope

● This is the final scope.

4.4.2   Guideline

● The development of the guideline recommendations will begin in March 2009.

5   FURTHER INFORMATION

● The guideline development process is described in:
  – 'The guideline development process: an overview for stakeholders, the public and the NHS'
  – 'The guidelines manual'.
These are available from the NICE website (www.nice.org.uk/guidelinesmanual). Information on the progress of the guideline will also be available from the website.

---

[85]This guideline was published as 'Alcohol-use disorders: diagnosis and clinical management of alcohol-related physical complications' (NICE, 2010b).

APPENDIX 2:
DECLARATIONS OF INTERESTS BY GUIDELINE DEVELOPMENT GROUP MEMBERS

With a range of practical experience relevant to alcohol dependence in the GDG, members were appointed because of their understanding and expertise in healthcare for people with alcohol dependence and support for their families and carers, including: scientific issues; health research; the delivery and receipt of healthcare, along with the work of the healthcare industry; and the role of professional organisations and organisations for people with alcohol dependence and their families and carers.

To minimise and manage any potential conflicts of interest, and to avoid any public concern that commercial or other financial interests have affected the work of the GDG and influenced guidance, members of the GDG must declare as a matter of public record any interests held by themselves or their families which fall under specified categories (see below). These categories include any relationships they have with the healthcare industries, professional organisations and organisations for people with alcohol dependence and their families and carers.

Individuals invited to join the GDG were asked to declare their interests before being appointed. To allow the management of any potential conflicts of interest that might arise during the development of the guideline, GDG members were also asked to declare their interests at each GDG meeting throughout the guideline development process. The interests of all the members of the GDG are listed below, including interests declared prior to appointment and during the guideline development process.

CATEGORIES OF INTEREST

- **Paid employment**
- **Personal pecuniary interest**: financial payments or other benefits from either the manufacturer or the owner of the product or service under consideration in this guideline, or the industry or sector from which the product or service comes. This includes holding a directorship, or other paid position; carrying out consultancy or fee paid work; having shareholdings or other beneficial interests; receiving expenses and hospitality over and above what would be reasonably expected to attend meetings and conferences.
- **Personal family interest:** financial payments or other benefits from the healthcare industry that were received by a member of your family.
- **Non-personal pecuniary interest:** financial payments or other benefits received by the GDG member's organisation or department, but where the GDG member has not personally received payment, including fellowships and other support

provided by the healthcare industry. This includes a grant or fellowship or other payment to sponsor a post, or contribute to the running costs of the department; commissioning of research or other work; contracts with, or grants from, NICE.

- **Personal non-pecuniary interest:** these include, but are not limited to, clear opinions or public statements you have made about alcohol dependence, holding office in a professional organisation or advocacy group with a direct interest in alcohol dependence, other reputational risks relevant to alcohol dependence.

Declarations of interest	
Professor Colin Drummond – Chair, Guideline Development Group	
Employment	Professor of Addiction Psychiatry and Honorary Consultant Addiction Psychiatrist, National Addiction Centre, Institute of Psychiatry, King's College London, and South London and Maudsley Foundation NHS Trust
Personal pecuniary interest	None
Personal family interest	None
Non-personal pecuniary interest	In receipt of research grants on alcohol research from the Medical Research Council, the European Commission, the Department of Health, the Home Office, the Scottish Government, and WHO (declared December 2008).
	A member of the WHO Expert Committee on Alcohol Problems and received travel and subsistence while working for WHO (declared December 2008).
	I have received an educational grant from Alkermes Inc. (manufacturers of Vivitrol) to the value of £5,000 in 2008 which is held at the Institute of Psychiatry (declared December 2008).
Personal non-pecuniary interest	None
Mr Adrian Brown	
Employment	Alcohol Nurse Specialist, Addiction Services Central and North West London NHS Foundation Trust, and St Mary's Hospital, Imperial College
Personal pecuniary interest	Consultancy- attending focus groups of professionals and acting as 'expert' on site at conference presentation. Archimedes Pharma- educational material for Wernicke-Korsakoff

	and Pabrinex. Received £250 + £550 and travel for two events (declared July 2009).
Personal family interest	None
Non-personal pecuniary interest	None
Personal non-pecuniary interest	None
Professor Alex Copello	
Employment	Professor of Addiction Research, University of Birmingham, and Consultant Clinical Psychologist, Addiction Services, Birmingham & Solihull Mental Health Foundation NHS Trust
Personal pecuniary interest	None
Personal family interest	None
Non-personal pecuniary interest	None
Personal non-pecuniary interest	None
Dr Edward Day	
Employment	Senior Lecturer and Consultant in Addiction Psychiatry, University of Birmingham Birmingham & Solihull Mental Health NHS Foundation Trust
Personal pecuniary interest	None
Personal family interest	None
Non-personal pecuniary interest	None
Personal non-pecuniary interest	I am a principal investigator on two grants in the substance misuse field (ACTAS study and COMBAT studies). I have published papers on alcohol detoxification, management of Wernicke-Korsakoff syndrome and liver transplantation for alcoholic liver disease (declared March 2009).
Mr John Dervan	
Employment	Lay member and retired Alcohol Treatment Agency CEO
Personal pecuniary interest	None
Personal family interest	None
Non-personal pecuniary interest	None

Personal non-pecuniary interest	Trustee, CASA Alcohol Services (declared January 2009).
Ms Jan Fry	
Employment	Carer representative and voluntary sector consultant
Personal pecuniary interest	None
Personal family interest	None
Non-personal pecuniary interest	None
Personal non-pecuniary interest	None
Mr Brendan Georgeson	
Employment	Treatment Coordinator, Walsingham House, Bristol
Personal pecuniary interest	None
Personal family interest	None
Non-personal pecuniary interest	None
Personal non-pecuniary interest	Individual member of The Federation of Drug and Alcohol Professionals (declared January 2009). Member of the Society for the Study of Addiction (declared January 2009). Associate Member of the Institute of Healthcare Management (declared January 2009). Trustee of Positive Images, a charity that uses film production to produce mentoring/training resources (declared April 2010).
Dr Eilish Gilvarry	
Employment	Consultant Psychiatrist (with specialist interest in adolescent addictions), and Assistant Medical Director, Northumberland, Tyne & Wear NHS Foundation Trust
Personal pecuniary interest	None
Personal family interest	None
Non-personal pecuniary interest	None
Personal non-pecuniary interest	None

Ms Jayne Gosnall	
Employment	Service User Representative and Treasurer of Salford Drug and Alcohol Forum
Personal pecuniary interest	None
Personal family interest	None
Non-personal pecuniary interest	None
Personal non-pecuniary interest	None
Dr Linda Harris	
Employment	Clinical Director, Wakefield Integrated Substance Misuse Services and Director, RCGP Substance Misuse Unit
Personal pecuniary interest	None
Personal family interest	None
Non-personal pecuniary interest	In receipt of an educational grant from Schering Plough to support clinical leadership development support across the health and social care stakeholder groups working in the Wakefield Integrated Substance Misuse Service. This is being delivered in the full knowledge of the local PCT and is being conducted within ABPI guidance (declared January 2009). A grant has been deployed to fund an independent management consultancy firm called Healthskills Consulting Ltd, who have supported leadership development and O & D of the drug misuse treatment system. ABPI rules obeyed and PCT aware (declared March 2009). Over the years RCGP SMU has been in receipt of educational grants to support special substance misuse workforce development and training standards (declared March 2009).
Personal non-pecuniary interest	None
Dr John Lewis (Co-opted specialist paediatric adviser)	
Employment	Consultant Community Paediatrician, Royal Cornwall Hospitals Trust

Personal pecuniary interest	None
Personal family interest	None
Non-personal pecuniary interest	None
Personal non-pecuniary interest	None
Professor Anne Lingford-Hughes	
Employment	Professor of Addiction Biology, Imperial College London and Honorary Consultant, Central North West London NHS Foundation Trust
Personal pecuniary interest	Bristol Myers Squibb, member of Core Faculty; current though no monies in last 12 months (declared January 2009).
	Janssen-Cilag-paid speaker: educational event, my talk on dual disorder was not about promoting one of their products (declared January 2009).
	CINP psychopharmacology certificate – two lectures on psychopharmacology of alcohol abuse: sponsored by Servier (declared January 2010).
	Meeting organised by pharmacology special interest group – presentation on comorbidity and managing substance misuse (declared March 2010).
	Lecturing on an educational programme about alcoholism for Pfizer (declared September 2010).
Personal family interest	None
Non-personal pecuniary interest	NIHR grant to study pharmacology in alcohol detox (declared July 2009).
Personal non-pecuniary interest	Co-ordinated British Association for Psychopharmacology guidelines which covered treatment of alcohol dependence. Published 2004 (declared January 2009).
	Leading revision of BAP guidelines in substance misuse and addiction (declared November 2009).
	Putting in a grant for an RCT involving baclofen (declared November 2009).

	Coordinating update of BAP guidelines in addiction (declared January 2010).
	Shortlisted for HTA grant for RCT of baclofen in alcohol dependence (declared January 2010).
	A meeting with Neurosearch (declared September 2010).
Mr Trevor McCarthy	
Employment	Independent Addictions Consultant and Trainer
Personal pecuniary interest	15 Healthcare - presenting at conferences, delivering training and national policy work at the National Treatment Agency for Substance Misuse (declared September 2010).
Personal family interest	None
Non-personal pecuniary interest	None
Personal non-pecuniary interest	Since September 2008 my employment has been as a self-employed consultant specialising particularly in work in the alcohol field. In this capacity I have worked with a voluntary sector provider; for a Drug & Alcohol Action Team and for Alcohol Concern, delivering services to PCTs and to the Regional Office on behalf of the Department of Health (declared January 2009).
	My previous role included managing the production of the *Review of effectiveness of treatment for alcohol problems* which includes the research evidence relevant to this guideline. I was also involved in the development of *Models of Care for Alcohol Misusers* (declared January 2009).
	I have also given presentations at conferences and other events which have included comment on the issues under consideration. The bulk of my employment experience has been gained in the non-statutory sector managing the delivery of community alcohol and drug treatment services (declared January 2009).

	It could be that some might interpret such activities as my having compromised my views and objectivity. My own view is that this experience qualifies me to make an application to the Institute and I do not believe that my past work could reasonably have been construed as contentious or biased (declared January 2009).
Dr Marsha Morgan	
Employment	Reader in Medicine and Honorary Consultant Physician, University of London Medical School
Personal pecuniary interest	I am a member of the Advisory board of the Institute of Alcohol Studies. I receive an annual stipend of £1,500 which I contribute to my University Research Account (declared January 2009).
	I have taken part in symposia both in the UK and abroad on the Pharmacotherapy of Alcohol Dependence. On some occasions my travel and subsistence have been covered by one of the Pharmaceutical companies but I have not accepted lecture fees (declared January 2009).
Personal family interest	None
Non-personal pecuniary interest	Between eight and 10 years ago I undertook pharmacotherapeutic trials in alcohol dependent patients for Du Pont Pharmaceuticals and Lipha Pharmaceuticals. Per capita fees were paid for recruited patients to the Royal Free Hospital Medical School for whom I worked (declared January 2009).
Personal non-pecuniary interest	None
Mrs Stephenie Noble	
Employment	Registered Manager/Nursing Manager, Broadway Lodge
Personal pecuniary interest	None
Personal family interest	None
Non-personal pecuniary interest	None
Personal non-pecuniary interest	None

Mr Tom Phillips	
Employment	Consultant Nurse in Addiction, Humber NHS Foundation Trust
Personal pecuniary interest	None
Personal family interest	None
Non-personal pecuniary interest	None
Personal non-pecuniary interest	PI on two projects, as stated in application for post. Both explore screening and brief interventions. SIPS trial and AESOPS. SIPS trial DH funded and AESOPS trial HTA funded (declared April 2009).
	NIHR – Clinical Doctoral Research Fellowship in area of alcohol research from January 2010 to 2015 (declared October 2009).
Dr Pamela Roberts	
Employment	Consultant Clinical and Forensic Psychologist, Cardiff Addictions Unit
Personal pecuniary interest	Small grant received from AERC with regard to small scale project studying the relationship between Pabrinex and cognitive functioning (declared March 2010).
Personal family interest	None
Non-personal pecuniary interest	None
Personal non-pecuniary interest	Welsh Representative for the BPS Faculty of Addiction (declared April 2010).
Dr Julia Sinclair	
Employment	Senior Lecturer in Psychiatry, University of Southampton and Honorary Consultant in Addiction Psychiatry, Hampshire Partnership NHS Foundation Trust
Personal pecuniary interest	None
Personal family interest	My husband, a psychopharmacologist has consulted for a number of companies who make treatments for anxiety or depression. His work does not include any treatments for alcohol-use disorders (declared January 2009).

Non-personal pecuniary interest	Part of research project funded by MRC piloting Assertive Community Treatment in alcohol dependence (declared March 2009).
Personal non-pecuniary interest	Gave a talk on non-promotional training course run by the 'Lundbeck Institute' on complex depression. Talk was on suicide and comorbidity (including alcohol) (declared June 2009).

National Collaborating Centre for Mental Health Staff

Professor Stephen Pilling – Facilitator, Guideline Development Group

Employment	Director, National Collaborating Centre for Mental Health; Professor of Clinical Psychology and Clinical Effectiveness; Director, Centre for Outcomes Research and Effectiveness, University College London.
Personal pecuniary interest	Funding of £1,200,000 p.a. from NICE to develop clinical guidelines (declared December 2008). Funding from British Psychological Society (2005 to 2011) £6,000,000 to establish the Clinical Effectiveness Programme at Centre for Outcomes Research and Effectiveness, UCL; with Professor P Fonagy and Professor S. Michie (declared December 2008).
Personal family interest	None
Non-personal pecuniary interest	RCT to evaluate multi-systemic therapy with Professor Peter Fonagy; Department of Health funding of £1,000,000 (2008 to 2012) (declared December 2008). RCT to evaluate collaborative care for depression; with Professor D. Richards; Medical Research Council Funding of £2,200,000 (2008 to 2012) (declared December 2008). Developing a UK Evidence Base for Contingency Management in Addiction with Professor J Strang; National Institute of Health Research Grant of £2,035,042 (2009 to 2013) (declared January 2009).
Personal non-pecuniary interest	None

Mr Matthew Dyer	
Employment	Health Economist, National Collaborating Centre for Mental Health
Personal pecuniary interest	None
Personal family interest	None
Non-personal pecuniary interest	None
Personal non-pecuniary interest	None
Ms Esther Flanagan	
Employment	Guideline Development Manager, National Collaborating Centre for Mental Health
Personal pecuniary interest	None
Personal family interest	None
Non-personal pecuniary interest	None
Personal non-pecuniary interest	None
Ms Naomi Glover	
Employment	Research Assistant, National Collaborating Centre for Mental Health
Personal pecuniary interest	None
Personal family interest	None
Non-personal pecuniary interest	None
Personal non-pecuniary interest	None
Dr Ifigeneia Mavranezouli	
Employment	Senior Health Economist, National Collaborating Centre for Mental Health
Personal pecuniary interest	None
Personal family interest	None
Non-personal pecuniary interest	None
Personal non-pecuniary interest	None
Dr Suffiya Omarjee	
Employment	Health Economist, National Collaborating Centre for Mental Health
Personal pecuniary interest	None

Personal family interest	None
Non-personal pecuniary interest	None
Personal non-pecuniary interest	None
Mrs Kate Satrettin	
Employment	Guideline Development Manager, National Collaborating Centre for Mental Health
Personal pecuniary interest	None
Personal family interest	None
Non-personal pecuniary interest	None
Personal non-pecuniary interest	None
Mr Rob Saunders	
Employment	Research Assistant, National Collaborating Centre for Mental Health
Personal pecuniary interest	None
Personal family interest	None
Non-personal pecuniary interest	None
Personal non-pecuniary interest	None
Ms Laura Shields	
Employment	Research Assistant, National Collaborating Centre for Mental Health
Personal pecuniary interest	None
Personal family interest	None
Non-personal pecuniary interest	None
Personal non-pecuniary interest	None
Ms Sarah Stockton	
Employment	Senior Information Scientist, National Collaborating Centre for Mental Health
Personal pecuniary interest	None
Personal family interest	None
Non-personal pecuniary interest	None
Personal non-pecuniary interest	None
Personal non-pecuniary interest	None

Dr Clare Taylor	
Employment	Senior Editor, National Collaborating Centre for Mental Health
Personal pecuniary interest	None
Personal family interest	None
Non-personal pecuniary interest	None
Personal non-pecuniary interest	None
Dr Amina Udechuku	
Employment	Systematic Reviewer, National Collaborating Centre for Mental Health
Personal pecuniary interest	None
Personal family interest	None
Non-personal pecuniary interest	None
Personal non-pecuniary interest	None

APPENDIX 3:
SPECIAL ADVISORS TO THE GUIDELINE
DEVELOPMENT GROUP

Dr John Lewis, Royal Cornwall Hospitals Trust

APPENDIX 4:

ALCOHOL ASSESSMENT TOOLS

The following assessment tools were referred to:
- Alcohol Problems Questionnaire (page 486)
- Alcohol Use Disorders Identification Test (AUDIT) (page 488)
- Clinical Institute Withdrawal Assessment of Alcohol Scale, Revised (CIWA-Ar) (page 490)
- The Leeds Dependence Questionnaire (page 491)
- Severity of Alcohol Dependence Questionnaire (SADQ) (page 493)

ALCOHOL PROBLEMS QUESTIONNAIRE

NAME:_____ DATE:_____

We would like to find out if you have experienced any of the difficulties which other people with alcohol problems sometimes complain of.
Below you will find a list of questions which we would like you to answer.
Read each box carefully and answer either YES or NO by putting a TICK in the appropriate box (e.g. YES)

	Yes	No
IN THE LAST SIX MONTHS	Yes	No
	✓	

PLEASE ANSWER ALL THE QUESTIONS WHICH APPLY TO YOU
ALL THE QUESTIONS APPLY TO YOUR EXPERIENCES IN THE LAST SIX MONTHS

---

1. Have you tended to drink on your own more than you used to? . . . .
2. Have you worried about meeting your friends again the day after a drinking session . . . .
3. Have you spent more time with drinking friends than other kinds of friends? . . . .
4. Have your friends criticised you for drinking too much? . . . .
5. Have you had any debts? . . . .
6. Have you pawned any of your belongings to buy alcohol? . . . .
7. Do you find yourself making excuses about money? . . . .
8. Have you been caught out lying about money? . . . .
9. Have you been in trouble with the police due to your drinking? . . . .
10. Have you lost your driving licence for drinking and driving? . . . .
11. Have you been in prison? . . . .
12. Have you been physically sick after drinking? . . . .
13. Have you had diarrhoea after a drinking session? . . . .
14. Have you had pains in your stomach after a drinking session? . . . .
15. Have you had pins and needles in your fingers or toes? . . . .
16. Have you had any accidents, needing hospital treatment after drinking? . . . .
17. Have you lost any weight? . . . .
18. Have you been neglecting yourself physically? . . . .
19. Have you failed to wash for several days at a time? . . . .
20. Have you felt depressed for more than a week? . . . .
21. Have you felt so depressed that you have felt like doing away with yourself? . . . . . .
22. Have you given up any hobbies you once enjoyed because of drinking? . . . .
23. Do you find it hard to get the same enjoyment from your usual interests? . . . .

PLEASE MAKE SURE YOU HAVE ANSWERED ALL THE QUESTIONS WHICH APPLY TO YOU PLEASE TURN PAGE

IF YOU HAVE NOT MARRIED, MISS OUT QUESTIONS 24–32, GO TO QUESTION 33.
(These questions apply to you if you have lived with your spouse or partner during the last six months)

IN THE LAST SIX MONTHS   Yes   No

24. Has your spouse complained of your drinking? . . . .

25. Has your spouse tried to stop you from having a drink? . . . .

26. Has he/she refused to talk to you because you have been drinking? . . . .

27. Has he/she threatened to leave you because of your drinking? . . . .

28. Has he/she had to put you to bed after you have been drinking? . . . .

29. Have you shouted at him/her when you have been drinking? . . . .

30. Have you injured him/her after you have been drinking? . . . .

31. Have you been legally separated from your spouse? . . . .

32. Has he/she refused to have sex with you because of drinking?..

IF YOU HAVE NO CHILDREN MISS OUT QUESTIONS 33-36, GO TO QUESTION 37.
(These questions apply if you have lived with your children during the last six months)

IN THE LAST SIX MONTHS: Yes No

33. Have you children criticised your drinking? . . . .

34. Have you had rows with your children about drinking? . . . .

35. Do your children tend to avoid you when you have been drinking? . . . .

36. Have your children tried to stop you from having a drink? . . . .

IF YOU HAVE BEEN UNEMPLOYED FOR THE LAST SIX MONTHS,
MISS OUT QUESTIONS 37-44

IN THE LAST SIX MONTHS   Yes No

37. Have you found your work less interesting than you used to? . . . .

38. Have you been unable to arrive on time for work due to your drinking? . . . .

39. Have you missed a whole day at work after a drinking session? . . . .

40. Have you been less able to do your job because of your drinking? . . . .

41. Has anyone at work complained about you being late or absent? . . . .

42. Have you had any formal warnings from your employers? . . . .

43. Have you been suspended or dismissed from work? . . . .

44. Have you had any accidents at work after drinking? . . . .

PLEASE MAKE SURE YOU HAVE ANSWERED ALL THE QUESTIONS
WHICH APPLY TO YOU

END OF QUESTIONNAIRE

THANK YOU FOR YOUR HELP

Copyright D.C. Drummond 1990

Appendix 4

CASAA Research Division*

AUDIT

FOR OFFICE USE ONLY

_____Study

_____ID

_____Point

_____Date

_____Raid

AUDOOO Revised 10/9/95 1 Page

Please circle the answer that is correct for you.

1. How often do you have a drink containing alcohol?

| NEVER | MONTHLY OR LESS | TWO TO FOUR TIMES A MONTH | TWO TO THREE TIMES A WEEK | FOUR OR MORE TIMES A WEEK |

NOTE: For answering these questions, one "drink" is equal to 10 ounces of beer, or 4 ounces of wine, or 1 ounce of liquor

---

2. How many drinks containing alcohol do you have on a typical day when you are drinking?

| 1 OR 2 | 2 OR 4 | 5 OR 6 | 7 TO 9 | 10 OR MORE |

3. How often do you have six or more drinks on one occasion?

| NEVER | LESS THAN MONTHLY | MONTHLY | WEEKLY | DAILY OR ALMOST DAILY |

4. How often during the last year have you found that you were not able to stop drinking once you had started?

| NEVER | LESS THAN MONTHLY | MONTHLY | WEEKLY | DAILY OR ALMOST DAILY |

5. How often during the last year have you failed to do what was normally expected from you because of drinking?

| NEVER | LESS THAN MONTHLY | MONTHLY | WEEKLY | DAILY OR ALMOST DAILY |

6. How often during the last year have you needed a first drink in the morning to get yourself going after a heavy drinking session?

| NEVER | LESS THAN MONTHLY | MONTHLY | WEEKLY | DAILY OR ALMOST DAILY |

7. How often during the last year have you had a feeling of guilt or remorse after drinking?

| NEVER | LESS THAN MONTHLY | MONTHLY | WEEKLY | DAILY OR ALMOST DAILY |

8. How often during the last year have you been unable to remember what happened the night before because you had been drinking?

| NEVER | LESS THAN MONTHLY | MONTHLY | WEEKLY | DAILY OR ALMOST DAILY |

9. Have you or someone else been injured as a result of your drinking?

| NEVER | YES, BUT NOT IN THE LAST YEAR | YES DURING THE LAST YEAR |

10. Has a relative or friend, or a doctor or other health worker been concerned about your drinking or suggested you cut down?

| NEVER | YES, BUT NOT IN THE LAST YEAR | YES DURING THE LAST YEAR |

Scoring Rules for the AUDIT Screening Questionnaire

Item 1	0 = Never
	1 = Monthly or less
	2 = Two to four times a month
	3 = Two to three times a week
	4 = Four or more times a week
Item 2	0 = 1–2 drinks
	1 = 3–4 drinks
	2 = 5–6 drinks
	3 = two to three times a week
	4 = four or more times a week
Item 3-8	0 = Never
	1 = Less than monthly
	2 = Monthly
	3 = Weekly
	4 = Daily or almost daily
Item 9-10	0 = No
	1 = Yes, but not in the last year
	2 = Yes, during the last year

Maximum possible score = 40

A score of 8 or more indicates a strong likelihood of hazardous or harmful alcohol consumption, and warrants more careful assessment.

Appendix 4

Clinical Institute Withdrawal Assessment of Alcohol Scale, Revised (CIWA-Ar)

Patient:_____ Date: _____ Time: _____ (24 hour clock, midnight = 00:00)

Pulse or heart rate, taken for one minute:_____ Blood pressure:_____

NAUSEA AND VOMITING -- Ask "Do you feel sick to your stomach? Have you vomited?" Observation.
0 no nausea and no vomiting
1 mild nausea with no vomiting
2
3
4 intermittent nausea with dry heaves
5
6
7 constant nausea, frequent dry heaves and vomiting

TREMOR -- Arms extended and fingers spread apart. Observation.
0 no tremor
1 not visible, but can be felt fingertip to fingertip
2
3
4 moderate, with patient's arms extended
5
6
7 severe, even with arms not extended

PAROXYSMAL SWEATS -- Observation.
0 no sweat visible
1 barely perceptible sweating, palms moist
2
3
4 beads of sweat obvious on forehead
5
6
7 drenching sweats

ANXIETY -- Ask "Do you feel nervous?" Observation.
0 no anxiety, at ease
1 mild anxious
2
3
4 moderately anxious, or guarded, so anxiety is inferred
5
6
7 equivalent to acute panic states as seen in severe delirium or acute schizophrenic reactions

AGITATION -- Observation.
0 normal activity
1 somewhat more than normal activity
2
3
4 moderately fidgety and restless
5
6
7 paces back and forth during most of the interview, or constantly thrashes about

TACTILE DISTURBANCES -- Ask "Have you any itching, pins and needles sensations, any burning, any numbness, or do you feel bugs crawling on or under your skin?" Observation.
0 none
1 very mild itching, pins and needles, burning or numbness
2 mild itching, pins and needles, burning or numbness
3 moderate itching, pins and needles, burning or numbness
4 moderately severe hallucinations
5 severe hallucinations
6 extremely severe hallucinations
7 continuous hallucinations

AUDITORY DISTURBANCES -- Ask "Are you more aware of sounds around you? Are they harsh? Do they frighten you? Are you hearing anything that is disturbing to you? Are you hearing things you know are not there?" Observation.
0 not present
1 very mild harshness or ability to frighten
2 mild harshness or ability to frighten
3 moderate harshness or ability to frighten
4 moderately severe hallucinations
5 severe hallucinations
6 extremely severe hallucinations
7 continuous hallucinations

VISUAL DISTURBANCES -- Ask "Does the light appear to be too bright? Is its color different? Does it hurt your eyes? Are you seeing anything that is disturbing to you? Are you seeing things you know are not there?" Observation.
0 not present
1 very mild sensitivity
2 mild sensitivity
3 moderate sensitivity
4 moderately severe hallucinations
5 severe hallucinations
6 extremely severe hallucinations
7 continuous hallucinations

HEADACHE, FULLNESS IN HEAD -- Ask "Does your head feel different? Does it feel like there is a band around your head?" Do not rate for dizziness or lightheadedness. Otherwise, rate severity.
0 not present
1 very mild
2 mild
3 moderate
4 moderately severe
5 severe
6 very severe
7 extremely severe

ORIENTATION AND CLOUDING OF SENSORIUM -- Ask "What day is this? Where are you? Who am I?"
0 oriented and can do serial additions
1 cannot do serial additions or is uncertain about date
2 disoriented for date by no more than 2 calendar days
3 disoriented for date by more than 2 calendar days
4 disoriented for place/or person

Total **CIWA-Ar** Score _____
Rater's Initials _____
Maximum Possible Score 67

The CIWA-Ar is not copyrighted and may be reproduced freely. This assessment for monitoring withdrawal symptoms requires approximately 5 minutes to administer. The maximum score is 67 (see instrument). Patients scoring less than 10 do not usually need additional medication for withdrawal.

Sullivan, J.T.; Sykora, K.; Schneiderman, J.; Naranjo, C.A.; and Sellers, E.M. Assessment of alcohol withdrawal: The revised Clinical Institute Withdrawal Assessment for Alcohol scale (**CIWA-Ar**). *British Journal of Addiction* 84:1353-1357, 1989.

The Leeds Dependence Questionnaire

On this page there are questions about the importance of alcohol and/or other drugs in your life.
Think about your drinking/other drug use in the last week and answer each question ticking the closest answer to how you see yourself.

	Never	Sometimes	Often	Nearly always
1. Do you find yourself thinking about when you will next be able to have another drink or take more drugs?				
2. Is drinking or taking drugs more important than anything else you might do during the day?				
3. Do you feel that your need for drink or drugs is too strong to control?				
4. Do you plan your days around getting and taking drink or drugs?				
5. Do you drink or take drugs in a particular way in order to increase the effect it gives you?				
6. Do you take drink or other drugs morning, afternoon and evening?				
7. Do you feel you have to carry on drinking or taking drugs once you have started?				
8. Is getting the effect you want more important than the particular drink or drug you use?				
9. Do you want to take more drink or drugs when the effect starts to wear off?				
10. Do you find it difficult to cope with life without drink or drugs?				

Appendix 4

Severity of Alcohol Dependence Questionnaire (SADQ)

S.A.D.Q. Name . . . .

Age . . . .

Sex . . . .

First of all, we would like you to recall a recent month when you were drinking heavily in a way which, for you, was fairly typical of a heavy drinking period. Please fill in the month and the year.

MONTH . . . . YEAR . . . . .

We would like to know more about your drinking during this time and <u>during other periods when your drinking was similar</u>. We want to know how often you experienced certain feelings. Please reply to each statement by putting a circle around ALMOST NEVER or SOMETIMES or OFTEN or NEARLY ALWAYS after each question.

First we want to know about the physical symptoms that you have experienced <u>first thing in the morning</u> during these typical periods of <u>heavy drinking</u>.

PLEASE ANSWER EVERY QUESTION

1. During a heavy drinking period, I wake up feeling sweaty.
   ALMOST NEVER   SOMETIMES   OFTEN   NEARLY ALWAYS

2. During a heavy drinking period, my hands shake first thing in the morning.
   ALMOST NEVER   SOMETIMES   OFTEN   NEARLY ALWAYS

3. During a heavy drinking period, my whole body shakes violently first thing in the morning if I don't have a drink.
   ALMOST NEVER   SOMETIMES   OFTEN   NEARLY ALWAYS

4. During a heavy drinking period, I wake up absolutely drenched in sweat.
   ALMOST NEVER   SOMETIMES   OFTEN   NEARLY ALWAYS

The following statements refer to moods and states of mind you may have experienced <u>first thing in the morning</u> during these periods of heavy drinking.

5. When I'm drinking heavily, I dread waking up in the morning.
   ALMOST NEVER   SOMETIMES   OFTEN   NEARLY ALWAYS

6. During a heavy drinking period, I am frightened of meeting people first thing in the morning.
   ALMOST NEVER   SOMETIMES   OFTEN   NEARLY ALWAYS

7. During a heavy drinking period, I feel at the edge of despair when I awake.
   ALMOST NEVER   SOMETIMES   OFTEN   NEARLY ALWAYS

8. During a heavy drinking period I feel very frightened when I awake.
   ALMOST NEVER   SOMETIMES   OFTEN   NEARLY ALWAYS

492

Severity of Alcohol Dependence Questionnaire (SADQ)

The following statements also refer to the recent period <u>when your drinking was heavy</u>, and to periods like it.

9. During a heavy drinking period, I like to have a morning drink.
   ALMOST NEVER   SOMETIMES   OFTEN   NEARLY ALWAYS

10. During a heavy drinking period, I always gulp my first few morning drinks down as quickly as possible.
   ALMOST NEVER   SOMETIMES   OFTEN   NEARLY ALWAYS

11. During a heavy drinking period, I drink in the morning to get rid of the shakes.
   ALMOST NEVER   SOMETIMES   OFTEN   NEARLY ALWAYS

12. During a heavy drinking period, I have a very strong craving for a drink when I awake.
   ALMOST NEVER   SOMETIMES   OFTEN   NEARLY ALWAYS

Again the statements refer to the <u>recent period of heavy drinking</u> and the periods like it.

13. During a heavy drinking period, I drink more than a quarter of a bottle of spirits per day (4 doubles or 1 bottle of wine or 4 pints of beer).
   ALMOST NEVER   SOMETIMES   OFTEN   NEARLY ALWAYS

14. During a heavy drinking period, I drink more than half a bottle of spirits per day (or 2 bottles of wine or 8 pints of beer).
   ALMOST NEVER   SOMETIMES   OFTEN   NEARLY ALWAYS

15. During a heavy drinking period, I drink more than one bottle of spirits per day (or 4 bottles of wine or 15 pints of beer).
   ALMOST NEVER   SOMETIMES   OFTEN   NEARLY ALWAYS

16. During a heavy drinking period, I drink more than two bottles of spirits per day (or 8 bottles of wine or 30 pints of beer).
   ALMOST NEVER   SOMETIMES   OFTEN   NEARLY ALWAYS

IMAGINE THE FOLLOWING SITUATION:
    (1) You have been COMPLETELY OFF DRINK for a FEW WEEKS
    (2) You then drink VERY HEAVILY for TWO DAYS

HOW WOULD YOU FEEL <u>THE MORNING AFTER</u> THOSE TWO DAYS OF HEAVY DRINKING?

17. I would start to sweat.
   NOT AT ALL   SLIGHTLY   MODERATELY   QUITE A LOT

18. My hands would shake.
   NOT AT ALL   SLIGHTLY   MODERATELY   QUITE A LOT

19. My body would shake.
   NOT AT ALL   SLIGHTLY   MODERATELY   QUITE A LOT

20. I would be craving for a drink.
   NOT AT ALL   SLIGHTLY   MODERATELY   QUITE A LOT

APPENDIX 5:

STAKEHOLDERS AND EXPERTS WHO SUBMITTED COMMENTS IN RESPONSE TO THE CONSULTATION DRAFT OF THE GUIDELINE

STAKEHOLDERS

Alcohol and Drug Service, The
Alcohol Education and Research Council (AERC) Alcohol Academy, The
Alcohol Focus Scotland
Association for Family Therapy and Systemic Practice (AFT)
Association of Higher Education Programmes on Substance Misuse
British Association for Counselling & Psychotherapy
British Association for Psychopharmacology
British Liver Trust
Children's Society, The
College of Mental Health Pharmacy
Department for Education
Department of Health
Drinksense
Kaleidoscope
Lundbeck
National Organisation for Fetal Alcohol Syndrome (NOFAS-UK)
National Treatment Agency for Substance Misuse
NHS Blackpool
NHS County Durham and Darlington
NHS Direct
NHS Lothian
National Institute for Health Research (NIHR) Evaluation, Trials and Studies Coordinating Centre – Health Technology Assessment
Nottinghamshire Healthcare NHS Trust
Public Health Wales NHS Trust
Royal College of General Practitioners, Wales
Royal College of Midwives
Royal College of Nursing
Royal College of Paediatrics and Child Health
Royal College of Physicians & British Society for Gastroenterology
Royal College of Psychiatrists
Royal Pharmaceutical Society of Great Britain

South Staffordshire & Shropshire NHS Foundation Trust
Specialist Clinical Addiction Network (SCAN)
St Mungo Housing Association Ltd
Turning Point
United Kingdom Clinical Pharmacy Association
Young Women's Christian Association (YWCA) England & Wales

EXPERTS

Professor Nick Heather
Dr Duncan Raistrick

APPENDIX 6:

RESEARCHERS CONTACTED TO REQUEST

INFORMATION ABOUT STUDIES

Dr Bert Aertgeerts
Dr Lynn Alden
Dr Gerard Connors
Dr David Foy
Dr Peter Friedmann
Dr J. C. Garbutt
Dr Ronan Hearne
Dr Rachel Humeniuk
Dr Hakan Kallmen
Dr David Kavanagh
Dr Mark Litt
Professor Richard Longabaugh
Professor Karl Mann
Proffessor John Monterosso
Dr Kathryn Rost
Janice Vendetti (Project MATCH coordinating Centre)
Dr Kim Walitzer
Professor Paul Wallace

APPENDIX 7:
REVIEW QUESTIONS

1. For people who misuse alcohol, what are their experiences of having problems with alcohol, of access to services and of treatment?
2. For families and carers of people who misuse alcohol, what are their experiences of caring for people with an alcohol problem and what support is available for families and carers?
3. In adults with alcohol misuse, what is the clinical efficacy, cost effectiveness, and safety of, and patient satisfaction associated with different systems for the organisation of care?
4. What are the most effective (a) diagnostic and (b) assessment tools for alcohol dependence and harmful alcohol use?
5. What are the most effective ways of monitoring clinical progress in alcohol dependence and harmful alcohol use?
6. To answer questions 4 and 5, what are the advantages, disadvantages, and clinical utility of:
   - the structure of the overall clinical assessment
   - biological measures
   - psychological/behavioural measures
   - neuropsychiatric measures (including cognitive impairment)
   - physical assessment?
7. In adults in planned alcohol withdrawal, what is the clinical efficacy, cost effectiveness, safety of, and patient satisfaction associated with:
   - preparatory work before withdrawal
   - different drug regimens
   - the setting (that is, community, residential or inpatient)?
8. In adults in planned alcohol withdrawal what factors influence the choice of setting in terms of clinical and cost effectiveness including:
   - severity of the alcohol disorder
   - physical comorbidities
   - psychological comorbidities
   - social factors.
9. In adults with harmful or dependent alcohol use what are the preferred structures for and components of community-based and residential specialist alcohol services to promote long-term clinical and cost-effective outcomes?
10. For people with alcohol dependence or who are harmful drinkers, is psychological *treatment x* when compared with *y*, more clinically and cost effective and does this depend on:
    - presence of comorbidities
    - subtypes (matching effects)

- therapist-related factors (quality, therapeutic alliance, competence, training, and so on).

11. What are the most effective (a) diagnostic and (b) assessment tools for alcohol dependence and harmful alcohol use in children and young people (aged 10–18 years)?

12. What are the most effective ways of monitoring clinical progress in alcohol dependence and harmful alcohol use in children and young people (aged 10–18 years)?

13. For children and young people with alcohol dependence or harmful alcohol use is *treatment x* when compared with *y* more clinically and cost effective and does this depend on the presence of comorbidities?

14. For people with alcohol dependence or harmful alcohol use, what pharmacological interventions are more clinically and cost effective? In addition:

(a) What are the impacts of severity and comorbities on outcomes?

(b) When should pharmacological treatments be initiated and for what duration should they be prescribed?

APPENDIX 8:
REVIEW PROTOCOLS

The completed forms can be found on the CD accompanying this guideline.

APPENDIX 9:
SEARCH STRATEGIES FOR THE IDENTIFICATION
OF CLINICAL STUDIES

The search strategies can be found on the CD accompanying this guideline.

APPENDIX 10:

CLINICAL STUDY DATA EXTRACTION FORM

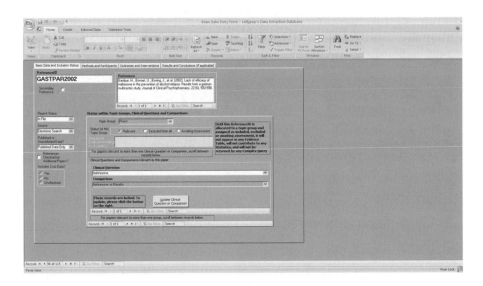

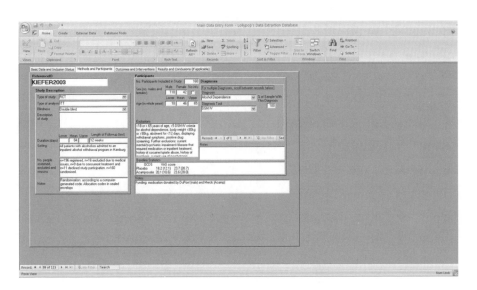

Appendix 10

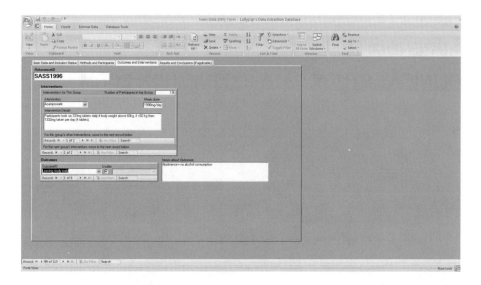

APPENDIX 11:
QUALITY CHECKLISTS FOR CLINICAL STUDIES AND REVIEWS

The methodological quality of each study was evaluated using dimensions adapted from SIGN (2001). SIGN originally adapted its quality criteria from checklists developed in Australia (Liddel *et al.*, 1996). Both groups reportedly undertook extensive development and validation procedures when creating their quality criteria.

Notes on the use of the methodology checklist: systematic reviews
and meta-analyses
Section 1 identifies the study and asks a series of questions aimed at establishing the internal validity of the study under review — that is, making sure that it has been carried out carefully and that the outcomes are likely to be attributable to the intervention being investigated. Each question covers an aspect of methodology that research has shown makes a significant difference to the conclusions of a study.

For each question in this section, one of the following should be used to indicate how well it has been addressed in the review:
● well covered
● adequately addressed
● poorly addressed
● not addressed (that is, not mentioned or indicates that this aspect of study design was ignored)
● not reported (that is, mentioned but insufficient detail to allow assessment to be made)
● not applicable.

Quality checklist for a systematic review or meta-analysis

Study ID:	
Guideline topic:	Key question no:
Checklist completed by:	
SECTION 1: INTERNAL VALIDITY	
In a well-conducted systematic review:	In this study this criterion is: *(Circle one option for each question)*
1.1 The study addresses an appropriate and clearly focused question.	Well covered Not addressed Adequately addressed Not reported Poorly addressed Not applicable
1.2 A description of the methodology used is included.	Well covered Not addressed Adequately addressed Not reported Poorly addressed Not applicable
1.3 The literature search is sufficiently rigorous to identify all the relevant studies.	Well covered Not addressed Adequately addressed Not reported Poorly addressed Not applicable
1.4 Study quality is assessed and taken into account.	Well covered Not addressed Adequately addressed Not reported Poorly addressed Not applicable
1.5 There are enough similarities between the studies selected to make combining them reasonable.	Well covered Not addressed Adequately addressed Not reported Poorly addressed Not applicable
SECTION 2: OVERALL ASSESSMENT OF THE STUDY	
2.1 How well was the study done to minimise bias? *Code ++ , + or –*	

1.1   The study addresses an appropriate and clearly focused question

Unless a clear and well-defined question is specified in the report of the review, it will be difficult to assess how well it has met its objectives or how relevant it is to the question to be answered on the basis of the conclusions.

1.2   A description of the methodology used is included

One of the key distinctions between a systematic review and a general review is the systematic methodology used. A systematic review should include a detailed description of the methods used to identify and evaluate individual studies. If this description is not present, it is not possible to make a thorough evaluation of the quality of the review, and it should be rejected as a source of level-1 evidence (though it may be useable as level-4 evidence, if no better evidence can be found).

1.3 The literature search is sufficiently rigorous to identify all the relevant studies

A systematic review based on a limited literature search – for example, one limited to MEDLINE only – is likely to be heavily biased. A well-conducted review should as a minimum look at EMBASE and MEDLINE and, from the late 1990s onward, the Cochrane Library. Any indication that hand searching of key journals, or follow-up of reference lists of included studies, were carried out in addition to electronic database searches can normally be taken as evidence of a well-conducted review.

1.4 Study quality is assessed and taken into account

A well-conducted systematic review should have used clear criteria to assess whether individual studies had been well conducted before deciding whether to include or exclude them. If there is no indication of such an assessment, the review should be rejected as a source of level-1 evidence. If details of the assessment are poor, or the methods are considered to be inadequate, the quality of the review should be down-graded. In either case, it may be worthwhile obtaining and evaluating the individual studies as part of the review being conducted for this guideline.

1.5 There are enough similarities between the studies selected to make combining them reasonable

Studies covered by a systematic review should be selected using clear inclusion criteria (see question 1.4 above). These criteria should include, either implicitly or explicitly, the question of whether the selected studies can legitimately be compared. It should be clearly ascertained, for example, that the populations covered by the studies are comparable, that the methods used in the investigations are the same, that the outcome measures are comparable and the variability in effect sizes between studies is not greater than would be expected by chance alone.

++	All or most of the criteria have been fulfilled. Where they have not been fulfilled, the conclusions of the study or review are thought **very unlikely** to alter.
+	Some of the criteria have been fulfilled. Those criteria that have not been fulfilled or not adequately described are thought **unlikely** to alter the conclusions.
−	Few or no criteria fulfilled. The conclusions of the study are thought **likely or very likely** to alter.

Quality checklist for an RCT

Study ID:	
Guideline topic:	Key question no:
Checklist completed by:	
SECTION 1: INTERNAL VALIDITY	
In a well-conducted RCT study:	In this study this criterion is: *(Circle one option for each question)*
1.1 The study addresses an appropriate and clearly focused question.	Well covered Not addressed Adequately addressed Not reported Poorly addressed Not applicable
1.2 The assignment of subjects to treatment groups is randomised.	Well covered Not addressed Adequately addressed Not reported Poorly addressed Not applicable
1.3 An adequate concealment method is used.	Well covered Not addressed Adequately addressed Not reported Poorly addressed Not applicable
1.4 Subjects and investigators are kept 'blind' about treatment allocation.	Well covered Not addressed Adequately addressed Not reported Poorly addressed Not applicable
1.5 The treatment and control groups are similar at the start of the trial.	Well covered Not addressed Adequately addressed Not reported Poorly addressed Not applicable
1.6 The only difference between groups is the treatment under investigation.	Well covered Not addressed Adequately addressed Not reported Poorly addressed Not applicable
1.7 All relevant outcomes are measured in a standard, valid and reliable way.	Well covered Not addressed Adequately addressed Not reported Poorly addressed Not applicable
1.8 What percentage of the individuals or clusters recruited into each treatment arm of the study dropped out before the study was completed?	
1.9 All the subjects are analysed in the groups to which they were randomly allocated (often referred to as intention-to-treat analysis).	Well covered Not addressed Adequately addressed Not reported Poorly addressed Not applicable

1.10	Where the study is carried out at more than one site, results are comparable for all sites.	Well covered	Not addressed
		Adequately addressed	Not reported
		Poorly addressed	Not applicable
SECTION 2: OVERALL ASSESSMENT OF THE STUDY			
2.1	How well was the study done to minimise bias? *Code* $++$, $+$ or $-$		

Section 2 relates to the overall assessment of the paper. It starts by rating the methodological quality of the study, based on the responses in Section 1 and using the following coding system:

Notes on the use of the methodology checklist: RCTs
Section 1 identifies the study and asks a series of questions aimed at establishing the internal validity of the study under review – that is, making sure that it has been carried out carefully and that the outcomes are likely to be attributable to the intervention being investigated. Each question covers an aspect of methodology that research has shown makes a significant difference to the conclusions of a study.

For each question in this section, one of the following should be used to indicate how well it has been addressed in the review:

● well covered
● adequately addressed
● poorly addressed
● not addressed (that is, not mentioned or indicates that this aspect of study design was ignored)
● not reported (that is, mentioned but insufficient detail to allow assessment to be made)
● not applicable.

1.1 The study addresses an appropriate and clearly focused question

Unless a clear and well-defined question is specified, it will be difficult to assess how well the study has met its objectives or how relevant it is to the question to be answered on the basis of its conclusions.

1.2 The assignment of subjects to treatment groups is randomised

Random allocation of patients to receive one or other of the treatments under investigation, or to receive either treatment or placebo, is fundamental to this type of study. If there is no indication of randomisation, the study should be rejected. If the description of randomisation is poor, or the process used is not truly random (for example, allocation by date or alternating between one group and another) or can otherwise be seen as flawed, the study should be given a lower quality rating.

507

1.3   An adequate concealment method is used

Research has shown that where allocation concealment is inadequate, investigators can overestimate the effect of interventions by up to 40%. Centralised allocation, computerised allocation systems or the use of coded identical containers would all be regarded as adequate methods of concealment and may be taken as indicators of a well-conducted study. If the method of concealment used is regarded as poor, or relatively easy to subvert, the study must be given a lower quality rating, and can be rejected if the concealment method is seen as inadequate.

1.4   Subjects and investigators are kept 'blind' about treatment allocation

Blinding can be carried out up to three levels. In single-blind studies, patients are unaware of which treatment they are receiving; in double-blind studies, the doctor and the patient are unaware of which treatment the patient is receiving; in triple-blind studies, patients, healthcare providers and those conducting the analysis are unaware of which patients receive which treatment. The higher the level of blinding, the lower the risk of bias in the study.

1.5   The treatment and control groups are similar at the start of the trial

Patients selected for inclusion in a trial should be as similar as possible, to eliminate any possible bias. The study should report any significant differences in the composition of the study groups in relation to gender mix, age, stage of disease (if appropriate), social background, ethnic origin or comorbid conditions. These factors may be covered by inclusion and exclusion criteria, rather than being reported directly. Failure to address this question, or the use of inappropriate groups, should lead to the study being downgraded.

1.6   The only difference between groups is the treatment under investigation

If some patients receive additional treatment, even if of a minor nature or consisting of advice and counselling rather than a physical intervention, this treatment is a potential confounding factor that may invalidate the results. If groups are not treated equally, the study should be rejected unless no other evidence is available. If the study is used as evidence, it should be treated with caution and given a low quality rating.

1.7   All relevant outcomes are measured in a standard, valid and reliable way

If some significant clinical outcomes have been ignored, or not adequately taken into account, the study should be downgraded. It should also be downgraded if the measures used are regarded as being doubtful in any way or applied inconsistently.

1.8   What percentage of the individuals or clusters recruited into each treatment arm of the study dropped out before the study was completed?

The number of patients that drop out of a study should give concern if the number is very high. Conventionally, a 20% dropout rate is regarded as acceptable, but this may vary. Some regard should be paid to why patients drop out, as well as how many. It should be noted that the dropout rate may be expected to be higher in studies conducted over a long period of time. A higher dropout rate will normally lead to downgrading, rather than rejection, of a study.

1.9   All the subjects are analysed in the groups to which they were randomly allocated (often referred to as intention-to-treat analysis)

In practice, it is rarely the case that all patients allocated to the intervention group receive the intervention throughout the trial, or that all those in the comparison group do not. Patients may refuse treatment, or contraindications arise that lead them to be switched to the other group. If the comparability of groups through randomisation is to be maintained, however, patient outcomes must be analysed according to the group to which they were originally allocated, irrespective of the treatment they actually received. (This is known as intention-to-treat analysis.) If it is clear that analysis is not on an intention-to-treat basis, the study may be rejected. If there is little other evidence available, the study may be included but should be evaluated as if it were a non-randomised cohort study.

1.10   Where the study is carried out at more than one site, results are comparable for all sites

In multi-site studies, confidence in the results should be increased if it can be shown that similar results have been obtained at the different participating centres.

Section 2 relates to the overall assessment of the paper. It starts by rating the methodological quality of the study, based on the responses in Section 1 and using the following coding system:

++	All or most of the criteria have been fulfilled. Where they have not been fulfilled, the conclusions of the study or review are thought **very unlikely** to alter.
+	Some of the criteria have been fulfilled. Those criteria that have not been fulfilled or not adequately described are thought **unlikely** to alter the conclusions.
−	Few or no criteria fulfilled. The conclusions of the study are thought **likely or very likely** to alter.

Quality checklist for a cohort study*

	Relevant questions:
Study ID:	
Guideline topic:	
Checklist completed by:	
SECTION 1: INTERNAL VALIDITY	
In a well-conducted cohort study:	In this study the criterion is: (*Circle one option for each question*)
1.1 The study addresses an appropriate and clearly focused question.	Well covered Not addressed Adequately addressed Not reported Poorly addressed Not applicable
SELECTION OF SUBJECTS	
1.2 The two groups being studied are selected from source populations that are comparable in all respects other than the factor under investigation.	Well covered Not addressed Adequately addressed Not reported Poorly addressed Not applicable
1.3 The study indicates how many of the people asked to take part did so, in each of the groups being studied.	Well covered Not addressed Adequately addressed Not reported Poorly addressed Not reported
1.4 The likelihood that some eligible subjects might have the outcome at the time of enrolment is assessed and taken into account in the analysis.	Well covered Not addressed Adequately addressed Not reported Poorly addressed Not applicable
1.5 What percentage of individuals or clusters recruited into each arm of the study dropped out before the study was completed?	
1.6 Comparison is made between full participants and those lost to follow-up, by exposure status.	Well covered Not addressed Adequately addressed Not reported Poorly addressed Not applicable
ASSESSMENT	
1.7 The outcomes are clearly defined.	Well covered Not addressed Adequately addressed Not reported Poorly addressed Not applicable

1.8	The assessment of outcome is made blind to exposure status.	Well covered Adequately addressed Poorly addressed	Not addressed Not reported Not applicable
1.9	Where blinding was not possible, there is some recognition that knowledge of exposure status could have influenced the assessment of outcome.	Well covered Adequately addressed Poorly addressed	Not addressed Not reported Not applicable
1.10	The measure of assessment of exposure is reliable.	Well covered Adequately addressed Poorly addressed	Not addressed Not reported Not applicable
1.11	Evidence from other sources is used to demonstrate that the method of outcome assessment is valid and reliable.	Well covered Adequately addressed Poorly addressed	Not addressed Not reported Not applicable
1.12	Exposure level or prognostic factor is assessed more than once.	Well covered Adequately addressed Poorly addressed	Not addressed Not reported Not applicable
CONFOUNDING			
1.13	The main potential confounders are identified and taken into account in the design and analysis.	Well covered Adequately addressed Poorly addressed	Not addressed Not reported Not applicable
STATISTICAL ANALYSIS			
1.14	Have confidence intervals been provided?		
SECTION 2: OVERALL ASSESSMENT OF THE STUDY			
2.1	How well was the study done to minimise the risk of bias or confounding, and to establish a causal relationship between exposure and effect? *Code* $++$, $+$ or $-$		

Note. *A cohort study can be defined as a retrospective or prospective follow-up study. Groups of individuals are defined on the basis of the presence or absence of exposure to a suspected risk factor or intervention. This checklist is not appropriate for assessing uncontrolled studies (for example, a case series where there is no comparison [control] group of patients).

Notes on the use of the methodology checklist: cohort studies

The studies covered by this checklist are designed to answer questions of the type 'What are the effects of this exposure?' It relates to studies that compare a group of people with a particular exposure with another group who either have not had the exposure or have a different level of exposure. Cohort studies may be prospective (where the exposure is defined and subjects selected before outcomes occur) or retrospective (where exposure is assessed after the outcome is known, usually by the examination of medical records). Retrospective studies are generally regarded as a weaker design, and should not receive a $2++$ rating.

Section 1 identifies the study and asks a series of questions aimed at establishing the internal validity of the study under review – that is, making sure that it has been carried out carefully, and that the outcomes are likely to be attributable to the intervention being investigated. Each question covers an aspect of methodology that has been shown to make a significant difference to the conclusions of a study.

Because of the potential complexity and subtleties of the design of this type of study, there are comparatively few criteria that automatically rule out use of a study as evidence. It is more a matter of increasing confidence in the likelihood of a causal relationship existing between exposure and outcome by identifying how many aspects of good study design are present and how well they have been tackled. A study that fails to address or report on more than one or two of the questions considered below should almost certainly be rejected.

For each question in this section, one of the following should be used to indicate how well it has been addressed in the review:
● well covered
● adequately addressed
● poorly addressed
● not addressed (that is, not mentioned or indicates that this aspect of study design was ignored)
● not reported (that is, mentioned but insufficient detail to allow assessment to be made)
● not applicable.

1.1   The study addresses an appropriate and clearly focused question

Unless a clear and well-defined question is specified, it will be difficult to assess how well the study has met its objectives or how relevant it is to the question to be answered on the basis of its conclusions.

1.2   The two groups being studied are selected from source populations that are comparable in all respects other than the factor under investigation

Study participants may be selected from the target population (all individuals to which the results of the study could be applied), the source population (a defined subset of the target population from which participants are selected) or from a pool of eligible subjects (a clearly defined and counted group selected from the source population). It is important that the two groups selected for comparison are as similar as possible in all characteristics except for their exposure status or the presence of specific prognostic factors or prognostic markers relevant to the study in question. If the study does not include clear definitions of the source populations and eligibility criteria for participants, it should be rejected.

1.3 The study indicates how many of the people asked to take part did so in each of the groups being studied

This question relates to what is known as the participation rate, defined as the number of study participants divided by the number of eligible subjects. This should be calculated separately for each branch of the study. A large difference in participation rate between the two arms of the study indicates that a significant degree of selection bias may be present, and the study results should be treated with considerable caution.

1.4 The likelihood that some eligible subjects might have the outcome at the time of enrolment is assessed and taken into account in the analysis

If some of the eligible subjects, particularly those in the unexposed group, already have the outcome at the start of the trial, the final result will be biased. A well-conducted study will attempt to estimate the likelihood of this occurring and take it into account in the analysis through the use of sensitivity studies or other methods.

1.5 What percentage of individuals or clusters recruited into each arm of the study dropped out before the study was completed?

The number of patients that drop out of a study should give concern if the number is very high. Conventionally, a 20% dropout rate is regarded as acceptable, but in observational studies conducted over a lengthy period of time a higher dropout rate is to be expected. A decision on whether to downgrade or reject a study because of a high dropout rate is a matter of judgement based on the reasons why people drop out and whether dropout rates are comparable in the exposed and unexposed groups. Reporting of efforts to follow up participants who drop out may be regarded as an indicator of a well-conducted study.

1.6 Comparison is made between full participants and those lost to follow-up by exposure status

For valid study results, it is essential that the study participants are truly representative of the source population. It is always possible that participants who drop out of the study will differ in some significant way from those who remain part of the study throughout.

A well-conducted study will attempt to identify any such differences between full and partial participants in both the exposed and unexposed groups. Any indication that differences exist should lead to the study results being treated with caution.

1.7   The outcomes are clearly defined

Once enrolled in the study, participants should be followed until specified end points or outcomes are reached. In a study of the effect of exercise on the death rates from heart disease in middle-aged men, for example, participants might be followed up until death, reaching a predefined age or until completion of the study. If outcomes and the criteria used for measuring them are not clearly defined, the study should be rejected.

1.8   The assessment of outcome is made blind to exposure status

If the assessor is blinded to which participants received the exposure, and which did not, the prospects of unbiased results are significantly increased. Studies in which this is done should be rated more highly than those where it is not done or not done adequately.

1.9   Where blinding was not possible, there is some recognition that knowledge of exposure status could have influenced the assessment of outcome

Blinding is not possible in many cohort studies. In order to assess the extent of any bias that may be present, it may be helpful to compare process measures used on the participant groups – for example, frequency of observations, who carried out the observations and the degree of detail and completeness of observations. If these process measures are comparable between the groups, the results may be regarded with more confidence.

1.10   The measure of assessment of exposure is reliable

A well-conducted study should indicate how the degree of exposure or presence of prognostic factors or markers was assessed. Whatever measures are used must be sufficient to establish clearly that participants have or have not received the exposure under investigation and the extent of such exposure, or that they do or do not possess a particular prognostic marker or factor. Clearly described, reliable measures should increase the confidence in the quality of the study.

1.11   Evidence from other sources is used to demonstrate that the method of outcome assessment is valid and reliable

The inclusion of evidence from other sources or previous studies that demonstrate the validity and reliability of the assessment methods used should further increase confidence in study quality.

1.12 Exposure level or prognostic factor is assessed more than once

Confidence in data quality should be increased if exposure level or the presence of prognostic factors is measured more than once. Independent assessment by more than one investigator is preferable.

1.13 The main potential confounders are identified and taken into account in the design and analysis

Confounding is the distortion of a link between exposure and outcome by another factor that is associated with both exposure and outcome. The possible presence of confounding factors is one of the principal reasons why observational studies are not more highly rated as a source of evidence. The report of the study should indicate which potential confounders have been considered and how they have been assessed or allowed for in the analysis. Clinical judgement should be applied to consider whether all likely confounders have been considered. If the measures used to address confounding are considered inadequate, the study should be downgraded or rejected, depending on how serious the risk of confounding is considered to be. A study that does not address the possibility of confounding should be rejected.

1.14 Have confidence intervals been provided?

Confidence limits are the preferred method for indicating the precision of statistical results and can be used to differentiate between an inconclusive study and a study that shows no effect. Studies that report a single value with no assessment of precision should be treated with caution.

Section 2 relates to the overall assessment of the paper. It starts by rating the methodological quality of the study, based on the responses in Section 1 and using the following coding system:

++	All or most of the criteria have been fulfilled. Where they have not been fulfilled, the conclusions of the study or review are thought **very unlikely** to alter.
+	Some of the criteria have been fulfilled. Those criteria that have not been fulfilled or not adequately described are thought **unlikely** to alter the conclusions.
−	Few or no criteria fulfilled. The conclusions of the study are thought **likely or very likely** to alter.

APPENDIX 12:
SEARCH STRATEGIES FOR THE IDENTIFICATION OF HEALTH ECONOMIC EVIDENCE

The search strategies can be found on the CD accompanying this guideline.

APPENDIX 13:

QUALITY CHECKLISTS FOR ECONOMIC STUDIES

This checklist is designed to determine whether an economic evaluation provides evidence that is useful to inform the decision-making of the GDG. It is not intended to judge the quality of the study *per se* or the quality of reporting.

Study identification *Including author, title, reference, year of publication*		
Guideline topic:		**Question no:**
Checklist completed by:		
Section 1: Applicability (relevance to specific guideline review question(s) and the NICE reference case). This checklist should be used first to filter out irrelevant studies.	**Yes/ Partly/ No/Unclear/ NA**	**Comments**
1.1	Is the study population appropriate for the guideline?		
1.2	Are the interventions appropriate for the guideline?		
1.3	Is the healthcare system in which the study was conducted sufficiently similar to the current UK NHS context?		
1.4	Are costs measured from the NHS and personal social services (PSS) perspective?		
1.5	Are all direct health effects on individuals included?		
1.6	Are both costs and health effects discounted at an annual rate of 3.5%?		
1.7	Is the value of health effects expressed in terms of quality-adjusted life years (QALYs)?		
1.8	Are changes in health-related quality of life (HRQoL) reported directly from patients and/or carers?		
1.9	Is the valuation of changes in HRQoL (utilities) obtained from a representative sample of the general public?		

1.10	Overall judgement: Directly applicable/ Partially applicable/Not applicable There is no need to use section 2 of the checklist if the study is considered 'not applicable'.		
Other comments:			

Section 2: Study limitations (the level of methodological quality). This checklist should be used once it has been decided that the study is sufficiently applicable to the context of the clinical guideline.	**Yes/Partly/ No/Unclear/ NA**	**Comments**
2.1	Does the model structure adequately reflect the nature of the health condition under evaluation?		
2.2	Is the time horizon sufficiently long to reflect all important differences in costs and outcomes?		
2.3	Are all important and relevant health outcomes included?		
2.4	Are the estimates of baseline health outcomes from the best available source?		
2.5	Are the estimates of relative treatment effects from the best available source?		
2.6	Are all important and relevant costs included?		
2.7	Are the estimates of resource use from the best available source?		
2.8	Are the unit costs of resources from the best available source?		
2.9	Is an appropriate incremental analysis presented or can it be calculated from the data?		
2.10	Are all important parameters whose values are uncertain subjected to appropriate sensitivity analysis?		

2.11	Is there no potential conflict of interest?		
2.12	Overall assessment: Minor limitations/ Potentially serious limitations/Very serious limitations		
Other comments:			

Notes on use of methodology checklist: economic evaluations
For all questions:
- answer 'yes' if the study fully meets the criterion
- answer 'partly' if the study largely meets the criterion but differs in some important respect
- answer 'no' if the study deviates substantively from the criterion
- answer 'unclear' if the report provides insufficient information to judge whether the study complies with the criterion
- answer 'NA (not applicable)' if the criterion is not relevant in a particular instance.
- For 'partly' or 'no' responses, use the comments column to explain how the study deviates from the criterion.

SECTION 1: APPLICABILITY

1.1   Is the study population appropriate for the guideline?

The study population should be defined as precisely as possible and should be in line with that specified in the guideline scope and any related review protocols. This includes consideration of appropriate subgroups that require special attention. For many interventions, the capacity to benefit will differ for participants with differing characteristics. This should be explored separately for each relevant subgroup as part of the base-case analysis by the provision of estimates of clinical and cost effectiveness. The characteristics of participants in each subgroup should be clearly defined and, ideally, should be identified on the basis of an *a priori* expectation of differential clinical or cost effectiveness as a result of biologically plausible known mechanisms, social characteristics or other clearly justified factors.

Answer 'yes' if the study population is fully in line with that in the guideline question(s) and if the study differentiates appropriately between important subgroups. Answer 'partly' if the study population is similar to that in the guideline question(s) but: (i) it differs in some important respects; or (ii) the study fails to differentiate between important subgroups. Answer 'no' if the study population is substantively different from that in the guideline question(s).

1.2   Are the interventions appropriate for the guideline?

All relevant alternatives should be included, as specified in the guideline scope and any related review protocols. These should include routine and best practice in the NHS, existing NICE guidance and other feasible options. Answer 'yes' if the analysis includes all options considered relevant for the guideline, even if it also includes other options that are not relevant. Answer 'partly' if the analysis omits one or more relevant options but still contains comparisons likely to be useful for the guideline. Answer 'no' if the analysis does not contain any relevant comparisons.

1.3   Is the healthcare system in which the study was conducted sufficiently similar to the current UK NHS context?

This relates to the overall structure of the healthcare system within which the interventions were delivered. For example, an intervention might be delivered on an inpatient basis in one country whereas in the UK it would be provided in the community. This might significantly influence the use of healthcare resources and costs, thus limiting the applicability of the results to a UK setting. In addition, old UK studies may be severely limited in terms of their relevance to current NHS practice.

Answer 'yes' if the study was conducted within the UK and is sufficiently recent to reflect current NHS practice. For non-UK or older UK studies, answer 'partly' if differences in the healthcare setting are unlikely to substantively change the cost-effectiveness estimates. Answer 'no' if the healthcare setting is so different that the results are unlikely to be applicable in the current NHS.

1.4   Are costs measured from the NHS and personal social services (PSS) perspective?

The decision-making perspective of an economic evaluation determines the range of costs that should be included in the analysis. NICE works in a specific context; in particular, it does not set the budget for the NHS. The objective of NICE is to offer guidance that represents an efficient use of available NHS and PSS resources. For these reasons, the perspective on costs used in the NICE reference case is that of the NHS and PSS. Productivity costs and costs borne by patients and carers that are not reimbursed by the NHS or PSS are not included in the reference case. The reference case also excludes costs to other government bodies, although these may sometimes be presented in additional analyses alongside the reference case.

Answer 'yes' if the study only includes costs for resource items that would be paid for by the NHS and PSS. Also answer 'yes' if other costs have been included in the study, but the results are presented in such a way that the cost effectiveness can be calculated from an NHS and PSS perspective. Answer 'partly' if the study has taken a wider perspective but the other non-NHS/PSS costs are small in relation to the total expected costs and are unlikely to change the cost-effectiveness results. Answer 'no' if non-NHS/PSS costs are significant and are likely to change the cost-effectiveness results. Some interventions may have a substantial impact on non-health outcomes or costs to other government bodies (for example, treatments to reduce illicit drug misuse may have the effect of reducing drug-related crime). In such situations, if the economic study includes non-health costs in such a way that they cannot be separated out from NHS/PSS costs, answer 'no' but consider retaining the study for critical appraisal. If studies containing non-reference-case costs are retained, use the comments column to note why.

1.5   Are all direct health effects on individuals included?

In the NICE reference case, the perspective on outcomes should be all direct health effects, whether for patients or, when relevant, other people (principally carers). This is consistent with an objective of maximising health gain from available healthcare resources. Some features of healthcare delivery that are often referred to as 'process characteristics' may ultimately have health consequences; for example, the mode of treatment delivery may have health consequences through its impact on concordance with treatment. Any significant characteristics of healthcare technologies that have a value to people that is independent of any direct effect on health should be noted. These characteristics include the convenience with which healthcare is provided and the level of information available for patients.

This question should be viewed in terms of what is **excluded** in relation to the NICE reference case; that is, non-health effects.

Answer 'yes' if the measure of health outcome used in the analysis excludes non-health effects (or if such effects can be excluded from the results). Answer 'partly' if the analysis includes some non-health effects but these are small and unlikely to change the cost-effectiveness results. Answer 'no' if the analysis includes significant non-health effects that are likely to change the cost-effectiveness results.

1.6   Are both costs and health effects discounted at an annual rate of 3.5%?

The need to discount to a present value is widely accepted in economic evaluation, although the specific rate varies across jurisdictions and over time. NICE considers it appropriate to discount costs and health effects at the same rate. The annual rate of 3.5%, based on the recommendations of the UK Treasury for the discounting of costs, applies to both costs and health effects.

Answer 'yes' if both costs and health effects (for example, QALYs) are discounted at 3.5% per year. Answer 'partly' if costs and effects are discounted at a rate similar to 3.5% (for example, costs and effects are both discounted at 3% per year). Answer 'no' if costs and/or health effects are not discounted, or if they are discounted at a rate (or rates) different from 3.5% (for example, 5% for both costs and effects, or 6% for costs and 1.5% for effects). Note in the comments column what discount rates have been used. If all costs and health effects accrue within a short time (roughly a year), answer 'NA'.

1.7 Is the value of health effects expressed in terms of quality adjusted life years (QALYs)?

The QALY is a measure of a person's length of life weighted by a valuation of their health-related quality of life (HRQoL) over that period.

Given its widespread use, the QALY is considered by NICE to be the most appropriate generic measure of health benefit that reflects both mortality and effects on HRQoL. It is recognised that alternative measures exist (such as the healthy-year equivalent), but few economic evaluations have used these methods and their strengths and weaknesses are not fully established.

NICE's position is that an additional QALY should be given the same weight regardless of the other characteristics of the patients receiving the health benefit.

Answer 'yes' if the effectiveness of the intervention is measured using QALYs; answer 'no' if not. There may be circumstances when a QALY cannot be obtained or where the assumptions underlying QALYs are considered inappropriate. In such situations answer 'no', but consider retaining the study for appraisal. Similarly, answer 'no' but retain the study for appraisal if it does not include QALYs but it is still thought to be useful for GDG decision-making: for example, if the clinical evidence indicates that an intervention might be dominant, and estimates of the relative costs of the interventions from a costminimisation study are likely to be useful. When economic evaluations not using QALYs are retained for full critical appraisal, use the comments column to note why.

1.8 Are changes in health-related quality of life (HRQoL) reported directly from patients and/or carers?

In the NICE reference case, information on changes in HRQoL as a result of treatment should be reported directly by patients (and directly by carers when the impact of treatment on the carer's health is also important). When it is not possible to obtain information on changes in patients' HRQoL directly from them, data should be obtained from carers (not from healthcare professionals).

For consistency, the EQ-5D is NICE's preferred measure of HRQoL in adults. However, when EQ-5D data are not available or are inappropriate for the condition or the effects of treatment, other multi-attribute utility questionnaires (for example, SF6D, Quality of Well-Being Scale or Health Utilities Index) or mapping methods from disease-specific questionnaires may be used to estimate QALYs. For studies not reporting QALYs, a variety of generic or disease-specific methods may be used to measure HRQoL.

Answer 'yes' if changes in patients' HRQoL are estimated by the patients themselves. Answer 'partly' if estimates of patients' HRQoL are provided by carers. Answer 'no' if estimates come from healthcare professionals or researchers. Note in the comments column how HRQoL was measured (EQ-5D, Quality of Well-Being

Scale, Health Utilities Index and so on). Answer 'NA' if the cost-effectiveness study does not include estimates of HRQoL (for example, studies reporting 'cost per life year gained' or cost-minimisation studies).

1.9 Is the valuation of changes in HRQoL (utilities) obtained from a representative sample of the general public?

The NICE reference case specifies that the valuation of changes in HRQoL (utilities) reported by patients should be based on public preferences elicited using a choice-based method (such as the time trade-off or standard gamble) in a representative sample of the UK population.

Answer 'yes' if HRQoL valuations were obtained using the EQ-5D UK tariff. Answer 'partly' if the valuation methods were comparable to those used for the EQ-5D. Answer 'no' if other valuation methods were used. Answer 'NA' if the study does not apply valuations to HRQoL (for studies not reporting QALYs). In the comments column note the valuation method used (such as time trade-off or standard gamble) and the source of the preferences (such as patients or healthcare professionals).

1.10 Overall judgement

Classify the applicability of the economic evaluation to the clinical guideline, the current NHS situation and the context for NICE guidance as one of the following:
- **Directly applicable** – the study meets all applicability criteria, or fails to meet one or more applicability criteria but this is unlikely to change the conclusions about cost effectiveness.
- **Partially applicable** – the study fails to meet one or more applicability criteria, and this could change the conclusions about cost effectiveness.
- **Not applicable** – the study fails to meet one or more applicability criteria, and this is likely to change the conclusions about cost effectiveness. Such studies would be excluded from further consideration and there is no need to continue with the rest of the checklist.

SECTION 2: STUDY LIMITATIONS

2.1 Does the model structure adequately reflect the nature of the health condition under evaluation?

This relates to the choice of model and its structural elements (including cycle length in discrete time models, if appropriate). Model type and its structural aspects should be consistent with a coherent theory of the health condition under evaluation. The selection of treatment pathways, whether health states or branches in a decision tree, should be based on the underlying biological processes of the health issue under study and the potential impact (benefits and adverse consequences) of the intervention(s) of interest.

Answer 'yes' if the model design and assumptions appropriately reflect the health condition and intervention(s) of interest. Answer 'partly' if there are aspects of the model design or assumptions that do not fully reflect the health condition or intervention(s) but that are unlikely to change the cost-effectiveness results. Answer 'no' if the model omits some important aspect of the health condition or intervention(s) and this is likely to change the cost-effectiveness results. Answer 'NA' for economic evaluations based on data from a clinical study which do not extrapolate treatment outcomes or costs beyond the study context or follow-up period.

2.2   Is the time horizon sufficiently long to reflect all important differences in costs and outcomes?

The time horizon is the period of analysis of the study: the length of follow-up for participants in a trial-based evaluation, or the period of time over which the costs and outcomes for a cohort are tracked in a modelling study. This time horizon should always be the same for costs and outcomes, and should be long enough to include all relevant costs and outcomes relating to the intervention. A time horizon shorter than lifetime could be justified if there is no differential mortality effect between options, and the differences in costs and HRQoL relate to a relatively short period (for example, in the case of an acute infection).

Answer 'yes' if the time horizon is sufficient to include all relevant costs and outcomes. Answer 'partly' if the time horizon may omit some relevant costs and outcomes but these are unlikely to change the cost-effectiveness results. Answer 'no' if the time horizon omits important costs and outcomes and this is likely to change the cost-effectiveness results.

2.3   Are all important and relevant health outcomes included?

All relevant health outcomes should include direct health effects relating to harms from the intervention (adverse effects) as well as any potential benefits.

Answer 'yes' if the analysis includes all relevant and important harms and benefits. Answer 'partly' if the analysis omits some harms or benefits but these would be unlikely to change the cost-effectiveness results. Answer 'no' if the analysis omits important harms and/or benefits that would be likely to change the cost-effectiveness results.

2.4   Are the estimates of baseline health outcomes from the best available source?

The estimate of the overall net treatment effect of an intervention is determined by the baseline risk of a particular condition or event and/or the relative effects of the intervention compared with the relevant comparator treatment. The overall net treatment effect may also be determined by other features of the people comprising the population of interest.

The process of assembling evidence for economic evaluations should be systematic – evidence must be identified, quality assessed and, when appropriate, pooled, using explicit criteria and justifiable and reproducible methods. These principles apply to all categories of evidence that are used to estimate clinical and cost effectiveness, evidence for which will typically be drawn from a number of different sources.

The sources and methods for eliciting baseline probabilities should be described clearly. These data can be based on 'natural history' (patient outcomes in the absence of treatment or with routine care), sourced from cohort studies. Baseline probabilities may also be derived from the control arms of experimental studies. Sometimes it may be necessary to rely on expert opinion for particular parameters.

Answer 'yes' if the estimates of baseline health outcomes reflect the best available evidence as identified from a recent well-conducted systematic review of the literature. Answer 'partly' if the estimates are not derived from a systematic review but are likely to reflect outcomes for the relevant group of patients in routine NHS practice (for example, if they are derived from a large UK-relevant cohort study). Answer 'no' if the estimates are unlikely to reflect outcomes for the relevant group in routine NHS practice.

2.5   Are the estimates of relative treatment effects from the best available source?

The objective of the analysis of clinical effectiveness is to produce an unbiased estimate of the mean clinical effectiveness of the interventions being compared.

The NICE reference case indicates that evidence on outcomes should be obtained from a systematic review, defined as the systematic location, inclusion, appraisal and synthesis of evidence to obtain a reliable and valid overview of the data relating to a clearly formulated question.

Synthesis of outcome data through meta-analysis is appropriate provided that there are sufficient relevant and valid data obtained using comparable measures of outcome.

Head-to-head RCTs provide the most valid evidence of relative treatment effect. However, such evidence may not always be available. Therefore, data from non-randomised studies may be required to supplement RCT data. Any potential bias arising from the design of the studies used in the assessment should be explored and documented.

Data from head-to-head RCTs should be presented in the base-case analysis, if available. When head-to-head RCTs exist, evidence from indirect or mixed treatment comparison analyses may be presented if it is considered to add information that is not available from the head-to-head comparison. This indirect or mixed treatment comparison must be fully described and presented in addition to the base-case analysis. (A 'mixed treatment comparison' estimates effect sizes using both head-to-head and indirect comparisons.)

If data from head-to-head RCTs are not available, indirect treatment comparison methods should be used. (An 'indirect comparison' is a synthesis of data from a network of trials that compare the interventions of interest with other comparators.)

When multiple interventions are being assessed that have not been compared within a single RCT, data from a series of pairwise head-to-head RCTs should be presented. Consideration should also be given to presenting a combined analysis using a mixed treatment comparison framework if it is considered to add information that is not available from the head-to-head comparison.

Only indirect or mixed treatment comparison methods that preserve randomisation should be used. The principles of good practice for standard meta-analyses should also be followed in mixed and indirect treatment comparisons.

The methods and assumptions that are used to extrapolate short-term results to final outcomes should be clearly presented and there should be documentation of the reasoning underpinning the choice of survival function.

Evidence for the evaluation of diagnostic technologies should normally incorporate evidence on diagnostic accuracy. It is also important to incorporate the predicted changes in health outcomes and costs resulting from treatment decisions based on the test result. The general principles guiding the assessment of the clinical and cost effectiveness of diagnostic interventions should be the same as for other technologies. However, particular consideration of the methods of analysis may be required, particularly in relation to evidence synthesis. Evidence for the effectiveness of diagnostic technologies should include the costs and outcomes for people whose test results lead to an incorrect diagnosis, as well as for those who are diagnosed correctly.

As for other technologies, RCTs have the potential to capture the pathway of care involving diagnostic technologies, but their feasibility and availability may be limited. Other study designs should be assessed on the basis of their fitness for purpose, taking into consideration the aim of the study (for example, to evaluate outcomes, or to evaluate sensitivity and specificity) and the purpose of the diagnostic technology.

Answer 'yes' if the estimates of treatment effect appropriately reflect all relevant studies of the best available quality, as identified through a recent well-conducted systematic review of the literature. Answer 'partly' if the estimates of treatment effect are not derived from a systematic review but are similar in magnitude to the best available estimates (for example, if the economic evaluation is based on a single large study with treatment effects similar to pooled estimates from all relevant studies). Answer 'no' if the estimates of treatment effect are likely to differ substantively from the best available estimates.

2.6   Are all important and relevant costs included?

Costs related to the condition of interest and incurred in additional years of life gained as a result of treatment should be included in the base-case analysis. This should include the costs of handling non-adherence to treatment and treating side effects. Costs that are considered to be unrelated to the condition or intervention of interest should be excluded. If introduction of the intervention requires additional infrastructure to be put in place, consideration should be given to including such costs in the analysis.

Answer 'yes' if all important and relevant resource use and costs are included given the perspective and the research question under consideration. Answer 'partly' if some relevant resource items are omitted but these are unlikely to affect the cost-effectiveness results. Answer 'no' if important resource items are omitted and these are likely to affect the cost-effectiveness results.

2.7 Are the estimates of resource use from the best available source?

It is important to quantify the effect of the interventions on resource use in terms of physical units (for example, days in hospital or visits to a GP) and valuing those effects in monetary terms using appropriate prices and unit costs. Evidence on resource use should be identified systematically. When expert opinion is used as a source of information, any formal methods used to elicit these data should be clearly reported.

Answer 'yes' if the estimates of resource use appropriately reflect all relevant evidence sources of the best available quality, as identified through a recent well-conducted systematic review of the literature. Answer 'partly' if the estimates of resource use are not derived from a systematic review but are similar in magnitude to the best available estimates. Answer 'no' if the estimates of resource use are likely to differ substantively from the best available estimates.

2.8 Are the unit costs of resources from the best available source?

Resources should be valued using the prices relevant to the NHS and PSS. Given the perspective of the NICE reference case, it is appropriate for the financial costs relevant to the NHS/PSS to be used as the basis of costing, although these may not always reflect the full social opportunity cost of a given resource. A first point of reference in identifying costs and prices should be any current official listing published by the Department of Health and/or the Welsh Assembly Government.

When the acquisition price paid for a resource differs from the public list price (for example, pharmaceuticals and medical devices sold at reduced prices to NHS institutions), the public list price should be used in the base-case analysis. Sensitivity analysis should assess the implications of variations from this price. Analyses based on price reductions for the NHS will only be considered when the reduced prices are transparent and can be consistently available across the NHS, and if the period for which the specified price is available is guaranteed.

National data based on healthcare resource groups (HRGs) such as the Payment by Results tariff can be used when they are appropriate and available. However, data based on HRGs may not be appropriate in all circumstances (for example, when the definition of the HRG is broad, or the mean cost probably does not reflect resource use in relation to the intervention(s) under consideration). In such cases, other sources of evidence, such as micro-costing studies, may be more appropriate. When cost data are taken from the literature, the methods used to identify the sources should be defined. When several alternative sources are available, a justification for the costs chosen should be provided and discrepancies between the sources explained. When appropriate, sensitivity analysis should have been undertaken to assess the implications for results of using alternative data sources.

Answer 'yes' if resources are valued using up-to-date prices relevant to the NHS and PSS. Answer 'partly' if the valuations of some resource items differ from current NHS/PSS unit costs but this is unlikely to change the cost-effectiveness results. Answer 'no' if the valuations of some resource items differ substantively from current NHS/PSS unit costs and this is likely to change the cost-effectiveness results.

2.9   Is an appropriate incremental analysis presented or can it be calculated from the data?

An appropriate incremental analysis is one that compares the expected costs and health outcomes of one intervention with the expected costs and health outcomes of the next-best non-dominated alternative.

Standard decision rules should be followed when combining costs and effects, and should reflect any situation where there is dominance or extended dominance. When there is a trade-off between costs and effects, the results should be presented as an ICER: the ratio of the difference in mean costs to the difference in mean outcomes of a technology compared with the next best alternative. In addition to ICERs, expected net monetary or health benefits can be presented using values placed on a QALY gained of £20,000 and £30,000.

For cost-consequence analyses, appropriate incremental analysis can only be done by selecting one of the consequences as the primary measure of effectiveness.

Answer 'yes' if appropriate incremental results are presented, or if data are presented that allow the reader to calculate the incremental results. Answer 'no' if: (i) simple ratios of costs to effects are presented for each alternative compared with a standard intervention; or (ii) if options subject to simple or extended dominance are not excluded from the incremental analyses.

2.10   Are all important parameters whose values are uncertain subjected to appropriate sensitivity analysis?

There are a number of potential selection biases and uncertainties in any evaluation (trial- or model-based) and these should be identified and quantified where possible. There are three types of bias or uncertainty to consider:
- Structural uncertainty – for example in relation to the categorisation of different states of health and the representation of different pathways of care. These structural assumptions should be clearly documented and the evidence and rationale to

support them provided. The impact of structural uncertainty on estimates of cost-effectiveness should be explored by separate analyses of a representative range of plausible scenarios.

- Source of values to inform parameter estimates – the implications of different estimates of key parameters (such as estimates of relative effectiveness) must be reflected in sensitivity analyses (for example, through the inclusion of alternative scenarios). Inputs must be fully justified, and uncertainty explored by sensitivity analysis using alternative input values.
- Parameter precision – uncertainty around the mean health and cost inputs in the model. Distributions should be assigned to characterise the uncertainty associated with the (precision of) mean parameter values. Probabilistic sensitivity analysis is preferred, as this enables the uncertainty associated with parameters to be simultaneously reflected in the results of the model. In non-linear decision models – when there is not a straight-line relationship between inputs and outputs of a model (such as Markov models) – probabilistic methods provide the best estimates of mean costs and outcomes. Simple decision trees are usually linear.

The mean value, distribution around the mean, and the source and rationale for the supporting evidence should be clearly described for each parameter included in the model.

Evidence about the extent of correlation between individual parameters should be considered carefully and reflected in the probabilistic analysis. Assumptions made about the correlations should be clearly presented.

Answer 'yes' if an extensive sensitivity analysis was undertaken that explored all key uncertainties in the economic evaluation. Answer 'partly' if the sensitivity analysis failed to explore some important uncertainties in the economic evaluation. Answer 'no' if the sensitivity analysis was very limited and omitted consideration of a number of important uncertainties, or if the range of values or distributions around parameters considered in the sensitivity analysis were not reported.

2.11   Is there no potential conflict of interest?

The BMJ defines competing interests for its authors as follows: 'A competing interest exists when professional judgment concerning a primary interest (such as patients' welfare or the validity of research) may be influenced by a secondary interest (such as financial gain or personal rivalry). It may arise for the authors of a BMJ article when they have a financial interest that may influence, probably without their knowing, their interpretation of their results or those of others.' Whenever a potential financial conflict of interest is possible, this should be declared.

Answer 'yes' if the authors declare that they have no financial conflicts of interest. Answer 'no' if clear financial conflicts of interest are declared or apparent (for example, from the stated affiliation of the authors). Answer 'unclear' if the article does not indicate whether or not there are financial conflicts of interest.

2.12 Overall assessment

The overall methodological study quality of the economic evaluation should be classified as one of the following:

- **Minor limitations** – the study meets all quality criteria, or the study fails to meet one or more quality criteria but this is unlikely to change the conclusions about cost effectiveness.
- **Potentially serious limitations** – the study fails to meet one or more quality criteria and this could change the conclusions about cost effectiveness.
- **Very serious limitations** – the study fails to meet one or more quality criteria and this is highly likely to change the conclusions about cost effectiveness. Such studies should usually be excluded from further consideration.

APPENDIX 14:
EXPERIENCE OF CARE: PERSONAL ACCOUNTS
AND THEMATIC ANALYSIS

The experience of care accounts can be found on the CD accompanying this guideline.

APPENDIX 15:
NETWORK META-ANALYSIS FOR THE ECONOMIC MODEL

This section outlines the network meta-analysis undertaken for the economic model assessing the cost effectiveness of pharmacological interventions for relapse prevention in people in recovery from alcohol dependence

Clinical data considered in the network meta-analysis
Clinical data for the network meta-analysis were derived from trials included in the guideline systematic literature review on pharmacological interventions for relapse prevention in people in recovery from alcohol dependence. This review included 33 RCTs that reported relapse data for one or more of the interventions assessed in the economic analysis. The evidence network constructed based on the available data is shown in Figure 12. Inspection of the network and the available evidence indicated that 32 studies contributed to provision of direct or indirect evidence on the relative effect between the three interventions assessed in the economic model, and thus should be considered in network meta-analysis. The time horizon of these studies ranged from 3 to 12 months. Table 108 provides the relapse data included in the network meta-analysis the studies, as well as the time horizons of the studies considered.

Figure 12: Evidence network for data on relapse to alcohol dependence

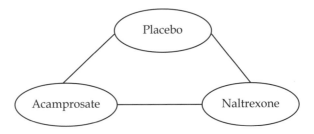

Appendix 15

Table 108: Summary of the data reported in the RCTs included in the guideline systematic review on rates of relapse to alcohol dependence used in the network meta-analysis

Study	Timepoint (months)	Comparators	Number of people relapsing	Number of people in each arm
1. ANTON1999	3	1) Placebo 2) Naltrexone	38 26	63 68
2. ANTON2005	3	1) Placebo 2) Naltrexone	47 33	80 80
3. ANTON2006	12	1) Placebo 2) Naltrexone 3) Acamprosate	126 122 117	156 155 151
4. BALLDIN2003	3	1) Placebo 2) Naltrexone	58 53	62 56
5. BESSON1998	12	1) Placebo 3) Acamprosate	47 41	55 55
6. CHICK2000A	3	1) Placebo 2) Naltrexone	61 64	85 90
7. CHICK2000B	6	1) Placebo 3) Acamprosate	242 245	292 289
8. GASTPAR2002	3	1) Placebo 2) Naltrexone	36 34	87 84
9. GEERLINGS1997	6	1) Placebo 3) Acamprosate	116 96	134 128
10. GUARDIA2002	3	1) Placebo 2) Naltrexone	19 8	99 93
11. HEINALA2001	3	1) Placebo 2) Naltrexone	54 52	58 63
12. HUANG2005	3	1) Placebo 2) Naltrexone	4 3	20 20
13. KIEFER2003	6	1) Placebo 2) Naltrexone 3) Acamprosate	32 21 22	40 40 40
14. KILLEEN2004	3	1) Placebo 2) Naltrexone	12 21	36 51
15. KRYSTAL2001	3	1) Placebo 2) Naltrexone	83 143	187 378
16. LATT2002	3	1) Placebo 2) Naltrexone	27 19	51 56

Continued

Table 108: (*Continued*)

Study	Timepoint (months)	Comparators	Number of people relapsing	Number of people in each arm
17. LEE2001	3	1) Placebo 2) Naltrexone	8 8	15 24
18. MONTI2001	3	1) Placebo 2) Naltrexone	21 18	64 64
19. MORLEY2006	3	1) Placebo 2) Naltrexone 3) Acamprosate	43 39 40	61 53 55
20. MORRIS2001	3	1) Placebo 2) Naltrexone	26 19	33 38
21. OMALLEY2008	3	1) Placebo 2) Naltrexone	28 22	34 34
22. OSLIN1997	3	1) Placebo 2) Naltrexone	8 3	23 21
23. OSLIN2008	6	1) Placebo 2) Naltrexone	76 73	120 120
24. PAILLE1995	12	1) Placebo 3) Acamprosate	144 113	177 173
25. PELC1992	6	1) Placebo 3) Acamprosate	43 35	47 55
26. PELC1997	3	1) Placebo 3) Acamprosate	46 31	62 63
27. POLDRUGO1997	6	1) Placebo 3) Acamprosate	79 58	124 122
28. SASS1996	6	1) Placebo 3) Acamprosate	105 73	138 137
29. TEMPESTA2000	6	1) Placebo 3) Acamprosate	61 49	166 164
30. VOLPICELLI1992	3	1) Placebo 2) Naltrexone	19 8	35 35
31. VOLPICELLI1997	3	1) Placebo 2) Naltrexone	26 17	49 48
32. WHITWORTH1996	12	1) Placebo 3) Acamprosate	139 129	224 224

Network meta-analysis – full random effects model
A full random effects model (model 1) was constructed to estimate the relative effect
between the $k = 3$ interventions assessed, using data from the 32 RCTs summarised
in Table 108. The data for each trial j comprised a binomial likelihood:

$$r_{jk} \sim \text{Bin } (p_{jk}, n_{jk})$$

where p_{jk} is the probability of relapse in trial j under treatment k, r_{jk} is the number of
people experiencing relapse in trial j under treatment k, and n_{jk} is the total number of
people at risk of relapse in trial j under treatment k.

The duration of the trials considered in the analysis varied from 3 to 12 months.
The model assumed constant hazards $\exp(\theta_{jk})$ acting over a period T_j in months. Thus,
the probability of relapse by the end of the period T_j for treatment k in trial j was:

$$p_{jk}(T_j) = 1 - \exp\left(-\exp(\theta_{jk})\, T_j\right)$$

Treatment effects were modelled on the log-hazard rate scale and were assumed
to be additive to the baseline treatment b in trial j:

$$\begin{aligned} \theta_{jk} &= \mu_{jb} && \text{for} \quad k = b; \\ \theta_{jk} &= \mu_{jb} + \delta_{jkb} && \text{for} \quad k \neq b \end{aligned}$$

where μ_{jb} is the log hazard of relapse for 'baseline' treatment b in trial j and δ_{jkb}
is the trial-specific log-hazard ratio of treatment k relative to treatment b.

The full random effects model took into account the correlation structure induced
by three multi-arm trials included in the 32 RCTs; this type of model structure relies
on the realisation of the bivariate normal distribution as a univariate marginal distribution and a univariate conditional distribution (Higgins & Whitehead, 1996):

$$\text{If} \begin{pmatrix} x_1 \\ x_2 \end{pmatrix} \sim N\left[\begin{pmatrix} \mu_1 \\ \mu_2 \end{pmatrix}, \begin{pmatrix} \sigma_1 & \sigma_1/2 \\ \sigma_2/2 & \sigma_2 \end{pmatrix}\right]$$

$$x_1 \sim N(\mu_1, \sigma^2), \text{ and } x_2\, |x_1 \sim N\left(\mu_2 + \frac{1}{2}(x_1 - \mu_1), \frac{3}{4}\sigma_2\right)$$

then

The trial-specific log-hazard ratios for every pair of interventions were assumed
to come from a normal random effects distribution:

$$\delta_{jkb} \sim Normal\ (d_{kb}, \sigma^2)$$

The mean of this distribution (d_{kb}) is the true mean effect size between k and b and
σ^2 is the variance of the normal distribution which was assumed to be common in all
pairs of treatments.

Vague priors were assigned to trial baselines, mean treatment effects and common variance:

$$\mu_{jb}, d_{kb} \sim Normal\ (0,\ 100^2); \qquad \sigma \sim Uniform\ (0,2)$$

A separate random effects model (model 2) was constructed to estimate the baseline placebo effect, using relapse data from the 32 trials with a placebo arm included in the guideline systematic review. The placebo effect (φ_j) was again modelled on a log hazard scale and was assumed to come from a normal random effects distribution:

$$\varphi_j \sim Normal\ (B,\ \omega^2)$$

$$B \sim Normal\ (0,\ 100^2);\ \omega \sim Uniform\ (0,\ 2)$$

$$p_j(T_j) = 1 - \exp\ (-\exp(\varphi_j)\ T_j)$$

Subsequently, the absolute log hazard θ_{jk} of each drug k was estimated based on the treatment effect relative to placebo (estimated in model 1) added to a random value of the absolute log hazard of placebo (estimated in model 2). The output of the model that was used in the economic analysis was the probability of relapse for each intervention by the end of 12 months.

Analysis was undertaken following Bayesian statistics principles and conducted using Markov chain Monte Carlo simulation techniques implemented in WinBUGS 1.4 (Lunn *et al.*, 2000; Spiegelhalter *et al.*, 2001). The first 60,000 iterations were discarded, and 300,000 further iterations were run; because of high autocorrelation observed in some model parameters, the model was thinned so that every 30th simulation was retained. Consequently, 10,000 posterior simulations were recorded.

The goodness of fit of the model to the data was measured by calculating the residual deviance defined as the difference between the deviance for the fitted model and the deviance for the saturated model, where the deviance measures the fit of the model to the data points using the likelihood function. Under the null hypothesis that the model provides an adequate fit to the data, it is expected that residual deviance would have a mean equal to the number of unconstrained data points (Cooper *et al.*, 2006). The residual deviance was calculated to be 44.86. This corresponds reasonably well with the number of unconstrained data points (67) of the model.

The WinBUGS code used to estimate the 12-month probability of relapse is provided in Table 109.

Table 110 provides summary statistics of a number of model parameters, including the log hazard ratios of the two drugs versus placebo and the between-trials variation. Results are reported as mean values with 95% credible intervals, which are analogous to CIs in frequentist statistics.

Table 109: WinBUGS code used for network meta-anlysis to estimate 12-month probability of relapse

```
model{
sw[1] <- 0
for(i in 1:67){
r[i] ~ dbin(p[i],n[i])                      #binomial likelihood
theta[i] < -mu[s[i]]+ delta[i]*(1-equals(t[i],b[i]))   #baseline and treatment effects
delta[i] ~ dnorm(md[i],taud[i])             #trial-specific log-hazard
                                            distributions
taud[i] <- tau * (1 + equals(m[i],3) /3)    #precisions of log-hazard
                                            distributions
md[i] <- d[t[i]] - d[b[i]] + equals(m[i],3) * sw[i]   #mean of random effect
p[i] <- (1-exp(-lam[i]*w[i]/360))           # pr of event (w = days; 360
                                            days = 12 mths)
log(lam[i]) <- theta[i]                     # log rates for each arm
rhat[i] <- p[i] * n[i]                      #predicted events
dev[i] <- -2 *r[i]*log(rhat[i]/r[i])        #deviance residuals for data i
}
resdev <-sum(dev[])                         #total deviance
for (i in 2:67) { sw[i] <- (delta[i-1] - d[t[i-1]]
+ d[b[i-1]] ) /2}                           #adjustment for 3 arm trials

#priors
for(j in 1:32){ mu[j] ~ dnorm(0,.0001)}     #vague priors for trial baselines
tau <- 1/(sd*sd)                            #precision
sd ~ dunif(0,2)                             # vague prior for random effects
                                            standard deviation
d[1] < -0
for (k in 2:3){d[k] ~ dnorm(0,.0001)        #vague priors for basic parameters
log(hazr[k]) <-d[k]                         #hazard ratios
}

#code for absolute effects on baseline (placebo, treatment 1)
for (i in 1:33) {
rb[i] ~ dbin(pb[i],nb[i])                   #binomial likelihood
pb[i] <- (1-exp(-lamb[i]*wb[i]/360))        # probability of event (w = days;
                                            360 days = 12 mths)
log(lamb[i]) <- mub[sb[i]]                  # log rate
}
```

```
for (j in 1:33) {mub[j] ~ dnorm(mb,tab)}            # priors for outcome and
                                                    trial-specific events
mb ~ dnorm(0,.001)
tab <- 1/(sdb*sdb)
sdb ~ dunif(0,2)


#code for predicted effects at 360 days, on a probability scale. Baseline risks in
mub[33] - new trial
d.new[1] <-0
for(k in 2:3)
{d.new[k] ~ dnorm(d[k],tau)}
for (k in 1:3)
{theta360[k] <-mub[33] +d.new[k]
log(lam360[k]) <-theta360[k]
p360[k] <- (1-exp(-lam360[k]))
}


# prob that treatment k is best
for (k in 1:3) { rk[k] <- rank(d[],k)
best[k] <- equals(rk[k],1) #Smallest is best (i.e. rank 1)
for (h in 1:3) { prob[h,k] <- equals(rk[k],h) }}
}


#initial values 1
list(
d = c(NA,0,0),sd = 1,mu = c(0,0,0,0,0, 0,0,0,0,0, 0,0,0,0,0, 0,0,0,0,0, 0,0,0,0,0, 0,0,0,0,0,
0,0),delta = c(0,0,0,0,0,  0,0,0,0,0,  0,0,0,0,0,  0,0,0,0,0,  0,0,0,0,0,  0,0,0,0,0,  0,0,0,0,0,
0,0,0,0,0, 0,0,0,0,0, 0,0,0,0,0, 0,0,0,0,0, 0,0,0,0,0, 0,0), sdb = 1,
mub = c(NA,0,0,0,0, 0,0,0,0,0, 0,0,0,0,0, 0,0,0,0,0, 0,0,0,0,0, 0,0,0,0,0, 0,0, NA),
mb = 1
)


#initial values 2
list(
d = c(NA,1,-1),sd = 1.2,mu = c(0,0.5,0,2,0,0, 1,-1,-1,0,0, -1,-1,-1,0,0, 1,1,1,0,-0.5,
0,1,-1,0,1, 0.5,2,1,0.3, 0.2, 0.1),delta = c(0.5,0.5,0.6,0.4,0.3, 1,-1,-1,-1,-1, 0,1,0.3,0.2,0, -
0.5,0,-1,-1,-1, 1,1,1,-1,0.1, 0.1,1,-1,-0.1,0, 0,1,1.5,0,-1, -1,0,1,1,1, 1,-0.1,0.5,0,1, 0,1,1,1,1,
-1,-1,-1,0,0,   1,1,1,0.5,0.5,   0,1,0,1,0,0,1),    sdb = 0.7,mub = c(NA,0.5,0.7,-1,0.2,
0.05,0.4,1,1,  1, -1,0.3,1,1,  0.2,0.3,0.4,-1,-1,  0.2,0.3,0.4,1.1,0.5,  -0.2,0,-1,0,-1,  0,0.4,-0.2,
NA),mb = 0.5
)
```

Table 110: Summary statistics estimated from network meta-analysis

Node	Mean	SD	MC error	25%	Median	75%	Start	Sample
p360[1]	0.8956	0.125	0.001383	0.5509	0.9433	1.0	60001	10000
p360[2]	0.8253	0.1656	0.001840	0.4095	0.8741	0.9997	60001	10000
p360[3]	0.8176	0.1691	0.001737	0.3894	0.8633	0.9996	60001	10000
sd	0.2043	0.05914	0.00084	0.0984	0.2011	0.3293	60001	10000
resdev	44.73	70.59	0.7011	−91.8	44.04	187.1	60001	10000

APPENDIX 16:

INCLUDED/EXCLUDED STUDY TABLES

The following appendices can be found on the CD accompanying this guideline:
- 16a – Experience of care study table
- 16b – Organisation of care study table
- 16c – Rehabilitation study table
- 16d – Psychological interventions study table
- 16e – Pharmacological interventions study table.

APPENDIX 17:

CLINICAL EVIDENCE FOREST PLOTS

The following appendices can be found on the CD accompanying this guideline:
● 17a – Organisation of care forest plots
● 17b – Rehabilitation forest plots
● 17c – Psychological interventions forest plots
● 17d – Pharmacological interventions forest plots.

APPENDIX 18:
GRADE EVIDENCE PROFILES

The following appendices can be found on the CD accompanying this guideline:
- 18a – Organisation of care GRADE tables
- 18b – Rehabilitation GRADE tables
- 18c – Psychological interventions GRADE tables
- 18d – Pharmacological interventions GRADE tables.

APPENDIX 19:
EVIDENCE TABLES FOR ECONOMIC STUDIES

This appendix can be found on the CD accompanying this guideline.

10   REFERENCES

Adamson, S. J. & Sellman, J. D. (2008) Five-year outcomes of alcohol-dependent persons treated with motivational enhancement. *Journal of Studies on Alcohol and Drugs*, *69*, 589–593.

Adamson, S. J., Sellman, J. D. & Frampton, C. M. (2009) Patient predictors of alcohol treatment outcome: a systematic review. *Journal of Substance Abuse Treatment*, *36*, 75–86.

Adamson, S. J., Heather, N., Morton, V., *et al.* (2010) Initial preference for drinking goal in the treatment of alcohol problems: II. Treatment outcomes. *Alcohol and Alcoholism*, *45*, 136–142.

Addolorato, G., Leggio, L., Ferrulli, A., *et al.* (2007) Effectiveness and safety of baclofen for maintenance of alcohol abstinence in alcohol-dependent patients with liver cirrhosis: randomised, double-blind controlled study. *The Lancet*, *370*, 1915–1922.

Addolorato, G., Leggio, L., Ojetti, V., *et al.* (2008) Effects of short-term moderate alcohol administration on oxidative stress and nutritional status in healthy males. *Appetite*, *50*, 50–56.

Adelstein, A. M., Marmot, M. G. & Bulusu, L. (1984) Migrant studies in Britatin. *British Medical Bulletin*, *40*, 315–319.

Agrawal, A., Hinrichs, A. L., Dunn, G., *et al.* (2008) Linkage scan for quantitative traits identifies new regions of interest for substance dependence in the Collaborative Study on the Genetics of Alcoholism (COGA) sample. *Drug and Alcohol Dependence*, *93*, 12–20.

AGREE Collaboration (2001) *Appraisal of Guidelines for Research and Evaluation (AGREE) Instrument*. London: St George's Hospital Medical School.

AGREE Collaboration (2003) Development and validation of an international appraisal instrument for assessing the quality of clinical practice guidelines: the AGREE project. *Quality and Safety in Health Care*, *12*, 18–23.

Ahles, T. A., Schlundt, D. G., Prue, D. M., *et al.* (1983) Impact of aftercare arrangements on the maintenance of treatment success in abusive drinkers. *Addictive Behaviors*, *8*, 53–58.

Ahmadi, J. & Ahmadi, N. (2002) A double-blind, placebo-controlled study of naltrexone in the treatment of alcohol dependence. *German Journal of Psychiatry*, *5*, 85–89.

Ahn, H. & Wampold, B. (2001) Where oh where are the specific ingredients? A meta-analysis of component studies in counseling and psychotherapy. *Journal of Counseling Psychology*, *48*, 251–257.

Aira, M., Kauhanen, J., Larivaara, P., *et al.* (2003) Factors influencing inquiry about patients' alcohol consumption by primary health care physicians: qualitative semi-structured interview study. *Family Practice*, *20*, 270–275.

Alcoholics Anonymous (2010) About Us: Membership. Available from: http://www. alcoholics-anonymous.org.uk/?PageID=54 [accessed May 2011].

Alden, L. E. (1988) Behavioral self-management controlled-drinking strategies in a context of secondary prevention. *Journal of Consulting and Clinical Psychology*, *56*, 280–286.

Alessi, S. M., Hanson, T., Wieners, M., *et al.* (2007) Low-cost contingency management in community clinics: delivering incentives partially in group therapy. *Experimental and Clinical Psychopharmacology*, *15*, 293–300.

Alexander, L. (1940) Wernicke's disease. Identity of lesions produced experimentally by B1 avitaminosis in pigeons with hemorhaggic polioencephalitis occurring in chronic alcoholism in man. *American Journal of Pathology*, *16*, 61–70.

Alexander, J. F., Waldron, H. B., Newberry, A., *et al.* (1990) The functional family therapy model. In *Family Therapy for Adolescent Drug Abuse* (eds A. S. Friedman & S. Granick), pp. 183–200. Lexington, MA: Lexington Books.

Allan, C., Smith, I. & Mellin, M. (2000) Detoxification from alcohol: a comparison of home detoxification and hospital-based day patient care. *Alcohol and Alcoholism*, *35*, 66–69.

Allen, J., Copello, A. & Orford, J. (2005) Fear during alcohol detoxification: views from the clients' perspective. *Journal of Health Psychology*, *10*, 503–510.

Allen, J. P. (2003) Assessment of alcohol problems: an overview. In *Assessing Alcohol Problems: A Guide for Clinicians and Researchers.* (eds J. P. Allen & V. B. Wilson). Bethesda, MD: National Institute on Alcohol Abuse and Alcoholism.

Allen, J. P. & Wilson, V. B. (eds) (2003) *Assessing Alcohol Problems: A Guide for Clinicians and Researchers.* Bethesda, MD: National Institute on Alcohol Abuse and Alcoholism.

Allen, J. P., Sillanaukee, P., Strid, N., *et al.* (2003) In *Assessing Alcohol Problems: A Guide for Clinicians and Researchers.* (eds Allen, J. P. & Wilson, V. B.). Bethesda, MD: National Institute on Alcohol Abuse and Alcoholism.

Allen, N. B., Chambers, R. & Knight, W. (2006) Mindfulness-based psychotherapies: a review of conceptual foundations, empirical evidence and practical considerations. *Australian and New Zealand Journal of Psychiatry*, *40*, 285–294.

Alterman, A., Hayashida, M. & O'Brien, C. P. (1988) Treatment response and safety of ambulatory medical detoxification. *Journal of Studies on Alcohol*, *49*, 160–166.

Altintoprak, A. E., Zorlu, N., Coskunol, H., *et al.* (2008) Effectiveness and tolerability of mirtazapine and amitriptyline in alcoholic patients with co-morbid depressive disorder: a randomized, double-blind study. *Human Psychopharmacology: Clinical and Experimental*, *23*, 313–319.

Altman, D. G. & Bland, J. M. (1994a) Diagnostic tests 1: sensitivity and specificity. *British Medical Journal*, *308*, 1552.

Altman, D. G. & Bland, J. M. (1994b) Diagnostic tests 2: predictive values. *British Medical Journal*, *309*, 102.

Alwyn, T., John, B., Hodgson, R. J., *et al.* (2004) The addition of a psychological intervention to a home detoxification programme. *Alcohol and Alcoholism*, *39*, 536–541.

References

American Academy of Child and Adolescent Psychiatry (2005) Practice parameter for the assessment and treatment of children and adolescents with substance use disorders. *Journal of the American Academy of Child and Adolescent Psychiatry*, *44*, 609–621.

Anderson, D. A. & Parker, J. D. (1997) The use of a mental status examination in a chemical dependence treatment program. *Journal of Substance Abuse Treatment*, *14*, 377–382.

Anderson, P. & Baumberg, B. (2005) *Alcohol in Europe. A Report for the European Commission*. London: Institute of Alcohol Studies.

Andreasson, S., Hansagi, H. & Österlund, B. (2002) Short-term treatment for alcohol-related problems: four session guided self change versus one session of advice – a randomized, controlled trial. *Addiction*, *28*, 57–62.

Annemans, L., Vanoverbeke, N., Tecco, J., *et al.* (2000) Economic evaluation of Campral (Acamprosate) compared to placebo in maintaining abstinence in alcohol-dependent patients. *European Addiction Research*, *6*, 71–78.

Annis, H. A. (1986) A relapse prevention model for treatment of alcoholics. In *Treating Addictive Behaviors. Processes of Change* (eds W. R. Miller & N. Heather), New York: Plenum Press.

Annis, H. M. (1996) Inpatient versus outpatient setting effects in alcoholism treatment: revisiting the evidence. *Addiction*, *91*, 1804–1807.

Anton, R. F. (2008) Naltrexone for the management of alcohol dependence. *New England Journal of Medicine*, *359*, 715–721.

Anton, R. F. & Moak, D. H. (1994) Carbohydrate deficient transferrin (CDT) and gamma-glutamyl transferase (GGT) as markers of heavy alcohol consumption: gender differences. *Alcoholism: Clinical and Experimental Research*, *18*, 747–754.

Anton, R. F., Moak, D. H., Waid, L. R., *et al.* (1999) Naltrexone and cognitive behavioral therapy for the treatment of outpatient alcoholics: results of a placebo controlled trial. *American Journal of Psychiatry*, *156*, 1758–1764.

Anton, R. F., Pettinati, H., Zweben, A., *et al.* (2004) A multi-site dose ranging study of Nalmefene in the treatment of alcohol dependence. *Journal of Clinical Psychopharmacology*, 24, 421–428.

Anton, R. F., Moak, D. H., Latham, P., *et al.* (2005) Naltrexone combined with either cognitive behavioural or motivational enhancement therapy for alcohol dependence. *Journal of Clinical Psychopharmacology*, *25*, 349–357.

Anton, R. F., O'Malley, S. S., Ciraulo, D. A., *et al.* (2006) Combined pharmacotherapies and behavioral interventions for alcohol dependence. *The Journal of the American Medical Association*, *295*, 2003–2017.

Anton, R. F., Kranzler, H., Breder, C., *et al.* (2008a) A randomized, multicenter, double-blind, placebo-controlled study of the efficacy and safety of aripiprazole for the treatment of alcohol dependence. *Journal of Clinical Psychopharmacology*, *28*, 5–12.

Anton, R. F., Oroszi, G., O'Malley, S., *et al.* (2008b) An evaluation of μ-opioid receptor (OPRM1) as a predictor of naltrexone response in the treatment of alcohol dependence: results from the Combined Pharmacotherapies and

Behavioral Interventions for Alcohol Dependence (COMBINE) study. *Archives of General Psychiatry*, *65*, 135–144.

APA (1987) *Diagnostic and Statistical Manual of Mental Disorders* (3rd edn, revised) (DSM–III–R). Washington, DC: APA.

APA (1994) *Diagnostic and Statistical Manual of Mental Disorders* (4th edn, revised) (DSM–IV). Washington, DC: APA.

APA (2010) *DSM–5 Development: Substance-Related Disorders.* Washington, DC: APA. Available from: www.dsm5.org/proposedrevisions/pages/substance-relateddisorders.aspx [Accessed 5 October 2010].

Army Individual Test Battery (1944) *Manual of Directions and Scoring.* Washington, DC: War Department, Adjutant General's Office.

Asplund, C. A., Aaronson, J. W., & Aaronson, H. E. (2004) 3 regimens for alcohol withdrawal and detoxification. *Journal of Family Practice*, *53*, 545–554.

Babor, T. F. (1996) Reliability of the ethanol dependence syndrome scale. *Psychology of Addictive Behaviors*, *10*, 97–103.

Babor, T. F., Higgins-Biddle, J. C., Saunders, J. B., *et al.* (2001). *AUDIT – The Alcohol Use Disorders Identification Test: Guidelines for Use in Primary Care* (2nd edn). Geneva: WHO.

Babor, T. F., Steinberg, K., Zweben, A., *et al.* (2003) Treatment effects across multiple dimensions of outcome. In *Treatment Matching in Alcoholism* (eds T. F. Babor & F. K. Del Boca), pp. 50–165. Cambridge: Cambridge University Press.

Bacchus, L. (1999) Client perceptions of inpatient treatment: a qualitative account with implications for service delivery. *Drugs: Education, Prevention and Policy*, *6*, 87–97.

Back, S. E., Brady, K. T., Sonne, S. C., *et al.* (2006) Symptom improvement in co-occurring PTSD and alcohol dependence. *The Journal of Nervous and Mental Disease*, *194*, 690–696.

Baekeland, F., Lundwell, L., Kissin, B., *et al.* (1971) Correlates of outcome in disulfiram treatment of alcoholism. *The Journal of Nervous and Mental Disease*, *153*, 1–9.

Bagrel, A., d'Houtaud, A., Gueguen, R., *et al.* (1979) Relations between reported alcohol consumption and certain biological variables in an "unselected" population. *Clinical Chemistry*, *25*, 1242–1246.

Bak, T. & Mioshi, E. (2007) A cognitive bedside assessment beyond the MMSE: the Addenbrooke's Cognitive Examination. *Practical Neurology*, *7*, 245–249.

Balldin, J., Berglund, M., Borg, S., *et al.* (2003) A 6-month controlled naltrexone study: combined effect with cognitive behavioral therapy in outpatient treatment of alcohol dependence. *Alcoholism: Clinical and Experimental Research*, *27*, 1142–1149.

Baltieri, D. A., & de Andrade, A. G. (2003) Efficacy of acamprosate in the treatment of alcohol-dependent outpatients. *Revista Brasileira de Psiquiatria*, *25*, 156–159.

Baltieri, D. A., Daró, F. R., Ribeiro, P. L., *et al.* (2008) Comparing topiramate with naltrexone in the treatment of alcohol dependence. *Addiction*, *103*, 2035–2044.

Banys, P. (1988) The clinical use of disulfiram (Antabuse): a review. *Journal of Psychoactive Drugs*, *20*, 243–260.

Barber, J. P., Crits-Christoph, P. & Luborsky, L. (1996) Effects of therapist adherence and competence on patient outcome in brief dynamic therapy. *Journal of Consulting and Clinical Psychology, 64*, 619–622.

Barber, J. P., Gallop, R., Crits-Christoph, P., *et al.* (2006) The role of therapist adherence, therapist competence, and the alliance in predicting outcome of individual drug counseling: Results from the NIDA Collaborative Cocaine Treatment Study. *Psychotherapy Research, 16*, 229–240.

Barnaby, B., Drummond, D. C., McCloud, A., *et al.* (2003) Substance misuse in psychiatric inpatients: comparison of a screening questionnaire survey with case notes. *British Medical Journal, 327*, 783–784.

Barrias, J. A., Chabac, S., Ferreira, L., *et al.* (1997) Acamprosate: multicenter Portuguese efficacy and tolerance evaluation study. *Psiquiatria Clinica, 18*, 149–160.

Barry, K. L. & Fleming, M. F. (1993) The Alcohol Use Disorders Identification Test (AUDIT) and the SMAST-13 predictive validity in a rural primary care sample. *Alcohol, 28*, 33–42.

Bart, G., Schluger, J. H., Borg, L., *et al.* (2005) Nalmefene induced elevation in serum prolactin in normal human volunteers: partial kappa-opioid agonist activity? *Neuropsychopharmacology, 30*, 2254–2262.

Bartu, A. & Saunders, W. (1994) Domiciliary detoxification: a cost effective alternative to inpatient treatment. *Australian Journal of Advanced Nursing, 11*, 12–18.

Bates, M. E., Barry, D. & Dowden, S. C. (2002) Neurocognitive impairment associated with alcohol use disorders: implications for treatment. *Experimental and Clinical Psychopharmacology, 10*, 193–212.

Beck, A. T., Wright, F. D., Newman, C. F., *et al.* (1993) *Cognitive Therapy of Substance Abuse.* New York, NY: Guildford Press.

Beich, A., Gannik, D., & Malterud, K. (2002) Screening and brief intervention for excessive alcohol use: qualitative interview study of the experiences of general practitioners. *British Medical Journal, 325*, 870–874.

Bell, D. C., Williams, M. L., Nelson, R., *et al.* (1994) An experimental test of retention in residential and outpatient programs. *American Journal of Drug and Alcohol Abuse, 20*, 331–340.

Bennett-Levy, J., Richards, D. A. & Farrand, P. (eds) (2010) *The Oxford Guide to Low Intensity CBT Interventions.* Oxford: Oxford University Press.

Berglund, M. (2005) A better widget? Three lessons for improving addiction treatment from a meta-analytical study. *Addiction, 100*, 742–750.

Berlin, J. A. (2001) Does blinding of readers affect the results of meta-analyses? *Lancet, 350*, 185–186.

Besson, J., Aeby, F., Kasas, A., *et al.* (1998) Combined efficacy of acamprosate and disulfiram in the treatment of alcoholism: a controlled study. *Alcoholism: Clinical and Experimental Research, 22*, 573–579.

Beullens, J. & Aertgeerts, B. (2004) Screening for alcohol abuse and dependence in older people using DSM criteria: a review. *Aging & Mental Health, 8*, 76–82.

Bien, T. H., Miller, W. R. & Tonigan, J. S. (1993) Brief interventions for alcohol problems: a review. *Addiction*, *88*, 315–335.

Bischof, G., Grothues, J., Reinhardt, S., *et al.* (2008). Evaluation of a telephone-based stepped care intervention for alcohol-related disorders: a randomised controlled trial. *Drug and Alcohol Dependence*, *93*, 244–251.

Bischof, G. H., Richmond, C. J. & Case, A. R. (2003) Detoxification at home: a brief solution-oriented family systems approach. *Contemporary Family Medicine*, *25*, 17–39.

Blondell, R. D. (2005) Ambulatory detoxification of patients with alcohol dependence. *American Family Physician*, *71*, 495–502.

Blondell, R. D., Looney, S. W., Hottman, L. M., *et al.* (2002) Characteristics of intoxicated trauma patients. *Journal of Addiction Disorders*, *21*, 1–12.

Boeijinga, P. H., Parot, P., Soufflet, L., *et al.* (2004) Pharmacodynamic effects of acamprosate on markers of cerebral function in alcohol-dependent subjects administered as pre-treatment and during alcohol abstinence. *Neuropsychobiology*, *50*, 71–77.

Boland, B., Drummond, D. C. & Kaner, E. (2008) Brief interventions for alcohol use disorders. *Advances in Psychiatric Treatment*, *14*, 469–476.

Bond, G. R. & McDonel, E. C. (1991) Assertive community treatment and reference groups: an evaluation of their effectiveness for young adults with serious mental illness and substance abuse problems. *Psychiatric Rehabilitation Journal*, *15*, 31–43.

Book, S. W., Thomas, S. E., Randall, P. K., *et al.* (2008) Paroxetine reduces social anxiety in individuals with a co-occurring alcohol use disorder. *Journal of Anxiety Disorders*, *22*, 310–318.

Booth, B. M. & Blow, F. C. (1993) The kindling hypothesis: Further evidence from a U.S. national survey of alcoholic men. *Alcohol and Alcoholism*, *28*, 593–598.

Booth, B. M., Ludke, R. L., Wakefield, D. S. *et al.* (1991). Nonacute inpatient admissions to department of veterans affairs medical centers. *Medical Care*, *29* (Suppl.), AS40–AS50.

Booth, B. M., Blow, F. C., Ludke, R. L., *et al.* (1996) Utilization of acute inpatient services for alcohol detoxification. *The Journal of Mental Health Administration*, *23*, 366–374.

Bordin, E. S. (1979) The generalizability of the psychoanalytic concept of the working alliance. *Psychotherapy: Theory, Research & Practice*, *16*, 252–260.

Bostwick, J. M. & Lapid, M. I. (2004) False positives on the Clinical Institute Withdrawal Assessment for Alcohol – Revised: is this scale appropriate for use in the medically ill? *Psychosomatics*, *45*, 256–261.

Bowden, S. C. (1990) Separating cognitive impairment in neurologically asymptomatic alcoholism from Wernicke-Korsakoff syndrome: is the neuropsychological distinction justified? *Psychological Bulletin*, *107*, 355–366.

Bowen, R. C., D'Arcya, C. A. & Keegana, D. (2000) A controlled trial of cognitive behavioral treatment of panic in alcoholic inpatients with comorbid panic disorder. *Addictive Behaviors*, *25*, 593–597.

References

Bowen, S., Witkiewitz, K., Dillworth, T. M., *et al.* (2006) Mindfulness meditation and substance use in an incarcerated population. *Psychology of Addictive Behaviors*, *20*, 343–347.

Bowen, S., Witkiewitz, K., Dillworth, T. M., *et al.* (2007) The role of thought suppression in the relationship between mindfulness meditation and alcohol use. *Addictive Behaviors*, *32*, 2324–2338.

Bower, P. & Gilbody, S. (2005) Stepped care in psychological therapies: access, effectiveness and efficiency. Narrative literature review. *British Journal of Psychiatry*, *186*, 11–17.

Bradizza, C. M., Stasiewicz, P. R. & Paas, N. D. (2006) Relapse to alcohol and drug use among individuals diagnosed with co-occurring mental health and substance use disorders: A review. *Clinical Psychology Review*, *26*, 162–178.

Brady, K. T., Myrick, H., Henderson, S., *et al.* (2002) The use of divalproex in alcohol relapse prevention: a pilot study. *Drug and Alcohol Dependence*, *67*, 323–330.

Brady, K. T., Sonne, S., Anton, R. F., *et al.* (2005) Sertraline in the treatment of co-occurring alcohol dependence and posttraumatic stress disorder. *Alcoholism: Clinical and Experimental Research*, *29*, 395–401.

Branchey, L., Davis, W., Lee., K. K., *et al.* (1987) Psychiatric complications of disulfiram treatment. *The American Journal of Psychiatry*, *144*, 1310–1312.

Brayne, C., Best, N., Muir, M., *et al.* (1997) Five-year incidence and prediction of dementia and cognitive decline in a population sample of women aged 70–79 at baseline. *International Journal of Geriatric Psychiatry*, *12*, 1107–1118.

Breslin, F. C., Sobell, M., Sobell, L., *et al.* (1997) Toward a stepped care approach to treating problem drinkers: The predictive utility of within-treatment variables and therapist prognostic ratings. *Addiction*, *92*, 1479–1489.

Breslin, F. C., Sobell, M., Sobell, L., *et al.* (1999) Problem drinkers: evaluation of a stepped-care approach. *Journal of Substance Abuse*, *10*, 217–232.

Brewer, C. (1984) How effective is the standard dose of disulfiram? A review of the alcohol-disulfiram reaction in practice. *The British Journal of Psychiatry*, *144*, 200–202.

British Association of Counselling (1992) *Code of Ethics and Practice for Counsellors*. Rugby: BAC.

British Medical Association and the Royal Pharmaceutical Society of Great Britain (2010) *British National Formulary, 59th edition (BNF 59)*. London: British Medical Association and the Royal Pharmaceutical Society of Great Britain.

Brosan, L., Moore, R., & Reynolds, S. (2007) Factors associated with competence in cognitive therapists. *Behavioural and Cognitive Psychotherapy*, *35*, 179–190.

Brotman, M. A., Strunk, D. R., & DeRubeis, R. J. (2009) *Therapeutic Alliance and Adherence in Cognitive Therapy for Depression*. (In preparation).

Brower, K. J. (2003) Insomnia, alcoholism and relapse. *Sleep Medicine Reviews*, *7*, 523–539.

Brower, K. J., Myra Kim, H., Strobbe, S., *et al.* (2008) A randomized double-blind pilot trial of gabapentin versus placebo to treat alcohol dependence and comorbid insomnia. *Alcoholism: Clinical & Experimental Research*, *32*, 1429–1438.

Brown, J. D. (1996) *Testing in Language Programs*, pp. 231–294. Upper Saddle River, NJ: Prentice Hall Regents.

Brown, M. E., Anton, R. F., Malcolm, R., *et al.* (1988) Alcohol detoxification and withdrawal seizures: clinical support for kindling hypothesis. *Biological Psychiatry, 23*, 507–514.

Brown, S., McGue, M., Maggs, J., *et al.* (2008) A developmental perspective on alcohol and youths 16 to 20 years of age. *Pediatrics, 121* (Suppl. 4), S290–S310.

Brown, S. A., Inaba, R. K., Gillin, J. C., *et al.* (1995). Alcoholism and affective disorder: clinical course of depressive symptoms. *American Journal of Psychiatry, 152*, 45–52.

Brown, S. A., Meyer, M. G., Lippke, L., *et al.* (1998) Psychometric evaluation of the customary drinking and drug use record (CDDR): a measure of adolescent alcohol and drug involvement. *Journal of Studies on Alcohol, 59*, 427–438.

Brown, T. G., Seraganian, P., Tremblay, J., *et al.* (2002). Process and outcome changes with relapse prevention versus 12-step aftercare programs for substance abusers. *Addiction, 97*, 677–689.

Bryant, M. J., Simons, A. D. & Thase, M. E. (1999) Therapist skill and patient variables in homework compliance: controlling an uncontrolled variable in cognitive therapy outcome research. *Cognitive Therapy and Research, 23*, 381–399.

Bucholz, K. K., Cadoret, R., Cloninger, C. R., *et al.* (1994) Semi-structured psychiatric interview for use in genetic linkage studies: a report on the reliability for the SSAGA. *Journal of Studies on Alcohol, 55*, 149–158.

Bullock, M., Umen, A., Culliton, P., *et al.* (1987) Acupuncture treatment of alcoholic recidivism: a pilot study. *Alcoholism: Clinical and Experimental Research, 11*, 292–295.

Bullock, M., Culliton, P. & Olander, R. (1989) Controlled trial of acupuncture for severe recidivist alcoholism. *Lancet,* 1 (June), 1435–1439.

Bullock, M. L., Kiresuk, T. J., Sherman, R. E., *et al.* (2002) A large randomized placebo controlled study of auricular acupuncture for alcohol dependence. *Journal of Substance Abuse Treatment, 22*, 71–77.

Burman, S. (1997) The challenge of sobriety: natural recovery without treatment and self-help groups. *Journal of Substance Abuse, 9*, 41–61.

Burns, D. D., & Nolen-Hoeksema, S. (1992). Therapeutic empathy and homework compliance in cognitive-behavioral therapy. *Journal of Consulting and Clinical Psychology, 60*, 441–449.

Burtscheidt, W., Wolwer, W., Schwarz, R., *et al.* (2001) Out-patient behaviour therapy in alcoholism: treatment outcome after 2 years. *Acta Psychiatrica Scandinavica, 106*, 227–232.

Burtscheidt, W., Wolwer, W., Schwarz, R., *et al.* (2002) Out-patient behaviour therapy in alcoholism: treatment outcome after 2 years. *Acta Psychiatrica Scandinavica, 106*, 227–232.

Bush, K., Kivlahan, D. R., McDonell, M. B., *et al.* (1998) The AUDIT alcohol consumption questions (AUDIT-C): an effective brief screening test for problem drinking. *Archives of Internal Medicine, 158*, 1789–1795.

References

Busto, U., Simpkins, J., Sellers, E. M., *et al.* (1983) Objective determination of benzodiazepine use and abuse in alcoholics. *British Journal of Addiction*, 78, 429–435.

Butterworth, R. F. (1989) Effects of thiamine deficiency on brain metabolism: implications for the pathogenesis of the Wernicke-Korsakoff syndrome. *Alcohol and Alcoholism*, 24, 271–279.

Cahill, J., Barkham, M., Hardy, G., *et al.* (2003) Outcomes of patients completing and not completing cognitive therapy for depression. *British Journal of Clinical Psychology*, 42, 133–143.

Campbell, N. C., Murray, E., Darbyshire, J., *et al.* (2007) Desigining and evaluating complex interventions to improve health care. *British Medical Journal*, 334, 455–459.

Caldwell, D. M., Ades, A. E. & Higgins, J. P. (2005) Simultaneous comparison of multiple treatments: combining direct and indirect evidence. *British Medical Journal*, 331, 897–900.

Carroll, K. M., Rounsaville, B. J. & Bryant, K. J. (1993) Alcoholism in treatment seeking cocaine abusers: Clinical and prognostic significance. *Journal of Studies on Alcohol*, 54, 199–208.

Carroll, K., Nich, C., Ball, S., *et al.* (1998) Treatment of cocaine and alcohol dependence with psychotherapy and disulfiram. *Addiction*, 93, 713–728.

Carroll, K., Nich, C., Ball, S., *et al.* (2000) One-year follow-up of disulfiram and psychotherapy for cocaine-alcohol users: sustained effects of treatment. *Addiction*, 95, 1335–1349.

Carroll, K. M., Fenton, L. R., Ball, S. A., *et al.* (2004) Efficacy of disulfiram and cognitive behavior therapy in cocaine-dependent outpatients: a randomized placebo-controlled trial. *Archives of General Psychiatry*, 61, 264–272.

Casswell, S. & Thamarangsi, T. (2009) Reducing harm from alcohol: call to action. *The Lancet*, 373, 2247–2257.

Chapman, P. L. H. & Huygens, I. (1988) An evaluation of three treatment programmes for alcoholism: an experimental study with 6- and 18-month follow-ups. *British Journal of Addiction*, 83, 67–81.

Charney, A. A., Paraherakis, A. M. & Gill, K. J. (2001) Integrated treatment of comorbid depression and substance use disorders. *Journal of Clinical Psychiatry*, 62, 672–677.

Cheeta, S., Drummond, C., Oyefeso, A., *et al.* (2008) Low identification of alcohol use disorders in general practice in England. *Addiction*, 103, 766–773.

Chick, J. (1999) Safety issues concerning the use of disulfiram in treating alcohol dependence. *Drug Safety*, 20, 427–435.

Chick, J., Ritson, B., Connaughton, J., *et al.* (1988) Advice versus extended treatment for alcoholism: A controlled study. *British Journal of Addiction*, 83, 159–170.

Chick, J., Gough, K., Falkowski, W., *et al.* (1992) Disulfiram treatment of alcoholism. *British Journal of Psychiatry*, 161, 84–89.

Chick, J., Howlett, H., Morgan, M. Y., *et al.* (2000a) United Kingdom multicentre acamprosate study (UKMAS): A 6-month prospective study of acamprosate versus placebo in preventing relapse after withdrawal from alcohol. *Alcohol and Alcoholism*, 35, 176–187.

Chick, J., Anton, R., Checinski, K., *et al.* (2000b) A multicentre, randomized, double-blind, placebo-controlled trial of naltrexone in the treatment of alcohol dependence or abuse. *Alcohol and Alcoholism, 35,* 587–593.

Chiesa, A. (2010) Vipassana meditation: systermatic review of current evidence. *Journal of Alternative and Complementary Medicine, 16,* 37–46.

Cho, S. H., & Wang, W. W. (2009) Acupuncture for alcohol dependence: a systematic review. *Alcoholism: Clinical and Experimental Research, 33,* 1305–1313.

Choudry, N. (1990). Medical treatment for problem drug takers. In *Treating Drug Abusers* (ed. G. Bennett). London: Routledge.

Christiansen, B. A., Smith, G. T., Roehling, P. V., *et al.* (1989) Using alcohol expectancies to predict adolescent drinking behavior after one year. *Journal of Consulting and Clinical Psychology, 57,* 93–99.

Christo, G., Spurrell, S. & Alcorn, R. (2000). Validation of the Christo Inventory for Substance-misuse Services (CISS): a simple outcome evaluation tool. *Drug and Alcohol Dependence, 59,* 189–197.

Chung, T., Colby, N., Barnett, D., *et al.* (2000) Screening adolescents for problem drinking and performance of brief screens against DSM–IV alcohol diagnoses. *Journal of Studies on Alcohol, 61,* 579–587.

Chung, T., Martin, C. S., Winters, K. C., *et al.* (2001) Assessment of alcohol tolerance in adolescents. *Journal of Studies on Alcohol, 62,* 687–695.

Chutuape, M. A., Katz, E. C. & Stitzer, M. L. (2001) Methods for enhancing transition of substance dependence patients from inpatient to outpatient treatment. *Drug and Alcohol Dependence, 61,* 137–143.

Cicerone, K. D., Dahlberg, C., Malec, J. F., *et al.* (2005) Evidence-based cognitive rehabilitation: updated review of the literature from 1998 through 2002. *Archives of Physical Medicine and Rehabilitation, 86,* 1681–1692.

Ciraulo, D. A., Sands, B. F. & Shader, R. I. (1988) Critical review of liability for benzodiazepine abuse among alcoholics. *The American Journal of Psychiatry, 145,* 1501–1506.

Clark, D. B., Lesnick, L. & Hegedus, A. M. (1997a) Traumas and other adverse life events in adolescents with alcohol abuse and dependence. *Journal of the American Academy of Child and Adolescent Psychiatry, 36,* 1744–1751.

Clark, D. B., Pollock, N., Bukstein, O. G., *et al.* (1997b) Gender and comorbid psychopathology in adolescents with alcohol dependence. *Journal of the American Academy of Child and Adolescent Psychiatry, 36,* 1195–1203.

Clark, D. B., Lynch, K. G., Donovan, J. E., *et al.* (2001) Health problems in adolescents with alcohol use disorders: self-report, liver injury, and physical examination findings and correlates. *Alcoholism: Clinical and Experimental Research, 25,* 1350–1359.

Clark, D. B., De Bellis, M. D., Lynch, K. G., *et al.* (2003) Physical and sexual abuse, depression and alcohol use disorders in adolescents: onsets and outcomes. *Drugs and Alcohol Dependence, 69,* 51–60.

Clark, D. M., Layard, R., Smithies, R., *et al.* (2009) Improving access to psychological therapy: initial evaluation of two UK demonstration sites. *Behaviour Research and Therapy, 47,* 910–920.

References

Cloninger, C. R., Bohman, M. & Sigvardsson, S. (1981) Inheritance of alcohol abuse. cross-fostering analysis of adopted men. *Archives of General Psychiatry*, *38*, 861–868.

Cochrane Collaboration (2004) *Review Manager (RevMan)* [Computer program]. Version 4.2.7 for Windows. Oxford: The Cochrane Collaboration.

Cochrane, M., Cochrane, A., Jauhar, P., *et al.* (2005) Acetylcholinesterase inhibitors for the treatment of Wernicke-Korsakoff syndrome- three further cases show response to donepezil. *Alcohol and Alcoholism*, *40*, 151–144.

Coffey, T. (1996) The process of teaching alcohol and opiod withdrawal management strategies to nursing staff in a new medical center. *Journal of Addictions Nursing*, *8*, 29–35.

Colby, S. M., Monti, P., Barnett, N., *et al.* (1998) Brief motivational interviewing in a hospital setting for adolescent smoking: a preliminary study. *Journal of Consulting and Clinical Psychology*, *66*, 574–578.

Collins, M. N., Burns, T., van den Berk, P. A. H., *et al.* (1990) A structured programme for outpatient alcohol detoxification. *British Journal of Psychiatry*, *156*, 871–874.

Connors, G., Carroll, K., DiClemente, C., *et al.* (1997) The therapeutic alliance and its relationship to alcoholism treatment participation and outcome. *Journal of Consulting and Clinical Psychology*, *65*, 588–598.

Connors, G. J. & Walitzer, K. S. (2001) Reducing alcohol consumption among heavily drinking women: evaluating the contributions of life-skills training and booster sessions. *Journal of Consulting and Clinical Psychology*, *69*, 447–456.

Conrad, K. J., Hultman, C. I., Pope, A. R., *et al.* (1998) Case managed residential care for homeless addicted veterans: results of a true experiment. *Medical Care*, *36*, 40–53.

Conrod, P. J., Stewart, S. H., Pihl, R. O., *et al.* (2000) Efficacy of brief coping skills interventions that match different personality profiles of female substance abusers. *Psychology of Addictive Behaviours*, *14*, 231–242.

Cook, C. C. H. (1994) Aetiology of alcohol misuse. In *Seminars in Alcohol and Drug Misuse* (eds J. Chick & R. Cantwell). London: Gaskell.

Cook, C. C. H. (2000) Prevention and treatment of Wernicke-Korsakoff syndrome. *Alcohol and Alcoholism*, *35* (Suppl. 1), 19–20.

Cook, C. C. H., Hallwood, P. M. & Thomson, A. D. (1998) B vitamin deficiency and neuropsychiatric syndromes in alcohol misuse. *Alcohol and Alcoholism*, *33*, 317–336.

Cook, P. (1990) Social costs of drinking. In *Expert Meeting on the Negative Social Consequences of Alcohol Use: 27–31 August 1990* (ed. O. G. Assland), pp. 49–94. Oslo: Norwegian Ministry of Health and Social Affairs.

Cooney, N. L., Kadden, R. M., Litt, M. D., *et al.* (1991) Matching alcoholics to coping skills or interactional therapies: two year follow up results. *Journal of Consulting and Clinical Psychology*, *59*, 598–601.

Cooper, D. B. (1994) *Alcohol Dome detoxification and Assessment.* Oxford: Radcliffe Medical Press.

Copeland, J. (1997) A qualitative study of barriers to formal treatment among women who self-managed change in addictive behaviours. *Journal of Substance Abuse Treatment*, *14*, 183–190.

Copello, A., Orford, J., Hodgson, R., *et al.* (2002) Social behaviour and network therapy: basic principles and early experiences. *Addictive Behavior, 27*, 345–366.

Copello, A. G., Velleman, R. D. & Templeton, L. J. (2005) Family interventions in the treatment of alcohol and drug problems. *Drug and Alcohol Review, 24*, 369–385.

Copello, A. G., Templeton, L. & Velleman, R. (2006) Family interventions for drug and alcohol misuse: is there a best practice? *Current Opinion in Psychiatry, 19*, 271–276.

Copello, A. G., Templeton, L., Orford, J., *et al.* (2009) The relative efficacy of two levels of a primary care intervention for family members affected by the addiction problem of a close relative: a randomized trial. *Addiction, 104*, 49–58.

Cornelius, J. R., Salloum, I. M., Thase, M. E., *et al.* (1998) Fluoxetine versus placebo in depressed alcoholic cocaine abusers. *Psychopharmacology Bulletin, 34*, 117–121.

Coulthard, M., Farrell, M., Singleton, N. & Meltzer, H. (2002) *Tobacco, Alcohol and Drug Use and Mental Health.* The Office for National Statistics, London: The Stationary Office.

Coulton, S., Drummond, C., James, D., *et al.* (2006) Opportunistic screening for alcohol use disorders in primary care: comparative study. *British Medical Journal, 332*, 511–517.

Cousins, M. S., Roberts, D. C., & de Wit, H. (2002) GABA(B) receptor agonists for the treatment of drug addiction: a review of recent findings. *Drug and Alcohol Dependence, 65*, 209–220.

Cox, G. B., Walker, D. R., Freng, S. A., *et al.* (1998) Outcome of a controlled trial of the effectiveness of intensive case management for chronic public inebriates. *Journal of Studies on Alcohol, 59*, 523–532.

Cox, W. M., & Klinger, E. (eds) (2004) *Handbook of Motivational Counseling: Concepts, Approaches, and Assessment.* New York, NY: John Wiley & Sons.

Craig, R., Mindell, J. & Hirani, V. (2009) *Health Survey for England 2008. Volume 1: Physical Activity and Fitness.* London: NHS Information Centre.

Crum, R. M., Anthony, J. C., Bassett, S. S., *et al.* (1993) Population-based norms for the Mini-Mental State Examination by age and educational level. *Journal of American Medical Association, 269*, 2386–2391.

Cummings, J. L. (1993) Mini-Mental State Examination: norms, normals and numbers. *Journal of American Medical Association, 269*, 2420–2421.

Currie, S. R., Clark, S., Hodgins, D. C., *et al.* (2004) Randomized controlled trial of brief cognitive–behavioural interventions for insomnia in recovering alcoholics. *Addiction, 99*, 1121–1132.

Curtis, L. (2009) *Unit Costs of Health and Social Care.* Canterbury: Personal Social Services Research Unit, University of Kent.

Curtis, J. R., Geller, G., Stokes, E. J., *et al.* (1989) Characteristics, diagnosis and treatment of alcoholism in elderly patients. *Journal of the American Geriatric Society, 37*, 310–316.

Daeppen, J. B., Gache, P., Landry, U., *et al.* (2002) Symptom-triggered vs fixed-schedule doses of benzodiazepine for alcohol withdrawal: a randomized treatment trial. *Archives of Internal Medicine, 162*, 1117–1121.

References

Dakof, G. A., Tejeda, M. & Liddle, H. A. (2001) Predictors of engagement in adolescent drug abuse treatment. *Journal of the American Academy of Child & Adolescent Psychiatry, 40,* 274–281.

Dansky, B. S., Brewerton, T. D. & Kilpatrick, D. G. (2000) Comorbidity of bulimia nervosa and alcohol use disorders: results from the National Women's Study. *International Journal of Eating Disorders, 27,* 180–190.

Dar, K. (2006) Alcohol use disorders in elderly people: fact or fiction? *Advances in Psychiatric Treatment, 12,* 173–181.

Davidson, D., Gulliver, S. B., Longabaugh, R., *et al.* (2007) Building better cognitive-behavioral therapy: is broad-spectrum treatment more effective than motivational enhancement therapy for alcohol-dependent patients treated with naltrexones? *Journal of Studies on Alcohol and Drugs, 68,* 238–247.

Davidson, K., Scott, J., Schmidt, U., *et al.* (2004) Therapist competence and clinical outcome in the prevention of parasuicide by manual assisted cognitive behaviour therapy trial: the POPMACT study. *Psychological Medicine, 34,* 855–863.

Davis, L., Uezato, A., Newell, J., *et al.* (2008) Major depression and comorbid substance use disorders. *Current Opinion in Psychiatry, 21,* 14–18.

Davis, W. T., Campbell, L., Tax, J., *et al.* (2002) A trial of "standard" outpatient alcoholism treatment vs. a minimal treatment control. *Journal of Substance Abuse Treatment, 23,* 9–19.

Davison, G. C. (2000) Stepped care: doing more with less? *Journal of Consulting and Clinical Psychology, 68,* 580–585.

Dawe, S., Rees, V. W., Mattick, R., *et al.* (2002) Efficacy of moderation-orientated cue exposure for problem drinkers: a randomized controlled trial. *Journal of Consulting and Clinical Psychology, 70,* 1045–1050.

Dawson, D. A., Grant, B. F., Stinson, F. S., *et al.* (2005a) Recovery from DSM–IV alcohol dependence: United States, 2001–2002. *Addiction, 100,* 281–292.

Dawson, D. A., Grant, B. F., & Stinson, F. S. (2005b) The AUDIT-C: screening for alcohol use disorders and risk drinking in the presence of other psychiatric disorders. *Comprehensive Psychiatry, 46,* 405–416.

Dawson, D. A., Grant, B. F., Chou, S. P., *et al.* (2007) The impact of partner alcohol problems on women's physical and mental health. *Journal of Studies on Alcohol and Drugs, 68,* 66–75.

Dawson, D. A., Goldstein, R. B., Chou, P. S., *et al.* (2008) Age at first drink and the first incidence of adult-onset DSM–IV alcohol use disorders. *Alcoholism: Clinical and Experimental Research, 32,* 2149–2160.

Day, E., Ison, J., Keaney, F., *et al.* (2005) *A National Survey of Inpatient Drug Treatment Services in England.* London: National Treatment Agency for Substance Misuse.

Day, E. J., Patel, J. & Georgiou, G. (2004) Evaluation of a symptom-triggered front-loading 27 detoxification technique for alcohol dependence: a pilot study. *Psychiatric Bulletin, 28,* 407–410.

DeCaroulis, D. D., Rice, K. L., Ho, L., *et al.* (2007) Symptom-driven lorazepam protocol for treatment of severe alcohol withdrawal delirium in the intensive care unit. *Pharmacotherapy, 27,* 510–518.

De Maeyer, J., Vanderplasschen, W. & Broekaert, E. (2008) Exploratory study on drug users' perspectives on quality of life: more than health-related quality of life? *Social Indicators Research*, 90, 107–126.

Deacon, L., Hughes, S., Tocque, K., *et al.* (2007) *Indications of Public Health in English Regions: 8. Alcohol.* York: Association of Public Health Observatories.

Deeks, J. J. (2002) Issues in the selection of a summary statistic for meta-analysis of clinical trials with binary outcomes. *Statistics in Medicine*, 21, 1575–1600.

Demirbas, H., Celik, S., Ilhan, I. O., *et al.* (2003) An examination of suicide probability in alcohol in-patients. *Alcohol and Alcoholism*, 38, 67–70.

Dennis, M., Titus, J., White, M., *et al.* (2002) *Global Appraisal of Individual Needs (GAIN): Administration Guide for the GAIN and Related Measures.* Bloomington, IL: Chestnut Health Systems.

Dennis, M., Godley, S. H., Diamond, G., *et al.* (2004) The Cannabis Youth Treatment study: main findings from two randomised trials. *Journal of Substance Abuse Treatment*, 27, 197–213.

Department for Children, Schools and Families, National Treatment Agency & Department of Health (2009) *Joint Guidance on Development of Local Protocols between Drug and Alcohol Treatment Services and Local Safeguarding and Family Services.* London: DCSF, DH & NTA.

Department of Health, Home Office *et al.* (2007) *Safe. Sensible. Social. The Next Steps in the National Alcohol Strategy.* London: Department of Health.

Department of Health (1995) *Sensible Drinking: the Report of an Inter-Departmental Working Group.* London: Department of Health.

Department of Health (1999) *National Service Framework for Mental Health: Modern Standards and Service Models.* London: Department of Health.

Department of Health (2006a) *Models of Care for Alcohol Misusers.* London: National Treatment Agency. Available at: http://www.dh.gov.uk/en/Publicationsandstatistics/Publications/PublicationsPolicyAndGuidance/DH_4136806 [Accessed January 2011].

Department of Health (2006b) *Clinical Management of Drug Dependence in the Adult Prison Setting.* London: Department of Health.

Department of Health (2007) *Best Practice in Managing Risk: Principles and Evidence for Best Practice in the Assessment and Management of Risk to Self and Others in Mental Health Services.* London: Department of Health.

Department of Health (2008a) *The Cost of Alcohol Harm to the NHS in England.* London. Department of Health.

Department of Health (2008b) *Pregnancy and Alcohol.* London: Department of Health.

Department of Health (2010) *NHS Reference Costs 2008–09.* London: Department of Health. Available from: http://www.dh.gov.uk/en/Publicationsandstatistics/Publications/PublicationsPolicyAndGuidance/DH_111591 [Accessed 11 May 2010]

Department of Transport (2009) *Reported Road Casualties in Great Britain: 2008 Annual Report.* London: Department of Transport.

DerSimonian, R. & Laird, N. (1986) Meta-analysis in clinical trials. *Controlled Clinical Trials*, 7, 177–188.

DeRubeis, R. J. & Feeley, M. (1990) Determinants of change in cognitive therapy for depression. *Cognitive Therapy and Research, 14*, 469–482.

DeRubeis, R. J., Hollon, S. D., Amsterdam, J. D., *et al.* (2005) Cognitive therapy versus medications in the treatment of moderate to severe depression. *Archives of General Psychiatry, 62*, 409–416.

De Sousa, A. & De Sousa, A. (2004) A one-year pragmatic trial of naltrexone vs disulfiram in the treatment of alcohol dependence. *Alcohol and Alcoholism, 39*, 528–531.

De Sousa, A. & De Sousa, A. (2005) An open randomized study comparing disulfiram and acamprosate in the treatment of alcohol dependence. *Alcohol and Alcoholism, 40*, 545–548.

De Sousa, A. A. & De Sousa, J. A. (2008) An open randomised trial comparing disulfiram and topiramate in the treatment of alcohol dependence. *Journal of Substance Abuse, 34*, 460–463.

DfES (2007) *Every Parent Matters.* London: Department for Education and Schools. Available from: http://publications.everychildmatters.gov.uk/eOrderingDownload/ DFES-LKDA-2007.pdf [Accessed May 2010].

Dick, D. M., Plunkett, J., Hamlin, D., *et al.* (2007) Association analyses of the serotonin transporter gene with lifetime depression and alcohol dependence in the Collaborative Study on the Genetics of Alcoholism (COGA) sample. *Psychiatric Genetics, 17*, 35–38.

DiClemente, C. C. & Hughes, S. O. (1990) Stages of change profiles in alcoholism treatment. *Journal of Substance Abuse, 2*, 217–235.

Donovan, D. M., Kivlahan, D. R., Doyle, S. R., *et al.* (2006). Concurrent validity of the Alcohol Use Disorders Identification Test (AUDIT) and AUDIT zones in defining levels of severity among out-patients with alcohol dependence in the COMBINE study. *Addiction, 101*, 1696–704.

Drake, R. E., McHugo, G. J., Clark, R. E., *et al.* (1998) Assertive community treatment for patients with co-occurring severe mental illness and substance use disorder: a clinical trial. *American Journal of Orthopsychiatry, 68*, 201–215.

Driessen, M., Meier, S., Hill, A., *et al.* (2001) The course of anxiety, depression and drinking behaviours after completed detoxification in alcoholics with and without comorbid anxiety and depressive disorders. *Alcohol and Alcoholism, 36*, 249–255.

Drobes, D. J., Anton, R. F., Thomas, S. E., *et al.* (2004) Effects of naltrexone and nalmefene on subjective response to alcohol among non-treatment-seeking alcoholics and social drinkers. *Alcoholism: Clinical & Experimental Research, 28*, 1362–70.

Drummond, C. (1990) The relationship between alcohol dependence and alcohol-related problems in a clinical population. *British Journal of Addiction, 85*, 357–366.

Drummond, C. (2009) Treatment services for alcohol use disorders. In *The New Oxford Textbook of Psychiatry* (eds M. Gelder, N. Andreasen, J. Lopez-Ibor, *et al.*), 2nd edn. Oxford: Oxford University Press.

Drummond, C., & Ghodse, H. (1999) Use of investigations in the diagnosis and management of alcohol use disorders. *Advances in Psychiatric Treatment, 5*, 366–375.

Drummond, D. C., Oyefeso, N., Phillips, T., *et al.* (2005) *Alcohol Needs Assessment Research Project (ANARP): The 2004 National Alcohol Needs Assessment for England.* London: Department of Health.

Drummond, C., Ghodse, H. & Chengappa, S. (2007) Use of investigations in the diagnosis and management of alcohol use disorders. In *Clinical Topics in Addictions* (ed. Day, E. J.). London: RCPsych Publications.

Drummond, C., Coulton, S., James, D., *et al.* (2009) Effectiveness and cost-effectiveness of a stepped care intervention for alcohol use disorders in primary care: pilot study. *The British Journal of Psychiatry, 195,* 448–456.

Drummond, D. C. (2000) What does cue reactivity have to offer craving research? *Addiction, 95* (Suppl. 2), S129–S144.

Drummond, D. C. & Phillips, T. S. (2002) Alcohol urges in alcohol-dependent drinkers: further validation of the Alcohol Urge Questionnaire in an untreated community clinical population. *Addiction, 97,* 1465–1472.

Drummond, D. C., Cooper, T. & Glautier, S. P. (1990) Conditioned learning in alcohol dependence implications for cue exposure treatment. *British Journal of Addiction, 85,* 725–743.

Drummond, L. M. & Chalmers, L. (1986) Prescribing chlormethiazole reducing regimes in an emergency clinic. *British Journal of Addiction, 81,* 247–250.

Dunn, M. E. & Goldman, M. S. (1998) Age and drinking-related differences in the memory organization of alcohol expectancies in 3rd, 6th, 9th, and 12th grade children. *Journal of Consulting & Clinical Psychology, 66,* 579–585.

Dukan, J. K., Reed, D. N., Looney, S. W., *et al.* (2002). Risk factors for delirium tremens in trauma patients. *Journal of Trauma, 53,* 901–906.

DVLA (2010) *For Medical Practitioners: At a Glance Guide to the current Medical Standards of Fitness to Drive.* Swansea: Drivers Medical Group DVLA. Available from: http://www.dft.gov.uk/dvla/medical/ataglance.aspx [accessed 16 February 2011].

Dyson, J. (2007) Experience of alcohol dependence: a qualitative study. *Journal of Family Health Care, 17,* 211–214.

Easton, C. J., Mandel, D. L., Hunkele, K. A., *et al.* (2007) A cognitive behavioural therapy for alcohol-dependent domestic violence offenders: an integrated substance abuse-domestic violence treatment approach (SADV). *The American Journal on Addictions, 16,* 24–31.

Eccles, M., Freemantle, N. & Mason, J. (1998) North of England evidence based guideline development project: methods of developing guidelines for efficient drug use in primary care. *British Medical Journal, 316,* 1232–1235.

Edwards, G. & Guthrie, S. (1966) A comparison of inpatient and outpatient treatment of alcohol dependence. *Lancet, 1,* 467–458.

Edwards, G. & Gross, M. M. (1976) Alcohol dependence: provisional description of a clinical syndrome. *British Medical Journal, 1,* 1058–1061.

Edwards, G., Brown, D., Oppenheimer, E., *et al.* (1988) Long term outcome for patients with drinking problems: the search for predictors. *British Journal of Addiction, 83,* 917–927.

Edwards, G., Marshall, E. J. & Cook, C. C. (2003) *The Treatment of Drinking Problems: A Guide for the Helping Professions* (4th edn). New York: Cambridge University Press.

Elkin, I. (1994) The NIMH treatment of depression collaborative research programme: where we began and where we are. In *Handbook of Psychotherapy and Behaviour Change*, 4th edn (eds A. E. Bergin & S. L. Garfield). New York, NY: Wiley.

Elkin, I., Shea, M. T., Watkins, J., *et al.* (1989) National Institute of Mental Health Treatment of Depression Collaborative Research Programme. General effectiveness of treatments. *Archives of General Psychiatry, 46,* 971–982.

Emrick, C. D. (1974) A review of psychologically oriented treatment of alcoholism: I. The use and inter-relationships of outcome criteria and drinking behaviour following treatment. *Quarterly Journal of Studies on Alcohol, 35,* 523–549.

Errico, A. L., Nixon, S. J., Parsons, O. A., *et al.* (1990) Screening for neuropsychological impairment in alcoholics. *Psychological Assessment: A Journal of Consulting and Clinical Psychology, 2,* 45–50.

Errico, A. L., Parsons, O. A. & King, A. C. (1991) Assessment of verbosequential and visuospatial cognitive abilities in chronic alcoholics. *Psychological Assessment: Journal of Consulting and Clinical Psychology, 3,* 693–696.

Eriksen, L. (1986a) The effect of waiting for inpatient alcoholism treatment after detoxification: An experimental comparison between inpatient treatment and advice only. *Addictive Behaviours, 11,* 389–397.

Eriksen, L., Björnstad. & Götestam, G. (1986b) Social skills training in groups for alcoholics: One-year treatment outcome for groups and individuals. *Addictive Behaviors, 11,* 309–329.

Escobar, J. I., Burnam, A., Karno, M., *et al.* (1986) Use of the Mini-Mental State Examination (MMSE) in a community population of mixed ethnicity: cultural and linguistic artifacts. *The Journal of Nervous and Mental Disease, 174,* 607–614.

Essock, S. M., Mueser, K. T., Drake, R. E., *et al.* (2006) Comparison of ACT and standard case management for delivering integrated treatment for co-occurring disorders. *Psychiatric Services, 57,* 185–196.

Evans, S. M., Levin, F. R., Brooks, D. J., *et al.* (2007) A pilot double-blind trial of memantine for alcohol dependence. *Alcoholism: Clinical and experimental Research, 31,* 775–782.

Everitt, B. J., Belin, D., Economidou, D., *et al.* (2008) Neural mechanisms underlying the vulnerability to develop compulsive drug-seeking habits and addiction. *Philosophical Transactions of the Royal Society (Series B) Biological Sciences, 363,* 3125–3135.

Evert, D. L., & Oscar-Berman, M. (1995) Alcohol-related cognitive impairments: an overview of how alcoholism may affect the workings of the brain. *Alcohol Health & Research World, 19,* 89–96.

Falk, D. E., Yi, H. Y. & Hiller-Sturmhofel, S. (2006) An epidemiologic analysis of co-occurring alcohol and tobacco use and disorders: findings from the National Epidemiologic Survey on Alcohol and Related Conditions. *Alcohol Research & Health, 29,* 169–171.

Fals-Stewart, W. & Klostermann, K. (2004). *Psychoeducational Attention Control Treatment for Alcoholism (PACT): A Guide.* Buffalo, NY: The Addiction and Family Research Group.

Fals-Stewart, W., Klosterman, K., Yates, B. T., *et al.* (2005) Brief relationship therapy for alcoholism: A randomized clinical trial examining clinical efficacy and cost-effectiveness. *Psychology of Addictive Behaviors*, *19*, 363–371.

Fals-Stewart, W., O'Farrell, T. J., Birchler, G. R., *et al.* (2004) *Standard Behavioral Couples Therapy for Alcoholism (S-BCT): A Guide.* Buffalo, NY: Addiction and Family Research Group.

Fals-Stewart, W., Birchler, G. R. & Kelley, M. L. (2006) Learning sobriety together: a randomized clinical trial examining behavioral couple's therapy with alcoholic female patients. *Journal of Consulting and Clinical Psychology*, *74*, 579–591.

Farrell, M., Cowing, L. R., Marsden, J., *et al.* (2001) Substitution treatment for opioid dependence: a review of the evidence and the impact. In: *Development and Improvement of Substitution Programmes: Proceedings. Seminar Organized by the Co-operation Group to Combat Drug Abuse and Illicit Trafficking in Drugs (Pompidou Group), Strasbourg, France, 8–9 October 2001.* Strasbourg: Council of Europe.

Farren, C. K., Scimeca, M., Wu, R., *et al.* (2009) A double-blind, placebo-controlled study of sertraline with naltrexone for alcohol dependence. *Drug and Alcohol Dependence*, *99*, 317–321.

Feeley, M., DeRubeis, R. J. & Gelfand, L. A. (1999) The temporal relation of adherence and alliance to symptom change in cognitive therapy for depression. *Journal of Consulting and Clinical Psychology*, *67*, 578–582.

Feldman, D. J., Pattison, E. M., Sobell, L. C., *et al.* (1975) Outpatient alcohol detoxification: initial findings on 564 patients. *American Journal of Psychiatry*, *132*, 407–412.

Fenwick, E., Klaxton, K., & Schulpher, M. (2001) Representing uncertainty: the role of cost-effectiveness acceptability curves. *Health Economics*, *10*, 779–787.

Ferguson, J. A., Suelzer, C. J., Eckert, G. J., *et al.* (1996) Risk factors for delirium tremens development. *Journal of General Internal Medicine*, *11*, 410–414.

Ferri, M., Amato, L. & Davoli, M. (2006) Alcoholics Anonymous and other 12-step programmes for alcohol dependence. *Cochrane Database of Systematic Reviews*, Issue 3. Art. No. CD005032.

Finney, J. W., Moos, R. H. & Brennan, P. L. (1991) The Drinking Problems Index: a measure to assess alcohol-related problems among older adults. *Journal of Substance Abuse*, *3*, 395–404.

Finney, J. W., Hahn, A. C. & Moos, R. H. (1996) The effectiveness of inpatient and outpatient treatment for alcohol abuse: the need to focus on mediators and moderators of setting effects. *Addiction*, *91*, 1773–1796.

Fiore, M. C., Jaen, C. R., Baker, T. B., *et al.* (2008) *Clinical Practice Guideline: Treating Tobacco Use and Dependence.* Rockville, MD: Department of Health and Human Services.

Fisher, P., Schaffer, D., Piacentini, J. C., *et al.* (1993) Sensitivity of the Diagnostic Interview Schedule for Children, 2nd Edition (DISC-2.1) for specific diagnosis of children and adolescents. *Journal of American Academy of Child and Adolescent Psychiatry, 32*, 666–673.

Flatley, J., Kershaw, C., Smith, K., *et al.* (2010) *Crime in England and Wales 2009/10. Volume 1. Findings from the British Crime Survey and Police Recorded Crime.* London: Home Office.

Fleming, M. F., Barry, K. L., MacDonald, R. (1991) The Alcohol Use Disorders Identification Test (AUDIT) in a college sample. *International Journal of the Addictions, 26*, 1173–1185.

Folstein, M. F., Folstein, S. E., McHugh, P. R. (1975) "Mini-mental state". A practical method for grading the cognitive state of patients for the clinician. *Journal of Psychological Research, 12*, 189–198.

Ford, P. (2003) An evaluation of the Dartmouth Assessment of Lifestyle Inventory and the Leeds Dependence Questionnaire for use among detained psychiatric inpatients. *Addiction, 98*, 111–118.

Foreman, M. D. (1987) Reliability and validity of mental status questionnaires in elderly hospitalized patients. *Nursing Research, 36*, 216–220.

Frank, D., DeBenedetti, A. F., Volk, R. J., *et al.* (2008). Effectiveness of the AUDIT-C as a screening tests for alcohol misuse in three race/ethnic groups. *Journal of General Internal Medicine, 23*, 781–787.

Freimanis, L. (1993) Alcohol and single homelessness: an outreach approach. In *Homelessness, Health Care and Welfare Provision* (eds K. Fisher and J. Collins), pp. 44–51. London: Routledge.

Fuller, E. (2008) *Drug Use, Smoking and Drinking Among Young People in England in 2007.* National Centre for Social Research, National Foundation for Educational Research.

Fuller, E., Jotangia, D. & Farrell, M. (2009) Alcohol misuse and dependence. In *Adult Psychiatric Morbidity in England, 2007 Results of a Household Survey* (eds S. McManus, H. Meltzer, T. Brugha, *et al.*). Leeds: NHS Information Centre for Health and Social Care.

Fuller, R. K., & Roth, H. P. (1979) Disulfiram for the treatment of alcoholism: An evaluation of 128 men. *Annals of Internal Medicine, 90*, 901–904.

Fuller, R. K., Branchey, L., Brightwell, D. R., *et al.* (1986) Disulfiram treatment of alcoholism: a veterans administration cooperative study. *Journal of the American Medical Association, 256*, 1449–1455.

Furieri, F. A. & Nakamura-Palacios, E. M. (2007) Gabapentin reduces alcohol consumption and craving: a randomized, double-blind, placebo-controlled trial. *Journal of Clinical Psychiatry, 68*, 1691–1700.

Furukawa, T. A., Barbui, C., Cipriani, A., *et al.* (2006) Imputing missing standard deviations in meta-analyses can provide accurate results. *Journal of Clinical Epidemiology, 59*, 7–10.

Gadalla, T., & Piran, N. (2007) Co-occurrence of eating disorders and alcohol use disorders in women: a meta-analysis. *Archives of Women's Mental Health, 10*, 133–140.

Gance-Cleveland, B. (2004) Qualitative evaluation of a school-based support group for adolescents with an addicted parent. *Nursing Research, 53*, 379–386.

Ganguli, M., Ratcliff, G., Chandra, V., *et al.* (1995). A Hindi version of the MMSE: the development of a cognitive screening instrument for a largely illiterate rural elderly population in India. *International Journal of Geriatric Psychiatry, 10,* 367–377.

Garbutt, J. C., Kranzler, H. R., O'Malley, S. S., *et al.* (2005) Efficacy and tolerability of long-acting injectable naltrexone for alcohol dependence. *The Journal of the American Medical Association, 293,* 1671–1625.

Garbutt, J. C., Osborne, M., Gallop., R, *et al.* (2009) Sweet liking phenotype, alcohol craving and response to naltrexone treatment in alcohol dependence. *Alcohol and Alcoholism, 44,* 293–300.

Gastpar, M., Bonnet, U., Boning, J., *et al.* (2002) Lack of efficacy of naltrexone in the prevention of alcohol relapse: Results from a german multicenter study. *Journal of Clinical Psychopharmacy, 22,* 592–598.

Gates, S., Smith, L. A., & Foxcroft, D. R. (2006) Auricular acupuncture for cocaine dependence. *Cochrane Database Systematic Review,* CD005192.

Gaval-Cruz, M. & Weinshenker, D. (2009) Mechanisms of disulfiram-induced cocaine abstinence: antabuse and cocaine relapse. *Molecular Interventions, 9,* 175–187.

Geerlings, P. J., Ansoms, C., & Van der Brink, W. (1997) Acamprosate and prevention of relapse in alcoholics. *European Addiction Research, 3,* 129–137.

Gelernter, J., Gueorguieva, R., Kranzler, H. R., et al. (2007) Opioid receptor gene (OPRM1, OPRK1, and OPRD1) variants and response to naltrexone treatment for alcohol dependence: results from the VA cooperative study. *Alcoholism: Clinical & Experimental Research, 31,* 555–563.

Gerrein, J. R., Rosenberg, C. M., & Manohar, V. (1973) Disulfiram maintenance on outpatient treatment of alcoholism. *Archives of General Psychiatry, 28,* 798–802.

Ghodse, H. & Royal College of Psychiatrists' Medical Working Group (2006) *Substance Misuse Detainees in Police Custody: Guidlines for Clinical Management* (3rd edn). Council Report CR132. London: Royal College of Psychiatrists.

Ghodse, H., Checinski, K., Drummond, C., *et al.* (1998*) St Georges Hospital Medical School Department of Psychiatry of Addictive Behaviour. Handbook* (4th edn). London: St George's Hospital Medical School.

Gilbert, F. (1988) The effect of type of aftercare of follow-up on treatment outcome among alcoholics. *Journal of Studies on Alcohol, 49,* 149–159.

Gilchrist, G. & Morrison, D. (2004) Prevalence of alcohol related brain damage among homeless hostel dwellers in Glasgow. *European Journal of Public Health, 15,* 587–588.

Giles, H. G. & Sandrin, S. (1990) Alcohol and deaths in police custody. *Alcoholism, 16,* 670–672.

Gill, B., Meltzer, H., Hinds, K., *et al.* (1996) *Psychiatric Morbidity among Homeless People. OPCS Surveys of Psychiatric Morbidity in Great Britain, Report 7.* London: Her Majesty's Stationary Office.

Gillen, R. W., Kranzler, H. R., Kadden, R. M., *et al.* (1991) Utility of a brief cognitive screening instrument in substance abuse patients: initial investigation. *Journal of Substance Abuse Treatment, 8,* 247–251.

Glasner-Edwards, S., Tate, S. R., McQuaid, J. R., *et al.* (2007) Mechanisms of action in integrated cognitive-behavioral treatment versus Twelve-Step Facilitation for substance-dependent adults with comorbid major depression. *Journal of Studies on Alcohol and Drugs*, *68*, 663–672.

Gleeson, D., Jones, J. S., McFarlane, E., *et al.* (2009) Severity of alcohol dependence in decompensated alcoholic liver disease: comparison with heavy drinkers without liver disease and relationship to family drinking history. *Alcohol & Alcoholism*, *44*, 392–397.

Goddard, E. (2006) *General Household Survey 2006, Smoking and Drinking Among Adults*. London: Office for National Statistics.

Goldman, D., Oroszi, G. & Ducci, F. (2005) The genetics of addictions: uncovering the genes. *Nature Reviews Genetics*, *6*, 521–532.

Goldstein, R. B., Dawson, D. A., Saha, T. D., *et al.* (2007) Antisocial behavioral syndromes and DSM–IV alcohol use disorders: results from the National Epidemiologic Survey on Alcohol and Related Conditions. *Alcoholism: Clinical and Experimental Research*, *31*, 814–828.

Gordon, D. A., Graves, K. & Arbuthnot, J. (1995) The effect of functional family therapy for delinquents on adult criminal behavior. *Criminal Justice and Behavior*, *22*, 60–73.

Gordon, H. W. (1986) The Cognitive Laterality Battery: tests of specialized cognitive function. *International Journal of Neuroscience*, *29*, 223–244.

Gossop, M. (2003) Withdrawal and detoxification. In *Drug Addiction and its Treatment*, pp. 115–136. Oxford: Oxford University Press.

Gossop, M., Marsden, J., Stewart, D., *et al.* (2003) The national treatment outcome research study (NTORS): 4–5 year follow-up results. *Addiction*, *98*, 291–303.

Gossop, M., Manning, V. & Ridge, G. (2006) Concurrent use of alcohol and cocaine: Differences in patterns of use and problems among users of crack cocaine and cocaine powder. *Alcohol & Alcoholism*, *41*, 121–125.

Grades of Recommendation Assessment, Development and Evaluation (GRADE) Working Group (2004) Grading quality of evidence and strength of recommendations. *British Medical Journal*, *328*, 1490–1497.

Grant, B. F., Stinson, F. S., Dawson, D. A., *et al.* (2004a) Prevalence and co-occurrence of substance use disorders and independent mood and anxiety disorders: results from the National Epidemiologic Survey on Alcohol and Related Conditions. *Archives of General Psychiatry*, *61*, 807–816.

Grant, B. F., Hasin, D. S., Chou, S. P., *et al.* (2004b) Nicotine dependence and psychiatric disorders in the United States. *Archives of General Psychiatry*, *61*, 1107–1115.

Gregg, E., & Akhter, I. (1979) Chlormethiazole abuse. *British Journal of Psychiatry*, *134*, 627–629.

Gregory, R. J., Chlebowski, S., Kang, D., *et al.* (2008) A controlled trial of psychodynamic psychotherapy for co-occurring borderline personality disorder and alcohol use disorder. *Psychotherapy: Theory, Research, Practice, Training*, *45*, 28–41.

Griffiths, R. R., & Wolf, B. (1990) Relative abuse liability of different benzodiazepeines in drug abusers. *Journal of Clinicial Psychopharmacology, 10,* 237–243.

Gual, A. & Lehert, P. (2001) Acamprosate during and after acute alcohol withdrawal: a double-blind placebo-controlled study in Spain. *Alcohol & Alcoholism, 36,* 413–418.

Gual, A., Segura, L., Contel, M., *et al.* (2002) AUDIT-3 and AUDIT-4: effectiveness of two short forms of the alcohol use disorders identification test. *Alcohol and Alcoholism, 37,* 61–66.

Guardia, J., Caso, C., Arias, F., *et al.* (2002) A double-blind, placebo-controlled study of naltrexone in the treatment of alcohol-dependence disorder: results from a multicenter clinical trial. *Alcoholism: Clinical and Experimental Research, 26,* 1381–1387.

Haddad, L. B. & Coffman, T. L. (1987) A brief neuropsychological screening exam for psychiatric geriatric patients. *Clinical Gerontologist, 6,* 3–10.

Happell, B. & Taylor, C. (1999) Drug and alcohol education for nurses: have we examined the whole problem? *Journal of Addictions Nursing, 11,* 180–185.

Hardern, R. & Page, A. V. (2005) An audit of symptom triggered chlordiazepoxide treatment of alcohol withdrawal on a medical admissions unit. *Emergency Medicine Journal, 22,* 805–806.

Harper, C. (1979) Wernicke's encephalopathy: a more common disease than realised. *Journal of Neurology, Neurosurgery, and Psychiatry, 42,* 226–231.

Harper, C. G., Giles, M. & Finlay-Jones, R. (1986) Clinical signs in the Wernicke-Korsakoff complex: a retrospective analysis of 131 cases diagnosed at necropsy. *Journal of Neurology, Neurosurgery, and Psychiatry, 49,* 341–345.

Harrell, A. & Wirtz, P. W. (1990) *Adolescent Drinking Index.* Odessa, FL: Psychological Assessment Resources.

Harrell, A. V. & Wirtz, P. W. (1985) *The Adolescent Drinking Index Professional Manual.* Odessa, FL: Psychological Assessment Resources.

Harrington, R., Kerfoot., M., & Verduyn, C. (1999) Developing needs led child and adolescent mental health services: issues and prospects. *European Child & Adolescent Psychiatry, 8,* 1018–8827.

Harrison, L. & Luck, H. (1997) Drinking and homelessness. In *Alcohol Problems in the Community* (ed. L. Harrison), pp. 53–75. London: Routledge.

Hartney, E., Orford, J., Dalton, S., *et al.* (2003) Untreated heavy drinkers: a qualitative and quantitative study of dependence and readiness to change. *Addiction Research and Theory, 11,* 317–337.

Hasin, D. S., Trautman, K. D., Miele, G. M., *et al.* (1996) Psychiatric Research Interview for Substance and Mental Disorders (PRISM): reliability for substance abusers. *American Journal of Psychiatry, 153,* 1195–1201.

Hawton, K., Bergen, H., Casey, D. *et al.* (2007) Self-harm in England: a tale of three cities: multicentre study of self-harm. *Social Psychiatry and Psychiatric Epidemiology, 42,* 513–521.

Hayashida, M., Alterman, A. I., McLellan, A. T., *et al.* (1989) Comparative effectiveness and costs of in-patient and out-patient detoxification of patients with mild-to-moderate alcohol withdrawal syndrome. *New England Journal of Medicine, 320,* 358–365.

Hays, R. D., Men, J. F. Nicholas, R. (1995) Response burden, reliability, and validity of the CAGE, Short MAST, and IT alcohol screening measures. *Behaviour Research Methods, Instruments & Computers, 27,* 277–280.

Head, J., Martikainen, P., Kumari, M., *et al.* (2002*)* Work Environment, Alcohol Consumption and Ill-Health. The Whitehall II Study. Norwich: HMSO.

Healy, D. & Nutt, D. (1998) Prescriptions, licenses and evidence. *The Psychiatrist, 22,* 680–684.

Heather, N. & Hönekopp, J. (2008) A revised edition of the Readiness to Change Questionnaire (treatment version). *Addiction Research and Theory, 16,* 421–433.

Heather, N., Luce, A., Peck, D., *et al.* (1999) Development of a treatment version of the Readiness to Change Questionnaire. *Addiction Research, 7,* 63–83.

Heather, N., Brodie, J., Wale, S., *et al.* (2000) A randomized controlled trial of moderation-orientated cue exposure. *Journal of Studies on Alcohol,* 61, 561–570.

Heather, N., Raistrick D., Tober, G., *et al.* (2001). Leeds Dependence Questionnaire: new data from a large sample of clinic attenders. *Addiction Research & Theory, 9,* 253–269.

Heather N., Adamson S. J., Raistrick D., *et al.* (UKATT Research Team) (2010) Initial preference for drinking goal in the treatment of alcohol problems: I. Baseline differences between abstinence and non-abstinence groups. *Alcohol & Alcoholism, 45,* 128–135.

Hecksel, K. A., Bostwick, M., Jaeger, T. M., *et al.* (2008) Inappropriate use of symptom-triggered therapy for alcohol withdrawal in the general hospital. *Mayo Clinic Proceedings, 83,* 274–279.

Heinala, P., Alho, H., Kiianma, K., *et al.* (2001) Targeted use of naltrexone without prior detoxification in the treatment of alcohol dependence: a factorial double-blind, placebo-controlled trial. *Journal of Clinical Psychopharmacology, 21,* 287–292.

Heinz, A. (2002) Dopaminergic dysfunction in alcoholism and schizophrenia-psychopathological and behavioral correlates. *European Psychiatry, 17,* 9–16.

Henggeler, S. W., Melton, G. B., & Smith, L. A. (1992) Family preservation using multisystematic therapy: an effective alternative to incarcerating serious juvenile offenders. *Journal of Consulting and Clinical Psychology, 60,* 953–961.

Henggeler, S., Pickrel, S., & Brondino, M. (1999) Multisystemic treatment of substance-abusing and dependent delinquent: outcomes, treatment fidelity and transportability. *Mental Health Services Research, 1,* 171–184.

Hershey, L. A., Jaffe, D. F., Greenough, P. G., *et al.* (1987) Validation of cognitive and functional assessment instruments in vascular dementia. *International Journal of Psychiatry in Medicine, 17,* 183–192.

Herz, A. (1997) Neurobiological principles of drug dependence. Exemplified by opioids and psychostimulants. *Der Nervenarzt, 66,* 3–14.

Hesse, M. (2004) Achieving abstinence by treating depression in the presence of substance-use disorders. *Addictive Behaviors, 29,* 1137–1141.

Hester, R. K., Squires, D. D., & Delaney, H. D. (2005) The Drinker's Check-up: 12-month outcomes of a controlled clinical trial of a stand-alone software program for problem drinkers. *Journal of Substance Abuse Treatment, 28,* 159–169.

Hibell, B., Guttormsson, U., Ahlström, S., *et al.* (2009) *The 2007 ESPAD Report: Substance Use Among Students in 35 European Countries.* Stockholm: The Swedish Council for Information on Alcohol and Other Drugs.

Higgins, J. P. T. & Thompson, S. G. (2002) Quantifying heterogeneity in a meta-analysis. *Statistics in Medicine,* 21, 1539–1558.

Higgins, J. P. T. & Green, S. (eds) (2009) *Cochrane Handbook for Systematic Reviews of Interventions.* Version 5.0.2 [updated September 2009]. The Cochrane Collaboration 2009. Available from: www.cochrane-handbook.org.

Higgins, J. P. T. & Whitehead, A. (1996) Borrowing strength from external trials in a meta-analysis. *Statistics in Medicine, 15,* 2733–2749.

Hingson, R. & Zha, W. (2009) Age of drinking onset, alcohol use disorders, frequent heavy drinking, and unintentionally injuring oneself and others after drinking. *Pediatrics, 123,* 1477–1484.

Hingson, R., Heeren, T. & Winter, M. (2006) Age of alcohol-dependence onset: associations with severity of dependence and seeking treatment. *Pediatrics, 118,* e755-e763.

HMSO (2004) *The Children Act 2004.* London: The Stationary Office. Available at: http://www.legislation.gov.uk/ukpga/2004/31/contents [Accessed April 2011].

Hodgson, R. J. & Rankin, H. J. (1976) Modification of excessive drinking by cue exposure. *Behaviour Research and Therapy, 14,* 305–307.

Hoffmann, N. G. & Harrison, P. A. (1995) *SUDDS-IV: Substance Use Disorder Diagnostic Schedule-IV.* St Paul, MN: New Standards, Inc.

Hoffman, P. L. & Tabakoff, B. (1996) Alcohol dependence: a commentary on mechanisms. *Alcohol & Alcoholism, 31,* 333–340.

Holder, H. D., Cisler, R. A., Longabaugh, R., *et al.* (2000) Alcoholism treatment and medical care costs from Project MATCH. *Addiction, 95,* 999–1013.

Hollis, V. (2007) *Reconviction Analysis of Programme Data using Interim Accredited Programmes Software (IAPS).* London: RDS/NOMS.

Hollon, S. D., Evans, M. D., Auerbarch, A., *et al.* (1988) *Development of a System for Rating Therapies for Depression: Differentiating Cognitive Therapy, Interpersonal Psychotherapy, and Clinical Management.* Unpublished manuscript. Nashville, TN: Vanderbilt University.

Horder, J. M. (1978) Fatal chlormethiazole poisoning in chronic alcoholics. *British Medical Journal, 1,* 693–694.

Horvath, A. O. & Symonds, B. D. (1991) Relation between working alliance and outcome in psychotherapy: meta-analysis. *Journal of Counseling Psychology, 38,* 139–149.

Huang, M. C, Chen, C. H., Yu, J. M., *et al.* (2005) A double-blind, placebo-controlled study of naltrexone in the treatment of alcohol dependence in Taiwan. *Addiction Biology, 10,* 289–292.

Hughes, J. R. (1995) Clinical implications of the association between smoking and alcoholism. In *Alcohol and Tobacco: From Basic Science to Policy. NIAAA*

Research Monograph vol. 30 (eds J. Fertig & R. Fuller), pp. 171–181. Washington, DC: US Government Printing Office.

Hughes, J. T. & Kalman, D. (2006) Do smokers with alcohol problems have more difficulty quitting? *Drug and Alcohol Dependence, 82*, 91–102.

Hunt, G. M., & Azrin, N. H. (1973) A community reinforcement approach to alcoholism. *Behavior Research and Therapy, 11*, 91–104.

Hunt, W. A., Barnett, L. W. & Branch, L. G. (1971) Relapse rates in addiction programs. *Journal of Clinical Psychology, 27*, 445–456.

Hyams, G., Cartwright, A., Spratley, T., *et al.* (1996) Engagement in alcohol treatment: the client's experience of, and satisfaction with, the assessment interview. *Addiction Research & Theory, 4*, 105–123.

Ilgen, M., Tiet, Q., Finney, J., *et al.* (2006) Self-efficacy, therapeutic alliance, and alcohol-use disorder treatment outcomes. *Journal of Studies on Alcohol, 67*, 465–468.

Institute of Medicine (1988) *Homelessness, Health, and Human Needs*. Washington, DC: National Academy Press.

Institute of Medicine (2003) *Reducing Underage Drinking: A Collective Responsibility*. Washington, DC: National Academy Press.

Iype, T., Ajitha, B. K., Antony, P., *et al.* (2006). Usefulness of the Rowland Universal Dementia Assessment Scale in South India. *Journal of Neurology, Neurosurgery, and Psychiatry, 77*, 513–514.

Jacobs, J. W., Bernhard, M. R., Delgado, A., *et al.* (1977). Screening for organic mental syndromes in the medically ill. *Annals of Internal Medicine, 86*, 40–46.

Jacobson, R. R., Acker, C. F. & Lishman, W. A. (1990) Patterns of neuropsychological deficit in alcoholic Korsakoff's syndrome. *Psychological Medicine, 20*, 321-334.

Jadad, A. R., Moore, R. A., Carroll, D., *et al.* (1996) Assessing the quality of reports of randomised clinical trials: is blinding necessary? *Controlled Clinical Trials, 17*, 1–12.

Jaeger, T. M., Lohr, R. H. & Pankratz, V. S. (2001) Symptom-triggered therapy for alcohol withdrawal syndrome in medical inpatients. *Mayo Clinic Proceedings, 76*, 695–701.

Jensen, P., Roper, M., Fisher, P., *et al.* (1995) Test-retest reliability of the Diagnostic Interview Schedule for Children (DISC-2.1), parent, child, and combined algorithms. *Archives of General Psychiatry, 52*, 61–71.

Jethwa, H. (2009) Social and psychological aspects of alcohol misuse and dependence. *Drugs and Alcohol Today, 9*, 29–35.

John, U., Veltrup, C., Driessen, M., *et al.* (2003) Motivational intervention: an individual counselling vs. a group treatment approach for alcohol-dependent in-patients. *Alcohol and Alcoholism, 38*, 263–269.

Johnson, B. A. (2008) Update on neuropharmacological treatments for alcoholism: scientific basis and clinical findings. *Biochemical Pharmacology, 75*, 34–56.

Johnson, B. A., Roache, J. D., Javors, M. A., *et al.* (2000) Ondansetron for reduction of drinking among biologically predisposed alcoholic patients: A randomized controlled trial. *The Journal of the American Medical Association, 284*, 963–971.

Johnson, B. A., Ait-Daoud, N., Bowden, C. L., *et al.* (2003) Oral topiramate for treatment of alcohol dependence: a randomised controlled trial. *The Lancet, 361,* 1677–1685.

Johnson, B. A., Rosenthal, N., Capece, J. A., *et al.* (2007) Topiramate for treating alcohol dependence: a randomized controlled trial. *The Journal of the American Medical Association, 298,* 1641–1651.

Jolliffe, N., Wortis, H., & Fein, H. D. (1941) The Wernicke syndrome. *Archives of Neurology and Psychiatry, 46,* 569–597.

Jones, L., Bellis, M. A., Dedman, D., *et al.* (2008) *Alcohol Attributable Fractions for England: Alcohol Attributable Mortality and Hospital Admissions.* Liverpool: North West Public Health Observatory.

Jordan, J. B. (2006) Acupuncture treatment for opiate addiction: a systematic review. *Journal of Substance Abuse Treatment, 30,* 309–314.

Joseph, A. M., Willenbring, M. L., Nudent, S. M., *et al.* (2004) A randomized trial of concurrent versus delayed smoking intervention for patients in alcohol dependence treatment. *Journal of Studies on Alcohol, 65,* 681–691.

Joyce, E. M. (1994) Aetiology of alcoholic brain damage: alcoholic neurotoxicity or thiamine malnutrition? *British Medical Bulletin, 50,* 99–114.

Kadden, R. M., Cooney, N. L., Getter, H., *et al.* (1989) Matching alcoholics to coping skills or interactional therapies: post treatment results. *Journal of Consultant & Clinical Psychology, 57,* 698–704.

Kadden, R., Carroll, K. M., Donovan, D., *et al.* (1992) *Cognitive-Behavioral Coping Skills Therapy Manual: A Clinical Research Guide for Therapists Treating Individuals with Alcohol Abuse and Dependence.* NIAAA Project MATCH Monograph, Vol. 3. Rockville, MD: National Institute on Alcohol Abuse and Alcoholism, 1995.

Kahan, M., Borgundvaag, B., Midmer, D., *et al.* (2005) Treatment variability and outcome differences in the emergency department management of alcohol withdrawal. *Canadian Journal of Emergency Medicine, 7,* 87–92.

Kahler, C. W., Read, J. P., Stuart, G. L., *et al.* (2004) Motivational enhancement for 12-step involvement among patients undergoing alcohol detoxification. *Journal of Consulting and Clinical Psychology, 72,* 736–741.

Kalant, H. (1996) Current state of knowledge about the mechanisms of alcohol tolerance. *Addiction Biology, 1,* 133–141.

Kalivas, P. W. & Volkow, N. D. (2005) The neural basis of addiction: a pathology of motivation and choice. *American Journal of Psychiatry, 162,* 1403–1413.

Källmén, H., Sjöberg, L. & Wennberg, P. (2003) The effect of coping skills training on alcohol consumption in heavy social drinking. *Substance Use & Misuse, 38,* 895–903.

Kalman, D., Hayes, K., Colby, S. M., *et al.* (2001) Concurrent versus delayed smoking cessation treatment for persons in early alcohol recovery: a pilot study. *Journal of Substance Abuse Treatment, 20,* 233–238.

Kalman, D., Kima, S., DiGirolamoc, G., *et al.* (2010) Addressing tobacco use disorder in smokers in early remission from alcohol dependence: the case for integrating smoking cessation services in substance use disorder treatment programs. *Clinical Psychology Review, 30,* 12–24.

Kaminer, Y., & Burleson, J. A. (1999) Psychotherapies for adolescent substance abusers: 15-month follow-up of a pilot study. *American Journal on Addictions, 8,* 114–119.

Kaminer, Y., Burkstein, O. G. & Tarter, R. E. (1991) The Teen Addiction Severity Index: rationale and reliability. *The International Journal of the Addictions, 26,* 219–226.

Kaminer, Y., Wagner, E., Plummer, B., *et al.* (1993) Validation of the Teen Addiction Severity Index (T-ASI): preliminary findings. *American Journal on Addictions, 2,* 250–254.

Kaminer, Y., Burleson, J., Blitz, C., *et al.* (1998) Psychotherapies for adolescent substance abusers: a pilot study. *Journal of Nervous and Mental Disease, 186,* 684–690.

Kaminer, Y., Burleson, J. & Goldberger, R. (2002) Cognitive behaviour coping skills and psychoeducation therapies for adolescent substance abuse. *Journal of Nervous and Mental Disease, 190,* 737–745.

Kaminer, Y., Burleson, J. A. & Burker, R. H. (2008) The efficacy of aftercare for adolescents with alcohol use disorders: a randomised controlled study. *Journal of the American Academy of Child and Adolescent Psychiatry, 47,* 1405–1412.

Kampman, K. M., Pettinati, H. M., Lynch, K. G., *et al.* (2009) Initiating acamprosate within-detoxification versus post-detoxification in the treatment of alcohol dependence. *Addictive Behaviors, 34,* 581–586.

Kandel, D., Chen, K., Warner, L. A., *et al.* (1997) Prevalence and demographic correlates of symptoms of last year dependence on alcohol, nicotine, marijuana and cocaine in the U.S. population. *Drug and Alcohol Dependence, 44,* 11–29.

Kaner, E. F. S. & Masterson, B. (1996) The role of general practitioners in treating alcohol dependent patients in the community. *Journal of Substance Misuse, 1,* 132 – 136.

Kaner, E., Rapley, T. & May, C. (2006) exploration of GPs' drinking and their alcohol intervention practices. *Family Practice, 23,* 481 – 487.

Kao, A. H., Lu, L. Y. (1974) Acupuncture procedure for treating drug addiction. *American Journal of Acupuncture, 2,* 201–207.

Karhuvaara, S., Simojoki, K., Virta, A., *et al.* (2007) Targeted nalmefene with simple medical management in the treatment of heavy drinkers: a randomized double-blind placebo-controlled multicenter study. *Alcoholism: Clinical and Experimental Research, 31,* 1179–1187.

Karno, M. P. & Longabaugh, R. (2007) Does matching matter? Examining matches and mismatches between patients attributes and therapy techniques in alcoholism treatment. *Addiction, 102,* 587–596.

Kaskutas, L. A., Ammon, L. N., Witbrodt, J., *et al.* (2005) Understanding results from randomized trials: use of program- and client-level data to study medical and nonmedical treatment programs. *Journal of Studies on Alcohol, 66,* 682–687.

Kaskutas, L. A., Bond, J. & Humphreys, K. (2002) Social networks as mediators of the effect of Alcoholics Anonymous. *Addiction, 97,* 891–900.

Katzman, R., Zhang, M. Y., Ouang-Ya-Qu, Wang, Z. Y., *et al.* (1988). A Chinese version of the Mini-Mental State Examination; impact of illiteracy in a Shanghai dementia survey. *Journal of Clinical Epidemiology, 41,* 971–978.

Kavanagh, D. J., Sitharthan, G., Young, R. M., *et al.* (2006) Addition of cue exposure to cognitive-behavior therapy for alcohol misuse: a randomized trial with dysphoric drinkers. *Addiction*, *101*, 1106–1116.

Kazantzis, N., Deane, F. P. & Ronan, K. R. (2000) Homework assignments in cognitive and behavioral therapy: A meta-analysis. *Clinical Psychology: Science & Practice*, *7*, 189–202.

Kelly, J. F. & Moos, R. H. (2003) Dropout from 12-step self-help groups: prevalence, predictors and counteracting treatment influences. *Journal of Substance Abuse Treatment*, *24*, 241–250.

Kelly, J. F., Magill, M., Slaymaker, V., *et al.* (2010) Psychometric validiation of the Leeds Dependence Questionnaire (LDQ) in a young adult clinical sample. *Addictive Behaviours*, *35*, 331–336.

Keso, L. & Salaspuro, M. (1990) Inpatient treatment of employed alcoholics: a randomized clinical trial on Hazelden-Type and traditional treatment. *Alcoholism: Clinical and Experimental Research*, *14*, 584–589.

Kessler, R. C., Nelson, C. B., McGonagle, K. A., *et al.* (1996) The epidemiology of co-occurring addictive and mental disorders: implications for prevention and service utilization. *The American Journal of Orthopsychiatry*, *66*, 17–31.

Kiefer, F., Helwig, H., Tarnaske, T., *et al.* (2005) Pharmacological relapse prevention of alcoholism: clinical predictors of outcome, *European Addiction Research*, *11*, 83–91.

Kiefer, F., Jahn, H., Tarnaske, T., *et al.* (2003) Comparing and combining naltrexone and acamprosate in relapse prevention of alcoholism. *Archives of General Psychiatry*, *60*, 92–99.

Killaspy, H., Bebbington, P., Blizard, R., *et al.* (2006) The REACT study: randomised evaluation of assertive community treatment in north London. *British Medical Journal*, *332*, 15–20.

Killeen, T. K., Brady, K. T., Gold, P. B., *et al.* (2004) Effectiveness of naltrexone in a community treatment program. *Alcoholism: Clinical and Experimental Research*, *28*, 1710–1717.

Kim, H., Ramsay, E., Hyewon Lee, H., *et al.* (2009) Genome-wide association study of acute post-surgical pain in humans. *Pharmacogenomics*, *10*, 171–179.

Kingdon, D., Tyrer, P., Seivewright, N., *et al.* (1996) The Nottingham study of neurotic disorder: influence of cognitive therapists on outcome. *British Journal of Psychiatry*, *169*, 93–97.

Kirby, K. C., Marlowe, D. B., Festinger, D. S., *et al.* (1999) Community reinforcement training for family and significant others of drug abusers: a unilateral intervention to increase treatment entry of drug users. *Drug and Alcohol Dependence*, *56*, 85–96.

Kissin, B., Platz, A. & Su, W. H. (1970) Social and psychological factors in the treatment of chronic alcoholism. *Journal of Psychiatric Research*, *8*, 13–27.

Kleber, H. D. (1985) Naltrexone. *Journal of Substance Abuse Treatment*, *2*, 117–122.

Knapp, G. & Hartung, J. (2003) Improved tests for a random effects meta-regression with a single covariate. *Statistics in Medicine*, *22*, 2693–2710.

Kodl, M., Fu, S. S., & Joseph, A. M. (2006) Tobacco cessation treatment for alcohol-dependent smokers: when is the best time? *Alcohol Health Research*, *29*, 203–207.

References

Koob, G. F. & Volkow, N. D. (2010) Neurocircuitry of addiction. *Neuropsychopharmacology*, *35*, 217–238.

Kopelman, M. D., Thomson, A. D., Guerrini, I., *et al.* (2009). The Korsakoff syndrome: Clinical aspects, psychology and treatment. *Alcohol & Alcoholism*, *44*, 148–154.

Kouimtsidis, C., Reynolds, M., Hunt, M., *et al.* (2003) Substance use in the general hospital. *Addictive Behaviours*, *28*, 483–499.

Kranzler, H., Abu-Hasaballah, K., Tennen, H., *et al.* (2004) Using daily interactive voice response technology to measure drinking and related behaviors in a pharmacotherapy study. *Alcoholism: Clinical and Experimental Research*, *28*, 1060–1064.

Kranzler, H., Tennen, H., Armeli, S., *et al.* (2009) Targeted naltrexone for problem drinkers. *Journal of Clinical Psychopharmacology*, *29*, 350–357.

Kranzler, H. R., Burleson, J. A., Brown, J., *et al.* (1996). Fluoxetine treatment seems to reduce the beneficial effect of cognitive-behavioural therapy in type B alcoholics. *Alcoholism: Clincial and Experimental Research*, *20*, 1534–1541.

Kranzler, H. R., Modesto-Lowe, V. & Van Kirk, J. (2000) Naltrexone vs nefazodone for treatment of alcohol dependence: a placebo-controlled trial. *Neuropsychopharmacology*, *22*, 493–503.

Kranzler, H. R., Armeli, S., Tennen, H., *et al.* (2003) Targeted naltrexone for early problem drinkers. *Journal of Clinical Psychopharmacology*, *23*, 294–304.

Kraemer, K. L., Mayo-Smith, M. F. & Calkins, D. R. (1997) Impact of age on the severity, course, and complications of alcohol withdrawal. *Archives of Internal Medicine*, *157*, 2234-2241.

Kraemer, K. L., Roberts, M. S., Nicholas, H. J., *et al.* (2005) Health utility ratings for a spectrum of alcohol-related health states. *Medical Care*, *43*, 541.

Krishnamurthy, R., VandeCreek, L., Kaslow, N. J., *et al.*(2004) Achieving competency in psychological assessment: directions for education and training. *Journal of Clinical Psychology*, *60*, 725–739.

Kristenson, H. (1995) How to get the best out of Antabuse. *Alcohol and Alcoholism*, *30*, 775–783.

Krug, I., Pinheiro, A. P., Bulik, C., *et al.* (2009) Lifetime substance abuse, family history of alcohol abuse/dependence and novelty seeking in eating disorders: comparison study of eating disorder subgroups. *Psychiatry and Clinical Neurosciences*, *63*, 82–87.

Krupski, A., Campbell, K., Joesch, J. M., *et al.* (2009) Impact of access to recovery services on alcohol/drug treatment outcomes. *Journal of Substance Abuse Treatment, 37*, 435–442.

Krystal, A. D., Thakur, M. & Roth, T. (2008) Sleep disturbance in psychiatric disorders: effects on function and quality of life in mood disorders, alcoholism, and schizophrenia. *Annals of Clinical Psychiatry*, *20*, 39–46.

Krystal, J. H., D'Souza, D. C., Petrakis, I. L., *et al.* (1999) NDMA agonists and antagonists as probes of glutamatergic dysfunction and pharmacotherapies in neuropsychiatric disorders. *Harvard Review of Psychiatry*, *7*, 125–143.

Krystal, J. H., Petrakis, I. L., Mason, G., *et al.* (2003) N-methyl-D-aspartate glutamate receptors and alcoholism: reward, dependence, treatment, and vulnerability. *Pharmacology & Therapeutics*, *99*, 79–94.

Krystal, J. H., Cramer, J. A., Krol, W. F., *et al.* (2001) Naltrexone in the treatment of alcohol dependence. *The New England Journal of Medicine*, *345*, 1734–1739.

Krystal, J. H., Staley, J., Mason, G., *et al.* (2006) Gamma-aminobutyric acid type A receptors and alcoholism: intoxication, dependence, vulnerability, and treatment. *Archives of General Psychiatry*, *63*, 957–968.

Kunz, S., Schulz, M., Lewitzky, M., *et al.* (2007) Ear acupuncture for alcohol withdrawal in comparison with aromatherapy: a randomized controlled trial. *Alcoholism: Clinical and Experimental Research*, *31*, 436–442.

Kushner, M. G., Sher, K. J. & Beitman, B. D. (1990) The relation between alcohol problems and anxiety disorders. *American Journal of Psychiatry*, *147*, 685–695.

Kuyken, W. & Tsivrikos, D. (2009) Therapist competence, comorbidity and cognitive-behavioral therapy for depression. *Psychotherapy & Psychosomatics*, *78*, 42–48.

Laaksonen, E., Koski-Jannes, A., Salapuro, M., *et al.* (2008) A randomized, multicentre, open-label, comparative trial of disulfiram, naltrexone and acamprosate in the treatment of alcohol dependence. *Alcohol and Alcoholism*, *43*, 53–61.

Ladewig, D., Knecht, T., Leher, P. *et al.* (1993) Acamprosate — a stabilizing factor in the long-term treatment of alcoholics. *Therapeutische Umschau*, *50*, 182–188.

Lam, W. K. K., Fals-Stewart, W. & Kelley, M. L. (2009) Parent training with behavioral couples therapy for fathers' alcohol abuse: Effects on substance use, parental relationship, parenting and CPS involvement. *Child Maltreatment*, *14*, 243–254.

Lambert, M. J., Whipple, J. L., Vermeersch, D. A., *et al.* (2002) Enhancing psychotherapy outcomes via providing feedback on client progress: a replication. *Clinical Psychology and Psychotherapy*, *9*, 91–103.

Landmark, C. J. (2007) Targets for antiepileptic drugs in the synapse. *Medical Science Monitor: International medical of Experimental and Clinical Research*, *13*, RA1–RA7.

Lange-Asschenfeldt, C., Muller, M. J., Szegedi, A., *et al.* (2003) Symptom-triggered versus 16 standard chlormethiazole treatment of inpatient alcohol withdrawal: clinical 17 implications from a chart analysis. *European Addiction Research*, *9*, 1–7.

Lapham, S., Forman, R., Alexander, M., *et al.* (2009) The effects of extended-release naltrexone on holiday drinking in alcohol-dependent patients. *Journal of Substance Abuse Treatment*, *36*, 1–6.

Larner, A. J. (2007) Addenbrooke's Cognitive Examination-Revised (ACE-R) in day-to-day clinical practice. *Age and Ageing*, *36*, 685–686.

Latendresse, S. J., Rose, R. J., Viken, R. J., *et al.* (2010) Examining the etiology of associations between perceived parenting and adolescents' alcohol use: common genetic and/or environmental liabilities? *Journal of Studies on Alcohol and Drugs*, *71*, 13–25.

References

Latt, N. C., Jurd, S., Houseman, J., *et al.* (2002) Naltrexone in alcohol dependence: a randomised controlled trial of effectiveness in a standard clinical setting. *Medical Journal of Australia*, *176*, 530–534.

Lawford, B. R., Young, R. M., Rowell, J. A., *et al.* (1995) Bromocriptine in the treatment of alcoholics with the D2 dopamine receptor A1 allele. *Nature Medicine*, *1*, 337–341.

Lechtenberg, R. & Worner, T. M. (1990) Seizure risk with recurrent alcohol detoxification. *Archives of Neurology*, *47*, 535–538.

Lee, A, Tan, S., Lim, D., *et al.* (2001) Naltrexone in the treatment of male alcoholics - an effectiveness study in Singapore. *Drug and Alcohol Review*, *20*, 193–199.

Leeman, R. F., Palmer, R. S., Corbin, W. R., *et al.* (2008) A pilot study of naltrexone and BASICS for heavy drinking young adults. *Addicitive Behaviors*, *33*, 1048–1054.

Leggio, L., Garbutt, J. C. & Addolorato, G. (2010) Effectiveness and safety of baclofen in the treatment of alcohol dependent patients. *CNS & Neurological Disorders Drug Trials*, *9*, 33–34.

Leichsenring, F., Rabung, S. & Leibing, E. (2004) The efficacy of short-term psychodynamic psychotherapy in specific psychiatric disorders: a meta-analysis. *Archives of General Psychiatry*, *61*, 1208–1216.

Leigh, G., Hodgins, D. C., Milne, R., *et al.* (1999) Volunteer assistance in the treatment of chronic alcoholism. *American Journal of Drug and Alcohol Abuse*, *25*, 543–559.

Lennings, C. J. (1999) An evalustaion of the Leeds Dependence Questionnaire. *Journal of Child & Adolescent Substance Abuse*, *8*, 73–87.

Leon, D. A. & McCambridge, J. (2006) Liver cirrhosis mortality rates in Britain from 1950 to 2002: an analysis of routine data. *Lancet*, *367*, 52–56.

Leontaridi, R. (2003) *Alcohol Misuse: How Much Does it Cost?* London: Cabinet Office.

Lesch, O. & Walter, H. (1996) Subtypes of alcoholism and their role in therapy. *Alcohol & Alcoholism*, *31*, 63–67.

Leung, A. (1977) Acupuncture treatment of withdrawal symptoms. *American Journal of Acupuncture*, *5*, 43.

Lezak, M. D. (1995) *Neuropsychological Assessment* (3rd edn). London: Oxford University Press.

Liddel, J., Williamson, M., & Irwig, L. (1996) *Method for Evaluating Research and Guideline Evidence*. Sydney: New South Wales Health Department.

Liddle, H. A. (1992) A multidimensional model for treating the adolescent drug abuser. In *Empowering Families, Helping Adolescents: Family-Centered Treatment of Adolescents with Mental Health and Substance Abuse Problems* (eds W. Snyder & T. Ooms), pp. 91–100. Washington, DC: U.S. Government Printing Office.

Ling, W., Weiss, D. G., Charuvastra, C., *et al.* (1983) Use of disulfiram for alcoholics in methadone maintenance programs. *Archives of General Psychiatry*, *40*, 851–854.

Lishman, W. A. (1998) *Wernicke's Encephalopathy. Organic Psychiatry. The Psychological Consequences of Cerebral Disorder* (3rd edn). Oxford, Blackwell Science.

Litt, M. D., Kadden, R. M., Cooney, N. L., *et al.* (2003) Coping skills and treatment outcomes in cognitive-behavioural and interactional group therapy for alcoholism. *Journal of Consulting and Clinical Psychology*, *71*, 118–128.

Litt, M. D., Kadden, R. M., Kabela-Cormier, E., *et al.* (2007) Changing network support drinking: initial findings from the network support projects. *Journal of Consulting and Clinical Psychology*, *77*, 229–242.

Litt, M. D., Kadden, R. M., Kabela-Cormier, E., *et al.* (2009) Changing network support drinking: network support project 2-year follow-up. *Journal of Consulting and Clinical Psychology*, *75*, 542–555.

Littleton, J. (2000) Can craving be modeled in animals? The relapse prevention perspective. *Addiction*, *95*, 83–90.

Liu, H. C., Teng, E. L., Lin, K. N., *et al.* (1994) Performance on a dementia screening test in relation to demographic variables. Study of 5297 community residents in Taiwan. *Archives of Neurology*, *51*, 910–915.

Lock, C. A. (2004) Alcohol and brief intervention in primary health care: what do patients think? *Primary Health Care Research and Development*, *5*, 162–178.

Lock, C. A., Kaner, E., Lamont, S., *et al.* (2002) A qualitative study of nurses' attitudes and practices regarding brief alcohol intervention in primary health care. *Journal of Advanced Nursing*, *39*, 333–342.

Loeber, S., Duka, T., Welzel, H., *et al.* (2009) Impairment of cognitive abilities and decision making after chronic use of alcohol: the impact of multiple detoxifications. *Alcohol & Alcoholism*, *44*, 372–381.

Longabaugh, R., McCrady, B., Fink, E., *et al.* (1983) Cost effectiveness of alcoholism treatment in partial vs. inpatient settings. *Journal of Studies on Alcohol*, *44*, 1049–1071.

Longabaugh, R., Mattson., M. E., Connors, G. J., *et al.* (1994) Quality of life as an outcome variable in alcoholism treatment research. *Journal of Studies on Alcohol*, (Suppl. 12), 119–129.

Lozano Polo, J. L., Guiérrez, M. E., Martínez, P. V., *et al.* (1997) Effect of methadone or naltrexone on the course of transaminases in parenteral drug users with hepatitis C virus infection. *Revista Clinica Espanola*, *197*, 479–483.

Lu, G. & Ades, A. E. (2004) Combination of direct and indirect evidence in mixed treatment comparisons. *Statistics in Medicine*, *23*, 3105–3124.

Luborsky, L., McLellan, T., Woody, G., *et al.* (1985) Therapist success and its determinants. *Archives of General Psychiatry*, *42*, 602–611.

Luborsky, L., Singer, B. & Luborsky, L. (1975) Comparative studies of psychotherapies: is it true that "everyone has won and all must have prizes"? *Archives of General Psychiatry*, *32*, 995–1008.

Lucey, M. R., Silverman, B. L., Illeperuma, A., *et al.* (2008) Hepatic safety of once-monthly injectable extended-release naltrexone administered to actively drinking alcoholics. *Alcoholism: Clinical and Experimental Research*, *32*, 498–504.

Lunn, D. J., Thomas, A., Best, N., *et al.* (2000) WinBUGS – a Bayesian modelling framework: concepts, structure, and extensibility. *Statistics and Computing*, *10*, 325–337.

References

Luxenberg, J. S. & Feigenbaum, L. Z. (1986) Cognitive impairment on a rehabilitation service. *Archives of Physical Medicine and Rehabilitation, 67*, 796–798.

Luykx, H. J., Dorresteijn, L. D., Haffmans, P. M., *et al.* (2008) Rivastigmine in Wernicke-Korsakoff's syndrome: Five patients with rivastigmine showed no more improvement than five patients without rivastigmine. *Alcohol and Alcoholism, 43,* 70–72.

Macdonald, J., Cartwright, A. & Brown, G. (2007) A quantitative and qualitative exploration of client-therapist interaction and engagement in treatment in an alcohol service. *Psychology and Psychotherapy: Theory, Research and Practice, 80,* 247–268.

Maisto, S. A., McKay, J. R. & Tiffany, S. T. (2003) *Diagnosis.* Bethesda, MD: National Institute on Alcohol Abuse and Alcoholism. Available from: http://pubs.niaaa.nih.gov/publications/Assesing%20Alcohol/maisto.pdf [Accessed 23 March 2010].

Majumdar, S. K. (1990) Chlormethiazole: current status in the treatment of the acute ethanol withdrawal syndrome. *Drug and Alcohol Dependence, 27,* 201–207.

Malcolm, R., Olive, M. F. & Lechner, W. (2008) The safety of disulfiram for the treatment of alcohol and cocaine dependence in randomized clinical trials: guidance for clinical practice. *Expert Opinion on Drug Safety, 7,* 459–472.

Malec, T. S., Malec, E. A. & Dongier, M. (2007) Efficacy of buspirone in alcohol dependence: a review: *Alcoholism: Clinical and Experimental Research, 20,* 853–858.

Mann, T. (1996) *Clinical Guidelines: Using Clinical Guidelines to Improve Patient Care within the NHS.* London: NHS Executive.

Mann, K. (2004) Pharmacotherapy of alcohol dependence: a review of the clinical data. *CNS & Neurological Disorders Drug Trials, 18,* 485–504.

Manikant, S., Tripathi, B. M., Chavan, B. S. (1993) Loading dose diazepam therapy for alcohol 35 withdrawal state. *Indian Journal of Medical Research, 98,* 170–173.

Mark, T. L., Kranzler, H. R., Poole, V. H., *et al.* (2003) Barriers to the use of medications to treat alcoholism. *American Journal of Addiction, 12,* 281–294.

Mark, T. L., Kassed, C. A., Vandivort-Warren, R., *et al.* (2009) Alcohol and opioid dependence medications: prescription trends, overall and by physician specialty. *Drug and Alcohol Dependence, 99,* 345–349.

Markou, A., & Koob, G. F. (1991) Postcocaine anhedonia: an animal model of cocaine withdrawal. *Neuropsychopharmaoclogy, 4,* 17–26.

Marlatt, G. A. & Gordon, J. R. (eds) (1985) *Relapse Prevention: Maintenance Strategies in the Treatment of Addiction Behaviors.* New York, NY: The Guilford Press.

Marmot, M., *et al.* (2010) *Fair Society, Healthy Lives: Strategic Review of Health Inequalities in England post-2010.* London: The Marmot Review.

Marques, A. C. P. R. & Formigoni, M. L. O. S. (2001) Comparison of individual and group cognitive-behavioral therapy for alcohol and/or drug-dependent patients. *Addiction, 96,* 835–846.

Marsden, J., Gossop, G., Stewart, D., *et al.* (1998). The Maudsley Addiction Profile (MAP): a brief instrument for assessment treatment outcome. *Addiction, 93,* 1857–1867.

Marsden, J., Farrell, M., Bradbury, C., *et al.* (2007) *The Treatment Outcomes Profile (TOP): A Structured Interview for the Evaluation of Substance Misuse Treatment.* London: National Treatment Agency for Substance Misuse.

Marshall, E. J., Edwards, G. & Taylor, C. (1994) Mortality in men with drinking problems: a 20-year follow-up. *Addiction*, *89*, 1293–1298.

Marshall, M. & Lockwood, A. (2004) Early intervention for psychosis. *Cochrane Database Systematic Review*, CD004718.

Martin, C., Kaczynski, N., Maisto, S., *et al.* (1995a) Patterns of DSM–IV alcohol abuse and dependence symptoms in adolescent drinkers. *Journal of Studies on Alcohol*, *56*, 672–680.

Martin, D. J., Garske, J. P. & Davis, M. K. (2000) Relation of the therapeutic alliance with outcome and other variables: A meta-analytic review. *Journal of Consulting & Clinical Psychology*, *68*, 438–450.

Martin, P. R., Adinoff, B., Lane, E., *et al.* (1995b) Fluvoxamine treatment of alcoholic amnestic disorder. *European Neuropsychopharmacology*, *5*, 27–33.

Martinez-Raga, J., Marshall, E. J., Keaney, F., *et al.* (2002) Unplanned versus planned discharges from inpatient alcohol detoxification: retrospective analysis of 270 first-episode admissions. *Alcohol and Alcoholism*, *37*, 277–281.

Martinotti, G., Di Nicola, M., Tedeschi, D., *et al.* (2008) Efficacy and safety of pregabalin in alcohol dependence. *Advances in Therapy*, *25*, 608–618.

Martinotti, G., Di Nicola, M., Di Giannantonio, M., *et al.* (2009) Aripiprazole in the treatment of patients with alcohol dependence: a double-blind, comparison trial vs. naltrexone. *Journal of Psychopharmacology*, *23*, 123–129.

Mason, B. J. & Lehert, P. (2010) The effects of current subsyndromal psychiatric symptoms or past psychopathology on alcohol dependence treatment outcomes and acamprosate efficacy. *The American Journal on Addictions*, *19*, 147–154.

Mason, B. J., Goodman, A. M., Dixon, R. M., *et al.* (2002) A pharmacokinetic and pharmacodynamic drug interaction study of acamprosate and naltrexone. *Neuropsychopharmacology*, *27*, 596–606.

Mason, B. J., Goodman, A. M., Chabac, S., *et al.* (2006) Effect of oral acamprosate on abstinence in patients with alcohol dependence in a double-blind, placebo-controlled trial: the role of patient motivation. *Journal of Psychiatric Research*, *40*, 383–393.

Mason, B. J., Light, J. M., Williams, L. D., *et al.* (2009) Proof-of-concept human laboratory study for protracted abstinence in alcohol dependence: effects of gabapentin. *Addiction Biology*, *14*, 73–83.

Mason, B. J., Salvato, F. R., Williams, L. D., *et al.* (1999) A double-blind, placebo-controlled study of oral nalmefene for alcohol dependence. *Archives of General Psychiatry*, *56*, 719–724.

Mathuranath P. S., Nestor, P. J., Berrios, G. E., *et al.* (2000). A brief cognitive test battery to differentiate Alzheimer's disease and frontotemporal dementia. *Neurology*, *55*, 1613–1620.

Mattick, R. P. & Hall, W. (1996) Are detoxification programmes effective? *The Lancet*, *347*, 97–100.

Mattson, M. E., Allen, J. P., Longabaugh, R., *et al.* (1994) A chronological review of empirical studies matching alcoholic clients to treatment. *Journal of Studies on Alcohol Supplement, 12,* 16-29.

Mayer, J. & Filstead, W. J. (1979) The Adolescent Alcohol Involvement Scale: an instrument for measuring adolescents' use and misuse of alcohol. *Journal of Studies on Alcohol, 40,* 291–300.

Mayo-Smith, M. F. (1997) Pharmacological management of alcohol withdrawal. A meta-analysis and evidence-based practice guideline. *Journal of American Medical Association, 278,* 144–151.

Mayo-Smith, M. F., Beecher, L. H., Fischer, T. L., *et al.* (2004) Management of alcohol withdrawal delirium. *Archives of Internal Medicine, 164,* 1405–1412.

McArdle, P. (2008) Alcohol abuse in adolescents. *Archives of Disease in Childhood, 93,* 524–527.

McCambridge, J. & Day, M. (2008) Randomized controlled trial of the effects of completing the Alcohol Use Disorders Identification Test questionnaire on self-reported hazardous drinking. *Addiction, 103,* 241–248.

McCance-Katz, E. F., Price, L. H., McDougle, C. J., *et al.* (1993) Concurrent cocaine-ethanol ingestion in humans: pharmacology, physiology, behavior, and the role of cocaethylene. *Psychophramacology, 111,* 39–46.

McCloud, A., Barnaby, B., Omu, N., *et al.* (2004) Relationship between alcohol use disorders and suicidality in a psychiatric population: in-patient prevalence study. *British Journal of Psychiatry, 184,* 439–445.

McCrady, B. S., Epstein, E. E., Cook, S., *et al.* (2009) A randomized trial of individual and couple behavioural alcohol treatment for women. *Journal of Consulting and Clinical Psychology, 77,* 243–256.

McCulloch, A., & McMurran, M. (2008) Evaluation of a treatment programme for alcohol-related aggression. *Criminal Behaviour and Mental Health, 18,* 224–231.

McGrew, J. G. & Bond, G. R. (1995) Critical ingredients of assertive community treatment: judgments of the experts. *The Journal of Behavioral Health Services and Research, 22,* 113–125.

McGrew, J. G., Bond, G. R., Dietzen, L., *et al.* (1994) Measuring the fidelity of implementation of a mental health program model. *Journal of Consulting and Clinical Psychology, 62,* 670–678.

McInnes, G. T. (1987) Chlormethiazole and alcohol: a lethal cocktail. *British Medical Journal (Clinical Research Edition), 294,* 592.

McInnes, G. T., Young, R. E. & Avery, B. S. (1980) Cardiac arrest following chlormethiazole infusion in chronic alcoholics. *Postgraduate Medical journal, 56,* 742–743.

McKay, J., Alterman, A., McLellan, A., *et al.* (1995) Effect of random versus non-random assignment in a comparison of inpatient and day hospital rehabilitation for male alcoholics. *Journal of Consulting and Clinical Psychology, 63,* 70–78.

McKinley, M. G. (2005) Alcohol withdrawal syndrome: overlooked and mismanaged? *Critical Care Nurse, 25,* 40–49.

McLachlan, J. F. C. & Stein, R. L. (1982) Evaluation of a day clinic for alcoholics. *Journal of Studies on Alcohol, 43,* 261–272.

McLellan, A. T., Luborsky, L., Woody, G., *et al.* (1980). An improved diagnostic instrument for substance abuse patients: the Addiction Severity Index. *Journal of Nervous and Mental Disease*, 168, 26–33.

McLellan, A. T., Luborsky, L., Woody, G., *et al.* (1983) Predicting response to alcohol and drug abuse. *Medicine*, *15*, 1005–1012.

McLellan, A. T., Hagan, T. A., Levin, M., *et al.* (1999) Does clinical case management improve outpatient addiction treatment. *Drug and Alcohol Dependence*, *55*, 91–103.

McLellan, A. T. & Alterman, A. I. (1991) Patient treatment matching: a conceptual and methodological review with suggestions for future research. *NIDA Research Monograph*, *106*, 114–135.

McLellan, A. T., Grissom, G. R., Zanis, D., *et al.* (1997) Problem-service "matching" in addiction treatment. *Archives of General Psychiatry*, *54*, 730–735.

McManus, S., Meltzer, H., Brugha, T., *et al.* (2009) *Adult Psychiatric Morbidity in England, 2007: Results of a Household Survey*. Leeds: NHS Information Centre for Health and Social Care.

Mee-Lee, D., Shulman, G. D., Fishman, M., *et al.* (2001) *ASAM Patient Placement Criteria for the Treatment of Substance-Related Disorders, Second Edition – Revised (ASAM PPC-2R)*. Chevy Chase, MD: American Society of Addiction Medicine, Inc.

Merikangas, K. R., Angst, J., Eaton, W., *et al.* (1996) Comorbidity and boundaries of affective disorders with anxiety disorders and substance misuse: results of an international task force. *British Journal of Psychiatry*, *168* (Suppl. 30), 58–67.

Merrill, J., Milner, G., Owens, J., *et al.* (1992) Alcohol and attempted suicide. *British Journal of Addiction*, 87, 83–89.

Meyers, R. J. & Miller, W. R. (eds). (2001) *A Community Reinforcement Approach to Addiction Treatment*. Cambridge: Cambridge University Press.

Meyers, K., McLellan, A. T., Jaeger, J. L., *et al.* (1995) The development of the Comprehensive Addiction Severity Index for Adolescents (CASI-A): an interview for assessing the multiple problems of adolescents. *Journal of Substance Abuse Treatment*, *12*, 181–193.

Meyers, R. J., Miller, W. R., Smith, J. E., *et al.* (2002) A randomized trial of two methods for engaging treatment-refusing drug users through concerned significant others. *Journal of Consulting and Clinical Psychology*, *70*, 1182–1185.

Microsoft (2007) Microsoft Excel [computer software]. Redmond, Washington: Microsoft.

Miller, D. K. & Homan, S. M. (1994) Determining transition probabilities: confusion and suggestions. *Medical Decision Making*, *14*, 52–58.

Miller, W., Benefield, G. & Tonigan, S. (1993) Enhancing motivation for change in problem drinking: A controlled comparison of two therapist styles. *Journal of Consulting and Clinical Psychology*, *61*, 455–461.

Miller, W. R. (1996) Motivational interviewing: research, practice and puzzles. *Addictive Behaviours*, *21*, 835–842.

Miller, W. R. & Hester, R. K. (1986) Inpatient alcoholism treatment. Who benefits? *American Psychologist*, *41*, 794–805.

Miller, W. R. & Marlatt, G. A. (1987). *Manual Supplement for the Brief Drinker Profile, Follow-up Drinker Profile, and Collateral Interview Form.* Odessa, FL: Psychological Assessment Resources.

Miller, W. R. & Munóz, R. (1976) *How to Control Your Drinking.* Englewood Cliffs, NJ: Prentice-Hall.

Miller, W. R. & Rollnick, S. (2002) *Motivational Interviewing: Preparing People for Change*, (2nd edn). New York, NY: Guilford Press.

Miller, W. R. & Tonigan, J. S. (1996) Assessing drinkers' motivation for change: the Stages of Change Readiness and Treatment Eagerness Scale (SOCRATES). *Psychology of Addictive Behaviors*, *10*, 81–89.

Miller, W. R. & Wilbourne, P. L. (2002) Mesa Grande: a methodological analysis of clinical trials of treatments for alcohol use disorders. *Addiction*, *97*, 265–277.

Miller, W. R., Zweben, A., Diclemente, C. C., *et al.* (1992) *Motivational Enhancement Therapy Manual: A Clinical Research Guide for Therapists Treating Individuals with Alcohol Abuse and Dependence.* Bethesda, MD: National Institute on Alcohol Abuse and Alcoholism.

Miller, W. R., Tonigan, J. S. & Longabaugh, R. (1995) *The Drinker Inventory of Consequences (DrInC): An Instrument for Assessing Adverse Consequences of Alcohol Abuse. Project MATCH Monograph Series, Vol. 4. DHHS Publication No. 95-3911.* Bethesda, MD: National Institute on Alcohol Abuse and Alcoholism.

Mills, E. J., Wu, P., Gagnier, J., *et al.* (2005) Efficacy of acupuncture for cocaine dependence: a systematic review and meta-analysis. *Harm Reduction Journal*, *2*, 4.

Mioshi, E., Dawson, K., Mitchell, J., *et al.* (2006) The Addenbrooke's Cognitive Examination Revised (ACE-R): a brief cognitive test battery for dementia screening. *International Journal of Geriatric Psychiatry*, *21*, 1078–1085.

Mohatt, G., Rasmus, S., Thomas, L., *et al.* (2007) Risk, resilience, and natural recovery: a model of recovery from alcohol abuse for Alaska natives. *Addiction*, *103*, 205–215.

Moncrieff, J., Drummond, D. C., Candy, B., *et al.* (1996) Sexual abuse in people with alcohol problems: a study of the prevalence of sexual abuse and its relationship to drinking behaviour. *British Journal of Psychiatry*, *169*, 355–360.

Monteforte, R., Estruch Valls-Solé, J., Nicolás, J., *et al.* (1995). Autonomic and peripheral neuropathies in patients with chronic alcoholism: a dose-related toxic effect of alcohol. *Archives of Neurology*, *52*, 45 – 51.

Monterosso, J. R., Flannery, B. A., Pettinati, H. M., *et al.* (2001) Predicting treatment response to naltrexone: the influence of craving and family history. *American Journal on Addictions*, *10*, 258–268.

Monti, P., Colby, S., Barnett, N. P., *et al.* (1999) Brief interventions for harm reduction with alcohol–positive older adolescents in a hospital emergency department. *Journal of Consulting and Clinical Psychology*, *67*, 989–994.

Monti, P. M., Abrams, D. B., Binkoff, J. A., *et al.* (1990) Communication skills training, communication skills training with family and cognitive behavioral mood management training for alcoholics. *Journal of Studies on Alcohol*, *51*, 263–270.

Monti, P. M., Rohsenow, D. J., Rubonis, A. V., *et al.* (1993) Cue exposure with coping skills treatment for alcoholics: a preliminary investigation. *Journal of Consulting and Clinical Psychology*, *61*, 1011–1019.

Monti, P. M., Rohsenow, D. J., Swift, R. M., *et al.* (2001) Naltrexone and cue exposure with coping skills training for alcoholics: Treatment process and 1-year outcomes. *Alcohol: Clinical and Experimental Research*, *25*, 1634–1647.

Moos, R. H., Moos, B. S. & Andrassy, J. M. (1999) Outcomes of four treatment approaches in community residential programs for patients with substance use disorders. *Psychiatric Services*, *50*, 1577–1583.

Moos, R., Schaefer, J., Andrassy, J., *et al.* (2001). Outpatient mental health care, self-help groups, and patients' one-year treatment outcomes. *Journal of Clinical Psychology*, *57*, 273–287.

Morgan, M. Y. & Ritson, E. B. (2009) *Alcohol and Health* (5th edn). London: The Medical Council on Alcohol.

Morgenstern, J., Bux, D. A., Labouvie, E., *et al.* (2003) Examining mechanisms of action in 12-step community outpatient treatment. *Drug and Alcohol Dependence*, *72*, 237–247.

Morgenstern, J., Irwin, T. W., Wainberg, M. L., *et al.* (2007) A randomized controlled trial of goal choice interventions for alcohol use disorders among men who have sex with men. *Journal of Consulting and Clinical Psychology*, *75*, 72–84.

Moriarty, K., Cassidy, P., Dalton, D., *et al.* (2010) *Alcohol-related disease. meeting the challenge of improved quality of care and better use of resources. A joint position paper on behalf of the British Society of Gastroenterology, Alcohol Health Alliance UK and the British Association for the Study of the Liver. Paper 9 C*, 31 March. London: British Society of Gastroenterology.

Morjaria, A. & Orford, J. (2002) The role of religion and spirituality in recovery from drink problems: a qualititative study of Alcoholics Anonymous members and South Asian men. *Addiction Research & Theory*, *10*, 225–256.

Morley, K. C., Teesson, M., Reid, S. C., *et al.* (2006) Naltrexone versus acamprosate in the treatment of alcohol dependence: a multi-centre, randomized, double-blind, placebo-controlled trial. *Addiction*, *101*, 1451–1462.

Morris, P. L. P., Hopwood, M., Whelan, G., *et al.* (2001) Naltrexone for alcohol dependence: a randomized controlled trial. *Addiction, 96*, 1565–1573.

Mortimer, D. & Segal, L. (2005) Economic evaluation of interventions for problem drinking and alcohol dependence: Cost per QALY estimates. *Alcohol & Alcoholism*, *40*, 549–555.

Mosher, V., Davis, J., Mulligan, D., *et al.* (1975) Comparison of outcome in a 9-day and 30-day alcoholism treatment program. *Journal of Studies on Alcohol*, *36*, 1277–1281.

Moyer, A., Finney, J. W., Elworth, J. T., *et al.* (2000) Can methodological features account for patient-treatment matching findings in the alcohol field? *Journal of Studies on Alcohol & Drugs, 62*, 62–73.

Moyer, A., Finney, J. W., Swearingen, C. E., *et al.* (2002) Brief interventions for alcohol problems: a meta-analytic review of controlled investigations in treatment-seeking and non-treatment-seeking populations. *Addiction*, *97*, 279–292.

References

Mueller, T. I., Pagano, M. E., Rodriguez, B. F., *et al.* (2005) Long-term use of benzodiazepines in participants with comorbid anxiety and alcohol use disorders. *Alcohol: Clinical & Experimental Research*, 29, 1411–1418.

Murphy, C. M., Winters, J., O'Farrell, T. J., *et al.* (2005). Alcohol consumption and intimate partner violence by alcoholic men: comparing violent and non violent conflicts. *Psychology of Addictive Behaviours*, 19, 35–42.

Murray, B. L. (1998) Perceptions of adolescents living with parental alcoholism. *Journal of Psychiatric and Mental Health Nursing*, 5, 525–534.

Naik, P. & Lawton, J. (1996) Assessment and management of individuals under the influence of alcohol is police custody. *Journal of Clinical Forensic Medicine*, 3, 37–44.

Najavits, L. M. & Weiss, R. D. (1994) Variations in therapist effectiveness in the treatment of patients with substance use disorders: an empirical review. *Addiction*, 89, 679–688.

Namkoong, K., Lee, B., Lee, P., *et al.* (2003) Acamprosate in Korean alcohol-dependent patients: a multicentre, randomized, double-blind, placebo-controlled study. *Alcohol and Alcoholism*, 38, 135–141.

Naranjo, C. A., Dongier, M. & Bremner, K. E. (1997) Long-acting injectable bromocriptine does not reduce relapse in alcoholics. *Addiction*, 92, 969–978.

National Audit Office (2008) *Reducing Alcohol Harm: Health Services in England for Alcohol Misuse*. London: National Audit Office.

National Institute on Alcohol Abuse and Alcoholism (1991) *Estimating the Economic Cost of Alcohol Abuse. No. 11 PH 293*. Bethesda, MD: National Institute on Alcohol Abuse and Alcoholism. Available from: http://pubs.niaaa.nih.gov/publications/aa11.htm [accessed May 2010].

National Treatment Agency (2009a) *National Alcohol Treatment Monitoring System*. Available from: http://www.alcohollearningcentre.org.uk/Topics/Latest/Resource/?cid=5120 [accessed 7 January 2010].

National Treatment Agency (2009b) *Residential Drug Treatment Services: A Summary of Good Practice*. London: National Treatment Agency.

National Treatment Agency and Department of Health (2010) *Statistics from the National Alcohol Treatment Monitoring System (NATMS) 1st April 2008 – 31st March 2009*. London: Department of Health.

National Treatment Agency for Substance Misuse (2002) *Models of Care for Treatment of Adult Drug Misusers: Promoting Quality, Efficiency and Effectiveness in Drug Misuse Treatment Services in England. Part 2: Full Reference Report*. London: National Treatment Agency for Substance Misuse.

National Treatment Agency for Substance Misuse (2006) *Models of Residential Rehabilitation for Drug and Alcohol Misusers*. London: National Treatment Agency.

National Treatment Agency for Substance Misuse (2007) *Drug Misuse and Dependence: Guidelines on Clinical Management*. London: National Treatment Agency for Substance Misuse.

National Treatment Agency for Substance Misuse (2010) *Treatment Outcomes Profile (TOP). The Protocol for Reporting TOP: a Keyworkers Guide*. London: National Treatment Agency for Substance Misuse.

NCCMH (2005) *Post-Traumatic Stress Disorder (PTSD): The Management of PTSD in Adults and Children in Primary and Secondary Care*. National Clinical Practice Guideline Number 26. Leicester & London: The British Psychological Society & The Royal College of Psychiatrists.

NCCMH (2008) *Drug Misuse: Psychosocial Interventions*. National Clinical Practice Guideline Number 51. Leicester & London: The British Psychological Society & The Royal College of Psychiatrists.

NCCMH (2009) *Attention Deficit Hyperactivity Disorder: Diagnosis and Management of ADHD in Children, Young People and Adults*. National Clinical Practice Guideline Number 72. Leicester & London: The British Psychological Society & The Royal College of Psychiatrists.

Nelson, A., Fogel, B. S. & Faust, D. (1986) Bedside cognitive screening instruments. A critical assessment. *Journal of Nervous and Mental Disease*, *174*, 73–83.

Nelson-Zlupko, L., Morrison-Dore, M. & Kauffman, E. (1996) Women in recovery: Their perceptions of treatment effectiveness. *Journal of Substance Abuse Treatment*, *13*, 51–59.

NHS Employers (2008) *Clinical Directed Enhanced Services (DES) Guidance for GMS Contract 2008/09: Delivering Investment in General Practice*. London: NHS Employers. Available from: http://www.alcoholpolicy.net/files/clinical_directed_enhanced_services.pdf [accessed May 2010].

NHS Information Centre & National Statistics (2009) *Statistics on Drug Misuse: England 2009*. London: The Health and Social Care Information Centre. Available from: http://www.ic.nhs.uk/webfiles/publications/drugmisuse09/Statistics_on_Drug_Misuse_England_2009_revised.pdf [accessed 4 February 2011].

Niaura, R. S., Rohsenow, D. J., Binkoff, J. A., *et al.* (1988) The relevance of cue reactivity to understanding alcohol and smoking relapse. *Journal of Abnormal Psychology*, *97*, 133–152.

NICE (2004) *Anxiety: Management of Anxiety (Panic Disorder, with or without Agoraphobia, and Generalised Anxiety Disorder) in Adults in Primary, Secondary and Community Care*. Clinical Guideline 22. London: NICE.

NICE (2006a) *Obsessive Compulsive Disorder (OCD) and Body Dysmorphic Disorder (BDD): Core Interventions in the Treatment of Obsessive-Compulsive Disorder and Body Dysmorphic Disorder*. Clinical Guideline 31. London: National Institute for Clinical Excellence.

NICE (2006b) *Brief Interventions and Referral for Smoking Cessation in Primary Care and Other Settings*. Public Health Intervention Guidance No. 1. London: NICE.

NICE (2007a) *Drug Misuse: Psychosocial Interventions*. Clinical Guideline 51. London: NICE.

NICE (2007b) *Drug Misuse: Opioid Detoxification*. Clinical Guideline 52. London: NICE.

NICE (2007b) *Community-Based Interventions to Reduce Substance Misuse Among Vulnerable and Disadvantaged Children and Young People*. Public Health Intervention Guidance No. 4. London: NICE.

References

NICE (2008a) *Antisocial Personality Disorder: Treatment, Management and Prevention.* Clinical Guideline 77. London: National Institute for Clinical Excellence.

NICE (2008b) *Social Value Judgements. Principles for the Development of NICE Guidance* (2nd edn). London: NICE.

NICE (2009a) *The Guidelines Manual.* London: NICE.

NICE (2009b) *Depression: The Treatment and Management of Depression in Adults.* Clinical Guideline 90. London: NICE.

NICE (2010a) *Alcohol-Use Disorders: Preventing the Development of Hazardous and Harmful Drinking.* Public Health Intervention Guidance No. 24. London: NICE.

NICE (2010b) *Alcohol-Use Disorders: Diagnosis and Clinical Management of Alcohol-Related Physical Complications.* Clinical Guideline 100. London: NICE.

NICE (2010c) *Pregnancy and Complex Social Factors: A Model for Service Provision for Pregnant Women with Complex Social Factors.* Clinical Guideline 110. London: NICE.

NICE (2011a) *Psychosis with Coexisting Substance Misuse: Assessment and Management in Adults and Young People.* Clinical Guideline 120. London: NICE.

NICE (2011b) *Common Mental Health Disorders: Identification and Pathways to Care.* Clinical Guideline 123. London: NICE.

NICE (2011c) *Generalised Anxiety Disorder and Panic Disorder (With or Without Agoraphobia) in Adults: Management in Primary, Secondary and Community Care.* Clinical Guideline 113. London: NICE.

Niederhofer, H. & Staffen, W. (2003a) Acamprosate and its efficacy in treating alcohol dependent adolescents. *European Child and Adolescent Psychiatry, 12,* 144–148.

Niederhofer, H. & Staffen, W. (2003b) Comparison of disulfiram and placebo in treatment of alcohol dependence in adolescents. *Drug and Alcohol Review, 22,* 295–297.

Niederhofer, H., Staffen, W. & Mair, A. (2003) Comparison of naltrexone and placebo in treatment of alcohol dependence of adolescents. *Alcoholism Treatment Quarterly, 21,* 87–95.

Nielsen, A. S. (2003) Alcohol problems and treatment: the patients' perceptions. European Addiction Research, 9, 29–38.

Nordqvist, C., Johansson, K. & Bendtsen, P. (2004) Routine screening for risky alcohol consumption at an emergency department using the AUDIT-C questionnaire. *Drug and Alcohol Dependence, 74,* 71–75.

North West Public Health Observatory (2010) *Local Alcohol Profiles for England.* Available from: http://www.nwph.net/alcohol/lape/ [Accessed 5 October 2010].

Nowinski, J., Baker, S. & Carroll, K. (1992) *Twelve Step Facilitation Therapy Manual: A Clinical Research Guide for Therapists Treating Individuals with Alcohol Abuse and Dependence.* NIAAA Project MATCH Monograph, Vol. 1, DHHS Publication No. (ADM) 92-1893, Washington, DC: Government Printing Office.

Nunnally, J. (1978) *Psychometric Theory.* New York: McGraw-Hill.

Nunes, E. V. & Levin, F. R. (2004) Treatment of Depression in Patients with alcohol or other drug dependence. *Journal of the American Medical Association, 291,* 1887–1896.

Nutt, D. (1999) Alcohol and the brain. Pharmacological insights for psychiatrists. *The British Journal of Psychiatry*, *175*, 114–119.

NVivo (2010) NVivo qualitative data analysis software. Version 9. Victoria, Australia: QSR International Pty Ltd.

O'Connell, H., Chin, A.-C., Cunningham, C., *et al.* (2003) Alcohol use disorders in elderly people: redefining and age old problem in old age. *British Medical Journal*, *327*, 664–667.

O'Connor, P. G. & Schottenfeld, R. S. (1998) Patients with alcohol problems. *The New England Journal of Medicine*, *338*, 592–602.

O'Connor, P. G., Gottlieb, L. D., Kraus, M. L., *et al.* (1991) Social and clinical features as predictors of outcomes in outpatient alcohol withdrawal. *Journal of General Internal Medicine*, *6*, 312–316.

O'Connor, P. G., Samet, J. H. & Stein, M. D. (1994) Management of hospitalized intravenous drug users: role of the internist. *American Journal of Medicine*, *96*, 551–558.

O'Donnell, W. E. & Reynolds, D. McQ. (1983) *Neuropsychological Impairment Scale (NIS) Manual*. Annapolis, MD: Annapolis Neuropsychological Services.

O'Donnell, W. E., DeSoto, C. B. & Reynolds, D. McQ. (1984a) Sensitivity and specificity of the Neuropsychological Impairment Scale (NIS). *Journal of Clinical Psychology*, *40*, 553–555.

O'Donnell, W. E., Reynolds, D. Q. & de Soto, C. B. (1984b) Neuropsychological impairment scale (NIS): initial validation study using trailmaking test (A & B) and WAIS digit symbol (scaled score) in a mixed grouping of psychiatric, neurological, and normal patients. *Journal of Clinical Psychology*, *39*, 746–748.

O'Farrell, T. J., Cutter, H. S. G., Choquette, K. A., *et al.* (1992) Behavioral marital therapy for male alcoholics: marital and drinking adjustment during the two years after treatment. *Behavior Therapy*, *23*, 529–549.

O'Hare, T., Sherrer, M., LaButti A., *et al.* (2006) Validating the Alcohol Use Disorders Identification Test in persons who have serious mental illness. *Research on Social Work Practice*, *14*, 36–42.

O'Malley, S. (Chair) (1993) *Naltrexone and Alcoholism Treatment 28: Treatment Improvement Protocol (TIP) Series 28*. Rockville, MD: Substance Abuse and Mental Health Services Administration (US). Available from: http://www.ncbi.nlm.nih.gov/bookshelf/br.fcgi?book=hssamhsatip&part=A51510 [accessed May 2010].

O'Malley, S. S., Jaffe, A. J., Chang, G., *et al.* (1992) Naltrexone and coping skills therapy for alcohol dependence: a controlled study. *Archives of General Psychiatry*, *49*, 881–887.

O'Malley, S. S., Jaffe, A. J., Rode, S., *et al.* (1996) Experience of a 'slip' among alcoholics treated with naltrexone or placebo. *American Journal of Psychiatry*, *153*, 281–283.

O'Malley, K. D. & Nanson, J. (2002) Clinical implications of a link between fetal alcohol spectrum disorder and attention-deficit hyperactivity disorder. *Canadian Journal of Psychiatry*, *47*, 349–354.

O'Malley, S. S., Rounsaville, B. J., Farren, C., *et al.* (2003) Initial and maintenance naltrexone treatment for alcohol dependence using primary care vs. specialty care. *Archives of Internal Medicine, 163,* 1695–1704.

O'Malley, S. S., Robin, R. W., Levenson, A. L., *et al.* (2008) Naltrexone alone and with sertraline for the treatment of alcohol dependence in Alaska natives and natives residing in rural settings: a randomized controlled trial. *Alcoholism: Clinical and Experimental Research, 32,* 1271–1283.

Office for National Statistics (2003) *Alcohol-Related Death Rates in England and Wales, 2001–2003.* London: Office for National Statistics.

Ofori-Adjei, D., Casswell, S., Drummond, C., *et al.* (2007) *World Health Organization Expert Committee on Problems Related to Alcohol Consumption, Second Report.* Geneva: WHO.

Okiishi, J., Lambert, M. J., Nielsen, S. L,. *et al.* (2003) Waiting for supershrink: an empirical analysis of therapist effects. *Clinical Psychology and Psychotherapy, 10,* 361–373.

Ojehagen, A., Berglund, M. & Hansson, L. (1997) The relationship between helping alliance and outcome in outpatient treatment of alcoholics: a comparative study of psychiatric treatment and multimodal behavioural therapy. *Alcohol and Alcoholism, 32,* 241–249.

Olive, M. F. (2009) Metabotropic glutamate receptor ligands as potential therapeutics for addiction. *Current Drug Abuse Reviews, 2,* 83–989.

Omer, H., Foldes, J., Toby, M., *et al.* (1983) Screening for cognitive deficits in a sample of hospitalized geriatric patients. a re-evaluation of a brief mental status questionnaire. *Journal of the American Geriatrics Society, 31,* 266–268.

Ooteman, W., Naassila, M. & Koeter, M. W. J. (2009) Predicting the effect of naltrexone and acamprosate in alcohol-dependent patients using genetic indicators. *Addiction Biology, 14,* 328–337.

Orford, J., Oppenheimer, E. & Edwards, G. (1976) Abstinence or control: the outcome for excessive drinkers two years after consultation. *Behaviour Research and Therapy, 14,* 409–418.

Orford, J., Natera, G., Davies, J., *et al.* (1998a) Tolerate, engage or withdraw: a study of the structures of families coping with alcohol and drug problems in South West England and Mexico City. *Addiction, 93,* 1799–1813.

Orford, J., Natera, G., Davies, J., *et al.* (1998b) Social support in coping with alcohol and drug problems at home: findings from Mexican and English families. *Addiction Research & Theory, 6,* 395–420.

Orford, J., Dalton, S., Hartney, E., *et al.* (2002) The close relatives of untreated heavy drinkers: perspectives on heavy drinking and its effects. *Addiction Research and Theory, 10,* 439–463.

Orford, J., Natera, G., Copello, A., *et al.* (2005) *Coping with Alcohol and Drug Problems: The Experiences of Family Members in Three Contrasting Cultures.* London: Taylor and Francis.

Orford, J., Hodgson, R., Copello, A., *et al.* (2006a) The clients' perspective on change during treatment for an alcohol problem: qualitative analysis of follow-up interviews in the UK Alcohol Treatment Trial. *Addiction, 101,* 60–68.

Orford, J., Korr, C., Copello, A., *et al.* (2006b) Why people enter treatment for alcohol problems: findings from UK Alcohol Treatment Trial. *Addiction*, *101*, 60–68.

Orford, J., Hodgson, R., Copello, A., *et al.* (2008) To what factors do clients attribute change? Content analysis of follow-up interviews with clients of the UK Alcohol Treatment Trial. *Journal of Substance Abuse Treatment*, *36*, 49–58.

Oroszi, G., Anton, R. F., O'Malley, S., *et al.* (2009) OPRM1 Asn40Asp predicts response to naltrexone treatment: a haplotype-based approach. *Alcoholism: Clinical & Experimental Research*, *33*, 383–393.

Oslin, D., Liberto, J. G., O'Brien, J., *et al.* (1997) Naltrexone as an adjunctive treatment for older patients with alcohol dependence. *The American Journal of Geriatric Psychiatry*, *5*, 324–332.

Oslin, D. W. & Cary, M. S. (2003) Alcohol-related dementia: validation of diagnostic criteria. *American Journal of Geriatric Psychiatry*, *11*, 441–447.

Oslin, D. W., Berrettini, W., Kranzler, H. R., *et al.* (2003) A functional polymorphism of the μ-opioid receptor gene is associated with naltrexone response in alcohol-dependent patients. *Neuropsychopharmacology*, *28*, 1546–1552.

Oslin, D. W., Lynch, K. G., Pettinati, H. M., *et al.* (2008) A placebo-controlled randomized clinical trial of naltrexone in the context of different levels of psychosocial education. *Alcoholism: Clinical and Experimental Research*, *32*, 1299–1308.

Oswald, L. M. & Wand, G. S. (2004) Opioids and alcoholism. *Physiology & Behavior*, *81*, 339–358.

Owens, D., Horrocks, J. & House, A. (2002) Fatal and non-fatal repetition of self-harm. *British Journal of Psychiatry*, *181*, 193–199.

Paille, F. M., Guelfi, J. D., Perkins, A. C., *et al.* (1995) Double-blind randomized multicentre trial of acamprosate in maintaining abstinence from alcohol. *Alcohol and Alcoholism*, *30*, 239–247.

Palmer, A. J., Neeser, K., Weiss, C., *et al.* (2000) The long-term cost-effectiveness of improving alcohol abstinence with adjuvant acamprosate. *Alcohol and Alcoholism*, *35*, 478–492.

Pani, P. P., Trogu, E., Vacca, R., *et al.* (2010) Disulfiram for the treatment of cocaine dependence. *Cochrane Database of Systematic Reviews*, *20*, CD007024.

Parrott, S., Godfrey, C., Heather, N., *et al.* (2006) Cost and outcome analysis of two alcohol detoxification services. *Alcohol and Alcoholism*, *41*, 84–91.

Passetti, F., Jones, G., Chawla, K., *et al.* (2008) Pilot study of assertive community treatment methods to engage alcohol-dependent individuals. *Alcohol and Alcoholism*, *43*, 451–455.

Patterson, D. G., Macpherson, J. & Brady, N. M. (1997) Community psychiatric nurse aftercare for alcoholics: a five-year follow-up study. *Addiction*, *92*, 459–468.

Pelc, I., Le Bon, O., Verbanck, *et al.* (1992) Calcium acetyl homotaurinate for maintaining abstinence in weaned alcoholic patients; a placebo controlled double-blind multi-centre study. In *Novel Pharmacological Interventions for Alcoholism* (eds C. Naranjo & E. Sellers), pp. 348–352. New York, NY: Springer Verlag.

Pelc, I., Verbanck, P., Le Bon, O., *et al.* (1997) Efficacy and safety of acamprosate in the treatment of detoxified alcohol-dependent patients. *British Journal of Psychiatry*, *171*, 73–77.

References

Pennings, E. J. M., Leccese, A. P. & de Wolff, F. A. (2002) Effects of concurrent use of alcohol and cocaine. *Addiction*, *97*, 773–783.

Perepletchikova, F., Krystal, J. H. & Kaufman, J. (2008) Practitioner review: adolescent alcohol use disorders: assessment and treatment issues. *Journal of Child Psychology and Psychiatry*, *49*, 1131–1154.

Petrakis, I., Ralevski, E., Nich, C., *et al.* (2007) Naltrexone and DIS in patients with alcohol dependence and current depression. *Journal of Clinical Psychopharmacology*, *27*, 160–165.

Petrakis, I. L., Carroll, K. M., Nich, C., *et al.* (2000) Disulfiram treatment for cocaine dependence in methadone-maintained opioid addicts. *Addiction*, *95*, 219–228.

Petrakis, I. L., Gonzalez, G., Rosenheck, R. *et al.* (2002) Comorbidity of alcoholism and psychiatric disorders : an overview. *Alcohol Research & Health*, *26*, 81–89.

Petrakis, I. L., Poling, J., Levinson, C., *et al.* (2005) Naltrexone and disulfiram in patients with alcohol dependence and comorbid psychiatric disorders. *BiologicalPsychiatry*, *57*, 1128–1137.

Petrakis, I. L., Leslie, D., Finney, J. W., *et al.* (2006) Atypical antipsychotic medication and substance use – related outcomes in the treatment of schizophrenia. *American Journal on Addiction*, *15*, 44–49.

Petry, N. M., Martin, B., Cooney, J. L., *et al.* (2000) Give them prizes, and they will come: Contingency management for treatment of alcohol dependence. *Journal of Consulting and Clinical Psychology*, *68*, 250–257.

Pettinati, H. M., Meyers, K., Jensen, J. M., *et al.* (1993) Inpatient vs. outpatient treatment for substance dependence revisited. *Psychiatric Quarterly*, *64*, 173–182.

Pettinati, H. M., Meyers, K., Evans, B. D. *et al.* (1999) Inpatient alcohol treatment in a private healthcare setting: which patients benefit and at what cost? *The American Journal on Addictions*, *8*, 220–233.

Pettinati, H. M., Volpicelli, J. R., Kranzler, H. R., *et al.* (2000) Sertraline treatment for alcohol dependence: interactive effects of medication and alcoholic subtype. *Alcoholism: Clinical and Experimental Research*, *24*, 1041–1049.

Pettinati, H. M., Kampman, K. M., Lynch, K. G., *et al.* (2008a) A double blind, placebo-controlled trial that combines disulfiram and naltrexone for treating co-occurring cocaine and alcohol dependence. *Addictive Behaviors*, *33*, 651–667.

Pettinati, H. M., Kampman, K. M., Lynch, K. G., *et al.* (2008b) Gender differences with high-dose naltrexone in patients with co-occurring cocaine and alcohol dependence. *Journal of Substance Abuse Treatment*, *34*, 378–390.

Pettinati, H. M., Oslin, D. W., Kampman, K. M., *et al.* (2010) A double-blind, placebo-controlled trial combining sertraline and naltrexone for treating co-occurring depression and alcohol dependence. *The American Journal of Psychiatry*, *167*, 668–675.

Piacentini, J., Shaffer, D., Fisher, P., *et al.* (1993). The Diagnostic Interview Schedule for Children-Revised version (DISC-R): III. Concurrent criterion validity. *Journal of the American Academy of Child and Adolescent Psychiatry*, *32*, 658–665.

Pittman, D. J. & Tate, R. L. (1972) A comparison of two treatment programs for alcoholics. *Journal of Social Psychiatry*, *18*, 183–193.

Poldrugo, F. (1997) Acamprosate treatment in a long-term community-based alcohol rehabilitation program. *Addiction, 92,* 1537–1546.

Poulsen, H. E., Loft, S., Andersen, J. R., *et al.* (1992) Disulfiram therapy – adverse drug reactions and interactions. *Acta Psychiatrica Scandinavica, 369,* 59–65.

Pragst, F. & Balikova, M. A. (2006) State of the art in hair analysis for detection of drug and alcohol abuse. *Clinica Chimica Acta, 370,* 17–49

Prati, D., Taioli, E., Zanella, A., *et al.* (2002) Updated definitions of healthy ranges for serum alanine aminotransferase levels. *Annals of Internal Medicine, 137,* 1–10.

Prendergast, M., Podus, D., Finney, J., *et al.* (2006) Contingency management for treatment of substance use disorders: a meta-analysis. *Addiction, 101,* 1546–1560.

Prime Minister's Strategy Unit (2003) *Strategy Unit Alcohol Harm Reduction Project Interim Analytic Report.* London: Cabinet Office.

Prime Minister's Strategy Unit (2004) *Alcohol Harm Reduction Strategy.* London: Cabinet Office.

Prochaska, J. O., DiClemente, C. C. (1983) Stages and processes of self-change of smoking: toward an integrative model of change. *Journal of Consulting and Clinical Psychology, 51,* 390–395.

Prochaska, J. J., Delucchi, K., & Hall, S. M. (2004) A meta-analysis of smoking cessation interventions with individuals in substance abuse treatment or recovery. *Journal of Consulting and Clinical Psychology, 72,* 1144–1156.

Project MATCH Research Group (1993) Project MATCH: rationale and methods for a multisite clinical trial matching patients to alcoholism treatment. *Alcoholism: Clinical and Experimental Research, 17,* 1130–1145.

Project MATCH Research Group (1997) Matching alcoholism treatments to client heterogeneity: Project MATCH posttreatment drinking outcomes. *Journal of Studies on Alcohol, 58,* 7–29.

Project MATCH Research Group (1998) Therapist effects in three treatments for alcohol problems. *Psychotherapy Research, 8,* 455–474.

Qatari, M., Shabeena, K., Barton, H., *et al.* (2001) Acamprosate is neuroprotective against glutamate-induced excitotoxity when enhanced by ethanol withdrawal in neocortical cultures of fetal rat brain. *Alcoholism: Clinical and Experimental Research, 25,* 1276–1283.

Raistrick, D. & Tober, G. (2003) Much more than outcomes. *Drug & Alcohol Findings, 8,* 27–29.

Raistrick, D., Dunbar, G. & Davidson, R. (1983) Development of a questionnaire to measure alcohol dependence. *Addiction,* 78, 89–95.

Raistrick, D., Bradshaw, J., Tober, G., *et al.* (1994) Development of the Leeds Dependence Questionnaire (LDQ): a questionnaire to measure alcohol and opiate dependence in the context of a treatment evaluation package. *Addiction, 89,* 563–572.

Raistrick, D., Heather, N. & Godfrey, C. (2006) *Review of the Effectiveness of Treatment for Alcohol Problems.* London: National Treatment Agency for Substance Misuse.

Ramayya, A. & Jauhar, P. (1997) Increasing incidence of Korsakoff's psychosis in the East End of Glasgow. *Alcohol & Alcoholism, 32,* 281–285.

References

Rampes, H., Pereira, S., Mortimer, A., *et al.* (1997) Does electroacupuncture reduce craving for alcohol? A randomized controlled study. *Complementary Therapies in Medicine*, *5*, 19–26.

Ramsay, M. (ed) (2003) *Prisoners' Drug Use and Treatment: Seven Research Studies.* Home Office Research Study 267. London: Home Office Research, Development and Statistics Directorate, HMSO.

Randall, C. L., Johnson, M. R., Thevos, A. K., *et al.* (2001) Paroxetine for social anxiety and alcohol use in dual-diagnosed patients. *Depression and Anxiety*, *14*, 255–262.

Regier, D. A., Farmer, M. E., Rae, D. S., *et al.* (1990) Comorbidity of mental disorders with alcohol and other drug abuse: results from the epidemiologic catchment area (ECA) study. *Journal of the American Medical Association*, *264*, 2511–2518.

Rehm, R., Room, K., Graham, M., *et al.* (2003) The relationship of average volume of alcohol consumption and patterns of drinking to burden of disease – an overview. *Addiction*, *98*, 1209–1228.

Rehm, J., Room, R., Monteiro, M., *et al.* (2004) Alcohol use. In *Comparative Quantification of Health Risks: Global and Regional Burden of Disease Attributable to Selected Major Risk Factors* (eds M. Ezzati, A. D. Lopez, A. Rodgers, *et al.*). Geneva: WHO.

Rehm, J., Ballunas, D., Brochu, S., *et al.* (2006) *The Costs of Substance Abuse in Canada 2002.* Ottawa: Canadian Centre on Substance Abuse.

Rehm, J., Mathers, C., Popova, S., *et al.* (2009) Global burden of disease and injury and economic cost attributable to alcohol use and alcohol-use disorders. *Lancet*, *373*, 2223–2233.

Reid, M. C. & Anderson, P. A. (1997) Geriatric substance use disorders. *Medical Clinics of North America*, *81*, 999–1016.

Reinert, D. F. & Allen, J. P. (2007) The Alcohol Use Disorders Identification Test: an update of research findings alcoholism. *Clinical and Experimental Research*, *31*, 185–199.

Reoux, J. P. & Miller, K. (2000) Routine hospital alcohol detoxification practice compared to 24 symptom triggered management with an Objective Withdrawal Scale (CIWA-Ar). *American Journal on Addictions*, *9*, 135–144.

Reuster, T., Buechler, J., Winiecki, P., *et al.* (2003) Influence of reboxetine on salivary MHPG concentration and cognitive symptoms among patients with alcohol-related Korsakoff's syndrome. *Neuropsychopharmacology*, *28*, 974–978.

Richardson, K., Baillie, A., Reid, S., *et al.* (2008) Do acamprosate or naltrexone have an effect on daily drinking by reducing craving for alcohol? *Addiction*, *103*, 953–959.

Robins, L. N., Wing, J., Wittchen, H. U., *et al.* (1989) The Composite International Diagnostic Interview: an epidemiologic instrument suitable for use in conjunction with different diagnostic systems and in different cultures. *Archives of General Psychiatry*, *45*, 1069–1077.

Robinson, T. E. & Berridge, K. C. (2008) Review. The incentive sensitization theory of addiction: some current issues. *Philosophical Transactions of the Royal Society of London (Series B) Biological Sciences*, *363*, 3137–3146.

Robinson, S. & Bulger, C. (2010) *General Lifestyle Survey 2008: Smoking and Drinking Among Adults, 2008.* Newport: Office for National Statistics.

Rogers, C. R. (1951) *Client-Centered Therapy; Its Current Practice, Implications, and Theory.* Oxford: Houghton Miffin.

Rohsenow, D. J., Monti, P. M., Hutchinson, K. E., *et al.* (2000) Naltrexone's effects on reactivity to alcohol cues among alcoholic men. *Journal of Abnormal Psychology*, *109*, 738–742.

Rolfe, A., Dalton, S. & Orford, J. (2005) On the road to Damascus? A qualitative study of life events and decreased drinking. *Contemporary Drug Problems*, *32*, 589–603.

Rolfe, A., Orford, J., Dalton, S., *et al.* (2009) Women, alcohol and femininity: a discourse analysis of women heavy drinkers' accounts. *Journal of Health Psychology*, *14*, 326–335.

Rollnick, S., Heather, N., Gold, R., *et al.* (1992) Development of a short 'readiness to change' questionnaire for use in brief, opportunistic interventions among excessive drinkers. *British Journal of Addiction*, *87*, 743–754.

Rollnick, S., Mason, P. & Butler, C. (1999) *Health Behavior Change: A Guide for Practitioners.* Edinburgh: Churchill Livingstone.

Room, R., Babor, T. & Rehm, J. (2005) Alcohol and public health. *Lancet*, *365*, 519–530.

Rosenblum, A., Cleland, C., Magura, S., *et al.* (2005a) Moderators of effects of motivational enhancements to cognitive behavioural therapy. *The American Journal of Drug and Alcohol Abuse*, *1*, 35–58.

Rosenblum, A., Magura, S., Kayman, D.J., *et al.* (2005b) Motivationally enhanced group counselling for substance users in a soup kitchen: a randomized clinical trial. *Drug and Alcohol Dependence*, *80*, 91–103.

Rosner, S., Leucht, S., Lehert, P., *et al.* (2008) Acamprosate supports abstinence, naltrexone prevents excessive drinking: evidence from a meta-analysis with unreported outcomes. *Journal of Psychopharmacology*, *22*, 11–23.

Roth, A. D. & Pilling, S. (2008) Using an evidence-based methodology to identify the competences required to deliver effective cognitive and behavioural therapy for depression and anxiety disorders. *Behavioural and Cognitive Psychotherapy*, *36*, 129–147.

Roth, A. D. & Pilling, S. (2011) The impact of adherence and competence on outcome in CBT and psychological therapies. In preparation.

Roth, A. D., Pilling, S. & Turner, J. (2010) Therapist training and supervision in clinical trials: Implications for clinical practice. *Behavioural and Cognitive Psychotherapy*, *38*, 291–302.

Roussaux, J. P., Hers, D. & Ferauge, M. (1996) Does acamprosate diminish the appetite for alcohol in weaned alcoholics? *Journal de Pharmacie de Belgique*, *51*, 65–68.

Royal College of Physicians (2001) *Alcohol: Can the NHS Afford It?* London: Royal College of Physicians.

Royal College of Psychiatrists (1986) *Alcohol: Our Favourite Drug.* London: Royal College of Psychiatrists.

Rubio, G., Jiminez-Arriero, M. A., Ponce, G., *et al.* (2001) Naltrexone versus acamprosate: one year follow-up of alcohol dependence treatment. *Alcohol and Alcoholism*, *36*, 419–425.

Rubio, G., Ponce, G., Rodriguez-Jiménez, R., *et al.* (2005) Clinical predictors of response to naltrexone in alcoholic patients: who benefits most from treatment with naltrexone? *Alcohol and Alcoholism, 40,* 227–233.

Rush, B. (1990) A systems approach to estimating the required capacity of alcohol treatment services. *British Journal of Addiction, 85,* 49–59.

Russell, M., Marshall, J. R., Trevisan, M., *et al.* (1997) Test-retest reliability of the Cognitive Lifetime Drinking History. *American Journal of Epidemiology, 146,* 975–981.

Ryan, L. & Ottlinger, A. (1999) Implementation of alcohol withdrawal program in a medical-setting: improving patient outcomes. *Journal of Addictions Nursing, 11,* 102–106.

Rychtarik, R. G., Connors, G. J., Whitney, R. B., *et al.* (2000a) Treatment settings for persons with alcoholism: evidence for matching clients to inpatient versus outpatient care. *Journal of Consulting and Clinical Psychology, 68,* 277–289.

Rychlik, R., Siedentop H., Pfiel, T., *et al.* (2003) Cost-effectiveness of adjuvant treatment with acamprosate in maintaining abstinence in alcohol dependent patients. *European Addiction Research, 9,* 59–64.

Sacks, L. (1975) Drug addiction, alcoholism, smoking, obesity, treated by auricular acupuncture. *American Journal of Acupuncture, 3,* 147–150.

Sacks, S., Sacks, J. Y., McKendrick, K., *et al.* (2004) Modified TC for MICA inmates in correctional settings: crime outcomes. *Behavioural Sciences and the Law, 22,* 477–501.

Saitz, R., Mayo-Smith, M. F., Roberts, M. S., *et al.* (1994) Individualized treatment for alcohol 13 withdrawal: a randomised double- blind controlled trial. *Journal of the American Medical Association, 272,* 519–523.

Saitz, R. & O'Malley, S. S. (1997) Pharmacotherapies for alcohol abuse. *Alcohol and Other Substance Abuse, 4,* 881–907.

Sandahl, C., Herlitz, K., Ahlin, G., *et al.* (1998) Time-limited group psychotherapy for moderately alcohol dependent patients: a randomized controlled clinical trial. *Psychotherapy Research, 8,* 361–378.

Sannibale, C., Hurkett, P., van den Bossche, E., *et al.* (2003) Aftercare attendance and post-treatment functioning of severely substance dependent residential treatment clients. *Drug and Alcohol Review, 22,* 181–190.

Santis, R., Garmendia, M., Acuña, G., *et al.* (2009) The Alcohol Use Disorders Identification Test (AUDIT) as a screening instrument for adolescents. *Drug and Alcohol Dependence, 103,* 155–157.

Specialist Clinical Addiction Network (2006) *Inpatient Treatment of Drug and Alcohol Misusers in the National Health Service.* London: SCAN.

Sass, H., Soyka, M., Mann, K., *et al.* (1996) Relapse prevention by acamprosate. *Archives of General Psychiatry, 53,* 673–680.

Schadé, A., Marquenie, L. A., van Balkom, A. J. L. M. *et al.* (2005) The effectiveness of anxiety treatment on alcohol-dependent patients with a comorbid phobic disorder: a randomized controlled trial. *Alcoholism: Clinical and Experimental Research, 29,* 794–800.

Schadlich, P. K. & Brecht, J. G. (1998) The cost effectiveness of acamprosate in the treatment of alcoholism in Germany. Economic evaluation of the Prevention of Relapse with Acamprosate in the Management of Alcoholism (PRAMA) study. *PharmacoEconomics*, *13*, 719–730.

Schmidt, A., Barry, K. L. & Fleming, M. F. (1995) Detection of problem drinkers: the Alcohol Use Disorders Identification Test (AUDIT). *Southern Medical Journal*, *J88*, 52–59.

Schmitz, J. M., Averill, P., Sayre, S., *et al.* (2002) Cognitive–behavioral treatment of bipolar disorder and substance abuse: preliminary randomized study. *Addictive Disorders & Their Treatment*, *1*, 17–24.

Schmitz, J. M., Stotts, A. L., Sayre, S. L., *et al.* (2004) Treatment of cocaine-alcohol dependence with naltrexone and relapse prevention therapy. *American Journal of Addictions*, *13*, 333–341.

Schmitz, J. M., Lindsay, J. A., Green, C. E., *et al.* (2009) High-dose naltrexone therapy for cocaine-alcohol dependence. *American Journal of Addictions*, *18*, 356–362.

Schuckit, M. A. (2009) Alcohol-use disorders. *Lancet*, *373*, 492.

Schultz, W. (2007) Behavioral dopamine signals. *Trends in Neuroscience*, *30*, 203–210.

Schumacher, L., Pruitt II, N. & Phillips, M. (2000) Identifying patients "At Risk" of alcohol withdrawal syndrome and a treatment protocol. *Journal of Neuroscience Nursing*, *32*, 158–163.

Schwab-Stone, M., Shaffer, D., Dulcan, M., *et al.* (1996) Criterion validity of the NIMH Diagnostic Interview Schedule for Children version 2.3 (DISC-2.3). *Journal of the American Academy of Child and Adolescent Psychiatry*, *35*, 878–888.

Schwamm, L. H., Van Dyke, C., Kiernan, R. J., *et al.* (1987) The Neurobehavioural Cognitive Status Examination and the Mini-Mental State Examination in a neurosurgical population. *Annals of Internal Medicine*, *107*, 486–491.

Schwan, R., Loiseaux, M. N., Schellenberg, F., *et al.* (2004) Multicenter validation study of the %CDT TIA kit in alcohol abuse and alcohol dependence. *Alcoholism: Clinical and Experimental Research*, *28*, 1331–1337.

Sellman, J. D., Sullivan, P. F., Dore, G. M., *et al.* (2001) A randomized controlled trial of motivational enhancement therapy (MET) for mild to moderate alcohol dependence. *Journal of Studies on Alcohol*, *62*, 389–396.

Schaffer, D., Fisher, P., Dulcan, M., *et al.* (1996) The NIMH Diagnostic Interview Schedule for Children (DISC-2): description, acceptability, prevalences, and performance in the MECA study. *Journal of the American Academy of Child and Adolescent Psychiatry*, *35*, 865–877.

Sereny, G., Sharma, V. & Holt, J. (1986) Mandatory supervised Antabuse therapy in an outpatient alcoholism program: a pilot study. *Alcoholism: Clinical and Experimental Research*, *10*, 290–292.

Shakeshaft, A. P., Bowman, J. A., Burrows, S., *et al.* (2002) Community-based alcohol counselling: a randomized clinical trial. *Addiction*, *97*, 1449–1463.

References

Shaw, G. K., Waller, S., Latham, C. J., *et al.* (1998) The detoxification experience of alcoholic in-patients and predictors of outcome. *Alcohol & Alcoholism, 33*, 291–303.

Shaw, C. M., Creed, F., Tomenson, B., *et al.* (1999) Prevalence of anxiety and depressive illness and help seeking behaviour in African Caribbeans and white Europeans: two phase general population survey. *British Medical Journal, 318*, 302–306.

Shaw, J., Appleby, L. & Baker, D. (2003) *Safer Prisons: A National Study of Prison Suicides 1999–2000 by the National Confidential Inquiry into Suicides and Homicides by People with Mental Illness.* London: Department of Health.

Sheehan, D. V., Lecrubier, Y., Sheehan, K. H., *et al.* (1998). The Mini-International Neuropsychiatric Interview (MINI): the development and validation of a structured diagnostic psychiatric interview for DSM–IV and ICD–10. *Journal of Clinical Psychiatry, 59* (Suppl. 20), 22–33.

Sher, L. (2006) Alcohol consumption and suicide. *Quarterly Journal of Medicine, 99*, 57–61.

Sinclair, J. M. A. & Green, J. (2005) Understanding resolution of deliberate self harm: qualitative interview study of patients' experiences. *British Medical Journal, 330*, 1112–1115.

Sinclair, J., Latifi, A. H. & Latifi, A. W. (2008) Co-morbid substance misuse in psychiatric inpatients: prevalence and association with length of inpatient stay. *Journal of Psychopharmacology, 22*, 92–98.

Sinclair, J., Hawton, K. & Gray, A. (2009) Six year follow-up of a clinical sample of self-harm patients. *Journal of Affective Disorders, 121*, 247–252.

Singleton, N., Meltzer, H. & Gatward, R. (1998) *Psychiatric Morbidity Among Prisoners in England and Wales.* London: Her Majesty's Stationery Office.

Sinha, R. & O'Malley, S. S. (2000) Alcohol and eating disorders: implications for alcohol treatment and health services research. *Alcoholism, Clinical & Experimental Research, 24*, 1312–1319.

Sisson, R. W. & Azrin, N. (1989) The community reinforcement approach. In *Handbook of Alcoholism Treatment Approaches: Effective Alternatives* (eds R. Hester & W. R. Miller), pp. 242–258. New York, NY: Pergamon Press.

Sitharthan, T., Sitharthan, G., Hough, M. J., *et al.* (1997) Cue exposure in moderation drinking: a comparison with cognitive-behavior therapy. *Journal of Consulting and Clinical Psychology, 65*, 878–882.

Skills for Health (2002) *Drugs and Alcohol National Occupational Standards (DANOS).* Bristol: Skills for Health. Available from: http://www.skillsforhealth.org.uk/service-area/~/media/Resource-Lbrary2/PDF/AD%20DANOS%20guide.ashx [Accessed February 2011].

Skinner, H. A. & Horn, J. L. (1984) *Alcohol Dependence Scale: Users Guide.* Toronto: Addiction Research Foundation.

Skinner, H. A. & Sheu, W. J. (1982) Reliability of alcohol use indices: the Lifetime Drinking History and the MAST. *Journal of Studies on Alcohol, 43*, 1157–1170.

Slattery, J., Chick, J., Cochrane, M., *et al.* (2003) *HTA Report 3: Prevention of Relapse in Alcohol Dependence; HTA Advice 3: Prevention of Relapse in Alcohol Dependence; Understanding HTBS Advice: Prevention Of Relapse in Alcohol Dependance.* Glasgow: Health Technology Board for Scotland (HTBS).

Small, B., Vitanen, M. & Bachman, L. (1997) Mini-Mental State Examination item scores as predictors of Alzheimer's disease: incident data from the Kungsholmen Project, Stockholm. *Journal of Gerontology*, *52A*, M299–M304.

Smart, R. G., Finley, J. & Funston, R. (1977) The effectiveness of post-detoxification referrals: effects on later detoxification admissions, drunkenness and criminality. *Drug and Alcohol Dependence*, *2*, 149–155.

Smith, M. (2004) The search for insight: clients' psychological experiences of alcohol withdrawal in a voluntary, residential, health care setting. *International Journal of Nursing Practice*, *10*, 80–85.

Smith, I. & Hillman, A. (1999) Management of alcohol Korsakoff syndrome. *Advances in Psychiatric Treatment*, *5*, 271–278.

Smith, M. O. & Khan, I. (1988) An acupuncture programme for the treatment of drug addicted persons. *Bulletin and Narcotics*, *XL*, 35–41.

Smith, K. L., Horton, N. J., Saitz, R., *et al.* (2006) The use of the mini-mental state examination in recruitment for substance abuse research studies. *Drugs and Alcohol Dependence*, *82*, 231–237.

Sobell, M. B. & Sobell, L. C. (1993) *Problem Drinkers: Guided Self-Change Treatment*. New York, NY: Guilford Press.

Sobell, M. B. & Sobell, L. C. (2000) Stepped care as a heuristic approach to the treatment of alcohol problems. *Journal of Consulting and Clinical Psychology*, *68*, 573–579.

Sobell, L. C. & Sobell, M. B. (2003) *Alcohol consumption measures*. Bethesda, MD: National Institute on Alcohol Abuse and Alcoholism. Available from: http://pubs.niaaa.nih.gov/publications/Assesing%20Alcohol/sobell.pdf [Accessed 23 March 2010].

Sobell, L. C., Maisto, S. A., Sobell, M. B., *et al.* (1979) Reliability of alcohol abusers' self-reports of drinking behavior. *Behavior Research Therapy*, *17*, 157–160.

Sobell, L. C., Sobell, M. B. & Leo, G. I. (2000) Does enhanced social support improve outcomes for problem drinkers in guided self-change treatment. *Journal of Behavior Therapy and Experimental Psychiatry*, *31*, 41–54.

Sobell, L. C., Sobell, M. B., Leo, G. I., *et al.* (2002) Promoting self change with alcohol abusers: A community-level mail intervention based on natural recovery studies. *Alcoholism: Clinical and Experimental Research*, *26*, 936–948.

South West London and St George's Mental Health NHS Trust (2010) *The Blue Book: Guidelines for the Management of Common/Selected Psychiatric Emergencies and Certain Trust Policies and Procedures* (13th edn). London: South West London and St Georges Mental Health NHS Trust.

Soyka, M. & Horak., M. (2004) Outpatient alcohol detoxification: implementation efficacy and outcome effectiveness of a model project. *European Addiction Research*, *10*, 180–187.

Spanagel, R., Zieglgansberger, W. & Hundt, W. (1996) Acamprosate and alcohol: III. Effects on alcohol discrimination in the rat. *European Journal of Pharmacology*, *305*, 51–56.

Spiegelhalter, D. J., Thomas, A., Best, N. G., *et al.* (2001) *WinBUGS User Manual: Version 1.4*. Cambridge: MRC Biostatistics Unit.

Spreen, O. & Strauss, E. (1998) *A Compendium of Neuropsychological Tests* (2nd edn). London: Oxford University Press.

Srivastava, A., Kahan, M. & Ross, S. (2008) The effect of methadone maintenance treatment on alcohol consumption: a systematic review, *Journal of Substance Abuse Treatment, 34,* 215–223.

Staner, L., Boeijinga, P., Danel, T., *et al.* (2006) Effects of acamprosate on sleep during alcohol withdrawal: A double-blind placebo-controlled polysomnographic study in alcohol-dependent subjects. *Alcoholism: Clinical and Experimental Research, 30,* 1492–1499.

StataCorp (2007) *Stata Statistical Software: Release 10.* College Station, TX: StataCorp LP.

Stein, L. I., Newton, J. R. & Bowman, R. S. (1975) Duration of hospitalization for alcoholism. *Archives of General Psychiatry, 32,* 247–252.

Stiles, W. B., Barkham, M., Twigg, E., *et al.* (2006) Effectiveness of cognitive-behavioural, person-centred and psychodynamic therapies as practised in UK National Health Service settings. *Psychological Medicine, 36,* 555–566.

Stinnett, J. L. (1982) Outpatient detoxification of the alcoholic. *International Journal of the Addictions, 17,* 1031–1046.

Stinson, D. J., Smith, W. G., Amidjaya, I., *et al.* (1979) Systems of care and treatment outcomes for alcoholic patients. *Archives of General Psychiatry, 36,* 535–539.

Stitzer, M. L., Iguchi, M. Y. & Felch, L. J. (1992) Contingent take-home incentive: effects on drug use of methadone maintenance patients. *Journal of Consulting and Clinical Psychology, 60,* 927–934.

Stockwell, T., Hodgson, R., Edwards, G., *et al.* (1979) The development of a questionnaire to measure severity of alcohol dependence. *British Journal of Addictions to Alcohol and Other Drugs, 74,* 78–87.

Stockwell, T., Murphy, D. & Hodgson, R. (1983) The severity of alcohol dependence questionnaire: its use, reliability and validity. *British Journal of Addictions, 78,* 145–155.

Stockwell, T., Bolt, E., & Hooper, J. (1986) Detoxification from alcohol at home managed by general practitioners. *British Medical Journal, 292,* 733–735.

Stockwell, T., Bolt, E., Milner, I., *et al.* (1990) Home detoxification for problem drinkers: acceptability to clients, relatives, general practitioners and outcome after 60 days. *British Journal of Addiction, 85,* 61–70.

Stockwell, T., Bolt, L., Milner, I., *et al.* (1991) Home detoxification from alcohol: its safety and efficacy in comparison with inpatient care. *Alcohol and Alcoholism, 26,* 645–650.

Stout, R., Rubin, A., Zwick, W., *et al.* (1999) Optimizing the cost-effectiveness of alcohol -treatment: a rationale for case monitoring. *Addictive Behaviours, 24,* 17–35.

Stouthard, M. E. A., Essink-Bot, M. L., Bonsel, G. J., *et al.* (1997) *Disability Weights for Diseases in the Netherlands.* Rotterdam: Erasmus University.

Strang, J., Marks, I., Dawe, S., *et al.* (1997) Type of hospital setting and treatment outcome with heroin addicts. *British Journal of Psychiatry, 171,* 335–339.

Sullivan, J. T., Swift, R. M. & Lewis, D. C. (1991) Benzodiazepine requirements during alcohol withdrawal syndrome: clinical implications of using a standardized withdrawal scale. *Journal of Clinical Psychopharmacology*, *11*, 291–295.

Sullivan, J. T., Sykora, K., Schneiderman, J., *et al.* (1989) Assessment of alcohol withdrawal: the revised Clinical Institute Withdrawal Assessment for Alcohol scale (CIWA-AR). *British Journal of Addiction*, *84*, 1353–1357.

Szapocznik, J., Perez-Vidal, A., Brickman, A. L., *et al.* (1988) Engaging adolescent drug abusers and their families in treatment: a strategic structural systems approach. *Journal of Consulting and Clinical Psychology*, *56*, 552–557.

Szapocznik, J., Rio, A., Murray, E., *et al.* (1989) Structural family versus psychodynamic child therapy for problematic Hispanic boys. *Journal of Consulting and Clinical Psychology*, *57*, 571–578.

Szapocznik, J., Hervis, O. & Schwartz, S. (2003) Brief strategic family therapy for adoelescent drug abuse. NIH Publication No. 03-4751, NIDA Therapy Manuals for Drug Addiction. Rockville, MD: National Institute on drug abuse.

Tabakoff, B., Cornell, N. & Hoffman, P. L. (1986) Alcohol tolerance. *Annals of Emergency Medicine*, *15*, 1005–1012.

Teasdale, J. D., Segal, Z. & Williams, J. M. G. (1995) How does cognitive therapy prevent depressive relapse and why should control (mindfulness) training help? *Behaviour Research and Therapy*, *33*, 25–39.

Tempesta, E., Janiri, L., Bignamini, A., *et al.* (2000) Acamprosate and relapse prevention in the treatment of alcohol dependence: a placebo-controlled study. *Alcohol and Alcoholism*, *35*, 202–209.

The NHS Information Centre, Lifestyles Statistics (2009) *Statistics on Alcohol: England, 2009*. The NHS Information Centre for health and social care. Available from: http://www.ic.nhs.uk/webfiles/publications/alcoholeng2009/Final%20Format%20draft%202009%20v7.pdf [accessed 31 March 2011].

Thevos, A. K., Thomas, S. E. & Randall, K. L. (1999) Baseline differences in social support among treatment-seeking alcoholics with and without social phobia. *Substance Abuse*, *20*, 1573–6733.

Thom, B. & Green, A. (1996) Services for women with alcohol problems: the way forward. In *Alcohol Problems in the Community* (ed. L. Harrison), pp. 200–222. London: Routledge.

Thomas, B. A. & McCambridge, J. (2008) Comparative psychometric study of a range of hazardous drinking measures administered online in a youth population. *Drug and Alcohol Dependence*, *96*, 121–127.

Thomson, A. D. & Cook, C. C. H. (1997) Parenteral thiamine and Wernicke's encephalopathy: the balance of risks and perception of concern. *Alcohol and Alcoholism*, *32*, 207–209.

Thomson, A. D. & Marshall, E. J. (2006) The treatment of patients at risk of developing Wernicke's encephalopathy in the community. *Alcohol and Alcoholism*, *41*, 159–167.

Thomson, A. D., Jeuasingham, M. & Pratt, O. E. (1987) Nutrition and alcoholic encephalopathies. *Acta Medica Scandinavica*, *717*, 55–65.

597

Thompson, K. S., Griffith, E. E. H. & Leaf, P. J. (1990) A historical review of the Madison Model of community care. *Hospital and Community Psychiatry, 41,* 625–634.

Timko, C. & DeBenedetti, A. (2007) A randomized controlled trial of intensive referral to 12-step self-help groups: one year outcomes. *Drug and Alcohol Dependence, 90,* 270–279.

Tober, G., Godfrey, C., Parrott, S., *et al.* (2005) Setting standards for training and competence: the UK Alcohol Treatment Trial, *Alcohol & Alcoholism, 40,* 413–418.

Tober, G. W., Brearley, R., Kenyon, R., *et al.* (2000) Measuring outcomes in a health service addiction clinic. *Addiction Research, 8,* 169–182.

Tonigan, J. S., Miller, W. R. & Brown, J. M. (1997) The reliability of Form 90: an instrument for assessing alcohol treatment outcome. *Journal of Studies on Alcohol, 88,* 358–364.

Tonigan, J. S., Connors, G. J., Miller, W. R. (2003) *Participation and involvement in Alcoholics Anonymous.* In *Treatment Matching in Alcoholism* (eds T. F. Babor. & F. K. Del Boca), pp. 184–204. New York, NY: Cambridge University Press.

Torrens, M., Fonseca, F., Mateu, G., *et al.* (2005) Efficacy of antidepressants in substance use disorders with and without comorbid depression: a systematic review and meta-analysis. *Drug and Alcohol DependenceDrug and Alcohol Dependence, 78,* 1–22.

Trepka, C., Rees, A., Shapiro, D. A., *et al.* (2004) Therapist competence and outcome of cognitive therapy for depression. *Cognitive Therapy & Research, 28,* 143–157.

Tripodi, S. J., Bender, K., Litschge, C., *et al.* (2010) Interventions for reducing adolescent alcohol abuse: a meta-analytic review. *Archives of Pediatrics & Adolescent Medicine, 164,* 85–91.

UKATT Research Team (2005) Effectiveness of treatment for alcohol problems: findings of the randomised UK alcohol treatment trial (UKATT). *British Medical Journal, 331,* 541–545.

UKATT Research Team (2007) UK alcohol treatment trial: client-treatment matching effects. *Addiction, 103,* 228–238.

United Nations (1977) *Convention on Psychotropic Substances, 1971.* New York: United Nations.

Upadhyaya, H. P. (2007) Managing attention-deficit/hyperactivity disorder in the presence of substance use disorder. *The Journal of Clinical Psychiatry, 68* (Suppl. 11), 23–30.

Ugarte, G., Iturriaga, H. & Pereda, T. (1977) Possible relationship between the rate of ethanol metabolism and the severity of hepatic damage in chronic alcoholics. *American Journal of Digestive Diseases, 22,* 406–410.

Vandermause, R. & Wood, M. (2009) See my suffering: women with alcohol use disorders and their primary care experiences. *Issues in Mental Health Nursing, 30,* 728-735.

Vandermause, R. K. (2007) Assessing for alcohol use disorders in women: experiences of advanced practice nurses in primary care settings. *Journal of Addictions Nursing, 18,* 187–198.

Vandevelde, S., Vanderplasschen, W., Broekaert, E., *et al.* (2003) Cultural responsiveness in substance-abuse treatment: a qualitative study using professionals' and clients' perspectives. *International Journal of Social Welfare*, *12*, 221–228.

Vargas, D. & Luis, M. A. V. (2008) Alcohol, alcoholism and alcohol addicts: conceptions and attitudes of nurses from district basic health centres. *Revista Latino-Americana de Enfermagem*, *16*, 543–550.

Vedel, E., Emmelkamp, P. M. G. & Schippers, G. M. (2008) Individual cognitive-behavioral therapy and behavioural couples therapy in alcohol use disorder: a comparative evaluation in community-based addiction treatment centres. *Psychotherapy and Psychosomatics*, *77*, 280–288.

Verheul, R., van den Brink, W. & Hartgers, C. (1998) Personality disorders predict relapse in alcoholic patients. *Addictive Behaviours*, *23*, 869–882.

Verheul, R., Lehert, P., Geerlings, P. J., *et al.* (2005) Predictors of acamprosate efficacy: results from a pooled analysis of seven European trials including 1485 alcohol-dependent patients. *Psychopharmacology*, *178*, 2–3.

Victor, M., Adams, R. D. & Collins, G. H. (1971) *The Wernicke-Korsakoff Syndrome.* Philadelphia, PA: F. A. Davis Company.

Victor, M., Adams, R. D. & Collins, G. H. (1989) *The Wernicke-Korsakoff Syndrome and Related Neurological Disorders Due to Alcoholism and Malnutrition.* Philadelphia, PA: F. A. Davis Company.

Villardita, C. & Lomeo, C. (1992) Alzheimer's disease: Correlational analysis of three screening tests and three behavioural scales. *Acta Neurologica Scandinavica*, *86*, 603–608.

Volpicelli, J. R., Alterman, A. I, Hayashida, M., *et al.* (1992) Naltrexone in the treatment of alcohol dependence. *Archives of General Psychiatry*, *49*, 876–880.

Volpicelli, J. R., Rhines, K. C., Rhines, J. S., *et al.* (1997) Naltrexone and alcohol dependence: role of subject compliance. *Archives of General Psychiatry*, *54*, 737–742.

Waldron, H. B. & Kaminer, Y. (2004) On the learning curve: the emerging evidence supporting cognitive-behavioral therapies for adolescent substance abuse. *Addiction*, *99* (Suppl. 2), 93–105.

Waldron, H. B., Slesnick, N., Brody, J. L., *et al.* (2001) Treatment outcomes for adolescent substance abuse at 4- and 7-month assessments. *Journal of Consulting and Clinical Psychology*, *69*, 802–813.

Walitzer, K. S. & Connors, G. J. (2007) Thirty month follow-up of drinking moderation training for women: A randomized clinical trial. *Journal of Consulting and Clinical Psychology*, *75*, 501–507.

Walitzer, K. S. & Dermen, K. H. (2004) Alcohol-focused spouse involvement and behavioural couples therapy: evaluation of enhancements to drinking reduction treatment for male problem drinkers. *Journal of Consulting and Clinical Psychology*, *72*, 944–955.

Walitzer, K. S., Dermen, K. H. & Barrick, C. (2009) Facilitating involvement in Alcoholics Anonymous during out-patient treatment: a randomized clinical trial. *Addiction*, *104*, 391–401.

Walsh, D. C., Hingson, R. W., Merrigan, D. M., *et al.* (1991) A randomized trial of treatment options for alcohol-abusing workers. *The New England Journal of Medicine, 325*, 775–782.

Walters, D., Connors, J. P., Feeney, F. X., *et al.* (2009) The cost effectiveness of naltrexone added to cognitive-behavioral therapy in the treatment of alcohol dependence. *Journal of Addictive Diseases, 28*, 137–144.

Walters, G. D. (2002) The heritability of alcohol abuse and dependence: a meta-analysis of behavior genetic research. *American Journal of Drug and Alcohol Abuse, 28*, 557–584.

Wasilewski, D., Matsumoto, H., Kur, E., *et al.* (1996) Assessment of diazepam loading dose therapy of delirium tremens. *Alcohol and Alcoholism, 31*, 273–278.

Watkins, K. E., Paddock, S. M., Zhang, L., *et al.* (2006) Improving care for depression in patients with comorbid substance misuse. *American Journal of Psychiatry, 163*, 125–132.

Weaver, M. F., Hoffman, H. J., Johnson, R. E., *et al.* (2006) Alcohol withdrawal pharmacotherapy for inpatients with medical comorbidity. *Journal of Addictive Diseases, 25*, 17–24.

Weaver, T., Madden, P., Charles, V., *et al.* (2003) Comorbidity of substance misuse and mental illness in community mental health and substance misuse services. *British Journal of Psychiatry, 183*, 304–313.

Wechsler, D. (1945/1997) *Wechsler Memory Scale: Third Edition (WMS-III)*. San Antonio: Harcourt Assessment.

Wechsler, D. (1981) *Manual for the Wechsler Adult Intelligence Scale—Revised*. New York, NY: Psychological Corporation.

Weithmann, G. & Hoffmann, M. (2005) A randomised clinical trial of inpatient versus combined day hospital treatment of alcoholism: primary and secondary outcome measures. *European Addiction Research, 11*, 197–203.

Webb, M. & Unwin, A. (1988) The outcome of outpatient withdrawal from alcohol. *British Journal of Addiction, 83*, 929–934.

Weisner, C., Ray, G. T. & Mertens, J. R. *et al.* (2003) Short-term alcohol and drug treatment outcomes predict long-term outcome. *Drug & Alcohol Dependence, 71*, 281–294.

Weiss, R. D. (1999) Inpatient treatment. In *Textbook of Substance Abuse Treatment* (eds M. Galanter & H. D. Kleber). Washington, DC: The American Psychiatric Press.

Weiss, R. D., Griffin, M. L., Kolodziej, M. E., *et al.* (2007) A randomised trial of integrated group therapy versus group drug counselling for patients with bipolar disorder and substance dependence. *American Journal of Psychiatry, 164*, 100–107.

Wen, H. L. (1979) Acupuncture and electrical stimulation (AES) outpatient detoxification. *Modern Medicine, 11*, 23–24.

Wen, H. L., Cheung, S. Y. (1973) Treatment of drug addiction by acupuncture and electrical stimulation. *Asian Journal of Medicine, 9*, 138–141.

Wetterling, T., Kanitz, R. D., Besters, B., *et al.* (1997) A new rating scale for the assessment of the alcohol withdrawal syndrome (AWS scale). *Alcohol and Alcoholism, 32*, 753–760.

White, H. R. & Labouvie, E. W. (1989) Towards the assessment of adolescent problem drinking. *Journal of Studies on Alcohol, 50,* 30–37.

White, A. R., Rampes, H. & Campbell, J. L. (2006) Acupuncture and related interventions for smoking cessation. *Cochrane Database Systematic Review,* CD000009.

Whitfield, C. (1980) Non-drug treatment of alcohol withdrawal. *Current Psychiatric Therapy, 19,* 101–109.

Whitworth, A. B., Fischer, F., Lesch, O. M., *et al.* (1996) Comparison of acamprosate and placebo in long-term treatment of alcohol dependence. *The Lancet, 347,* 1438–1442.

WHO (1992) *The International Classification of Diseases*: *Classification of Mental and Behavioural Disorders: Clinical Descriptions and Diagnostic Guidelines* (10th edition). Geneva: WHO.

WHO (2000) *International Guide for Monitoring Alcohol Consumption and Related Harm.* Geneva: WHO.

WHO (2004) *Global Status Report on Alcohol 2004.* Geneva: WHO.

WHO (2010a) *Lexicon of Alcohol and Drug Terms Published by the World Health Organization.* Geneva: WHO.

WHO (2010b) *Screening and Brief Intervention for Alcohol Problems in Primary Health Care.* Geneva: WHO.

Wilcox, H. C. Conner, K. R. & Caine, E. D. (2004) Association of alcohol and drug use disorders and completed suicide: an empirical review of cohort studies. *Drug & Alcohol Dependence, 76,* S11–S19.

Wilens, T. E., Adler, L. A., Weiss, M. D., *et al.* (2008) Atomoxetine treatment of adults with ADHD and comorbid alcohol use disorders. *Drug & Alcohol Dependence, 96,* 145–154.

Willems, P. J. A., Letemendia, F. J. J & Arroyave, F. (1973) A categorization for the assessment of prognosis and outcome in the treatment of alcoholism. *The British Journal of Psychiatry, 122,* 649–654.

Williams, B. T. R., & Drummond, D. C (1994) The Alcohol Problems Questionnaire: reliability and validity. *Drug & Alcohol Dependence, 35,* 239–343.

Winters, K. & Henly, G. (1993) *Adolescent Diagnostic Interview (ADI) Manual.* Los Angeles, CA: Western Psychological Services.

Winters, K., Stinchfield, R., Fulkerson, J., *et al.* (1993) Measuring alcohol and cannabis use disorders in an adolescent clinical sample. *Psychology of Addictive Behaviors, 7,* 185–196.

Winters, K. C. & Henly, G. A. (1989) *Personal Experience Inventory (PEI) Test and Manual.* Los Angeles, CA: Western Psychological Services.

Winters, K. C., Stinchfield, R., Opland, E., *et al.* (2000) The effectiveness of the Minnesota Model approach to the treatment of adolescent drugs abusers. *Addiction, 95,* 601–612.

Winters, L. & McGourty, H. (1994) *Alcohol Services in Chester and Ellesmere Port.* Observatory Report Series No. 22. Liverpool: Liverpool Public Health Observatory.

Wiseman, E. J., Henderson, K. L., & Briggs, M. J. (1997) Outcomes of patients in a VA ambulatory detoxification program. *Psychiatric Services, 48,* 200–203.

Witbrodt, J., Bond, J., Kaskutas, L. A., *et al.* (2007) Day hospital and residential addiction treatment: Randomized and nonrandomized managed care clients. *Journal of Consulting and Clinical Psychology*, *75*, 947–959.

Woody, G. E. (2003) Research findings on psychotherapy of addictive disorders. *American Journal on Addictions*, *12* (Suppl. 2), S19–S26.

Worner, T. M., Zeller, B., Schwarz, H., *et al.* (1992) Acupuncture fails to improve treatment outcome in alcoholics. *Drug and Alcohol Dependence*, *30*, 169–173.

Wu, L. T., &. Ringwalt, C. L. (2004) Alcohol dependence and use of treatment services among women in the community. *American Journal of Psychiatry*, *161*, 1790–1797.

Velleman, R. & Orford, J. (1999) *Risk & Resilience: Adults who were the Children of Problem Drinkers*. London: Harwood.

Xin, X., He, J., Frontini, M. G., *et al.* (2001) Effects of alcohol reduction on blood pressure: a meta-analysis of randomized controlled trials. *Hypertension, 38*, 1112–1117.

Yeh, M. Y., Che, H. L. & Wu, S. M. (2009) An ongoing process: a qualitative study of how the alcohol-dependent free themselves of addiction through progressive abstinence. *BMC Psychiatry, 9*, 76.

Yoon, S. J., Pae, C. U., Namkoong, K., *et al.* (2006) Mirtazapine for patients with alcohol dependence and comorbid depressive disorders: a multicentre, open label study. *Progress in Neuro-Psychopharmacology and Biological Psychiatry, 30*, 1196–1201.

Yoshida, K., Funahashi, M., Masui, M., *et al.* (1990) Sudden death of alcohol withdrawal syndrome – a report of a case. *Japanese Journal of Legal Medicine*, *44*, 243–247.

Zahl, D. & Hawton, K. (2004) Repetition of deliberate self harm and subsequent suicide risk: long term follow up study of 11583 patients. *British Journal of Psychiatry*, *185*, 70–75.

Zarkin, G. A., Bray, J. W., Aldridge, A., *et al.* (2008) Cost and cost-effectiveness of the COMBINE study in alcohol-dependent patients. *Archives of General Psychiatry*, *65*, 1214–1221.

Zeigler, D., Wang, C., Yoast, R., *et al.* (2005) The neurocognitive effects of alcohol on adolescents and college students. *Preventive Medicine*, *40*, 23–32.

Zemore, S. E. & Kaskutas, L. A. (2008) Services received and treatment outcomes in day-hospital and residential programs. *Journal of Substance Abuse Treatment, 35*, 232–44.

Zgierska, A., Rabago, D., Zuelsdorff, M., *et al.* (2008) Mindfulness meditation for alcohol relapse prevention: a feasibility pilot study. *Journal of Addiction Medicine*, *2*, 165–173.

Zweben, A., Pearlman, S. & Li, S. (1988) A comparison of brief advice and conjoint therapy in the treatment of alcohol abuse: the results of the marital systems study. *British Journal of Addiction*, *83*, 899–916.

11   ABBREVIATIONS

5HT(1A, 3)	5-hydroxytryptamine (subtypes)
AA	Alcoholics Anonymous
AAF	alcohol-attributable fraction
AAIS	Adolescent Alcohol Involvement Scale
ACAM	acamprosate
ACE (-R)	Addenbrooke's Cognitive Evaluation (– Revised)
ACT	assertive community treatment
ADHD	attention deficit hyperactivity disorder
ADI	Adolescent Drinking Index
ADS	Alcohol Dependence Scale
AfC	Agenda for Change
AFCS	alcohol-focused coping skills
AFLS	alcohol-focused life skills
AFPSY	alcohol-focused psychoeducation
AFSI	alcohol-focused spousal involvement
AGREE	Appraisal of Guidelines for Research and Evaluation Instrument
AHRQ	Agency for Healthcare Research and Quality (United States)
ALT	alanine amino transferase
AMED	Allied and Complementary Medicine Database
ANARP	Alcohol Needs Assessment Research Project
ANOVA	analysis of variance
APA	American Psychiatric Association
APQ	Alcohol Problems Questionnaire
AQ	Alcohol Questionnaire
ASAM	American Society of Addiction Medicine
ASI	Addiction Severity Index
ASPD	antisocial personality disorder
AST	aspartate amino transferase
ATR	Access to Recovery
AUD	alcohol-use disorder
AUDIT (-C)	Alcohol Use Disorders Identification Test (– Consumption)
AVI	Swedish Alcohol Use Inventory
AWS	Alcohol Withdrawal Syndrome Scale
BCE	behavioural cue exposure
BCT	behavioural couples therapy
BMJ	British Medical Journal
BNF	British National Formulary

BRT	brief relationship therapy
BSCT	behavioural self-control training
BSM(T)	behavioural self-management (training)
BST	broad-spectrum treatment
BT	behavioural therapy
Ca	calcium
CAD	cumulative abstinence duration
C/AF	couples therapy–alcohol focused
CAMHS	child and adolescent mental health services
CASI-A	Comprehensive Addiction Severity Inventory for Adolescents
CBMMT	cognitive behavioural mood management training
CBT	cognitive behavioural therapy
CCSE	Cognitive Capacity Screening Examination
CCM	clinical case management
CCoun1	advice counselling (couples counselling)
CDDR	Customary Drinking and Drug Use Record
CDP	Comprehensive Drinker Profile
CDT	carbohydrate-deficient transferrin
CD-ROM	compact disc – read-only memory
CDSES	Controlled Drinking Self-Efficacy Scale
CDSR	Cochrane Database of Systematic Reviews
CDU	chemical dependency unit
CE	cue exposure
CENTRAL	Cochrane Central Register of Controlled Trials
CEO	Chief Executive Officer
CG	control group
CI	confidence interval
CIDI	Composite International Diagnostic Interview
CINAHL	Cumulative Index to Nursing and Allied Health Literature
CISS	Christo Inventory for Substance Misuse Services
CIWA-AD	Clinical Institute Withdrawal Assessment
CIWA-Ar	Clinical Institute Withdrawal Assessment Scale for Alcohol, revised
CLB	Cognitive Laterality Battery
CLDH	Cognitive Lifetime Drinking History
CM	case management
CMA	Canadian Medical Association
COMBINE	combining medications and behavioural interventions
CONT	control
COPD	chronic obstructive pulmonary disease
COPSK	coping-/social-skills training group
COUNS	counselling

CPN	community psychiatric nurse
CRD	Centre for Reviews and Dissemination
CRFT	community reinforcement and family training
CrI	credible interval
CS	coping skills
CSPRS	Collaborative Study Psychotherapy Rating Scale
CST	communication skills training
CSTF	communication skills training with family therapy
CT-8	conjoint therapy (eight sessions)
CTS	Cognitive Therapy Scale
CYT	Cannabis Youth Trial
DANOS	Drug and Alcohol National Occupational Standards
DARE	Cochrane Database of Abstracts of Reviews of Effects
DCU	drinker's check-up
DDD	drinks per drinking day
df	degrees of freedom
DfES	Department for Education and Skills
DISC	Diagnostic Interview Schedule for Children
DIS–IV	Diagnostic Interview for DSM–IV
Disulf	disulfiram
DM	Deutschmark
DPI	Drinking Problems Index
DRD2	dopamine receptor D2
DrInC	Drinker Inventory of Consequences
DS	directed social support
DSM (–III, –IV, –R, –V)	*Diagnostic and Statistical Manual of Mental Disorders* of the American Psychiatric Association (3rd edition, 4th edition, Revised, 5th edition)
DSML	Drinking Self-Monitoring Log
DSSI	Delusions-Symptoms-States Inventory
DTs	delirium tremens
DVLA	Driver and Vehicle Licensing Agency
ECE	emotional cue exposure
EconLIT	economics literature search (the American Economic Association's electronic bibliography)
EDNOS	eating disorder not otherwise specified
EDS	Ethanol Dependence Syndrome scale
EED	Economic Evaluation Database
EMBASE	Excerpta Medica Database
EQ-5D	European Quality of Life – 5 Dimensions
FAST	Fast Alcohol Screen Test
FC	full care

FD	fixed-dosing
FN	false negative
FP	false positive
FRAMES	feedback, responsibility, advice, menu, empathy, self-efficacy
FT	full time
GABA (-A, -B)	*gamma*-aminobutyric acid (type A, type B)
GABRA (A2, A6)	*gamma*-aminobutyric acid subunit receptor (alpha 2, alpha 6)
GAIN	Global Appraisal of Individual Needs
GBL	gamma-butyrolactone
GDG	Guideline Development Group
GGT	*gamma*-glutamyl transferase
GHB	*gamma*-hydroxybutyric acid
G-I-N	Guidelines International Network
GMI	relapse prevention with motivational enhancements
GP	general practitioner
GRADE	Grading of Recommendations: Assessment, Development and Evaluation
GRP	Guideline Review Panel
GSH	guided self-help
HCHS	Hospital and Community Health Services
HDRS	Hamilton Depression Rating Scale
HMIC	Health Management Information Consortium
HRG	Healthcare Resource Group
HRQoL	health-related quality of life
HSD	Honestly Significant Difference
HTA	Health Technology Assessment
IAA	indulgence, ambivalence and attempt
IATP	individual assessment treatment program
IBT	individual-based treatment
ICD–10	*International Classification of Diseases*, 10th Revision
ICER	incremental cost-effectiveness ratio
ICP	integrated care pathway
ICQ	Impaired Control Questionnaire
ICT	interactional couples therapy
ICP	integrated care pathway
INT	intensive
Int V Nor-AFLS	Intensive versus normal AFLS
IV	inverse variance
k	number of studies
KP	Korsakoff psychosis

LDH	Lifetime Drinking History
LDQ	Leeds Dependency Questionnaire
LOCF	last observation carried forward
LS	life skills
LT	long term
M/m	mean
MANOVA	multivariate analysis of variance
MAP	Maudsley Addiction Profile
MAST	Michigan Alcohol Screening Test
MATCH	Matching Alcoholism Treatments to Client Heterogeneity
MD	mean difference
MEDLINE	Medical Literature Analysis and Retrieval System Online
MET	motivational enhancement therapy
mGLuR	metabotropic glutamate receptor
M-H	Mantel-Haenszel estimate
MIND	Minnesota Detoxification Scale
MINI-CR	Mini International Neuropsychiatric Interview-Clinician Rated
MM	multi-modal treatment
MMSE	Mini-Mental Status Examination
MoCAM	*Models of Care for Alcohol Misusers*
MOCE	moderation-oriented cue exposure
MSQ	Motivational Structure Questionnaire
MTC	mixed treatment comparison
n	number of participants in a group
N	total number of participants
n/a or NA	not applicable
NACOA	National Association for Children of Alcoholics
NALX/NLT/NX	naltrexone
NATMS	National Alcohol Treatment Monitoring System
NCCMH	National Collaborating Centre for Mental Health
NDRL	non-directive reflective listening
NHMRC	National Health and Medical Research Council
NHS	National Health Service
NIAAA	National Institute on Alcohol Abuse and Alcoholism
NICE	National Institute for Clinical Excellence
NIHR	National Institute for Health Research
NIS	Neuropsychological Impairment Scale
NLH	National Library for Health
NMB	net monetary benefit
NMDA	N-methyl D-aspartate
NNT(B; H)	number needed to treat (for benefit; for harm)

NOR	normal
NS	network support
NSF	National Service Framework
NTA	National Treatment Agency
OB	office-based
OCD	obsessive-compulsive disorder
OCDS	Obsessive Compulsive Drinking Scale
OLS	ordinary least squares
OR	odds ratio
OT	occupational therapy
p	probability
PACT	psychoeducational attention control treatment
PAT	Paddington Alcohol Test
PCBT	packaged CBT program
PCM	primary care management
PDA	percent days abstinent
PEI	Personal Experience Inventory
PI	psychological intervention
PICO	Patient, Intervention, Comparison and Outcome
PLB	placebo
PRISM	Psychiatric Research Interview for Substance and Mental Disorders
PS	problem solving
PSBCT	BCT and parental skills training
PSS	Personal Social Services
PSY	psychoeducational
PsycINFO	Psychological Information Database
PSYDY	short-term psychodynamic therapy
PSYEDU	bibliotherapy/drinking guidelines
PTSD	post-traumatic stress disorder
QALY	quality-adjusted life year
q.d.s.	*quater die sumendus* (four times a day)
QF	Quantity–Frequency
RAPI	Rutgers Alcohol Problem Index
RCGP	Royal College of General Practitioners
RCQ (-TV)	Readiness to Change Questionnaire (– Treatment Version)
RCT	randomised controlled trial
RESULT	routine evaluation of the substance use ladder of treatments
ROC	receiver operating characteristic
RP	relapse prevention'
RPME	RP and MET

RR	risk ratio/relative risk
RTCQ–TV	Readiness to Change Questionnaire Treatment Version
SADD	Short Alcohol Dependence Data
SADQ (–C)	Severity of Alcohol Dependence Questionnaire (– Community)
SADV	Substance Abuse Domestic Violence
SASQ	Single Alcohol Screening Question
S-BCT	standard behavioural couples therapy
SBNT	social behaviour and network therapy
SC	stepped care
SCAN	Specialist Clinical Addiction Network
SCID SUDM	Structured Clinical Interview for the DSM Substance Use Disorders Module
SCL-90	Symptom Checklist-90
SD	standard deviation
SERT	sertraline
SG	standard gamble
SHM	self-help manual
SIGN	Scottish Intercollegiate Guidelines Network
SMART	Self-Management and Recovery Training
SMAST	Short Michigan Alcohol Screening Test
SMD	standardised mean difference
SOCRATES	Stages of Change Readiness and Treatment Eagerness Scale
SPC	Summary of Product Characteristics
SSAGA	Semi–Structured Assessment for the Genetics of Alcoholism
SSRI	selective serotonin reuptake inhibitor
ST	symptom triggered (means 'standard treatment' or 'short term' in Appendix 16e)
SUDDS-IV	Substance Use Disorders Diagnostic Schedule
SWLSTG	South West London and St George's
T-ASI	Teen Addiction Severity Index
TAU	treatment as usual
t.d.s.	ter die sumendum (three times a day)
TLFB	TimeLine FollowBack
TN	true negative
TOP	Treatment Outcomes Profile
TP	true positive
TPQ	Tridimensional Personality Questionnaire
TRIP	Turning Research Into Practice
(I-, S-)TSF (dire, mot)	(intensive, standard) 12-step facilitation (– directive approach and coping skills, – motivational approach and coping skills)
TTO	time trade-off

Abbreviations

UKATT	UK Alcohol Treatment Trial
URICA	University of Rhode Island Change Assessment
USD	United States dollar
VA	Veterans Affairs vs versus (in Appendices)
VS	volunteer support
WAIS (-III, -R)	Wechsler Adult Intelligence Scale (– 3rd edition, – Revised)
WE	Wernicke's encephalopathy
WHO	World Health Organization
WKS	Wernicke–Korsakoff syndrome
WMD	weighted mean difference